A
LONG
STRANGE
TRIP

A LONG STRANGE TRIP

The Inside History of the Grateful Dead

Dennis McNally

BROADWAY BOOKS

NEW YORK

BOOK DESIGN BY CAROLINE CUNNINGHAM

The Library of Congress has cataloged the hardcover edition as follows:
McNally, Dennis.
A long strange trip : the inside history of the Grateful Dead / Dennis McNally — 1st ed.
p.   cm.
Includes bibliographical references.
1. Grateful Dead (Musical group) 2. Rock musicians—United States—Biography.
3. Rock musicians—United States—Interviews. I. Title.
ML421.G72 M36 2002
782.42166'092'2—dc21
[B]   2002025561

ISBN 0-7679-1186-5

1   3   5   7   9   10   8   6   4   2

A Long Strange Trip is dedicated to the memories of

Jerry Garcia and Dick Latvala

When the going gets weird, the weird turn pro.

—HUNTER THOMPSON

Look, there are two curves in the air: the air
That man's fate breathes: there is the rise and fall of
    the Christian culture-complex, that broke its dawn-
    cloud
Fifteen centuries ago, and now past noon
Drifts to decline; and there's the yet vaster curve, but
    mostly in the future, of the age that began at Kitty-
    hawk
Within one's lifetime.—The first of these curves passing
    its noon and the second orient
All in one's little lifetime make it seem pivotal.
Truly the time is marked by insane splendors and ag-
    onies. But watch when the two curves cross: you
    children
Not far away down the hawk's nightmare future: you
    will see monsters.

—ROBINSON JEFFERS, "Diagram"

That's why the Lord gave us three ears.
An invisible one for what is not said.

—ROBERT HUNTER

Contents

Preface   xiii

Acknowledgments   xvii

1. Introduction: Power. The Stage as Alembic (mid-1980s)   1

2. Children of the American Decades (1940–1960)   6

3. Roots (1961–2/62)   22

4. A Fine High Lonesome Madness (3/62–12/63)   41

5. Interlude: A Meeting of Minds (Company Meetings, 1984)   55

6. Something New (12/31/63–10/64)   62

7. The Warlocks (11/64–6/65)   76

8. A Very Loud Bar Band (6/10/65–11/12/65)   85

9. Interlude: Albert Hofmann's Discovery (the Psychedelic World)   102

10. The Bus Came By (11/13/65–2/5/66)   107

11. Hollywood and Home Again (2/6/66–5/1/66)   129

12. Psychedelic Indians (5/1/66–9/29/66)   144

13. The Hippest City Hall Ever (9/30/66–10/31/66)   158

14. The San Francisco Scene (11/1/66–1/29/67)   169

15. Before the Fall (1/30/67–5/31/67)   181

16. The Prodigals (6/1/67–9/15/67) 196

17. Interlude: The Crew 213

18. Dark Anthem (9/16/67–12/31/67) 219

19. Interlude: Purifying the Elements (Setting the Stage) 237

20. Independence and Its Price (1/1/68–6/30/68) 247

21. Interlude: The Promoters 267

22. Forward into the Fog (7/68–2/15/69) 273

23. Interlude: The Circus Is in Town (the First Set Begins) 291

24. No Turn Left Unstoned (2/19/69–6/20/69) 299

25. Interlude: "When the Music Plays the Band" (the Dead Talk About Playing Music) 313

26. If My Words Were Gold (6/20/69–8/15/69) 316

27. Interlude: "Eastbound and Down" (End of Set One) 326

28. Bethel to Sears Point (8/16/69–12/4/69) 332

29. Trouble All Around (12/5/69–3/70) 343

30. Interlude/Intermission: "Waits Backstage While I Sing to You" (1980s) 356

31. Might as Well Work (3/70–7/70) 360

32. An American Beauty (8/4/70–12/31/70) 374

33. Interlude/Intermission II: Uncle John's Children 385

34. Dreams and All (1/71–7/71) 391

35. Dealing Solo Aces and the New Guy (7/71–3/72) 403

36. Interlude: The Home Front: Money and Management (1980s and Beyond) 418

37. Bozos Abroad (3/72–12/72) 424

38. Megadead (1973) 445

39. Interlude: Into the Zone (Second Set Begins) 461

40. The Wall (1/74–10/20/74)   468

41. The Hiatus (10/21/74–6/76)   480

42. The Monster Revives (6/76–8/78)   493

43. Dark Moon over Gizeh (9/78)   508

44. Interlude: The Rhythm Devils (Drum Break)   517

45. Shakedown (10/78–10/80)   521

46. Interlude: Beyond the Zone (End of Second Set)   536

47. After Heaven (11/80–7/86)   541

48. A Suitable Touch of Grey (8/86–12/89)   558

49. Interlude: "Noble but Lame" (the Grateful Dead on the G.D.)   577

50. A Deadicated Life (1/90–9/92)   579

51. Interlude: "Can't Stop for Nothin' " (Encore/New Year's Eve)   594

52. Interlude: Packed and Gone (Load-Out)   597

53. "I Guess It Doesn't Matter, Anyway" (10/92–4/96)   600

54. Finale: Metaphysics and Other Humorous Subjects   617

Notes   621

Bibliography   639

Interviews   661

Index   667

Permissions   683

Preface

A s I came of age in the 1960s, I defined two fundamental intellectual orientations in my life. The first, born of modest participation in and deep sympathy for the civil rights and antiwar movements, and in the antimaterialist aspects of "hippie," was an affinity for elements of culture outside the mainstream. The second, by instinct and the blessing of having wonderful teachers, was a profound respect for the study of history. So when I arrived at graduate school in 1971 and discovered that it was more a professional training center than a hall of scholars, I chose a topic of study that would maintain my identification with that first orientation: a biography of Jack Kerouac, my intellectual forefather.

Six months after I began in 1972 what became *Desolate Angel: Jack Kerouac, the Beat Generation, and America* (Random House, 1979), a friend took me to my first Grateful Dead concert, introduced me to the psychedelic experience, and changed my life. A few months later, it occurred to me that I wanted to write a two-volume history of post–World War II American bohemia, volume one via the life of Kerouac and volume two through the lives of the Grateful Dead. It was my great good fortune (and intuitive correctness about the fundamental connections between the two phenomena) that Jerry Garcia shared my vision. I sent him a copy of *Desolate Angel* on publication, and eventually we met. Shortly after, he said, "Why don't you do us?" At one of our first meetings, we chatted in his dressing room, which was decorated with two pictures, one of his late friend and musical cohort, Pigpen, and one of Jack Kerouac.

At one of our first interviews, he commented, "For the sake of history, or whatever, as a member of the Grateful Dead, and as a person who's consciously involved in some kind of historical process, right, it's very important to me that somehow some essence of what we're doing is accurately . . . that it conforms to my bias"—he laughed—". . . that some representation of us is undertaken . . . your sensitivity with Kerouac and Cassady and the resonance of me having known Cassady and so forth, that resonance tells me that your work at the second level—I mean you weren't there when it was happening, but your sensitivity and selectivity and so forth, on the second level away from it was accurate enough it hit my recognitions, and the fact that you're interested in us—I mean that eminently qualifies you, as far as I'm concerned."

That conversation was in 1981. In 1984, the Grateful Dead Productions company receptionist complained at a meeting that reporters were annoying her because no one was dealing with them, and Garcia remarked, "Get McNally to do it. He knows that shit." So from then until the end of the road for the band in 1995, I was the band's publicist, adding a new layer of knowledge, intimacy, and detail to my study. Among many other things, the Dead was a spiritual experience, a musical phenomenon, and a business, and it is my hope that I have included all these facets in my portrait. It is for that reason that there are two sorts of chapters in *A Long Strange Trip*. It is largely a linear narrative that spans the early 1940s (the childhoods of Jerry Garcia and Phil Lesh) to 1996, when we scattered Garcia's ashes. In between these chapters, you will find "interlude" chapters that describe a hypothetical year in the 1980s and '90s, the era in which the band was an established success, the time that I witnessed directly, and within that year a hypothetical or perhaps more ideally archetypal concert. These interlude chapters describe subtopics in the music business as well as life on the road as the Grateful Dead—and the Dead Heads—experienced it.

Being the biographer (as well as the publicist) of the Dead was not a job, it was an adventure. But that was true for all the participants—the band, the employees, the audience. It was, to quote Phil Lesh, "definitely long, definitely strange—and definitely a trip." Together we all joined in on a quest, and I'd follow that path anytime. In Robert Hunter's words,

Midnight on a carousel ride
Reaching for the gold ring down inside

Never could reach
It just slips away but I try

Acknowledgments

This sort of project is of necessity collaborative; my love and thanks to: Chris Byrnes (who started me), John and Gerry Hurley and Steve Buccieri (first companions), Danny Hupert, Maria Maloney, and Maya Maloney Hupert (younger brother and sister, plus), Lisa Biasi and Sandy Melloy (ace legwomen), Stu (ace legman) and Robin Nixon, Paul Grushkin (who helped introduce me to San Francisco, Joe Moss (keeper of the wheels), Jan Simmons (a gem of a sister), Quilley Powers (transcribing demon & savior), Michael Vosse (good buddy), Michael Bailey (ditto), Marty and Yvonne Martinez (Jersey siblings), Barry Alterman and June Omura (life is a dance), Phil, Arden, Sam, and Max Coturri, Jeff Briss and Dorothy Fullerton, Tom, Maggie, and Anthony Pinatelli, Felina Tambakos, Jon Korchin, Bernice Millman, the late Gertrude McNally, Alex Krutsky and Maggie McNally (just plain lovely family).

My thanks to the Grateful Dead family, most especially the late Bobby Petersen (start-up), Sue Stephens (guidance), Harry Popick (sonic advice), Ram Rod and Frances Shurtliff (senses of humor), Eileen Law (heart & soul), Cassidy Law (and unto the second generation), Mary Knudsen (critical support), Sue Swanson, Connie Bonner, Danny Rifkin,

Alan Trist, Cameron Sears, Hal Kant, Bill Belmont, Wavy Gravy, Willy Legate and Carolyn Garcia (examples), Robert Hunter (mind), Bill Kreutzmann, Phil Lesh, Mickey Hart, Bob Weir, and Jerry Garcia (for making it interesting). Although the whole band read the manuscript, Mickey Hart and Robert Hunter were exceptionally giving of time and knowledge—many thanks.

During the writing, Joel Selvin generously shared his research files, and Nicholas Meriwether proved a first-rate fact-checker. Jeremy Weir Alderson gave me access to a superlative unpublished interview he conducted with Garcia. Blair Jackson and Regan McMahon were the cosmic readers—I'm responsible for the mistakes, but they, especially, know how many aren't here. David Gans also contributed an extremely valuable reading. Susana Millman was a fabulous photo editor for a visually challenged writer.

One day, I'm very happy to say, Stacey Kreutzmann said, "You need Sarah Lazin as your agent." And Sarah, bless her, brought me to an equally superb editor, Gerry Howard. My gratitude to them.

One cannot travel in the Dead's trail without friends; Sandy Rosen, Barbara Lewit, and Lou Tambakos were the very special road crew—not possible without.

Nine bows to the imps of synchronicity who sent me to Season Ray and Susana Millman—I don't know why I'm lucky, but I'm glad.

San Francisco, 9/2001

Introduction:
Power. The Stage
as Alembic

(MID-1980s)

hortly before every Grateful Dead concert, there is a luminous, suspended moment. The doors are still closed. The band has not yet arrived. Bathed in the subliminal hum of the stage's electric potential, you smell the ozone of 133,000 burning watts and realize that the elegantly arranged castle of equipment around you is *alive*—not just stuff, but a sentient alchemical sculpture. You are surrounded by an enormous electronic beast that can link the group consciousness of six musicians and an audience of thousands to transmute notes, thoughts, and volts, fusing boogie dancing, high-tech doodah, and the act of performance into a subtle, profoundly human ritual of celebration. This stage is a giant alembic, the fabled alchemical chamber where the magical transformation took place. It is a portal to the mysterious world beyond daily life.

This monster lives. The equipment cases that define the rear stage are its skeleton, extruded daily as it is assembled for its labors. It breathes through the pulsating speaker diaphragms, the interconnecting cables are its nerves, and it hears through a $30,000 harmonic analyzer originally designed by NASA to evaluate the aerodynamic strength of metals. The ears and the brain, a forty-eight-channel sound mixing board, are positioned in a booth eighty-five feet away in the center of the hall. From there, the stage seems a smooth, powerful monolith, its base draped in black, the undecorated equipment atop it set in a symmetric arc. Backstage, the seams are more evident.

From the top of the center-rear stage stairs, you stand behind and between the two glistening drum sets that anchor the setup. At far left front-of-stage sit Brent Mydland's Hammond B-3 organ, a Yamaha synthesizer, and his own small mixing board. Next to Mydland's corner, moving toward the center, is guitarist Jerry Garcia's equipment cabinet, essentially a frame that holds a sound effects rack, a preamplifier, a McIntosh 2300 amplifier, and four JBL speakers. A floor strip with two foot pedals and seven switches, labeled "Mutron, Oct, Boss, Wah, Dist, Phase, Delay," sits in front of Garcia's vocal microphone. It is secured to the worn Afshar-style stage carpet with gaffer's tape, the unique product of a small New Hampshire company, which is the secret ingredient that binds together all live rock and roll. Some seven hundred pounds of Sonar drums and Zildjian cymbals make up each of the two trap sets played by Mickey Hart on the left and Bill Kreutzmann on the right. An exotic array of other percussion instruments is set up behind them. The front row, the "amp line," continues to the right with rhythm guitarist Bob Weir's Godzilla 1000 amplifier and a cabinet holding eight Gauss ten-inch speakers. Phil Lesh's Godzilla and a sound processor bass monitor, essentially a small computer, define the right side. A mixing board for the monitors, the floor speakers facing the musicians which allow them to hear themselves, fills the stage's right front corner. Both sides of the stage are walled off by the boxes that carry the ninety steel-jacketed NASA surplus cables ("snakes") and twenty-seven Crest power amplifiers that energize the system.

An aisle behind the amp line gives access to each cluster of instruments and equipment, and the space behind the lane is defined by each crew member's tool case, surrounded by a fort of empty cases. Production manager Robbie Taylor's case stands at the top of the stairs. The left-hand drum set is backed by Ram Rod Shurtliff, crew chief since 1967, chatting with basketball star and NBC basketball analyst Bill Walton as he lays out some of Hart's "instruments"—an infant's windup toy, whistles, a kazoo. The left rear corner of the stage is the redoubt of Steve Parish, stage manager and squire to the two guitarists, just now catching a hasty nap on the crew bus. The other drum roadie, Billy Grillo, sits changing drumheads behind Kreutzmann's setup. The far right rear is the territory of Bill "Kidd" Candelario, who cares for the keyboards and bass.

Above, 144 state-of-the-art Meyer Sound Lab (MSL) loudspeakers hang five-deep from the ceiling. Still higher is a giant pentagonal truss holding two hundred lights. Though they absorb far more power than all of the stage gear and sound equipment, the Dead's lights are still only a fraction of the normal design for a rock band; Van Halen, for instance, carries fifteen hundred lights. Scrib (as in scribbler), the band's publicist and biographer, half listens as Taylor gleefully harasses the local union steward and reflects on his, Scrib's, conversation with Taylor during the previous night's drive. Taylor had interpreted his muttered "House lights"—the last command before a show begins—as a demand to resume an interview. Taylor replied, "How'd you know that 'House lights' means the beginning?"

"I just want to see what I'm rolling," said Scrib, "but getting back to what we were talking about, I was chewing on what you said about the crew last time. They come on so cynical, but if anything weird ever threatened Garcia, they'd probably attempt something silly and heroic, y'know, just because they'd have to."

"Yeah," Taylor had agreed. "And you know how embarrassed he'd be?"

Which is why this concert is more than entertainment, why the star syndrome doesn't exactly apply here, why the Grateful Dead isn't really a rock band and is only tangentially part of the American music industry. Garcia is indeed charismatic, but not the least remarkable of his contributions to the group is his general refusal to run it. "You can call me boss," he once said, chuckling, "just don't ask me to make any decisions." That is why the fans, the colorful, exuberant Dead Heads gathered outside, are members of a cult that at its best serves Dionysus rather than individual performers, and why the police, veterans of these parking lot festivals, understand the benign nature of their guests and are smiling at them.

A few days earlier the gig had been at a music theater out in the country. The endless sleepy commute, a forty-five-minute spin on an unfamiliar road from a generic RamadaMarriottSheraton, through endless geometrically identical cornfields, to a resort nowhere in particular, induced a feeling of absolute random disassociation. Conversation was desperately required, and centered on Lesh's newly purchased book about the anthropic principle, which posited the universe as a mind.

Obeying an unspoken protocol, Scrib had left the front seats to the band and retreated to the back of the van—limousines are thought too conspicuous—to consider the band's personalities in archetypal terms. Garcia is a powerful bohemian visionary, a shaman of a sort, and his personal style has largely defined the band's social and musical structure. Yet his role is nothing like that suggested by the automatic attention paid to a virtuoso rock guitarist or the guru figure the media have fabricated in his name. The band's candidate for Handsome Rock Star is Weir, the eternal Younger Brother. But on a day-to-day basis, the psychic pivot to the Dead is Phil Lesh, the most aggressive purist, the anti-philistine Artist. It is he who most often and most loudly demands that they dance as closely as possible to the edge of the nearest available precipice. Intellectual, kinetic, intense, he was once nicknamed Reddy Kilowatt in recognition of his high mental and physical velocity. Twenty years later his mind is still exceedingly agile, although on this day he was content to let Garcia dominate the rap.

"Why would the universe go through the trouble of evolving consciousness?" inquired Garcia. "If it wanted life that would succeed, just to create the most effective living thing, it could have stopped at bacteria. Or it could have stopped at vertebrates or sharks. But consciousness goes a quantum step further than just life. It might be that consciousness is the whole reason there is a universe. There might not be a universe apart from consciousness." Garcia lit another Pall Mall. "And who knows what it's like elsewhere in the universe? Local realities change enough, locally, that those Hindu guys can walk through huge, blazing fires and not get burned. It's got to be that consciousness modulates reality. Besides, the truth can't only be here, or you could stare at your toes and figure it all out."

"Yeah, but that's just solipsism, man, useless," interjected Lesh. "All you do is climb up your own verbal asshole."

"The real black hole," snickered Kreutzmann as Scrib reached for his pen while trying to imagine the members of Led Zeppelin in a rapt discussion of teleology and human consciousness.

Today the vans arrive at the usual 6 P.M. as Taylor finishes with the steward and sends Scrib to the crew bus to inform Parish that the band is onstage. Blond and sophisticated, tour manager Jon McIntire emerges from the lead van and heads for the stage. Wise to his rhythm guitarist's fondness for preshow tinkering, he tells Taylor, "Let's get the doors open. Weir might want to *do* something." Not all band arrivals have been so orderly. Once in the early 1970s, Weir and Ram Rod's wife, Frances, equipped with a guitar, identification, and sincerity, were unable to persuade a guard at one venue of their legitimacy. Ever polite, Weir waited until the gentleman no longer stood in front of the gate, then drove his rented car through it to the backstage area. Taylor turns to the promoter's security chief, whose shaven head and earring suggest a fierceness that is fortunately never displayed, and signals for the doors to be opened.

By 7 P.M. the crew members have taken their places onstage as most of the musicians digest dinner in a common dressing room. The drummers drill away on rubber practice pads and Weir works at his own exercise/étude, "Sage and Spirit." Garcia warms up in the opposite corner, his small, grubby hands bulging with muscle as they run endless scales up and down his custom Irwin guitar. Lesh sits onstage talking with his wife, Jill. A few minutes before showtime, a security guard shepherds Dan Healy and Candace Brightman, directors of sound and lights respectively, to their enclosure out in the audience. The anticipatory roar goes up several decibels as the crowd spots sound engineer Harry Popick taking his position at the onstage monitor soundboard.

McIntire finds his various charges and announces, "Time, guys." Weir has still not traversed the étude to his satisfaction, and calms his anxiety with a shot of brandy. Mydland gulps glycerin to coat his vocal cords and gets the usual reaction; the final backstage signal of an oncoming Dead concert is the sound of retching. Straggling out more or less in line, the musicians drift onto the stage.

Taylor leans over and murmurs into his headset, "House lights."

Children of the
American Decades

(1940–1960)

ut on the edge of the Western world, the Golden Gate channel cuts through the coastal range to link the Pacific Ocean and a bay, creating a haven called San Francisco. In 1492, the greater region was the fertile home to the most populous place in what would become the United States. When it was colonized and named for St. Francis of Assisi in 1776, some ineffable but authentic connection linked the name source to the spirit of the land and kept it a place that wasn't quite like the rest of the continent. The gold rush that began in 1848 filled it with marginalized seekers from the rest of the United States and the world, and ever after, it was a sanctuary for the odd and eccentric. As Robinson Jeffers put it, "For our country here at the west of things / Is pregnant of dreams."

Near the end of World War I, it welcomed Manuel Garcia, an electrician from La Coruña, Spain, who bought a home in the outer Mission District and settled there with his wife and four children. In 1935 his second son—baptized Jose, but commonly called Joe—a swing-band leader and reedman, married for the second time, to Ruth Marie "Bobbie" Clifford, a nurse. Their first child, Clifford ("Tiff"), was born in 1937, and their second and last child was born on August 1, 1942, at Children's

Hospital in the city. They named him Jerome John Garcia, after Jerome Kern, Bobbie's favorite composer. From all accounts, Joe and Bobbie were both easygoing and benevolent, and it was a happy home. By now, Joe had leased a building on the corner of 1st and Harrison Streets near the waterfront, with a tavern, Joe Garcia's, downstairs and rooms for rent above, and they were financially comfortable. Their house on Amazon Street was filled with music, as Joe kept up with his clarinet and Bobbie played the piano. At the age of four or five, Jerry dug into a box in the attic of his maternal grandparents' country place and discovered a windup Victrola phonograph, some steel needles, and the first recorded music he would be able to recall, a handful of dusty, one-sided old records of folk songs like "Sweet Betsy from Pike." No one showed him how, but he played them over and over, "a compulsion almost," as he later put it.

It was a miserable irony that the Garcia family was irremediably shattered while on vacation. In the summer of 1947, they were enjoying themselves near Arcata, in Northern California. Joe went fishing, and drowned. Jerry later claimed to have witnessed his father's death, though it seems more likely that this was a memory formed from repeated tellings. A bit paradoxically, he also recalled being unable to listen to stories about his father until he was ten or eleven. In any event, their wounds were grievous.

In the absence of his father, Jerry naturally depended on his mother for support. But Bobbie had never been a particularly domestic woman. Artistic and a student of opera, she was also a follower of Velikovsky, astrology, and palm reading. More pressingly, she had a living to earn, and as she came to spend the bulk of her time down at Joe Garcia's at 1st and Harrison, the care of her children fell more and more to her parents, Tillie and Bill Clifford, "Nan" and "Pop." Jerry in particular felt deprived and deserted, especially when he and Tiff moved in with Nan and Pop at 87 Harrington Street, in the Excelsior neighborhood of the outer Mission District, while Bobbie lived in a cottage across the street. In later years he would relate a specific traumatic memory of being left behind on the street one day by his mother, of frantically searching for her until he was finally found by his grandmother. He was bereft, and he would always carry a feeling that he was not loved or cared for, that he was not worthy. These scars would never fade.

Jerry's relationship with his mother would sour further when Bobbie, as Tiff put it, "started getting married a lot." There was a brief marriage to one Ben Brown in 1949, seemingly because Ben was a construction foreman whose labors Bobbie employed to improve her cottage. The extended

Garcia family did not approve of the marriage, and any support they might have given the boys fell away. Years later, as a teenager, Jerry even made nasty remarks about his mother's morals. Fair or not, the damage was done. His self-esteem and capacity for trust in women had been permanently damaged.

A few months before his father's death, Jerry suffered another loss. He and Tiff were at Nan and Pop's country house in the Santa Cruz mountains south of San Francisco. Tiff was chopping wood, and Jerry was being his little helper when his right hand got in the way of the descending ax. His enduring memory was of a buzzing sound he would come to associate with shock, then jumping around not looking at his wound, then a long drive to the doctor's, the world vibrating in his ears. It was only when the last bandage fell off in the bathtub one night that he discovered to his surprise that he had lost the top two joints of his middle finger.

Harrington Street was only a block long, connecting Mission Street at one end and a major thoroughfare, Alemany Boulevard, at the other. In the 1940s, the center of the block was not yet developed, and there was a small open field, with a barn, trees, and an informal playground. Mission Street was lined with stores, including a hobby and model train shop. It was an Italian and Irish working-class neighborhood, with the Jewish Home for the Aged just a block or two down Mission. Despite their Latin last name and Tillie's own Swedish heritage, the Garcia boys thought of their ethnicity as deriving largely from Pop and saw themselves as Mission (District) Irish, a standard San Francisco ethnic classification. Around the corner on Alemany was Corpus Christi Church, which they attended regularly. The Church's theater of hell served as usual to tinge Jerry's later sexuality with guilt, but even more important, he realized later, it gave him a sense of the mysterious spiritual world beyond the material one.

Life with Nan and Pop had its rewards. For Tiff, who at ten was supposed to be the man of the family (at least as this applied to his mother and brother), there was a good role model in Pop, a taciturn man who liked his beer, the fights, and puttering with a wide array of hobbies. His independent laundry delivery business brought him home early, in time to keep an eye on the boys. Jerry, by contrast, thought of Pop as a "bump on a log," and instead turned to Nan, whom he resembled in charm and gregariousness. Tillie Clifford was a fascinating and formidable woman. A founder and the secretary/treasurer of the local Laundry Workers' Union, she was an expert politician who always dressed well and seemingly knew everyone in San Francisco. She was not to be trifled with. In 1916, she had filed charges against her husband for assault. He was contrite, and the judge had taken his side. "You will run for office again," she warned the court. "I shall see to it that you don't get some votes." Her threat did not seem to have any effect, but she remained unabashed. Jerry would recall her as a beautiful woman with a spiritual quality, an authentic socialist who was either "a fabulous liar or she just genuinely loved everybody." She was also a second-generation San Franciscan, independent of conventional mores as she openly attended out-of-town union meetings with her extramarital boyfriend.

Periodically bedridden by asthma attacks as a young boy, Jerry passed his time reading and watching television. Their nearly first-on-the-block set—the people with the first one had a child with polio, so no one could visit and watch it—confirmed him as a child of the fifties. He also loved drawing, for which he showed an early talent. Perhaps it was true, as his palm-reading mother had told him, that he had "the hands to be an artist." In the third grade he had the good fortune to have a young bohemian teacher, Miss Simon, who encouraged him to be involved in every possible art project. Soon he felt not only a blossoming identity as an artist, but also a general sense of being different from most other people. His favorite reading became the comics which Tiff swiped on Mission Street, especially E.C. ("Entertaining Comics") comic books, like the classic *Tales From the Crypt*. Though the gory Old Testament tales of retribution revolted parents across the nation, their German expressionistic silent-movie graphic style introduced young Jerry unconsciously to fundamental lessons in art and form.

Whatever needs the horror genre satisfied for Jerry, and it would appeal to him all his life, he soon found a new medium in which to explore them. He went to the Granada Theater at Ocean and Mission to see *Abbott and Costello Meet Frankenstein*, and both horror movies and film in general permanently captured his attention. On his first visit, he was so frightened that he couldn't look at the screen, and instead found the pattern of the fabric on the back of the seats engraved in his memory. Striving to master his fear with knowledge, he began to study the classic film monsters—Frankenstein's, Dracula, and the Wolf Man. When his reading graduated to novels, his first selection was Mary Shelley's *Frankenstein*. Horror also influenced his artwork, and his favorite subject for years was Boris Karloff in the Jack Pearce Frankenstein's monster makeup. It was his first taste of the weird, and he loved it. Always.

———

In 1953 Bobbie remarried, the boys moved back in with her, and for Jerry, life went straight to hell. Wally Matusiewicz was a stocky blond sailor, a hardworking man who expected his stepsons to work alongside him on home projects; but physical labor was never going to be Jerry's idea of a good time. His relationship with Wally went swiftly downhill, for a variety of deeply emotional reasons. In a confused, never-understood way, Jerry had never entirely forgiven his mother for the death of his father, nor for remarrying. Now hormones swept over him in the usual tidal wave, crashing into the retaining wall of his Roman Catholicism and creating a jumbled mess. As an adult he would concede that sex and women were never his primary concern, "except for when it really runs you around crazy, when you're around fourteen or so." Add to puberty his alienation from his mother and you had a recipe for torment. Twenty years later he would read an underground comic book called *Binky Brown Meets the Holy Virgin Mary* and grasp profoundly that it described exactly the hell of his early teens, as captured in the rays of light, lust, guilt, that emanated from Binky's crotch, up toward the Virgin, down to hell, and out toward the entire world. Coping with sexuality is tough; dealing with the guilt of the Roman Catholic Church regarding sex is tougher; doing both when confused by an absent father and a mother perceived as disloyal—this for Jerry was impossible. He would love and be loved, but he would stay painfully confused about himself and women for all his days.

That year Union Oil bought the property on which Joe Garcia's was located, and while Bobbie waited for the company to build her a new bar on the opposite corner, she decided to move her family twenty-five miles south of the city to Menlo Park. The Garcias were part of a social tidal wave. In the aftermath of World War II, millions of veterans had used the G.I. Bill to move from working-class to middle-class lives, and from renting city apartments to owning suburban homes. Their prosperity was one consequence of the permanent war economy that the Cold War demanded. Another result was suburban conformity. Jerry would first become conscious of racism and anti-Semitism in Menlo Park, and he didn't like them. His new friends were determinedly diverse, ranging from a classmate and early sweetheart, Mary Brydges, to Will Oda, the son of a Nisei gardener at Stanford, to his best friend, Laird Grant, a working-class borderline hoodlum. One of the other ways that he countered the suburban blahs was with music. As the predominant culture of the fifties grew ever more bland, the discerning ear could find escape in the riches of African American music.

In the Bay Area, that meant the rhythm and blues station KWBR, to which Tiff introduced him. An obscure street-corner tune by the Crows called "Gee" set him to listening to the cream of American popular music, and Ray Charles, John Lee Hooker, Jimmy Reed, B.B. King, and Muddy Waters kept him company all day and half the night long. Initially a solo acoustic form from the Mississippi Delta, the blues evolved through boogie-woogie piano and Kansas City big-band vocal shouting to Chicago, where Muddy Waters found acoustic guitar inaudible in forties clubs. His transition to electric guitar defined a new urban blues, which evolved yet again into the R&B of the late forties and the fifties. Each mode contained a high realism that knew life as a solitary confinement sometimes comforted by sexuality or even love but inevitably succeeded by a death sentence. In all of American popular music, only the blues spoke truthfully of love and death. Enthralled, Jerry absorbed not only chords and rhythms but a certain vision. It was not the psychopathology of Norman Mailer's "White Negro" that he acquired, but hipness, the authentic wisdom eternally found at the edges and bottom of the social pyramid.

In 1955, rock and roll—rhythm and blues with a backbeat—emerged to enliven a torpid America. First came Bill Haley and the Comets' "Rock Around the Clock," a no. 1 hit a year after its release when it served as the theme song of a classic film of youthful rebellion, *Blackboard Jungle.* The producers of the film displayed their understanding of the music's importance and violated film custom by mixing the song at high volume. The audience grasped that decision perfectly. The resistance to adult authority depicted in the film and in the contemporary career of James Dean attracted Jerry, though not the song itself. Most of the early rock tunes were the product of small regional labels, like Little Richard Penniman's bizarre, manic "Tutti Frutti" on Specialty. Inevitably, the larger companies moved to co-opt the rock and roll fad, releasing Pat Boone's acceptably bland cover version of "Tutti Frutti" among many other covers to even greater commercial success. It was a critical moment for Jerry, who swiftly came to understand that there was frequently an authentic black version, and then "there's the lame white version." Two unquestionably genuine tunes from Chicago's small Chess Records caught his ear. Bo Diddley's self-named tune established the fundamental shave-and-a-haircut beat, and Chuck Berry's "Maybellene" melded country guitar riffs with the backbeat and melody of rhythm and blues and defined rock's fundamental structure and attitude. To Jerry it seemed like a cowboy song, "only nastier," and to a thirteen-year-old with surging hormones, nasty was very, very good. For the first time in history, large masses of young white Americans were listening and dancing to black musicians.

Another aspect of black American life stirred at this time, the precise connections to the music uncertain but impossible to dismiss. In December 1955, a young Birmingham, Alabama, minister named Martin Luther King Jr. united his passionate nonviolent moral leadership with the organizational genius of the city's local civil rights leader and the communications system of television to sustain an antisegregation bus boycott. It would trigger the greatest American social movement since the organization of labor. Not least of the civil rights movement's effects would be to give the future politics of American protest a spiritual rather than an ideological base. And the spirit was in the songs.

Jerry had been a bright but fairly indifferent student to this point, excelling in art and the occasional subject that took his interest, but an underachieving "wise guy" the rest of the time. He seemed to his friend Mary Brydges to be pretty much "in his own world," doodling skulls and crossbones and monsters, always funny and fun, sarcastic but not cruel, somehow "more worldly, faster" than the rest of the kids, but also a little lonelier. Then in the fall of 1955 he entered the Fast Learner Program in the eighth grade at Menlo Oaks school. His new teacher, Dwight Johnson, an iconoclastic bohemian who was regularly in trouble with the school administration, was the perfect inspiration for students like Jerry. When Mr. Johnson roared up to school on his Vincent Black Shadow motorcycle or MG TC, he instantly drew his students' attention, and when he threw open the class to discussion and introduced them to D. H. Lawrence and George Orwell, Jerry delightedly followed him into the intellectual world. Johnson noticed Jerry's facility as an artist, and soon the boy was absorbed in murals, the sets for school plays, and the school newspaper. He did not exactly become a well-behaved Good Student, however, and continued with one of his favorite games, mock switchblade duels in the school corridor with his buddy Laird Grant. When he dug in his heels over retaking certain tests toward the end of the year, he was required to repeat the eighth grade. Finally, in June 1957 he graduated from Menlo Oaks and moved back to San Francisco, where he lived some of the time with Nan and Pop and some of the time with his mother and stepfather at their new apartment above the new bar at 1st and Harrison.

Bobbie's fifteenth-birthday present to him that summer would turn out to be quite special, although at first it was a giant disappointment. She'd purchased a lovely Neapolitan accordion for him from one of the sailors at the bar, but after plenty of adolescent moans and whines, she agreed to swap it for the Danelectro guitar he'd spotted in a pawnshop window at the corner of 3rd and Folsom, a few blocks from the bar. He'd had years of piano lessons before the move to Menlo Park, but his personality resisted formal teaching, and he'd lost interest. Now music consumed him. Whatever his other deficiencies were, Jerry's stepfather happened to have mandolins and other stringed instruments around the house, even electrical instruments, amplifiers, and a rare (for that time) tape recorder. Mr. Matusiewicz tuned the Danelectro to some odd open tuning, or perhaps it merely became that in Jerry's hands. Working only with his ear and the Chuck Berry tunes on the bar jukebox, Garcia began the practice that would turn out to be the focus of his life.

His cousin Danny saw him with the guitar and followed suit, going to the same pawnshop for his own. Though Danny, Joe's brother Manuel's son, had been part of Jerry and Tiff's life from their earliest days, music proved an especially unifying common bond in their mid-teens. Jerry's father had not been the only musical Garcia. Their grandfather "Papuella" (Joe's father) had insisted that his sons and grandsons learn to play an instrument and sing, and though, as Danny recalled it, "it wasn't an option," the boys liked music anyway. Jerry, Tiff, and Danny would spend a good part of their teens singing on street corners, learning how to harmonize. Now Danny, who knew some music theory, taught Jerry the conventional tunings for rock, and he found them "a revelation . . . the key to heaven." He began to gobble up the styles of Eddie Cochran, Jimmy Reed, Buddy Holly, Bo Diddley, and, as always, Chuck Berry.

The summer of 1957 was a memorable one. In addition to the guitar, Jerry discovered cigarettes, a lifelong habit, and marijuana, two joints shared with a friend that sent them laughing and skipping down the street. Tiff had graduated from high school in 1956 and enlisted in the Marine Corps, so Jerry was more on his own now, and his world began to expand. He and Danny would take the 14 Mission bus downtown to see movies, go shopping at the Emporium, sometimes with a "five-finger discount" (shoplifting), or out to the Cliff House, a restaurant and sightseeing complex that overlooked the ocean, and the Playland amusement park down the hill. Jerry spent the ninth grade at Denman Junior High School in the outer Mission, and then in the fall of 1958 began tenth grade across the street at Balboa High School. Balboa was frequently a rough place, filled with Barts ("Black Bart" Italians with "greaser" haircuts) and Shoes (Pat Boone white-shoe-wearing prep types). Later, Garcia would tell more than a few tall tales about his career as a street fighter, but his family and friends of the era didn't recall it that way.

His more natural environment was at Joe Garcia's, where he worked "pearl diving" (washing) dishes and "decorating" (stocking) the joint with beer. Music remained his passion, and he often worked with a transistor radio earplug wedged firmly in his ear. Just as often he'd take a break and play along to the jukebox with his guitar. Although the old-fashioned original Joe Garcia's had been replaced by a modern fifties circular bar with mirrored columns for glasses, slick Naugahyde booths, and chrome fixtures, it remained a lively place, its clientele a mixture of longshoremen and sailors from the Sailors Union of the Pacific on one corner, and Union Oil executives from the other corner. It was a verbal ambience, one that welcomed Joe Garcia's son as an equal. He was gregarious by nature, but this aspect of his personality was greatly encouraged by example. "I've always wanted to be able to turn on people," he said later, "and also I've always taken it for granted that if I like something, that other people will like it, too . . . the bar world established that kind of feeling; it engulfed me like a little community." He joined the conversational mix with pleasure, listening to tales of the 1934 general strike, Harry Bridges, and other local legends. The founder of the Longshoremen's Union, Bridges was an Australian and former Communist Party member who was a hero in San Francisco, but only there, and only in San Francisco were the latest rebels, the members of the Beat Generation, a source of civic pride.

In fact, San Francisco had an institution that served as a direct channel into this alternative world, the California School of Fine Arts (later the San Francisco Art Institute). It was the only school Garcia would ever be proud of attending. On Saturdays the school had an extension program, Pre-College Art, taught by its regular faculty. Garcia's teacher was the well-known funk (assemblage) artist Wally Hedrick, who would serve Jerry as a model not only as a painter but as an expositor of a way of life. He taught the boy, remembered Garcia, that "art is not only something you do, but something you are as well." A working-class military veteran who'd once, on the strength of his beard, gotten a job sitting in the front window of the Beat North Beach bar Vesuvio's, Hedrick had found his first conventional job as a teacher at the School of Fine Arts. It was he who had asked poet Michael McClure to organize the 1955 Six Gallery reading that introduced Allen Ginsberg's "Howl" to the world. Struck by Garcia's native intelligence and sense of hipness, Hedrick told Jerry that he and his friends were the real Beat Generation, and sent them down the hill to North Beach and its coffeehouses to, as Garcia said later, "pick up my basic beatnik chops," listening to Lawrence Ferlinghetti read at the Coexistence Bagel Shop, along with other poets at other clubs.

And on the way, Hedrick sent Garcia over to City Lights Bookstore to pick up Jack Kerouac's *On the Road,* a book that changed his life forever. Kerouac's hymn to the world as an explorational odyssey, an adventure outside conventional boundaries, would serve as a blueprint for the rest of Garcia's life. And it plugged him consciously into a continuous line of alternative American culture going back to Thoreau and Walt Whitman and up through the current eminence of Bay Area bohemia, Kenneth Rexroth, the master of ceremonies of that seminal Six Gallery reading. As McClure, one of the other Six readers, put it, Rexroth promoted "serious Buddhism, Eskimo poetry, radical social movements, physics, and even esoteric Christianity. He was a mountain climber, a hiker, and he knew how to fix his own car." It was a very different vision of life and culture than one might find in the heavily intellectualized New York City of the same period.

As one of Garcia's classmates in Pre-College Art, Ann Besig, would later recognize, he was more mature and "comfortable" in the bohemian environment than most of the other students. Hedrick described Garcia's work as "figurative but with freewheeling brushwork . . . strongly painted, heavily textured . . . not talented, but [he had] understanding." To Laird Grant, Jerry's best painting was of a man sitting destitute in the gutter, a jug in his hand. Aside from introducing the exalted mysteries of art, the school was a direct connection to fun, like the costume party they attended, Jerry as a vampire and Laird as a monster. They arrived in time to see a young woman, nude under a fur coat, step out of a limo to enter the gathering. The raisin in her navel identified her as a cookie.

Despite the stimulation of art school, Garcia continued to get into trouble. Many of his friends from before Menlo Park were now hoodlums, and though he probably wasn't all that involved in violence or crime, he was certainly diverging from the straight and narrow. More often than not, his journey to Balboa High School concluded instead downtown at the movie theaters on Market Street, where he stoked his lifelong fascination with film. Formal education became increasingly irrelevant, and his rare appearances at Balboa were chiefly punctuated by getting caught— for smoking in the boys' room, minor fights, or cutting classes, all the usual dreary detritus of high school life. In the summer of 1959, Bobbie Garcia made a last-ditch effort to restore her son to conventional behavior and moved the family to Cazadero, a tiny town in the redwoods eighty miles north of San Francisco. It was futile, of course. Garcia's problems were centered on his boredom with regimented life, and adding a lengthy commute to his day at Sebastopol's Analy High School did not help.

However, Analy did have a band called the Chords, and Jerry soon joined it. Their business card read "featuring the Golden Saxes," and their material was largely 1940s big-band tunes, including "Misty" and songs by Billy Vaughn. It was, Garcia would say, "kind of easy-listening stuff. Businessman's bounce, high school version." They played at youth canteens, high school dances, and once at a Sea Scouts graduation ceremony. With only limited experience at playing with others, Garcia was an extremely primitive musician, so crude that his bandleader had to shift the capo on his guitar so that he could transpose keys. Jerry's attitude didn't always help, either. He played a great deal with his cousin Danny at this time, and Danny was a sober, steadying influence who wanted to rehearse regularly and learn chords and structure. But Jerry's invariable response was "Let's just play, man." Years later Garcia would, inevitably, regret his lack of formal knowledge and discipline. But even in 1959 he showed an ability to play convincing rock and roll on the Chords' occasional contemporary tunes. The band even won a contest and got to record a song, Bill Doggett's "Raunchy."

Garcia's facility with rock was ironic, because the form was at a low ebb, with each of its creators distracted by circumstances: Elvis Presley was in the army, Chuck Berry was on his way to jail for a Mann Act violation, and Little Richard had entered the ministry. The predominant institution in pop music at the time was Don Kirshner and Al Nevins's Aldon Music, which focused on the songwriting of Barry Mann and Cynthia Weill, Gerry Goffin and Carole King. Highly professional New York City production-oriented pop had replaced the original performer-created rock.

Early in 1960, Jerry got into his final bit of trouble, as he would recall it, by stealing his mother's car. In the tradition of the era, his options were simple—jail or the army. Though Tiff begged Jerry to delay his enlistment until he could get home from the marines and talk his younger brother out of it, Jerry was in no mood to wait; he decided to join the army and see the world. He got about 150 miles away from San Francisco, to Fort Ord, near Monterey, where he endured basic training. Somehow, it was not terribly surprising that his squad leader turned out to be a jail veteran who happened to be able to fingerpick acoustic guitar. Jerry had first heard acoustic music from Jimmy Reed on the radio, and then again when Wally Hedrick played Big Bill Broonzy during class, and now he started to listen to Joan Baez's incredibly beautiful voice, which sent him into old-time southern white music. It was a move in line with hip taste.

Folk music had entered the American mainstream a year before in San Francisco, at a club called the Purple Onion, with a group of good-looking college boys in striped shirts called the Kingston Trio. With five no. 1 albums and hits like "Tom Dooley" and "Scotch and Soda," they knocked off traditional tunes with smooth harmonies and good humor, and started a rage. Rock had been professionalized and made boring, whereas folk was direct and authentic, seemingly the genuine product of a community rather than a manufactured commodity. It was part of a continuum that included the New Deal, Woody Guthrie, and the ongoing civil rights movement, and it swept the country.

It was easy for Garcia to observe the San Francisco folk scene, since it had moved to North Beach's hungry i, the hippest club in America, and after basic training at Fort Ord he'd landed in the choicest duty in the entire United States Army, the Presidio of San Francisco. He might just as well have been back hustling on Mission Street, because the army was just a party. In between working at menial tasks, he would sit up all night with the armorer filing the serial numbers off .45 automatics in order to sell them. Surrounded by old army characters now safely ensconced in the heavenly confines of the Presidio, he correctly saw his military career as a joke best expressed by the old saw "the incompetent leading the unwilling to do the unnecessary in an unbelievable amount of time." His inglorious military career revealed an utter lack of talent for either mindless obedience or artful dodging, and it was bound not to last. His friend the squad leader had taken up with the sister of one of Garcia's former girlfriends, and late in 1960 he was holed up in a Palo Alto hotel threatening suicide as well as trying to sell Garcia a Fender Jazzmaster guitar he'd stolen somewhere. Garcia spent more time sitting up with his friend than making it back to the Presidio in time for roll call, and he began to collect multiple counts of AWOL (absent without official leave).

As his life slid further and further out of control, music became the only stabilizing force available to him. The one thing that he could hold on to was the guitar, which he played constantly. But his music was handicapped, and not by the missing portion of the middle finger on his right hand; almost from the first, he'd chosen to use a pick (although he did acknowledge later that with a full hand he'd have played piano or classical guitar). No, his limit as a musician at that time was his lack of a partner. Very early on, he intuitively realized that he needed someone else to play with, a companion, a musical cohort. Over the years he would have many collaborators, but in terms of playing music, as apart from composing it, there would be one supreme pal, and he hadn't met him just yet.

Phil Lesh found his future one Sunday in 1944 at the age of four, when his grandmother discovered him intently listening from the next room to the New York Philharmonic's broadcast. Having already taught him to read, she was happy to expose her grandson to more. The next week she inquired, "Philip, would you like to come and listen to the nice music on the radio?" Bruno Walter conducted Brahms's First Symphony, and from then on, Lesh's life had focus. His father, Frank, was an office equipment repairman, and their lives were generally comfortably middle-class, except for a rather rarefied taste in music. From the third grade on, Phil took violin lessons, and when his braces were removed at fourteen, he took up the trumpet. Except for a fascination with racing cars, music occupied most of his life. He was not athletic, and his intelligence had set him apart from his peers. In the second grade, word had gotten out at a PTA meeting that Phil Lesh had the highest I.Q. in school, and more than a few of his classmates were asked why they couldn't be as smart as he was. He would never hear the end of it, and it made for an extremely difficult adolescence. The incident turned him inward, and the combination of brilliance and isolation made him focus powerfully on his own values, in the tradition of an elite artist.

His parents, Frank and Barbara, supported the musical ambitions of their only child, and in the middle of his junior year in high school the family moved so that he could transfer from El Cerrito High School to Berkeley High School, where the music program was infinitely better. He seized the opportunity, joining the band, the orchestra, the dance band, and the Pro Musica. He also acquired an affectionate surrogate musical father in Bob Hanson, the conductor of the distinguished Golden Gate Park Bandshell unit. Eventually, Lesh would play second trumpet for Hanson in the Oakland Symphony and earn the first chair in Hanson's Young People's Symphony Orchestra. Hanson would remember a thin, restless boy with a marvelous ear who lacked wind, but not persistence. By graduation in June 1957, Lesh's ability to transpose keys on sight would earn him the first chair at a high-quality college-sponsored music camp and send him that fall to San Francisco State University. Less developed as a personality than as a musician, he soon dropped out of State and returned home.

As demanding and critical of the world as he was of himself, Phil was troubled by what he perceived as the raw deal that life had given his father, who had worked brutally hard and had little to show for it. At this juncture Lesh was certain that whatever he did with his future, he didn't want to be stuck in his father's trap. Commitment to anything conventional was to be avoided, and he fully identified with the artistic tradition.

A year later, in September 1958, he resumed his studies, this time at the College of San Mateo (CSM), on the peninsula twenty miles south of San Francisco. An eccentric, intellectual loner, Lesh found his first good friend in a local young man named Mike Lamb, the son of a Stanford administration staff member who had become acquainted with the local cognoscenti. Lamb groomed him a bit socially, and then a succession of intellectual encounters further opened Lesh's life. First, Morse Peckham's *Beyond the Tragic Vision* defined the philosophical underpinnings to his inner certainty that only the arts could be free of the fraud that was society: "Absorbed in the work of art, we can for a moment experience life as pure value . . . Aesthetic contemplation is our only innocence." Then Peckham made these words visible by introducing him to the pre-impressionist English painter J. M. W. Turner, whose hellish, prophetic *Rain Steam and Speed* depicted light as a shining thing in itself, the music of the spheres put down on canvas. When Lesh's student job turned out to be evaluating new records at the library, his intellectual menu was complete. He discovered the experimental *Music Quarterly,* and learned that music could be created, stored on tape, and fully controlled by the author. Beethoven and Charles Ives were his heroes. He wanted to be a Komposer.

Meantime, he was caught up in the highly competitive world of the CSM music department. The school's contest-winning jazz band, a powerhouse group that played the cool West Coast jazz exemplified by Stan Kenton's arranger, Bill Holman, featured five trumpets, saxophones, and trombones each, plus four rhythm instruments. In his pursuit of the first trumpet chair, Lesh generally found himself behind William "Buddy" Powers, who would take eight years to graduate from CSM due to his habit of dropping out to work with groups like the Woody Herman and Benny Goodman bands. Still thin and lacking the blasting lung power the genre demanded, Lesh increasingly experimented with composition. Fortunately, the band's rehearsals were wildly open. He would create ten-bar exercises for bizarre orchestrations like the "mother chord," a dissonant blast that included all twelve chromatic tones, or his first chart, in which the bass player had to tune down his instrument for the first line and then retune it for the remainder, while the brass players began in the highest register, and each section of the band was in a different key. He would recall the piece as resembling "blocks of granite sliding together . . . pretty weird for a junior college."

His best exercise title, at least, came from James Joyce's *Finnegans Wake:* "The Sound of a Man Being Habitacularly Fondseed" (i.e., being tapped upon the third eye). Lesh had gone down the coast to Partington Ridge in Big Sur to look for Henry Miller, but the master proved not at home. In a ritualistic way, Phil decided to pay homage to the act Miller described in *Big Sur and the Oranges of Hieronymus Bosch,* and pissed off the ridge. Standing in Miller's metaphorical shoes, he experienced an epiphany, one that he was able to replicate aurally in a four-bar exercise for the largest orchestra he'd ever get to write for. After writing out the parts on tiny exercise pages, he brought it to the band, which, after protesting, "Fuck you, Lesh, we need a magnifying glass on this stuff," fought through it, produced an obscene chord, and received his thanks. He'd been able to hear what he'd written, and that was a singularly fulfilling experience.

His jazz composing career peaked in May 1959, when the annual CSM jazz band "Expressions in Jazz" concert at San Mateo High School featured his lead on the Bill Holman chart of "I Remember April" and "Jeff's Jam," and the band's performance of his own tune "Wail Frail." Shortly before this time he'd encountered a diminutive ex-convict blues poet named Bobby Petersen, who turned him toward poetry and Allen Ginsberg–style illuminated (spiritual) politics, essentially inducting him into the Beat Generation. Petersen was an experienced hipster who wrote poems about Billie Holiday and the "high sad song of spade queens / in pershing square / hipsters of melrose fade / into wallpaper." They became roommates, and their first sharing came when Bobby stole a volume of Henry Miller from City Lights Bookstore, and they went home and read it aloud to each other. Petersen introduced Phil to pot, and to the broad sweep of avant-garde and Beat literature. Allen Ginsberg's "Howl" so consumed Lesh that he began to set it to music. They also studied James Joyce, which gave Phil the title for his last tune at CSM.

In spring 1960, Lesh at least mentally completed his stay at CSM when the band performed his tune "Finnegan's Awake." He had moved up to the first chair by then, but would later admit with his typically brutal self-honesty that he never played as well as Powers, and consequently quit playing the trumpet after his graduation in June. He celebrated his graduation in the tradition of another of those City Lights authors, taking a Kerouacian journey to Calgary in search of work in the oil fields. Though he made it only as far as Spokane before riding the rails back to

Seattle and then taking a bus home, the experience confirmed for him his place outside the conventional American life. He was a part of the Beat Generation, too.

Back at the Presidio in December of that year, Garcia's multiple absences caught up with him. An army psychiatrist decided that his priorities were neurotic, and a superior officer asked him if he'd like to leave the army with a general discharge. "I'd like that just fine, sir." It marked his last attempt to fit in.

Roots

(1961–2/62)

Discharged from the army in January 1961, Garcia moved down to East Palo Alto, the African American side of Palo Alto, where his friend since junior high school, Laird Grant, was staying. Jerry had acquired a 1950 Cadillac with one of his last army paychecks, and the heap made it to Laird's place just before it died, there being no money left for gas. In between couches and garages and other donated beds, the car became Garcia's apartment. Getting by in Palo Alto was easy. The weather was warmer than in foggy San Francisco, and people were kind to a charming minstrel, especially the (female) residents of Stanford's Roble Hall, who could frequently be counted upon to smuggle minstrels into the dining commons. His first new friend was Dave McQueen, a black man who was a neighbor and friend of Laird Grant's, and for a little while they hustled odd jobs together, becoming what Garcia later thought of as "the Laurel and Hardy of East Palo Alto." "Here, take the heavy end." "No, goddamm it! You take it." "No, no, no, no, oh! Lookout for that—" Then McQueen heard Garcia play some blues. McQueen said, "I never heard a white man with . . . soul like you got, man. Come on, I'm going to take you around." Very quickly, Garcia was a comfortable citizen of East Palo Alto, and with its allied party circles, including a bunch of guys who lived on the other side of Palo Alto near the Stanford University campus at a rooming house called the Chateau.

The Chateau sheltered a bizarre collection of young black and white bohemian proto-artists, musicians, and weirdos, and parties there more closely resembled a Fellini film than a campus sock hop. A visit in 1961 typically included being greeted by the nonresident Joe Novakovich, a lunatic vagabond known to wear a hangman's noose for a necktie, who happened to be missing half his fingers and consequently insisted on shaking hands with everyone. Or one might meet John "Page" Browning, who had just left the U.S. Marine Corps equipped with a bullwhip and a double set of fast-draw handguns, or John "the Cool" Winter, whose favorite occupation, when not playing Lord and Master of Chance at the kitchen poker games, was to sit in his black cloth-lined room reading flagellant novels while sipping white port and cherry Kool-Aid. John F. Kennedy had been in office for a month and the rising energy of the new decade could already be felt, but these lads were ahead of their time in many ways, bentness perhaps foremost. The gathering of February 20, 1961, had a particular edge to it, caused oddly enough by a visitor, an actor named Gary who had wandered about the party relating intimations of imminent disaster to all who cared to listen. He'd finally narrowed down his premonitions to four guys who ignored him and climbed into a Studebaker Golden Hawk to scare up some pot or go home, whichever.

In the backseat was Paul Speegle, who three years before at the age of fifteen had quit high school to paint and liked to observe, as he extinguished a candle, "That's the way I'm going to go." Flamboyant wearing a cape and carrying a silver-tipped walking stick, he was a prominent figure in the Palo Alto art scene, working on sets at the Commedia Dell'arte Theater as well as making jewelry and painting. Next to him sat Alan Trist, a tweedy Anglo-American student spending a year's pre-Cambridge holiday with his father, then on sabbatical as a fellow at Stanford's Center for Advanced Studies in the Behavioral Sciences. Just before leaving the Chateau, Speegle and Trist had been acting out what Trist later called "death charades," Paul in his dramatic black cloak fencing with Alan, who was using a fireplace poker for a sword. Their driver was the Chateau house manager, Lee Adams, a smooth-talking black man whose taste for expensive suits and Alfa Romeos had earned him the nickname "Reginald Van Gleason," after a suave television character played by Jackie Gleason. Jerry Garcia rode shotgun next to him.

Lee had a heavy foot on the accelerator and Speegle encouraged it as they drove down toward campus from their start on the first ridge of the coastal range between Palo Alto and the Pacific Ocean. The grade was gentle and the evening pleasant, but as they passed the Menlo Park Veterans Hospital, there was one wicked curve. The Hawk was cruising at around 90 mph when it slammed into the curve and clipped the chatter bars, fishtailed, and took off like a fast but clumsy bird. Whirling end over end, it ejected three of its passengers before landing in the field next to the hospital. Speegle remained in the car and died, the smash reputedly breaking every bone in his body but those of his hands.

Lee's abdomen was laid open and Trist suffered a compression fracture of the back that would cost him some height. Garcia limped away with a broken collarbone and bruises after being blown through the windshield by a crash so violent and furious he would never be able to recall it. All he knew was that he had been seated in a car and next found himself squatting barefoot in a field. A hundred feet away he could see the car, a lump of twisted metal which closely resembled a flattened beer can, sod and dirt drilled into its roof. His shoes were underneath the front seat. No one seemed to be responding to the accident, so he eventually walked over to the hospital and reported it. A little later Gary (no one could ever recall his last name), the psychic party guest, left the Chateau and on his way home had to pull over for an ambulance. He knew immediately whom it was for.

Since Garcia had no veteran's benefits, he spent a long and painful night without medication reading ancient copies of *Life*. Eventually, an ambulance took him to a local clinic, where X rays ascertained nothing was too horribly smashed. Executing a swift exit before someone tried to make him pay, he laid up on a friend's couch for a few days and healed.

Not the least of the reasons Garcia had been attracted to Speegle was that, of his new Palo Alto crowd, Paul had developed his art the most deeply. The excitement of a new comrade and brother was replaced by grief, a slingshot that whirled Garcia into a new seriousness and gave his life a profound sense of urgency and purpose. The delayed gratification of painting lost its meaning, and he gravitated to the real-time immediacy and dynamic interplay possible in making music. This second of the deaths in his life had an enormous impact. Instead of crippling him, as had his father's death, Speegle's death gave him focus. His life after the accident would be a lucky bonus to be cherished. Even though there were no obvious immediate changes in his behavior, the accident marked a fundamental turning point in his life. Garcia would remain an amusing, gregarious bum, living a life as far from the nine-to-five pattern as possible.

He would still be undisciplined, but now he would become obsessive. The guitar would become an extension of his hands, ears, and mind, and for years few would remember him without an instrument in his hands. Implicitly, Paul Speegle would be memorialized with every song.

It was a normal afternoon in the spring of 1961 at St. Michael's Alley, a coffeehouse on University Avenue in Palo Alto. Vern Gates, the owner, was tired of Jerry Garcia, Alan Trist, and their new friend Robert Hunter, their long conversations and infrequent purchases. Named after the location of the first London coffeehouse, the Alley was media bohemia for the early sixties, offering chess, a lovely and aloof young woman singing esoteric folk songs, and instant coffee sold from an elaborate brass pot. The three friends were working on a play.

As Hunter depicted it in a contemporary but never-published *roman à clef*, "The dialogue's beginning to drag a little," Trist said, "so we've decided to write in the eruption of Mount Vesuvius for act twelve." Then he described how amid decadence and enough action for ten normal plays, a small black beetle at center stage would contemplate the eternal truths until, about to utter them, it would be squished by an elephant.

"We expect to run through several beetles in rehearsals," Garcia admitted.

"The essential strategy will be to charge no admission but lock the doors and charge a fee to get out," concluded Alan.

"You all sit here and don't buy anything," griped Gates. "That alone costs me more than you're all worth . . . but you not only scare away potential customers, you *drive away* any that have been paying."

"But look at it this way," Jerry answered. "It's your *business,* but it's *our home.*"

Alan added, "Besides, sir, the colossal scheme of things seems to dictate that we sit here, which, in due course, we do. You stand in danger of jeopardizing the whole structure of destiny by your rash proclamations."

It was just sixteen years after World War II, and leaders from that era like Charles de Gaulle and Chiang Kai-shek remained in power. There was a young new U.S. president, elected among other reasons because he had made a phone call to the wife of that imprisoned Birmingham minister, Martin Luther King Jr. In his inaugural speech that January, John F. Kennedy had spoken of letting the oppressed go free, of assuring the "survival and success of liberty," of exploring the stars, these deeds to be accomplished by a "new generation of Americans." A world that had seemed so glacially predictable in the 1950s was rapidly shifting. Sexual mores would be challenged by the just-introduced birth control pill. Technology would begin to evolve at an exponential pace, beyond the wildest dreams of the average citizen, in ways even the science-fiction visionaries could not imagine. All bets were off, and these young men intuitively knew it.

Early in March Garcia had volunteered as a lighting technician for a production of *Damn Yankees* at Palo Alto's Commedia Dell'arte Theater, and was introduced to a young man named Robert Hunter. A couple of days later, Hunter walked into St. Michael's Alley and came upon Garcia and his friend Alan Trist. The three of them began a conversation that would last their lifetimes. Though it was neither obvious nor immediate, Garcia and Hunter were perfect collaborators, two halves of a creative process.

Born Robert Burns on June 23, 1941, near San Luis Obispo, California, Hunter had grown up a child of the West and of World War II. His father, said Robert, was a "potentially good man ruined by World War II, the navy, his subsequent alcoholism and inability to keep a family or a job." Robert and his mother followed him to various navy assignments up and down the West Coast before he deserted them when Robert was seven. His parents divorced when Robert was nine. For two or three years he lived in a string of foster homes, and the period scarred him deeply. Add to that the dozen different schools of a rootless life, and the result was a boy—and man—who had major problems getting along with people. In his own words, "I had probably more than the usual load of sensitive bullshit as a young man." He found solace in the Roman Catholic Church as a substitute for the family he lacked, but it did not last. On a different social plane, he tried the Boy Scouts, but was kicked out for calling the scoutmaster a son of a bitch.

Books and music would be his salvation. At eight he read Steinbeck's *The Red Pony,* then Howard Pyle's *Robin Hood,* Robert Louis Stevenson, all the usual children's adventure material, and later science fiction. He also went through a period of reading up on Wyatt Earp, marinating himself in the imagery of the West. It was an authentic impulse, since one of his grandfathers was a cowboy who occasionally lassoed him as Robert ran about the yard. What marked Robert as unusual was the novel that he began to write at eleven, a fifty-page handwritten fairy tale. He saw himself as a novelist. Even as an adult, though he would concede that his gifts as a writer were more suited to lyrics than to prose, he would maintain that "I have a novelist's mentality." He began playing music at age nine, when his grandmother gave him a Hawaiian steel guitar. In his teens he picked up cello, violin, and trumpet.

Robert's life improved considerably when his mother remarried when he was eleven. His stepfather, Norman Hunter, whose surname he adopted, was a national sales manager for the McGraw-Hill publishing firm, a stern and severe Scottish disciplinarian who would mark Robert's life heavily with one incident. Mr. Hunter looked at a piece of Robert's writing and saw the phrase "merciless north." "He absolutely turned livid. He took my report and threw it across the room and said, 'I don't ever want to see you attributing human attributes to nature again.'" Hunter laughed. "He busted me on the pathetic fallacy, which is the absolute sine qua non of the poor writer." The short-term result of his improved writing was an F on a book report because the teacher said it was far too good for a seventh grader. Mr. Hunter had edited William Saroyan and could recall seeing T. S. Eliot in the office, and he brought to Robert's life not only stability but a stimulating intellectual atmosphere. When McGraw-Hill considered putting out *Animal Farm* in a children's series, Robert was asked to read it to see if he could comprehend it. With a little help—he was told that Snowball the Pig represented Trotsky—he did fine. Though Mr. Hunter was conservative in his private life, the political atmosphere at home was liberal.

They settled first in San Francisco and then in Palo Alto, where Robert attended Wilbur Junior High and then Cubberly High School for the tenth and eleventh grades. Slowly, he began to fit in, joining the band and orchestra, and the Free Thinkers Club. It was "the first I'd heard of atheism," and it gave him a fascinating new idea to play with. Even better for a young man wanting to be accepted, he discovered that he was a good wrestler and got some peer "credit for being an okay guy at that point, maybe the first time that ever happened to me." Then his world turned upside down again, as he and his family moved to Stamford, Connecticut, and he went from Palo Alto's superb and liberal school system to "conservative Connecticut, where you learned everything by rote and wore suits and ties to school." An outsider once more, he passed a dismally unhappy senior year, ameliorated only by being able to play trumpet in his first band, the Crescents. It was a rather old-fashioned combination of Dixieland and rock and roll, and Hunter's trumpet models were Harry James, Ray Anthony, and Louis Armstrong—he'd yet to hear of Miles Davis.

Graduating in June 1958, he went off to the University of Connecticut, where he joined the Folk Music Club and became a Pete Seeger fan. College did not engage him, and in his second semester he drifted away.

He worked for a while and then decided to return to Palo Alto, largely because of an old flame from high school days. He considered taking the bus, then flew, dreaming of plane crashes all the way to the West Coast. Back in his old hometown, he found and soon left his no-longer-true love, and fell in with a fairly dubious lot of old friends. He felt himself sinking into potentially serious trouble, and escaped by enlisting in the National Guard, where he spent six months training at Fort Ord and then Fort Sill, first in the artillery and then as a Teletype operator. In March 1961, about ten days after Paul Speegle's death, he completed his initial six-month tour of duty and returned to Palo Alto.

In the course of their first conversation at St. Michael's Alley, Garcia and Trist learned that Hunter had a functioning car, and the next morning they were *bangbangbang* on his hotel room door. The '40 Chrysler took them to Berkeley, where they searched for the animated film *Animal Farm*. They never did find the movie, but it mattered not at all. Not long after, the Chrysler came to rest next to Garcia's Cadillac, and for a time that spring, they shared the same vacant lot in East Palo Alto. Hunter had liberated several enormous tins of crushed pineapple from the National Guard, while Garcia's car was stuffed—in the glove compartment, under the seats, everywhere—with plastic forks and spoons. As though from an O. Henry story, but for real, spoon met pineapple and helped the two young men bond. Along with Alan Trist, they became inseparable.

"Like any proper Englishman," Trist later observed, "I was a bit of a renegade." A bohemian literary intellectual who was up on Rimbaud and Dylan Thomas and had not only read the Beat bible, Don Allen's *New American Poetry*, but had visited the legendary Beat Hotel in Paris, Trist was enthusiastic, stylish, and catalytic. Hunter would recall the thrill of absorbing "Howl" for the first time at Alan's, thinking "someone was going to bust in and arrest me for reading it." Enjoying a year off between prep school and Cambridge, Alan had time and a twenty-five-dollar weekly allowance that left him free to pursue whatever he chose, and that meant a daily circuit of Kepler's Bookstore in the daytime, St. Mike's in the evening, and a coffee shop called Stickney's for the late hours.

Kepler's was a wonderful place. Probably the second paperback bookstore in America, it was a faithful reproduction of City Lights, and was founded in the mid-1950s by Roy Kepler, a onetime Fulbright scholar who had been a founder of the left-wing radio station KPFA and national secretary of the War Resister's League. With his close friend and fellow pacifist Ira Sandperl, Roy ran a store that featured unlimited browsing, coffee, and hang-out rights, even for the bedraggled young beatniks like

Garcia, who became, he said, "a fixture . . . a bum, virtually." Instead of ejecting this bum, Roy felt he "could protect him." Kepler was more political than most Beats, but the store welcomed the poets Ferlinghetti, Rexroth, and William Everson for readings. It was a lovely, nurturing institution, closely linked to Ira's other occupation, which was running the Palo Alto Peace Center, home to one of the strangest and most interesting persons in the whole scene, Willy Legate. Garcia and company paid almost no attention to the politics of the Peace Center. Rather, it was, as Hunter said, "Willy's gift to us." "We were like the back door of the Peace Center," said Garcia. "The front door was Joan Baez, Willy, and Ira." Later, Garcia would reflect that "we all learned how to think a certain kind of way from Willy . . . things that come out of sequence—nonlinear, Zen, synchronistic thinking. How to think funny, the cosmic laugh."

Willy Legate was tall and stooped, with an enormous head, a bulging forehead, and thick glasses. Raised in Arkansas, he'd begun reading up on psychic research, the Rosicrucians, the theosophist Annie Besant, and yoga in high school, and while in college in 1959 he learned how to elicit vials of LSD from the manufacturer, Sandoz Pharmaceutical. He never, Hunter wrote around that time,

> said a great deal, or, if he did, it was mainly incomprehensible. He smoked many cigarettes and attempted to write books which were, if anything, as incomprehensible as Willy . . . When asked a question of greater or lesser import, he was prone to answer "Won't tell ya," but he could, on occasion, wax eloquent . . .
>
> "For Christ's sake, must you always be so damned difficult?" [Hunter] asked, becoming irritated.
>
> "Difficult . . ." [Willy] muttered . . . "D-i-f-f-i-c-u-l-t. D as in diphthong, I as in ichthyology, F as in flagellation and again as in fornication, I as in infantile paralysis, C as in communist, U as in Ukrainian Soviet Socialist Republic, L as in lacerations of the head and kidneys, T as in Chinese Religion."
>
> "Chinese Religion?"
>
> "Taoism, obviously."
>
> "Oh; and what is this all supposed to be indicative of, other than an obvious crying need for psychiatric assistance?"
>
> "You'll find it in Zechariah 2.6: 'Ho ho, saith the Lord.' "
>
> . . . if Willy had a bed, everyone had a bed; if Willy had cigarettes, everyone had cigarettes . . . maybe even more of them than Willy took. Willy was the kind of person who somehow made you wonder

just who you were and where you were going, and if maybe he didn't have the right idea after all.

It was a sweet time. Garcia and his circle were too poor to have much of anything, so they cherished what they found. The occasional taste of pot was memorable, leading to fabulous conversations and movable parties. They'd gather up a gang, perhaps a couple of the Chateau's wastrels or some of the people from Norman "Pogo" Fontaine's house in East Palo Alto. Pogo was an artist and a conga player, a bit older than they, and a fine party-giver. They'd load a pickup truck with people and go off to the beach at Half Moon Bay on the other side of the coastal range, or to San Francisco, to the Beat scene in North Beach, or to see the Vatican organist play Bach on the Grace Cathedral organ, or to feed Garcia's cinephilia with strange art-house movies, especially Jan Potocki's *Saragossa Manuscript*. Both Jerry and Robert read the book it was based on before going up to the Cento Cedar cinema to see the film, in which story after story unfolded in a perfectly mythic world. There were potent forerunners of their lives in the film; characters drink magic potions from a skull, as door after door opens to an ever more surreal world.

Their cultural tastes fed a continuous stream of conversation, for all of them had something to say and an exquisite joy in listening. Many years later a friend of Garcia's would call him quite possibly the world's greatest conversationalist, and he surely took immense delight in the art, recognizing, as the friend put it, that "thought is the most ductile source of pleasure, because you can construct all pleasures from it." Hunter and Trist would sit with their notebooks open, each capturing the moment in some prose or poetic fashion, while Garcia sat with a guitar, always a guitar.

There were lots of young women in their scene, including Alan's friend Karen "K.K." Kaplan, an ardent Zionist, and Hunter's love, Christie Bourne, a flamenco dancer with an exotic Brigitte Bardot aura. But soon there would be a woman who, though quite young, would be a peer. Barbara "Brigid" Meier was an extraordinarily beautiful fifteen-year-old high school student when she met Garcia in March on her way to a hike in the Los Trancos Woods with Jerry's friend Sue. When Sue invited him along, Garcia was quick to join them, and on the way home, he sat in the backseat playing a song to Brigid from Joan Baez's first album, "Don't Sing Love Songs, You'll Wake My Mother." Brigid had read Kerouac the year before, and this daughter of left-wing bohemians whose lives closely resembled Zelda and F. Scott Fitzgerald's was totally ready for the Garcia-Hunter-Trist scene. It did not represent "coupling," as she later put it, but "mayhem. Where's the scene tonight?" After school she'd go to Kepler's, and then to who-knows-where. She met one of Garcia's other friends, an older woman named Grace Marie Haddy, who seemed like someone from a Doris Lessing novel. Grace Marie lived alone and was, Brigid recalled, "arch, erudite, practiced free love, smoked pot, drank wine, and had something to say about everything." It was at this point a very literary group, and Garcia was reading all the time: *Finnegans Wake*, poetry from the Beats and Kenneth Patchen, science fiction, and lots of other things that fell off Kepler's shelves. Naturally, Brigid expressed it in a poem.

> *He [Patchen] speaks of angels and snowy hillsides*
> *But I am in rapture of the thing*
> *where we are all in love*
> *with life and each other*
> *Never before and perhaps again*
> *will it be so*
> *with such youthful vigor*
> *and wild eyes*
> *He who creates such magical music [Garcia]*
> *radiates it upon us*
> *The one of poetic words [Trist]*
> *encourages*
> *and overwhelms us with faith*
> *The blind man in the corner [Hunter, in his glasses] sees all*
> *even though he believes not in himself today*
> *and I, follower of each*
> *cry beautiful tears of joy.*

Something was happening, and they knew it. It would be presumptuous, thought Brigid later, to even call it avant-garde. But there was a wave, and they were riding it. It was May 1961, and the image of the moment was "Camelot." Representing youth, style, and virile Hemingwayesque manhood, John Kennedy and his beautiful, elegant wife defined a current that suggested change, though Kennedy's politics were as much a part of Cold War rationalism as his opponent Nixon's. Americanism and technology would see us through, and on May 5 Alan Shepard became the first American in space. Other, even more powerful events were not entirely controlled by the government. On May 4, the civil rights movement, its leadership taken over by youth, sent the Freedom Riders into the deep South to challenge segregation in bus stations. When they arrived in Anniston, Alabama, on May 14, their bus was attacked and later firebombed, and the Freedom Riders were beaten. Attorney General Robert Kennedy intervened, and National Guard troops and helicopters flanked the riders as they proceeded to New Orleans. A change could be felt, and it was captured in a song: "We Shall Overcome."

Faddish dance songs like "The Twist" dominated pop music, and to many, folk music seemed more authentic. A purist approach had catalyzed itself out of the commercial adaptations of the Kingston Trio, first in 1958 in Boston's Club 47 through its house band, the Charles River Valley Boys. Soon after, Palo Altan Joan Baez became a regular at the club, and when she captivated the Newport Folk Festival in 1960, she became an icon. There was always a collegiate link between Cambridge and Berkeley, and shortly after Club 47 opened, Rolf Cahn, a young radical musical heir to Woody Guthrie who was married to the folksinger Barbara Dane, moved West and began the Blind Lemon there. The Lemon joined a couple of other Berkeley institutions that encouraged Bay Area folk music. There was the annual folk music festival, which began on a large scale in 1958. Most important was *The Midnight Special,* a live, late-Friday-night hootenanny on the radical Berkeley radio station KPFA.

Not long after they'd met, Hunter and Garcia were at a party and Robert picked up a guitar, playing about half a song before, Hunter recalled, "Jerry said, 'Hey, give me that,' and grabbed it away from me and kept it. That's how it's been ever since. He could play better than I could." Garcia was clearly the dominant musical partner. The political side of folk—Woody Guthrie, Pete Seeger, Leadbelly—did not move him. From the beginning, Garcia was an apolitical artist, certainly pro–civil rights and intuitively liberal, but at heart concerned only with music and its performance. He and Hunter would sit in the back of Kepler's all day, at first playing what he would later shamefacedly dismiss as "dippy folk songs" like "Michael Row the Boat Ashore" or "Banks of the Ohio" or tunes from early Joan Baez albums. Hunter and Garcia even wrote a song together, "Black Cat."

> *Tell you a story about my old man's cat*
> *A cat whose hide was uncommonly black*
> *Fame and fortune and good luck hath*
> *the man who would cross the black cat's path . . .*
> *My old man's cat went out one night*
> *the moon and stars were shining bright*
> *crossed the path upon his way*
> *of the man who's president today.*

But in those days, folk music was to be taken from the masters, not newly created, and they didn't write any more songs.

Instead, Garcia and Hunter turned to a fundamental source, Harry Smith's magical and peculiar *Anthology of American Folk Music,* on Folkways Records. Early in the 1950s, Smith had tapped into American popular culture from the twenties and thirties to assemble the anthology, selecting songs that had been commercial enough to release on record, exotic but not esoteric. He put eighty-four tunes on six long-playing discs, then wrapped them in alchemical quotations and decoration. In so doing, he gave young folkies like Garcia and Hunter a passageway into the heart of the old, eccentric, gnarly, lovely America. A homosexual dope fiend whose body was stunted and humped, Smith was the ultimate outsider, the ideal person to introduce a new generation to something *truly* authentic. Garcia and Hunter would be indebted to him for life.

Their real scene remained the back room at Kepler's, but on May 5, 1961, Bob and Jerry made a foray into public performance, playing for the Peninsula School's graduation. Willy's girlfriend, Danya, got them the gig, for which they earned five dollars. Later in the month they got another job, this time lined up by some fans who asked them to come to their Stanford dormitory to play. Hunter would remember the sweet sound of the applause, and Garcia's jocular introduction. "The next number is an old Indian work song, translated from the original Slavic by the head of the Hebrew department at Sacred Heart University."

As it happened, Hunter was an extremely limited guitarist. In his own words, Garcia was already "getting serious. I was getting to be more and more impatient with Hunter's guitar playing." The turning point of his life that past February had begun to take solid hold of him. "I was just playing all the time," Garcia recalled. "I just wanted to conquer that stuff. For me, it was little discoveries. I was just hungry to meet people to play. I was out on a limb like a motherfucker." To another friend he remarked, "Man, all I wanna do is live my weird little life my weird little way—all I wanna do is play." Hunter was a writer, already working on a novel about their lives, and wasn't really interested in being a professional musician. Their sessions at Kepler's and their friendship continued, but the duo billed as "Bob and Jerry" did not.

That June, Garcia met someone who could teach him. Marshall Leicester had just finished his sophomore year at Yale, where he'd been part of one of the first collegiate purist folk scenes, disciples of the New Lost City Ramblers (NLCR). Garcia was playing "Everybody Loves Saturday Night" as he strolled into Kepler's, and though Leicester hated the song, he recalled Garcia from their seventh-grade class together at the

Menlo Oaks school and borrowed his guitar to show him some real picking. They soon fell in together, with Garcia staying at Marshall's home
when Mrs. Leicester could be so persuaded. Like many moms, she
thought Jerry was "shiftless." Dazzled with Jerry's verbal facility, Marshall
enjoyed their relationship hugely. Together they followed Harry Smith
and the NLCR's lead and reveled in the manifold joys of the Carter Family songbook. Simple and expressive, A. P. Carter's popular modulations of
the mountain culture—since the material was recorded and then broadcast on radio, it was popular by definition—took folk music into the modern era with "Wabash Cannonball," "Wildwood Flower," and Mother
Maybelle's unique guitar technique (the "Carter Scratch"). Marshall also
lent Jerry a copy of Flatt and Scruggs's "Foggy Mountain Breakdown,"
and he fell in love with it.

As summer came in, Garcia briefly followed Brigid to San Francisco,
where she was living with her Aunt Muriel and modeling at I. Magnin's
department store while attending Jerry's alma mater, the California
School of Fine Arts, on weekends. He stayed for a while with John "the
Cool" Winter at the Cadillac Hotel, in the seedy Tenderloin District, living largely on potatoes and carrots they stole from the produce market on
the Embarcadero. Brigid fed him and gave him cigarette money, and
occasionally Garcia gave lessons to an odd man named Bruce "the
Nerd" Warendorf, who'd acquired an unusual semi-mandolin called a
Waldzither and adopted Jerry as a mentor. Somehow Garcia had acquired
a portable phonograph, and he spent the summer studying Elizabeth
Cotten–style guitar, as well as Flatt and Scruggs.

Before going off to the Cadillac Hotel, Garcia had gotten an offer he
couldn't refuse. As usual, he was sitting in Kepler's and playing—"Railroad Bill," as it happened—when a young man named Rodney Albin approached him. As Rodney's younger brother Peter and his friend David
Nelson watched, peeking between shelves of books, Rodney asked Jerry if
he'd care to perform at his new folk music club, the Boar's Head. They were
pleasantly surprised when Garcia, already possessed of an imposing local
reputation, said, "Sure, man." "Great," said Rodney. "Can you bring anybody else? Tell everybody." It was characteristic of Rodney Albin that the
first Peninsula folk club would be his idea. An eccentric intellectual who
carried a briefcase at the age of nineteen and was notorious for the dried
bat hanging off his bedroom lamp at home, Rodney was definitely a leader.

The Boar's Head was a tiny loft seating perhaps thirty or forty people
above the San Carlos Book Stall, a metaphysical bookstore in a town
halfway up the Peninsula between Palo Alto and San Francisco. There

was a miniature triangular stage, with lighting provided by bulbs masked by cut-up coffee cans. Donations covered the cost of the coffee, and the musicians were unpaid, mostly performing hootenanny style—that is, one song per person or group at a time, with few long sets. A surviving tape captures what people recalled as a fairly typical night. Garcia, with Leicester on autoharp, played "Wildwood Flower," and with both men on guitar and Hunter on mandolin, they covered "Brown's Ferry Blues," and so forth. They were more than competent, though not yet any threat to the Carter Family.

The Boar's Head was small but popular, and Garcia adopted it as his home, bringing along Hunter, Leicester, David McQueen, and Truck Driving Cherie Huddleston to play. A local electric guitarist, Troy Weidenheimer, might play some Ventures or Jimmy Reed. A few nonlocals performed, including a calypso singer named Walt Brown, and the East Bay blues singer Jesse "the Lone Cat" Fuller. It was a highly sociable environment, not least because it had an "annex," the Belmont home of Suze Wood, Leicester's girlfriend. Their enormous house, built at the turn of the century by the magnate William Ralston for his daughter, sheltered a rowdy, individualistic household, and they welcomed the Boar's Head gang to spread blankets in the backyard, drink wine, talk, and play. The Boar's Head would also be significant as the place where Garcia's East Palo Alto friend and future musical partner Blue Ron McKernan first performed in public, as a member of the Second Story Men, a one-night group with Rodney and Peter Albin and their friend Ellen Cavanaugh.

Ron McKernan always had depths. He was a serious child, and his mother, Esther, would recall that when she took him on carnival rides, he would sit stone-faced. She could never tell if he was truly enjoying himself or just pleasing her, because he was always sweet and considerate. "He'd throw me." His father, Phil, played boogie-woogie piano until Ron was born in 1945, and then was a rhythm and blues disc jockey at KRE under the name "Cool Breeze" until the mid-fifties, when he went to work at Stanford as an electronics engineer. After an early fondness for Elvis Presley, Ron followed his father's tastes into Presley's black roots, and the early exposure to African American music became central to his life. He was a serious student of blues lore, well up on the musicians and the labels long before there were any reference books available. But his interest went far deeper than a taste for music. By the time he showed up at the Boar's Head at the age of sixteen, he had left white middle-class life entirely behind. His first nickname was "Rimms," as in the rim of a wheel, like steel. He had a motorcycle chain permanently bolted to his wrist and wore oily jeans, Brandoesque T-shirts, and greasy hair. He was never violent or mean, but the ugly boil on his cheek seemed to at least one friend to have made him a sensitive disfigured artist figure, like the Phantom of the Opera. He was certainly set apart in his bodily funkiness, so extreme that the officials of the local pool would not let him swim there. Along with his friend Roger Williams, also nicknamed Cool Breeze, he'd clack through high school with horseshoe taps on his shoes, such a sure sign of depravity in that era that his expulsion from Palo Alto High School seemed almost foreordained. He'd always played piano, though he refused lessons, but few knew that he wrote poetry, painted, and read science fiction.

What everyone did know was that he was the white kid who practically lived in black East Palo Alto, hanging out with a black man named Tawny Jones, who had a Harley-Davidson motorcycle as well as a bread truck that they called the Seventh Son. It came with a mattress in the back, and their sexual exploits went far beyond the average teen's. It was also useful for their trips to a bootlegger in La Honda, in the mountains above Palo Alto, where they bought whiskey at $1.50 a gallon. That, a horrid cheap sweet wine called Hombre, white port and lemon juice, and anything else they could find were their drinks of choice—Ron claimed to have begun drinking at the age of twelve. Satisfactorily lubricated, he and Tawny would go down by the railroad tracks and write songs. They took to hanging out at the Anchor Club and the Popeye Club in East Palo Alto and the Aztec Lounge in San Mateo, listening to old blues players, corroding their stomach linings with booze and hot links while they absorbed the blues life. Ron picked up harmonica and acoustic guitar, and connected with Garcia for some impromptu lessons, which he quickly absorbed. He always had the feel of the blues, even before he acquired the technique. One of the Chateau guys, a black saxophone player named Lester Hellum, was their friend, and he later recalled taking Ron to see T-Bone Walker at a San Mateo club. Ron sat staring at T-Bone's hands and then said to him, "I'll see you in twenty years." Aside from being known to steal any blues album not nailed down (Tawny took the jazz albums), he generally avoided breaking the law. Once a friend offered to sell him a nine-millimeter automatic pistol. Ron was fascinated by guns and borrowed it, saying he wanted to show it to his father. A few days later, he returned it, pleading, "Don't tell anybody I had it." Beneath the fairly fearsome exterior was what Garcia called a "real pixie quality. [He] was just really lovable, really fun. He was a sweetheart."

In September 1961, Alan Trist returned from a month of hiking the

John Muir Trail in the Sierras, and before leaving for Cambridge had what he remembered as a long, "apocalyptic" talk with Garcia. They walked about in San Francisco near the Palace of the Legion of Honor, on a bluff overlooking the Golden Gate and the Pacific, kicking pebbles and baring their hearts as young men will. What impressed Alan then and after was the positiveness of their outlook. He wasn't too sure of the rest of the "hip" United States, with its emphasis on angst and torment, but in San Francisco they concluded, "this is a positive place, this planet," rather in the sense that Kerouac derived the honorific "Beat" from "beatific." They felt blessed. Hunter and Garcia saw Alan off at the bus station, and though they were not good correspondents, they would manage to stay in touch.

In October, Garcia returned to Palo Alto and moved into the Chateau. Though it was only a rooming house, it had a certain free-spirited quality that made it exceptional. Perhaps it sprang from the owner, Frank Serratoni, who liked to water the yard in a brief bathing suit, his old man's paunch hanging out. Lee Adams was there first, then a drummer named Danny Barnett, then Rudy Jackson, a trumpet player. Rudy unfortunately made himself memorable by asking Miles Davis if he could sit in one night at the Blackhawk. "Hey, babe, want to do something together?" he inquired. Miles replied, "What you want to do, babe, fuck?" There was Page Browning, John the Cool, Robert Hunter, Willy Legate, and at times, Jerry's old friend Laird Grant. The furnishings ran from fine Chinese antique pieces in the living room to a refrigerator empty but for rotting mustard and moldy bread. David McQueen and Lester Hellum were regular visitors, joyfully slandering each other in ways that left on-lookers gasping with laughter. And there were plenty of female visitors, like Suze Wood, Cherie Huddleston, and Joan Simms.

And, of course, Brigid Meier. That fall, her relationship with Garcia changed dramatically. She had been "part of the cement of our scene," Garcia thought, reminding him of his grandmother in her ability to love everyone. Now she enthusiastically gave up her virginity to Garcia. Per-haps because she was so exceptionally beautiful, Garcia would always cherish the relationship as the height of romance, twenty years later de-scribing her as "the love of my life, really, in a way," astonishingly still re-morseful over the lust that had made their relationship a physical one. Their new romantic status bothered Hunter, who thought of Brigid in a protective way. Now in the throes of writing a novel about their group, Hunter used his feelings as an artistic goad, referring to himself as a "prophet of melancholy." He took his title, *The Silver Snarling Trumpet*, from Keats's "The Eve of St. Agnes," and in its first draft it was a good first novel. Unfortunately, he decided that the taut original version was too short, and he rewrote it, waxing ever longer and more philosophical.

Sometime in 1961, John the Cool brought around a new guy by the name of Phil Lesh. Impressed by his sheer speed of mind and obviously forceful intelligence, Winter told Hunter that Lesh "could walk on your mind in three minutes," which made for a bad first impression. But Lesh turned out to be less intimidating than that, and his musical gifts bridged the gap. He blew a little trumpet with Lester Hellum on alto, and his enthusiasm for music was endearing. He was then much more involved with composition than playing, and when Hunter and Garcia saw him sitting at a card table at work on "The Sun Cycle," a piece planned for three orchestras, writing it out of his head without even a piano, they were stunned. At the time, one of his party parlor tricks was to turn his back and challenge guitarists, as one of the crowd recalled, to "come up with knuckle-busting perverse chords, seventeenths with flatted eighths with augmented—he'd tell me the notes, the order, whether or not my guitar was tuned standard."

Lesh had graduated from the College of San Mateo that June of 1961, and while taking an entrance examination for the U.C. Berkeley musicology department that spring, had met Tom "T.C." Constanten, who would become his lifelong friend. Speaking with a young woman about serial music, Lesh was charmed when T.C. interjected, "Music stopped being created in 1750 but it started again in 1950." Lesh's only response was to stick out his hand. Immediate partners in musical crime, the two of them took up residence in Berkeley, with Phil's troll friend the con artist/poet Bobby Petersen as a regular visitor. For such a skinny fellow, Lesh had a remarkable facility for shoplifting, and in his persona as "Phil the Coat" he made sure, as he later put it, that "we ate pretty well for poor folks." However, Lesh was less adept in his dealings with bureaucracy. He got into Cal by taking dictation, listening to a piece of music by Chopin and transcribing it. Alas, he wrote down what he heard, and he cared not how Chopin might have originally written it. When told that he would still have to take Ear Training, he concluded that university music departments were more oriented to obedience than creativity. By midsemester he'd dropped out to spend the winter reading Joyce and listening to Mahler, his and T.C.'s favorite composer. Then, early in 1962, they learned that Luciano Berio, the young (then thirty-seven) Italian modernist composer, a distinguished associate of Karlheinz Stockhausen, was about to begin teaching a graduate-level course in composition at

Mills College in Oakland, a small women's school with a classy reputation in the arts. Too nervous even to apply, Lesh was ecstatic when T.C. got them both in the class, which included the cream of the Bay Area's young composers, among them John Chowning and Steve Reich. It would be a formative experience.

Berio was omnivorous about his sources, using jazz and Dante among many streams. His "Omaggio a Joyce" had established him as a leader in avant-garde composition, and Lesh was even more stunned when he came in with the actual "fuckin' five-channel tape that Stockhausen made for performances" of "Gesang der Jüngliche," a composition in which boys' voices were electronically modified. There was a performance at Mills that also involved five channels. "We only had four in the room, so we put one in the hall. I got to run the knobs. The fifth speaker was supposed to be out there, somewhere . . . I got to control the positions of all the music in space, which meant trying to learn this piece, just from hearing it. No score, just the tape." Lesh did so again at a performance of a Berio piece at the Ojai Festival. His own contribution to the class was a small piece that went over poorly in formal performance, but he'd heard it done beautifully in rehearsal, which was all that mattered to him. While taking Berio's class, he also volunteered as an engineer at KPFA so that he could continue his involvement in music even without performing.

One Saturday night in the spring of 1962, Lesh and Garcia connected. They'd seen each other around, but at a party at Pogo's, Lesh remarked, "Jerry, you sing and play good, I work for KPFA, how'd you like to be on the radio?"

"Why not? What do we have to do?"

Lesh replied, "Well, first, my roommate has a tape recorder, and as long as you're sittin' here pickin' and singin', and the party is yet early, I'll go up to Berkeley and get this tape recorder, and we'll make what amounts to a demo, and I'll play it for Gert [Chiarito, the producer of *The Midnight Special* folk show]."

Jerry agreed and added, "Well, shit, I'll ride with you."

Out to T.C.'s Oldsmobile they went, and by the time they'd returned to Palo Alto they were lifelong partners. Lesh would remark that Garcia had a "raw," really powerful personality, "and people were just awed by him, sitting at his feet—and I'm the kind of guy who distrusts people like that." But they bridged their mutual barricades of personality, and something important happened between them, a lovely flowering of trust and connectedness that they would celebrate two months later on the ides of March on Lesh's twenty-second birthday, sitting in Garcia's room at the

Chateau as they smoked the entire bag of weed Page Browning had brought to celebrate.

On the night of Pogo's party, they returned and recorded the demo. Gert Chiarito was so impressed that she had Garcia do an entire show solo, a virtually unprecedented event on *The Midnight Special.* She interviewed him about his music, and then he played. He was just nineteen, and yet somehow musically mature. His voice was not a great instrument, but it was evocative and right for his material. She remembered that he sang "Long Black Veil," and the "sad, distant country" tone of it moved her. Normally she had a dozen people in the studio for the show, but she could concentrate at this solo session, so she was particularly startled toward the end of the hour to notice his missing finger. "He was playing as though he had everything and a few extras."

A Fine High
Lonesome Madness

(3/62–12/63)

en Frankel was a U.C. Berkeley physics student and guitar player who lived across the street from Lundberg's Fretted Instruments, the Berkeley store that was a locus for acoustic music in the Bay Area. Touring professionals stopped by for strings and repairs, and everyone else who was interested would visit for talk and the swapping of tapes, which they made in the back of the store. One day Frankel heard a young picker named Garcia making a tape he coveted. It was easy to initiate a conversation, and when Garcia remarked that he was looking for a fiddler, Ken claimed experience he actually lacked. A couple of weeks later, he was a member of the Thunder Mountain Tub Thumpers.

A year and more of constant practice had qualified Garcia to obey the central drive of his entire musical career, which was to play with other people. From the very beginning, he sought communication and collaboration, not performance-as-theater. He'd already come across Joe and Jim Edmonston, who were a few years older than he. They were regular working guys, union men, but they loved to play, which was what counted. It didn't hurt that their mother was a terrific cook. On May 11, 1962, the Tub Thumpers, with Joe Edmonston on banjo, Frankel on fiddle, Garcia on guitar, and Hunter chucking chords on the mandolin on three days' practice, led off the Stanford University Folk Festival. Under various names and with a shifting cast of characters that included Marshall Leicester and Jim Edmonston, they played wherever else they could, including the Boar's Head. Lacking any financial motive, the musicians simply enjoyed each other's company and playing. "Everybody took the time to listen to everybody else," said Jim. Garcia took most of the vocals and was dominant, but he also listened, and his bandmates recognized him as their most capable member. Their best gig came as the Hart Valley Drifters. With Frankel on banjo, Garcia on guitar, Hunter on mandolin, and Jim Edmonston on bass, they went to work in the interests of one Hugh Bagley, a candidate for Monterey County sheriff. Playing on the back of a flatbed truck, their job was to attract a crowd for Hugh to speechify and handshake. It was a hilarious, goofy day, and when they couldn't even find Bagley's name in the election results, it mattered not at all.

Just at this time Hunter underwent a most extraordinary experience. He'd been making some money by taking psychological tests at Stanford, and somehow that gave him the opportunity to earn $140 for four sessions, one per week, taking psychedelic drugs at the V.A. Hospital under the auspices of what would prove to be the CIA. He received LSD (lysergic acid diethylamide, commonly called acid) the first week, psilocybin the second, mescaline the third, and a mixture of all three on the fourth. Danny Barnett told him he was crazy, but he ignored the doubts. Instead, he told Ken Frankel, "It'll be fun! I'll take my typewriter and no telling what'll come out."

Indeed. He'd read a bit of Huxley and tried the notorious cough syrup Romilar, but otherwise this was the first expedition into the world of the psychedelic by any of them, and what he brought back transfixed them all. His first session generated six single-spaced pages of notes, a remarkable document of a mind trying to remember paradise. "Sit back picture yourself swooping up a shell of purple with foam crests of crystal drops soft nigh they fall unto the sea of morning creep-very-softly-mist . . . and then sort of cascade tinkley-bell like (must I take you by the hand, ever so slowly type) and then conglomerate suddenly into a peal of silver vibrant uncomprehendingly, blood singingly, joyously resoundingbells." Other people were enmeshed in "the most GODAWFUL prison of concrete and veins and consciousness," while he could feel "PURE WHITE SPIRIT" pouring from each vein. It was not all ooh and ahh. He saw that "from this peak of Darien" he could unravel any riddle, but if it was brought to him and stripped down, "it would reveal itself to be simply its own answer . . . By my faith if this be insanity, then for the love of God permit me to remain insane." On his second test, he went beyond the "Lord I'm high" rhapsodies and straight into linguistics, Joycean word sounds, the play of vowel and syllable. His ability to articulate hallucinations would serve him well in the future.

His friends passed around his notes and then took him for coffee, pumping him for details. Garcia's reaction was simple: "God, I've *got* to have some of that." Hunter was not the only person they knew who had access to this experience. Palo Alto had its very own bohemian neighborhood, eight shacks on Perry Avenue, and one of its residents, Vic Lovell, was a psychology graduate student who kept his friends well supplied with this interesting new stuff, especially his pal Ken Kesey, a graduate student in writing who happened to work as a janitor at the V.A. Hospital. Older and more sophisticated than the Chateau gang, "Kesey and the wine drinkers," as Garcia would call them, were not impressed with the youngsters who tried to crash their parties, the annual Luwow and the Perry Lane Olympics ("Lane" sounded sooo much more aesthetic than "Avenue" to them), and gave them the boot.

Lesh, who'd been brought over to Lovell's by his friend Mike Lamb, had at first thought of Kesey as a "blustering asshole," until Lamb snuck in and read what was on Ken's typewriter, afterward telling them all to look out for his book. Kesey's seminar with Malcolm Cowley, the distinguished editor of Faulkner, Hemingway, and Kerouac, and a remarkable group of young writers which later included Robert Stone, Ed McClanahan, Gurney Norman, and Larry McMurtry, combined with psychedelics to produce something extraordinary. His fable of liberation from an authority-bound society, *One Flew Over the Cuckoo's Nest,* had been published to glorious reviews that February 1962. It was a masterpiece.

June meant Marshall Leicester's annual return from Yale. This year they would call themselves the Sleepy Hollow Hog Stompers, a tribute to the 1920s group Fisher Henley and His Aristocratic Pigs, which had been sponsored by Armour Ham. Suze Wood made them some snappy red-trimmed black vests, and they were ready to play. But there was a major difference this summer. Marshall had returned from school with one suitcase and six instrument cases, and the upshot was that Garcia began to play the devil's own fiendish twanger, the banjo. In all of acoustic music there is nothing quite like it. There is fire in a banjo, an intrinsic speed and intensity. He was drawn to what he described as "that incredible clarity . . . the brilliance" of the instrument. It consumed him, and as with nothing in his life to that point, he enslaved himself to his practice. His model was Earl Scruggs, and Garcia treated Scruggs's fingering as though it was the master lock, studying it by playing back his records at slow speeds, trying to crack the combination. His devotion to music would be central to his life, and it came at a price. Brigid Meier was talented, beautiful, and interested in literature and jazz, but now Garcia's idea of a great time was to find someone who could teach him a new song, and their romance sputtered. As 1962 passed, he continued to meet her every day for lunch across the street from school, and they even discussed marriage, when she was eighteen and he twenty-one, but the bloom was off.

The Hog Stompers were followers of the New Lost City Ramblers, and Garcia's banjo playing was at first in the old-timey tradition. The Boar's Head had found new quarters at the Peninsula Jewish Community Center in Belmont, and they played there regularly. But the banjo and Scruggs led Jerry inexorably from old-time music to bluegrass, a very different thing. Bluegrass was not folk music. It had been created in the 1940s by superbly gifted professionals, starting with Bill Monroe, and it required considerable skill to play. Bluegrass had a limited but important history in the Bay Area, beginning with Garcia's heroes, the Redwood Canyon Ramblers. Neil Rosenberg, Mayne Smith, and Scott Hambly were all classmates of Phil Lesh's at Berkeley High School and veterans of *The Midnight Special.* Neil and Mayne had come upon authentic bluegrass while attending Oberlin College, and their Bay Area shows in 1959 and 1960 brought the form to the region and inspired a second generation of East Bay players who would come to be Garcia's friends, including Butch Waller, Sandy Rothman, and Rick Shubb. Most Berkeley folkies had little use for bluegrass players, dismissing them as technicians concerned with speed rather than taste, and rejected bluegrass itself as "social tyranny," due to its difficulty. There was even a Berkeley band called the Crabgrassers; the name served as a pointed joke.

The atmosphere of the fall of 1962 was dominated by the tensions of the Cuban missile crisis. Hunter was taking classes at the College of San Mateo in philosophy and astronomy, which was certainly appropriate: John Glenn had orbited the earth that February, the Telstar communications satellite had been launched in July, and the best-selling book in America, *Silent Spring,* was concerned with pesticides and damage to the environment. For Hunter, this single vivid memory of the missile crisis involved going outdoors to scan the horizon for mushroom clouds at the time when Russian ships were required to turn back from the blockade. The crisis, thought one historian, "imbued the sixties generation with an apocalyptic cast of mind, a sense of the absurdity of politics, and a suspicion of politicians." True.

With Marshall back in New Haven, Garcia organized a new band. This version of the Hart Valley Drifters included Hunter on mandolin, Rodney and Peter Albin's young friend David Nelson on guitar, Jerry on banjo, and a new guy, Norm Van Maastricht, on bass. Nelson, who had graduated from high school in 1961, owned a motorcycle and a twenty-five-dollar '48 Plymouth, which immediately became band transportation. The Drifters practiced Tuesdays and Thursdays, and their big day came on November 10, when they debuted in the afternoon at an art gallery opening at San Francisco State and then headlined that night at the College of San Mateo Folk Festival. It was Nelson's first paid gig, and he would remember every detail. At their dress rehearsal the night before, they'd worked into the night and all night. As the show approached, David and Norm began to tire. Grumbling genially about "the rookies in my band," Garcia produced some Dexamyl, and their energy returned. They arrived at the art gallery, but no one met them. Seeing some microphones, they set up, and after stalling, finally had to play. Nelson suddenly wondered, "Good God, what's the tune?" Knowing that it would be a banjo instrumental, he looked at Garcia, who had his own nerves to deal with. Digging into the strings too hard with his picks, Garcia suddenly felt a string slide underneath the flap of the pick and send it twirling around. "Heh, heh," he snickered embarrassedly, and began again. By then, Nelson was "fucking terrified, paralyzed." But they kicked off without further interruption, and the music settled them. The audience liked what it heard, and filtered in. There were intentional laughs for their between-songs patter, some applause, and before they knew it, they were on break in a closet-size dressing room.

The CSM Folk Festival was actually a device for the Art Students Guild to raise money for beer, and with one giant poster at the cafeteria, they managed to sell out. It was partly luck: that very week, the cover of *Time* acclaimed Joan Baez a "Sibyl with Guitar." The audience expected something on the order of the Kingston Trio's "Scotch and Soda," but they got a lot more first. One student contributed a protest tune called "The Atom Song." An Indian student, Ramesh Chan, played Indian folk songs. Rodney Albin played "The IRT." Then Garcia played two solo banjo tunes, "Little Birdie" and "Walking Boss," extremely obscure material for this audience. "We make music in the tradition," said Garcia as he then introduced the Hart Valley Drifters' first set. "It says so right here in the program." But he didn't merely jest, going on to inform his audience of the historical roots and record-label contexts of the tunes they were playing.

After some comments on the Carter Family and the song, he and Nelson, "who more than anything else wants to be a real boy," played "Deep Ellum Blues." With Hunter, they played "Will the Circle Be Unbroken" ("The first code of the banjo is to get it into the proper tune . . . since our band is a strict adherent to this rule, we can take hours to tune," Garcia explained), and then Garcia gave them "Man of Constant Sorrow," solo and *a cappella*. They closed with two bluegrass tunes, "Pig in a Pen" and "Salty Dog." It was authentic and skilled and more than the audience could appreciate, although the Drifters' performance was very good indeed. Dean Hammer and His Nails closed the show with a few snide remarks about being made to wait, then sang "Scotch and Soda," and the audience went home happy.

So did the band. In the middle of the show, Nelson noticed something fall from Hunter's pocket, an object he thought was a white-wrapped Stickney's toothpick. Hunter assumed David knew that it was, in fact, a joint. At the postshow party at Suze Wood's, Nelson and his friend Rick Melrose said to Hunter, "Let's get loaded," as in "Have a drink." Since they were underage, Hunter's reluctance didn't surprise Nelson, but eventually Hunter talked to Garcia, and the four of them went to the car. A joint appeared, and Melrose asked, "What's that?" Nelson muttered to himself, "Shit, we'll blow our chance to smoke pot."

Hunter began to grumble about underage kids who weren't cool, but Garcia reassured and disarmed him, then gave lessons in smoking to the rookies, and before long they'd gone back to the Chateau and buzzed their way through Hunter's entire stash. At which point the rookies asked, "When does this stuff take effect?" Hunter resumed fuming, mostly silently, about the waste of scarce pot, and Garcia interceded again. "Here's what we do. Let's just talk about what a great guy Hunter is for getting us all stoned. What a great, great guy, he really put himself out for us, and isn't it just the nicest world . . ." And Hunter came out of his snit. "Aww, you guys, it was worth it, okay, okay." And Nelson began to think that they were talking a little funny. Garcia was beginning to giggle like crazy. Nelson turned to Melrose and said, "Too bad it didn't work, but we'll have a good time."

By now they were back at Suze's, and as they crossed her front lawn, they began to notice the dewdrops in the grass, and the moon, and the beauty of the night, and Rick turned to Nelson and whispered, "David, have you noticed this lawn? David, you know what I think? I think this stuff works."

The Tangent started as an amusement for two bored young doctors, but it became, for two years, the home of folk music on the Peninsula. Stu Goldstein and David Schoenstadt were Stanford Hospital residents who knew nothing about folk music, but Max and Bertha Feldman's Palo Alto deli had a room upstairs, and it occurred to Stu and David to open a club there, using Pete Seeger's songbook, *How to Make a Hootenanny,* as their blueprint. They opened in January 1963, with open hoots on Wednesdays and the winners playing weekends. The charge was a dollar fifty, and the performers got five or ten dollars. It quickly became Garcia's new musical home, "a little community . . . a sweet scene." It also produced some remarkable music. One night in a moment of boredom, Rodney Albin and Garcia gathered up four other guitarists, broke out some sheet music, crowded onto the stage, and played Tchaikovsky's "March Slav." On another night, a new woman blues singer from Texas, Janis Joplin, was a no-show. Her accompanist, a guitarist from Santa Clara by the name of Jorma "Jerry" Kaukonen, allowed as how he could play some blues, and proved it. Both became regulars, and part of a widening folk network. Joplin had read about Jack Kerouac in *Time* back in her hometown of Port Arthur, Texas. After apprenticing in Austin at a club called Threadgill's, she'd hit the road, eventually getting to San Francisco. Her circles of association included the North Beach scene and also a crew of young folkies at the Charles Van Dam houseboat in Sausalito that included Dino Valenti, Paul Kantner, and David Crosby, all of whom would come to be famous in due course.

The Tangent was part of an informal network of folk clubs that included Coffee and Confusion in San Francisco and the Cabale in Berkeley. The Cabale had more national acts, including Lightnin' Hopkins, though it was largely dominated by an in-group purism. Ego was also not unknown at the Tangent. One visiting musician, Herb Pedersen, thought of himself and Garcia as "two gunfighters" when they met, warily checking out each other's skills. Butch Waller, then of the Westport Singers, saw Garcia as "the surly guy drinking coffee who wouldn't talk to us" at first, although once Garcia saw their essential seriousness, he loosened right up. On February 23, 1963, Garcia brought his band, now named the Wildwood Boys, to its new home.

Shortly after that appearance, Jerry returned to the Tangent with a new friend, Sara Ruppenthal. After a year of what she termed "playing second fiddle to a banjo," Brigid Meier had had enough. There was a new young man in her life, one her family even approved of—her dates with Garcia had been undercover—and in the fall of 1962 Jerry had found the two of them together, producing an ugly, near-violent scene. Garcia had no money, so they couldn't go anywhere. He was prey to black moods, and as Brigid remarked, "I'm just sitting and he's playing, and he's playing and I'm sitting. I was seventeen and a lot of people wanted to take me out." At Christmas she joined her family in Mexico for a vacation and enjoyed a flaming new romance, which she inevitably disclosed to Jerry on her return. Garcia spent the season sitting on the Chateau porch drinking, and though they theoretically still saw each other in January, he hooked up with Sara Ruppenthal in February, and his romance with Brigid was history.

The daughter of a former airline pilot who'd served on the Palo Alto City Council and then taught at Stanford's business school, Sara grew up in the pacifist/bohemian tradition, listening to folk music as well as a recording of the House Un-American Activities Committee's hearings, and reading Kerouac and Zen philosophy. She entered Stanford in 1961, an extremely lovely Earth Mother beatnik in sneakers, tights, and a turtleneck, her hair in a braid. She had gotten to know Joan Baez through Ira Sandperl at the Peace Center, and spent time at Baez's shack in Big Sur. "I used to take great pleasure in signing Joan Baez as the person responsible for me while I was gone from my dorm . . . I wanted nothing more than to be just exactly like her." One day in late February she wandered into Kepler's, and Garcia caught her eye. He had a mustache and goatee, longish hair, and a dashing, "renegade" quality. "A channel opened up between us," she said, "and we both fell in." She ended up at the musicians' table at St. Michael's that night with Garcia, Hunter, and Legate, laughing so hard her stomach hurt. "It was just like falling into a whole 'nother world, but that was the world I wanted." She spent the night at Garcia's grubby shack behind the Chateau, and while it lacked electricity, the candles seemed romantic to her. The next morning she enjoyed a "funny cigarette" with Hunter and Legate as they walked around the garden. Sara had a "Wendy complex," as in *Peter Pan,* and the Chateau was full of lost boys.

The first complication in their lives came early in April, when Joan Baez invited Sara to accompany her as a secretary/assistant on a tour of Europe. Garcia was jealous of Baez, both emotionally in connection to

Sara and professionally as a competing musician. As a picker, he told Sara, "I'm king." In the end, romance won, in more ways than one. Around that time Jerry's co-resident at the Chateau, David Nelson, loaned them his room for the night, complete with a double bed, clean sheets, and central heat. Shortly after Sara turned down Baez's invitation, she discovered that she was pregnant. Her parents were no more impressed with Garcia than Brigid's had been, and offered Sara a round-the-world trip as an alternative to marriage. The young couple—he was twenty, she nineteen—had no idea of what they were getting into, but after missing out on a complete family life as a child, Jerry was willing to take the chance, and Sara was eager to be a mother. So they decided to get married.

Shortly before the wedding, they went to see Bobbie Garcia, Jerry's first visit with his mother in years. She was very sweet to her daughter-in-law-to-be, taking her to her heart. In a fox fur collar and high heels, she seemed "a real sport" to Sara, a woman who "liked a good drink" and wasn't terribly maternal. After a delightful visit, Bobbie stopped at the bank and sent each of them home with a hundred-dollar bill in their pockets. By now, Jerry's grandmother Tillie Clifford was senile, so for Jerry the feminine side of his life was going to have to come from his wife.

Jerry and Sara were married on April 27, 1963, at the Palo Alto Unitarian Church, with a reception following at Rickey's Hyatt House that included the music of the Wildwood Boys. It was the sort of wedding, several friends later observed, where the groom's friends could be found stuffing their empty bellies at the food line, while the bride's family members soothed their shaken nerves with drinks at the bar. The wedding was "tense," Garcia recalled. "As far as the parents of my girlfriends . . . I've always been like Satan." Sara "was such a delicate fawn in my jungle." His best man was David Nelson, who felt scruffy around the Ruppenthals, although Willy Legate trumped him by attending in a T-shirt.

For Garcia, one of the best aspects of the wedding was that it brought Phil Lesh back to the Bay Area. Late the previous year Phil had moved to T.C.'s home in Las Vegas, and after being instantly evicted by Mrs. Constanten, moved in with T.C.'s friend Bill Walker, whom they dubbed "the ambassador plenipotentiary from the land of zonk." Their slogan, "It's always ten to six in the land of zonk," would endure as a sly reference to their pot-smoking habits. Lesh was briefly a keno marker at the Horseshoe Club on the graveyard shift, and then found work at the post office. He had torn up his "Sun Cycle" as derivative plagiarism, but continued his efforts to compose, working on a monstrous polytonal piece called "Foci for Four Orchestras," which would have required 125 musicians and four conductors and included a chord in four keys at once. It required sixty-stave music paper. One of his favorite places to compose was the post office latrine, where he would sit nodding his head in contemplation before going home to write it down. With "Foci" finished, he took the bus to Palo Alto, staggered into Kepler's, then landed at the Chateau, the only refuge he could imagine, just a bit before the wedding.

Five days after their ceremony, Jerry and Sara played together at the Tangent, singing tunes like "Deep Ellum Blues," "Will the Weaver," "Long Black Veil," and "The Man Who Wrote Home Sweet Home." Sara had a good voice and they blended nicely, although she lacked Garcia's obsessiveness, which he demonstrated by playing, in the course of the evening, guitar, banjo, mandolin, and even a decent fiddle. Two weeks later the Hart Valley Drifters, with Garcia on banjo, Ken Frankel on mandolin, Hunter on bass, and Nelson on guitar, performed at the Monterey Folk Festival in the amateur division, winning Best Group. Garcia was also awarded Best Banjo Player.

The focus of the festival was on Peter, Paul and Mary, a group assembled by its manager, Albert Grossman, to promote the work of one of his other clients, a new singer named Bob Dylan. Dylan had scandalized the purist Garcia by writing new songs outside the folk canon, including "Blowin' in the Wind," which would turn into a radio hit in the next month. Dylan also performed at the festival, and Garcia would recall leaving early in his set. Hunter attributed their departure to the lousy sound system, though Garcia's sententious purism may well have played a part. It was the first time they'd really heard of Dylan, though it would certainly not be the last.

Born Robert Zimmerman in 1941 in Minnesota, Dylan had grown up listening to Hank Williams and the great Shreveport, Louisiana, disc jockey Gatemouth Page, who played Muddy Waters, Howlin' Wolf, and Jimmy Reed on the night radio waves, and then early rock, especially Little Richard. Arriving in New York in 1961, he created a fantasy identity with his new name, and soon became the most important artist the folk scene would ever know. In April of that year he opened for John Lee Hooker at Gerde's Folk City, and ten months later he had his own eponymously titled album, though it sold only five thousand copies in the first year. In 1962 he wrote "Blowin' in the Wind," and it quickly became one of the anthems of the burgeoning civil rights movement. Just as he appeared at Monterey, Columbia Records released his second album, the immediately successful *The Freewheelin' Bob Dylan*, which included the topical yet brilliantly universal "Oxford Town," "Masters of War," and "A Hard Rain's A-Gonna Fall."

The summer of 1963 saw Garcia make a certain effort to be a family man, distancing himself for a brief while from his friends. Hunter was convinced that Sara was trying to "make something of him," and the two men drifted apart. Garcia even took something resembling a job, teaching guitar at Dana Morgan's music store in Palo Alto. His timing was impeccable. *Hootenanny*, a television folk music program, had debuted in April, and kids were flocking to learn guitar. Physical fitness was all the rage, especially one's capacity for a fifty-mile hike. In April, the United States had sponsored an aborted and failed invasion of Cuba at a place called the Bay of Pigs. News from Vietnam dominated television with images of monks immolating themselves to protest the local regime. In June, Medgar Evers, an NAACP field-worker in Jackson, Mississippi, was murdered, and shortly after, President Kennedy proposed a Civil Rights Act. In Palo Alto the Chateau was sold, sending Nelson, Hunter, and Legate fleeing to a new home at 436 Hamilton Street, a block away from St. Michael's Alley.

Steeped in domesticity, the Garcias lived in suburban Mountain View, with Jerry hitching to work carrying his instrument cases. His tiny, smoky room at Dana Morgan's had two chairs and a music stand, which seemed quite sufficient. He was a good, if unconventional, teacher. "I tried to teach them how to hear," he said, making tapes of relatively easy but good-sounding material like the Carter Family for his students. Benignly encouraging, he answered the stock question "How long should I practice?" with "Play when you feel like it." At least one student was so delighted by that response that he played all the time. Some of the lessons would involve simply listening to Garcia play and then asking questions. His sense of time as it applied to lessons was unreliable. A student would knock, Garcia would call out, "I'll be with you in a minute," and half an hour later the student's mother would be there, and he'd still be enthusiastically describing something new to his first student.

Morgan's led him to another musical diversion, his first foray into rock and roll since the Chords. Dana Morgan's store manager was Troy Weidenheimer, an electric guitarist whom Jerry had known since the Boar's Head. Troy had a band called the Zodiacs, and that summer he invited Garcia to join it—as the bass player. It was great fun, Jerry would say, despite the fact that he was "out of my idiom" playing rock and out of his instrument with the bass. But "Troy taught me the principle of 'hey—stomp your foot and get on it.' He was a great one for the instant arrangement . . . fearless for that thing of 'get your friends and do it,' and 'fuck it if it ain't slick, it's supposed to be fun.' He had a wide-open style of playing that was very, very loose, like when we went to play gigs at the

Stanford parties, we didn't have songs or anything, and he would just say play B-flat, you know, and I'd play bass, and we'd just play along and he'd jam over the top of it, so a lot of my conceptions of the freedom available to your playing really came from him. He would like take chorus after chorus, but he directed the band like right in the now . . . we never rehearsed or anything ever, we would just go to the shows and play—and he was so loose about it, he didn't care, he just wanted it cookin' so he could play his solos, and he was just a wonderful, inventive, and fun, good-humored guitar player. One of the first guys I ever heard who exhibited a real sense of humor on the guitar. He was quite accomplished. I mean, in those days he was certainly the hot-rod guitar player of P.A., as far as electric guitar was concerned. While I was a folkie and all that . . ." The band also included a young local drummer named Bill Kreutzmann, and Jerry's old friend Ron McKernan, on harmonica.

Rock and roll was only a passing fancy, however, and Garcia remained serious about bluegrass. In September the Wildwood Boys evolved into the Black Mountain Boys, at a cost. One day at the house on Hamilton Street, Hunter came to a rehearsal and realized that everyone was looking at him in a guiltily embarrassed way. It gradually dawned on him that he'd been dropped from the band, although no one could bring himself to tell him directly. It wasn't an unreasonable decision, because his replacement, Eric Thompson, was a far better instrumentalist, but it hurt. Hunter wasn't a devoted picker, but he loved playing bluegrass, and of course he enjoyed being part of the band. Shortly after, he moved to Los Angeles.

Originally called Elves, Gnomes, Leprochauns *(sic)* and Little People's Chowder and Marching Society Volunteer Fire Brigade and Ladies Auxiliary String Band, the Black Mountain Boys was fun for all, and it produced high-quality bluegrass. The players even had vague professional hopes. One of the Tangent bands, the Westport Singers, was now managed by Dave and Stu, the Tangent's doctor owners, and had won a hoot in Los Angeles. They were cutting a record before joining a package tour that would play Carnegie Hall. Jerry kept asking Dave and Stu why they wouldn't work with the Black Mountain Boys, but the answer was obvious. His purist bluegrass was not commercial, and Garcia was, said Dave with a smile, "resistant to suggestions."

In November, the Black Mountain Boys briefly flirted with commerce when they met an agent and promoter named Stan Leed. He had an idea for a tour called the Bay City Minstrels, which would include the Black Mountain Boys and David [Freiberg] and Michaela, a folk duo, bound for schools in the Northwest. Sara wrote to Stu, by now away in the military, that Stan was "sort of a weasel, and much disliked. However, he's doing good things for our boys, so we don't mind him." Unfortunately, a few weeks later her letter would relate that Stan had skipped town owing everyone at least sixty dollars. Far more their style was the newest club around, the Offstage, in San Jose. It was run by Paul Foster, a dropout computer programmer who'd been known to attend political demonstrations with a sign that read "Now." Foster had fallen in with a group of Santa Clara–area folkies that included Paul Kantner, David Freiberg, and Jorma Kaukonen, and created a club that would give them a home. The charge was a dollar, except for drunks, in which case it was four dollars. There was, of course, no liquor, and even the coffee had to be consumed before the music began so there would be no clinking of cups. They sold pot under the counter to make the rent, and it became a regular stop for Garcia and company.

It was a difficult fall. Phil Lesh had settled in Palo Alto, but a romantic entanglement had encouraged his swift departure. He went off to San Francisco, where he moved in with T.C. and dabbled with amphetamines. His active participation in music seemed to have come to an end. Garcia was painfully learning the demands of being a husband. Because of her pregnancy, Sara couldn't tolerate drugs, tobacco, or alcohol, not only for herself but for anyone around her. In her own words, she "made life miserable for poor Jerry," trying to "domesticate him." "He'd come home silly and I'd get pissed." It did not occur to her that her hormonal mood swings were natural, and she shoved her anxiety on her husband, whom she described as a "traditional sexual redneck." "He was moody and I was critical."

In the country at large, a glorious coming-together was followed by two great tragedies. In August, hundreds of thousands of Americans had gathered at the Lincoln Memorial to hear Dr. Martin Luther King Jr. give one of the masterpieces of American oratory, the "I Have a Dream" speech. And not only did the younger generation join the March on Washington, but its minstrels, Bob Dylan and Joan Baez, were able to participate, singing "Blowin' in the Wind" there. Not since Woody Guthrie had song joined moral purpose so persuasively; the dream was vivid and alive. Three weeks after the march, unspeakable horror struck down four little girls in Birmingham, Alabama. Addie Mae Collins, Denise McNair, Carol Robertson, and Cynthia Wesley died when the 16th Street Baptist Church was bombed. And on November 22, 1963, there was further madness, with the murder of President John F. Kennedy.

Like so many Americans, Phil Lesh turned "into a robot" on Friday the twenty-second, and he was still in shock on Sunday morning. Driving down McAllister Street in his post office van, he heard music coming out of a barroom door, parked the van, and went in. It was the funeral march from Beethoven's *Eroica* Symphony, conducted by Leonard Bernstein. "That was the day that my illusions were blown away, one hundred percent. The only gleam of light was Beethoven . . . things shifted an octave, like consciousness rather than political control. Good-bye everything we ever believed in. Welcome to the modern world, where a coup d'état is everyday business."

Two weeks later, on December 8, Sara Garcia gave birth to Heather, named after the folksinger Hedy West. It was a natural childbirth, so Sara was conscious and could inquire, halfway through the process, "Is it a boy or a girl?" "Only the head's out, honey." "If she's smiling," Sara replied, "it's a girl." Garcia charged down the hospital corridor, yelling to Hunter, who would be Heather's godfather, "It's a broad, it's a broad."

"I can't describe to you the feeling," he said, grinning, shrugging, shaking his head. However unready, he was a father. Sara came down with an infection, and had to return to the hospital for a little while. When she got out on December 18, she had to fend for herself, because Garcia had gotten an impromptu out-of-town gig at the Ashgrove, Southern California's premier folk club. Marshall Leicester, Ken Frankel, a returned Robert Hunter, and Garcia were the Badwater Valley Boys, and they were opening for the God and creator of bluegrass, Bill Monroe, as well as bluegrass's finest younger band, the Kentucky Colonels. Nervous, Hunter began to spin a yarn as Badwater Bob, and someone yelled, "Shut up and play bluegrass." So they did.

5

Interlude:
A Meeting of Minds

(COMPANY MEETINGS, 1984)

It is a California corporation that grosses over eight figures annually, carries an employee pension fund and a health insurance plan, and retains two attorneys. It owns office and sound equipment and a Mack truck, but no stocks, real estate, or diamond mines. It is run by monthly board (primarily band member) meetings, where the president of the corporation is a crew member with nineteen years' seniority, and the putative manager has no vote. Roughly once a month, there is an all-employee "band meeting" at the rehearsal hall, where everyone gathers around a sixteen-foot-long Victorian Gothic Revival table found in Europe by Alan Trist during the 1972 tour. The opinions expressed there carry weight. The shape of the Grateful Dead, lyricist Robert Hunter once said, reflects the shape of Jerry Garcia's mind. Hunter described the band as an "anarchic oligarchy." Garcia once said, "I am not an artist in the independent sense, I'm part of dynamic situations, and that's where I like it." The band's social organization flows from precisely the same principle.

Since he is philosophically antisystematic, his perspective, said one friend, is "a matter of sensibility rather than system," and he leads only

subtly and by example. The result is an intelligent and functioning anarchy, with responsibility so diffused that the essential is accomplished, but
only that, and in which, as Lesh once said, "Avoidance of confrontation is
almost a religious point with us." Or, as manager Rock Scully put it, "Default and digression [are] the principal modus operandi of the band." Although seniority often resolves conflicts, building a consensus is the usual
deciding political factor. There is a hierarchy, but it changes constantly,
and the considered optimum is for everyone to lead as they feel their moment. It is in fact a conservative democracy, often disorganized because it
is quite genuine. The most negative vote carries. "The question is," Garcia
told one interviewer, "can we do it and stay high? Can we make it so our
organization is composed of people who are like pretty high, who are not
being controlled by their gig, but who are actively interested in what
they're doing? . . . Wisdom is where you find it, every point of view at its
very worst will see something that you don't see . . . It would be a terrible
bummer not to be able to go through life with your friends anyway—
that's what the very start was about, you know . . . But as a life problem,
the Grateful Dead is an anarchy. That's what it is. It doesn't have any . . .
stuff. It doesn't have any goals, plans, or leaders. Or real organization. And
it works. It even works in the straight world. It doesn't work like General
Motors does, but it works okay. And it's more fun."

The subtext of anarchism is surrealism, and the Dead's best political
statement came in a 1974 letter from Ron Rakow, then president of the
Grateful Dead Record Company, to President Richard Nixon. Rakow
offered the threatened officeholder an idea on how to continue his administration. "We pass our solution along to you with only the remotest expectation that you will carry it out. Since, while it is brilliant, it is not
extremely logical. We have concluded that the problems referred to above
would disappear, as if by magic, were you to chrome the entire White
House."

In fact, the one dependable structure in the scene is the calendar of
the tour year. Three tours of seventeen shows in three and a half weeks—
one in March–April, one in June–July, one in September–October—plus
Bay Area and other West Coast shows and short runs in February, May,
and December. This added up to about eighty shows a year, and for the
best part of the eighties and nineties it is the one constant in an otherwise
swirling universe.

It worked well when the band was relatively small and relatively poor.
But that anarchy, which worked as a horizontal hierarchy—the band at
the center, then the crew and other senior employees in the next ring

out—began to suffer when the scale became distended by the addition of a million fans in the third ring. For anarchy disdains authoritarianism, and the pressure exerted by a million people is enormous. Lyricist John Barlow once endured a spell as road manager and then wrote, "I think you are all operating under pressures which generally exceed human specifications."

Eccentricity is often encouraged—certain very obnoxious people are considered necessary, the irritant that generates pearls. But this sometimes smug tolerance applies only to family. Once Bob Seidemann, an old friend but a fast-track photographer and art designer, grumbled about some of his billings. Earlier that day booker Danny Rifkin had told him that Dead employee qualifications started with loyalty, honesty, and compatibility . . . but Seidemann heedlessly blasted forward about commercial values as though he were talking to a band seriously concerned with making money, say, a group from Los Angeles. When he reached the point of being very slightly rude to bookkeeper Janet Soto-Knudsen, the president of the corporation (as well as crew chief) could stand it no longer. An Oregon country boy, Ram Rod is the conscience of the band, in Garcia's words the "highwater integrity marker." Ram Rod spoke up and put Seidemann in his place. Once again, Seidemann learned the hard way the complexities of doing business with the Dead.

This loose yet complex style can also create a cranky selfishness that lyricist Robert Hunter once defined in "The Ten Commandments of Rock & Roll," a sort of open letter he wrote to the band after he went along on a tour. Although it came out of a completely different context, it identifies the least-charitable aspects of life in the Grateful Dead hierarchy.

1. Suck up to the Top Cats.
2. Do not express independent opinions.
3. Do not work for common interest, only factional interests.
4. If there's nothing to complain about, dig up some old gripe.
5. Do not respect property or persons other than band property or personnel.
6. Make devastating judgments on persons and situations without adequate information.
7. Discourage and confound personal, technical and/or creative projects.
8. Single out absent persons for intense criticism.
9. Remember that anything you don't understand is trying to fuck with you.

10. Destroy yourself physically and morally and insist that all true brothers do likewise as an expression of unity.

As a meeting collects around the table, it occurs to Scrib that sometimes Hunter comes off as an optimist.

Minutes of the Meetings

1/ Present: Janet Soto-Knudsen [bookkeeper], Harry Popick [engineer], John Cutler [studio engineer], Willy Legate [studio superintendent], Eileen Law [Dead Heads], Patricia Harris [merchandising], Steve Marcus [Ticket Office], Maruska Nelson [assistant to booker], Mary Jo Meinolf [accountant], Sue Stephens [administrative assistant], Mickey Hart [percussion], Steve Parish [crew], Phil Lesh [bass], Kidd [Bill Candelario, crew and merchandising manager], Bill Kreutzmann [drums], Ram Rod [crew chief, president], Hal Kant [attorney], Robbie Taylor [production manager], Scrib McNally [publicity], Jon McIntire [booker, road manager], Dan Healy [director of sound], Jerry Garcia [lead guitar, vocals], John Meyer [guest, founder of Meyer Sound Labs], Bob Weir [rhythm guitar, vocals], Paul Roehlk [truck driver], Candace Brightman [director of lights], Dan Rifkin [booker, road manager], Bill Grillo [crew], Brent Mydland [keyboards, vocals]. Called to order at 2:45 p.m. by Chairman Phil Lesh.

2/ Backstage: per D. Rifkin, Bob and Peter Barsotti [Bill Graham Presents' house and stage managers] think our backstage is too loose. There needs to be more discipline in number of laminates issued. Graham wants us to play in New Orleans on Mardi Gras. J. Garcia: "They don't need us." No.

3/ John Meyer came with a proposal for going ahead with research—cost ultimately could be $1 M . . . using digital, can now adjust sound to *any* room. A whole new level—an organic, not systemic, approach. Band says prepare laundry list and begin. D. Healy: "The game is getting very deep, fellas . . ."

3/ Per S. Marcus, allotment for Berkeley Community Theater benefit series will be 4 purchase tickets per employee per night.

3/ Bammies [Bay Area Music Awards]. PL won best bassist. "I'll do the show this time if you promise never to put me on the ballot again."

3/ Merchandising: up to now, the building has received high % [e.g., Nederlander gig—building received 35%—we got about 20%]. Del Furano at Winterland Productions [T-shirt manufacturers] will give us some guidelines to lower building %. Discussion of a T-shirt bootlegger, 5,000 shirts at least. R. Hunter says don't bust, BW says tell him they're ugly. Kidd: not allowed to sell within 3-block radius of show. Per J. Garcia, we need to be evenhanded with policy. Per Hal Kant, we are required to take reasonable steps to protect our copyright . . .

3/ M. Hart suggested maternity leave for Janet. Approved at full salary and for whatever time she needs. Janet will have phone hookup and will be able to do books at home!

3/ [Attorney] B. Stilson has an offer for use of our recording of "Ripple" in a movie entitled *Mask* with Cher and Sam Elliott. J. Garcia and R. Hunter have already okayed the start of negotiations. Approved.

4/ Ice Nine/David Gans Book . . . Per B. Stilson, Hal says usual industry usage fee is $100–$200 per song. R. Hunter said he doesn't see any reason to charge anything at all . . . No charge.

4/ Irvine Hotels suffered damage from alleged Dead Heads—we are not welcome at any of them. Note that this year's Irvine hotel is part of the same chain as our New York hotel—we lose, we lose big. S. Parish: "Is there a problem?" Ram Rod: "If they'll let us in, there's no problem."

5/ Red Rocks Amphitheater, Denver: B. Weir stated he was willing to do about anything to facilitate our playing there in the future. Although advance crew notified Feyline, the local promoter, of our requirements prior to our last appearance, we didn't get satisfaction; general feeling is that problem is with them rather than unwillingness on city's part. Changes have to be made, i.e., [JG]: "Take away the dumb side panels and dumb roof." . . . Security: policy, whenever possible, will be accountable security [ID# or name]. We issue cautionary statements with all tickets we sell . . .

7/ Taper Section: they feel dead center thirty feet from stage is ideal—the area in front of sound booth. We would like to set aside a section for them behind the booth . . . doing this not so much for the tapers, but for the others in the audience . . . Do we want to stop the taping? Do we want to enforce the clause in our contract rider? Philosophical aspects tabled until the next meeting.

8/ Rex Foundation: Scrib has been approached by the SF Blues Festival re sponsoring Little Milton Campbell—yeah, you remember that tune. Sure.

8/ Zena Heard, former crew member Sonny Heard's widow, will be sent a contribution—Eileen will see that gold records are sent to Sonny's mom.

8/ Fall tour: Rifkin: as of now, we have a tour in the South, two weeks off, and then a tour of the NE. Our extreme popularity has cost us many venues of late—Carrier Dome at Syracuse, Blossom, Saratoga—and he suggests dropping the South after Hampton and going to the Northeast twice—i.e., saturating the area to the point where perhaps we'll not have sellouts. Ram Rod: "If it doesn't work we'll have more money." J. Garcia: "It's a way to find out." Schedule: Shoreline Amphitheatre is tentative. M. Hart: Bill [Graham]'s squirming—"No prisoners, Rifkin."

10/ Per W. Legate, Dick Latvala's services working as vault archivist have been invaluable. Suggests he keep track of his hours and be paid . . . Approved.
Computerization of office: J. Cutler has set the Macintoshes up and is giving lessons.

11/ New Year's: J. Cutler will book NPR satellite for radio broadcast. Opening act suggestions: M. Hart: Mapenzi, Big City. J. Garcia: Los Lobos. B. Weir: Freaky Executives.

Several moments stick with Scrib. One is when multimillion-dollar corporate executive Bill Graham visited the meeting because he is a board member of the band's charitable arm, the Rex Foundation. He made a suggestion, and had it dismissed as "commercial" by Willy Legate. Everyone plainly agreed with their building superintendent. Graham looked away, presumably muttering to himself, "The janitor?"

This janitor once wrote a note to the band and pinned it on the bulletin board at the studio:

> Bad-mouthing someone in his absence is an art form, deliberately cultivated here . . . Optimistic descriptions of situations are sometimes passed out to anyone nearby who is prepared to play the role of patronized fawning multitude. The optimistic description is given with the understanding by all concerned that if it should change within the next hour or week, that adjustment will not be relayed; in other words, that anything good you're told is meaningless. In the words of the prophet: if you don't know by now, don't mess with it. And I want you to know that there is no hope. Insanity, sickness and death are coming.

The second moment came when John Cutler protested the manner in which an employee had been let go. Struggling to express himself without giving in to rage, this man who had been rescued from depression by some of the brothers in the room politely chewed out band members—and they sat and took it.

A final moment, this from the band's attorney, Hal Kant. At a meeting about crew bonuses, comment was solicited from Ram Rod, who said, "Well, I can't say anything logical about it." Lesh replied, "Just ramble. Just rave awhile." A patient encouragement of communication is not part of the average set of business procedures.

Something New

(12/31/63–10/64)

Late on the afternoon of December 31, 1963, three teenagers named Bob Weir, Bob Matthews, and Rich McCauley were aimlessly wandering around the streets of Palo Alto when they heard the sound of a banjo coming from Dana Morgan's store. They followed the notes in and began to talk with Jerry Garcia. When they pointed out that it seemed unlikely for any of his students to appear on New Year's Eve, he agreed, then opened the front of the store and lent them some instruments. They began to jam. It was an appropriate beginning; for much of the rest of his life, Garcia would have Weir off to his side. One was homely, one was handsome. One was a self-educated intellectual, one was severely dyslexic and though intelligent, barely literate. One was physically lethargic, the other athletic. One was born to the laundry workers' union, and one grew up in Atherton, an extremely wealthy enclave south of San Francisco. Yet they were brothers.

The adopted son of Frederick Utter and Eleanor Cramer Weir, Robert Hall Weir was born October 16, 1947, and grew up in a world of wealth (earned, not inherited), forever carrying himself, as he put it, "like a Republican." An engineering graduate of Annapolis, Frederick Weir was a "mild-mannered and easygoing" father, with an extremely dry sense of humor he passed on to his son. Unable to serve aboard a ship due to deathly seasickness, Lieutenant Commander Weir had returned to San Francisco to establish the engineering firm of Beyah, Weir and Finato, eventually settling at 89 Tuscaloosa Avenue in Atherton with Eleanor, his son Bob, another adopted son, John Wesley, and their natural daughter, Wendy, born in 1949. Eleanor was a strong woman, "driven," as Bobby put it, and "not about to let the kids . . . be anything but successful." She was a volunteer at San Francisco's de Young Museum and its symphony, and the family was listed in the city's social register.

Atherton's single greatest virtue, in young Bob Weir's eyes, was that it was essentially an oak forest, and it was in the trees that he grew up. A childhood bout with spinal meningitis left him with a lifelong inclination to spaced-out dreaminess, something he described as the occasional need to sit and stare at a TV screen, turned on or off, and "bubble my spit." Thirty years later, a writer would note that his "eyes open wide when he talks, like he's experiencing a revelation, or there's a murder going on over your left shoulder and he's too polite to interrupt the conversation." The meningitis also, Weir thought, burned an early horrible temper out of him. This, combined with an upbringing that expected him to be pleasant and civil, made him an extraordinarily nice person to be around. But not necessarily an obedient one. His sense of fun was highly developed and his respect for rules was not. "It wasn't like he was a sociopath," said his best friend, John Barlow, somewhat later, "he just did not understand [the rules of conventional behavior] . . . he could never quite get the idea that fun was wrong." And so he became, Weir said, the "only guy I ever knew who was drummed out of the Cub Scouts." He also managed to be ejected from preschool.

From early on he was an athlete, inspired by the local legends, Willie Mays of the baseball Giants and Y. A. Tittle of the football 49ers. He ran track, played football, and enjoyed a rather normal childhood with summers in a cabin above Donner Lake in the Sierra Nevada. He and his slightly older brother wrestled and generally got along, while sister Wendy was "Mama's little angel." The family was not musical, and Bobby's most stimulating early exposure to music came from his nanny, a black woman named Luella, who shared with him Duke Ellington, big-band music, and a little bop. He briefly took piano lessons, but when his teacher showed him a boogie-woogie bass line for the left hand and a simple pattern for the right hand, he proceeded to hammer it so incessantly that his parents soon disposed of the piano. They got him a trumpet, but he practiced outside and the neighbors complained. His life changed totally at the age of thirteen, when the son of a family friend stopped by the house one day carrying a guitar. An acoustic guitar could be practiced quietly in one's room, and this time his parents approved. His first was a seventeen-dollar Japanese model, bought to celebrate his graduation from junior high school, and he christened it with the Kingston Trio's tune "Sloop John B."

Guitar did nothing for his problems at school. Dyslexia was not a recognized syndrome in 1962, and although bright enough to fake his way through his classes, he was barely able to sit still as he did so. After public school in Atherton and then two years at the private Menlo School, he was sufficiently difficult that his parents decided to send him to Fountain Valley, a school in Colorado Springs, Colorado, that specialized in boys with behavioral problems. There he encountered John Perry Barlow, his pal for life, and teachers who were idiosyncratic enough to keep up with him. The choir leader, Mr. Kitman, had once water-skied in a tuxedo, and that was enough to impress the boys. Mr. Barney, the English literature teacher, inspired Weir with a reverence for the clean "economy of speech" of Twain, Hemingway, and Steinbeck. Even though Weir had a problem with reading, he'd worry his way through the classics. He had a great year in Colorado, but his behavior remained problematic: the legendary biology lab spitball war in which the spitballs were frog internal organs was definitely initiated by Weir. In May the school administration concluded that either he or Barlow, his partner in crime, could return—but not both. Barlow elected to return, but first, Weir spent that summer of 1963 with the Barlow family at the Bar Cross Ranch in Cora, Wyoming. Even there, he had problems with his span of attention. He drove the scatter raker, and because of his habit of amusing himself by jumping off the still-running tractor to chase field mice, it had a tendency to wind up in a ditch. He was sufficiently faster than the machine to get away with it most of the time, but "about every fiftieth time, there'd be a little drainage ditch that I hadn't foreseen."

His summer's labors earned him a Harmony classic nylon string guitar and a Mexican twelve-string, and they evolved into a seventy-nine-dollar steel string Harmony Sovereign. Showing the first signs of a tinkering mentality, he shaved down the inside struts to make it boomier, later impressing the great folksinger Doc Watson with its tone at a jam session at Lundberg's. His new school was Pacific High School, a progressive school in Los Altos Hills, but he lasted only six months because his entire program there consisted of "playing guitar and chasing chicks." Other than conveying a certain sense of beatnik life, Pacific was useful only for giving him time to practice his instrument. His next school, the public Menlo-Atherton High School, was considerably less welcoming. He entered M-A in the spring of 1964, and his guitar and longish hair marked him as an oddball at a high school that worshiped madras clothing and fitting in. Shy, a little peculiar, he was nicknamed Blob Weird, and he delighted in proving his nickname true. As always, he was popular with the girls, taking the head cheerleader to the prom, but the boys didn't know what to make of him, and his gadfly tactics with the teachers put off most of his classmates. A natural-born iconoclast, he had read the *Communist Manifesto,* and his year at Fountain Valley had taught him a great deal about Native American history. The civics teacher would turn him loose just to get the class stirred up, and his new friend, Sue Swanson, liked to egg him on. "Traitor. Traitor," she'd whisper from the seat behind him. Actually, he came to realize, he was an aspiring beatnik.

Now sixteen, he had his own gang, which included his friends Bob Matthews and Rich McCauley and his girlfriend, Debbie Peckham. McCauley and Peckham also had guitars, and they all played together. Their main influences were a mix of (mostly) folk and rock, with an emphasis on fine vocalists: Joan Baez, the Kingston Trio, the Everly Brothers, and John Herald of the Greenbriar Boys. Lessons were out. Guilty over the trumpet fiasco, his parents had hired Troy Weidenheimer to teach him guitar. But Troy taught a straight-ahead big-band style, and it did not appeal to Weir. Instead, he studied with his ears, down the street at the Tangent, and the player he followed most closely was Jorma (though still known as Jerry) Kaukonen. He and his friends circulated tapes of Jorma, learning and trading licks, he later said, like "baseball cards." Garcia was also around, but banjo was too exacting, too rigorous, for Weir. He correctly concluded that "you can't just blow" with Scruggs-style banjo, and although he listened closely to bluegrass singing, it was the guitar players Eric Thompson and David Nelson that he most appreciated. One hoot night that spring at the Tangent, he even stepped up and performed in public for the first time. The Uncalled Four, with Weir, Debbie Peckham, and their friends Rachel Garbet and Michael Wanger, played two or three tunes, including a Carter Family version of "Banks of the Ohio." What Weir would remember was a paralyzing stage fright that only dissolved after he had embarrassed himself as much as possible. His bright orange thumb pick fell off, and it seemed to him that every eye in the audience tracked its slow-motion flight to the floor. After that abyss, their turn onstage was a delight.

One reason that it had been easy for Weir, Matthews, and McCauley to barge into Morgan's on New Year's Eve was that Matthews was one of Garcia's banjo students, although admittedly an extremely lazy one. Matthews did contribute a good idea to the circle—it was he who suggested they begin a jug band. Raucous, frequently lecherous, always fun, jug music was a black dance form that came out of Memphis and other southern party spots in the 1920s. Among the leading bands were Will Shade's Memphis Jug Band and Cannon's Jug Stompers, featuring Noah Lewis on harmonica. In 1963, Jim Kweskin had assembled a group from the Cambridge-Berkeley folk network that included Geoff Muldaur and Fritz Richmond, and their ensuing Vanguard album was something of a hit. Consequently, Sara would write, she and Jerry "practically lived in Berkeley the week" in January 1964 that the Jim Kweskin Jug Band was at the Cabale. Playing in a jug band was a relaxing and amusing interlude for Garcia from the rigors of bluegrass banjo, although he remained serious about musical quality. As Matthews recalled his own less-than-spectacular career in the band, he began on banjo at the first rehearsal, moved to washboard for the second, then kazoo, and was then fired. At least twenty-two people had passed through the band by May.

Among the main settled personnel were Garcia on guitar and vocals, Weir on washtub bass and jug, for which he had an unusual facility, his friend Tom Stone on banjo, and another pal, Dave Parker, on washboard. With Garcia and Weir, the third regular was Jerry's friend Ron McKernan, on harmonica and vocals. Ron's semibestial persona had only ripened since the Boar's Head days just three years before. Now eighteen, he was beefy, grubby, and fearsome-looking, although Weir swiftly realized that he was the sweetest guy around. To top things off, he'd acquired a new nickname. One night at the JCC Boar's Head, milling about in the post-show consideration of where to go next, Truck Driving Cherie Huddleston lifted a line from the *Peanuts* cartoon and cracked, "All right for you, Pigpen," and Blue Ron was "Pigpen" forevermore.

Studying the canon of jug was enormously entertaining. They began with Kweskin's records, and then his Folkways sources. Then Weir's friend Michael Garbet discovered a trove of original Bluebird Record Company 78s in his mother's attic. Their repertoire soon included Cannon's "Goin' to Germany," the Memphis Jug Band's "Stealin' " and "Overseas Stomp," and two tunes that they'd play for a long time, Noah Lewis's "Viola Lee Blues," and his version of "Minglewood Blues." Other blues classics filtered in, like Howlin' Wolf's "Little Red Rooster" and Sonny Boy Williamson's "Good Morning Little Schoolgirl." Tom Stone brought in records by the East Bay one-man-band blues singer Jesse Fuller, and "Beat It on Down the Line" and the "Monkey and the Engineer" became Weir staples. Later they would add Chuck Berry's "Memphis" and Jimmy Reed's "Big Boss Man." Whatever the material, Weir was ecstatic, barely able to believe his good luck in finding musicians who could teach him. Sara thought of him as "real pretty, real eager," and so he was. David Nelson gave them their name, dubbing this new band Mother McCree's Uptown Jug Champions. Just to keep it loose, they changed the spelling with each gig.

Their first show was at the Tangent on January 25, 1964, and their performances throughout that year were always down-home, with a "certain level of chaos and disorganization, slightly loony and chaotic," said David Parker, much funkier than Kweskin's band. Weir he saw as goofy but lovable, well meaning, the baby of the bunch and the main butt of the traditional male ribbing. Pigpen, on the other hand, needed to get slightly, but only slightly, drunk to perform. Oddly enough, or perhaps not, the band began to grow in popularity. "Somehow," Jerry mused, "the sheer fun of it made it successful." Lacking the anxiety-producing perfectionism demanded by bluegrass, jug certainly had that effect on him.

Fun is always a popular commodity, but early in 1964 it was especially desirable. Still reeling emotionally from the assassination of John Kennedy, a significant portion of the entire country, 70 million people, glued itself to a television on the night of Sunday, February 9, to watch the new British musical sensation, the Beatles, on *The Ed Sullivan Show*. Even muggers watched: police reported the lowest crime rate in fifty years for the hour of the program. By the end of the following month, the top five songs on the *Billboard* charts were all by the Beatles, with seven more in lower positions. The word "phenomenal" was actually an understatement. Four boys from Liverpool, heavily exposed to American rhythm and blues music brought home by their town's sailors, had created their name in homage to Buddy Holly's Crickets and John Lennon's social heroes, the Beats, and reenergized the rock and roll music that had fallen quiet in 1960. Their timing was exquisite. On the heels of the Profumo scandal and the great mail train robbery, Britain, too, needed a happy diversion, and its newspapers were entirely ready to collaborate in creating one. In October 1963 the papers covered the Beatles' appearance on the top English TV entertainment program, *Sunday Night at the London Palladium*, as though it were a riotous second coming, though in fact the audiences outside had been well behaved. When Fleet Street was finished, Britain was awash in what they dubbed Beatlemania, and by the time it reached the United States, Beatlemania was real. The media adored the lads' cheeky wit and recognized their basic wholesomeness, and were happy to run with a good story. It swept young America, although not, initially, Garcia and his friends. Jerry was a purist folkie, and he and his peers were skeptical of any fad.

Besides, they were busy. Hunter, Nelson, and Legate, for instance, had briefly settled in Los Angeles, where they were studying Scientology, looking for what they later described as science-fiction magical powers. For some time they had been experimenting with Legate's e-meter, a primitive type of lie detector, and it had been fascinating to monitor their own inhibitions and limits. Down at Scientology headquarters in Los Angeles, complete with security checks and rules about things like pot smoking, the game grew less interesting to everyone. As Legate said, "I didn't feel myself accountable to them, and walked away." Hunter was also sampling various other spiritual practices, including Subud, a neo-yogic form of meditation with modern origins in Java, and the Gurdjieff Fellowship, essentially looking for a nonchemical version of what he'd found in the V.A. Hospital drug tests. He got an invitation to join the jug band from Garcia, but he decided that he couldn't play jug well. Truth be told, he was still nursing something of a grudge over his ouster from the Black Mountain Boys—grudge-holding being one of his obdurate character traits—and so he declined. Instead, he grew deeply involved with amphetamines and prose word-painting, trying to create an Ur-language, a language beyond language.

Lesh, too, disdained the Beatles for lacking in intellectual substance. Living in San Francisco and driving his mail truck, he joined his Berio classmate Steve Reich and worked on a hip project, Event III, which brought together their music, the light projections of artist Elias Romero, and the theater of the San Francisco Mime Troupe. The evening was a fundraising benefit for the civil rights activists then seeking to integrate the workforce of the Sheraton Hotel, a protest that came to involve two major sit-ins, hundreds of arrests, and the hotel's complete capitulation. Reich was part of a number of avant-garde collaborations at this time, including the Tape Music Center, founded by Ramon Sender and Morton Subotnick, located first at the San Francisco Conservatory of Music, then at a site on Divisadero Street, and later at Mills College. The center allowed electronic composers to work in an open, nonacademic atmosphere, and one of its programs might include a reading by Beat poet Michael McClure, a performance by the Mime Troupe, and tape music. For Event III, the musicians wore white sweaters on which their age appeared in numbers. Lesh played a bit of trumpet, and the music was a combination of tape and live performance, as well as a section for multiple pianos. They were followed by the Mime Troupe. Founded by R. G. "Ronnie" Davis, the troupe was highly political theater out to challenge the power structure, but it was saved from extremist tedium by its sense of humor. A collection, in one member's words, of "dockworkers, college students, socialist organizers, market analysts, musicians, opera singers, vegetarians, drug addicts, ballet dancers, criminals, and bona fide eccentrics . . . It was the troupe's expectation that America should live up to her promises and play by her stated rules—and we intended to provoke her until she did." It would have a considerable impact on San Francisco, although at Event III, when Davis took questions from the audience, Reich and Lesh found them so obtuse that they felt the need to repeat their performance, and did so.

Working with Reich had been stimulating, and it inspired Lesh's last Komposition, a part of the "New Music" series held late in May at the Capp Street performance space in San Francisco. Lesh would dismiss his piece, "6⅞ for Bernardo Moreno," as *Gebrauchsmusik,* or filler, something he'd done only because not participating was unthinkable. He described it as a questing piano in the midst of a cosmic background of strings. Zenlike and relatively simple, it was performed by a group that included Reich, with the piano played by Tom Constanten, who thought it resembled middle Stockhausen, a "Zeitmasse" or "Time Measures" type of piece in twelve-tone serial technique. What was most amusing for T.C. was that during the performance, thumps from the judo classes upstairs intruded, and T.C. was able to find a pattern in the score that resembled the thumps, blending them nicely. The same intersection of music and reality was repeated when car sounds outside faded into the piece. It seemed to T.C. a most synchronous evening, perhaps because the day before, he and Phil had taken LSD for the first time, spending the night listening to their beloved Mahler's complete symphonies with extremely fresh ears. For Lesh, it was his father's teasing remark that absolutely made his evening at the New Music event. "Hat size, huh? For a pinhead? 6⅞ is pretty small." Lesh later reflected, "I don't think I ever loved him more."

As the summer of 1964 came in, Garcia confronted his love affair with bluegrass. He'd gotten exceptionally good as a player. Moreover, the first nonsouthern, nonrural, "citybilly" picker, Bill "Brad" Keith, had already passed through Bill Monroe's band, so the idea of an outsider "making it" in bluegrass no longer seemed ridiculous. In March, the Black Mountain Boys had played the Tangent with Jerry Kaukonen opening, and one of their best tunes was Keith's "Devil's Dream." Although the Black Mountain Boys were inclined to play too fast, much of their show was technically excellent. Garcia had a wonderful ear and great sensitivity to what others were playing, although at times he was perhaps a bit too pyrotechnical and overconfident in his abilities. In May they played at the San Francisco State Folk Festival, meeting two Ozark pickers then living in Stockton, Vern Williams and Ray Park. Vern would recall Garcia as a "damn good banjo picker," although he did think it strange for a "Mexican" to play bluegrass. The problem was, there was no significant audience for bluegrass in the Bay Area, and even when bodies filled a room, it was not a sophisticated group of patrons. There weren't enough high-caliber musicians to go around, and there certainly wasn't enough money to be made to support Sara and Heather. If he was going to be serious about it as a career, he'd have to consider leaving San Francisco. First, though, he had to investigate the home of the art form, the American South.

His friend Sandy Rothman had spent the previous summer around the Valhalla of bluegrass, Bill Monroe's "Bean Blossom" facility, and was looking for a companion to accompany his return, so Garcia had a travel partner. Sandy was four years younger than Jerry, a Berkeley kid who'd played guitar since the age of eleven, and who'd heard the Redwood Canyon Ramblers in junior high school. When Eric Thompson had gone off to the East Coast late in 1963, Sandy had replaced him in the Black Mountain Boys. As his and Sandy's departure approached, Garcia turned over the bulk of his students to Bob Weir, who would enjoy the challenge of teaching young kids with small hands. Early in May, Garcia and Rothman bought a bunch of blank seven-inch tapes for Jerry's Wollensak recorder, climbed into Garcia's car, and hit the road.

The summer of 1964 was a hell of a time for a Jew and a "Mexican" driving a car with California plates to go into the deep South. It was the Freedom Summer, and the South was writhing with change—and danger. A month after Jerry and Sandy passed through the region, three civil rights workers—James Chaney, Andrew Goodman, and Michael Schwerner—would vanish near Meridian, Mississippi. Their bodies would be found in August. For reporters and other visiting outsiders, the car of choice that season was the biggest, heaviest vehicle possible, with windows and doors controlled from the driver's seat, and that meant a Chrysler Imperial. Jerry's '61 Corvair wasn't remotely in that league. Still, he shaved his goatee and cut his hair short, and in his new windbreaker he looked, Sara thought, like a gas station attendant. He and Sandy managed to traverse the South without overt incident, but Jerry would remember it as "creepy," based on the reactions they got to their license plates and "foreign-sounding" names. His first sight of "colored" drinking fountains and bathrooms was shocking, and grew no easier with repetition. He realized he was naive in his San Francisco tolerance, and the South's legacy of bigotry and fear overwhelmed him. Garcia and Rothman's timing was remarkable, for they passed through the South at a pivotal time in American political history, as a southern president directed the passage of the Civil Rights Act in May and then listened to socialist Michael Harrington and ramrodded the Economic Opportunity Act through Congress in August, creating what he called the Great Society, the apotheosis of American liberalism.

More concerned with music, Garcia and Rothman went first to Los Angeles, where they saw Hunter and David Nelson, and then met up with their friends the Kentucky Colonels, the bluegrass band that featured Clarence White. They crossed the country together in a small caravan, and their first memorable stop was a trailer park near St. Louis, where they met an old friend of the Colonels named Slim, a big handsome hillbilly of French Canadian descent, the king of the trailer park, and the kind of character one might find in a book half *On the Road* and half *The Grapes of Wrath*. They spent the night picking and singing in a Cajun-like party atmosphere, and then Jerry and Sandy broke off and headed for their first stop, Bloomington, Indiana, home of Neil Rosenberg, the original banjo player of the Redwood Canyon Ramblers and now a graduate student in folklore at Indiana University, and his wife, Ann.

After a few days they decided to give the Rosenbergs a break and took off for Tyndall Air Force Base in Panama City, Florida, the current duty station of Neil's friend Scott Hambly, also of the Redwood Canyon Ramblers. Scott was impressed with Garcia, who was by then "gobbling up" every bluegrass banjo lick possible, "boiling away" as he spent four to five hours a day practicing alone, analyzing and recasting finger positions with a "tremendous power of attention." After that, the three of them would play for four or five hours, and although Hambly felt that Garcia sometimes neglected the "holistic concept of bluegrass as a united sound," he was extremely taken with Jerry's development. The three of them even played a show at the Noncommissioned Officers' Club at Tyndall, but after a few days the vicious insect life of Florida drove Jerry and Sandy away, and they set off for Dothan, Alabama, to hear the well-known players Jim and Jesse McReynolds.

Around May 20, they returned to Bloomington. Neil, too, was impressed with Garcia's musical growth, and enthralled him with his sweetness and generosity. Neil took the boys, armed with Jerry's Wollensak, to a treasure vault, Marvin Hedrick's radio-TV repair shop. Marvin also sold tape recorders and had been doing so since the fifties, a seminal time for bluegrass. Tape recorders were then a rare commodity, so his tapes of early bluegrass were a precious trove. Jerry and Sandy spent what Jerry recalled as several days dubbing tapes like kids in a candy store with no stomachache to follow.

On May 24 they arrived at bluegrass Valhalla, Bill Monroe's Brown County Jamboree, otherwise known as Bean Blossom, after its location in that tiny town near Bloomington, Indiana. Shows were at 3 and 8 P.M. on Sunday, price one dollar. The parking lot was really part of the show, and it appeared that half the audience brought instruments to jam with before the performance. Bean Blossom the facility was in fact a long, low horse barn, heated by coal-fired stoves, the floor half gravel and stained by the end product of Bill's free-roaming roosters. Bill was frugal, but he was still the Creator, and seeing him up close and not onstage struck them speechless. They were too terrified to take out their instruments in front of him, and Garcia's charm evaporated into a tongue-tied shyness that left him incapable of promoting himself. Garcia never would be able to bring himself to apply for the job, although later that same summer Sandy would join Monroe on guitar. Aside from treasured memories and a rich educational experience, the only thing Garcia would get out of the day at Bean Blossom was the tape he and Sandy made, and it turned out to have an electronic hum that ruined it.

They did much better a few days later. Garcia would always feel that in the course of his journey he saw some essential essence of bluegrass, "the where-it-comes-from hit," and one of the best moments was in Dayton, Ohio, home to many displaced Appalachians, where they recorded the Osborne Brothers at the White Sands Bar. Early in June they reached Sunset Park, Pennsylvania, a bluegrass showplace. Among the many Amish who crowded the place, Garcia spotted a young man by the name of David Grisman walking across the parking lot with his mandolin case. He knew about Grisman from Eric Thompson, and they quickly fell in with each other, picking a few tunes. It was an excellent start to a friendship. But Garcia and Rothman were still on the road and headed for their last two stops, Marshall Leicester in New Haven and Bill Keith in Boston. There was an interlude when they got lost and found themselves on the streets of Manhattan, but it was exceedingly brief. "We left *immediately,*" Garcia said, laughing. "I didn't want to drive in that mess."

After seeing Marshall, they wound up sharing a Cambridge attic room with the Kentucky Colonels, who'd managed to beat them to New England. They spent some richly fulfilling time with Bill Keith, one of Garcia's primary hopes for the trip, and then Jerry realized his odyssey was over. His letters home had been detailed, full of his encounters and emotions, complete with pictures in the margins for little Heather. Now he wired home to Sara for funds, hopped into the Corvair, said good-bye to Sandy in Bloomington, and drove straight back to the Bay Area, stopping only for gas and naps. He would play more bluegrass upon his return, with two different bands. The first was the Asphalt Jungle Mountain Boys, with Eric Thompson and his friend Jody Stecher, and then what Garcia thought was his best bluegrass playing yet, a December gig at the Offstage with Sandy and Scott Hambly in a one-night band that combined members of the Black Mountain Boys with a member of the Redwood Canyon Ramblers. But his dream was over. There was no way for him to be a San Franciscan and a full-time bluegrass musician, and life in the South was simply not a practical possibility for him.

There was still the jug band, and it remained satisfying, but a couple of nonperforming activities also enriched his life that August. The dark genius/social critic/humorist Lenny Bruce was then being pursued by a coalition of local police and elements of the Roman Catholic Church for his use of "obscenity" in his act, and he needed transcripts of his shows to use in the many legal cases he was confronting. Joe Edmonston's wife was Lenny's lawyer's secretary, and she thought of Garcia. After all the time he'd spent with old music tapes, his ear was acute, and he became a transcriber. "[Lenny] had a shorthand way of talking when he was mumbling like a speed freak, but it was real content, real stuff," Garcia said. "I learned so much, it was incredible. What a mind. He'd thumb through a magazine and riff. I'd find the article . . . I swear to God, he could condense all the key stuff in like three or four paragraphs . . . It would be a mumble in seven syllables but it had bits and pieces of everything in the article." It was an extraordinary opportunity for Garcia, and he enjoyed it to the fullest. It placed him in the very heart of American cultural criticism from an absolutely unique perspective. He was already a full-fledged American outsider—one cover of *Life* that month concerned the unprecedented prosperity then sweeping America, and he certainly had no part in that. But he also stood outside the intellectual culture of that time, centered on *Evergreen* magazine, which was all existential coolness and

detachment—Beckett, Genet, Ionesco, and Warhol. Lenny Bruce's cruci-
fixion was about passion and caring, not alienation, and Garcia knew it.
Not that he was humorless.

The other high point of his August was the opening of the Richard
Lester Beatles film *A Hard Day's Night.* A wondrous combination of antiauthoritarian humor, fabulous music, and simple, leaping joy, it was, Jerry
thought, a "little model of good times," fun, but consciously artistic, with a
simple message: "You can be young, you can be far-out, and you can
still make it." Suddenly, rock and roll made a little more sense to him,
although he did not attend the Beatles' show at the Cow Palace on
August 19.

Sara was then attending film classes at Stanford, and they borrowed
an eight-millimeter camera from David Parker to make their own
movies. Humor was their keynote: Garcia filmed Parker and Eric
Thompson pushing Eric's motorcycle around town, grunting and groaning until at the end they hopped on and sped off. Garcia shot Hunter
spinning in circles in stop-action at the zoo, Pigpen fooling around down
by the bay, and a stop-action chalkboard cartoon that was quite funny.
The only nonhumorous piece documented something going on across
the bay, at U.C. Berkeley. It was called the Free Speech Movement.
Berkeley was supposed to be the American dream fulfilled, a great university that was public and effectively free. But the students, some of
them civil rights movement veterans, felt that they were being treated
like factory product. They demanded that Sproul Plaza, traditionally a
free-speech area for students, remain open, and in the course of the fall
brought the university to its knees with a strike. In December at yet
another gathering in the plaza, student Mario Savio said, "There's a time
when the operation of the machine becomes so odious, makes you so sick
at heart, that you can't take part . . . and you've got to put your bodies
upon the gears and upon the wheels and you've got to make it stop." As
Joan Baez sang "Blowin' in the Wind," a thousand students, many of
them the academic cream of the school, illegally entered the administration building. More than six hundred were arrested for trespassing, but
the American educational system would be reacting to the Free Speech
Movement for the next decade.

Hunter had a delivery job that brought him into Berkeley every day,
and though he felt it was "too violent-feeling," he sympathized with the
demonstrators. Less sensitive to violence, Weir directly modeled his point
of view on Savio. Sara had been part of the peace movement since her
teens and was making antiwar placards throughout the fall. And Garcia

watched, fascinated. Though always on the side of the dispossessed, he was apolitical, distrusting demonstrations on principle. That fall he voted for Lyndon Johnson against Barry Goldwater. It would feel morally wrong to him, and he would not vote again. Instead, he figured, he would live a life that was a daily vote for freedom.

The Warlocks

(11/64–6/65)

The new band was primarily Pigpen's idea. He'd been telling Garcia for months that they should start an electric blues band, and as the fall of 1964 passed, Jerry came to agree. Pig's point was that much of the jug band's blues material could easily be electrified, on the model of his favorite new rock band, the Rolling Stones. The Beatles had turned out to be the forerunner of what came to be called the British Invasion, and although all the new English bands played a music derived from American rock and roll, the Stones were the closest in spirit and playing to the root blues that preceded rock. At age twelve, Mick Jagger had lived near an American army base, where a black cook introduced him to rhythm and blues. Keith Richard heard Elvis Presley's "Heartbreak Hotel" and fell straight out of his choirboy suburban London childhood. Childhood friends, Keith and Mick heard Brian Jones play Elmore James material at the Ealing Club in 1962, added Charlie Watts on drums and Bill Wyman on bass, and became the Rolling Stones.

Despite the initial outcry over the Beatles' stylized haircuts—American males had kept their hair short for the previous seventy years or so—U.S. opinion had largely come to see the Beatles as charming if irreverent, lovable, and surely no threat. The Stones' manager, Andrew Loog Oldham, decided to sell his clients with a darker, more controversial vision. Mixing bohemian rebelliousness with "campy" sexual ambiguity, Oldham challenged current mores with a wink and a snicker. Should one not have the purchase price of their first album, *England's Newest Hitmakers,* he wrote in the liner notes, "see that blind man, knock him on the head, steal his wallet, and lo and behold, you have the loot." That was worth a chuckle to Pigpen and Garcia, but the material was of greater importance—Buddy Holly's "Not Fade Away," Willie Dixon's "I Just Wanna Make Love to You," Slim Harpo's "King Bee." The harsh, driving sound took Garcia back to the twin guitar rhythm and blues radio sounds of his childhood, the sound of Jimmy Reed, Muddy Waters, and Howlin' Wolf.

Rock and roll was in the air. Night after night, they'd close up Dana Morgan's, borrow from the new instrument stock in front, and play. Pigpen was now the janitor at Morgan's, and his voice and harmonica ("harp") were as good as any rock and roller's. He also began to pick away at a little Farfisa organ. Bob Weir, Garcia's summer teaching replacement, had stuck around and was thoroughly absorbed by the Beatles. Electric instruments were fun and, he thought, "seductive." He picked up the rhythm guitar. It seemed to him that "we just knew an electric band was coming, and then Dana Morgan's son, Dana Junior, picked up the bass." The band seemed about complete when they turned to one of their fellow teachers, Bill Kreutzmann, who was Palo Alto's hottest drummer. "The only drummer I had really played with around that area that I thought really had a nice feel was Bill," said Garcia. "By now he's eighteen, so I talked to him and he was just as weird as ever, and I really, really didn't understand anything he said. He was just like 'Rcty rcty shdd.' You know, what? 'Rrrrou.' Okay, you know. I asked him if he wanted to play and he was delighted. He was all over the place, so we played and it was great, you know. He worked out fine. I didn't realize what a truly straight person he was until we finally got high together and that was a whole other Bill jumped out, you know. That Bill was a total imp."

Grandson of the famed Chicago Bears football coach Clark O'Shaughnessy, Bill Kreutzmann was born on May 7, 1946, and grew up in a prosperous home on the Peninsula. His father was an attorney with the Emporium, a San Francisco department store, who for some reason listened to the black radio station KDIA. His mother taught dance at Stanford University, and from his earliest years Bill would pound a little Indian drum for her as she prepared choreography for her classes. His career had its bumps: in the sixth grade, his music teacher told him, "Bill, you have to leave class because you can't keep a beat." But he persevered, and the beat became part of him. He was the sort of kid who never stopped practicing his drumming, whacking on the handlebars of his bike as he delivered newspapers.

In 1959, in the eighth grade, he found his savior in a drum teacher named Lee Anderson, a Stanford graduate student in physics, and he began taking lessons every Saturday. A resident of Perry Lane, Anderson also acted as a raffish bohemian role model for the boy, teaching him how to mix elaborate drinks at his home bar, draped in Hawaiian nets, and exposing him to the creative graduate-student bohemians who were his neighbors, like the writer Ken Kesey, the psychology student Vic Lovell, and the dancer Chloe Scott. Kreutzmann's homelife was difficult, and his parents eventually divorced after years of dissension. Meantime, the drums offered relief. "When I was a kid, I'd have fights with my parents, then . . . beat the shit out of my drums for hours." And when it counted, the folks came through. During one of those drum marathons in the garage, Kreutzmann became aware that a neighbor, objecting to the racket, was pounding on the side of the garage with a bat, "out of time and everything . . . I'd stop, it'd stop. I'd begin, he'd hit some more." Dad came out and confronted the neighbor. "Leave my son alone—and that's *my* garage you're hitting."

Family tensions finally made it best for Bill to go away to school, and he spent a year at the Orme School in Arizona. He found it difficult, until his parents sent out his drums and he was able to resume daily practice. One day, the headmaster brought that night's distinguished visiting lecturer into the auditorium where Kreutzmann was practicing, and signaled for him to stop. But Aldous Huxley asked the boy to continue, and although Kreutzmann didn't particularly understand that night's lecture on the impact of psychedelic drugs on human culture, he would remember the validation the man had given him.

Big, sometimes aggressive, Kreutzmann was also a reader, from Kerouac's *On the Road* to Mezz Mezzrow's white hipster guidebook, *Really the Blues,* to John Steinbeck, whose character Lenny in *Of Mice and Men* became an important personal reference point to him. His reading also helped him with the other prime activity at Morgan's, which was the ongoing seminar in everything, led by Garcia, insatiably curious about the world around him and ways to understand it. In addition to riffs and jams, they discussed Martin Heidegger and existentialism. Initially, the younger guys, Weir and Kreutzmann, would mostly listen, and Pigpen would periodically flap his wings and crow "bullshit," just to keep things real.

Kreutzmann was already a working band veteran when he joined them at Morgan's, having played for a local band called the Legends for some time. Fronted by a black vocalist named Jay Price, the Legends were more a rhythm and blues than a rock band, covering James Brown, Junior Walker, Freddie King, the Isley Brothers' "Shout," and Ray Charles's "What'd I Say." They wore red coats, black pants, and black ties, and played YMCA dances, fraternity parties, and shows at the local navy airstrip, Moffett Field, which frequently ended in brawls. Though he was only eighteen that fall, and a senior at Palo Alto High School because he'd stayed back a year, Kreutzmann was already married and a father. At sixteen he'd met a young woman named Brenda at a Legends dance. Neither had much of a family life at home, and it brought them together. After their daughter, Stacey, was born in July 1964, they married, moving into a tiny apartment near East Palo Alto. Brenda went to work at the phone company, and since she was legally an adult because she'd graduated from high school, she was able to sign for Bill's absences from school. He worked in a wig shop and taught drumming at Morgan's and sometimes at people's homes, with Brenda and Stacey waiting in the car. They seemed an utterly conventional couple.

Having a drummer catalyzed the young group as a band, and although they were all broke, Dana Morgan, Jr.'s participation as the bass player solved the immediate problem of paying for electric instruments. They set to work. One day in December Randy Groenke, one of Garcia's banjo students, came into Dana Morgan's and was stunned almost to tears to see Jerry playing an electric guitar. The change had come. In fact, change seemed positively to accelerate as the new year 1965 began. Early in January Mother McCree's Uptown Jug Champions played its last gig at yet another College of San Mateo Folk Festival. In one of the first overt post-Beatles signs that big business was coming to recognize rock's financial power, the archetypal Fender Guitar Company was purchased by CBS for $13 million. *Hullabaloo,* the first national rock television show, began broadcasting on January 8. At the end of the month there was a typical-for-the-era rock show at the Cow Palace in San Francisco, featuring the Righteous Brothers, the local Beau Brummels, the Supremes, the Temptations, Sonny and Cher, the Ronettes, and several other bands, each doing three to five tunes in front of a packed house whose aisles were patrolled by sheriffs waving flashlights. The truly important events of the early year were in the realm of civil rights: the assassination on February 21 of Malcolm X, the March 7 attack by Alabama State Police on civil rights marchers in Selma that killed a visiting Boston minister, and the response by President Johnson, who quoted the anthem of the civil rights movement, "We Shall Overcome," and pushed a voting rights bill through Congress. The South that Garcia had visited only the previous summer would never be the same.

Early in April in Palo Alto, Jerry Garcia and David Nelson were helping their friend and former jug band mate David Parker and his girlfriend, Bonnie, move. One of their banjo buddies, Rick Shubb, had scored a bottle full of LSD and had shown up that day with Butch Waller, Herb Pedersen, and Eric Thompson. When the move was over, Jerry grabbed two doses, ran home, and gave one to Sara. The day turned magical. "Mostly it was that wonderful feeling you get of 'suspicions confirmed,' " said Garcia. "*Haha hahahahaha.* A perfectly wonderful time, that soft psychedelia, sweet, great fun . . . tremendous affirmation and reassurance." At another time, he spoke of the day in terms of destiny. "Yeah, this is what I've been looking for. You know I've been a seeker all along, and this is at least part of what it was I was looking for and maybe even more." And again, "There's more than anybody ever let on. We *know* that." As the trip evolved, Sara entered a period of doubt, and then looked in the mirror and grew uneasy. Separately, so did David Nelson. Instinctively, both Sara and David turned to the experienced Hunter for reassurance, walking over to his home at different times. Hunter told Nelson, "Do you always jump out of airplanes without a parachute?" but was kindlier to Sara, smiling: "It's all right." And it was.

LSD's impact on all of them would be positive and liberating, Garcia most of all. Bluegrass banjo was a massive exercise in precision and control, and the combination of LSD and electricity would set him free. He reflected later that he'd been too serious before the LSD experience, and that his vision of music had been too small. The essence of his approach to playing had always been rhythmic, and now that the strictures of his own limited imagination were gone, he would enter a more fluid realm, where anything was possible.

This included something never before contemplated: rock music with intellectual content. In February, Bob Dylan had played on *The Les Crane Show,* singing "It's All Over Now, Baby Blue," and Garcia had thought it beautiful. His folkie prejudices against Dylan started to melt. Then Dylan began to talk with Crane, "and just rapped insanely. Beautiful mad stuff. And that like turned us all on," Garcia told a friend. "We couldn't believe it. Here was this guy, it was almost like being in the South and seeing a spade on television." A few days after the acid trip, Garcia dropped by Eric Thompson's house and heard Dylan's new album, *Bringing It All Back Home,* for the first time, playing it over and over. "Using a blowtorch in the middle of the candle," said one critic, "is less aesthetic than burning it at both ends, but more people see the flame." "Subterranean Homesick Blues," "Mr. Tambourine Man," "Love Minus Zero/No Limit," "She Belongs to Me," and "Baby Blue" were not just songs, but lightning bolts that illuminated their lives.

> *That he not busy being born*
> *Is busy dying . . .*
> *While them that defend what they cannot see*
> *With a killer's pride, security*
> *it blows their minds most bitterly*
> *For them that think death's honesty*
> *Won't fall upon them naturally*
> *Life sometimes*
> *Must get lonely.*

Garcia and his friends understood, in their minds, their hearts, their souls.

Jammed into a tiny, dark rehearsal room at Morgan's, they practiced away, setting the snare drums that hung on the wall to rattling. Garcia was studying Freddie King as he began the process of translating precision bluegrass playing into blues-based guitar licks. From the beginning, his style would retain the clarity of the banjo note, but electric guitar allowed for a freedom of expression, particularly of rhythm, and for emphasizing individual notes, in a way that bluegrass banjo never could. One reason the room was crowded was their audience. The first rehearsal had been closed, but a friend of Weir's, veteran Beatlemaniac Sue Swanson, had elected herself fan for life and found a corner from which to watch the second rehearsal, and those that followed. She was soon joined by her sister in Beatleism, Connie Bonner. Fairly soon, Sue also found herself a job, that of playing the 45s from which the band learned new songs. At length, it came time to choose their name. Weir was reading Tolkien's *Lord of the Rings*, and there was much talk of wizards and magic. Some combination of Weir, Garcia, and Pigpen came up with the name "Warlocks," and it stuck. On May 5 the Warlocks played their first public show, at Magoo's Pizza Parlor in Menlo Park. It was a quiet night, with an audience that was primarily Menlo-Atherton High School students, since Sue, Connie, and another of Weir's friends, Bob Matthews, had talked up the show there.

By the second gig, on May 12, the joint was packed, and the response was fabulous. Hunter, for one, thought the show was "wonderful." They were a basic cover band, playing Chuck Berry, "Stealin'," Dylan's "Baby Blue," "King Bee," "Walkin' the Dog," "Wooly Bully," and other hits. Afterward there was the usual party, and Jerry and Phil Lesh, who'd arrived late and missed the gig, went out to Weir's friend's car to get stoned. It was a slightly nervous situation, since Weir was not only underage but incapable of dissimulation. But pot was pot, and this baggie came from a special source, a friend of Weir's having purchased it from the legendary Neal Cassady, "Dean Moriarity" of Kerouac's *On the Road*. This was an exceptional pedigree, and they all appreciated it.

Lesh remarked casually that he might take up bass, but it was only an idle remark. He'd pretty well left the music world as a participant by now, but *A Hard Day's Night* had made him a rock music fan, and he took a transistor radio along with him in his post office truck. When he heard Dylan's "Subterranean Homesick Blues" on the Top 40 station KFRC, he was so startled that he pulled over and forgot about his route for a while. He'd grown his hair out, and someone complained in a letter to his boss that he looked like an "unkempt monkey," a compliment he of course thoroughly cherished. Although he cut his hair once, it was still too long, and he was ordered to do so again. Enough—he began collecting unemployment. On May 14 he joined some of the hipper people in San Francisco, including many of the Beat poets and the people who would create at least three significant new bands in the next few months, at the Rolling Stones' concert at the Civic Auditorium. It was a seminal event, thought poet David Meltzer: "We are witness to the emergence of a song-culture." The show was in a fifties-style format, with many bands, including the Byrds, doing three or four songs each. Despite the trite structure, when it was over, many of those hip young people left the show by snake-dancing down the aisle.

On May 27 Phil and his friends Hank Harrison and Bobby and Jane Petersen took some acid and went down to Menlo Park to see what Jerry's band could do. Hunter was also there, as were Bonnie and David Parker. His imagination seized by Pigpen's harmonica on "Little Red Rooster," Lesh began to dance, and was told by the pizza parlor management to stop. Kreutzmann would recall his long blond hair shaking away, and the ensuing argument. Weir knew that Garcia had plans for his old friend. The bass player, Dana Morgan, wasn't really a musician, and he couldn't make weekend gigs because of a National Guard obligation. Moreover, his wife didn't particularly care for the other Warlocks. Consequently, after the first set Garcia pulled Lesh into a booth, put a beer in his hand, and told him, "Listen, man, you're gonna play bass in my band." It was a statement, not a question or invitation. "I was so excited," Lesh said, "that I didn't have to think about it . . . but I knew something great was happening, something bigger than everybody, bigger than me for sure." Afterward they went over to Garcia's home, where Bobby Petersen told Garcia that they'd all taken LSD. "Gee," Jerry replied, "if I'd known you were doing acid, I'd have taken you on a better trip . . . I could never play doing acid." It would be a while before he'd be confident enough to get high and play, and the first time was accidental.

Lesh went back to San Francisco, where his girlfriend, Ruth Pahkala, bought him his first bass, an inexpensive Gibson, with a "neck like a telephone pole," he thought. "Kinda like a flashlight." He demanded a lesson from Garcia, who said, "See those bottom four strings on my guitar? They're tuned just like the bass, only an octave higher."

"Yeah, I know that already, Jerry."

"Well, didn't you used to play the violin?"

"Sure."

"Here you go, man."

Later, Lesh would say that his first practice session lasted seven hours, and he could not sleep that night. He'd listened to and loved the great jazz bass players like Scott La Faro and Charlie Haden, but this instrument involved electricity, and that created something altogether special. His style was unique, because he had almost no electric role models and essentially made it up from scratch. On June 7 Laird Grant helped Phil move down to Palo Alto. As a way of acknowledging the significance of the moment, he injected the psychedelic drug DMT and found out, as he put it later, whom the joke was on. "Oh my God, here comes the invisible mind circus" was the day's slogan, and he laughed all the way to Palo Alto. "It was perfect, too perfect," Lesh thought some twenty years later. "There's that core of perfection that runs through the whole thing, that thread, we're still sliding along it."

With Dana out of the band, Mr. Morgan Sr. "decided I just hated the noise they were making . . . I put them out in the carport, but they kept sneaking back in. Finally I got so tired of them I sold the instruments." Jerry had to ask his mother for money to buy a guitar and amp, and they borrowed instruments from Swain's and Guitars Unlimited. They rehearsed anywhere they could find, from Sue Swanson's house to Lesh's to wherever. But this was the kind of practice that was fun. Phil became the guy who would crawl through the window to wake up Pigpen, never a reliable soul that way, and they were off.

On June 18 they played their first show with Lesh, at a teen rock club in Hayward across San Francisco Bay called Frenchy's. It was a fairly wobbly night. Their sound was "wooden," thought Phil, "real stiff." "Our most endearing quality was how rough and raunchy we were . . . noisy," said Garcia.

It must have been rough. When they returned for the second night of their engagement, they found out they'd been replaced by an accordion and clarinet duo. They never did get paid for that first night.

A Very Loud
Bar Band

(6/10/65−11/12/65)

The summer of 1965 was probably the best in history for listening to Top 40 rock. Two days before Lesh had seen them in San Francisco in May, the Rolling Stones had gone to a studio in Los Angeles to lay down what was Keith Richard's first classic chromed buzz-saw chord progression, a perfect, murderous ode to adolescent frustration called "(I Can't Get No) Satisfaction." By late June and for the rest of the summer it was no. 1. It had displaced "Mr. Tambourine Man," the Dylan tune covered by the Byrds, the first of the American folk rock responses to the British Invasion. Smart enough to get ex-Beatles press agent Derek Taylor as a cohort, the Byrds were miles ahead of the Warlocks in ambition and sophistication, but they were also all former folkies turned on to rock by the Beatles, and Byrd David Crosby was part of the same Bay Area folk scene as Garcia.

The live rock and roll moment of the summer took place in July, on a stage at Newport, Rhode Island. Bob Dylan's *Bringing It All Back Home* had been a complex album with electric instruments, but this was something else. After his normal solo acoustic set, Dylan took to the stage of the Newport Folk Festival in late July with Mike Bloomfield on guitar, Harvey Brooks on bass, Al Kooper on organ, and Sam Lay on drums, all of them recruited and rehearsed that very afternoon. He plugged in his own electric guitar and proceeded to lay waste to the temple of folk with amplified versions of "Maggie's Farm" and "Like a Rolling Stone." The saintly Pete Seeger called for an ax, threatening to cut the power cables. Once the audience recovered from its shock, it booed. Dylan returned solo to sing what would, in time, become obvious: "It's All Over Now, Baby Blue." "Like a Rolling Stone" had been released as a single in June, had entered the charts the day before Newport, and would replace "Satisfaction" at no. 1 in September. The album *Highway 61 Revisited* would be released in early August. The future of rock had arrived.

Like most new bands just getting a start, the Warlocks were scuffling through a series of bar gigs. There was the Fireside Club in San Mateo, and Big Al's Gas House and the Cinnamon A-Go-Go in Redwood City. The band celebrated Garcia's twenty-third birthday on August 1 with a group LSD trip. Acid wasn't Pigpen's thing, and he declined. Kreutzmann was not yet ready. But Jerry, Phil, Bobby for the first time, and various others dropped, and then everyone went off to run around the hills, leaving Weir with his cheerleader girlfriend, who hadn't taken any but wanted to watch. It was a telling moment for his future when the car zoomed back and his friends tossed him in the car, smiled at the cheerleader, shrugged apologetically, and took off. He ended the day with his buddies Sue Swanson and Connie Bonner in the hills above Palo Alto, gazing down at the twinkling lights as he intoned, "If I've had any major realizations, it's that I want to be a musician." Just as LSD separated Weir from his girlfriend, it brought Garcia to a new reality. "The whole world just went kablooey . . . my little attempt at having a straight life," he told an interviewer, "was really a fiction."

That August, the Garcia family moved into a communal house on Waverly Street in Palo Alto with David Nelson, Robert Hunter, Rick Shubb, and David and Bonnie Parker. Heather and Piro, the son of Hunter's friend Chris, shared a room, and it all seemed to work well.

The same week, on August 4, the gang went up to San Francisco to see another band of folk veterans, the Lovin' Spoonful, at Mother's, advertised as the "world's first psychedelic nightclub." Painted by the Psychedelic Rangers of Big Sur in layers of plastic and fluorescent paint, the colors crawled across the walls, and "the bathrooms alone," recalled the manager, "were just a *trip*, you know." The Spoonful included John Sebastian and Zal Yanovsky, New York folk veterans who tickled Sara by acknowledging Garcia as a respected musician. Their hit song "Do You Believe in Magic" was one of Lesh's favorites, and became part of the Warlocks' repertoire.

Culturally speaking, it was a busy and prophetic summer. On August 7, members of the Mime Troupe were arrested in San Francisco's Lafayette Park for performing *Il Candelaio,* a bawdy commedia dell'arte piece, without a permit. On the same day, a considerable portion of the Hell's Angels motorcycle club met Ken Kesey and his friends, who'd come to be known as the Merry Pranksters, at Kesey's house in La Honda. August 13 saw the debut of the *Berkeley Barb,* the first of the alternative "underground" weeklies, which covered political rallies, the Sexual Freedom League, the Hell's Angels, and anything else weird enough to interest its publisher, Max Scherr. On August 11, the first major urban American riot in many years ripped through South-Central Los Angeles. Before it was over, the Watts riot would kill 33, injure 812, and cause 3,000 arrests and $175 million in damage. Robert Hunter was among the National Guardsmen called out to "keep order." None of these events were isolated; all of them would have many consequences.

August 13 also witnessed the debut of yet another band, this time at a new club called the Matrix, on Fillmore Street in San Francisco's Marina neighborhood. Marty Balin had been a printer, dancer, and artist, and a member of the Town Criers, a slick professional folk act. Then he saw the Beatles and began to assemble a rock band, often choosing members for inscrutable reasons. He encountered Paul Kantner at a folk club called the Drinking Gourd, and, based on Paul's long hair and old cap, invited him to join. Somewhat later he saw a guitarist named Skip Spence auditioning for yet another group and divined that Spence would make a good drummer. Kantner called his old San Jose buddy Jerry, now Jorma, Kaukonen, but Jorma was still an acoustic blues purist, and declined. But hanging out with Kesey one day demonstrated to him that electricity could produce fascinating sounds, and he changed his mind. Later still, when they decided to replace the original bassist, he would put in a call to his old friend Jack Casady, a veteran of Washington, D.C., rhythm and blues bands, who happened not to have played bass in six months. "You better be able to play," Jorma told him, "or I'm gonna kill you." Jack lived. With vocalist Signe Toly Anderson, they were a band. Their search for a name would be involved. Utterly taken by Robert Heinlein's *Stranger in a Strange Land,* Kantner wanted to call the band the Nest, but was overruled. Their friend Steve Talbott spoofed the entire name game and offered "Blind Lemon Thomas Jefferson Airplane." Another friend cut it down, and the Jefferson Airplane took flight.

They had an invaluable ally. Bill Thompson was a copyboy at the *San Francisco Chronicle* as well as a poet and a painter who'd gotten to know Balin, and had eventually come to share a house with him. Tipped by

Thompson, Ralph Gleason, the *Chronicle*'s legendary jazz critic, presented himself at the Matrix on opening night. Gleason had always had an affection for rock, and his approval and support were gold. His piece "Jefferson Airplane—Sound and Style" appeared on August 15 and was the first public announcement of what would become the San Francisco music scene. As Gleason added a couple of days later, it was "entirely possible that this will be the new direction of contemporary American pop music." He was right. And more than just music was emerging. On September 5, the *San Francisco Examiner* ran a piece called "A New Paradise for Beatniks," about the Haight-Ashbury, a neighborhood named after a street intersection, where writers, painters, musicians, civil rights workers, crusaders, homosexuals, and marijuana users had gathered. But these weren't exactly beatniks. The paper called them "Hippies," the first time the word, a derivation of "hipsters," was applied to the San Francisco scene.

At the same time, six thousand miles east, another cultural pot was on a rolling boil. More stylistic and fashion-oriented than philosophical, Swinging London, as the media dubbed it, seemed to be the emergence of a hip, happening new generation of Londoners finally outgrowing the pinched legacy of World War II. It created a new aristocracy—of rock stars like the Beatles, the Stones, and the Who, fashion models like Jean Shrimpton, photographer David Bailey, designer Mary Quant, and actresses Julie Christie and Diana Rigg. Carnaby Street was style central, and the television show *The Avengers,* and especially the films *Blowup* and *Help!,* documented the mood. For the first time, youth-oriented styles began to have widespread artistic and commercial influence.

The Warlocks had found a home at a club halfway between Palo Alto and San Francisco in the town of Belmont. The In Room was a heavy-hitting divorcée's pickup joint, the sort of swinging bar where real-estate salesmen chased stewardesses and single women got plenty of free drinks. Dark, with red and black as the color scheme, it was the kind of place that sold almost nothing but hard liquor. The Warlocks' agent at this time, Al King, booked the headliners, like the Coasters, Jackie De Shannon, and Marvin Gaye. Managed by Donald Johnson, also known as Whitey North, and Dale O'Keefe, it was a hot room, with bouncers escorting the waitresses through the crowd. At first the Warlocks seemed a mistake, playing too loud and too strangely. As O'Keefe saw it, the band would be okay for the first two of their five fifty-minute sets, but by the third they'd be high, and by the fifth they'd be "barbaric." But in some sort of mysterious transference, they began to develop their own audience, and held their own, avoiding the management of the bar, except for Larry, their favorite bartender. Each night they'd show up with their equipment stuffed into Kreutzmann's Pontiac station wagon, set up, and get to work. One of the complications to their lives was that Kreutzmann and Weir were not only considerably but obviously underage. Bobby Petersen stole some draft cards that somehow passed muster, and the cops would look at the ID, chuckle, and warn them not to drink. O'Keefe swore that he did not pay off the cops, so such tolerance could only be ascribed to providence.

For six weeks the Warlocks worked six nights a week, five fifty-minute sets a night, earning $800 weekly at most, and began to learn how to be a band. They surely didn't look like anyone's idea of the sort of group that would keep the booze flowing and the action hot. The lead guitarist was bespectacled, round-faced, acne-scarred, and lank-haired. Though longhaired, the bass player looked as though he should have a slide rule in a holster, a plastic pocket protector, and twelve pens. The rhythm guitarist looked like a longhaired fourteen-year-old angelic choirboy. This left the drummer and the keyboard player. Ed McClanahan, one of Kesey's Stanford friends, saw them around this time and thought that Kreutzmann "looked so young and innocent and fresh-faced that one's first impulse was to wonder how he got his momma to let him stay out so late." And then there was Pigpen, "the most marvelously ill-favored figure to grace a public platform since King Kong came down with stage fright . . . bearded and burly and barrel-chested, jowly and scowly and growly . . . long, Medusalike hair so greasy it might have been groomed with Valvoline . . . motorcyclist's cap, iron-black boots . . . the gap between the top of his oily Levi's and the bottom of his tattletale-gray T-shirt exposed a half-moon of distended beer belly as pale and befurred as a wedge of moldy jack cheese . . . But the ugly mother sure could *play*! . . . Verily, he was wondrous gross, was this Pigpen, yet such was the subtle alchemy of his art that the more he profaned love and beauty, the more his grossness rendered him beautiful."

They began their run backing up Cornell Gunther and the Coasters, and for the first set their rhythm guitarist was a guy named Terry, who taught them the songs. It was not really necessary for Garcia, who loved the Coasters and knew the material. Weir took the slight in seeming good humor, watching Terry so closely that he not only learned the chords but absorbed unconsciously how to cue a band with the neck of his guitar as a baton. From then on, when he sang a song, he became the bandleader, a democratic development not common to most bands. "We knew Weir could cut it then," said Lesh. "And after that it went much better, of course."

As the weeks went on, things began to get . . . stranger. The word "weird" derives from *wyrd,* "controlled by fate," and it was the Warlocks' fate to incline in the direction of strangeness. They would spend the day romping about the Peninsula high on LSD, come down, and go to the In Room to smoke pot and play. The songs began to get "longer and weirder and louder," Garcia said, and the early audience would run outside "clutching their ears." The bartenders loved it and wanted it louder. Larry was a striking man, six foot four, with a glass eye he'd take out on the odd interesting occasion. As the sets mounted and it grew late, he would fill the drain on the inside of the bar with lighter fluid, touching it off at a good crescendo. "So then he was our man," said Kreutzmann. One night there actually was a grease fire in the kitchen, and after everyone evacuated the bar, Kreutzmann ran back in to rescue his kit, they put out the conflagration, and the band returned for the last set.

A few years later, Phil Lesh would read a book by the distinguished science fiction writer Theodore Sturgeon, *More Than Human,* that would portray for him exactly what happened at the In Room: the development of a gestalt, a rapport, a group mind. It was not a consequence of LSD. Whatever acid did for them later, their bond was first musical. Weir recalled playing on acid once at the In Room, but was quite sure he was alone that night. Lesh never did, and the one time that Garcia came in a little too high, he concluded that LSD and a bar atmosphere simply didn't jibe. *More Than Human* describes a small group of people in a postapocalyptic setting, each member deeply flawed or damaged in some fashion. Baby is a mongoloid; two little black girls, Bonnie and Beanie, are tongue-tied; Lone is mentally damaged; Alicia is the emotionally distraught daughter of a sadist. As the novel progresses, they come together, blend and mesh. And in "bleshing," as Sturgeon put it, they have "a part that fetches, a part that figures, a part that finds out, and a part that talks." Weir learned the word "gestalt" that fall, and came to realize that the five of them were one hand with fifty fingers. One day during this time, he looked down at his hand during an acid trip and saw the claw of a dragon, in itself a symbol of a collective. It would be a year before he concluded that this was indeed a symbol of the same unity Lesh would later identify as bleshing. As for Garcia, being in the Warlocks was about commitment and liberation. "Surrendering your own little trip . . . [being] willing to stop caring about what you've already got . . . We just thought . . . why not?" At another time, he remarked, "Bluegrass music was formal . . .

[this] music was not formal, not traditional, and when it got to that place and did that thing, it was something incredible. It took off."

Part of that liftoff was the act of playing together night after night, learning how to stretch out tunes because, in Weir's words, "we weren't done playing, but the tune was over." The folk world they'd mostly emerged from treated performance as a recital. Their decision to play improvisationally was never consciously discussed, and was an ingrained fact long before they stopped to think about it. But as soon as they began to play, the idea of opening up the music to variation became essential. There were various sources for the impulse. For Garcia, one prized example was a night he'd seen Scotty Stoneman play. Despite the traditional formal rigidity of bluegrass, on this night Stoneman began to play, Garcia said, in "longer and longer phrases, ten bars, fourteen bars, seventeen bars—and the guys in the band are just watching him! They're barely playing, going ding-ding-ding, while he's burning." They stretched the tune to twenty minutes, "unheard of in bluegrass." "It was like those incredible excursions that Coltrane and those guys took, where all of a sudden you're hearing traffic on the streets . . . with Scotty it was diesel trucks and the highway. It was all there. And burnin', like a forest fire . . . Instead of playing the tune he would play some crazed idea that stretched clear across it . . . [He was the] model of the demon fiddler, the guy that has hell snapping at his heels, he was playing to save his soul . . . That's the first time I had the experience of being high, getting high from him, going away from it like 'what happened?' and just standing there clapping till my hands were sore."

For most of the Warlocks, the man who taught them how to improvise was John Coltrane. The great tenor player had entered the jazz world after World War II, and until the mid-1950s was only a competent sideman. Then he worked with the great composer of postwar jazz Thelonious Monk, and something emerged in his playing and composition that was so profound he became a fundamental influence, "one of the reasons," wrote Leroi Jones, "that suicide seems so boring." Phil Lesh had observed that transition in the San Francisco jazz clubs Coltrane had played in the late fifties—one of the special moments of his life was shaking Coltrane's hand after seeing him play with the Miles Davis Quintet—and heard it in the albums *My Favorite Things, Africa/Brass,* and *A Love Supreme.* So had Garcia. The guitarist and the bassist were instantly at one in an essential vision of how to play, and from the beginning, they taught Trane's lessons to their bandmates. "It was the simplest thing to do," said Lesh, "because you didn't have to remember any chords." Or, as the student Weir put it,

"The first thing we learned was to rattle on in one chord change for a while, until we were done punching it around. That was good for me, because I didn't know many chords." Lesh introduced Kreutzmann to the work of Coltrane's great drummer, Elvin Jones, and Bill's world expanded mightily. Further, Coltrane's band worked up a collective improvisational approach, with every musician improvising, not just the soloist. His influence on the Warlocks was omnipresent and permanent. Interestingly, that same fall John Coltrane experienced LSD and came to very similar conclusions about it as had the Warlocks. But that was only an addendum. No rock band in that era or after would take the lessons of John Coltrane more to the soul of their playing than the Warlocks.

There were, of course, many other influences. One that Garcia would cite was a Junior Walker instrumental called "Cleo's Back." "There was something about the way the instruments entered into it in a kind of free-for-all way, and there were little holes and these neat details in it—we studied that motherfucker. We might have even played it for a while, but that wasn't the point—it was the conversational approach, the way the band worked, that really influenced us."

As their music grew more bizarre to the average listener, the atmosphere of the In Room followed suit. "We were a bar band with abnormal features," said Weir, and there among the stewardesses would appear people with orange hair and feathers, or Page Browning, of the Chateau gang, with face putty and paint distorting his ears, chin, and nose. The Warlocks began to write their first song, and it was definitely not "Satisfaction." The In Room was located quite near the railroad tracks that run up the Peninsula to San Francisco, and as the band grew more and more attuned to the schedule, they learned to play with, instead of against, the sound of the trains as they rumbled by. One day, going from somewhere to somewhere, they heard the Them song "Mystic Eyes" on the car radio, and a fragment germinated in their minds. Eventually, they locked it into the sound of the trains, and "Caution: Do Not Stop on the Tracks" was born. It was a long, modal ramble, really only an excuse to jam, with a fragmentary, half-improvised lyric by Pigpen about "the gypsy woman." It was not In Room material. By the end of October, it became clear that the In Room could get along without them and vice versa, and they brought the run to a close. As they packed their gear into the Pontiac on the last night, the manager offered them a consensus professional critique of their act: "You guys will never make it. You're too weird."

———

On October 16, two weeks before the Warlocks' departure from the In Room, the future of rock and roll presentation had appeared in San Francisco. Produced by the Family Dog, "A Tribute to Dr. Strange" was the first adult rock dance, and it featured the Charlatans, the Jefferson Airplane, the Great Society, and the Marbles at Longshoremen's Hall. The roots of the Family Dog, which established dancing as the medium for music presentation over the rest of the decade, lay in a peculiar institution called the Red Dog Saloon. Early in 1965, at a cabin in the Sierra Nevada called the Zen Mine, while playing the board game Risk high on LSD, Mark Unobsky, Don Works, and Chandler "Chan" Laughlin, the former manager of the Cabale folk club, conceived the idea of a rock and roll club in the old mining town and now tourist destination of Virginia City, Nevada. It would be called the Red Dog Saloon. They imported some Beat Sausalito carpenters and began to patch up an abandoned building. Chan went to San Francisco to buy pot and whorehouse red velvet drapes, and to inveigle his friend Luria Castell and another friend to join them as go-go dancers.

Virginia City sits on the eastern flank of the Sierra Nevada, and from the wooden boardwalk in front of the Red Dog, one can see a hundred miles across Nevada. The combination of cowboy atmosphere and LSD made it a special theater. "We were the bad guys' saloon down at the end of the street," reflected Laughlin. "The ground rules were that from the time your feet hit the floor in the morning, you're in a grade B movie— play it! And it worked." On opening night, June 29, 1965, the sheriff stopped by, handed his gun to the bartender, and said, "Check my gun." The bartender fired a round into the floor and handed it back. "Works fine, Sheriff." Everyone carried guns, including the lead waitress, imported from a strip club on Broadway in San Francisco, who had a Walther PPK in a black leather thigh holster over her net stockings. And everyone lived in the combination of cowboy and Victorian dress that the Charlatans embodied. But they were cowboys on acid, and the Red Dog included an early light show created by San Franciscans Bill Ham and Bob Cohen, a light box that changed with the music.

In the course of the spring, a friend had played Unobsky a tape of a band that had formed around George Hunter, a hanger-on at San Francisco State who worked with electronic scores. Although he could not really play an instrument, George had an amazing sense of style, and in his long hair and Beatle boots, he thoroughly looked the part of a musician. It was generally true that the Charlatans were longer on style than musical skill—Laughlin said that George "got them together and started taking pictures. They never actually rehearsed as an entire band until the day they arrived up here," an understandable if not entirely correct assertion. Thus they were Charlatans. But the psychedelic theater that was the Red Dog took care of that. More an impresario than a musician, Hunter had gathered up Mike Ferguson, who'd created the Magic Theater for Madmen Only on Divisadero Street in San Francisco. The name was taken from Hermann Hesse's *Steppenwolf*, but the enterprise was actually a combination art gallery and small store that sold Victoriana, rolling papers, pipes, and, if you looked cool, pot. Ferguson's sense of style coalesced with Hunter's, and the result was the Victorian look of things that came pouring out of San Francisco attics. With Hunter on autoharp and Ferguson on piano, they added Dan Hicks on drums, Mike Wilhelm on guitar, and Richie Olsen on bass, played an energized, improvisatory electric folk music, and began a most delightful summer.

When the people who'd enjoyed the scene at the Red Dog returned to San Francisco in the fall, they found that they did not dig what they termed the "plastic" bars on Broadway where the Byrds and the Spoonful had recently played, and wanted to support their friends the Charlatans. They decided to throw a dance. The prime mover was Luria Castell, a political science major at S.F. State, a HUAC protester, Fair Play for Cuba committee member, and a onetime organizer for the W. E. B. Du Bois Club. She also loved to dance. With her housemates Alton Kelley, his lover, Ellen Harmon, and Jack Towle, they decided to name their little production company in tribute to Ellen's recently deceased dog, Animal. Luria was the mouthpiece; Jack took care of the money; Ellen stayed home, read comic books, and answered the phone; and Kelley did the posters. Through Luria's radical connections they found a union hall near Fisherman's Wharf and began. They were serious about things, if not themselves. "Not only did we want to have a good time, we felt a potential," said Luria later, "a positive change in the human condition . . . almost a religious kind of thing, but not dogma, unlocking that tension and letting it come out in a positive way with the simple health of dancing and getting crazy once a month or so." These earliest hippies lived a fairly austere life in cheap buildings, with cheap clothes. They had no holy men, philosophies, or politics, said Kelley, they just wanted a good time. They visited Ralph Gleason, and he faithfully reported their goal: "San Francisco can be the American Liverpool," said Luria. It was a "pleasure city," unlike the too-large New York and the "super-uptite plastic" Los Angeles.

It was an era of parties, and they were about to get bigger. By now, students at S.F. State had moved into the Haight-Ashbury neighborhood, and there were a dozen parties every Friday and Saturday night. One regular site was a large rooming house at 1090 Page Street, where an antiques and pot dealer and Lemar ("legalize marijuana") activist named Chet Helms had lovingly eyed the rosewood-paneled ballroom in the basement and decided it would be a great place to have parties and jam sessions. The building manager was Rodney Albin, their old friend from the Boar's Head and now a student at S.F. State, and he thought it a fine idea. The door charge was fifty cents.

The Gleason article, some posters tacked up around the old beatnik neighborhood of North Beach, the Haight-Ashbury, and at the Matrix, and a few ads on the Top 40 station KYA were enough to sell out the October 16 show at Longshoremen's Hall, a concrete hexagon that resembled an umbrella, where Louis Armstrong, Count Basie, and Ray Charles had all played. The Dog didn't bother with city permits, but they certainly brought together a community. At the Stones' show that summer, the older members of the audience didn't really know each other, said Tom Donahue, a KYA disc jockey. Now they did, and the dance was informed by a collective shock of recognition, as hundreds of slightly longhaired freaks in thrift-shop clothing styles that ranged, as Gleason put it, "from velvet Lotta Crabtree to Mining Camp Desperado, Jean Laffite leotards, I. Magnin beatnik, Riverboat Gambler, India Import Exotic, [to] Modified Motorcycle Racer," their eyes shining with the light of LSD, converged on the hall. "They can't bust us all," thought Chet Helms. The sound was terrible and Bill Ham's light show was still primitive, but it was a marvelous night.

The Charlatans and the Airplane were already stars in the small world of San Francisco, and they were joined by the Great Society. Formed by a guitarist, Darby Slick, his film student brother, Jerry, and Jerry's wife, Grace, after seeing an Airplane show at the Matrix, the Great Society had played in public for the first time the day before, October 15. That night at the Longshoremen's Hall, the seeds of yet another band would germinate as a guitarist from Marin County, John Cipollina, met some out-of-towners named Greg Elmore and Gary Duncan. In a while, they would be the Quicksilver Messenger Service. The next day, on the afternoon of October 16, the Instant Action Jug Band performed for the first time, part of anti–Vietnam War demonstrations in Berkeley, leading the demonstrators from a flatbed truck in the chant "1-2-3, what are we fightin' for?" Of that band, Country Joe McDonald and Barry "the Fish" Melton were both red diaper children of left-wingers, and their activist politics were much more Berkeley than San Francisco, but they were definitely imbibing the spirit of rock and roll. The missing element from the first night at Longshoremen's Hall was the Warlocks, either as audience members or as performers. They'd auditioned for Alton Kelley and Ellen Harmon at the In Room, but their lack of original material identified them as a mere cover band, and they were rejected.

Being at liberty from the In Room had certain rewards. Saturday, October 30, was a beautiful day, as Indian-summer days in San Francisco tend to be, and the Warlocks went off to Marin County, just north of the city, to drop acid and enjoy themselves. On the road to Fairfax, a little town on the border between eastern, urbanized Marin and its rural western reaches, they fell in behind a gasoline tank truck with a damaged transmission that made the most remarkable sound. Lesh was in good form that day, and the sound sang to him. "It was in phase," he said, "the real sound, and I fell in love with a broken transmission." He was riding shotgun in the front car, owned by Sue Swanson and nicknamed George, and leaned out of the car window listening to the sound modulate his brain waves, pointing at the truck and generally being transfixed. "There's more going on than we even suspected," they thought, even in truck transmissions. It was, Garcia said later, the first psychedelic music he'd heard, even if it was not precisely music. Later that fall they'd be larking about in Los Trancos Woods as a jet passed overhead and split the universe with a "cataclysmic" sound. Garcia would try to make his guitar sound like a jet engine for a good while. But on October 30, still quite high, they came into the city, stopped for burgers at a good dive called Clown Alley, and headed over to the Longshoremen's Hall to see the second Family Dog show, "A Tribute to Sparkle Plenty," with the Loving Spoonful and the Charlatans. Weird people and strange rock and roll— just what they wanted. Metaphorically frothing at the mouth in glee, Lesh recognized Luria Castell and stopped her. "Lady, what this little séance needs is us." Quite so. Later, Chet Helms would see Garcia and remark, "This is great. Every hippie in town is here tonight, in drag." And Garcia thought, "Right on, this *is* a hell of a trip." It was the first time that LSD and music had mixed appropriately for them.

In his wife's words "a piano player in the whorehouse of life," Tom "Big Daddy" Donahue was more than three hundred pounds of charm and love of music. He'd begun his career as a disc jockey in Philadelphia, been run out of town by the late-fifties payola scandals, and settled in San Francisco at KYA. Soon he and his fellow D.J. and partner, Bobby Mitchell, had expanded into a variety of businesses, including a radio tip sheet, band management, show promotion, a psychedelic nightclub called Mother's, and, finally, a record label called Autumn Records. With the help of a gifted record producer, Sylvester "Sly" Stewart, they'd scored hits with local musicians Bobby Freeman ("C'mon and Swim") and the Beau Brummels ("Laugh, Laugh"). On November 3 Autumn Records auditioned the Warlocks, who were calling themselves the Emergency Crew for the day. The session took place at Golden State Recorders, a cheap studio down by the train station south of Market Street, and it was not a priority event, since they had only an engineer, and no producer. They recorded six tracks as a sample, or demo, of their work, including Gordon Lightfoot's "Early Morning Rain," the traditional "I Know You Rider," and four originals: "Caution," "I Can't Come Down," "Mindbender" (aka "Confusion's Prince"), and "The Only Time Is Now." They had been playing together for only five months, and the tape showed it. It was poorly recorded, and only Garcia's strong leads and Pig's vocals were clearly audible. Lesh's bass skills were still primitive, and Kreutzmann and Weir were rarely present in the mix. Their originals were pop-oriented, and showed that they listened to the Beatles as well as the Stones. They had the right mood and feeling, but lacked pop hooks, and they simply weren't very good. The tunes were not especially original, the best being "The Only Time Is Now," written by Garcia and sung by Lesh. "Oh I come to you a ragged and open stranger / And you come to me an angel of the night / so I'll dance and we will sing but it doesn't mean a thing / To remember that the only time is now."

As Garcia would concede later, "I'm really a jive lyricist. My lyrics come from right now—put pencil on paper, and what comes out, if it fits, it fits. I didn't think about them, I just made the first, obvious choices and never rewrote. It took me a long time to sing them out, because they embarrassed me." "I Can't Come Down" was in many ways worse because it was more ambitious, a clear pilfering from Dylan: "With secret smiles like a Cheshire cat and leather wings like a vampire bat / I fly away to my cold water flat and eat my way through a bowl of fat." Donahue liked the Warlocks, but his partner was ill and the record company was already foundering, and nothing came of their demo. For Weir, the day's most arresting moment came when he wandered next door, to a room where another band's gear was stored. They had Fender Showman amps, and he craved one to replace his mere Fender Bandmaster amp. Amp lust was a popular emotion in young musicians.

Through November they remained a regular fledgling rock band.

Phil's friend Hank Harrison became their manager for about a week, and got them a gig at Pierre's, a strip joint on San Francisco's Broadway. By then, Broadway was the legendary home of Carol Doda, who the year before had become famous by having her breasts enlarged and going to work as a go-go dancer in a topless Rudi Gernreich bathing suit. Before that, the street had been known as the home of the Jazz Workshop, where Miles Davis, John Coltrane, Art Blakey, and Horace Silver played after the Blackhawk closed in 1963. Earlier in 1965, Lenny Bruce had broken both ankles after taking a dive out the window of his room at the Swiss American Hotel, just up Broadway from Pierre's. It was an altogether odd street, and Pierre's fit in. The club was six times as long as it was wide, which made it small. It was high-ceilinged, and all bricks and concrete, so it sounded awful. The audience asked the Warlocks to turn down, but to no effect. There were two topless go-go dancers, one nice, one not. As Lesh put it, "We'd play for twenty minutes and the chick would come out and she'd be onstage a total of five minutes and it would take her four minutes to get her jacket off, so out of every thirty-minute set, when they changed the audience over, you got one minute of tit." Their old friend Peter Albin came to see them and noticed some sailors behaving with the usual testosterone-induced blindness until the dancer left, and the navy boys found themselves staring fixedly at Garcia's hands.

The Warlocks were excited that month by their first national publicity, even if it came as a gift from a buddy. Garcia's New York bluegrass friend, David Grisman, had come out that summer to visit Eric Thompson and had seen the Warlocks play. On his return he mentioned them to his friend Israel Young, whose November "Frets and Frails" column in the prestigious folk magazine *Sing Out!* reported, "David Grisman found the Warlocks to be the best rock-and-roll group he heard in California. He especially liked a song written by their lead guitarist, Jerry Garcia, titled 'Bending Your Mind.' " It was a good start, Garcia said, because the readership of *Sing Out!* was an elite.

Another first that month was a photo session. Their photographer, Herb Greene, was a friend they'd met through his wife, Maruska, who was a seamstress at the Mime Troupe and knew Phil. It was his first music shoot, too; his usual subjects were fashion models at the I. Magnin store. The Warlocks briefly dreamed of Beatle-type suits but couldn't afford them and decided to appropriate some of the striped French sailor sweaters that the Spoonful had taken to wearing. They also went to Flagg Brothers, a surplus store on Market Street, to buy black, pointy-toed boots with a zipper up the back—Beatle boots. Greene took them to some old army artillery positions under the Golden Gate Bridge at Fort Point in the Presidio and lifted the visual motif from *Help!*, the recently released second Beatle movie. The results were charming, although the Warlocks lacked the good looks of the originals. They bought a new, just-like-the-Beatles Vox organ at Swain's in Palo Alto, and eventually managed to pay for it. Since Mr. Swain had once been a professional children's social worker and made a practice of employing juvenile delinquents as clerks, there was a measure of tolerance that they could count on.

On November 6, two rock and roll currents collided in San Francisco. At Longshoremen's Hall, the Family Dog put on a dance featuring a band from Los Angeles led by Frank Zappa, while the Mime Troupe was sponsoring a benefit at their loft on Howard Street, near the *San Francisco Chronicle* building. The Family Dog event was a mess. Gangs of teenagers from the nearby housing projects had found out about the dances, and the hall had far too many doors to make it securable. Luria found herself flailing at two boys who were fighting, shouting, "How dare you fuck up my dance!" By now the musicians' union had taken notice of the Dog's activities, even if the city never got around to it, asking the hall why it was housing a nonunion event. Shortly after, Luria decided to take a little vacation in Mexico.

The people at the Howard Street loft had a better time. The brainchild of Bill Graham, the troupe's business manager, the Appeal was designed to raise money to defend the Mime Troupe's leader, Ronnie Davis, who'd been found guilty on November 1 of performing in the park without a permit. Graham's main act was the Jefferson Airplane, a band he knew of only because they rehearsed at the Mime Troupe's warehouse. The show also boasted a New York band called the Fugs, a guitarist named Sandy Bull, the satirical troupe the Committee, and poets Lawrence Ferlinghetti and Allen Ginsberg, whom Graham knew from New York's 92nd Street YMHA (Young Men's Hebrew Association) readings. Bill knew nothing of rock and had no background in promotion, but his instincts were superb. He decorated the dumpy warehouse by hanging bunches of fruit and chewing gum from the rafters, and greeted patrons with gifts of what one participant recalled were "coins and raisins and whistles and clicking noisemakers and little mirrors all individually wrapped in Christmas gift papers." The door charge was on a sliding scale, from those making $100,000, who paid forty-eight dollars—several people did so—to those with a part-time job paying less than twenty dollars weekly, who could "come on in" gratis. For most, the charge was a dollar. Graham stocked egg rolls and fried chicken for two hundred, which was the audience he expected, and at three in the morning was still bringing people up in the elevator. When police took notice of the gross violation of capacity, he told them, "Frank [Sinatra]'s flying in," and they left him alone. Appeal I ended at 6 A.M. with Ginsberg leading chants; it had raised more than $4,000 and triggered a collective social orgasm. As Graham pulled up to the warehouse at the beginning of the evening after taking a dinner break, he'd seen the line around the block and yelped, *"This* is the business of the future." So it was.

The following week the Warlocks, or at least Weir, Kreutzmann, Lesh, and Garcia, met to consider a problem. Phil Lesh had been thumbing through a record rack and came across a single put out by another group called the Warlocks, probably not the New York City band that featured Lou Reed, John Cale, Sterling Morrison, and Maureen Tucker (later this band would find a new moniker in the title of a sadomasochistic novel and became the Velvet Underground), but most likely a Texas band that included guitarists who would become known as ZZ Top. The San Franciscans decided they needed a new name, and they began to evaluate possibilities. Kreutzmann lobbied for a black club band name, like the "Vikings" or the "Crusaders." Garcia wanted to be whimsical and threw out "Mythical Ethical Icicle Tricycle." Weir suggested "His Own Sweet Advocates," his softened version of the term "devil's advocate." Finally, on November 12, a cold gray windy day, the four of them gathered at Lesh's house on High Street. Garcia had smoked DMT before coming over, but the others were sober. Garcia and Lesh sat on the couch as Weir and Kreutzmann hovered behind them. They paged through a *Bartlett's,* read out a thousand possibilities, rejected them all. Then Garcia opened Phil's girlfriend Ruth's *Funk and Wagnall's New Practical Standard Dictionary* (1956), shook it open, and stabbed it with his finger. "Everything else on the page went blank," he later said, "diffuse, just sorta *oozed* away, and there was GRATEFUL DEAD, *big* black letters *edged* all around in gold, man, blasting out at me, such a stunning combination." "Hey, man. How about the Grateful Dead?" Lesh began to jump up and down, shouting, "That's it! That's it!" Weir didn't like it, thinking it morbid. "It held us back for years and years," he would say much later. As soon as he thought about it, even Garcia found it "kinda creepy." Hanging out at Swain's Music Store, Jerry asked Evie, a clerk there, how to spell "grateful." "However you spell it," she sniffed, "you'll never make it with that name."

Innocent as babes, they had connected with a motif that twined itself throughout human history. The definition in the dictionary referred specifically to the nineteenth-century musicologist Francis Child's term for a type of ballad. The grateful dead ballad or folktale concerns a hero who comes upon a corpse being refused a proper burial because it owes a debt. The hero resolves the debt and thus the corpse's destiny without expectation of reward, often with his last penny. Soon he meets a traveling companion who aids him in some impossible task, who, of course, turns out to be the spirit of the corpse he aided. This motif is found in almost every culture since the ancient Egyptians. Unknowingly, the Warlocks had plunked themselves into a universal cultural thread woven into the matrix of all human experience. The term "grateful dead" is about karma, and asserts that acting from soul and the heart guarantees that righteousness will result. It is about honor, compassion, and keeping promises. It precedes and suggests "Cast thy bread upon the waters," and "No man is an island," and "What goes around comes around." The very fact of a good-time rock band selecting a name that involved death created a gap that automatically separated the sheep from the goats. You had to be at least a little bent just to appreciate it. It confused some and appalled others—and what could be better for a rock band? It implied layers and layers of depth, unique among all rock band names in that era, and suggested that something very powerful indeed happened on High Street that day. In the end, they did not choose their name. It chose them.

9

Interlude:
Albert Hofmann's
Discovery
(THE PSYCHEDELIC WORLD)

ollowing close behind survival and procreation, the pursuit of spiritual transcendence seems to be a universal human need. The three-hundredths-of-a-second neural gap between reality and our apprehension of it dooms us to see our lives in images forever newly obsolete and to grasp only the tiniest fraction of what is available. It is the chasm that Plato described as the difference between shadow and fact. The methods chosen for the pursuit, from the Roman Catholic mass to whatever the Dionysians used to the raptures of southern Pentecostalists induced by gospel music to LSD-25, are merely a matter of cultural taste. Lumping LSD and other psychedelics, including the milder marijuana, with other drugs is simply ignorant, and largely reflects Western cultural shibboleths about the loss of control and fear of sensuality. The Dead and their peers in the Haight, unlike the lawmakers and their supporting cast of medical opinion makers, actually chose to investigate psychedelics in an empirical, if informal, way. They sought what T. S. Eliot called in "The Dry Salvages" "the primitive terror," the place where a foundering Western civilization might be renewed.

The Grateful Dead were always about music, not drugs, and if there is an alpha element to their gestalt, it is improvisation, as a social as well as musical technique. If the Dead's social and intellectual structure was, in Robert Hunter's words, a reflection of Jerry Garcia's mind, that structure began with a healthy skepticism directed at all cant, all received wisdom, all assumptions. From that clean slate came improvisation. But after improvisation, the single largest element in the Dead's *weltanschauung* was their pursuit of group mind under the influence of LSD, which in its celebration of the moment, of be-here-nowness, confirmed improvisation as a life- as well as musical performance-guiding choice. Much of what followed, whether we are discussing Dead philosophy, the psychedelic experience, or improvisational music, was frequently beyond words, so that any formula created would be long after the event. In point of fact, almost any analysis of this experience is potentially antithetical to the essence of the experience itself. Yet a consideration of this alternative universe is worth the effort, if only to lessen the fears of those trapped by the "Just Say No" nonsense. It is worth noting that much of the legal furor over drugs in the United States in the last century or so has a racial and/or social basis. As opium became connected with the "yellow peril," it became demonized. When marijuana was associated with African American jazz musicians, despite the benign conclusions of the La Guardia Commission's report, ditto, and so forth. A little dispassionate thinking seems called for.

Looking back, the critic Paul Williams theorized that the variations in critical receptivity to the Dead's music were based on one's openness to the psychedelic experience. Those who got high understood, and those who didn't, didn't. This would suggest to some that "you can't like this music without being stoned," which would obviously imply a very limited music. On the other hand, one might argue that while choosing to not ingest psychedelics is an inarguable right, being so emotionally constituted as to be unable to experience the psychedelic world is at least equally limiting.

On April 16, 1943, Albert Hofmann touched his hand to his mouth and accidentally absorbed some of the twenty-fifth version of LSD he had produced—the first twenty-four derivations showed no great value—and discovered that the most remarkably tiny dosage had a powerful psychic impact. As LSD use spread, several conclusions about it emerged. Put simply, it seemed that evolutionary survival needs had required the limiting of the mind's capacity for sensory input, and LSD reopened the valve. For a few hours, reality became a flood instead of a trickle. Haight Street philosopher Stephen Gaskin quoted a critic as saying, "Acid lowers your powers of discrimination until everything seems important." On the contrary, Gaskin replied: "No. Acid *raises* your powers of *integration* until everything *is* important." "It's a language, that's all, without words—just the images themselves," wrote Art Kleps, an early associate of LSD researcher Timothy Leary, and one of the few to consider LSD in Western philosophical terms. LSD, he argued, lays waste to supernaturalism, since, ironically, much of the LSD experience lies in the realm of the absurd, and there is "no room for the absurd in the cosmologies of the occultists and supernaturalists." The simple materialism of the lower reaches of scientific thought also had to go: "It is materialism that is destroyed by these overwhelming demonstrations of the limitless power of the imagination, not, necessarily, as those who like to disparage nihilism and solipsism assume, empiricism, logic, or honor. It is not one's experience or character that is intimidated, but only certain abstract concepts about the organization of experience."

Very few things come out of *every* acid trip. As Garcia remarked, "When LSD hit the streets finally, that was like, 'You're looking for more? Here it is. This is more. This is more than you can imagine' . . . [Acid trips] have that way of being individual . . . people don't experience exactly the same effects. They experience themselves, and sometimes it turns out to be utterly delightful, sometimes it turns out to be a total bummer, but either way, you've got more of it to work with when you've taken psychedelics and seen the bigger picture, you know? . . . after that, for me, in my life, there was no turning back. There was no back, not just a turning back, but the idea of backness was gone. It was like all directions were forward from there . . . conventional wisdom won't accept this subjective of an overview."

Most people come out of LSD trips believing in the oneness of all life, the interconnectedness of things, and from that, the philosophically disposed frequently hit on Jungian synchronicity, the notion that things can be connected on a non-cause-and-effect basis, as in dreams. "If one's thesis is that ordinary life is a dream," wrote Art Kleps, "then anything that can happen in a dream in sleep can happen in waking life also, without disproving the thesis. If you can see that, you can see everything."

After synchronicity, the essentially mental (solipsistic) nature of reality suggested a second realm of thought, that of alchemy. Owsley "Bear" Stanley, the finest large-scale producer of LSD in the world, was the Dead's best-known alchemist. But after Bear, the Dead's favorite mental divertissement was the psychedelic adventures and theorizing of Terence and Dennis McKenna. Sometime in the middle 1970s, Alan Trist went to the bookstore, bought about ten copies of their *The Invisible Landscape*, and handed them around to the attendees at a band meeting. The McKennas' work theorizes that evolution will accelerate and end in the year 2012. Garcia loved it as a mental exercise, finding it "incredibly optimistic."

Terence McKenna's *True Hallucinations* describes the journey that led to the theory. In February 1971, the McKennas traveled to La Chorrera, Colombia, in the Amazonian jungle, where they ingested *Stropharia* mushrooms that "spun a myth and issued a prophecy, in quite specific detail, of a planet-saving global shift of consciousness." Said shift was to take place on December 22, 2012, the end of the world in the Mayan calendar. The book describes a sort of sci-fi vision of a shamanic quest, wherein they would pass the doorway of death and find as living men "a kind of hyperspatial astral projection that allows the hyper-organ, consciousness, to instantly manifest itself at any point in the space-time matrix, or at all points simultaneously." In other words, they sought "a modern transdimensional alchemical philosopher's stone." This is a worthy twentieth-century version of Faust's quest. In the end, Terence concluded that time is a bumpy, not continuous, thing, and further developed the notion of the time wave, "a kind of mathematical mandala describing the organization of time and space." "The timewave theory is like the score of the biocosmic symphony." This is the Dead's kind of thinking, bold and fascinating, off the wall but a good deal further along than "Gee, I'm ripped." The book served as a creative source of conversation for years.

A related meditation on the metaphysical implications of the psychedelic experience was Robert Anton Wilson's satirical *Illuminati* series. Wilson began with the Bavarian Illuminati, who supposedly secretly ruled the world, and before he was done touched on the territory occupied by the collector of inexplicable events Charles Fort, the satanist Aleister Crowley, the occult, cattle mutilations, crop circles, UFOs, Bell's theorem, which posits the underlying unity of all physical phenomena, the metaphysical paradox of Schrödinger's cat, and—for no entirely clear reason—the number 23. He also posited a philosophy that worshiped chaos, "Discordianism," which held meta-beliefs called *catma* (as opposed to dogma). Garcia particularly cherished catma as a concept; it is a delicious pun.

LSD was, in the Dead world, a catalyst. For Lesh the highest he would ever get was during the Dead's 1966 sojourn in Los Angeles, when he and his lover, Florence, Garcia and his lover, Diane Zellman, and a friend called "Heddie the Witch" went to a canyon on Mount Wilson and experienced telepathy. Information came in extraordinarily fast bursts, ten minutes of material exploding into each brain in a few moments. It would be the closest Lesh would ever feel to Garcia off the stage, and it staggered him. They were well and truly connected. And then a test rocket at the nearby Rocketdyne facility exploded through the sky, severing their gestalt. It was, Garcia said, "a reality butt splice." Suddenly, their trip was over. "Sorry, kids. Go home."

To Kreutzmann, LSD "wasn't a drug, it was an endless roller-coaster ride, and I guess if you had any percentage of imagination . . . you wanted to get on this roller coaster and ride on it, because pretty soon it went over this big hill and it didn't stay on this track. Pretty soon it went through the whole amusement park and then it cruised the waves for a little while, went up and down the boardwalk, and then it went out to everywhere, right? So we were not afraid, is what I'm saying. And we'd get back."

The Bus
Came By

(11/13/65–2/5/66)

eal. Neal Leon Cassady, "Dean Moriarity" of *On the Road*, a
fundamental document of the cultural odyssey that all the
members of the Grateful Dead would travel. Having taken
sex, car driving, drugs, stress, and torment well beyond the limits of human tolerance, Cassady was the "one hundred per cent commu-
nicator . . . the furthest out guy" Garcia would ever know. Neal had been
an essential part of Garcia's psychic life since Jerry had hit the North
Beach Beat scene at age fifteen, but for his mates, school was about to
begin.

The members of the Grateful Dead had taken their first steps. They
had sampled psychedelia, played together night after night, and studied
an adept in John Coltrane. Now they were about to undertake, many
times, the acid test, and define themselves in an extreme psychedelic environment with a life master. The media, for instance Tom Wolfe, whose
The Electric Kool-Aid Acid Test was superior journalism but still the product of an outsider, would imagine that the scene centered on Ken Kesey.
The Dead knew better. Disguised as a loony, mad-rapping speed freak,
Neal Cassady was very possibly the most highly evolved personality they
would ever meet, and was certainly among their most profound life influ-

ences other than the psychedelic experience itself. "He seemed to live in another dimension," Weir said, "and in that dimension time as we know it was transparent." Consciousness, Garcia thought, consisted of knowing when you're on and when you're off. To learn that, you adopt a discipline and focus on it. Neal's practice was car driving, and there were dozens of witnesses who testified that from behind the wheel, Neal could see around corners and take his car through spaces that didn't exist. Once, Lesh recalled, they were going up Highway 101 past San Francisco's Candlestick Park as a ball game was letting out. Neal's car simply flowed through the traffic in a series of waves, and by the time the city skyline appeared, Lesh felt that it was a privileged state of grace to be with him in action. Neal had his own art, his own medium, and it involved the way he moved through space. It was "an art form that hasn't been discovered yet . . . something between philosophy and art," thought Garcia, an action, not a meditation, but "a Western model for getting high." He'd eliminated the tool of discipline and simply *was*. "If you imagine human beings as having many surfaces, all of his surfaces were on that edge of off-ness and on-ness and being conscious."

Talk was one of his primary tools, and there were no simple chats with Neal Cassady. Stopped by the police, he'd bring out his wallet and begin to explain the rain of items pouring out. Before long, whatever reasons the officers had for initiating the encounter would be washed away. Standing in a circle at a party, he'd carry on a separate conversation with each person, going into the cultural image bank and relating the present to several other dimensions. His friend Paul Foster later wrote, "Others can talk fast but slowed down it's poppycock . . . play Neal at 33 and it's interesting, voluminous, humorous, often rhyming and intimidatingly encyclopedic in that he was enormously well read and he could handle simultaneously eight channels of audio interchange, including items from all radios and televisions he had turned on, random street noise, conversations within earshot and several secret thoughts, it would all enter the fabric, the nap of his rap." Hunter once taped a conversation with Neal and then remarked, "I'd *swear* that every time I played [it] that there would be a different conversation with me on it. He was flying circles about me." Kreutzmann thought of him as a "friendly swarm of bees all over your body that never bite. It was a little scary, but it never hurt—you were only feeling your own feelings."

The son of an alcoholic Denver barber, Neal grew up, among other places, in a transients' flophouse hotel. His teenage life combined multiple auto thefts with reading Proust and Schopenhauer. A Columbia University graduate, Justin Brierly, adopted him as a protégé and connected him with Allen Ginsberg and Jack Kerouac in New York, and the life described in Kerouac's *On the Road*. His other reality, that of marriage to Carolyn, their three children, a suburban home in Mountain View, and a steady job with the Southern Pacific Railroad, was shattered in 1960 when he was arrested for possession of two joints of marijuana and sentenced to two years in San Quentin. Years later Ken Kesey wrote of Neal that his was "the yoga of a man driven to the cliff edge by the grassfire of an entire nation's burning material madness. Rather than be consumed by this he jumped, choosing to sort things out in the fast-flying but smog-free moments of a life with no retreat."

Shortly after his release from San Quentin, Neal turned up at Kesey's home on Perry Lane. He'd read *One Flew Over the Cuckoo's Nest* and felt a spiritual kinship with Randle Patrick McMurphy, the novel's protagonist, and indeed there was a bond. "Speed Limit" became his nickname, and he became an integral part of Kesey's circle.

In 1964 Kesey completed his second novel, *Sometimes a Great Notion*, and needed to go to New York on business. He happened to be encumbered with more money than he considered good for him, and he'd retained his profound interest in LSD. These facts revealed to him a new medium for his talents, one that was social and magical. The medium would coalesce in a journey to New York, the great bus trip of 1964, which one critic called his third novel. He and his friends, the Merry Pranksters, climbed aboard a 1939 International Harvester school bus with "Furthur" on the destination placard and crossed the country, Neal Cassady at the wheel (of course!).

It was not an ordinary bus. Wired inside and out, it could broadcast to the neighborhood over speakers, while microphones brought the outside world in, usually processed through time lag and electronic manipulation. The barrel of a Laundromat clothes dryer was welded on top to make a turret. A modestly understated sign reading "Caution: Weird Load" festooned the bus's rear. Splashed in Day-Glo colors, it was not merely transportation but something more akin to Don Quixote's steed Rosinante, for they were on a mythic quest, as Kesey said, to "stop the coming end of the world." They also planned to film their quest. Mike "Mal Function" Hagen, Ken "the Intrepid Traveler" Babbs, Paula "Gretchen Fetchin'" Sundsten, Ken's brother Chuck and his cousin Dale: they were "Astronauts of Inner Space." They crossed the country, filming and recording their adventures, more interior than overt events, which ranged from a romp in a slimy pond to a truly loony day at the beach, the black section of a stretch of Lake Pontchartrain. Once in New York, one of their specific intentions had been to visit that year's world's fair in Flushing, Queens, and to chronicle their stoned interactions with the regular citizenry. As was so often the case with the Pranksters, they arrived, pranked around for the ten-minute duration of the first film reel, and then, while the camera was being reloaded, disappeared. On their return to California, they would discover that most of the film, shot with hands and eyes from another dimension, was blurred and unusable. The $70,000 spent on the odyssey left wonderful still pictures by Ron "Hassler" Bevirt and memories of a mythic journey that would reverberate through a large section of the American culture for the next decade.

Kesey's place at La Honda was no ordinary California coastal range home. There were speakers in trees, Day-Glo paint was splashed everywhere, and the people were . . . different. One of them was Paul Foster, who'd been known to leap to his feet after a good performance of *As You Like It* shouting, "Author, author," and who once spent an entire summer wearing ice skates. "You're either on the bus," went the phrase from the summer of '64, "or you're off the bus." The metaphorical bus began to take on more passengers. After their return from New York, Neal Cassady had met a striking young woman named Carolyn Adams, who would become a central figure of future events. The daughter of an entomologist and a botanist, she was a rebellious teen who'd moved to Palo Alto to live with her brother, who worked at Stanford. She'd been sitting in St. Michael's Alley when she met Neal, who invited her to smoke a joint. They'd gotten into his car, and he'd backed up University Avenue to the railroad tracks, then driven to Menlo Park on the Southern Pacific rails, leaving the track at precisely the right time to avoid being demolished by a train. Neal was as attuned as ever to the rhythms of the world and of the S.P. Carolyn loved it, bursting into laughing hysterics. "Crazy people, oh boy!" She soon became part of the La Honda scene.

On August 7, 1965, some even weirder people showed up. Hunter Thompson was a Kentucky-born local journalist who'd been working on a book about the motorcycle club called the Hell's Angels. Having more than an incidental interest in any form of derangement, chemical or social, he'd thought to introduce the Angels and the Pranksters. On August 7, a Cadillac showed up at La Honda, its muffler dragging in the dirt, bringing eight giant ogres, including Frisco Pete and Freewheelin' Frank, to visit. With their badges, patches, tattoos, earrings, nose rings, and finger rings, "these guys were way further out than we were," thought Carolyn, who'd by now acquired the nom de prank of "Mountain Girl," or

"M.G." Allen Ginsberg and Ram Dass, the former Richard Alpert, who'd been Timothy Leary's associate at Harvard and afterward, also attended the party, which despite the occasional tensions induced by the Angels' propensity for violent physical solutions to disagreements, was a fabulous success.

Einstein had transcended Newtonian physics with another order of perception, and it seemed to the Pranksters that acid was doing the same to ordinary human social consciousness. The Pranksters were searching for a way to communicate the meaning of the new psychic world order. "Secret meanings hid coyly in bowls of alphabet soup and Major Clues hung on every tree just out of reach," wrote Paul Foster. Or, as Kesey was wont to say, "We're working on many levels here." Since the Pranksters were also big fans of Saturday night parties, the bash that welcomed the Angels had many successors. There were those who suspected that Kesey wanted the parties to stop so that he could go back to writing, but no one would let him. Instead, the parties grew, and emerged into the larger world. The first of those special parties was at Ken Babbs's place in Soquel, near Santa Cruz, on the coast south of Palo Alto, on November 27, 1965. Such public notice as there was of the event came through a posting at Lee Quarnstrom and Peter Demas's Hip Pocket Bookstore in Soquel. The Pranksters were joined by Allen Ginsberg and his lover, Peter Orlovsky, and Garcia, Lesh, Weir, Sue Swanson, and Connie Bonner among others, and the night basically involved hanging out and tripping together.

Lesh would always recall the capsules they took that night, completely transparent except for the tiniest of scratches on the inner surface that marked the LSD that was their transport to another world. He spent much of the evening staring at the stars with Swanson, but at length decided that he'd like to play the electric guitar that Kesey was banging on. Kesey didn't want to give it up, but Phil was not dissuaded, and learned one of his early lessons in the subtleties of tripping. He proceeded to glue-hiseyesonKesey, and in a while Ken got up and shoved the guitar at him. "Here." Weir, on the other hand, had another sort of adventure. Although he had read "Howl," he did not recognize Allen Ginsberg, and saw only that he "was pretty damned amazing, the stuff he would say and do. So I figure, okay, I'm gonna sit next to this guy. Which was okay with him"—if not with Peter Orlovsky, who would be cautiously jealous of the utterly hetero Weir in the future.

A day or two later there was a Prankster meeting at La Honda attended by Phil Lesh and Bob Weir, representing the Dead. They sat around Kesey's kitchen table and planned a somewhat larger party for the following Saturday in San Jose, one that would include the music of the Grateful Dead. They weren't entirely sure what they were doing, beyond throwing a party and having a good time. Spreading consciousness of what LSD might teach you was one notion; getting good and crazy and spreading the virtue of *that* was another. Making money was definitely out. For the members of the Grateful Dead, it was first of all an opportunity to play the way they wanted. "We knew we had something," Lesh said later, "but we didn't know how deep it was. We directed and focused it through these parties." By now, someone—no one recalled who—had designed ID cards for the sessions, with the traditional recruiting picture of Uncle Sam posing a new and dicey question: "Can YOU pass the Acid Test?" And so the parties became the acid tests.

The Dead sensed, quite correctly, that the Pranksters were onto something powerful. Kesey and Babbs were "living myths" to Lesh, and Neal Cassady, well, he was Neal Cassady. The Pranksters loved the Dead, seeing them as younger and slightly junior partners but definitely "on the bus." "History had kicked [Garcia] between the eyes and you could see it," said Kesey. "We always thought of the Grateful Dead as being the engine that was driving the spaceship we were traveling on," thought Babbs. And the combination was much greater than the sum of its parts. "We plugged in to take it to the next level," said Lesh, and thus Kesey came to call them the Faster-Than-Light Drive. The people producing the acid tests were not trying to be "far out." They were going far in.

The second acid test took place on December 4 in the living room of a black man Kesey nicknamed Big Nig—Ken was always interested in obliterating expectations of correctness, political or otherwise—near the San Jose State University campus, and was not terribly successful, largely because the space was far too small. Everyone paid a dollar, including the members of the Dead and the Pranksters, and they communistically divvied up the take at the end of the night. Practical Bill Kreutzmann, recalled Weir, made sure the Dead did okay. Paul Foster was wrapped in gauze like a mummy and went about pouring sugar into people's hands. They thought it was dosed with LSD, but it wasn't. At one end of the living room was the Dead's equipment, at the other the Prankster's projectors, tape recorders, and electronics. "The idea," Garcia said later, "was of its essence formless. There was nothin' going on. We'd just . . . make something of it." Coincidentally, the Rolling Stones were playing just down the street that night, and Sue Swanson, Connie Bonner, and Neal went off to "bring back the Stones." Unfortunately, the girls rushed the stage in the general melee occasioned by Mick Jagger's shirt coming un-buttoned, and were ejected. Sara Garcia would remember the night as fre-netic, with people milling around a terribly loud environment occasioned by the Dead's playing in too small a room. One thing was clear from this night: they needed a bigger place. A number of the attendees were relative strangers, including a U.C. Berkeley student and *Daily Cal* columnist named Jann Wenner. The grapevine had begun to function, and acid awareness was spreading.

They scheduled the next acid test for Saturday, December 11, but be-fore that the Dead had promised to do a benefit for the San Francisco Mime Troupe on Friday the tenth. The overwhelming success of the warehouse benefit had emboldened Bill Graham to seek a larger venue. Acting on a tip from either one of the Family Dog people or Ralph Glea-son, he'd booked this event into a San Francisco ballroom called the Fill-more Auditorium, on the second floor at the corner of Fillmore and Geary, in a black neighborhood halfway to the beach. Once called the Majestic Hall, then the Majestic Academy of Dancing, the Fillmore had headlined Ray Charles and Count Basie and was now run by a man named Charles Sullivan. Graham was already ingenious and indefatigable as a promoter. The week before, Bob Dylan had held a press conference at the public TV station KQED to promote his own show, and at one point displayed a poster Graham had given him that announced, "Appeal II, For Continued Artistic Freedom in the Parks." Appeal II cost $1.50 and fea-tured the Great Society, the Jefferson Airplane, the Mystery Trend, and "Many Other Friends." The handbill quoted Hamlet regarding the "inso-lence of office," promised dancing, and noted that "the place is huge [ca-pacity 1,000], and, like, it's there. Till dawn, we hope."

When the Dead arrived, they discovered that Graham had placed an easel on the side of the stage for each act's picture and name. Bill had asked Lesh, whom he knew from the Mime Troupe, for a picture, but they couldn't manage to produce one. Worse still, from Bill's point of view, was their new name, which perplexed, even angered, him. It gave him the creeps, he said, and he demurred at putting it on the easel. It was the be-ginning of a long series of arguments over many years. Phil replied, "Bill, I'm sorry. This is the decision we've made. Here's what you do. Put 'for-merly the Warlocks' in the space where the picture would go." And so he did. It was another tremendously successful event. At 9:30 there was a block-long double line, and it was just as long at 1 A.M. Signs with "Love" in three-foot-tall letters were at each end of the hall. The costumes, Glea-son reported, were "Goodwill cum Sherwood Forest," and in addition to raising $6,000 (which suggested sales of more than four thousand tickets) for the Mime Troupe, everyone had a great time.

The Dead had an even better time at the next night's acid test, held at the Big Beat club in Palo Alto, on the mudflats down by Highway 101. It was an L-shaped room, and the Dead were at the bend of the L. At one end was the Prankster setup, which looked like a cockpit, with its Day-Glo organ, tape recorders, microphones, and such. It was the first time the Pranksters had donned their quasi-military uniforms, and they looked even stranger as a result. By now, the audience was sufficiently large that they put a liquid form of LSD in a medium, which turned out to be Kool-Aid, both because it was inexpensive—and amusingly cool. As an experiment, Kreutzmann decided not to take LSD that night, though he pretended to, and discovered that it didn't seem to matter: everybody else was so high he had a terrific time. The Dead's music was probably not as strange as people recalled it, the context lending it a sheen that was somewhat more exotic than the slightly mutated modal rock and roll they played at the time. The weirdness was in the ears and the situation more than the music itself, which would take a while to evolve.

Once the Dead collected a quorum—"Where's Pigpen?"—they straggled out to play. The Dead and the Pranksters played at the same time, one band playing, the other, as Kreutzmann said with a chuckle, "kinda playing." Prankster music was "like pigs being slaughtered, like a parrot-peacock donnybrook," wrote Paul Foster. "Antimusic, antiplaying," thought Weir. "Of course, we couldn't really hear them, since we were louder. We had them outgunned." Prankster music, Sara explained, "was anybody picking up anything and doing anything they wanted . . . to break down barriers." As Kesey put it, "Suddenly people were stripped before one another and behold! as we looked on, we all made a great discovery: we were beautiful. Naked and helpless and sensitive as a snake after skinning, but far more human than that shining nightmare that had stood creaking in previous parade rest. We were alive and life was us. We joined hands and danced barefoot amongst the rubble. We had been cleansed, liberated! We would never don the old armors again."

The glory of an acid test for the Dead was that it wasn't a show and they weren't the night's entertainment. *Everybody* was the show, and Lord knew everybody was entertaining. "Freedom had a lot to do with it," Garcia said, "and the synergy, the thing of lots of things happening at once. Having no specific focus meant that there was a kind of pattern beyond randomness, that would emerge, and with no order at all, a deeper level of order would surface, something like Mandelbrot equations and chaos theory today. There were no performers and no audience, or rather everybody was both. The performance and the reality outside the performance are one. That's why I paid to get in." Another time he said of the acid tests that they were "tremendously funny and good and entertaining—what life should be, really." The Prankster equipment generated its own magic. "Voices coming out of things that weren't plugged in and, God . . . sometimes they were like writhing and squirming." There was a figure-eight tape-lag setup, connecting a speaker with a microphone in front at each end of the room. Thus sound would come out of a speaker, go into a microphone, back into the sound system, into the other speaker, and out. The result would be a continuous echo. What you heard was a matter of synchronicity, the Jungian notion of non-cause-and-effect connections among events, karma, or the luck of the draw. "Either you needed to hear it," Weir realized, "wanted to hear it, or didn't want to hear it."

In addition to the two bands, the night included Stewart Brand, a local anthropologist and friend of Kesey's who had a multimedia show he took around called "America Needs Indians." His tepee, which served as the screen for a slide show, was set up at one end of the club. The owners, two conventional middle-aged ladies, hovered, fascinated, at the bar all night. And there were bums and hoboes and truck drivers who'd wandered in off the street, having no idea of what was going on in this utterly surreal environment.

Finally, of course, there was Neal. He had a small sledgehammer that he used as his wizard's wand, "slinging it around like a fancy gunslinger," said Sara, "rapping to everyone in the room, seemingly, about what they were thinking, wrapping everybody's secret trip into this whole eloquent bubble." "He would pick stuff up off the floor," recalled one new Prankster, Hugh Romney (later known as Wavy Gravy), "cigarette packs or whatever, and he would read it like Native Americans read meaning in natural things . . . the world as *I-Ching*." Less romantically, Neal reminded Garcia of "the guy who was out picking pockets while the man on the platform was selling snake oil." Then Neal joined a group under a strobe light. Roy Sebern, an artist, had brought in a roll of paper towels, and people began to tear them into tiny fragments and throw them into the strobe flash, over and over, until it became what Stewart Brand called a "flickering flashing dazzling snowstorm. Pure magic." Then it was dawn outside, the equipment stopped humming, and they were done. But Garcia went home with a bonus, although it later became slightly annoying. Ducking out for a breath of air, he'd been standing in the parking lot with Denise Kaufman, a Prankster and later part of the band Ace of Cups, when a police officer came by to check out the scene. After passing the time, he departed, and Garcia tipped his hat with the comment "The tips, Captain." And up through the vapors of Denise's mind bubbled the words "Captain Trips." Garcia had acquired his Prankster nickname.

By now, of course, the Grateful Dead had entirely dropped out of anything remotely resembling the music business. After all, exploring inner space was a great deal more interesting. The next test was scheduled for Stinson Beach, a little town on the coast just north of San Francisco. Somewhat isolated by the extremely twisting road, Stinson seemed a good place, but at the last second the test was moved to a lodge a few miles back up the highway, at Muir Beach. The setting was beautiful, with flowers and a lawn going down to the beach. It turned out to be a fairly weird night, odd even by acid test standards. As Weir put it, they dosed and then went into a horse race to get set up before the LSD came on. Some of them lost the race. Kreutzmann went into a time warp. His acid came on, "all of a sudden, boom, that's it, set's over. And I proceeded to tear down my drum set for two hours, and the night was just begun." The Pranksters were screening part of the film they'd shot on the bus ride, and Babbs was narrating: "Are you in the movie, or are you watching the movie? Are you in the movie, aren't we all in the movie?" And Kreutzmann got lost in the rap. "I'm watching it, and I realize that I'm as much *that*—there's no difference. Einstein's theory again. You're the same, in our mind it's the same." Though it would take a while, he eventually managed to set up his equipment and play.

A young local woman named Goldie Rush had heard about some hippie party at the lodge and came out with a couple of girlfriends to see what was up. Since she didn't take any acid, she found the goings-on, which seemed to involve much seriousness and lots of fiddling with knobs, quite boring. "Nothing happening," she thought, and left. Contrarily, it was one of Lesh's most interesting acid tests. A woman named Florence Nathan, who worked for Tom Donahue, had come to the acid test looking for her friend Lenny Bruce. Lenny not being there, she wandered around, locked eyes with Lesh, and without a word they embraced. It was the beginning of a long-term relationship.

That night the band played the Reverend Gary Davis's song "Death Don't Have No Mercy" for the first time, and as Kesey and Babbs stood in front of Lesh, "just sweating like pigs, jaws dropped with raving enthusiasm and affirmation in their faces," Phil realized that if they could move these legends, "I sort of figured we were onto something." All that was the least of it. At some time during the night, a man began to freak out. He later said that he was hearing extremely high-pitched screeching sounds from the band, and in his anxiety he responded in kind, by pushing a chair along the floor until it made a similar horrible scraping screech, the sound of fingernails on a blackboard, cubed. Eventually, one of the Pranksters tripled the chair man's paranoia level by seeing some conventionally dressed people and thinking they were the police. The chair man had a pocketful of LSD, and even though it was still legal, he decided to leave, leaped into his car, and proceeded to crash it, although he emerged unscathed. It was not the easiest of introductions between Owsley "Bear" Stanley and the Grateful Dead, but it didn't ultimately matter; the man who produced LSD for the Bay Area and the band that played to the experience were destined to unite.

Born Augustus Owsley Stanley III on January 19, 1935, Owsley was named for his grandfather, a U.S. senator from and governor of Kentucky, and the father of the St. Lawrence Seaway. His father was a government bureaucrat whose wartime service had left him with a bad case of alcoholism. The end result, Bear—he said he acquired the nickname when he developed a hairy chest at quite a young age—was a man who combined brilliance and charisma with social dysfunction, a genius who would fascinate the Grateful Dead, but at the same time a southern aristocrat who could, Weir noted, "abuse a waitress like no one else in the world," a man isolated from others by intelligence and personality to the point of extreme elitism, so that while he was not genteel, he remained gentry. As one of his housemates later said, "If Bear decided that X brand toothpaste was *it,* you'd better switch to X, or you'd never hear the end of it." His pursuit of quality was part of his gift to the Grateful Dead, but it came with baggage.

After a dismal high school educational experience epitomized, he said, by getting a D for pointing out that his physics teacher contradicted the textbook, he briefly attended the University of Virginia engineering school, where he discovered that engineers generally sat at desks and used slide rules. He wanted to make things, and over the decade of the fifties he spent time in the air force, where he learned that he was ill suited to take orders as an enlisted man. On his return to civilian life, he had various technical electronics jobs at Rocketdyne and the Jet Propulsion Laboratory, worked at radio and television stations as an announcer and engineer, and studied Russian, ballet, and almost anything else that caught his fancy. In 1963 he moved to Berkeley to take classes and found himself living near campus in a rooming house called the Brown Shoe. He'd tried pot, then grew interested in psychedelics, and one day a friend gave him some authentic Sandoz Laboratory LSD. Since he wanted to take more, he concluded that he'd have to make it himself. His inexhaustible curiosity led him to the U.C. Berkeley chemistry library, and he began serious research. Needing money for the process, he first sold morning glory seeds, then traded some seeds for some amphetamine ("speed"). He needed a scale to weigh the speed and went into the U.C. chemistry building, walked up to a chemistry student named Melissa, and asked to borrow hers. They grew friendly, became lovers, and after a while they began making speed in the laboratory, which gave them enough money to make LSD.

Owsley's subtle approach to LSD making was unique, and critical to the history of psychedelia, because what he made was an immense quantity of extraordinarily pure LSD. Without him, there simply wouldn't have been enough acid for the psychedelic scene of the Bay Area in the sixties to have ignited. Owsley had a personality that wanted to dominate, to "gain mastery over" whatever it was that interested him, said Melissa, "to penetrate into things," as he put it himself. When he was twenty, he'd been very ill and had spent some time analyzing religion, reading everything from the *Book of Mormon* to the texts of High Church Anglicans. It all seemed like the hypocritical work of priests to him. Then he met a lifelong friend, Bob Thomas, who led him to alchemy. Having by now read the Rosicrucians and theosophy, the psychedelic experience made utter sense to him. Alchemy teaches that the universe is a mind, or in the language of quantum physics, a set of vibrations. All reality is a series of standing waves and can be modulated by the mind. Since LSD itself modulated the mind, Owsley assumed that it was profoundly sensitive to the atmosphere in which it was made, and he approached making it as an alchemical act, with a fanatical concern for purity of both heart and chemistry. His standards were so exacting that he rejected a significant proportion of his yield. Between 1965 and 1967 he made about 450 grams of crystalline LSD. A gram produces 3,600 quite strong (250 microgram) doses, so his total was around 1,250,000 hits. He gave away at least half.

Sometime before the Muir Beach Acid Test, a friend of Owsley's had taken him to La Honda to meet Kesey, and their encounter was a revelation to Bear. Owsley thought he'd understood psychedelics, but this was another level of experience. Then he went to Muir Beach, where he was completely overwhelmed and terrified, primarily by "Garcia's guitar, which seemed to come out of the universe and try to eat me alive." It occurred to him that there was a metaphorical barrier in the mind, like the literal hymen of a virgin woman, and that the Prankster group mind psychedelic experience tore through it. "I let totally go, went off into the universe, and there was no one running my body, which was running around doing crazy goofy things because I had left. I had gone off into a part of the universe that was just a spiral, and every so often I would be presented with some fantastic scene." Kesey, the Pranksters, and the Grateful Dead had gotten into his head, and he would have to come to grips with this, and to dominate it. The whole point of the acid test, it seemed to Bear, was to "expose you right down to your infinite detail, exposing you to forces of the universe that [Kesey and the Pranksters] didn't thoroughly understand." All the demons and spirits that are part of mythology and part of alchemical lore were "part of that real other reality which you fall right into with things like the acid test . . . They had discovered on their own the secret rituals of the ancient witchcraft rites and alchemical rites of human history that had been lost, suppressed by the Christian church among other things." Bear, too, would help them take it to another level.

Leaning on the top rail of a driftwood fence outside the lodge at dawn, Garcia, Kesey, and Babbs chatted about the glorious futures they saw arising from their experiences. "Just like the big time," thought Babbs. "It is, it is the big time! Why, we could cut a chart-busting record to-fuckin-*morrow!*" "Hey, we taped tonight's show," said Kesey. "We could *release* a record tomorrow." Alone among them, Garcia stayed grounded. "Yeah, right. And a year from tomorrow be recording a 'Things Go Better with Coke' commercial."

The acid tests had a much more enduring legacy than this momentary megalomania, for they would serve as the template that permanently defined the Grateful Dead's view of its audience. The bond between virtually all theatrical or musical performers and their audience is romantic; the artist seeks love, the audience gives it. The Grateful Dead certainly sought to entertain and move its audience, but the root basis of their relationship was that of a partnership of equals, of companions in an odyssey. Ironically enough, these young people, in both the band and the audience, would go on to achieve an incredibly mature bond. The only parallel in American music might be the relationship of certain jazz musicians to their audience. Coltrane had truly left his mark.

As the year turned over into 1966, the Dead enjoyed a special Neal Cassady road adventure, taking the acid test to Portland, Oregon. The main road from the Bay Area to Portland crosses a shoulder of Mount Shasta and then the Siskiyou mountain range, and in January it is no casual drive.

The bus broke down in far northern California, and they proceeded to take psychic hostages at a gas station, intimidating the locals with Dead-Prankster flash. They rented a U-Haul truck and stuffed the Dead, the Pranksters, their equipment, and a generator into the back for a ride without chains on a road coated by black ice and effectively closed by a blizzard to all vehicles driven by sane people. "You did this?" someone asked Kreutzmann, incredulous. "Shit yeah," he said. "I wouldn't have missed it." Because of the generator, they had an intercom to the cab, which resulted in an expedition with Cassadyan commentary. When Lesh fell out for a nap, Pigpen took the shotgun seat, tranquilly watching I-5 flow by at 70 mph as they passed the occasional truck still out, but seeing damn little else in the near-zero visibility. The radio was playing as loud as possible, the raving went on nonstop. No problem: Neal was driving.

Compared to that, the Portland Acid Test was unsurprisingly anticlimactic, although Weir had an extraordinary personal experience. At some point in the evening, he suddenly felt as though he couldn't play a wrong note. "I felt golden," he said, as his hands played effortlessly without him in control, or needing to be. It was a humbling and joyful moment. The next morning was just the opposite. They were rehearsing on headphones, and M.G. and George Walker, the Prankster technicians, began feeding them a delayed sound signal. For the longest time, Weir couldn't get anything right, and blamed himself.

On returning to the Bay Area, they had a couple of gigs at the Matrix, where the Airplane had begun. It was a tiny bar with a capacity of perhaps one hundred, so small that the lighting booth was built over the toilet fixtures. There were noise complaints even without performers, and then the Dead moved in. Lacking a permit, the Matrix could not allow dancing, so it was not a particularly comfortable show. Nonetheless, Garcia loved it, because they were only a few blocks from the bay, and it was possible to hear the foghorns. In addition to Chuck Berry, the jug material, Pig's blues tunes, and the originals, they'd added a couple of covers—Bobby Bland's "(Turn on Your) Lovelight" and the Olympics/Young Rascals' "Good Lovin'"—and three more originals: "You Can't Catch Me," "The Monster," and "Otis on a Shakedown Cruise."

Came Saturday, January 8, and things got a little complicated in San Francisco's rock world. The Dead were playing an acid test at the Fillmore. Over at Longshoremen's Hall, radio station KYA was sponsoring a "teen dance" with the Vejtables. And the Family Dog had revived itself to put on the Jefferson Airplane and the Charlatans at California Hall on Polk Street, a Heidelberg castle look-alike which had been Das Deutsche

Haus until World War I. Luria Castell had returned from her vacation in Mexico and was living at a boarding house at 710 Ashbury Street in the Haight-Ashbury, where the house manager was a semistudent named Danny Rifkin. Rifkin was working at the post office, and with free rent, his $200 in savings "seemed to be gobs," so he gladly lent it to Luria for the show. He also helped her put up posters promoting the gig, and was rewarded with the Coca-Cola concession. His friend Rock Scully, also an S.F. State student, was now the Charlatans' manager, so he, too, was part of that night's show. When they learned about the acid test from Kesey, who had visited a State philosophy class, they decided to combine forces, and agreed that tickets to each show were good for both. They had even planned a shuttle bus between buildings—the Dead had mentioned it the night before at the Matrix—but it fell through. The California Hall show was a success, although Rifkin actually made more on the Cokes than Luria did on the entire show, because the poster artist, George Hunter of the Charlatans, had put the Coke logo on the poster, and Rifkin got a tremendous discount when he went to the bottling plant to stock up. What happened after the show, however, was more important. Danny and Rock went to the Fillmore.

Ralph Gleason's column reported that the people at the Fillmore were "like the backstage crowd at the California Hall dance." There were the usual costumes, strobe lights, balloons, TV cameras, electronic equipment, and so forth. Paul Foster now had a white mechanic's suit with a black cross on the front and a message that read "Please Don't Believe in Magic" on the back. There were giant Frisbees, and girls with four-inch eyelashes. Sara Garcia's job was to draw designs on everyone's hand as a method for marking people as having paid. At concerts later, it would be a split-second process with an ink stamp, but at the acid test, Sara would do a reading of the person and then translate it into an elaborate design.

The evening passed through the usual divine madness. Brian Rohan, a local attorney and an old University of Oregon friend of Kesey's, had put up the seventy-five dollars for the hall rental and was mortified when the show started late. For some reason, the spiked Kool-Aid, complete with a dry-ice float, didn't come out until nearly 10 P.M., and the band didn't go on until 11:30. It was Rock Scully's first Grateful Dead show, and he would be impressed. "An hour or so into the set and something very odd starts to happen. It's the room, doctor. The room is *breathing*. Breathing deeply, like a great sonic lung from which all sounds originate and which demands all the oxygen in the world. We inhale and exhale with it as if to the great collective heartbeat of an invisible whale. We are all under the hypnotic spell of this ghostly pulse." John Warnecke, a close friend of Kreutzmann's, ascended into the heavens and found himself in sync with the drums at the same time that he found himself in front of the power controls for the entire hall. He began to flash the switches in time to the beat, which proved somewhat disconcerting to the rest of the conclave. In time, Billy came and settled John down near the drums.

It was the ending that everyone would recall. Around 2 A.M. the police came by to close the show, although in the absence of alcohol they lacked any legal authority to do so. Their first question was the usual "Who's in charge here?" Since the idea of anyone being in charge at an acid test was among the funniest thoughts imaginable, various participants began chanting, "Hug the heat." There wasn't a shred of paranoia in the room that night, and to Garcia the cops were "buffoons, dog police." An officer came out onstage and motioned for the band to stop, and was duly ignored. The cops grew perplexed. Everyone was acting weird, but confusingly so. "They're pretty fast for drunks," they thought. "Pretty quick-witted, too." They tried to use the house P.A. to announce closing, but their voices came out sounding peculiar, particularly after Warnecke offered them a little Kool-Aid. They began to pull power cords out of the wall, and M.G. followed them and plugged things back in. At length the band stopped playing and the police dutifully began shooing everyone out, although it was a slow process.

It occurred to Lesh and Weir that when a TV station goes off the air, it plays "The Star-Spangled Banner," so they began an *a cappella* duet. Spotting a twenty-foot ladder, and always part monkey, Weir swarmed up to continue his end of the duet from on high. A too-many-donuts cop eyed the rickety thing and decided on discretion, refusing to follow Weir and merely barking, "Come on down off that ladder, kid."

"No."

"Come down or you're gonna really be in trouble."

"Now I'm really not gonna come down."

Eventually, the officer gave up. But there was another bit of fallout from the Fillmore Acid Test. Since the benefit on December 10, Bill Graham had coveted the Fillmore as a dance hall, and he was working on his game plan. Bill Kreutzmann, the most practical member of the Dead, and therefore the de facto business manager, had gone through Graham to get the building for the acid test. One of the side aspects of the evening had been the spontaneous repainting of the Fillmore's bathrooms. And so on the day after the test, leaseholder Charles Sullivan came in to find his sleek chrome and black and yellow replaced with electric Day-Glo pastels.

He was disturbed. Bill Graham grew disturbed, and decided to share his feelings with Kreutzmann. It was by no means the last time the Dead would disturb Bill Graham.

Graham mollified Sullivan, the initiation passed quickly, and the Dead joined the Great Society and other bands in yet another Mime Troupe benefit on January 14, Graham's swan song with the troupe. The Dead also played that week at the Matrix. All of it, however, was only a buildup to the "big show," which had been in the planning for some time and scheduled for late in January, the Trips Festival. The previous summer, Ramon Sender of the Tape Music Center had broached an idea to the light artist Tony Martin about some sort of "crazy ceremonial." Tony suggested talking to Stewart Brand, the anthropologist. In December, Prankster Mike Hagen visited Brand and began, as Brand put it, "blathering how there was going to be [i.e., should be] an acid test at Longshoremen's Hall or some such high-viz venue in San Francisco. I knew there was no way the Pranksters could actually bring off the preparation for such an ambitious occasion, but it seemed eminently worth doing, so I just picked up the phone and started doing it." It was to be a mixed-media event, an "electronic circus," a synthesis of all the various vectors of artistic change zipping around the Bay Area into one combined event. Years before, Kesey had posited a "Neon Renaissance" that connected the work of Ornette Coleman, the Bay Area choreographer Ann Halprin, Lenny Bruce, William Burroughs, and Jerry's old art teacher, Wally Hedrick. With a little discreet chemical help, it could happen. They'd selected the entire third weekend of January as the time and Longshoremen's Hall as the place. Rock bands would also be a part of the action. At first Ramon thought of inviting the Charlatans, but they'd rented space at the Tape Music Center and damaged the ceiling. In the end, the rock component would be the Dead and a new band, Big Brother and the Holding Company.

The buildup to the Trips Festival was a rich stew. The organizers were media-savvy, and as early as January 9 an *Examiner* piece on Marshall McLuhan had a plug for the festival. On the eighteenth the *Chronicle* ran an article called "Glorious Electricity," which revealed that "in his infinite wisdom the Almighty is vouchsafing visions in certain people in our midst along side which the rapturous transports of sweet old St. Theresa are but early Milton Berle shows on a ten inch screen." The psychedelic underground was beginning to surface. On January 16 Kesey went to court to resolve a pot bust at La Honda from the previous April, receiving six months on a work farm and six months probation, but was set free on bail pending appeal. On the nineteenth, just two days before the festival was due to begin, Kesey and Mountain Girl were smoking a joint on the roof of Stewart Brand's North Beach apartment and managed to get arrested, making the front pages of every afternoon paper in the Bay Area. Out on bail once again, thanks to their very good attorney, Brian Rohan, Kesey and Mountain Girl helped hype the festival with a ceremony in downtown San Francisco's Union Square, releasing balloons that read "Now" and playing on Ron Boise's *Thunder Machine,* a sculpture of metal, wires, and springs. Kesey's white Levi's carried a message: one side of his derriere read "Hot," one "Cold"; the middle was marked "Tibet."

The Trips Festival began on Friday the twenty-first, with Brand's "America Needs Indians" slide show, the Open Theater, a comedy troupe called the Congress of Wonders, the Jazz Mice, liquid projections, and so forth. The Dead went to get a feel for the place. The night was not without its amusements. Vera Mae Frederickson, an assistant at the Lowe Anthropology Museum at U.C. Berkeley, was part of Brand's scene. She took part as an 1870 acculturated Apache, complete with a tepee on the floor. A Hell's Angel approached her and said, "Well, I'm an Angel, and we all get along real well with oppressed people." When he offered her a joint, he was welcomed right into the tent.

Saturday offered work from the Tape Music Center, the Acid Test (i.e., Kesey and the Pranksters), Ann Halprin's Dancer's Workshop, the Dead, and Big Brother and the Holding Company. There were five screens on the walls, a center platform with projectors, and a pair of traffic lights blinking away. The Beat poet Michael McClure read, avant-garde filmmakers John Korty and Bruce Conner showed their work, Kesey emceed, and all hell broke delightfully loose. Up on the scaffolding, Stewart Brand felt "the pure juiciness" of being in the middle of "a sea of high weirdness, with a full sense of initiation and none whatever of control—that combination was tonic." Some bits of theater—a shadow play on his tepee, for instance—failed, Brand recalled, and other parts worked incredibly. He'd hired a world-class gymnast, Dan Millman, to dive off the balcony onto a trampoline under a strobe light. "In his ski mask he did Olympic-quality flips and spins and visions of flashing human flight that ignited psychedelic dazzlement in all who saw him. I imagine that most remember him as hallucinogenic rather than real. His act was utterly in the midst—it was never advertised, announced, or reported. Seeming spontaneous, its impact helped inspire an evening of, and a generation of, boundless spontaneity."

"By Saturday I felt as though I was a priestess," said Sara. She had always been a dancer, and now costumes were part of the event, fantasy clothing. She wore sleazy tight neon green leopard-print satin bell-bottoms and declared that the "whole room just went into orbit." Kesey was at an overhead projector in the middle of the room, writing messages to one and all, she said, and "you'd look up and see your thoughts magically on the ceiling. Everyone was so open, ready to go on." Hunter had momentarily been a bit uncomfortable, lost in some dreary rut, and then looked up to see Kesey's message, "Outside is inside, how does it look?" and instantly, his mood rose and everything was great. "Lights flashing . . . everything would be demolished, spilled, broken, affected, and after that another thing would happen, maybe smoothing out the chaos," said Garcia. "What you said might come out a minute later on a tape loop in some other part of the place . . . Thousands of people, man, all helplessly stoned, all finding themselves in a roomful of other thousands of people, none of whom any of them were afraid of. It was magic, far out, beautiful magic." Another time, he added, "It was open, a tapestry, a mandala—it was whatever you made it . . . the quest is to extend the limit, to go as far as you can go. In the Acid Test that meant to do away with old forms . . . everybody was creating . . . [there was a] willingness for everybody to be constantly on the lookout for something new."

There were simply more tripping people in one room—between three thousand and five thousand—than anyone had ever seen before. "Nobody knew there were so many freaks," said Lesh. "Nobody could have guessed that you could give thousands of people acid in one room and not have it blow up from the psychic energy. My main visual image was the sea of people, with waves rippling through it. It was a higher stage than we were used to. There was an incredible variety of dress, color, and lighting. Waves of light, waves of light which turned out to be people. It reminded me of the Boccioni painting *The City Rises*—he was a Futurist—this picture of a team of horses pulling construction gear in turn-of-the-century Milan. The energy and light of it, people became light, the light solidified into people. My other image of that night was that the cords of our equipment were literally jumping out of the wall sockets, there was so much energy."

And it was the Dead that played to it, although Big Brother briefly preceded them. Big Brother was a new band whose bassist, Peter Albin, was their old friend from the Boar's Head. It had begun as a group of jammers at 1090 Page Street, where Chet Helms, the pot dealer, organized parties. He'd introduced guitarist Jim Gurley, a friend of his from Detroit, to the jam scene, and they'd taken shape as a band. But the night of the festival was part of their first week of existence, and they weren't ready. The Dead, thought Ramon Sender, more or less gently pushed them off the stage, and the night did indeed go into orbit: "It was obvious that the Dead had what the audience wanted," said Sender, "and they played the shit out of their instruments." "It was music," Lesh added, "that was seriously intended to get you high. Not deadpan but high farce . . . and it was music that actually changed people's personalities. It was warping." The fact that the building was concrete and sounded awful actually helped, reverberating the sound through everyone, pounding the music into their bones. Someone dosed some ice cream and encouraged the security guards to partake. Soon, the doors were open to all. An ordinary citizen/tourist had just flown in from Southeast Asia, heard the music, and wandered in. Eventually, he asked Sara Garcia what was going on. Being that sort of soul, she tried to tell him: "Oh, this is where we're just brothers and sisters and join God here on earth." It really did feel heavenly.

One of the physiological limits of LSD is that one tends to react less intensely by the third night in a row. Sunday the twenty-third was subdued, as tiredness set in. The idea for the evening was to take the various elements of the first two nights, have everybody do everything at once, and have a cosmic pinball machine choose, randomly, what everyone would hear. It didn't work, and for the Grateful Dead there was a more significant problem. At some point in the evening, Kesey wrote on his overhead projector, "Garcia, plug in." Jerry looked down at his guitar only to discover that the bridge was flattened and the strings had rolled up the neck; it required serious surgery. A man carrying a clipboard and wearing a cardigan sweater that would have been appropriate on a golf course ran up. "What's the matter?" he said. Garcia was stoned and having a good time, and, after all, this was an acid test; he was free to play or not play. "Well, my guitar . . . ," he said vaguely, shrugging. The stranger, Bill Graham—to this point, his contacts with the band had been with Lesh and Kreutzmann, and Garcia was, after all, quite stoned—sat down and frantically began trying to fix the guitar, a task for which he was heroically unqualified. But his desire to be helpful would leave an indelible impression on Garcia. "It was so sweet—I loved Bill from then on. I'll always love him for that. What does he know about a guitar? He was so earnest, there in the midst of total chaos. It was just the nicest gesture."

In the week before the festival, with the energy mushrooming and then Kesey being arrested, the de facto producers, Ramon Sender and Stewart Brand, grew a little nervous and decided they needed someone to help manage the event. They called Graham, then in the process of leaving the Mime Troupe and striking out on his own, and offered him the job. He said sure, asking for a percentage, which would turn out to be $800, his first paying job as a producer. Running about the Trips Festival with his watch and clipboard, he tried to create order out of chaos and not surprisingly failed. He also annoyed some of the participants. Weir's memory of that night was "Who's this asshole with the clipboard?" This was a not-uncommon reaction. When Graham found Kesey, wearing a space suit complete with spherical helmet, letting in some Hell's Angels by a side door, he confronted him, screaming, "What the fuck do you think you're doing?" Kesey simply closed his bubble helmet.

The media response to the Trips Festival was fairly predictable. The *Examiner* story patronizingly reported that the supposed orgy had gone silent when interrupted by an announcement of a missing child. "In the clutch, the mantle [of social responsibility] fell back into place." In the *Chronicle*, Ralph Gleason criticized the production for failing to deliver all the things it promised, dismissed Friday and Sunday as bores, and held that the success of Saturday night was directly related to the rock music. The *Daily Cal*'s rock critic, "Mr. Jones" (Jann Wenner), agreed. "The Acid Test is at its best as a dance, but once the music stops, it becomes very dull." Both *Newsweek* and *Time* covered the event, and the latter was particularly feeble. "Happenings Are Happening" reported that "a woman in a negligee was bombarded with raw eggs," that "a stark-naked Negro beat the drums," and that "pounding music exploded in the eardrums and blurred reason." Nonetheless, it was the first pebble of what would become a landslide of national media coverage of San Francisco's rock/psychedelic culture.

The Dead followed up the festival with more work at the Matrix, and also a small acid test at Sound City, a studio in the South of Market neighborhood. Ray Andersen, the Matrix soundman, was at Sound City, and recalled that Kreutzmann and his wife were fighting, that Bear was irritating everyone not in the Dead and seemed primarily concerned with making sure that the man who owned the studio did not get a copy of anything recorded. Garcia went around saying, "Cut out this craziness, we're going to play again." And Lesh spent the best part of the evening sitting with Owsley, with whom he fell in love. "Hanging around with him was like being in a science-fiction movie," Lesh said, and Phil was a sci-fi fan. In a sense, he felt he already knew Bear, since any artist puts himself into his art, and by now they knew Owsley's art quite well. Phil had asked Owsley if he'd like to be their manager. "No, I wouldn't like that." "How about soundman, we need one of those." "Well, I don't know anything about that, either, but I guess I could probably learn. It sounds like more fun." Bear was on the bus.

And the bus was pulling out. Late in January the Pranksters met, and Kesey asked a Ouija board for advice regarding his legal problems. The message he gleaned was: leave. Being a novelist, he was constitutionally unable to do it simply, so he concocted a fake suicide. A friend took a Prankster truck up the coast and left it near Eureka, along with a pair of Kesey's shoes and a note that read in part, "Ocean ocean I'll beat you in the end," while Kesey headed for Mexico. Bereft of their leader, the Pranksters decided to follow, with a stop in Los Angeles. Now rehearsing with their new soundman at a Berkeley club called the Questing Beast, the Dead were inclined to join them in Los Angeles, with vague plans to investigate the music business headquartered there. Bear didn't particularly like it, but he was overruled, and they decided to go. Just as they were leaving town, Phil drove past the Fillmore Auditorium, now run by Bill Graham, and read the marquee: "Jefferson Airplane, with sights and sounds of the Trips Festival." Since the Airplane hadn't even been part of the festival, he was annoyed. "Asshole," he thought. "Now who's gonna reap the harvest of what the acid test has sown? The Jefferson Airplane and Bill Graham? Who's gonna clean up now?"

Hollywood
and Home Again

(2/6/66–5/1/66)

wsley had other business, so the band flew to L.A. without him. They were met at the airport by his friend Jean Mayo Millay, a scholarly schoolteacher who'd made a documentary movie called *The Psychedelic Experience* and consequently met Tim Leary, Dick Alpert, and Bear. Though she was intellectually up on LSD, Jean was relatively conservative, and she was nonplussed at her first sight of the Dead as they came crashing down the airport stairs, Phil riding the banister, all of them now quite longhaired, Pigpen just plain frightening. "A motlier crew I had never seen." That night, February 6, there was a small acid test at the Northridge Unitarian Church, out in the San Fernando Valley. Paul Sawyer, the minister, had met Kesey at an Esalen conference and was happy to welcome the remaining Pranksters. "Great to see you. We've got a great place for you to hide the bus," he told Julius Karpen, a new Prankster. "We don't hide," replied Julius.

On February 12, the Pranksters and the Dead threw the Watts Acid Test at a dirty, dusty warehouse in Compton, and for various reasons it became legendary. Apparently, two people independently arranged the Kool-Aid that night, and it was a very strong dose. It was hot in the warehouse, so everyone was thirsty, and there was only one thing to drink.

There was also the Bear factor. His sound system was essentially experimental and usually caused long delays in the setup process. This was the case at Watts, and everyone got terrifically high while waiting for the band to play. Even the band got weirded out, and Kreutzmann recalled it as the first time that he ever felt uncomfortable playing while high. It certainly did not help that the test seemed to become the evening's most popular topic on the Los Angeles Police Department's radio system, and there were a considerable number of police cars around. When the police entered, they displayed the traditional charm of the LAPD, shining flashlights in people's faces. Naturally, at least one participant obliged them with a rant: "I'm so high, I am so far out. Where I am, my consciousness is so far beyond anything you can comprehend." Though undoubtedly true, it was hardly diplomatic.

The Pranksters went into survival mode, taking an occasional breather outside on the railroad tracks. Mike Hagen, who was part jackrabbit, leaped over a six-foot fence in back of the building and landed in a garbage can. Everyone laughed, until he looked up and saw police everywhere. Paul Foster, his face painted half black and half silver, was arrested, which would inspire the infamous "Blue Boy" episode of everyone's favorite advertisement for the LAPD, *Dragnet*. Eventually, the warehouse was surrounded by wooden sawhorses. Outside the sawhorses was a ring of helmeted men holding billy clubs.

In these circumstances, it was not surprising that there was a significant freak-out in Watts. A young lady had a fight with her boyfriend, Ray, who stalked off. Lost in the ozone, she began to wail, "Ray? Ray? Who cares? Who cares?" Babbs decided to involve everyone, and put a microphone in front of her face with the comment "Freak freely." Of course, her cries ran into a figure-eight time-delay loop, which only succeeded in further disorienting her. It fell to new Prankster Hugh Romney to comfort her, which he was magnificently equipped to do. Romney had been the poetry director of the Gaslight Cafe in New York, and for a while his roommate in his apartment upstairs had been Bob Dylan, who'd written "A Hard Rain's A-Gonna Fall" on Hugh's typewriter. Romney had read his poetry as an opening act for Thelonious Monk, worked in improvisational comedy with the Committee in San Francisco, and then had come to Los Angeles, where he was at that time working with brain-damaged children. Hugh took over with the "Who cares?" lady, and then he got some help from the stage.

A cappella, Pigpen began to sing. "I wanna know, do you feel good? . . . I wanna know, can you find yo' mind?" The audience responded

"*Oh, yes,*" and Pig—possibly the only person in the room not tripping—snickered, "If you can, you better get on out of this place." But the young lady kept on, and Pigpen and Hugh were there for her. "I wanna tell everybody in da house right now—[audience:] *Yeah!*—there's many many things you got to do one more time—*Yeah!*—You gotta think about yo' neighbors—*Yeah!*—You got to think about yo' friends—*Yeah!*—You got to think about yo' brothers . . . You got to think about everybody that means something . . . I'm talkin' 'bout somebody who lost a little bit of love—*Yeah!*—Somebody lost a little bit of friendship!—*Yeah!*—I wanna know, do you know what I'm talking about now?—*Yeah!*—You know what I'm talkin' about now." Ray returned from his snit, and the night proceeded from there with more ups than downs. When the test concluded about sunrise, a giggling Neal Cassady took the garbage can of Kool-Aid outside—it was the first time they'd ever had any left over—to pour into a storm drain. As he poured, it began to dawn on an officer that whatever caused the oddness happening that night was literally going down the drain. Just as the thought was fully realized, it was too late.

It had been a harsh and demanding night. Sara and Jerry, who'd been estranged for some weeks, he having taken a lover and she having followed suit, were discussing their daughter Heather's future when two cops walked in. Sara approached them and asked if she could help them. They wondered aloud what a nice girl like her was doing in a place like this, "and I tried to explain it to them." After this particularly futile conversation, she and Jerry wandered outside, where George Walker was parking the bus, directed by Neal, who was so remarkably high that no one would let him drive—a virtually unprecedented event. Neal was always both mentally and physically humorous, a combination, Garcia had said, of Lenny Bruce and Buster Keaton, but this morning he surpassed himself on the Keaton side, slooowwwly directing the backing bus into a signpost, which it knocked over. He began to joke with the post physically, acting like a drunk hanging off it, wobbling about. By now it was early Sunday morning, and as two elderly women passed by on their way to church, he mimed hiding the pole behind his back. Afterward, he oh-so-very-slowly drove Garcia home.

When they passed the Watts Towers, a peculiar local artistic monument to junk sculpture, Garcia had an epiphany. The Towers was the work of one person, Simon Rodia, and it was concrete, which is to say material. Early on February 13, Sunday morning coming down, nerves shredded by a grueling night, he gazed at the Towers and came to several conclusions. One was that material artifacts made no sense to him; whatever art he could participate in would have to be intangible, something that left behind only memories. In other words, music. And it had to be a group effort. The individual artist, as epitomized in Rodia or even more extremely in Neal Cassady, wasn't going to work for Garcia. Neal was his own brilliant, if demented, artist, and his own product as well. But he was also isolated. Something "dynamic" had a chance, Garcia thought, something cooperative but leaderless, and operating in real time, in the present moment. "This isn't strictly recreational," he decided. "This is really important. And that's when I started paying attention."

The members of the Grateful Dead settled down in Los Angeles to conquer the music business; how, they hadn't a clue. Someone found them a stucco home off Western Avenue on the outskirts of Watts which would be dubbed the Pink House. On one side was a den of iniquity, variously described as a home for gambling and/or prostitution, and on the other, the home of an elderly woman. It was never clear who complained more about the noise their practicing made. A year later they'd describe their sojourn to friends:

GARCIA: "And then we went to L.A. and suffered for three months. Didn't accomplish much. It wasn't all bad. There were some high lights, some low lights."

PIG: "Sitting on the front porch. Riding them little kids' bicycles."

GARCIA: "We had some fun, I must say, come to think of it. Hah. We've never failed to have *some* fun."

PIG: "Watched a lot of TV."

GARCIA: "Watched a lot of TV, ate a lot of steak."

PIG: "The only good thing about L.A. is they've got about a thousand television stations."

GARCIA: ". . . nothing much else going on. We stayed in the house there, afraid to go out on the streets."

The Pink House was a bizarre place. There was no furniture other than a few mattresses and cartons, although Weir somehow managed to procure a brass bed for himself and his girlfriend, Barbara Lee. Instruments and equipment filled the living room, their bedrooms were on the second floor, and Owsley had the whole top floor. But the twistiest aspect of the Pink House was the cuisine. As a young man, Bear had been overweight, but in his twenties he'd come across a book on the Eskimo all-meat diet. It worked for him, and he espoused it with the same fervor he used for

LSD. Bear ate meat. Bear ate *only* meat. Since he was their patron and their sole source of income, controlling the money and LSD, and since he theorized that meat generated the most calories for the dollar and was therefore financially efficient, there was nothing in the house to eat but meat and milk. They ate standing up in the kitchen, cutting off steaks from a side of beef and frying them.

The women involved were less than impressed. Sara, already living apart from Garcia, felt that the band was "in captivity," that the house felt "perverse, evil." Bear was "obviously a wizard, obviously a madman," but . . . Brenda Kreutzmann would recall having to fight hard to get oatmeal for her baby, Stacey. What women did do at the Pink House was laundry. One run to the Laundromat involved thirty-seven washing machine loads. Sara had finally become Wendy to the Lost Boys, but fairly soon she decided that she'd rather be Peter Pan. Early on, she and Garcia had a last talk, after which she and toddler Heather returned to the Bay Area. The other women visitors were equally skeptical. Phil's girlfriend, Florence Jean Nathan, came to join them and remembered a night in which Bear had decided that all would take LSD. Phil was tired, and declined. Somewhat later, Bear charged in. "The band is my body. You are my left leg. My left leg is asleep. You must get high." With a sigh, Phil got up and got high.

Not that they were puppets. Aside from searching out an alternative diet with clandestine visits to Canter's, the famed L.A. deli, the members of the family could always float a dissenting viewpoint about Owsley, or anything else, for that matter. Brenda Kreutzmann, for instance, mocked his short stature and penchant for patchouli, high-heeled boots, and excessively trendy taste in clothing, calling him a "hippie Sonny Bono." Within the band, Bob Weir kept his own counsel on Bear. "He had Phil's mind, so much that Jerry wasn't about to fight it," recalled Weir. "And if Jerry wasn't about to fight it, then I wasn't about to fight it. Billy couldn't give a shit. Billy saw, 'Here's this guy with some bucks, and he's going to bankroll us.' Made sense to Billy. I'm thinkin', we could go out and play strip bars, we can do that. But the older guys want to go with this Bearzeebub guy. As far as I was concerned, Owsley was the devil. I'd just as soon have him living on the top floor than not know where he is."

One of Weir's essential memories of Owsley involved his nickname. Owsley would have it that "Bear" came from his teen years, but to Weir it involved the considerable volume Bear lent to his carnal pursuits. When Weir would have to ascend to Bear's third-floor lair to tell him there was a phone call, he would hear from the other side of the door a "combination of a flying saucer invasion and some sort of demonic hoedown" that would leave him "dumbstruck."

Bear had two other significant effects on the band at this time, one technological, the other business-oriented. Even before they'd left San Francisco, he'd invited Rock Scully, the manager of the Charlatans, to assume management of the band. Scully agreed, asking if he could bring along his partner, Danny Rifkin. Scully had only a limited knowledge of the music business, but he had nerve and vision, and just as the band slowly learned how to play, he slowly learned how to promote. He'd grown up in Carmel, part of the bohemian artistic scene that included Henry Miller and Ansel Adams. His stepfather, Milton Mayer of the War Resisters League (WRL), had a show on NBC radio called *Voices of Europe*, and Rock had spent some of his childhood holding Milton's tape recorder, meeting Bertrand Russell among others.

After studying with Kurt Adler at the University of Vienna, Rock graduated in 1963 from a Quaker school in Indiana, Earlham College. He entered San Francisco State to work on a graduate degree, mixing a WRL-inspired antiwar social consciousness with the psychedelics he'd discovered in Europe. His income came from dealing pot in five-dollar matchboxes and ten-dollar "lids" in Prince Albert tobacco cans. He also got to know people like Luria Castell through a series of civil rights demonstrations that had begun at State and spread across the city to Auto Row and the Sheraton Hotel. Running backstage errands at the Monterey Jazz Festival had been his first introduction to the music business, and on January 8 he'd left the Family Dog show at California Hall and gone to the Fillmore Acid Test, where he "had the distinct sensation that the roof was lifting off. I was totally taken aback." He told Bear that he thought the Dead "were extraordinarily ugly and would probably never make it commercially, but I'd never heard a more amazing band musically." When his thesis was rejected at State, he had the perfect excuse to get on the bus, and moved to Los Angeles.

Danny Rifkin, his partner, was a little more cautious and first came to the Pink House as a visitor, then instantly became an integral part of the band's gathering momentum. On his initial visit, everyone took LSD together, and another guest, a marine just about to leave for Vietnam, grew terrified. Rifkin's compassion for the marine made Weir "fall in love with Danny the day I met him. He entered my whole world at the top rung of the ladder." Simple trustworthiness was sufficient for Weir at that point, since the two new managers had succeeded Hank Harrison, who'd gotten them the gig on Broadway just three months before. But Hank was patently a "shuck and jivester," thought Weir, while Rifkin's essential righteousness was equally obvious. Appropriately, Rifkin's first ambition had been that of a street youth worker. Now he had some other youths to try to help. Born and raised in New York City, an official red diaper baby—his parents were members of the Communist Party—he learned social responsibility from his father, a printer and later writer and teacher. The family moved to Los Angeles, and Danny briefly attended UCLA, then Berkeley, then flunked out and moved to the Haight-Ashbury. He became the building manager at 710 Ashbury and so met first Rock and then Luria Castell, and his circle of acquaintances at his post office job included Tom Constanten, Phil Lesh, and Steve Reich, among other familiar names. In later years he would quote a friend that it was "not a small world, but a big family."

Rock and Danny had a third friend. One of the odder touches of the early Grateful Dead was their tendency to appear at places in a Cadillac convertible, which many would incorrectly recall as a limousine. The car was owned by a friend of Rifkin and Scully's named Cadillac Ron Rakow, a former stock trader who'd been brought West to advise a woman named Natalie Morman on financial matters. Late in 1965 he arrived in San Francisco with his wife and two children, checking into the Hilton Hotel. Within a few days he'd encountered rock and roll and an attractive friend of Natalie's named Lydia d'Fonsecca, which caused him to run out on his wife, children, and the hotel bill. Rakow was a stereotypical hustler, always looking for an interesting financial proposition, even as LSD brought him into a rather different culture. When he saw Danny Rifkin profit on the Coca-Cola concession on January 8, he insisted on participating in the next California Hall gig, where he took on the hot dog sales. What he had not yet learned was that tripping people rarely ate, and it was one gamble he lost on, although he and Lydia got to eat the unsold stock. With Lydia as his secretary, he took over a glossy-looking office at Van Ness and Lombard in San Francisco, but it was a dubious enterprise. Danny and Rock, inured to conventional business ethics, once spent the night helping him forge signatures on real estate documents, and on another occasion found it hilarious when he asked them to leave by the window so that an arriving visitor wouldn't see them. At any rate, he had the Cadillac. He was also a very fine amateur photographer, and he began to hang around the Dead's scene.

Owsley's primary official responsibility was as soundman, and he had serious ambitions for making technology serve music. At the Trips Festival he'd been struck by the thought that, once upon a time, the "pinnacle of technology" on planet earth had been a musical instrument, namely the pipe organ in the era of Mozart. Whatever was presently at the techno-logical pinnacle almost certainly served war, and he wanted to reverse the trend. Shortly before he'd met the Dead, he'd purchased a new home hi-fi. It was inordinately powerful, with an eighty-watt McIntosh amplifier and Voice of the Theater A-7 speakers. His hi-fi became the Grateful Dead's sound system. Unfortunately, it was not made for knockabout touring, and proved delicate and undependable.

Though Owsley had experience in various facets of electronics, he was not a design engineer, so before they left Berkeley he'd found a hard science assistant, Tim Scully (no relation to Rock). In the seventh grade Tim had won a science fair by designing a primitive computer, and his prize had been a tour of the Berkeley radiation lab. A job there later fos-tered a heroic ambition to change mercury into gold with a linear acceler-ator—twentieth-century alchemy. Early in 1965 he took LSD, and his life was transformed. He had long thought that technology could solve social problems, and now he was certain that LSD was the answer. Seeking to spread the word, he tracked down the source of his dose. When Bear learned of Tim's technical skills, he concluded that they made a nearly perfect match. In the parlance of the era, Scully was a "nerd." His father had taught him to avoid anything that might endanger a security clear-ance on the way to a Ph.D., so meeting the Dead, Tim thought, was like "running off to join the circus." Bear brought him to the Trips Festival to see how he'd react. When he reported experiencing "group mind telepa-thy," he was welcomed onto the metaphorical bus and soon after left for L.A.

Bear and Tim's first project was to modify the guitars. The cables that connected the guitars to the amplifiers were high-impedance, which made them pick up noise and limited the clarity of the signal. By installing a transformer, they could use a low-impedance cable and clean up the sig-nal. Then they began to build a panel with gain, tone, and mixing con-trols, which would allow them to create a stereo mix. They used Sennheiser microphones, quite advanced for the time, recorded every-thing so that they could critique the performances, and acquired an oscil-loscope to monitor the amplifiers' output.

Unfortunately, their ambitions vastly overshot their knowledge. The equipment was extremely heavy, and the band coined the term "lead sled" to describe the experience of hauling it around. It took considerable time to set up, and once set up, it worked only intermittently. All of them had much to learn about sound systems, but Bear's intransigent personality made him slow to acknowledge that. Early on, Phil Lesh found himself standing onstage waiting for Bear and Tim to fix something. Never the most patient of men, he looked down at their derrieres and imagined his right foot in a swift kick. There was the band, ready to play, and there was the "crew," once again soldering a transformer box on his amplifier. Given their psychedelicized mental state, it was not terribly surprising that they weren't very efficient. The combination of stonedness and Owsley's demand for perfection at all costs resulted in endless repetition and delay. They'd err, even a little, and then clip out their work and start all over again. Lesh looked on and reflected, "This is the way it's going to be."

Though their announced intention in going to L.A. was to "make it in the record business," they accomplished little in that realm. They had no connections in the music business, so they made no contact with record companies. Their few gigs were independent and promoted with handbills passed out from Rakow's Cadillac, an effective tactic in San Francisco, which had a specific district to home in on, but not in diffuse L.A. In addition to the Northridge and Watts Acid Tests, the Dead and the Pranksters staged two other acid tests, the Sunset Acid Test at the Empire Studios, and one at the Cathay Theater, the Pico Acid Test. They were not terribly successful. In Kesey's absence, Ken Babbs had taken over as Chief Prankster, and acid had not put a dent in the authoritarian tendencies he'd absorbed as a Marine Corps helicopter pilot. His reign spread dissension. It was a difficult time. The Pranksters were in the process of leaving L.A. to join Kesey in Mexico, but not everyone would be allowed to go, and Babbs was the decision-maker. Neal, for instance, would be left behind, because his relationship with his current girlfriend, Ann Murphy, was so explosively messy that even the Pranksters couldn't stand it. As the Pranksters seethed within, there was ongoing friction between Bear and the Pranksters. At the Pico Acid Test, Julius Karpen recalled an argument with Owsley over money, "and *he* [Bear] was on acid." In fact, the Bear-Prankster dance generally amused the band members, who saw it as charming. Ironically, Owsley's priority at this time was the Dead and its music, not spreading acid consciousness. Besides, the acid tests were getting harder and harder to bring off, because their utter anarchy scared too many people.

The Dead put on two regular shows in March, one at the Danish Center and one at Trooper's Hall, producing amusement but no income. As their time in L.A. wound down, the Dead enjoyed one charming incident. Their neighbors had often complained about the volume of their practicing, and one day the lady next door struck back. After a particularly late night of rehearsal, the musicians were awakened early in the morning by a discordant blare from next door. Their neighbor had lined up every noisemaking device in her home—radios, TV, hi-fi, tape recorder—set them at the windows facing the Pink House, and cranked them up. Her error was that they were all making different sounds, and the result was so bizarre it fascinated them. "If they'd all been on one thing, the stock market report, maybe we'd have been bummed," thought Weir. Instead, they came out to the driveway, took in the situation, laughed, went over, and made friends.

Their real problem was their utter poverty. Bear was a brilliant chemist but not a profit-driven businessman. Where acid was concerned, he was primarily a messianic true believer, giving away at least half of what he made. He had promised the band that he would concentrate on them and their music and not make LSD while he worked for them, and until the pinch came, he honored his pledge. As March rolled into April, they hit a financial crunch, and the only thing he could do was encapsulate his remaining "stash." Contrary to popular mythology, there were no capping machines or pill presses in the attic. Instead, Bear made up around three thousand hits by hand, making a paste from the crystalline LSD that was rubbed onto titrate boards. It was called Blue Cheer, and he sold it immediately. In the nature of such things, it instantly generated paranoia. The young lady with whom Bear did business happened to brag to mutual friends about her source, and within a few hours of the sale, Bear heard about it. Having sampled the day's work, one and all became convinced that the police were on the way. They scurried about the house collecting anything illegal, put it in the trunk of the car, and proceeded to drive around L.A. being very stoned and paranoid, acting so weird that even the denizens of Venice Beach asked them to leave. Miraculously, they managed to get home that night in one piece.

The sale of the Blue Cheer was only a stopgap, and they reached financial bottom. At their last show, at Trooper's Hall, Weir managed to rip out the seat of his pants. Lacking underwear or a replacement for his trousers, he spent the night facing the audience, sidestepping over to Tim Scully to tell him how to adjust his sound. It turned out not to be so bad. That night he also met a *Playboy* Playmate, a cordial redhead, and she didn't seem to mind the state of his wardrobe. Finally, Rock lined up a booking back home at the Longshoremen's Hall that would pay them the respectable sum of $375. It required no persuasion for everyone to pack up and flee Los Angeles. They ascended California in a strenuous trip occasioned by malfunctioning vehicles and a heavy deadline, but when they began to hear San Francisco radio stations, they knew they were almost home, and glad of it.

They got to Longshoremen's Hall, fell out of their cars, and immediately goofed. The sound system was feeding back and squeaking, so they decided to go to someone's nearby apartment to wait while Bear and Scully worked on it. As Kreutzmann told the story, they got to the apartment, and then Bear was there, too. "He had a baggie full of white caps . . . it was still going to be a half hour, so a number of us popped at least three more. One and then three . . . 'Hey, you ready to go?' 'Okay, you're on.' Everything was just melting, man, we were just blown away . . . everything's doing what I can think of. I learned that one real early. Anything I can think of, I can see it . . . making my own Technicolor movies. We played, I don't know how long, and we came off the stage, and this black guy [the promoter] walks up to me and says, 'You know, you guys are all right, you really sound like a black band.' " Under the circumstances, it was no surprise that their time sense was seriously warped, and they would all remember that that night's "Midnight Hour" would stop and start according to the vagaries of the muse. Sick with the flu, Weir played part of the gig while kneeling.

Much had happened in San Francisco's burgeoning rock community during their absence, with new bands popping up and a new facility to hear them in. The Fillmore Auditorium was clearly the best room in the city, and initially, Bill Graham and the Family Dog, whose name had been appropriated by Chet Helms, shared it. Their contrasting personalities, business practices, and social awareness guaranteed that this would not endure. With his long hair and beard, Helms resembled popular portraits of Jesus, and in truth he was a man with a cause. The grandson of a Baptist minister, preaching the gospel came easy to him, but his sermons were devoted to LSD and dancing. Texas-born, he was a member of the Young People's Socialist League at the University of Texas, and after visiting San Francisco, he stayed. He got to know the Family Dog people by doing pot business with them, and when Luria went off to Mexico, he simply took over the name. With his friend John Carpenter, a protégé of Tom Donahue's and the booking agent for the Great Society, he began to put on shows at the Fillmore in cooperation with Graham, who did not have control of the building's lease. In late March they brought in the Butterfield Blues Band of Chicago. Graham and Helms were already divided by the issue of pot, with Chet heartily in favor and Graham flatly against permitting smoking at the Fillmore. But that weekend they at least agreed on how fantastically the Butterfield Band had played.

On Sunday night Graham set his alarm for 6 A.M., 9 A.M. in New York. Butterfield's manager was Albert Grossman, who sent Graham to the agent, and after a normal negotiation, they set a price, made a deal for the band's next appearance in San Francisco, and Bill went back to sleep. Eventually—as with many of the stories of Bill Graham's earliest days, the facts are in dispute—Chet called and complained. "Hey, man, like you know, that's not quite fair." Graham was proud of his response: "I get up early." True as that was, the issues were considerably more complex. He was in a partnership with Helms at the time, and though it was simply not meant to last, Graham certainly leaped the moral fence. Without Chet and John, he would never have known of Butterfield, nor would the earliest shows have sold so well without their promotional contributions. Bill Graham was tougher and stronger—and more gifted as a promoter—than anyone in the San Francisco rock music business, and he ate his opposition alive. He said he was "trying to be an artist . . . [in the] production end," and he was absolutely right. In fact, he defined the rock and roll promotion business at its creative peak. That he was at times also a bully and a thief did not erase his achievements.

Born Wolfgang Grajonza in Berlin in 1931, he was sent to a Parisian orphanage ahead of the Nazis in 1939, soon joining sixty-three other children in a terrifying escape from Paris to Lisbon by foot, bus, and train. From Lisbon they traveled to Casablanca, from there to Dakar, then to New York. Only eleven children survived the trip. At that, he was luckier than many of his relatives, some of whom died, or his sister Ester, who endured and somehow survived the concentration camp at Auschwitz. In New York he grew up to be a pugnacious Bronx hustler, interested in sports, Latin dancing, and gambling. He waited tables and ran a gambling sideline in the Catskills, then served in Korea, where he earned one Bronze Star for bravery and two courts-martial for insubordination. He spent the fifties bumming around the United States and Europe, alternating between office jobs and trying to break in as an actor. In the end, he would take his act to the production side. He settled in San Francisco as an office manager for the Allis Chalmers company before quitting to be the business manager of the Mime Troupe, where he could be close to the muse. Then he saw rock and roll and was reborn.

The dispute over booking the Butterfield Blues Band ended the sharing of the Fillmore, and Chet Helms moved on. But Graham had other problems, primarily with the San Francisco Police Department. On

March 14, Ralph Gleason described the "Dance Renaissance at the Fill-more" as "peaceful as a Sunday school picnic and a lot more fun." Two days later Graham was denied a dance permit, supposedly due to neighborhood objections about trash. He kept operating under Sullivan's permit, and the *Chronicle* came to his support. "He is ambitious, aggressive, imaginative, responsible, hard working, opinionated," wrote Gleason's associate, John Wasserman, "the best entrepreneur, in my opinion, of public entertainment in San Francisco." The clippings helped, and so did the lawyer he hired. To complicate matters, he was also the target of suspicion from the hip community. At thirty-five, he was older than they were, and even more to the point, he wasn't stoned. In Berkeley, *Daily Cal* columnist Jann Wenner opined that the "dances are being promoted by a little man named Bill Graham [as] money-making schemes first and foremost. Whatever fun one has is strictly incidental to, almost in spite of, Bill Graham."

A legendary encounter between Bill and Luria Castell was characteristic. She appeared one night at the Fillmore with what she said were three friends, local musicians. As Bill told it, after a brief conversation with her, he invited her in, and she added, "Wait a minute, I've got a friend . . . These are the Charlatans and these are my soul brothers . . . two of Ken Kesey's people." Bill concluded, "I became my real self! I yelled 'fuck you!' . . . eleven people and it tore me apart but I let 'em in." Bill never worried about the facts of a good story, and he told this one for the rest of his life, but the clash of styles was unmistakable.

He attributed the police antipathy to the Fillmore to its attracting white youth into a black neighborhood, causing more work. Whatever the reasoning, the police fought his application for a dance permit, collecting signatures of local merchants on a petition of opposition. The most important foe was the Fillmore's neighbor, the rabbi of the synagogue next door. Having promised not to put on shows during Jewish holidays, Bill won him over. On April 21, the *Chronicle* ran an editorial about the "misdirected and highly unfair malevolence toward the innocent and highly popular entertainment" at the Fillmore. The next day, clipping in hand, two very dumb cops arrived at the Fillmore and arrested fourteen young people for being underage under an obscure ordinance banning people below the age of eighteen from being in a dance hall, even where no alcohol was served. "Why are you arresting me?" asked one of the fourteen kids. "I'm arresting you for being under eighteen and for being in attendance at a public dance." "But is that illegal?" "I don't want to tell you right now because there's a newspaper reporter standing right here." Only a limited amount of flagrant stupidity can be tolerated in San Francisco, and after enduring the gibes of the entire city, the police dropped the charges. Graham eventually got his permit.

The scene in San Francisco involved a great deal more than just the Fillmore. Over on Haight Street, businesses that would make the neighborhood a center for countercultural activity had begun to open. The most important was Ron and Jay Thelin's Psychedelic Shop. The Thelins had grown up in an all-American small-town environment in San Luis Obispo, but Ron had always been a rule breaker. Three years in the army in Asia had given him multicultural interests, and after reading Kerouac's *On the Road,* he'd traveled around the United States. The brothers' psychedelic journeys made them true believers, and their store was a way of giving people information about the experience, via both reading—they stocked Aldous Huxley, Joseph Campbell, and Timothy Leary—and experience, with rolling papers, roach clips, Lava Lites, color wheels, and music by Ravi Shankar, John Coltrane, and Archie Shepp. Down Haight Street there was also Mnasidika, a hip clothing store owned by Peggy Caserta, the health food store nicknamed Blind Jerry's, actually Far Fetched Food, and the Blue Unicorn coffeehouse.

There were also plenty of new bands. Quicksilver Messenger Service had begun when Marin County guitarslinger John Cipollina had formed a band with his friend Jimmy Murray to back a folkie named Dino Valenti (real name Chet Powers), but Valenti had been sent to jail for marijuana possession. As Dino went in, their friend David Freiberg, once of the David and Michaela folk duo, came out—he, too, had been arrested for pot possession—and joined them on bass. Cipollina had met Greg Elmore and Gary Duncan, two musicians from Modesto, at the first Longshoremen's Hall dance back in October. A couple of days later they were all jamming on the Bo Diddley song "Mona." They chose their name in homage to the fact that they were all Virgos, ruled by the planet Mercury, the speedy messenger of the gods.

Big Brother and the Holding Company was working around town. The Jefferson Airplane had acquired a manager, Matthew Katz, and the first recording contract of any of the San Francisco bands, with RCA. That spring they'd gone to the RCA studios in Hollywood to record their first album, *Jefferson Airplane Takes Off.* The Charlatans were playing at a Broadway strip joint, the Roaring 20s. And Country Joe and the Fish had added Bruce Barthol on bass, John Gunning on drums, and David Cohen on guitar, and were starting to play rock and roll. Cohen was a bluegrass guitarist and a friend of Garcia's, so the entire Dead attended their debut as an electric band, at that spring's Berkeley Folk Festival. Naturally, there were many other bands, most of which didn't click at all, and at least one, the Sopwith Camel, that had an entirely different ethos and left town for New York intending to cut commercial hits.

The week after the Dead's return to San Francisco was, at least for Garcia, a "walking horror." They had sent ahead Phil's girlfriend, Florence, and Bear's lover, Melissa, to find some sort of place to live, and the two had succeeded, but the lease did not begin until May 1. The band separated, each member finding a place to stay wherever he could. Garcia passed the week until then "staying with all kinds of strange people and getting really [financially] strung out, walkin' around."

It was a very long week.

12

Psychedelic
Indians

(5/1/66–9/29/66)

round A.D. 500 the Miwok Indians settled at a site near present-
day Novato, north of San Francisco in Marin County, which
they called Olompali, meaning either "south village" or "southern people." It was a salubrious place, sheltered from the cold
ocean breezes by the coastal range, carpeted by madrone oaks, and close to
the fertile shores of the bay. By 1100 it was a sizable trading village, and in
1300 the general region was probably the most densely populated single
place north of the Rio Grande. Even after the arrival of the Spanish con-
quistadores, Olompali remained in native hands, and the Miwok leader
Camilo Ynitia built a twenty-six-room adobe house there. In 1948 the
house was purchased by the University of San Francisco. Up from Los
Angeles, Florence and Melissa went to a real estate agent, and with blind,
loving good fortune, Florence said, "managed to rent paradise" at the rate
of $1,100 for six weeks. Sentimentality would never be a popular emotion
in the world of the Grateful Dead, but if ever there was an exception,
Olompali was it. They simply loved the place.

The first sign of their luck was Lady, a marvelous black Labrador who
adopted them all upon their arrival. They'd gone from Watts to heaven,
with a week of independent, separated limbo in between. Their nearest

neighbors were miles in any direction. Their home was a large adobe house, cool in the summer heat. To the side was a swimming pool. A mile or two away in one direction, San Francisco Bay shone blue. In the other, the golden hills of California were broken up by the dark oaks. It was authentically beautiful. At the end of the driveway, Highway 101 took them to the city in half an hour. Olompali was freedom. Even if they were broke, they could hunt deer for the cooking pot, and did. Of course, being the Dead, this involved some risks. One night they were practicing, and it went so poorly that Weir grew frustrated and took off up the hill. They called it quits for the evening, at which point Pigpen spotted a deer in the driveway. Bill got out their .22 and then told Pigpen to turn a light on, which would freeze the deer so he could shoot it. Just after he fired, the deer bolted and then they heard Weir, up the hill, cry out. Kreutzmann moaned, "Oh, fuck." Pigpen ran away and croaked, "You did it." Fortunately, the bullet landed near but not in Weir, and sure enough, when they found the deer's corpse a week later, it had been shot through the head.

As soon as they settled in, their thoughts turned to sharing their good fortune, and that meant a party. Life at Olompali always felt like a party, but there were two in particular that no participant would ever forget. For the first one, late in May, they actually mailed out invitations to all their friends, which boiled down to the rock community of San Francisco. It was, Danny Rifkin decided, "an incredibly free, open celebration about nothing special." The media would identify the next summer, that of 1967, as the "summer of love." But for the original settlers, the summer of 1966, at Olompali in particular, was as good as it could ever get.

Everybody came to the party. Jorma Kaukonen was, along with the rest of the Jefferson Airplane, on the verge of prosperous stardom. A couple of months later the Airplane would open for a Rolling Stones show at the Cow Palace, sneaking Garcia in as one of their crew. But that summer, record contract or no, Jorma was living in a crummy, rat-infested flat on Divisadero Street. He got to Olompali for the party, and as he approached the house, his jaw dropped. The adobe building looked like a mansion, and the pool was filled with naked maidens. There was an attractive striped awning to the side, and under it was a mountain of Bear's best and shiniest electronic equipment. There was also a jug with Bear's best and shiniest chemistry, and it all made for a happy day. Sitting with his old folk music mate Janis Joplin, who'd recently returned from Texas, his bass-playing musical partner Jack Casady, and Garcia, he was dazzled. It was "rock star heaven." "Who'da thought," Jorma mused much later, "that playing a coffeehouse could come to this—the magnificence

of Olompali . . . Garcia was saying that we were all going to be arche-
types of a sort," and Jorma was laughingly doubting him. "But of course
it turned out to be true."

Though she would not make a general habit of being nude in public—it was just that sort of time and place—one of those nymphs in the
pool was Julia Dreyer. The sixth child after five brothers, she'd been nicknamed Girl. The daughter of what she called a "spaced-out intellectual"
socialite mother, Girl had grown up in Sausalito, where by the age of fifteen she was running free with the folkies from the Charles Van Dam
houseboat, like Dino Valenti and David Crosby. At sixteen she'd run away
alone to Mexico for five months, where she'd encountered acid at Timothy Leary's compound. Threatened with arrest for being underage and on
the loose when she returned to San Francisco, she decided to get married
in order to stay out of juvenile hall, and chose as her husband the nicest
guy in the music scene, David Freiberg of Quicksilver. For her, the hit of
the day at the Olompali party was Neal Cassady, there with his hammer
and raps. Though clearly a nice person, Weir struck her as an interloper,
because of his clean-cut, preppy appearance. Young or not, Julia was quite
conscious that something special was going on that day, something innocent, free, and happy. It felt like "a period of grace," as though "some alien
force was moving consciousness along, to benefit mankind. That might
sound presumptuous, but we felt it." It was a positive, loving, and intelligent vision. Another of the wandering young women was Tangerine, a
Marin girl who also remembered Neal and his hammer, though to Tangerine he looked so conventional, so "straight," that she thought he was an
accidentally dosed neighbor. She also noticed Rock, who wore Beatle
boots, pegged pants, and a collegiate shirt. By the end of the day, they'd
fallen in love.

Not everyone was quite so free and easy. George Hunter of the Charlatans fell prey to an insane jealousy of his lover, and came into the middle
of the party with a rifle. "Just because Garcia has that aura of being somebody," thought Kreutzmann, "he was a great target. They weren't more
than twenty yards apart. Streetwise ol' Jerry just bolted and ran—you
couldn't see no dust." In the meantime, Weir had stepped in front of
George, and eventually talked him out of his gun. Rifkin then talked him
down. Brenda Kreutzmann did not fit in at all at Olompali parties, and
the nudity upset her. Generally, she stayed in her room.

Among the more neurotic guests were the members of the Great Society, a strange romantic triangle that included Darby Slick, who was in
love with his brother Jerry's wife, Grace. "Grace really couldn't seem to

stand parties," Darby wrote later. "It was either [drink until] blackout and rage, or split." As they arrived, Grace saw Pigpen leaning on the gate and the nude Girl running around behind him. Neal was raving, and Phil turned to Grace with the remark "That's Neal Cassady, and if you stand here long enough, you'll catch up with all seven of the conversations he's having with himself." Though Grace didn't stay long, she left an indelible mark with her presence. About as beautiful as any woman could be and a graduate of the very social Finch College, she had been a model at I. Magnin, one of the premier San Francisco department stores. She'd grown up not liking the real world very much, and in what she later declared was an "exercise in counterprogramming," centered her childhood on fantasy costumes for characters like Robin Hood, Snow White, Peter Pan, and Prince Valiant. As an adult, she held the real world at bay with alcohol and sarcasm, and her hero was Lenny Bruce. Not being fond of LSD, Slick did not enjoy the Olompali ambience and left early.

Another guest, Barry Melton, came to check out his old Berkeley friend Bear's sound system, but it didn't seem to want to work that day. The police arrived, more likely to check out the bare breasts than the mysterious complaint about some parked cars in the road. Confused by Neal, nudity, and Weir's ingenuous smile, they did not stay long.

The second party was actually occasioned by a visit from the outside world. The Dead threw it for the benefit of the BBC, which had sent a film crew to San Francisco, gathering up their friends by word of mouth. The Beeb's stiff upper lip melted at what they saw, and they fled, cameras in hand. Phil felt that "we were on the tip of the arrow of human consciousness flying through time." The BBC wasn't arrow-ready.

The rural setting made Olompali a trusted place for psychedelic exploration, although what almost everyone perceived as the shades of the Native Americans that lingered in the adobe walls complicated things, spiritually speaking. Once, Lesh said, he "made contact with the spirits of what I thought were the Olompali Indians. They asked, 'What are you doing here, white boy?' " Nonetheless, Olompali was acid-drenched, and it would be Garcia who would remember his trips in greatest detail. One day he lay down on the grass by the pool, having consumed a mixture of mescaline and some of Owsley's finest. "I closed my eyes and I had this sensation of perceiving with my eyes closed. It was as though they were open, I still have this field of vision and the field of vision had kind of a pattern in it partly visible and then I had this thing that outside the field of vision was like starting to unravel like an oldtime coffee can, you know that little thing that you spin around and it takes the little strip of metal off. It was like that and it began stripping around the outside of the field of vision until I had a three hundred and sixty degree view, and it revealed this pattern and the pattern said 'All' in incredible neon . . . I had one where I thought I died like multiple, it got into this thing of death, kind of the last scene, the last scene of hundreds of lives and thousands of incarnations and insect deaths . . . last frames of my life . . . I run up the stairs and there's this demon with a spear who gets me right between the eyes. I run up the stairs and there's this woman with a knife who stabs me in the back. I run up the stairs and there's this business partner who shoots me . . . there was one time when I thought that everybody on earth had been evacuated in flying saucers and the only people left were these sort of lifeless automatons that were walking around, and there's that kind of sound of that hollow mocking laughter, when you realize that you're the butt of the universe's big joke."

Even in paradise, they were still a working band. Rock and Danny had retained a room at 710 Ashbury Street as an office, and when necessary they would go into the city. The gigs began to come, first a couple in Berkeley in early May, and then one at the Family Dog's new location, the Avalon Ballroom, upstairs at Sutter and Van Ness Avenue, in San Francisco. The Avalon was an old swing ballroom once called the Puckett Academy of Dance, with good acoustics, a wonderful sprung wooden dance floor, mirrors, columns, red flocked wallpaper, and lots of gilt. The Dead's first show there was to raise money for the Straight Theater, a dance hall on Haight Street that some local young people were trying to open. Two weeks later, on May 27, the Dead played their first regular show for the Family Dog.

The differences between the Fillmore and the Avalon were at once glaringly obvious and terribly subtle. For Jerry, they lay between Chet, "who never appeared to be doing anything, as opposed to Bill, who appeared to be doing everything." The Avalon was "a good old party," the Fillmore was "the thrill of opening night." Bill Graham could yell, but he listened equally well, and spent a great deal of time soliciting the local musicians for suggestions as to whom they wanted to see. He also wanted to challenge his audience, and so he booked the avant-garde pianist Cecil Taylor to open for the British band the Yardbirds, among other interesting combinations. To the Beat poet Michael McClure, the Fillmore sounded better and had a better dance floor, but the Avalon's superior light shows made him feel "like I was part of a massive work of art." The first time they played the Avalon, Garcia recalled, the Dead's speakers were in front of the screen and blocked Bill Ham's lights. The next day they painted the speakers white.

Chet Helms was a prophet, not a businessman, and life at the Avalon could be disorganized, especially when he got bands to commit to shows without talking to their management. But he had a profound understanding of his audience, and they listened to his message. He saw the scene that was arising in the Haight-Ashbury as primarily one of simple "self-determination," as young people strove to exchange a spiritually unsatisfying, earth-despoiling straight life for something better. There were some politics involved, an early environmental awareness, a romanticized vision of peasant life and finding roots. But what was going on at his dance hall combined two things—electronics and the need for social ritual. Electronics—the bands and their loud music—*"commands* attention," as Helms saw it, and made new social rituals all the more powerful. The modern world had blurred the old rites of passage. In a world of birth control pills, for instance, parenthood was not an immediate given. So it was time to develop new rites, and this happened at the ballrooms. In dancing one had a nonverbal method of saturating the senses, participating in a ritual death of an old consciousness to move on to a new one; it was the cult of Dionysus in 1966. Dance enough and one sweats, literally purging and cleansing the body, which is the meaning of the Greek *katharsis.* The result might be *abraxas,* joining the godhead, or *ekstasis,* flight from the body.

Outside the ballrooms, there were other changes in American life that summer. In June, the Supreme Court ruled in *Miranda v. Arizona* that prisoners must actually be warned of their rights. Civil rights leader James Meredith and four friends began a march through Mississippi, and when he was shot and wounded on the second day, it became a "march against fear." In the North, urban black people reacted more violently, and in July riots ripped through Chicago, Brooklyn, and Cleveland. On August 3 Lenny Bruce died of a heroin overdose, a martyr to years of legal harassment.

In the world of music, the Mamas and the Papas, fine singers from the commercial end of the folk movement, had giant hits with "California Dreamin' " in the spring and "Monday, Monday" in the summer. *Time* reported on July 1 that rock lyrics were "no longer down with the P.T.A. and conformism, but—whee! onward with LSD and lechery." (Dylan's "Mr. Tambourine Man" was supposed to be a pusher.) On July 2, the *Saturday Evening Post* ran a story called "Daddy Is a Hippy" *(sic),* probably the first national use of the word. On July 29, Bob Dylan went for a ride on his Triumph motorcycle in Woodstock, New York, dumped it, and reportedly broke his neck. On August 5, John Lennon remarked that the Beatles might be "more popular than Jesus." On the same day, the Beatles released their album *Revolver;* its last song had a remarkable bond with what the San Francisco bands were doing at the same time. Earlier that summer Lennon had stopped by Indica, a store in London much like the Psychedelic Shop, which sold weird art, Beat writing, and other books, including Leary, Metzner, and Alpert's *The Psychedelic Experience,* which he purchased. Having tripped once and not enjoyed it much, Lennon put into practice the authors' advice, tried again and had a much better time, and encapsulated it all in "Tomorrow Never Knows," the final song on their new album.

One further effort to translate the progressive mood of the summer in San Francisco came from the Mime Troupe's Ronnie Davis, who established the Artist's Liberation Front, a loose collective of artists in all sorts of media whose goal would be a free outdoor trips festival. Naturally, the ALF turned to the musicians for a benefit, and on July 17 the Dead, the Airplane, and Sopwith Camel played the Fillmore, capping the evening with a "Midnight Hour" that included Marty Balin, Pigpen, Joan Baez, and Mimi Fariña trading vocals. The ALF would not accomplish much, but it planted a seed in various minds. "Free" was a very powerful idea.

Back home at Olompali, the Dead's lease on paradise came to an end. Brenda Kreutzmann would recall that people in Novato were "having a fit" at the idea of hippies occupying a historic landmark. Then and after, there were two Marin Counties. Eastern Marin was known as a cluster of generally wealthy suburbs near San Francisco such as Sausalito, Tiburon, Belvedere, Mill Valley, and Ross, along with the more middle-class towns of San Rafael and Novato somewhat to the north. But to the west, past the bohemian town of Fairfax and over White's Hill, along Sir Francis Drake Boulevard, it was rather too far for the average commuter to settle. Western Marin was mostly dairy country, and through Woodacre, Forest Knolls, and Lagunitas to the coast and north to Olema, Point Reyes, and Marshall, it became the promised land for hippies. That summer of 1966, bands led the way. Late in June the Dead left Olompali and resettled at a former Girl Scout camp on Arroyo Road, in the town of Lagunitas.

Farther up the highway, Quicksilver Messenger Service—sometimes called, said Girl Freiberg, the "good-looking Grateful Dead"—had acquired a ranch in Olema. Big Brother and the Holding Company lived

five minutes away from the Dead in Lagunitas, and they became particularly friendly. Not only did Big Brother's bassist, Peter Albin, go back to
the Boar's Head days in Garcia and Pig's circle of friendship, but they'd
added a new lead singer, Jorma's buddy Janis Joplin. She'd performed her
first show with Big Brother on June 24 and had settled in with the band.
That summer she also had a hot romance going with Pigpen. He introduced her to Southern Comfort, a whiskey-based cordial, and they'd sit
and play guitars and the piano in the camp dining hall, where the Dead's
equipment was set up. At some point they'd be loaded enough to retire to
bed and noisily consort with each other, in between restorative breaks in
the swimming pool.

The atmosphere at the Lagunitas camp reminded many of Middle
Earth, the world of J. R. R. Tolkien's hobbits. A creek ran through the
property, which was carpeted with redwood trees; it was lovely. Phil and
Florence drew the basement room at the main house, Rock and Tangerine
had part of the bunkhouse, and Rifkin lived in the former arts and crafts
shack, which had only three walls and was open to the air. The one complication to life on Arroyo Road was their next-door neighbor, the county
sheriff, so the main house rule, said Lesh, involved never hollering
" 'dope,' 'fuck,' or the names of young girls."

Business, in the form of Local 6, American Federation of Musicians,
intruded on their life that summer. The local was hassling Bill Graham
about his hiring policies, requiring him to retain a quantity of Local 6
members to balance the out-of-town, frequently English, bands that
headlined. The local also insisted that Graham pay the acts through the
union on the previous Wednesday. It would then subtract fees and pay the
designated leaders of the band by check the following Wednesday. Since
hardly anyone had a bank account, this presented problems. Quicksilver's
John Cipollina and Garcia joined a group of bandleaders in a visit to the
Local 6 offices one day, and their protest developed an amusing quality.
There was a glassed-in meeting room in the center of the office, and when
the board looked up and saw Cipollina, Garcia, and company filling up
the main room, it seemed as though the barbarians had breached the
outer defenses. There were more than a dozen young longhairs, and they
were, as Cipollina put it, "cocky." The members of the board sat tight in
their glass cocoon, with no intention of ending their meeting. At length,
John and Jerry began an "Oh yeah?" mock argument, partly to amuse
themselves and the other guys, partly to send shivers up the spines of the
union bureaucrats hiding so nakedly behind glass. The mock argument
escalated.

"My band says your band eats shit," said Cipollina.

"Oh yeah?" And then Garcia had a sweet inspiration. The Dead lived in a camp in the woods with an archery range, arts and crafts room, and so forth, and Danny Rifkin was not alone among them in his interest in Native American crafts. By contrast, the members of Quicksilver lived on a horse ranch and had taken to wearing cowboy hats. So Garcia segued into a whole new riff. "Indians are better than cowboys." After a suitable period, the bandleaders left for the day.

Eventually, Local 6 was approached by Ron Polte, Quicksilver's manager and a former union guy from Chicago, and Julius Karpen, ex-Prankster, manager of Big Brother, and a former union business agent, who convinced them to loosen up. But on the day of the barbarian invasion, the leaders left with the cowboy-Indian riff as the highlight, at least to John and Jerry. At home, they told their bandmates the story, and each resolved to "get" the other band. Quicksilver had been nicknamed the Quicksilver Consumer Service for their massive ingestion of pot, and after supper, they were vulnerable. Members of the Dead dressed up in feathers and variations on war paint—Garcia painted "Tippecanoe and Tyler too" across his face—picked up bows and arrows, and snuck up on the Quicksilver ranch house. Accompanied by popping firecrackers, they burst in and found the cowboys with their metaphorical pants down. Quicksilver offered a swift and honorable surrender, and everyone sat down to smoke the peace pipe.

Of course, Quicksilver couldn't take this lying down, and they plotted revenge. The Dead were playing that week at the Fillmore with Jefferson Airplane, and Quicksilver conspired with Graham to prank the Indians. While the Dead played, Quicksilver would go onstage dressed as cowboys, their faces covered with bandanas, stick up the Dead, tie them to their amps, play Hank Williams's "Kaw-Liga Was a Wooden Indian," and leave. They began rehearsing "Kaw-Liga" with special enthusiasm. On the appointed evening, Quicksilver gathered outside the Fillmore. They went to the door, but Graham hissed at them that it was too early, and to wait, so they returned to their van to get stoned. Unbeknownst to them, what was commonly called the "long hot summer" of racial unrest of 1966 had reached San Francisco, and a fairly small but nonetheless real race-based riot had begun in the Fillmore neighborhood in response to the police shooting of a young black man. People living near the Fillmore Auditorium observed white men with rifles getting out of a car, and called police. The members of Quicksilver were enjoying themselves when a gun poked into the front door of the van. Freiberg said, "Aaah, come on, you guys," then looked again and realized that it was a very real .357 Magnum. "And all we had was cap pistols." Poor Quicksilver. Arrested for the pot, they went off to jail and never got their revenge.

After their thin economic pickings in L.A., the Dead enjoyed a busy and relatively prosperous time that summer. There were gigs on most weekends, at either the Fillmore or the Avalon, or somewhere within reasonable commute. Unable to rehearse in Lagunitas for noise reasons, they found space first at the Straight Theater in San Francisco. When that fell apart, Jerry's old friend Laird Grant, now their roadie, found them a spot at the Heliport, a warehouse area in the houseboat district of Sausalito. That summer they also had their first recording experience, with a man named Gene Estribou, who had built a studio in his home at 737 Buena Vista West, a few blocks from the Dead's office at 710 Ashbury. Estribou's building was spectacular. It had been built in 1897, and in the course of its history, Ambrose Bierce had lived there and Jack London had written *White Fang* on the premises. Unfortunately, the studio was on the fifth floor, and most of Weir's memories of the session centered on hauling the lead sled up four flights of stairs. To Lesh, Estribou seemed to be a wealthy "dilettante" who wanted to break into the business, but the session was at least an opportunity to get something on tape. They recorded the old jug songs "Don't Ease Me In" and "Stealin'," and other songs, including a Pigpen number called "Tastebud," and one by Lesh called "Cardboard Cowboy." The first two were duly released as a 45 rpm single on Scorpio Records that August. Garcia later guessed that not more than 150 copies were pressed, and since they were sold only on Haight Street, primarily at the Psychedelic Shop, the record made little impression.

That summer they left the Bay Area for their first out-of-town shows, and their trip swiftly went sour. They began in late July with three shows at the British Columbia Festival, at the rather large Pacific National Exhibition Garden Auditorium, in Vancouver. On their way up they lost their crew member Laird, who was turned away at the border because he had an arrest record. Then the Dead made the fundamental mistake of forgetting that they had a show to do. That afternoon they'd all gone to the coast to take LSD, and at some time late in the day they all came to the adrenaline-surging realization that showtime was only an hour away. They stuffed themselves into the one car available, but the overloaded vehicle blew its clutch and it took a lot of angst to find cabs and get to work. When they got to the gig, Garcia recalled, they were told they could play only one set a night and "got screwed around one way or another." He found the stage to be so inordinately high that he insisted their equipment be moved back so they could avoid the edge. Members of the audience were trying to climb up the front of the stage, and in sufficient numbers to shake it. Nothing sounded right that night, and their patience with Owsley dwindled. After the festival dates, they spent several days in a motel with no money, playing Monopoly and bemoaning their lack of marijuana, and on the next weekend played a couple of nights at a small club called the Afterthought, which, while fun, did not make up for the generally miserable week.

They straggled back to Lagunitas and convened a meeting. Bear had not been quite so potent a figure in their lives since they'd gotten to Olompali, where he'd had a room but still lived in Berkeley. Their tolerance for the delays endemic to his sound experiments had run out. Bear himself was tired of being broke and wanted to return to his other art. Besides, since he'd joined the Dead, the whole Bay Area scene was experiencing a drought in the psychedelic realm, so it was time for him to go back to work. Tim Scully later attributed the change in the band's relationship with himself and Bear to the impending criminalization of LSD, set to take place in October, but neither Bear nor anyone else remembered it that way. Bear told the band, "Fine. Tell you what. Go to Leo's [music store], pick out whatever you want, and send me the bill." He took back his system and sold it to Bill Graham for the Fillmore, where as a permanent installation it worked much better. Bear went off to his laboratory, but left behind a legacy, one of alchemical "purification" in whatever one might do, "a really solid consciousness," Garcia said, "of what quality was."

Shortly after Bear's departure, the band played at the Fillmore, and Phil Lesh's amp went on the fritz. In one of the lovely moments of serendipity that always carried the Dead, they looked up from the amp and found in the audience one Dan Healy, a friend of John Cipollina's who worked at a radio station and was able to solve the problem. Later that night he remarked that he'd not been able to hear the vocals, and was instantly invited to do better. Blessed with a consummate pragmatic troubleshooter's gift, Healy could, in fact, do better. A self-described "Gyro Gearloose kid," he was an ugly duckling growing up in the town of Weott, on the Eel River in Northern California. His father was a jukebox, vending machine, and slot machine operator, so Dan had plenty of access to records. His mother had been a big-band stride pianist, and he inherited a subtle ear from her. After a flood during his childhood, he found a Webcor tape recorder and radio parts in the debris, and created his own low-power radio station. Graduating from high school in 1963, he got a job at Commercial Recorders, a jingle/advertising business studio in San Francisco. As he got to know the Dead, he would sneak them into the studio for late-night off-the-books recording sessions. Challenged by the band to improve their live sound, he went to McCune Audio, the primary local source of equipment, rented a bunch of stuff, blew it up, and rented some more. Eventually, he forced McCune to go to the manufacturers for better equipment. On an ascending scale of sophistication, he would do this off and on for the next three decades. He would be essential to the Dead for a very long time.

With their more conventional and functional new equipment and a new soundman in Healy, the Dead went to work, taking any gig, as a young band must. But often their jobs seemed to be more fun than the average young band's. Late in August they played two nights at the Grange Hall in the coastal village of Pescadero, thirty miles south of San Francisco, as part of the Tour del Mar three-day bicycle race. The pre-race/concert hype was also fun, since it involved the band and some *Playboy* bunnies riding around the San Francisco Civic Center in convertibles. The female members of the Dead's scene, like Sue Swanson and Connie Bonner, were excluded by the band, which was not popular. At the end of the car ride, the band and bunnies were delivered to City Hall, where they were to meet the mayor. He sent an assistant, who came out to encounter Phil Lesh. In his best Prussian manner, Lesh clicked his Beatle boot heels, offered his hand, and said, "People are starving." What the Dead would remember of the shows themselves was that Pescadero was simply carpeted in strawflowers, and it was vividly beautiful. One of the people they met at the show was Gary Fisher, who would later invent the mountain bike.

Their next gig, on September 2, was a debutante party at La Dolphine, in the exceedingly wealthy neighborhood of Hillsborough. Garcia would recall being treated as though he was "unclean." Lesh said it was "boring . . . we weren't allowed to fraternize with the natives." Naturally, Weir's sister, Wendy, who'd arranged the booking, managed to catch Phil smoking a joint in the backyard. A much better gig was one of the endless benefits they played that year, this time for the Both/And jazz club, which Ralph Gleason called "the most successful show since Bill Graham has been operating." Unannounced and on borrowed equipment, they joined a lineup that featured Jon Hendricks, Elvin Jones, Joe Henderson, the Jefferson Airplane, and the Great Society among others. As Darby Slick remembered it, the Society delivered a truly great performance that night, but afterward his brother Jerry told him that Grace had been invited to join the Airplane, and Jerry had advised her to do so. Darby would feel betrayed for many years.

Early in September, artists Alton Kelley and his partner Stanley "Mouse" Miller went to the stacks of the San Francisco Public Library in search of inspiration. They had a second commission from Chet Helms to do a poster for the Avalon, and they wanted it to be good; after all, they'd misspelled Grateful Dead ("Greatful") on their first effort, which depicted a member of the undead called Frankenstein's monster. They were an interesting pair. Mouse had grown up in Detroit, first pinstriping cars and then airbrushing T-shirts for the hot-rod scene. Arriving in San Francisco on the night of the Trips Festival, he'd walked into Longshoremen's Hall and found a new home. He was quiet and smiling, in contrast to his more extroverted friend. Raised in Maine, Kelley had hitchhiked to North Beach and the Coexistence Bagel Shop in 1959 at the age of nineteen. He'd run pot from Mexico up and down the coast and been part of the scene at the Red Dog Saloon before producing the first Family Dog posters. At first, Kelley did the layout and Mouse the lettering, but as they went along, they worked up designs together, trading licks like musicians. At the very beginning of the ballroom scene, Wes Wilson had drawn posters for both Bill and Chet, but in June Graham had insisted that he work exclusively for the Fillmore, and Kelley/Mouse succeeded him at the Avalon. Their artistic influences were varied, but started with psychedelics, popular entertainment, and the earthy bohemian style embodied by Wally Hedrick and the eclectic "funk" assemblage art of the fifties. Mostly, they did what they liked, since there were no rules. They created, Mouse said, "20th century teenage hip Americana . . . electrical age folk art."

Looking for stimulation and/or a piece to begin a collage, they haunted the public library's stacks, and one afternoon they came across the classic 1859 edition of *The Rubáiyát of Omar Khayyám*, translated from the Persian by Edward FitzGerald, with graphics by Edmund Sullivan. They opened it, and found the twenty-sixth quatrain.

> *Oh, come with old Khayyám, and leave the Wise*
> *To talk; one thing is certain, that Life flies;*
> *One thing is certain, and the Rest is Lies;*
> *The Flower that once has blown for ever dies.*

They barely noticed the marvelous poetry. Next to it was Sullivan's wonderful work, a skeleton crowned in roses, and they surged with inspiration. "Look at this, Stanley," whispered Kelley. "Is that the Grateful Dead or is that the Grateful Dead?" They did a bigger drawing of the image, which was in the public domain, worked up lettering and a ribbon border around it, and it became an Avalon poster.

At first, Garcia didn't realize that it was taken from *The Rubáiyát;* he only knew it was "brilliant." The Grateful Dead had its first great visual metaphor. Flowers and bones, grateful and dead. Now it was possible to see it.

The Hippest
City Hall
Ever

(9/30/66–10/31/66)

The Dead's sojourn at Camp Lagunitas was pretty much idyllic, until the shit almost literally hit the fan. The septic system backed up, and as usual there were noise complaints, so they moved again, this time into San Francisco, where late in September they settled at Rifkin's rooming house at 710 Ashbury Street. For the first month, Phil, Florence, Jerry, and his then girlfriend, Guido, shared a room. There was a Chinese paper screen for privacy, but Garcia's snores were profound and not about to be blocked by something so flimsy. With relief, Phil and Billy and their ladies soon moved to an apartment a couple of blocks up the hill on Belvedere Street. Garcia, Weir, Pigpen, Danny, Rock, and Tangerine were the main complement at 710, but at least one or two visitors were usually around.

Home at last. In L.A. they'd flopped on the floor, and both their Marin stays had had the feeling of summer camp. This was the real thing. They were a family, and they settled down. Danny was a nurturing presence. Jerry was the generally benign, occasionally grumpy paterfamilias. Weir, of course, was the kid. Pigpen was the crusty uncle. Everyone who lived there, and this included several more people over the coming eighteen months, made their living from the band, and all contributed to its needs. Once, Florence did some bookkeeping and asked to be paid. Rifkin was dumbfounded. "Nobody gets paid. How ridiculous." Life was communal, but utterly without ideology; they lived together because it was all they could afford. It was also fun. Life at 710 wasn't exactly conventional, but it wasn't as outrageous as some might imagine. Although there were exceptions, they generally went to bed early. Garcia was usually up at 6:30, and after coffee, he had a guitar in his hand for the rest of the day.

The living room centered on a large desk, once Rakow's, which was the band office. They never quite got around to buying chairs, so Rock and Danny would each sit on it, playing good cop, bad cop games with promoters. "I'd be the hippie and be sweet and nice to everybody," said Rock, although his routine often concluded, ". . . but I don't know what my partner, Danny, will say." Danny had a halo of curls that made him resemble, at least to one friend, Beardsley's David, and Rock looked to some like an Apache with his headband. They were synced up, and very tight. At one point the two managers even had shares equal to that of band members of whatever the Dead made, but Kreutzmann's father, an attorney, got them to drop it. It didn't matter. They were on a mission, and they, too, were true believers. They wanted to get the band exposed to more people, not as a means of making money, but to influence the times. Their goal was "to create events," Rifkin would say, "not to manage the band, but they were a vehicle that was part of something going on that made events. All of a sudden, you had all these people kinda like us—psychedelic radicals. It was fun to be together, do stuff together—flash the straight world, that kind of thing." The desk was never locked, and for that matter, neither was the front door, so whatever paperwork filled the desk was available to the entire Haight-Ashbury. At times, a good chunk of the neighborhood seemed to pass through the house, usually through the front door, except for Willy the Doorman, who tended to use the front window if it was open.

Seven-ten was a creative center for what was in the fall of 1966 a charming neighborhood. In the early 1950s, urban renewal had razed much of the nearby Western Addition, and the mostly black evictees had spread into the Haight, which also had a sizable Russian immigrant population. The result was an integrated community that in the late fifties welcomed refugees from North Beach fleeing too much media and tourist attention. The Haight was inexpensive, and the combination of older Beats and San Francisco State students, who had good transit service to school, added up to a very hip community. Early in 1966 the city's voters rejected a freeway that would have destroyed the Haight, and it stayed popular. Something special grew there, a new attitude. There was "a fantastic universal sense that whatever we were doing was *right*," wrote the journalist Hunter Thompson, "that . . . our energy would simply *prevail*." America had once been about freedom and possibility, and now it was choked in bureaucracy. Dropping out had become a most reasonable social statement. Yet the Haight was the sort of neighborhood in which poet Michael McClure could give his eleven-year-old daughter a dime to go down to the Psychedelic Shop in utter security to buy a bead or stick of incense. And the Shop was joined by other stores, like the I and Thou bookstore and In Gear, whose owner, Hyla Strauch, lived down the street from 710.

On September 20, just before the Dead moved to Ashbury Street, the neighborhood raised a metaphorical but ineluctably colorful flag with the first edition of the *Oracle*. The local poet Allen Cohen, one of Rifkin's pals, had dreamed of a newspaper covered with rainbows being read all over the world. He'd gone to Ron Thelin of the Psychedelic Shop, who pledged to help finance it. "The *Oracle* is an attempt," Cohen wrote in the first issue, "to create an open voice for those involved in a 'life of art,' as Dr. Timothy Leary calls it . . . a cybernetic/chemical revolution." It wasn't really a newspaper but a psychedelic magazine, one that broke normally linear columns into sensuous shapes and used split-fountain, varicolored printing to make each page beautiful as well as informative. They wanted it to have, Allen said, a "direct effect on consciousness." It was another link in the chain of a conscious bohemian tradition, and in the end, the most influential and stimulating piece in the *Oracle* would be the "House Boat Interview" with elders Alan Watts, Allen Ginsberg, Gary Snyder, and Timothy Leary.

As with any family, there was a wide range of interests and behaviors at 710. Weir had found his intake of LSD very difficult. It had left him quite dazed at times, running into mike stands onstage or sitting isolated in a corner at Olompali. When he began to hallucinate aurally, he concluded that he needed no chemical assistance to get any dreamier, and he ceased deliberate use of LSD on August 1, 1966, the one-year anniversary of his first trip. Although he'd get the occasional accidental or intentional dose in the future, his psychedelic career was done. He embraced a vegetarian diet, initially a macrobiotic one, and his early experiments in the kitchen produced exploding rice pots and boiled-over miso soup. He also, his housemates noticed, had a serious problem with flatulence. By way of contrast, Pigpen preferred whiskey, bad wine, and hot links. Though a gentle soul, he tended to sit up late in his room behind the kitchen, drinking and singing with Janis Joplin or some other blues-inclined friend, or perhaps more quietly writing Beat-influenced poetry.

> *We'll talk and screech madly through the night*
> *in heated arguments about the Witch doctors of Africa*
> *as versus*
> *the Hindus of India and Voodoo men of the West Indies.*
> *We'll howl through eons*
> *whilst Charlie Mingus puts it down . . .*
> *Why doesn't the middle class put up?*
> *because they've got their all holy standards warped!*

That fall he also met the love of his life, Veronica "Vee" Barnard. A traditionally raised young black woman, Vee had left her strict Seventh-Day Adventist household in Vallejo to sample the San Francisco scene, where she bumped into Pigpen on Haight Street at the Blue Unicorn coffeehouse. He invited her to a party at Olompali, and they began keeping company. Sometime that fall, Vee lost her roommate and asked Pig for a place to stay. When she overheard him say, "My old lady's moving in," she knew she wasn't going anywhere. Their lives were generally homebound, Pig sitting in his little red chair, receiving guests like Janis, Elvin Bishop, Vince Guaraldi, and John Lee Hooker. He was a regular customer at the A-1 Deli on Haight Street for his daily bottle of booze, but otherwise he left home only for band business or after midnight for a run to Leonard's Hickory Pit Barbecue on Fillmore. When he didn't make music, he read—science fiction mostly, Ray Bradbury like everyone at 710, fantasy stuff like Doc Savage, and English history and Arthurian legends.

Seven-ten's visitors tended to be charming. LuVell Benford was a tall, striking black man from Oakland, a businessman with a most enlightened air about him, whom Weir first recalled seeing at Olompali riding a white BMW motorcycle with white saddlebags, a big white cowboy hat on his head. He was noticeably warm and generous, more monklike than any trader could reasonably be. Another regular for a time was Michael McClure, at eighteen the youngest of the Beat poets at the seminal 1955 Six Gallery reading that introduced "Howl" to the world, and now a young elder statesman who lived a couple of blocks away on Downey Street. In 1965 he'd noticed a gaggle of longhairs rehearsing in a house on his block, and came to find out that they were called the Charlatans. One night at a party at 710, he got to talking with Garcia, and they naturally contemplated collaborating on a song. He brought Garcia a stanza of his poem

"Love Lion," and though Jerry looked a little doubtful, he set to work, picking out a "beautiful, beautiful tune." But, McClure realized later, "it didn't look like a song on a page to him. My work is all over the page, centered, and then off-centered—I think that was throwing him. Because he wanted something that, like Dylan's work, was countable and repetitive. At least he did in those days. We worked back and forth, he suggested, I made some changes, he suggested . . . I would say we were halfway through." Unfortunately, when McClure called him about finishing, Garcia let the energy dribble away, and Michael let it go.

Sometimes their visitors came for simpler reasons. Mary Ann Pollar, a friend of Garcia's from Berkeley folk days, recalled coming to 710 to cook paella for everyone and having a delightful time. The string of beads Rock gave her was a gift she'd cherish. Sometimes their visitors stayed. The whole household took in a little boy named Jason McGee because his mother, they thought, was unable to care for him.

A day or two after they got to 710 in late September, Phil Lesh was walking down Haight Street when a jeep filled with National Guardsmen armed with loaded, bayonet-tipped rifles roared past and a police sergeant said to him, "You guys, get the fuck out of here." A police officer in the black neighborhood of Hunter's Point had shot a young man, and the black men of San Francisco had had enough. The result was six days of curfews and the guard in the streets.

Among other reactions, certain members of the Mime Troupe decided that formal street theater was an insufficient response to times as stark as these. They were also reacting to what they perceived as the softness of the *Oracle's* psychedelic chat and the swelling tide of consumerism on Haight Street. They seceded from the Troupe and formed, insofar as an intellectually antiorganization group can be said to form at all, the Diggers. Their central members were Emmett Grogan, Peter Berg, Kent Minault, and Peter Cohon (later Coyote). Though they would rapidly become known for feeding the hippies of the Haight and other hungry people, they were by no means a hip Salvation Army. They were, wrote Peter Coyote, later nationally known as an actor, "far more dangerous than that. It was a radical anarchist group that was really about authenticity and autonomy . . . Because we knew the real problem was the culture. The problem wasn't capitalism. The problem wasn't Communism. The problem was the *culture.*" They took as their central tenet the idea of "free," and for a while they made it work. The one thing that the endlessly flexible and adaptive American culture could not absorb or co-opt was something, anything, that didn't involve profit. The Diggers were mostly actors, and now they became what Berg called "life actors," people who consciously choose their roles in life and help others break out of their imposed roles. "The antidote to [societal] conditioning," Coyote wrote, "was personal authenticity: honoring one's inner directives and dreams by living in accord with them, no matter the consequences."

Early in October the Diggers circulated through the Haight a broadside signed by the alias "George Metesky," the New York City "mad bomber." It preached the "Ideology of Failure." "To show love is to fail. To love to fail is the Ideology of Failure. Show Love. Do your thing. Do it for FREE. Do it for Love. We can't fail. And Mr. Jones will never know what's happening here." Their message was freedom—freedom from money, and freedom from fame, which they interpreted as anonymity, so that all Diggers were George Metesky. Shortly after, they began their free food program, scrounging and stealing supplies from wholesalers, cooking it in someone's apartment, and serving it on the Panhandle, a block-wide extension of Golden Gate Park that marked the northern border of the Haight. Before the hungry got their food, they stepped through an open wooden square, the "Free Frame of Reference," because, as John Cage said, if you put a frame on something, it's art. The Diggers embodied brilliant social criticism and frequently wonderful street theater, though they were handicapped by various lunacies. They were extremely macho, wanting to "measure ourselves against the toughest of the tough," by which Coyote meant the Freedom Riders. Unfortunately, these nonviolent but truly tough heroes were soon replaced as role models by the Hell's Angels, whose toughness boiled down to plain old excesses of physical intimidation and bodily abuse. The Diggers' later notion of heroin use as a heroic challenge to the state was only sad.

The initial encounter of the Diggers and the Dead was not propitious. The band was playing a show at the giant former ice-skating rink called Winterland, a couple of blocks away from the Fillmore, for promoters who everyone assumed were mob-affiliated. As the Dead pulled up in Rakow's Cadillac, they ran into a Digger picket line with drums, tambourines, and music, and were handed a broadside. "It's yours. You want to dance, dance in the street. You don't need to buy it back." Rifkin and Coyote began a serious argument, and even the old communist Rifkin reached the point of spluttering, "Money is sacred." They did the gig, but the Diggers had created a new notion of what was hip, and the Dead had to answer the challenge. A few days later Emmett Grogan and Peter Berg visited 710. Grogan was a former burglar from Brooklyn who was authentically charismatic, "a mature street person at a time when there were so many novices," said Bill Graham, who knew whereof he spoke.

At 710, Grogan mesmerized Rifkin and Garcia with stories of organizing black people and the Mafia to pick up the garbage during the recent New York City sanitation strike. He came on like a "Robin Hood superhero," thought Rifkin, and soon became "one of my most revered dudes, teaching me another level of sophistication—lying," he said with a laugh. Grogan finished his persuasive rave with a suggestion: "Why don't you guys play free?" The Diggers would organize a flatbed truck to act as stage and acquire permits from the city. Simple home extension cords strung from someone's apartment over the street to a light pole could deliver power to the Panhandle. And suddenly, there *was* dancing in the streets. Free was "social acid," and it worked.

The Digger-Dead relationship wasn't always smooth. Coyote would sense a tension generated by the fact that the Dead had some (if very little) money, while the Diggers had none. "Of all the bands," Coyote said later, "the Dead were the most intellectual, they were the most cutting-edge, they were the ones we were really close to; but it was like siblings." Weir appreciated the Digger ideology, but sensed a "vindictive" streak in Grogan that put him off. "There was an edge to him that I didn't care for, and he didn't like me because I didn't follow him. But Danny wrapped Emmett's rap in compassion and made it palatable to us. We understood it as promotion, but the point of everything was to make enough money so we could play for free." The Dead existed to play, and now they could do it three blocks from home. It became an absolutely essential part of their cosmology; other bands played free, but none took it to heart the way the Dead did.

In part, that was because playing in the Panhandle was just an extension of living in the neighborhood. Their across-the-street third-floor neighbor, Marilyn Harris, was impressed by that. A Daly City schoolteacher, Marilyn was no hippie, but had lived in the Haight for a couple of years and watched it change. "It happened in the shops" at first, she noticed, "and then when the music went into the parks." Marilyn thought highly of the Diggers and gave a major portion of her time to working on the free food project, but she felt that Peter and Emmett "assumed that no one else knew what they knew." In contrast, "one of the things that the Dead pulled off, which was actually remarkable, was to not get involved with being the center of the universe. There wasn't a lot of ego around them. They didn't act as though they had just created the Second Coming." They were just neighbors, if a little eccentric.

Pigpen was especially fond of Marilyn and not always comfortable with the ongoing intensity of life at 710, so he would occasionally put on his bathrobe, walk across the street, and ask if he could use her shower. Other times, Marilyn might be correcting papers, and he'd come over and sit with her, sipping away on a bottle. It was also true that life on Ashbury Street could get distinctly odd. One rainy night Marilyn was seeing off her boyfriend, who happened to be wearing a trench coat. Suddenly, she heard a "ping," followed by another, and realized that someone was shooting at her with a pellet gun. LuVell and Pigpen, both inebriated, had succumbed to paranoia and assumed that anyone on Ashbury Street in a trench coat must be the law. Another time, Glenn McKay, then doing light shows for the Airplane, decided to play a joke on the Dead. Glenn had moved into 715 Ashbury, across the street from 710. He projected a film of fire on the front of 710, then had Gut, a Hell's Angel who was everyone's friend, run into the street shouting "Fire, fire!" The occupants of 710 came flying onto Ashbury Street, got the joke, and enjoyed themselves.

Good neighbors or not, they were first a band, and a certain kind of professionalism came with the territory. Money was not a major goal, but getting better as musicians was. Garcia was profoundly concerned with legitimately earning their fee by putting on a good show, and belabored Rock, the world's least punctual human, with the importance of the band being on time. Then there was Weir, whom LSD had rendered temporarily immobile onstage. "Garcia would hammer me and hammer me, calling me the 'wooden guitar player. You've gotta fuckin' move,'" said Weir, although he noticed Garcia was much more diplomatic on the subject of musical development. In his typically quirky fashion, Weir addressed that issue by studying the great jazz pianist McCoy Tyner rather than any guitarist. As a band, they began to submit to conventional promotional practices, including interviews and photo sessions. One of their first group interviews had appeared that summer in a Haight Street fan magazine called *Mojo Navigator*, and revealed them as casual and utterly open, Garcia shushing Weir at will, and with a trademark group humor they'd always reserve for the media, this time in a prolonged riff on Pigpen's age and appearance. In September they were part of *I.D., the Band Book*, a listing of Bay Area bands that included lots of the never-to-be-famous, suburban Beatles imitators like the Baytovens, Jack and the Rippers, and the London Taxi Cab, but also their peers, Quicksilver, the Charlatans, and Big Brother. Their own ad cited Kesey's description of them as "the faster than light drive," and listed their management as Frontage Road, Ltd., a joke based on the fact, as Rifkin put it, that "wherever you go, there's a frontage road—and we didn't even have a car."

I.D. also ran an ad for the clothing store Mnasidika with the Dead as models. The embarrassingly stiff portrait made it clear their futures would lie elsewhere. They would never like posing for pictures, even when it was a new experience, although one set of sessions at least became classic, well worth their investment of time. Their friend Herb Greene's roommate was studying Egyptology at S.F. State and had illustrated their kitchen wall with hieroglyphics. Over time, Herb would shoot almost every prominent person in the local music scene in front of that wall, but he and his wife, Maruska, would especially recall the Dead's visit. The sound from the stairs was like an earthquake. First through the door was Pigpen, who said to Maruska, "Got any juice [as in alcohol]?" "I think I've got some orange juice," she said, and took him back to the kitchen.

Early in October, Stewart Brand produced a second, somewhat more modest, Trips Festival, in the cafeteria at San Francisco State. For a price of one dollar (two for nonstudents), participants had "enter" stamped on their foreheads as they passed through an archway at the commons. Called Whatever It Is?, the event offered, in addition to the Dead, the Only Alternative (with Mimi Fariña), a Bill Ham light show, the Mime Troupe, the Congress of Wonders, Ann Halprin's Dancers Workshop, and so forth. It ran from Friday afternoon to Sunday morning and had the dazzling elements of an acid test, but set in an extremely dramatic context. After eight months in Mexico, Ken Kesey had returned to the Bay Area, and he made an appearance at the State acid test by remote control, broadcasting into the event from the safety of the campus radio station. Another subplot was the tension one new Prankster, Larry Shurtliff, sensed between some Pranksters and some Dead members, though when Page Browning arrived, he and Pigpen hugged warmly. There was at least one other warm greeting, between Garcia and Mountain Girl. As a performance, the State test was a lost opportunity for the Dead, because they were without their anchor. Someone had dosed Pigpen, totally incapacitating him. Rock took him home, but Pig's lover, Vee, was pissed: "You're the manager, you can't let this happen." The show finally began around midnight, and given Pig's absence, the music lacked energy and focus, although the audience was treated to Garcia playing organ behind Kesey.

The rest of the Dead's week was busy. On October 6 the State of California made LSD illegal, and *Oracle* editor Allen Cohen and artist Michael Bowen, a Timothy Leary associate, decided to respond with a celebration rather than a protest. Their Love Pageant Rally parade down

Haight Street, which included the fugitive Kesey in a cowboy suit, attracted hundreds to the Panhandle, where the Dead and Big Brother played. It was one of the first of their free performances there, and it delighted the band. Out in the street, playing was "pure," Jerry realized. "You weren't posing for a picture in some magazine of the future." Laird Grant, their equipment guy, was the only one with reservations. The occasional street person just had to get onstage, and it was up to Laird to keep him off, establishing early on a gruff reputation for the Dead's road crew.

October passed: the Dead opened for the Butterfield Blues Band and the Airplane at Winterland, played at the Mount Tamalpais Peace Festival, at Stanford, in Sausalito, at the Avalon for the Family Dog's one-year anniversary, at a high school in suburban Walnut Creek, and with Lightnin' Hopkins at the Fillmore, a doubly significant occasion for Pigpen, who revered the blues singer and was nervously proud to share the stage with the master. It was at these shows that the Dead unveiled their first exercise in merchandising, the Pigpen T-shirt, made by Kelley/Mouse and sold in three colors for $2.50 at the Pacific Ocean Trading Company, POTCO, on Haight Street. The Dead also served as entertainment at the opening of the North Face Ski Shop in a tiny hole in the wall next to the Condor Club, the North Beach topless joint where Carol Doda's breasts were on display. Over the next few years, North Face would become a fabulously successful chain, as would its successor company, Esprit, but at this time founders Doug and Suzie Tompkins were so poor that they made ends meet by stealing electricity from their next-door neighbor. The event included Mimi Fariña as a skiwear model and Joan Baez as a guest attraction. Two Hell's Angels acted as security to the invitation-only crowd. Afterward, the store owners took the Dead and the Angels to a local restaurant for dinner, where a slightly sozzled local attorney bought wine for the party. "He was really delighted," said Garcia, "as an old San Franciscan, because of the fact that, at least, there was this little thing he could talk about or look at, somebody was taking a fucking chance on the streets."

As the month came to an end, taking a chance became a major issue. After appearing on television to boast of rubbing "salt in J. Edgar Hoover's wounds," Ken Kesey had been apprehended after a chance sighting on the Bayshore Freeway on October 8. He faced three felony charges, including the La Honda possession rap, the San Francisco possession charge, and unlawful flight. His attorneys got the last charge dropped and Kesey free on $35,000 bail, then worked out a deal with the judge to moderate any possible sentence if Kesey would persuade youth to go "beyond acid" at some sort of Prankster Acid Graduation Ceremony, to be held under Bill Graham's auspices at Winterland on Halloween with, of course, the Grateful Dead.

There were a number of problems with this. Along with Quicksilver, the Dead already had a booking for that night at California Hall with a promoter named Bob McKendricks. McKendricks called Quicksilver's manager, Ron Polte, and said, "The Dead are pulling out, are you firm? I just saw a poster that says you guys are playing Winterland for Kesey." Polte flipped and called Garcia, who said that they'd play both gigs. Ron replied, "That's not right. The guy [McKendricks] will lose his ass. Where are our ethics?" Then his old Chicago friend, Prankster Julius Karpen, brought him disturbing news, a rumor that spread instantly throughout the Haight: that the Graduation Ceremony would be Kesey's last and greatest prank, with LSD being introduced into the water system at Winterland. Polte began to work on Graham, who'd only that year gotten his own dance hall permit. If the rumor came true, Graham's career in San Francisco was over. Then Polte and Karpen met with Danny Rifkin and Kesey's attorney, Brian Rohan, at 710. At first Danny tried to change Polte's mind, but Julius began to express his concerns. As Rifkin remembered it, it seemed to him that Julius had almost been held prisoner by the Pranksters. "It was like they were dosing him every day, and he didn't want to be [dosed], and he said, 'These people will stop at nothing, and they'll put it in the water supply.' 'Julius, is this serious?' 'Yes.' " As it happened, Rifkin loved being dosed, but disapproved of dosing, and had never entirely approved of Kesey, whom he felt was a "power tripper." Danny was the moral center of the Dead's scene, and when he changed his mind, so did the band. The Dead would play on Halloween at California Hall with Quicksilver. The Acid Graduation Ceremony was held at a warehouse South of Market for a small group of people, and Kesey would then face a few months at a work farm for his legal problems.

Considering these issues seven years later, Garcia dismissed the pro- and anti-nature of the graduation ceremony as moot. "That whole [acid test] scene was over. It had already caused what it was going to cause and those waves are still spreading out now." As Lesh said, "We were always more aware of ourselves as a unit, as a band, than as representatives of the culture, or any other abstract—that's why we didn't stick with the acid tests, because we wanted to be the Grateful Dead and not the acid test house band . . . I remember that being an unspoken but totally conscious thought." Afterward Karpen compared it all to a snake molting, a mitosis. The scene would go on, if somewhat more discreetly.

The
San Francisco
Scene

(11/1/66–1/29/67)

What was happening socially in San Francisco was an extension of the bohemian tradition in which, as Dan Healy later put it, rock music had become the "agreed medium." For the musicians, the focus would be on making a statement, rather than addressing tradition or form. The statement was at root a cry for freedom and the need for a spiritual rebirth. "There is no new morality," wrote journalists David Felton and David Dalton a bit later, "as *Time* and *Life* would have us believe, but a growing awareness that the old morality has not been practiced for some time. The right to pursue different goals, to be free of social and economic oppression, the right to live in peace and equity with our brothers—this is Founding Fathers stuff." Succeeding revisionist rock historians, wrote the estimable critic Robert Christgau, would be "anxious to believe that the sixties were an aberration rather than an aborted spiritual necessity."

All the people who didn't fit in anywhere else came to San Francisco, where they could be "out of step together," said Spencer Dryden, the Airplane's new drummer. It was "the longest party I ever went to," thought Alton Kelley, "unselfconscious, completely on the natch." Acid and fellowship melted intellectual and sexual shackles, and much that had been proscribed was suddenly attractive. Because of LSD, it was especially visual and aural. It was a dance scene, and the Dead was a dance band, then and forever. Naturally, it happened in San Francisco, the home of the mental frontier, too individualistic and idiosyncratic to be an industry town like Los Angeles, and among other distinctions, a more beautiful city much closer to nature, and with far better-tempered cops than its southern neighbor. "Everybody looked like a rock star," wrote reporter Michael Lydon, "and rock stars began to look and act and live like people, not gods on the make. The way to go big time was to encourage more people to join the community or to make their own."

The many bands were affiliated by friendship, but their musical approaches were wildly divergent. For instance, the Jefferson Airplane's superbly crafted songs and glamorous lead singers were a world apart from the Grateful Dead. The noted producer David Rubinson would identify a few general characteristics of the San Francisco sound, including multi-guitar voicings based on folk guitar styles, eclecticism, an ensemble orientation, and "no reliance on outsiders or overdubs, no use of strings or brass." But after that, each band created as it chose. That past summer of 1966, Marty Balin had told Ralph Gleason that he thought it was time for the Airplane to move to L.A., " 'cause we know we need that hit record. 'Cause nobody'll really give you a break without it." The Dead loved the Airplane, but always felt that *they,* the Airplane, had it together, while the Dead were just stoned hippies, one step away from a banana peel.

So it was deliciously ironic that Garcia helped the members of the Airplane attain their first great success. Early in November he went to Los Angeles to assist them with recording their second album, *Surrealistic Pillow.* The producer, Rick Jarrard, later denied Garcia's influence, leading Jorma Kaukonen to speculate that they had possibly smuggled Jerry in after hours to evade the union rules at RCA. Studio logs confirmed that Garcia played the high electric lead on "Today" and acoustic guitar on "Plastic Fantastic Lover," "My Best Friend," and "Coming Back to Me." He also set the arrangement for "Somebody to Love," adding chords to the less interesting song Grace had brought from the Great Society. It would be the Airplane's first hit single. Recorded in only thirteen days at a cost of $8,000, the album became a classic. Garcia even named it. Trying to describe the songs, he said, "it's as surrealistic as a pillow." In thanks, although the Airplane did not list him with specific song credits, they acknowledged him as their "Musical and Spiritual Advisor," a private joke that would unfortunately further an unwanted reputation for profundity that never did quite go away. Oddly, his impact on Jorma *was* rather spiritual. Though they were in theory rival guitarslingers, they were old friends and had little real sense of competition. Jorma had been a solo musician for a long time, and felt that Garcia taught him and the Airplane a sense of how to interact as a band. Of course, the Airplane's internal dynamics, which were always high on the Richter scale in terms of friction, might not commend Garcia's advice. But one thing he said privately to Jorma did stick: "It's not what you play, it's what you don't play that counts." It wasn't a terribly original thought, but then, good advice rarely is.

Always slightly skeptical about outside institutions, the Dead did not pursue a record deal with quite the avidity of most young bands. Garcia, in particular, had an acute appreciation for the way the record companies had defrauded rhythm and blues musicians in the recent past. Yet, eyes wide open, and with a little help from a trusted friend, they were prepared to follow the conventional process. The friend was Tom Donahue, who had by now folded Autumn Records but was still a D.J. and still a proponent of the Dead. One of Tom's old pals was a man named Joe Smith, then president of Warner Bros. In August Tom had gotten Joe to attend a gig at the Avalon. Joe was a Yale graduate, and dressed like it. He and his strikingly elegant wife, Donnie, had dinner at Ernie's, an appropriately posh restaurant, and then went over to the Avalon, where Joe had his mind seriously roiled, if not blown. "Tom," he said, "I don't think Jack Warner will ever understand this. I don't know if I understand it myself, but I really feel like they're good." He sat and talked with the band at intermission. Although he mostly met with suspicion, the band agreed they wanted to record, and when they returned to the stage, Joe shook hands with Rock and Danny.

In the coming decades, Warner Bros. would become a musical megacorporation. This was not yet the case in 1966. Warner's had begun in 1958, and was first known for albums by Connie Stevens, the Everly Brothers, Bob Newhart, and Allen Sherman. In an attempt to entice Frank Sinatra into Warner Bros. Pictures, the record company acquired his personal label, Reprise, and got Reprise President Morris "Mo" Ostin in the bargain. Mo had been an accountant but he wasn't a bean counter, and he took as his business model the cinema mogul Irving Thalberg, who let his directors direct. Mo's protégé was A&R man Lenny Waronker, who would bring superb players like Randy Newman and Van Dyke Parks into the company's circle as studio musicians. Still, in the summer of 1966 Warner's most profitable acts ranged from Dean Martin,

Trini Lopez, and Petula Clark to Peter, Paul and Mary. Then Stan Cornyn, who would dub himself Warner's "official speller" because he wrote the liner notes, was asked by Warner Pictures to write a screenplay about the San Francisco Beat scene. He strolled Grant Avenue and saw some Kelley and Mouse posters and grew fascinated. Cornyn and Tom Donahue convinced Joe Smith to sample the San Francisco rock music scene. Quickly concluding that it was musically genuine, Joe told his boss, Mike Maitland, that for $100,000 they could sign every band, and at least some of them would be profitable. Maitland would not okay such a large sum. After all, Warner Bros. was then located in two thousand square feet of dumpy space above the old film company machine shop, with linoleum on the floors and used, scrambled furniture. This was not the big time—yet.

When they learned that Joe Smith wanted to offer them a contract, the Dead turned to the only lawyer they trusted, even though he knew nothing about the music business. Having saved Kesey from prison, Brian Rohan certainly had credentials as a first-rate defense attorney. More important, he was a brother. A San Franciscan, he had briefly attended the University of Oregon, where in 1958 he'd met Kesey and Prankster Mike Hagen. A feisty Irish drinker, he was no hippie, but his lifelong hatred of bullies made him a good attorney, and he was in the right place, having joined the San Francisco firm of the legendary socialist, atheist, and all-around noble rabble-rouser Vincent Hallinan. In 1965 Rohan bumped into Hagen, and soon after became Kesey's counsel. Rock and Danny asked him to conduct the negotiations, and when he demurred, they pointed out, "We like you, we trust you, and we think we can get straight answers from you." The three of them tried to educate themselves, talking with Ron Polte about how to avoid being screwed, and through him with Paul Butterfield. Rohan also called his law school friend Mike Maloney, Dave Brubeck's attorney, who told him, "Brian, keep the publishing. If they got kids, give up the kids, kids cost money. Keep the publishing. That's all you have to remember in this business."

Rohan met with Joe Smith, and between August and October, they worked out a deal. It gave the Dead creative freedom, and what would turn out to be an effectively unlimited budget for studio time, although the costs would be deducted from their royalties, as custom dictated. There was also a commitment to promote the album. But contrary to legend, it was not an especially remarkable deal. Their publishing rates were based on time rather than on a per-song basis ("jazz rates"—thus an album with a few long songs rather than many short ones was not discriminated against), but that was not new. They kept their publishing, something the Beatles, Rolling Stones, and Bob Dylan had failed to do, but this had more to do with Warner Bros.' weakness and Rohan's honesty than their own shrewdness. According to Joe Smith, he never asked the Dead or any other band for publishing, because "I was totally unaware of the value of publishing." Though that seems hard to believe, their contract, dated September 30, 1966, and revised in December, did not mention publishing and boiled down to a $10,000 advance and an 8 percent royalty. A fair part of the advance went to buy Kreutzmann a new car to replace the Pontiac station wagon that had been consumed by its service as the band's equipment transport. Of course, the Mustang he selected was of no use to the band, but a combination of his insistence, the band's inertia, and the fact that Garcia didn't care where the money went put Bill behind the wheel.

The deal did Warner Bros. a lot of good. The Grateful Dead was Warner's first rock band, and they instantly raised Warner's hipness quotient. Over the next few years, it would earn a legitimate reputation as an artist-friendly company. From Rifkin's point of view, Smith "was straight, but he wasn't an asshole. He never quite got us, but he knew we were part of what was happening. Warner Bros. was really nice. They didn't have a clue—and we had an attitude because they were corporate. But they were pretty decent people. They were kinda lame—college newspaper kind of people." Lame or no, Warner's would certainly get an education over the next few years. In Rock Scully's eyes, they were a little more problematic. "It's like dealing with aliens. They all have the same uniform, the spooky Southern California leisure wear that is affected by most of the industry at the time: V-neck velour sweaters with high collars . . . Very slick, cheery, ultra-tanned faces, and all topped off with the de rigueur Jay Sebring haircut, a type of razor cut so immaculate it looks sprayed into place. These record execs look like golfers without the spikes on their shoes. The spikes are in their teeth! Out for us! Out for blood!" At first, the band's name alone, much less the possibility of actually meeting Pigpen, was enough to intimidate most of the staff. At one early meeting, Cornyn recalled, the band expressed some concerns regarding Kreutzmann. Stan piped up, "You know, we could get a studio drummer." In the silence that followed, "they kind of stared at me," and his words melted away into silence.

Shortly after they signed their contract, the band had a side adventure in recording, spending a couple of days with the distinguished jazz vocalist Jon Hendricks, who'd been commissioned to produce the sound track of a radical film about the Vietnam Day Committee's antiwar demonstrations called *Sons and Daughters*. Hendricks had grown up in Ohio, five doors down from Art Tatum, then formed the preeminent jazz vocal group Lambert, Hendricks and Ross. He was a genuine hero, and the Dead leaped at the chance to work with him. Weir was not familiar with Lambert, Hendricks and Ross, and Garcia and Lesh gave him an education. The session was hard for him, and he felt considerable pressure. Hendricks enjoyed himself: "Pigpen was the one that I was told I was going to have so much trouble from. He was like a child, he was very sweet." Jon had heard of Jerry, and said much later that Garcia had the respect of some of the local jazz musicians. The band as a whole "seemed to feel like they were in training. And I didn't realize it myself until about the end of the first day. They didn't seem to want any latitude at all. Garcia said, 'Look, anything you want us to do, just let us know. And we'll do it.' And when it got to the singing, Pigpen was brilliant on the vocals."

Interestingly, when the film was being prepared for showing, the Dead asked that their name be removed from the credits. To Rifkin, they were about music, not politics. Weir remembered, "We were getting a lot of heat then." The FBI had a tendency to stop by 710 looking for Bear or other well-known "underground" people, and "they knew our names . . . As far as we were concerned," Weir continued, "the war was their business—the people who were fighting it. We wanted nothing to do with it, and that was that. We weren't into protesting it—we were realistic enough to realize that there was nothing we could do that was going to change anything. In our hearts, we were against it." The Dead's attitude about politics would stay consistent, if unique. They probably did more benefits than any band ever, and frequently for explicitly political groups, but they'd sign nothing. They put their time where their beliefs were, but not their mouths. It was a policy designed to make "Grateful Dead" something separate, above life's daily shuffle. "It's our responsibility to keep ourselves free of those connotations," said Garcia years later. "I want the Grateful Dead experience to be one of those things that doesn't have a hook. We're all very antiauthoritarian. There's nothing that we believe so uniformly and so totally that we could use the Grateful Dead to advertise it."

Late in the year the Dead entered the world of national publicity. In November the respected music monthly *Crawdaddy!* reported in "San Francisco Bay Rock" that the Dead were "rapidly gaining prominence and ascending from their underground status to a position close to the Airplane." Garcia's leads were "exciting, sustained genius." It also commended Bill "Sommers," which had been the name on Kreutzmann's phony draft card. Of the mainstream national press, *Newsweek* covered San Francisco best. Rick Hertzberg, a relatively young reporter in the local bureau, was attuned to what was happening in the Haight, and his enthusiasm yielded a December 19 article called "The Nitty Gritty Sound." Music in San Francisco was "the newest adventure in rock 'n' roll. It's a raw, unpolished, freewheeling, vital and compelling sound. And it's loud." Although sprinkled with clichés regarding the light shows and dress—"bead necklaces, the high sign of LSD initiation"—the article was not only positive but less silly than most. The Dead, "second in popularity [to the Airplane] are blues oriented, and so far unrecorded. Their hard, hoarse, screeching sound is pure San Francisco . . . Mostly untrained, the top groups boast skilled and intuitive musicians in whom a depth of genuine feeling and expressive originality is unmistakable."

The Dead family had much to give thanks for, and they celebrated Thanksgiving Day 1966 from the heart. They borrowed chairs and tables, opened the room dividers, and ran a table from the front door back to Pigpen's room, seating forty to fifty people, including the Airplane, Quicksilver, the *Oracle* people, the Thelins, and many others. Kreutzmann's friend John Warnecke brought two kilos of pot, and there was pot tea, pot cookies, and pot stuffing. Jack Casady, a highly dexterous roller, left a souvenir joint at each place setting. Lesh rose and toasted the moment: "These are the good old days." It was a sign of the impending times, however, that one friend inappropriately brought along to the family gathering a photographer from *Paris-Match;* the stranger was politely asked to leave. The next night they enjoyed a second celebration at the Fillmore, where Bill Graham threw a bash for musicians, friends, and regulars. Appropriating a green onion as a sword, Pig fenced with a friend, and Jerry declared, "This is the bossest." Afterward, the Dead played a set that Ralph Gleason lauded. They had achieved a particular kind of status within their world. They'd been a band for less than two years, yet there was an apartment at the corner of Stanyan and Alma in the Haight whose tenants sold buttons that read "Good Ol' Grateful Dead."

The musical year crested later in December, with one of the most incredible runs the Fillmore would ever see. Bill Graham didn't listen to the radio, but he always listened to the musicians, and they were unanimous in telling him that he needed to book Otis Redding. For three nights, Otis and an eighteen-piece band held court, with the Dead opening one show. Each day, Janis Joplin would come in the afternoon to secure a central position in front of the stage. The Dead were there each night, rapt. Once Danny took some of Otis's backup singers for a walk, and shocked them when he announced he was going to smoke a joint. In 1966 it was a long way, culturally, from Macon to San Francisco.

The year ended with what would become a tradition, a Bill Graham Presents New Year's Eve concert, with the Airplane, Quicksilver, and the Dead. The new year's baby, diaper and all, was Jim Haynie, Graham's stage manager. Tripping happily, Haynie lay on a litter and pitched flowers to the audience as security guards hauled him up to the stage, where he danced long enough to lose the diaper. Haynie would keep the role for years, even after he left Graham's employ. Country Joe and the Fish were at the Avalon that night, and when they were finished, they went over to the Fillmore to join in a memorable jam that included Garcia, Lesh, John Cipollina, and Barry Melton, the "Dead Silverfish." At some point, Melton looked around at the light show screen, and sure enough, there was an image of a cartoon bug, its legs in the air.

The year 1967 was ushered in by *Time* with an article that chose people under twenty-five years of age as "Man of the Year." Lieutenant Norbert "the Nark" Currie of the San Francisco narcotics squad noted that there had been 163 drug arrests in the Haight in 1966, double the previous year. On January 3 the *Chronicle* began a major series with a banner front-page headline, "Life with the Hippies." The accompanying photo was captioned, "One stop on [a young hippie named] Diana's route—dirt, crowded bedrooms, and more risks than you'd imagine." *Life* reported on Francis Cardinal Spellman's twenty-first annual Christmas visit to the troops, this time in Vietnam, where more than 200,000 were stationed; "Less than victory is unthinkable," he intoned. On the tenth, Chester Anderson, a friend of the Diggers then working at *Ramparts* magazine, secured financing from some dope dealers and acquired a Gestetner 366 stencil machine to establish the Communications Company, or com/co. It would become a Haight Street–specific medium of information.

The Dead began the year by playing in the Panhandle with Big Brother for a New Year's Day party that the Hell's Angels were throwing for the Diggers. Two weeks before, the Diggers had sponsored a "Death of Money" event in which member Phyllis Wilner rode down Haight Street on the back of a motorcycle carrying a banner that read "Free." The day ended with the arrest of Chocolate George, a Hell's Angel, who was thereupon bailed out through the efforts of the Diggers. Now the Angels were saying thank you. Garcia would identify it as the day that the Angels adopted him and the Dead. Though the Angels certainly shared with the hippies a sense of alienation from the norm, their predisposition toward violence, their general suspicion of all non-Angels, and their political conservatism had always made for uneasy relationships with the hip community. During the fall 1965 Vietnam Day marches from Berkeley to the Oakland Naval Base, Angels had sided with police and beaten demonstrators. Allen Ginsberg and Ken Kesey had negotiated with them, and in the end the Angels had announced that they would not soil their hands with these un-American peaceniks. But the Dead's personal gesture of playing for their party seemed to matter.

The park and Panhandle gatherings grew. Starting with the first October rally, various members of the community led by Allen Cohen and Michael Bowen had begun meeting at the *Oracle* office to plan an event that would assemble all of the various elements of the larger "freak" community of Northern California and beyond. The first stumbling point was politics. As Rock Scully put it, the suit-and-tie Berkeley politicos wanted a political platform and "kept busting into our meetings." They wanted to rouse the rabble—"Rabble-rousing is their very raison d'être," said Rock, while his and the Dead's view was "Let's make it fun, not misery. We've won already, we don't have to confront them [the government and other prowar forces]. Why go on their trip? Why battle? Dissolve. Disappear. Let them be the ones looking for a fight." Conversely, the politicals distrusted drugs and rock and roll as hedonistic and antirevolutionary, and truly despised the hippies' lack of overt political sensibility. Perhaps they also resented the way that the hippies had stolen their thunder with the media. The meetings did not resolve any differences, except to allow Vietnam Day Committee activist Jerry Rubin three minutes on the stage at the big event. A second sticking point was the Diggers, who had become suspicious of almost everything. The greatly esteemed poet Gary Snyder interceded and convinced Peter Berg that a group celebration was called for. The organizers took the event's name from Richard Alpert, who had chortled, on first observing a Panhandle rock show, "It's a human be-in."

Early in January the *Oracle* published a Stanley Mouse poster for "A Gathering of the Tribes for a Human Be-In" featuring Allen Ginsberg, Timothy Leary, Richard Alpert, Michael McClure, Jerry Ruben [sic], Gary Snyder, and "All S.F. Rock Groups," to take place Saturday afternoon, January 14, at the Polo Field in Golden Gate Park. The central image was a picture of an (Asian) Indian holy man with a third eye. It would be "a union of love and activism previously separated by categorical dogma and label mongering . . . the joyful, face to face beginning of the new epoch." Another poster, by Rick Griffin, depicted a Native American with a guitar. Otherwise, there was little publicity, except for a piece in the *Chronicle* and a few mentions on the radio.

A LONG STRANGE TRIP

The Be-In weekend was good and crazy for the Dead. They were booked for those three nights at the Fillmore with Chicago blues star Junior Wells and a new, as-yet-unknown band from Los Angeles, the Doors. On Friday afternoon the Dead got a call from Bill Graham, who also had the Mamas and the Papas playing at the Berkeley Community Theater, with Jose Feliciano booked to open. But Jose couldn't make it, and Bill asked the Dead to rush over to Berkeley to fill in, which they did. Then to the Fillmore, where they listened to the Doors. Garcia was ordinarily a generous man and would almost never bad-mouth any musician who honestly tried, but Jim Morrison struck him as the embodiment of Los Angeles, which meant the triumph of style without substance. The Doors had no bassist and consequently sounded thin to him, and Morrison's imitation of Mick Jagger did not impress him. Androgyny, Garcia thought, had been fulfilled by James Dean. Morrison would have considerably greater success with other audiences. The son of a U.S. Navy admiral, he was a raving antiauthoritarian who had been set on his path by Kerouac's *On the Road*, Nietzsche, and Rimbaud, and formed the band after meeting keyboardist Ray Manzarek at the UCLA film school. Their name was taken from William Blake, by way of Aldous Huxley. Much of the Doors' thinking was parallel to the Dead's, but stylistically and emotionally they were oceans apart.

Saturday, January 14, had been identified as propitious by astrologer and eminent Haight citizen Ambrose Hollingsworth, and he was right. Early in the day, Danny Rifkin and Jay Thelin went to scout out the site at the Polo Field, and found the road to the berm, an earth wall that surrounded the field, chained shut. A little surgery with a bolt cutter, and the road was clear. As the Dead family walked from 710 to the park, it slowly dawned on them that more and more people were joining them, and everyone had a secret, stoned smile. As Charles Perry put it later, it was the "unique Be-In smile, at once conspiratorial, caressing, astonished, and beaming with stoned-out optimism . . . a giddy high. Except the puzzling thought: what were we doing here? Was this a political demonstration? A religious gathering? A party? . . . such a big unspoken secret we shared." "My God," thought Florence. "There's so many of us." The tribes had indeed gathered, and at least twenty thousand people were there. Garcia was blown away. "I'd never seen so many people in my life. It was really fantastic. I just didn't believe it almost. It was a totally underground movement. It was all the people who were into dope of any sort."

People settled down on the grass, gathering in little affinity groups, the Dead family here, a Big Sur tribe there. Bear ran around passing out tabs from his latest batch, which he had named "White Lightning" after the bolts on Rick Griffin's Be-In poster, and the afternoon assumed a certain glow. At length, Gary Snyder picked up a conch shell and blew a long blast and the ceremony began, with bands and poets alternating.

Fairly early in the day, as Quicksilver played, the stage power was interrupted, the reasons unclear. The Angels took responsibility for guarding the lines, which kept them pleasantly occupied, and there was a half-hour pause. Later, Ron Polte decided that it was this half hour that really made the day, because the audience became the show, sharing fruit and smiles, bonding. It was "early Christianity without the lions," thought Julius Karpen, and everyone caught the mood. When Julius had arrived at the Polo Field, he saw a lady approach one of the two mounted policemen on duty and say, "I've lost somebody, please help me go down in that crowd." The cop replied, "I can't go down in that crowd, lady. All those people are smoking grass."

The crowd was not interested in gurus or politicians, and neither Leary nor Rubin got much attention. As he went on to speak, Rubin told Rifkin, "Now, pay attention. What I'm going to say is very important." Garcia found his message at best laughable and at worst fascistic. "Like, all that campus confusion seemed laughable too. Why enter this closed society and make an effort to liberalize it when that's never been its function? Why not just leave it and go somewhere else?" When Rubin began a standard antiwar harangue, "The words didn't matter. It was that angry tone. It scared me, it made me sick to my stomach." Timothy Leary's rap was equally off-putting. Weir listened closely, "trying to get with it," but he failed. Leary's hierarchical and ritualistic inclinations were utterly incongruent with the Dead's democratic approach. Even Leary's fans at the *Oracle* conceded that his talk that day simply didn't fly. A week later the Dead would go down to Santa Barbara and open for a Leary lecture, and it would be a different matter. He brought with him Ralph Metzner's elaborate slide show, which Rifkin would find "quite gorgeous."

The Dead's set at the Be-In got people up and dancing, so of course the band felt great. They played a folk tune they'd electrified called "Morning Dew," "Viola Lee Blues," and, with saxophonist Charles Lloyd sitting in on flute, "Good Morning, Little Schoolgirl." As they played, a parachutist drifted down and landed in the crowd. A toothless speed freak with a harmonica leaped onstage and sat in until Laird got there, but it was a very brief distraction. For the band, the best thing was that Dizzy Gillespie, there with Ralph Gleason, thought they were "swinging."

"No fights. No drunks. No troubles. Two policemen on horseback and

20,000 people," wrote Gleason. "The greatest non-specific mass meeting in years, perhaps ever."

Allen Ginsberg chanted a mantra at sunset, and the crowd left the field spotless.

"My day was full," said Rifkin on his way home.

Before the Fall

(1/30/67–5/31/67)

On January 30, 1967, the Dead flew to Los Angeles to begin recording their first album at RCA Studio A, because there wasn't a professional quality studio at home. Their producer was Dave Hassinger, whom they had requested because he'd engineered the Stones' "Satisfaction" and the Airplane's *Surrealistic Pillow*. Lacking any studio experience, and most probably due to first-time nerves, they were deferential and utterly cooperative with Hassinger and the RCA staff engineers. It was a mistake that they would never repeat. Weir later denied that they were intimidated, arguing they were simply respectful of experience. For him the problem with the first album was that the engineers were certain that the only way to record was to play quietly, and that didn't work for the Dead. "It didn't fill out the same way." Everyone but Weir and Pigpen was taking Ritalin, a stimulant, and the drug was reflected in the speeded-up—and sometimes slowed-down—versions of their material. They certainly failed to take advantage of their artistic freedom, and instead hyperactively recorded the bulk of the album in four days and mixed it on the fifth. It was not surprising that only a few tunes came out well, and those were the longer ones where they could jam.

The album material was from their normal repertoire, including Weir on Jesse Fuller's "Beat It on Down the Line," and Pigpen's take on H. G. Desmarais's "Good Morning, Little Schoolgirl." Pigpen's tune was particularly rushed in the recording, and failed to capture the richness of his voice, although his harp playing was brilliant. The album version of the traditional "Cold Rain and Snow" showed the way they'd totally adapted someone else's tune, changing the melody and the rhythm, but the sound of the recording did not do them justice. "Sitting on Top of the World" had first been a hit for the Mississippi Sheiks jug band, but the Dead's version was taken from Bob Wills by way of Carl Perkins. The album was essentially live. Because it was recorded on four-track, there would be more than one instrument on each track, eliminating the possibility of dynamic changes among the instruments.

The album was redeemed partially by three really good takes. Their one original tune (tune by the band, lyrics by Garcia), "Cream Puff War," came out well, with Garcia singing the Dylanesque piece with a certain nasty panache. "Your constant battles are getting to be a bore / So go somewhere else and continue your cream puff war." And the two tunes on which they stretched out, "Morning Dew" and "Viola Lee Blues," showed what the band could do. During "Viola Lee," Hassinger was in the studio with the musicians, puffing on a cigar, sparks flying as he grew excited by their performance, but he reverted to standard music practice by telling them and the engineers to fade out. In one of the few challenges to Hassinger's wisdom, Rifkin can be heard on the tape saying, "Let them play."

When they returned home, Joe Smith called and told management, as record companies will, "We don't hear a strong single here." The band chorused in reply, "A strong single, sure." They sat down and worked up a tune, and not a bad one, but then made the fatal error of being literal, writing a song about what was happening just outside their door on Haight Street. Sue Swanson had suggested "The Golden Road to Unlimited Devotion" as a name for the fan club she was in the process of organizing, and they lifted it to make a song title. They combined an archetypal dancing girl with the Haight scene and chorused, "Hey hey, come right away / Come and join the party every day." Ironically, the sound of this track, recorded in San Francisco, was vastly superior to the sound of the material recorded in Los Angeles.

Perhaps it was his beautiful new lover that Garcia was writing and singing about in "Golden Road." He had long admired Carolyn "Mountain Girl" or "M.G." Adams, thinking her, his first wife Sara said, "a lot like a man in her competence and fearlessness." After all, it was M.G.

who dealt with much of the equipment at the acid tests, since she somehow managed to stay focused. At Watts she'd worn the red, white, and
blue of Wonder Woman, and the outfit seemed perfectly apt. What
neither Sara nor Jerry knew at the time was that she was pregnant, running to vomit every half hour or so. Late in 1966 M.G. left the
Pranksters, and with Sunshine, her daughter by Kesey, she fetched up at
710. The house had just acquired a kilo of Acapulco Gold, she recalled,
"the best dope you could ever dream of." Encouraged by such hospitality,
mother and child came to rest for a while. By the time the band went to
L.A. to record, she and Jerry had become lovers and moved in together.
As grounded and organized a woman as someone not entirely of this
planet could be, M.G. was from the beginning a slightly larger-than-life
presence with the Grateful Dead. "Everybody loved her," Weir recalled.
"Although not everybody knew what to do about her."

A band is a very fragile social institution. Musicians tend toward
artistic self-doubt, and their ability to have mature relationships is frequently handicapped. With its cult of celebrity, the very nature of rock
and roll breeds ego of the negative sort, and the celebratory setting results
in a dangerous and seemingly inevitable flirtation with drug and alcohol
abuse. Setting aside issues of sexism and the generally male nature of rock
and roll for the moment, *anyone* of either gender who becomes close, sex-
ually or otherwise, to a band member is almost always viewed with suspicion by other band members.

When M.G. arrived, the band had already established what Weir
would call "I won't say hierarchy—our social dynamics." It was based on
seniority and included only the musicians, with a little room for Rock and
Danny. None of the lovers/wives at that time—Florence, Vee, Brenda—
had any known impact on band decisions. Then in waltzed M.G., who
didn't fit the criteria. She had plenty to say, and "she wasn't about to be denied," said Weir. His analysis was that she rapidly concluded that the
group was too tight to interfere with. "She very quickly retreated, not by
dint of any defeats. She just realized that these guys have enough work to
do to get it together to do this or that, and they don't need another opinion." It was one thing to work directly on one's partner and quite another
to work on the whole band. It was Weir's opinion that the Dead's behavior was neither misogynistic nor even paternal, just tightly bound with
each other. "Those five opinions, maybe Rock and Danny, was about all
we could handle." It was frequently too much for the women. Late the
previous year, Tangerine had correctly concluded that the Dead had a
greater claim on Rock than she did, and departed. Just as M.G. arrived,

Brenda Kreutzmann did the same. "The band always came first, and I was always in competition with it." Taking her daughter, Stacey, with her, Brenda returned to her childhood home. It was also significant that over the years the women in the scene generally treated each other with affection and respect. The legendary nastiness and infighting among the wives of so many bands had no place at 710 or after.

The Be-In had been an almost perfect day, but it had enormous consequences, quite a lot of them negative. Their cover was blown, and their sweet little neighborhood scene was about to be inundated, first by waves of media sweeping in to investigate the emerging story, and then by the children and tourists who heard the news. Inevitably, some of the reporters were quite dense, but not all of them. Michael Lydon, an ambitious Irish kid who'd gotten into Yale and then covered "Swinging London," came to San Francisco in January for *Newsweek*. He arrived just in time for the Be-In and loved it, and then exercised the reporter's right to talk to anyone, showing up at 710, where he found Garcia a reporter's dream as a quote machine, but also a positive, encouraging individual, a real person. Garcia opined that if he could live life on his own terms, so could Lydon. When Michael muttered that his secret ambition was to play the harmonica, Garcia replied, "Whyn't you try it, get yourself a harmonica." The encouragement worked, and over time Lydon became a musician. Their talk would turn into another *Newsweek* piece, "Drop Outs with a Mission." Confident that it would be positive, the Dead even posed for a picture.

Late in January Jann Wenner showed up to talk with Garcia. Their conversation focused on the local music scene, which had once been "underground," said Garcia, and "now everybody in the world knows who we are." Touching on *A Hard Day's Night*, Dylan, and Allen Ginsberg, Garcia expressed approval of even the teenyboppers Wenner wanted him to mock, and spoke of "hoping . . . that the people on the scene will start using their creative resources instead of a formula that works." And, of course, he talked about drugs, as he would be required to do for many years. "I don't think LSD is where it's at, but it's a symptom of where it's at . . . There is something spiritual in everything that's going on these days, and especially in rock and roll . . . A dance is a kind of celebration of the mind and the body and the senses. Music might be the one thing the earth has in the expanses of the cosmos."

The March issue of the San Francisco–based radical magazine *Ram-*

parts, with a cover picture of Mouse holding an elaborate silver pipe, featured Warren Hinckle's synoptic "A Social History of the Hippies." *Life* followed suit with a piece by Loudon Wainwright that concluded, "Those I met use the word 'love' a lot . . . It is a weapon of astonishing powers." On February 21, a stunning new ingredient became visible in the Bay Area's social brew. Betty Shabazz, Malcolm X's widow, came to the *Ramparts* office in San Francisco that day for an interview. She was escorted by members of the Black Panthers, a new political group from Oakland. Since they were dressed in black pants, black leather jackets, and black berets, and were quite legally and highly visibly armed to the teeth, they caused a sensation. Police, reporters, and TV crews converged on the office, and as the Panthers exited, the leader of the group, Huey Newton, confronted a belligerent police officer. "Man, you gonna draw it? Go ahead and draw it, you big fat motherfucking pig." The cop was seized with discretion, and the Panthers left without further incident. Newton and his partner Bobby Seale had written their manifesto, "What We Want/What We Believe" ("We want land, bread, housing, education, clothing, justice and peace") while listening to Dylan's "Ballad of a Thin Man," and had already become friendly with the Diggers. They would practice street theater with a vengeance.

The Dead played on, visiting the outskirts for paying gigs and doing benefits at the Fillmore. The Invisible Circus, a planned Digger event at San Francisco's interracial Glide Church, was supposed to feature Pigpen on organ, but he couldn't make it. One weeklong booking that spring meant something personal to Garcia. A friend of theirs had started a nightclub in the Mission District, not terribly far from where Jerry had grown up. "I walked past the place a million times," he said. "Near the funeral homes, the mystery part of my neighborhood." His mother came one night during the run, and it was sweet to have her at the show. She asked him how he got his guitar to sound like a horn, and he was pleased, though not surprised, by her perceptive ear. He'd always played with the saxophone in mind, but it was especially easy that week. The opening act was the Charles Lloyd Quartet, with Jack DeJohnette and Keith Jarrett.

On St. Patrick's Day, March 17, Warner Bros. released *The Grateful Dead.* They had left the album's visual design to the band, which was wise though unheard-of, and the cover was a collage by Kelley that incorporated pictures by Herb Greene and Gene Anthony. In a display of intuitive good taste, the band vetoed Kelley/Mouse's notion of putting a quotation, "In the land of the dark, the ship of the sun is drawn by the Grateful Dead," across the top of the cover. Variously attributed to the

Tibetan or Egyptian *Book of the Dead*, but seemingly a piece of Haight Street apocrypha, it had been floating around the neighborhood for a while. As part of their small-*c* communism, their publishing credits were all attributed to McGannahan Skjellyfetti, one of Pigpen's private jokes, derived from a Kenneth Patchen poem. For the single, Warner's released "Golden Road" backed by "Cream Puff War." Three of the album's reviews stood out. Gleason noted correctly that it wasn't as good as the band live, as did the magazine *Crawdaddy!*, where Paul Williams said that "only 'Viola Lee' has any of the fantastic 'this is happening *now!*' quality of a good Dead performance." In the *Village Voice*, Richard Goldstein was balanced and reasonable: "Straight, decent rhythm and blues . . . feels spontaneous; it sounds honest . . . leaderless cooperation you seldom find in rock and roll."

As the album was being released, Garcia amiably participated in two more interviews, the first with his old banjo student Randy Groenke, then with Ralph Gleason. Perhaps because Groenke was an old friend, their talk was exceptionally revealing. The night before, the Dead's equipment truck had been stolen, and Garcia's refusal to fuss about the theft was an example of the detached wisdom millions would come to attribute to him. He dismissed concern as "pointless," hoping that no one would have to go to jail, and speculated that "maybe there's some sort of spiritual due that we paid because we're being successful, that means that now somebody can steal our equipment and not feel guilty about it." No guru, he came across as modest, rational, compassionate, and sober. Asked to define "hippie," he replied, "somebody who's turned on . . . who's in forward motion, uh, they might have been called progressive at one time . . . creative energy at its best." The Dead scene is "more inclusive than exclusive" and "has to do with integrity . . . The point is, we're not trying to be famous or rich, we're just trying to make our music as well as we can, and get it out." As to the music scene, San Francisco was "just a good place to live," while "we're trying to change the whole atmosphere of music, the business part of it . . . by dealing with it on a more humanistic level because it's a valuable commodity."

As the conversation drifted into politics, Garcia stayed sane. "The war is an effort on the part of the establishment to keep the economic situation in the United States comparatively stable . . . would I go? I would not go. I am totally against war. I'm against it not on any religious principles, but just because I could never kill anybody. And I don't expect that in the natural course of things I would ever be brought to a situation in my head where I would want to kill anybody, or where I'd actually be able to do it. I

just don't want to do it. It's a sin. It might be the only 'sin' tl
like anti-life . . . I don't feel like I'm any kind of subver
know; I feel like an American, and I'm really ashame
Groenke was obviously wrestling with his own attitude
pursued the question, asking about the causes of the war, which Garcia attributed to the pursuit of power, which he found meaningless. "Like having lots of money, or having a huge corporation, or something like that, it
all represents power, but the kind of power it is is illusory, it's not real
power, it's worthless. If you're gonna die, you're gonna die, and all the
things that you've done in terms of your power and your money are of absolutely no value."

His refusal to be a leader in any verbal way was already established
and clear. "We are trying to make music in such a way that it doesn't have
a message for anybody. We don't have anything to tell anybody. We don't
want to change anybody. We just want to give people a chance to feel a little better . . . The music that we make together is something that's an act
of love and an act of joy, and we like it . . . If it says something, it says it in
its own terms at the moment we're playing it . . . we're not telling people
to get stoned, or to do something different, or to drop out . . . We started
all of this [Haight-Ashbury scene] from nothing, just people moving in,
and decided, 'Let's get a little bit friendly, and let's get a little bit closer together, and let's just see what we're trying to do.' And what we're trying to
do is live a good life and have things happen in a good way and not put
anybody uptight."

The interview came to a happy close. Jason McGee, the 710 adoptee,
came in and demanded a dime, and Garcia dismissed him. Then from the
front room came the sound of Rifkin on the phone, shouting, "Incredible!
Too much!" Bear and Laird had cruised around the alleys near their rehearsal hall and found some street kids who'd led them to the truck. Their
equipment was safe.

His conversation with Gleason stayed on music. Garcia remarked that
they'd only been playing electric instruments for the two years the band
had been together, so they were all novices. He thought of himself as a
"student guitarist." "I'd say that we'd stolen freely from everywhere! Re-
morselessly . . . and we have no bones about mixing our idioms . . . so you
might hear some very straight traditional counterpoint, classical-style
counterpoint popping up in the middle of some rowdy thing." One of
their newest compositions, "New Potato Caboose," was especially interesting because it lacked the normal verse/chorus form. Such new approaches were in their immediate future.

The media interest and their new album led to three rich visual images. In connection with a *Look* article, the Dead were part of a gathering on the Panhandle that included the Airplane, Quicksilver, the Charlatans, and Big Brother, where Jim Marshall snapped a picture of all the bands together, the 1967 Haight-Ashbury music team. On a more amusing note, he also got Bill Graham and all the managers to line up, each with a hand in the next man's pocket. Later in the year, Marshall took some formally posed pictures of the band, Lesh shoeless, Weir in white Kabuki makeup, for *Teen Set*. For his pains, the band dosed him with LSD, which only annoyed him until he was finished with the shoot. The Dead were also the subject of a more elaborate and abstract portrait. Bob Seidemann was a New York photographer who'd come to San Francisco and been brought over to 710 by his friend Mouse. A picture Seidemann had taken of Pigpen became a popular poster at Louis Rapaport's Berkeley Bonaparte poster shop, so he came back with a second idea. They tried to shoot it, but it required standing in the street, and the police ran them off. Finally, Seidemann cajoled them all back to the location, a suburban Daly City block that perfectly represented Malvina Reynolds's "Little Boxes"—"and they're all made out of ticky tacky and they all look just the same." The sun was behind them, and a red filter darkened the sky. Each musician was therefore in black, except for a light on each face reflected by a mirror held by Seidemann's helpers. They looked, thought Seidemann, like "mutant transplants from Jupiter, fresh out of their flying saucer." It was the first metaphorical photograph of the band, and the poster sold like crazy.

On March 20 Warner Bros. threw an album release party at Fugazi Hall, a small club in North Beach. Hippies and businessmen met in a stereotypical clash of cultures; Joe Smith and his "chief speller," Director of Creative Services Stan Cornyn, came wearing their natty blazers, "WR" (Warner Reprise) on the breast pocket, custom-made by Carroll & Company, Beverly Hills. The first thing Stan saw was a woman sitting on the floor swaying to music, her head wreathed in dry-ice vapors. The straights sat on one side drinking, the hippies on the other side smoking. The hippies would pass joints to Joe and Stan, who would politely return them unsmoked. A former disc jockey, Joe Smith would become a legendary speaker, but that night he fell into cliché. "I want to say what an honor it is for Warner Bros. Records to be able to introduce the Grateful Dead and its music to the world." Blah blah blah blah. Garcia rose. "I want to say what an honor it is for the Grateful Dead to introduce Warner Bros. Records to the world." It was the last time Stan would remember wearing the blazers.

From the time of the Be-In, it was obvious that the Haight-Ashbury was about to be inundated by pilgrims, certainly by summer and perhaps sooner. In January the Thelins, Tsvi Strauch, and some of the other Haight Street business owners had formed HIP (Haight Independent Proprietors), and in a conventional liberal way, were trying to pressure the police to be more friendly. They met with Chief of Police Tom Cahill, who observed, "You're sort of the Love Generation, aren't you?" The term stuck, but the police continued to grow ever more irritated with the problems of overpopulation. The city installed ugly yellow crime lights and made Haight Street one-way, and the police pursued a regular policy of rousting the young. On March 24 Mayor John F. Shelley asked the Board of Supervisors for an official declaration that the hippie migration was "unwelcome." The board ignored him. On the twenty-fifth, City Health Director Ellis D. Sox (a name too good not to be true) announced a review of the Haight-Ashbury that claimed his forces had in one day visited 691 buildings and issued sixty-five notices, of which he said sixteen recipients might be presumed to be hippies. Since he had eight teams, this suggested that they were able to visit ninety buildings per day per team, or more than eleven buildings per hour. The hippies ignored him.

On March 24, an anonymous rock band played from a corner apartment at the intersection of Haight and Ashbury. A crowd gathered and the police moved in. Two hundred hippies, the *Chronicle* reported, then surrounded a paddy wagon, cutting the valve stems on the tires. Sixteen people were arrested, and by the end of the scuffle, there were fifty police, five paddy wagons, and two thousand people on the scene. March 26 was Easter Sunday, and the street was set for an encore. As people began to gather, Allen Cohen of the *Oracle* went to the supervising captain and said, "You don't want to hurt anybody, man, it's Easter Sunday. Let the people have the street." "It's an illegal rally, and we have to get them off the street." Yet the captain was not itching for trouble. Cohen sent a messenger up to 710 and then got a bullhorn from the police. Mounting a police car, he announced to the growing crowd that the Dead were going to play in the Panhandle, and to go there, because after all, "It's ridiculous to have more crucifixions on Easter Sunday." Sure enough, the Dead came down Masonic Avenue waving, went down to the Panhandle, plugged in, and played. A week later they were not available, and 150 riot police arrested thirty-two hippies when they shut down the street simply by walking around.

Two moments involving the media enlivened the month of April. Early in the month, Jerry and Phil went off to promote the new album on radio station KMPX, but this was not the average radio station visit. In the middle 1960s the urban AM airwaves had begun to fill up, and the FCC decreed that FM stations generate original programming instead of re-peating, or simulcasting, material from AM stations. Until then, FM had been virtually ignored, since few people owned FM receivers and the rare FM stations tended to be foreign-language or generally obscure. Tom Donahue fixed that. Early in 1967 he called every FM station in San Francisco until he found KMPX, which was so broke that its phone was disconnected. Donahue took over the evening slot, and subsequently the whole station. He gathered up friends, including a few languishing in jail, pooled their record collections, and basically started "underground FM" radio, one of the first creative adaptations of mass media in America. Just as the Haight was beginning to sink beneath a flood of overpopulation, some of its best aspects were magically available on the radio.

Garcia and Lesh visited Donahue only days after he'd taken over his air shift, and brought with them a selection of material that was singularly eclectic and indubitably hip: the Swan Silvertones, Charles Mingus's "Wednesday Night Prayer Meeting," Blind Willie Johnson, Ray Charles, James Brown's "It's a Man's Man's Man's World" and "Ain't That a Groove," Bob Dylan's "Maggie's Farm," the Ensemble of the Bulgarian Republic's "The Moon Shines," Charles Lloyd Quartet's "Dream Weaver," the second movement of Charles Ives's Symphony no. 4 conducted by Leopold Stokowski, Ian and Sylvia, Skip James, Aretha Franklin, the Righteous Brothers, Ike and Tina Turner, Lou Rawls, the Rolling Stones, and Otis Redding. Oh, and two cuts from their own new album. Albums were ex-pensive, but if you had a radio, good, varied music was now free. KMPX became a part of people's lives and an integral part of the community.

The whole band shared the next adventure, which was their first ap-pearance in a movie. *Petulia* starred George C. Scott and Julie Christie in a romance set in San Francisco, but the real attraction, especially for cinephile Garcia, was director Richard Lester, of *A Hard Day's Night* and *Help!* fame. It was a tremendous learning experience. Although it was a big-budget Hollywood film, *Petulia* was shot by Lester, a cameraman, a script girl, and a recordist. All sound was "wild," or live, rather than re-recorded afterward. Their friends at the satirical troupe the Committee, who were also in the movie, had recommended them, and the shoot was a fine opportunity for good talk, even if the interminable delays of movie-making were a bore. Lester was funny and accessible, jamming with them on organ during one break.

What happened after the filming was quite extraordinary. In order to be in the movie, they had to join the Screen Actors Guild, and in order to join SAG, they were required to sign a loyalty oath. Danny Rifkin had prepared a rousing speech for why they shouldn't sign, but he'd barely begun when the band unanimously agreed. Film fame was not worth hypocrisy. They'd already rejected the opportunity to work in the James Coburn film *The President's Analyst* because ABC-Paramount would not give them creative control over their part. Just a month or two before, Otto Preminger had visited 710, ostensibly to discuss a film, only to be greeted by M.G., Sue, Connie, and Weir, armed with water balloons and firecrackers. Shouting what M.G. recalled as "vile epithets" on the subjects of mogulism and Hollywood, they sent the famous director scurrying back to his limousine. Weir wasn't even sure who Preminger was, but he welcomed any opportunity to exercise his superior throwing arm. Having rejected the SAG loyalty oath, they assumed they'd land facedown on the cutting room floor. Remarkably, this did not happen. SAG's board of trustees met, and sanity prevailed. Perhaps they feared a right-to-work lawsuit, little knowing that the Dead had neither the money nor the inclination for such a thing. Seemingly, they realized that the oath, instituted in 1953, was irrelevant. Perhaps a few members even understood the essentially un-American nature of a loyalty oath. For whatever reason, the board voted to make the oath optional, and seven years later it was deleted. The apolitical Grateful Dead had struck a blow for freedom.

Still resolutely apolitical, they played a benefit on April 9 at Longshoremen's Hall for the Spring Mobilization to End the War. The evening was supposed to be a big homecoming for the headlining band, Sopwith Camel, which had gone to New York and recorded the song "Hello, Hello," currently a radio hit. This did not particularly impress the Dead, who were moved by the spirit that night, playing quite late. The Camel got through half of one song and were shut down by union stagehands. This was not the only time a band grew upset with the Dead. Late that month they played a show in Santa Barbara with the Doors. When Ray Manzarek noticed that he and Pigpen had the same Vox organ, he suggested to Pigpen that they save the roadies work and use the same instrument. "No way, man," grunted Pig. "Nobody plays my organ." "What difference does it make?" "It makes a big difference."

The San Francisco music business was beginning to show the effects of success. All feathers and beads, Janis Joplin was zipping around town in a Sunbeam convertible. Moby Grape, with whom the Dead would play yet another Mime Troupe benefit on April 12, was just about to release its first album. In an act of inspired hubris, they and their record company announced that there would be five singles from the album and a $100,000 promotional budget. Just as it came out, various band members were arrested with pot and underage women, and their future dimmed.

The Grape's approach contrasted vividly with the Dead's, whose promotional vehicle was a mimeographed newsletter, *The Olompali Sunday Times*, put out to about 150 people by Sue Swanson, Connie Bonner, and Bob Matthews. The first issue, in March, gushed. Lesh: "reads extremely fast . . . energetic!" Kreutzmann: "has a shiny new Mustang . . . used to sell wigs." Garcia: "talented, talented . . . has a lot to say . . . digs girls, girls . . . loves orange juice . . . hates dishonesty (they all do) . . . owns a pedal steel guitar . . . Leo." Pigpen: "rides a BSA . . . walks around the house in strange outfits . . . washes his hair a lot . . . afraid of bees." Weir: "on Zen macrobiotic diet . . . super nice guy . . . nickname Mr. Bob Weir Trouble." Their second issue grew more wry, as the band took to contributing tall tales: Garcia was Captain Trips because he had once piloted boats on the Sacramento River, while Phil Lesh was known to kids as "the lovable Miss Frances of 'Ding Dong School.'" "We inherited the evil and wars, but chose to ignore them to death rather than to try and kill off everyone who does not see Utopia as we do. The movement of Joy is spreading, and we are glad to be a part of it."

On the afternoon of April 16 Garcia wandered down to Haight Street and came across the latest missive from com/co: "Pretty little 16 yr old middle-class chick comes to the Haight . . . gets picked up by a . . . street dealer who spends all day shooting her full of speed . . . feeds her 3000 mikes & raffles off her temporarily unemployed body . . . Rape is as common as bullshit on Haight Street." Garcia was sickened, not only by the rape but by the focus. The positive avenue that had been the Haight and its ways was not naive or innocent, he thought, but honest. And now "this guy took it upon himself to print up bad news and put it up. We had no bias for positive or negative, only some real reasonable stuff about freedom, and fun was the filter. We had to have laughs." Laughs were getting harder to find on Haight Street in April. By now, Weir noted, the atmosphere on the street was the product of police and very young kids, often strung out on speed.

The band members responded, as usual, by playing. The free Panhandle shows were their last-ditch gift to their community. Bert Kanegson was a War Resisters League activist who'd been putting on benefits for the WRL at the Anchor Steam Brewery, which was owned by a WRL member. He occupied what he thought of as the gentle end of the Diggers, as the more famous and angry Diggers began to spend more time doing heroin than on the street. That spring he helped get permits for the free shows, working from an office at 715 Ashbury. The building had been owned by Don McCoy, a wealthy young hippie, and then by his ex-wife, Paula, who became involved with the Diggers. Kelley and Mouse, Ron Rakow, Sue Swanson, and other friends lived there as well.

Now that they had an album, the Dead began to make plans to go to New York in June. Meantime, they played locally and in Los Angeles. Even with an album, they were still sufficiently small-time that many of their shows remained something of an adventure. In May they began a brief series of Monday nights at the Rendezvous Inn, a gay bar on Geary Street where Weir insisted that Sue and Connie accompany him at all times. Laird, Pigpen, and Phil's pal Bobby Petersen suddenly betrayed an inclination to pat him on the ass, and the nickname "Candy" was bruited about, but as Lesh put it, "I thought it was going to be freaky, but it wasn't." They journeyed down to Fresno one day, played a fairgrounds another, and then worked a high school assembly in Mountain View, a gig set up by Garcia's banjo student Randy Groenke. Under the pretext of a dentist's appointment, Kesey and Neal Cassady snatched up Neal's son John from school and took him to the show. When they arrived, the band was hanging out in the teachers' lounge. "Jerry's got his Les Paul out, and he's talking philosophy with the principal," wrote John. "Bob Weir and Phil Lesh were babbling to the teachers."

Back home, the band heeded Brian Rohan and played another benefit for their community. On the night of the Be-In, police had arrested more than a hundred people on charges of failure to disperse as the crowd flowed through the Haight on its way home. Rohan and his partner, Michael Stepanian, had gone to the D.A. and proposed a bargain. Promising to tie up the courts for years if necessary, they suggested taking a small group and trying them. "If they're guilty, we'll plead the others," said Rohan. "If not, you'll drop." "We picked fourteen of the smartest, most polite, best-looking, most articulate defendants you have ever seen in a courtroom." At four counts per defendant, they got acquittals on fifty-five of fifty-six charges (one man admitted taking a minor into a bar). "From then on," Rohan said, "judges had to recognize hippies as human. Bail bondsmen, too."

Soon after, the two attorneys founded the Haight Ashbury Legal Organization, HALO, which was run from the downstairs room at 710. On May 30 all the major San Francisco bands played at Winterland and raised $12,000, which would finance the HALO office for the summer. After a day at the Hallinan office, Rohan and Stepanian would pull up at

710, double-park, go in, and take every case, no matter what the crime. In Rohan's memory, HALO had 265 clients that summer, and only one—a kid who flipped off the judge and had many, many traffic tickets—went to jail.

The HALO concert would be the only time that the Airplane, the Dead, Quicksilver, Big Brother, and the Charlatans all played on the same bill, and in some ways, it was the Haight's last gasp. Summer made it clear that the scene simply couldn't endure on such a scale. The Haight had developed because a group of young adults, not children, had found themselves in a quiet spot, flying under the cultural radar while they worked out some ideas about freedom during a time of such prosperity that it was possible to live easily on the fringe of the mainstream culture. But the war in Vietnam was about to end that prosperity, and the social divisions over the war would produce a mood completely opposite to what the Haight had stood for. "I never was that optimistic," Garcia said later. "I never thought that things were going to get magically better. I thought that we were experiencing a lucky vacation from the rest of consensual reality to try stuff out. We were privileged in a sense . . . Our world certainly changed. Our part of it did what it was supposed to do, and it's continuing to do it, continuing to evolve. It's a process."

The Haight had broadcast a message of a revolution of consciousness such that, as one historian wrote, "personal liberation had become a mass movement rather than the privilege of small cadres of bohemians." The Haight was indeed a brief vacation, a fragment of time when there seemed to be grounds for faith—faith in freedom, in the ultimate benevolence of humans, in the chance that racism might be replaced with mutual respect. It was part of a long parade of dreamers that heard a different song, from Thoreau and Whitman to Rexroth and Kerouac. Much of what would be perceived, for better or worse, as "New Age" began or was influenced there. Yoga, meditation, biofeedback, astrology, the occult, all of these alternative spiritual approaches were simply LSD without the acid. Hippie antiviolence sentiments challenged sexual roles and contributed mightily to feminism and gay liberation. Perhaps more important than social developments was the evolution of the environmental movement in this country. If humans manage to avoid destroying the earth, it will be hippies and their heirs who will be significantly responsible.

Late in May, the band fled the city to John Warnecke's family ranch on the Russian River north of San Francisco near Healdsburg. Too many fans and too much negativity on Haight Street had left them somewhat burned-out—710, for Chrissake, was now a stop on a Gray Lines bus tour. They had a platform over the riverbank where they set up their instruments, a campfire, and a mix of tents and cabins. It was a reflective and spiritual moment. An avant-garde filmmaker, Robert Nelson, had expressed interest in working with them, and during their time on the river he made a ten-minute film, most memorably as they fooled around in a canoe.

They'd been working on a new blues tune for Pigpen for some time, but they got some extra help during their stay on the river. Robert Hunter had spent the previous couple of years ingesting methedrine and mostly writing experimental Joycean poetry, but he'd come up with one thing that wasn't too complex. "Sleepy alligator in the noonday sun / Sleepin' by the river just like he usually done / Call for his whiskey / He can call for his tea / Call all he wants but he can't call me." Hanging out on the platform by the river, they'd watch people slide by, and then, said Kreutzmann, "we'd get freaky, get high, and make weird sounds. Frogs, invading Martians, whatever, the P.A. turned up all the way . . . We could almost turn over canoes." Back on the city streets, some dreams were dying, but out in the country, new ones were just taking shape.

16

The Prodigals

(6/1/67–9/15/67)

few minutes into the Dead's first set on the East Coast, at a free concert in Tompkins Square Park on the Lower East Side of Manhattan, in an area that had recently come to be known as the East Village, someone threw a framed portrait of Jesus onto the stage. It landed on the drums, scattering fragments of glass, and native New Yorker Danny Rifkin was bemused. "We didn't know whether we were pelted or blessed." Weir thought of it as a challenge: "One of those New Yorkers tossed it up there and said, 'Waddya think about *that*?'" New York was not only the Western world's media headquarters, it was a place where every citizen was a critic by right. The essence of being a New Yorker required a pride in coping with the sheer difficulty of life in the city. To New Yorkers, life in San Francisco was simply too easy to be meaningful. In Rock Scully's view, the press never covered the Dead as a band but as a social phenomenon, "some artifact from the decadence of the West Coast." As the *Village Voice*'s Richard Goldstein wrote of their visit, they "functioned not only as missionaries of the San Francisco sound but as emissaries from the Haight."

Goldstein was the first full-time rock critic at a major American publication. A longhaired Columbia journalism school graduate, he'd gone to work for the *Voice* the previous year, and was fascinated with San Francisco and London, the era's twin psychedelic capitals. He'd written a book about drugs while in journalism school, thought the acid scene was "important and world-changing," and saw San Francisco as "the center of whatever new culture was going to emerge." He'd taken it seriously enough to visit the city early in 1967, where he went by the Digger house and stayed for several days, sleeping on the floor and watching the Diggers distribute food. When he returned to New York, he wrote a story, "In Search of George Metesky," that in March brought the first published news of the Diggers to Manhattan. He'd also visited 710 and was fascinated with its openness, people wandering in and out at all times, so unlike New York with its paranoia and Fox police locks. He felt welcome in the Dead's home, yet felt "shy about being around such incredible people," and they reacted by being "solicitous." Weir's heterosexual androgyny was also new to him. "San Francisco has the vanguard because it works hard to keep it."

But Goldstein was a New Yorker, and couldn't really trust what he saw. He quoted Wier (as he spelled it) that "if the industry is gonna want us, they're gonna take us the way we are," and speculated, "It will be interesting to visit the Bay Area when the breadmen have gutted every artery." "I always had very mixed feelings," Goldstein mused later. "And the Dead apotheosized this for me because on the one hand I felt that scene was extremely naive and apolitical and completely without substance and tradition . . . and very middle-class. And I wasn't middle-class, because I'd grown up in housing projects and had a kind of working-class upbringing. So I held some contempt for it on those grounds. On the other hand, it worked. It was a really functioning community. All the hierarchies of status that applied in New York weren't there, and the way the Dead lived was sort of the essence of this notion, and that's what I regarded as so heroic and romantic."

The Dead arrived in New York on May 31. They were met at the airport by their initial hosts, the Group Image, a band and a surrounding arts collective led by an old friend of Rifkin's named Artie Schlachman. The Dead settled in at the dumpy Van Rensselaer Hotel, where Weir almost came to tears over the traces of broken dreams that he could imagine "humming and buzzing in the elevator cage." Meanwhile, Rock hurried off to consult with East Village district captain Joseph Fink, the man Mayor John Lindsay called "my favorite hippie," about their free show at Tompkins Square Park the next day. Friction between Puerto Ricans and the hippies in the East Village was Fink's immediate problem, and the

Dead's show would perhaps help alleviate it. It was preceded by a hippie parade down St. Marks Place to the park, where Pigpen graciously accepted a white carnation key to the East Village. Richie Havens opened for them, and the band got its feet wet on a new coast. Goldstein stood there thinking that it seemed as though they'd been "parachuted in, that there was a kind of gap between them and the audience." He wondered if the difference was drugs, because while everyone in the park was probably on something, the New Yorkers were more likely to be doing speed than LSD. There was a "lack of edge and definition in New York terms in their music," which might be interpreted as a lack of hostility and aggression. Eventually, Goldstein noted, they would create their own "innocent, as compared to New York," milieu.

Lacking an agent, Rock and Danny had booked this tour on their own, and the linchpin was a week at the Cafe au Go Go, where the owner, Howard Solomon, was attuned to the West Coast music scene and would bring a number of the bands to New York. As a way of laying off his risk, Solomon had joined forces with Howie Klein, chairman of the Student Activities Board at Stony Brook, a State University of New York campus some fifty miles east on Long Island. Consequently, the Dead's first paying East Coast gig was at Stony Brook, widely considered to be the stonedest campus in the East. They earned $750. Klein was also a D.J. at the campus radio station, and his close friend was Sandy Pearlman, the student body president and an editor of *Crawdaddy!*, the seminal rock magazine. Pearlman was plugged into a growing network of insiders that yielded him prerelease tapes of music, and he shared them with Klein and another Stony Brook student and *Crawdaddy!* editor, Richard Meltzer. Klein loved the Dead's first album and worked hard promoting the group at every college on Long Island; the region would be Dead territory for many years to come.

At the time, the Cafe au Go Go was *the* important club for rock in New York, the music otherwise being largely confined to the Scene, the Electric Circus, the efforts of the Group Image at the Cheetah and other places, and the Dom, home of Andy Warhol's "Exploding Plastic Inevitable" events with Nico and the Velvet Underground (formerly the Warlocks). The Velvet's first album, the "Banana album" (so called because of Andy Warhol's pop art cover), had been released in March, and it defined New York's rock attitude, which was, of course, the polar opposite of the Dead's. Its most memorable song was called "Heroin," written under the influence of William Burroughs and Hubert Selby's *Last Exit to Brooklyn,* and the music was all hard edges, with a dark, nihilistic attitude that hated not only something as soft as hippies but its own audience as well. It was then and forever a complete success with the generally New York–based critics. Howard Solomon's taste was somewhat more varied, but the Cafe au Go Go was certainly dark enough to feel like New York to the Dead. It was a dingy little cave with horrible acoustics that did not allow dancing and charged a pricey three-dollar cover plus a one-drink minimum. Frank Zappa and the Mothers of Invention played upstairs, and the band's roadie Laird was known to join Zappa's audience in pelting the Mothers with fruits and vegetables.

On opening night, after a big announcement from the house manager, the lights came up on the Dead, and there stood Garcia, tuning. He looked up, nodded, murmured "That's right," and resumed his task. *Time* sent a stringer to the show, and his notes, never used for an article, were revealing. His very thoughts were clichés: the band was "a shaggy lot who would prefer making music to most anything. Except, perhaps, making 'luv' and strewing flowers." Yet the Dead got to him, and he concluded that the music was "sensory, piercing right to the blood, and you become one with the music."

Pleased with their Tompkins Square gig, Captain Fink passed the Dead on to City Parks Commissioner Thomas Hoving, and they received permission to play at the Central Park Bandshell one afternoon. One member of the audience was Charles Mingus, who sat watching them while sipping from a thermos of martinis. Lesh was delighted to meet the great man, who charmed him with the observation that "the way to make a woman love you is to fuck her for an hour and not come." Along with the Group Image, the Dead played free for a few hundred people, and the *New York Times* duly reported that "hippies armed with electric guitars occupied the bandshell" as dancers bounced around "like rag dolls being jerked by wires." That same afternoon, a few hundred yards across Central Park on a lawn in back of the Metropolitan Museum of Art, Lower East Side political activist Abbie Hoffman was married in a wedding so perfectly media-designed that a picture of it was part of the July 7 *Time* cover story on hippies. Hoffman had correctly intuited something very powerful. A Brandeis graduate and civil rights activist, he was then running Liberty House, a store that sold Poor People's Corporation handcrafts in New York. But the gritty day-to-day of hard street politics didn't really suit him. His real gift lay in the imaginative manipulation of the media via the "put-on." It occurred to him that it would be more fun to use those gifts to organize the hippies, using the Lower East Side as a base and the Digger message as the vehicle.

After Richard Goldstein's initial *Voice* article, Digger philosophy had come to New York in a series of reprints of the com/co papers by a man named Linn (later Freeman) House, who published a psychedelic review called *Inner Space* from the Group Image loft. In April, Peter Berg and Emmett Grogan had visited New York. Peter appeared on the *Alan Burke Show* and did a masterful job of taking over the program. He refused to answer Burke's questions, changed the subject to his own concerns, and concluded by walking off the stage and up the aisle. Beckoning to the camera to follow him, he told the home audience, "I am leaving this black box of a studio; you can leave the black box of the TV by turning it off." Impressed, House became the first New York Digger, making his 23rd Street loft available to the Diggers to begin a New York Free Store. Emmett still preached Digger anonymity, or freedom from media identity, but that was something Abbie would never grasp. Although he promised House, who would perform the wedding ceremony, that he would keep it private, Abbie turned it into a photographers' field day.

An old pal of Weir's popped up at one of the Cafe au Go Go shows and made an interesting connection for the Dead. Weir and John Perry Barlow hadn't really stayed in touch since leaving prep school, but the instant they saw each other, they were close again. With Weir's current flame, Mireille, they wandered around the city, managing to attract the attention of some suburban thugs, who rudely introduced Weir to New York with a hippie-bashing. The thugs poured out of a car, and foggy as he was, Weir chirped, "I sense violence, and when I feel violence in myself, there's something I sing that calms me." He set into "Hare Krishna," and for a fragile moment it worked. Then the leader grunted, "What the fuck?" and led his friends in punching out Weir and Barlow.

Barlow was then attending Wesleyan University, and he'd connected with LSD in a manner very different from the cheerful chaos of the Dead-Prankster world. He'd gotten to know Timothy Leary, who was headquartered in a mansion north of New York City called Millbrook, and in the middle of the run at the Cafe au Go Go, Barlow took Lesh, Garcia, and Weir to visit.

Millbrook was owned by the Hitchcock family, including Billy, a budding stockbroker, and his sister Peggy, a "colorful patroness of the livelier arts," wrote Leary, "and confidante of jazz musicians, race car drivers, writers, movie stars. Stylish, with a wry sense of humor, Peggy was considered the most innovative and artistic of the Andrew Mellon family." Millbrook was extravagantly enormous. It was fully a mile from the gatehouse, complete with sallyport and portcullis, to the main house, which had four stories, sixty-four rooms, and two towers. A mile across the fields lay "the bungalow," a more modern mansion. Leary's underlying authoritarianism, born of an Irish Catholic and military background, was immediately observable to the band members, and they were not impressed. What they would remember of their visit to Millbrook was psychedelic, but had nothing to do with Leary. It was the first place they heard the new Beatles album, *Sgt. Pepper's Lonely Hearts Club Band*.

For any number of reasons, *Sgt. Pepper* was an extremely important piece of music. It distinguished the album—versus the single—as the defining mode in rock. It was assumed to be psychedelic because of tunes like "Lucy in the Sky with Diamonds," although it lacked the improvisational guitar previously thought to represent psychedelia. *Sgt. Pepper* was psychedelic in its costumes and spectacle and words, what one critic would call "vaudeville for the mind," but the music was still English music-hall mixed with rock. In any case, it was a wonderful album, something to unify all rock fans in pleasure. It became ubiquitous, and that fall it was not possible to pass through a college dormitory, day or night, and not hear it being played.

The Dead's stay at the Cafe au Go Go passed pleasantly. They played a final show with the Group Image at the Cheetah and headed home. It had been a good run, a successful introduction to the big time that is New York, although the critical take on them would be a frequent handicap in the coming years. *Crawdaddy!* had served as the field of germination for what would be many critical points of view in the next few years. Begun early in 1966 by a Swarthmore freshman named Paul Williams, it was the first rock magazine, and it brought together many bright minds. In the magazine's pages, as critic Sandy Pearlman would put it later, criticism ranged from his own "technogothic" vision to Richard Meltzer's "philosophochaotic" version to Jon Landau's "scholastically rigorous style of exegesis" to Paul Williams's "morally engaged ethos." The dominant view came to be that of Landau and *Esquire*'s Robert Christgau, and it focused on two things: technical excellence and the primacy of the African American roots of the music. As Christgau wrote, "the problem is that when poetry, musical complexity, and psychedelic basso-profundity come into the music, its original values—simplicity, directness, charm—are often obscured." This became code for limiting rock to three-minute songs with clever hooks, and the Dead clearly failed that test. That spring, Christgau wrote, "Most hippie rock and roll musicians exhibit the same in-group pretentiousness that characterized the folk and jazz purists who were their predecessors." Though Christgau himself would be more flexible in the future, Landau would not. In his defining critical manifesto, "Rock and Art," Landau declaimed, "Rock was not intended to be reflective or profound." Where this left Bob Dylan went unsaid, but this essentially reactionary attitude became the prevailing orthodoxy in rock's critical establishment.

Alan Pariser was an heir to the Sweetheart Paper fortune who happened to sell superior marijuana and consequently had gotten to know various musicians, and he had a good idea: he wanted to replicate the popular Monterey Jazz Festival with a rock and roll version. He hired the Beatles' former and future press agent, Derek Taylor, and began to line up bands. They approached Ralph Gleason for his blessing, but it came back "Judgement reserved." Shortly after, the festival became nonprofit, to be run by John Phillips of the Mamas and the Papas and his record company president, Lou Adler. From the beginning, it was clear that a successful Monterey Pop Festival would need the style and cachet of the music from the two psychedelic cities, San Francisco and London. And immediately there was conflict, because almost nothing could be more instantly repugnant to any San Francisco musician in 1967 than an ultrahip Los Angeles record producer like Lou Adler, whose instincts were superbly commercial. Early on in the process, Derek Taylor, who'd stayed with the project, filled a slow news day by floating a notion that the festival would benefit the Diggers. Not appreciating being so used, Peter Berg, Emmett Grogan, Bill Fritsch (a Digger and Hell's Angel commonly called Sweet William), and Peter Coyote drove to Los Angeles to meet with Adler at Phillips's mansion. Emmett disappeared, wrote Coyote, "to rifle the coatroom, we later discovered," while the other three laid down a simple message: the festival could not charge money for anything associated with the Diggers. Free was not an L.A. concept. Coyote "said it nicely, Berg said it coldly, and Bill made it dangerous." Then Derek Taylor got up and ended the meeting, "announcing over his shoulder breezily as he walked out the door: 'That's it, I'm out of here. These guys have always been the hippest. If they say it's not happening, it's not happening.'"

But the notion of the festival had assumed an enormous momentum. There was so much wonderful new music around, and showcasing it in one spot for three days made sense. There was also money involved. ABC-TV had put up $250,000 for film rights, with the distinguished documentary director D. A. Pennebaker to direct. The producers forged ahead, leaving the good name of the Diggers out of the mix. Still needing the San Francisco hipness/integrity quotient, they recruited Paul Simon, a member of the nonprofit board that theoretically ran the festival, to act as an emissary. Rock and Danny spent a day with Simon, taking him around San Francisco and to a free show in the park while explaining their fears of being co-opted by Adler. Simon said, "I get it," recalled Rifkin, and established a personal relationship with Danny so cordial that he later gave Rifkin the keys to his New York apartment.

At length, Adler and Phillips flew up to meet with the San Francisco bands at the Fairmont Hotel. The festival had a number of groups signed, but they were all from Los Angeles, and hardly cutting-edge. They needed San Francisco. The San Franciscans were simultaneously skeptical and naive. They wanted to know where any expected profit would go, and Adler was vague. They wanted to know who would end up owning the film, and Adler was vague. Fair questions. But they also ingenuously wanted to know why it couldn't be a free show and why the musicians were being flown in first-class. Rifkin asked, "Are you gonna let the people on the fairgrounds, Lou? What do you mean, for a buck? Music should be for everyone, Lou; those prices are ridiculous. These bands are all rich, why do you have to pay expenses?"

Adler would later say that it was only the calming influence of Ralph Gleason and Bill Graham that kept him from walking out, especially when Rifkin floated the notion of a free antifestival, to be held a few miles up the road at Fort Ord. Aside from the improbability of an army commandant welcoming a full-on hippie festival, the idea lost all momentum when Rifkin and Emmett went to check out Fort Ord as a campsite and Emmett developed an allergic reaction to military police and fenced-in compounds. Rock braced his former employer, the local state representative Fred Farr, and the hippies were able to get the use of the Monterey Peninsula College football field for camping and a free stage. With that, most of the hippie bands threw in the towel and agreed to play. The movie was the one place where the San Francisco bands drew the line. Correctly apprehending that the film would be the final prize to the whole event, the Dead, Quicksilver, and Big Brother united in refusing to sign performance releases. They would play for Adler's pop festival, but giving Adler control over their image on film was too much. The Jefferson Airplane, influenced by their manager, who was now Bill Graham, didn't seem to care.

In between jousting with the San Francisco bands and negotiating with the city of Monterey, John Phillips decided to write a song that would promote the festival and put out the message "to come in peace and stay cool." Phillips couldn't miss. In half an hour he had a tune and gave it to his old friend Scott McKenzie, who then recorded "San Francisco (Be Sure to Wear Some Flowers in Your Hair)." Released the last week of May, it was an instant hit. The song and Derek Taylor's efforts combined to give the Monterey Pop Festival a fabulous velocity as opening day, Friday, June 16, approached. "1,100 people who said they were media," wrote Taylor, "and we allowed them all in, all . . . the best-covered pop event in history—and for the first time the straight press had to realize that there was another sort of press . . . Every plane skimming low over the Pacific, bright with fresh cargoes of acid heads and amps and coats of many colors." Bear whipped up a special batch called Monterey Purple, and assumed a visible and respected presence backstage. There were nicely decorated booths selling beads, bells, flowers, underground papers, and so forth in the fairgrounds. One hundred thousand orchids were flown in from Hawaii, and every attendee got a flower. Tickets were relatively expensive, ranging from three to six dollars, but the number of people without tickets was manageable, and loudspeakers outside the seating area helped. The hippies slept at the college football field, were fed by the Diggers, saw some free music, and stayed peaceful. The police ignored the smell of pot and stayed relaxed, and for three days it really was a living "Sgt. Pepper summer of love." The face of American music was about to change.

On Friday night 7,500 people filled the seating area, with Goddard Lieberson and Clive Davis of Columbia, Mo Ostin of Warner Bros., Jerry Wexler of Atlantic, and Jerry Moss of A&M in the dress circle, along with celebrities like Candice Bergen. Backstage, Brian Jones of the Rolling Stones mingled with the performers, and rumors of the imminent arrival of the Beatles swirled everywhere. The slick pop-folk group the Association kicked off the festival with its tune "Enter the Young," followed by the Paupers, a Canadian band brought in by Dylan's manager, Albert Grossman, then Lou Rawls. Johnny Rivers, a Lou Adler act backed by the house band that included Jimmy Webb and Hal Blaine, the king of the L.A. studio session drummers, came next, followed by Eric Burdon, with Jerry Abrams's Head Lights splashing visuals behind him. Simon and Garfunkel closed the show. If the festival had ended after one day, no one would have ever remembered it.

The Dead had played on Friday in Los Angeles, where Phil's bass was stolen. They flew up Saturday morning and enjoyed meeting Ravi Shankar at the airport, then scattered around the fairgrounds to pass the day before their performance on Sunday night. Weir found himself in the

Guild Guitars tent on the concourse. Paul Simon was there, and some black guy. There weren't many amps, so Weir and the black guy plugged into the same Standell amp, while Simon strummed on his acoustic. "You won't be able to hear me," said Paul, "but you'll be able to feel the vibrations." They began to jam on a Miles Davis riff, and Weir proceeded to feed back his guitar, and then the black guy joined him. "We're both right up on the amp, crawling on it like a couple of monkeys, having our way with the amplifier, both of us, and we got close." It was that sort of day. The police were covered in flowers, and by afternoon, Chief Marinello sent most of them home, especially when Chet Helms and Danny Rifkin defused the last potential glitch by giving the Hell's Angels free tickets—to Ravi Shankar, on Sunday.

Onstage, the music began to heat up, first with Canned Heat, then with Big Brother and the Holding Company. With "Down on Me," "Combination of the Two," and "Ball and Chain," Janis ripped glory out of her tortured larynx, and the audience stood screaming in disbelief as chills slithered up 7,500 spines. Every showbiz cliché of ecstatic success she or the band could ever have dreamed cascaded down on them like the flowers. And when their music was done, the mental cash registers went *ka-ching,* and Albert Grossman, even then looking to sign Big Brother, suggested to Janis that she really should be in the movie. Big Brother's manager, ex-Prankster Julius Karpen, had held out for creative control, but Janis wanted her triumph Now. As the arguments raged, the music continued. Country Joe and the Fish, the Butterfield Blues Band, Quicksilver Messenger Service, Steve Miller, and the first public performance of the Electric Flag, with Harvey Brooks, Buddy Miles, Nick Gravenites, and Michael Bloomfield, completed the afternoon. It was a gooood afternoon.

But magic happens in the dark. As the sun set, a Head Lights light show flickered behind the entire night's program. Moby Grape opened, then Hugh Masekela in a too-long set, the Byrds in one of their last performances, featuring David Crosby rambling about JFK's assassination, Laura Nyro, who exited crying, and then the Jefferson Airplane, at the top of its game. "Somebody to Love" was just leaving the Top Ten, "White Rabbit" was climbing, and they whipped the crowd. The night came to a thundering climax with Otis Redding, Booker T. and the MGs, and the Bar-Kays, in a set as triumphant as Big Brother's. It was a fabulous night, and afterward, some musicians went over to the Peninsula College football field and played on, most notably Eric Burdon. Oddly, the Dead did not join them.

Sunday afternoon was reserved for Ravi Shankar, and he entranced the entire fairgrounds with his perfection. Though he did not approve of LSD, the audience certainly found Indian music suitable to trip to. Sunday evening opened calmly with the Blues Project, then Big Brother. Janis had gotten her way with the band, and they had overruled Julius; they would be filmed. Buffalo Springfield, without Neil Young but with David Crosby, followed. Backstage, the Dead stood around, not particularly familiar with the band they would follow, the Who, or the band that would follow them, the Jimi Hendrix Experience. Weir knew Hendrix could play, because he was the black guy he'd jammed with at the Guild tent the day before. Otherwise, they were blissfully ignorant. The Who's Pete Townshend had followed Hendrix before, and he didn't care to repeat the experience, so John Phillips flipped a coin, and the Who went on first. It was only the Who's second American performance, and while they'd had success in England, they hadn't really hit in the United States. Though they were closely identified with the mods, an English youth social group that was central to Swinging London, they'd come through much the same material as the Dead, blues like "Big Boss Man" and "Smokestack Lightning." In personality and performance, they were miles apart. Sometime before, they'd been playing in a low-ceilinged room when Townshend took one of his trademark leaps and broke his guitar neck against the ceiling. It became part of the act.

At Monterey they followed a strong but poorly received set with high theater. As smoke bombs went off, Townshend rubbed his guitar against the mike stand, then smashed it repeatedly until he stabbed the amp with the neck. Keith Moon kicked over his bass drum, sound techs ran to rescue microphones, and the audience went crazy. Standing at the side of the stage with Florence, Lesh muttered, "We have to follow this?" Kreutzmann threw up and became convinced his hand was frozen. In the melee, Weir grabbed the neck of Pete's guitar, briefly thinking to give it to Sue Swanson, then gave it up to a member of the Who's crew. Garcia thought the choreography of the destruction was beautiful, but he knew that following it was going to be hell.

"You know what foldin' chairs are for," drawled Weir as they hit the stage. "They're for folding up and dancin' on." It was a good opening line, and deeper than the usual showbiz work-the-crowd throwaway. It revealed a fundamentally different philosophy of performance. The Dead really *were* a dance band, and "felt that we weren't there to put on a show," as Weir said later. "We were there to play, and the people were there to put on the show." Following the Who's destructo-derby with good but unatheatrical music was almost impossible. They were also trying to follow an epic moment with several handicaps. Because of the theft, Phil was playing on a backup instrument, and since it was a festival situation, they had no time to warm up together onstage. With the cameras pointing down to the floor, the Dead opened with "Viola Lee Blues," and people began to dance, first on the stage, then out in the audience. Adler personally moved to clear the dancers from the stage, while ushers did the same out in the house. It was exactly the sort of thing the Dead didn't like, and there was more. Imaginary Beatle sightings had been floating around the fairgrounds since Friday, and now kids on the concourse were trying to sneak in, both to see stars and to hear the music. Adler sent out Peter Tork, one of the Monkees, a faux television band that lip-synched rather good pop material, to talk to the audience at a moment between songs. "People," Tork said, "this is me again. I hate to cut things down like this, but, uh, there's a crowd of kids . . . um, these kids are like crowding over the walls and trying to break down doors and everything, thinking the Beatles are here."

Phil Lesh was full up with the situation. Tork was annoying, but the audience was more his concern. "This is the last concert," Lesh barked. "Why not let them in anyway?" The audience clearly sided with Lesh, and Tork limped away. The doors opened, kids filled the back of the space, and the Dead played a set that contained what at least one critic would declare the best guitar playing of the weekend. As though anyone would ever remember it.

Introduced by Brian Jones, the Jimi Hendrix Experience presented itself to America with a colossal bang. "Killing Floor," "Foxy Lady," "Like a Rolling Stone," "Hey Joe," and what Jimi called "the English and American combined anthem," "Wild Thing," ripped through the audience. The Experience's first album, just then arriving in the stores, was superb, and Jimi's showmanship was unbelievable. All his years of backing up Little Richard and the Isley Brothers paid off; he combined unique guitar playing with moves and style that were simply awesome, and then came his finale: "I just want to grab you, man, and just ummm kiss you, but dig, I just can't do that . . . so what I want to do, I'm going to sacrifice something right here that I really love . . . don't get mad, don't get mad, no." And with the help of a little lighter fluid, he set his guitar on fire. In a wonderfully superfluous anticlimax, the Mamas and the Papas, who hadn't performed in three months, came onstage to close the night and the festival.

After all the machinations over film rights, ABC-TV took one look at the Jimi Hendrix footage and lost interest, suddenly realizing it was a family network. Pennebaker's movie would become a staple on the art-house circuit, and over the years, as half owner, he would profit. Although they violated their promises and Pennebaker did shoot the Grateful Dead for a minute or two, Lou Adler was never able to get the Dead to approve their footage. When he went back to the town of Monterey the next year for permits, he was denied, and he dropped the application.

The Dead would depart Monterey with a considerable stack of pur-loined amps and speakers and bring them to San Francisco, where they used them as part of the sound system at a summer solstice celebration in Golden Gate Park on June 21. The members of Mad River, a band from Antioch College that had recently moved to Berkeley, got to the park that day and were flabbergasted when Rock offered them some first-rate equipment. Unused to such quality, they got so excited and played so loudly that they drowned out Big Brother, playing at the same time across the way. A few days later Julius went by 710 and convinced Rock and Danny that it would be bad karma to keep the gear, which they were stashing at the Diggers' Free Store. After Emmett Grogan wrote a suit-ably obnoxious letter to Adler telling him that the hippies had taken his equipment and would return it if he would come "and wear some flowers in your hair," Danny and Grogan returned it to the music store in Mon-terey where it had been rented, minus one amp, which had disappeared in the process.

But Monterey would be memorable for much more than a movie. "Promoters, hustlers, narks, con men," wrote Hunter Thompson, "all sell-ing the New Scene to *Time* magazine and the Elks Club. The handlers get rich while the animals either get busted or screwed." The prize at Monterey was Big Brother, and Albert Grossman grabbed the brass ring, convincing the band to dump Julius and hire him. The other big winner at Monterey was Clive Davis, who went for social reasons and discovered his future. Soon he would sign Big Brother, and later other bands that would become essential to his career as the most successful recording industry executive of his era.

Three weeks later *Time* put hippies on its cover, which was created by the artists of the Group Image collective. The issue quoted the theologian Bishop Pike, who thought that hippies evoked the early Christians, and identified Thoreau, Jesus Christ, Buddha, St. Francis, Gandhi, Huxley, and hobbits as hippie heroes. One of the more interesting aspects of the piece was its coverage of Lou Gottlieb's Morningstar Ranch, an open commune in Sonoma County, north of San Francisco, which was essen-tially based on the Digger principles of "1. Open Earth 2. Open Air 3.

Open Fire 4. Open Water: . . . Exclusive ownership of land is Original Sin." Like the Haight, it was soon overflowing with bodies, but meantime, people there grew food for the people back in town. The *Time* article also had a picture of the Dead. Awash in a media sea, they had by now concluded that talking to reporters was pretty much a hopeless waste of time. That summer, when future *Washington Post* columnist Nicholas von Hoffman visited, Garcia and Bobby Petersen made a point of bullshitting him. On a visit to Vancouver that month they gave their names to the local newspaper as "Pigpen, Captain Trips, Kid Decibel, Reddy Kilowatt, and Captain Credit."

On July 24 *The Love-Ins,* starring James MacArthur and Susan Oliver, opened at theaters across the country. Said Sam Katzman, the producer, "We start off sympathetic with them, making it look glamorous. Then we prove how wrong it is, we expose it." Outside the world of pop culture, it was racially and politically another "long hot summer." Newark, New Jersey, went up in flames in July, leaving twenty-six dead and one thousand arrested, followed by Detroit, where forty-three died as order was imposed by 8,000 National Guardsmen and 4,700 U.S. Army paratroopers. John Coltrane, the band's musical hero, died on July 17.

Life at 710 was sufficiently hectic that horrible summer of love that the band at least briefly decided to move to New Mexico. Sue Swanson, Kreutzmann's new lady friend, Susila, M.G., and Vee went as scouts. Since their van was stocked with a coffee can full of hash and Acapulco Gold, they enjoyed their trip. They camped near the Four Corners and even found a lovely place near Taos, but were unable to pin down a lease. They also found themselves running out of money and were forced to wire home for more. At some point Vee grew suspicious when the band didn't seem all that thrilled with what the scouts had found, and concluded that they "had just wanted us out of the house." They returned home in time to join the band on a special jaunt.

Bill Graham had decided to take "the San Francisco Scene"—the Airplane, the Dead, and Head Lights—to the O'Keefe Centre in Toronto for a week. The O'Keefe Centre was Toronto's Carnegie Hall, a high-end room built for classical music that was not ready for dancing, an issue that would consume a lot of energy for the Dead and other bands over the next few years. After the show on opening night, Graham had the bands play again as a gift for the O'Keefe's employees. It established a good relationship, and after that it was only the newspaper writers who had any problem. To the *Globe and Mail* the Dead were "simian." "Not volume, not intensity, but noise . . . like a jet taking off in your inner ear, while the mad scientist was perversely scraping your nerves to shreds." Most of the other reviews focused on the hit-making Airplane, which was perhaps just as well. For Garcia, they were terrible shows in which everyone played badly, there was a buzz in the sound system that was louder than the music, the band was in complete turmoil, and he was ready to fire Weir for his insensate playing.

Life in the other band may have been worse. By now at least comparatively wealthy from *Surrealistic Pillow*, the Airplane was doing its best to experience every problem of success, rock star category, by (a) lavishing money on their latest recording project, *After Bathing at Baxter's*, and (b) spending the rest of their energy on internal bickering. Jack and Jorma picked on Marty's show business pretensions, the lovers Grace and Spencer squared off against the world, and Paul managed somehow to dominate everyone from the middle.

Their Toronto hotel, the Royal York, was pleasant enough. The two bands took over one entire floor, and madras bedspreads, candles, incense, and Persian carpets made things more homey. Almost everyone on the trip would recall the hotel's specialty, hot apple pie with apricot brandy sauce. Jerry and M.G. and Jorma and his wife, Margaretta, took a side trip to Niagara Falls together, but, Jorma said, "it was just classic. Each couple fought the entire way." There was another regret to the week. Out in the audience one night was a woman to whom the Dead would owe much over the years, the author of "Morning Dew," Bonnie Dobson. She was too shy to come backstage, and the band never knew of her visit.

After their last night in Toronto, the two bands climbed into a bus for a ride to Montreal, where they would play two more shows. Jack Casady had rigged speakers in the back, M.G.'s golden-haired daughter, Sunshine, crawled up and down the aisle, and the bus was blue with pot smoke, so that even Bill Graham developed a contact high. In Montreal they played a free show downtown on a postage-stamp-size stage in front of what the *Montreal Gazette* said was "25,000 hippies, teenyboppers, adults and squares [for] Montreal's first large-scale love-in." Then they played another free show, at the Youth Pavilion on the Expo '67 site. It was a futuristic setting, with a monorail snaking through a geodesic dome, and it was perhaps a little intimidating. Everyone except Weir and Pig dropped acid, and as the Airplane's road manager, Bill Thompson, recalled it, Rock and Danny vanished, and he worked for both bands that day. Unfortunately, the Expo police got nervous. As the audience began to dance, the cops lined up in front of the stage, arms locked, putting off the band no end. From the back of the stage Graham was hyperactively telling them to "stop playing so exciting," exactly the wrong thing to say. "That's what we're here for," thought Garcia. "That's what the crowd is here for, nobody's gonna get hurt, it was all little girls anyway." It was a most unsatisfactory day.

The Dead were not without a sense of drama. When they got downtown after the Expo show, they twisted Graham's tail by abruptly announcing that they were getting off the bus. No one would later recall what the alternative was, but members of the Airplane plaintively inquired, "Are you sure you don't want to come with us?" The Dead didn't have a gig for another ten days, had very little money, and were in a foreign country. They did have a couple of aces in the hole. One was their favorite scammer, Ron Rakow. The year before, when they'd separated from Owsley, Rakow had lent them some money, knowing he'd never get it back, which would make him, he thought, "a patron, entitled to respect." He'd become involved with an investment called Circlephonics, a revolutionary new loudspeaker design, and raised around $40,000 from investors. Nothing came of it, recalled his lady friend, Lydia. In Montreal, however, Rakow was running around with another woman friend, and she was the other ace in the hole. Her name was Peggy Hitchcock, and with her help they rented a couple of cars, loaded up, and drove to her estate, Millbrook, which was certainly a nice hideout, although it seemed to Rifkin, at least, that the residents generally saw the Dead as invading barbarians, there to "smoke their dope and fuck their women."

Soon enough, the band was off to New York, for the first of a series of odd and interesting gigs. On August 10 they played on the roof of the Chelsea Hotel for the Diggers' Trip Without a Ticket, a party Grogan had arranged in an effort to hustle some funds from avant-garde New Yorkers like their hostess, Shirley Clark, the director of the play *The Connection,* and Andy Warhol, who was one of the guests. From Manhattan the Dead headed west, and after a couple of paying gigs played free at West Park, in Ann Arbor, as part of Warner Bros.' promotion of the album. It was just a month after the Detroit riots, so their timing was distinctly problematic, particularly when someone used an American flag to wipe the stage dry. More appropriately, Garcia and Rock Scully went off to hang out and inhale nitrous oxide with John Sinclair, a poet, jazz critic, marijuana activist, and sponsor of Detroit's MC [Motor City] 5.

It should have been nice to get home, but it wasn't. The Haight's atmosphere was poisoned. The main local headlines concerned an acid dealer named John Kent Carter, whose body had been found minus an arm, presumably because that arm had been handcuffed to a briefcase full of cash or merchandise. The Dead were to play on August 20 at a gathering on beautiful, holy Mount Tamalpais, but when they got to the mountaintop, they discovered that there was no power, and the event turned into what Rifkin would call "a bongofest." On August 22 the band members were unanimously embarrassed by their first nationwide TV appearance, on ABC's *The Hippie Temptation*. As Harry Reasoner sanctimoniously intoned, "at their best they are trying for a kind of group sainthood . . . saints running in groups are likely to be ludicrous," Garcia reminded himself—again!, and not for the last time—of the futility of talking to the press. A few days later they learned that their good friend Chocolate George had died in a car accident.

In a one-night repeat of the Toronto run, Graham took the Airplane and Dead to the Hollywood Bowl in mid-September. Garcia would have better memories of the Bowl than Toronto, however. Over Labor Day, they'd gone up to Rio Nido, a small resort town north of San Francisco in the redwoods on the Russian River, for a couple of gigs. One night they played a blistering thirty-one-minute "Midnight Hour" that even the critical Phil Lesh would treasure many years later. And in the afternoons, they'd begun working on a new, as-yet-untitled song. Since their mood was always based on the last show, there was still hope.

17

Interlude: The Crew

 magine an extreme in male bonding, on the order of the front four of an NFL defense, or perhaps some elite military unit. In the world of the Grateful Dead, it is the crew, one of the most remarkable elements in the band's saga. The history of rock will record that Dead crew chief Lawrence "Ram Rod" Shurtliff was undoubtedly the longest-term employee of any group ever, and many of his companions stayed nearly as long. Their bond was sufficient that when Mickey Hart fired Steve Parish as his drum roadie, Ram Rod—for the good of the crew as a whole— swapped his longtime role as Jerry Garcia's guitar roadie with Steve and went to work for the far more demanding Hart. The record will also show that the Dead's crew was undoubtedly the only road crew ever to have its own charter plane, a Learjet. The crew had better pay, better working conditions, and more influence on the band's decisions—their dislike for the demands of crossing borders had much to do with the rarity of Dead visits to Canada or Europe—than any employees of any music group ever. They were not employees, really, but de facto band members. Jerry Garcia's role as the leader who wouldn't lead extended maximally to the people who helped his band to play. Without them, no stage, and therefore no

music. This was a two-pronged responsibility: not only did the crew set up the stage and hand it over to the band members so that they could play, but during performances, it devolved upon them, like it or not, to maintain order on the stage. This made for the occasional rub.

The Dead's stage was not a conventional performance space. It was their living room. They did not trot out onstage with a show; they made music that defined their lives and shared it with friends. So the stage was not separate from everyday life; it was where they lived. Which was why the playing area had no theatrical decorations, and why dozens of people—friends, family, women friends for the night or a lifetime—had access to the stage during a performance. This made for complications. As sound crew member Dennis "Wizard" Leonard once remarked, "The stage is a very fragile bubble. Music reflects consciousness, and the crew was responsible for protecting that bubble, and that consciousness." It was a profound responsibility, and they took it quite seriously. There really was an occasion in which a young woman stumbled, kicked out a plug, and plunged one entire side of the stage into darkness. Another time, a completely crazed young man leaped onstage from an overhanging balcony, shouting, "Fuck me, Garcia, fuck me." Handicapped by their unwillingness to hit him, it took three roadies twenty minutes to wrestle him off the stage, although no one in front of the stage ever saw the struggle. One night early in Steve Parish's career, a naked man leaped onstage, fell on a power box, and crushed a connection, rendering it useless. At six foot five and 250-plus pounds, Parish was a most imposing figure and was able to hustle him off so quickly that Garcia never saw the man. He looked up and yelled, "What happened to all my stuff?" Parish said, "This naked guy just came running up—" "*What* naked guy?" Parish smiled. "[Jerry] thought we were nuts."

The Grateful Dead scene was a horizontal, not vertical, hierarchy, with the band at the center. The crew was the next layer out. More than a million people occupied the succeeding layers, and the social pressure they generated led to what could at times be a very difficult attitude. As Joe Winslow was warned when he joined the crew, "Everyone is gonna be your fuckin' friend." There hadn't been any "idols" in his hometown of Pendleton, Oregon, and he realized later the crew role left him with a considerably swelled head for a good while. In the interim, the combination of male bonding and road stress was a killer. "The road turns you into gristle," he said. "If you're looking for comfort," Garcia told an interviewer, "join a club or something. The Grateful Dead is not where you're going to find comfort. In fact, if anything, you'll catch a lot of shit. And if you don't get it from the band, you'll get it from the roadies. They're merciless. They'll just gnaw you like a dog. They'll tear your flesh off. They can be extremely painful." Aside from verbal abuse, the crew fraternity practiced hazing as an art form, of which the sine qua non was being seized and held down by two or three members and then being mummified in gaffer's tape. The skilled application of the hotfoot made it inadvisable to fall asleep around them. Heaven help the visitor who got to the stage on a day when Parish and his brother-in-crewness Kidd Candelario were particularly bored. The destruction of one's shirt was a minimum price.

Though they were not infrequently sexist and/or difficult, the woman they worked with for twenty years, lighting designer Candace Brightman, took a benign, if qualified, view of them as coworkers. "I didn't have trouble because I forgot that I was a woman . . . You see, I liked playing that game. I was always ready for a little [metaphorical] fisticuffs." Going on to describe a passing quarrel with Dan Healy, she remarked that she was "elated" when the gauntlet was flung down. "I don't have any normal fear for those people [guys who think women can't work]. One time Steve banged my head into the drum kit a number of times, and I ruined it by breaking out laughing. I love a certain amount of lighthearted physical violence. I know this sounds a little sick, but . . . you had to be kind of thick-skinned around my house, growing up."

The band's unwillingness to be authority figures had consequences. "[The crew] became so powerful," said Mickey Hart, "and we just said whatever. That was one of our big downfalls, not taking a stand with the crew. They didn't want to work, and we said, okay, whatever. It was one of the stupidest things we've ever done, letting the crew run the show . . . Rifkin and Ram Rod were the great spirit of the Grateful Dead, the real souls, but some of the other guys had other agendas, partying animals . . . We let it go down. It was our cross to bear. We spotted it. We thought it was endearing and cute, letting the quippies run the show. That's what I thought. What an odd thing. Everything else is so odd, why shouldn't this be odd? Maybe they're protecting us from some evil . . . I liked all of them. I got along with Heard. Even Candelario, before he turned into a monster . . . Me me me. He wouldn't step outside of his area code to help. I noticed that once. Something happened on the stage, and he stood there." The tolerance of the band could be abused, as when a crew member insisted that caterers bring him a thousand-dollar bottle of brandy to take home, and another crew member demanded an equally expensive gift, which turned out to be a fishing rod. But in the end, if there was a truly legitimate criticism to put to the crew, it was their treatment of each other, which was as testosterone-driven as everything else, and especially of production manager Robbie Taylor, who bore the brunt of being the efficient, meticulous front man who had to deliver the stage to the band while placating periodically foul-tempered coworkers.

The crew generally showed another, more noble face. In 1982 the prime minister of Jamaica arrived to address the crowd at the World Music Festival, and the captain of his bodyguards ordered the stage cleared. The Uzis his men carried were very shiny, but the captain was informed by the Dead's crew that when their equipment was on the stage, they did not leave. The prime minister spoke with the Dead's crew behind him.

There were always grumbles from people who thought they should be onstage and weren't, a completely futile exercise when one remembers that Garcia once chuckled that Parish had ordered Jerry's own brother, Tiff, offstage. But in later years there was only one real challenge to the crew's primacy, and their reaction to it was brilliant. Various members of the crew, primarily Parish, made a habit of reading over the guest list for tickets and passes and occasionally amending it, removing people's names from the backstage-pass column, and sometimes, if the person had annoyed them, entirely from the list. Their premise was that these people were generally guests of office staff who were not present to supervise them. One person was brave enough to protest, and that was Eileen Law, the angel and guardian of the Dead Heads. One too many of her guests had not received their promised tickets, much less backstage passes, and she raised the point at a company meeting. A thin-skinned bunch, the crew was mightily offended at being challenged, and at the next concert, they brilliantly confused the issue by quitting *all* their security functions. Though Law's objections had focused solely on the guest list, the crew members abdicated their essential stage-guarding functions, in fact inviting backstage passersby onstage to watch the show. When a complete stranger wandered so far out on the playing area that she blocked Phil Lesh's sight line of Harry Popick, the monitor mixer, Lesh grew enraged, berating Parish and gripping Steve's massive arm with his bass-playing fingers of steel hard enough to leave five vividly distinct bruises. The stage was cleared of strangers, and no one ever felt like messing with the crew again on the subject.

The crew developed an extraordinary tradition. It began with Laird Grant, Garcia's junior high school friend and their first roadie. "For sure he could fix the snakes of wirings at the acid tests, with a gas hose in his mouth and a chick humping on his left leg," wrote one observer, and the elements of functioning in the middle of sex, drugs, and rock and roll never changed. Laird quit in 1967, and five months later Ram Rod became the rock of the band for its career. Quiet, ethical, the soul of decency, he was always the One. Rex Jackson came the next year, a brashly confident man who had a certain glow about him. He had "a drive to express some spark," thought Joe Winslow, but was "frustrated in how to do it." A little larger than life, Rex was, as one band member noticed, better-looking than anyone in the band, and his eventual loss was a grievous one. The crew member who would be most visible and last the longest, after Ram Rod, was Steve Parish, a New Yorker who met the band in 1969, and eventually came to define the crew to many. "We knew we were a vanguard," he said. The band and crew were so close that a number of times, after long periods of sleep deprivation on the road, they would finally get to a hotel and a decent quantity of sleep and find, comparing notes the next day, that their dreams were remarkably similar.

As Parish also put it, "We're part of the Dead. You really put your whole heart into the system, right from the vibration of a guitar string out to the back of the hall." Larger than life both literally and metaphorically, Parish is loud, theatrical, demonstrative, and utterly committed to the band. A splendid example of that took place on December 27, 1989, when the Oakland branch of the International Alliance of Theatrical and Stage Employees, commonly called the IA (and also known as IATSE), contemplated a strike against Bill Graham Presents (BGP), to be carried out on the first night of a Dead new year's run at Oakland Coliseum. The Dead's crew were also IA members, both because it smoothed their relations with stagehands across the country and because they anticipated needing such credentials whenever the band got around to retiring. The Oakland branch of the IA had not had a contract with Bill Graham Presents for eighteen months, and they had finally decided to strike BGP because they thought the Dead's crew would back them. Certainly, they knew that BGP would gladly have sacrificed any given show to crush the union, even though the Oakland hands were getting five dollars an hour less than the San Francisco local.

By early afternoon of the twenty-seventh, the first show of the run, negotiations were at a stalemate, and the Dead's staff walked out of the building. Truck driver Mike Fischer was ordered to move the truck off the ramp and into the parking lot, which he proceeded to do with Bill Graham pleading/screaming at him to stop. Bill could tolerate much in life, but not losing a Grateful Dead New Year's run. His argument to the band that he was saving them money was useless; the band never minded paying good wages for good work. At this point Parish went to Graham and told him that he was betraying the Dead and its audience, and he had to negotiate. Calls to band members and manager Danny Rifkin indicated their support. Graham was not quite good enough a poker player to wait out the Dead's bluff, if bluff it was, and he folded. The final twist came when the IA members refused to trust Graham without a signed contract. By then it was 3 P.M., two hours late for load-in, and for the second time, Parish went crazy-as-a-fox berserk. Fischer brought the truck back, and Steve began to unload it by himself. Twenty-one IA stagehands looked at each other, shrugged, and went back to work.

Joe, Jerome John, and Ruth "Bobbie" Garcia,
San Francisco, 1942.

Wendy, Bob, and John Weir at
home in Atherton, 1956.

Mickey Hart, graduation from
air force basic training, 1961.

Jerry Garcia's music-teaching job
portrait, Dana Morgan studio, 1962.

Jerry Garcia and Robert Hunter in
bluegrass days, 1962.

The Warlocks at the In Room, October 1965.

The Warlocks/Grateful Dead, Fort Point, San Francisco, November 1965.

Pranksters at an acid test.

Trips Festival setup, Longshoremen's Hall, San Francisco, January 1966.

Neal Cassady at Olompali, June 1966.

Tangerine, Rock Scully, Girl Freiberg, and George Hunter at Olompali, June 1966.

In front of 710A Ashbury Street, fall 1966. Back row: Pigpen, Jerry Garcia, Phil Lesh, Florence Nathan, Laird Grant, Bill Kreutzmann. Front row: Rock Scully, Tangerine, Danny Rifkin, Bob Weir.

The Diggers at City Hall, fall 1966. Sculptor La Mortadella, Emmett Grogan, Slim Minnaux, Peter Berg, and Butcher Brooks.

Pigpen at the Be-In, Golden
Gate Park, January 1967.

The children's pilgrimage arrives on
Haight Street, spring 1967.

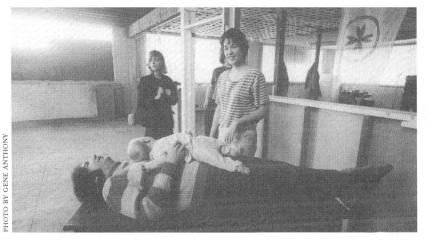

Jerry Garcia, Sunshine Kesey, and Carolyn "M.G." Adams, at a rehearsal break,
spring 1967.

First visit to New York, June 1967. Phil Lesh and Bob Weir at the Cafe au Go Go in Greenwich Village.

Jerry Garcia, Phil Lesh, and Ralph Gleason backstage at the Monterey Pop Festival.

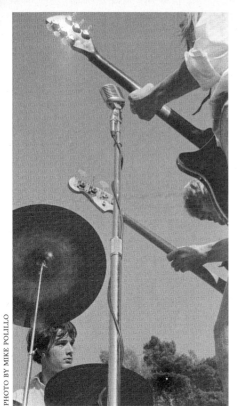

Bill Kreutzmann, Golden Gate Park,
June 21,1967.

Jerry Garcia, Golden Gate Park,
June 21,1967.

The Grateful Dead as mutants, Daly City, 1967.

Jim Marshall *Teen Set* magazine band photo, San Francisco, Fall 1967.

After the bust of 710 Ashbury Street, the culprits at the Hall of Justice, October 2, 1967: Bob Weir, Bob Matthews, Rock Scully, Sue Swanson, Pigpen, Veronica Grant, Toni Kaufman, Danny Rifkin.

Dead on Haight Street, March 3, 1968;
a man going to work.

Early 1968 Dead; just foolin' around.

Phil Lesh, Bill Kreutzmann, and Jerry Garcia, well and truly on Haight Street.

Dead at Columbia University during student strike, May 4, 1968.

Jerry Garcia playing live in Central Park, June 1968.

Pigpen as cowboy, part of life at
Mickey Hart's ranch, 1969.

Mickey on Snorty converses with manager Lenny Hart.

Jerry Garcia and Owsley "Bear" Stanley, on the road, 1969.

Home away from home: the Dead at the Fillmore East, January 2, 1970.

Pigpen sings, with Bill Graham as bonus percussionist, Fillmore East.

Jerry Garcia plays pedal steel,
December 1970.

The Grateful Dead with the New Riders. David Nelson, Jerry Garcia, Pigpen, Bob Weir,
David Torbert (hiding behind Weir), Mickey Hart, John Dawson (behind Phil Lesh),
Phil Lesh, Bill Kreutzmann, at Mickey Hart's barn late 1970.

18

Dark
Anthem

(9/16/67–12/31/67)

One day at dawn in August 1967, Robert Hunter set out hitchhiking from near Taos, heading home to San Francisco. Thin and worn, he looked not unlike Don Quixote. He was not in the best of shape, having come to New Mexico some weeks before to get away from the methedrine he was ingesting too much of back in Palo Alto. Like Sherlock Holmes, he craved mental stimulation, and speed led him to poetry that would endure. Unfortunately, the physical consequences of speed had left him with a bad case of hepatitis and the nickname "Yellow Angel." His monthlong sojourn in Santa Fe had sorted out his problem with methedrine, but it was not otherwise serene. There were various disasters involving housing, the breakup of a long-term relationship with his lover, Judy, and an excess of drinking to ease the methedrine withdrawal. In his own words, he was a "lost puppy" after the breakup with Judy, but an hour after their final denouement, his friend Carl Moore showed up and took him to Carl's place in San Cristobal, on the road to Taos.

He stayed there a week, and during that time he heard from Garcia, who informed him that the band was working with his lyrics on a song called "Alligator" and that he should join them. One night in San Cristobal he took LSD, and in the morning set out for San Francisco with twenty dollars in his pocket and a brain full of what he later realized were the fumes of borderline lunacy. It would take him several weeks to get home. Wobbling through a phantasmic mindscape, it would seem to him that he lived the entirety of Kerouac's *On the Road* during the journey. He began by wearing a hole in his boots while walking in the wrong direction across the Rio Grande. He tried to sleep under a train trestle one night but was routed by a blizzard of mosquitoes. Still pointed in the wrong direction, he caught a ride in a truck hauling carnival equipment to Denver, Neal Cassady's old hometown, where he wandered for days in a purgatory of confusion. One morning he saw the Dead's first album in a supermarket cutout rack, which reminded him that he was supposed to be going to San Francisco. He set out once again, and by Nevada he was down to his last dime, which he naturally put in a slot machine, winning enough to call the band and let them know he was coming.

On his arrival in San Francisco, Phil picked him up and took him to Rio Nido on the Russian River, where they had a weekend's worth of gigs at the Dance Hall, a funky shack hanging over the water that held perhaps two hundred people. That afternoon, Hunter sat recovering from the road on the lawn outside the little joint, and listened to them rehearse a new song. Garcia had come up with the first lick, which was a modal development of a simple figure with a line against it. It was a song made to go anywhere. It came from nowhere and from many places, from several psyches, from the larger collective unconscious. Hunter understood instantly, and began to scribble lyrics. He had only been working with poetry for a year, having been inspired by Lew Welch, a young Beat poet who was part of Gary Snyder's circle, but he had always been what he called "the most lucid hallucinator in the group," and now his practice bore fruit. In addition to "Alligator," he had sent them some other work, including one particularly abstract hallucination that began, "Look for a while at the china cat sunflower," ran through material that would appear in future songs, asked, "Ever been to see a comical collection of gears, grinding out galactical illusions of years?" and returned to the "china cat sunflower." At Rio Nido, even though he was treating a transcendental experience, he kept his language and images crystalline, even paying formal tribute to so classic a poem as T. S. Eliot's "The Love Song of J. Alfred Prufrock": "Shall we go, then, you and I." In a little while, he ran into the shack and handed Garcia the lyrics.

> *Dark star crashes*
> *pouring its light*
> *into ashes*

Reason tatters
the forces tear loose
from the axis

Searchlight casting
for faults in the
clouds of delusion

Shall we go,
you and I
while we can?
Through
the transitive nightfall
of diamonds

Jerry smiled. "Yeah, that scans, that works." Hunter felt so good that he reached up and started swinging from the rafters, giving himself a ripe splinter. As he listened to them apply his words to the music, he knew he had found his life's work. A few days later he was sitting in Golden Gate Park working on the second verse and a hippie passed by, noticed him writing, and handed him a joint with the comment "Maybe this will make things easier for you." Hunter lit it and replied, "Thanks a lot, man." He toked and added, "In case anything ever comes of it, this is called 'Dark Star.'" The Dead had found their fulcrumatic song; "Dark Star" was to be their magic carpet, a vehicle that allowed them to approach music as an unfolding dance. "Caution" had been that sort of song, but "Dark Star" was simply much better and more beautiful. The Dead had also found their voice.

After a foray to Colorado to christen the Family Dog's new branch establishment, the Denver Dog, the band returned to San Francisco to help open, at long last, the Straight Theater, on Haight Street, just three blocks from 710. The event was a hoot and a half. The young men who had worked to create the Straight Theater were not without connections, but they had faced tough opposition from the police and community business types, especially one Matthew Boxer, the executive manager of the San Francisco Council of District Merchants, who felt threatened by a third ballroom in the city. Ironically, the Diggers also opposed the Straight, claiming it would "rip off the people." "Ridiculous," said Hillel Resner, one of the organizers. "We *were* the people."

The Straight had opened in June and had put on several concerts, but couldn't get a dance permit. In September, the organizers went to the Board of Permit Appeals, where Dame Judith Anderson, among others, testified on their behalf. Even with such distinguished support, they were rejected. Then one of the theater's organizers, Luther Green, got terribly clever. The City of San Francisco did not require permits for dance *schools*. For September 29 and 30, the Straight announced, the Dead would play for dance lessons. "Learn body movement, muscle tone, physical exercises, expanded space perception—this and whatever else not listed here to happen at Straight Dance Lessons." With TV cameras and attorney Terence Hallinan in the lobby looking on, and a big blowup of the Declaration of Independence hanging on the wall behind him, Lieutenant James Ludlow of the SFPD decided to do nothing. The "registration fee" was $2.50, and "dance students" filled out membership cards at a table. The joke of the night was, "Do I get a student discount?" On the stage, an associate of Ann Halprin's named Peter Weiss began the class: "What I would like everyone to do is close your eyes and relax, and note how you breathe and how your heart is pumping." The Dead ripped into "Dancing in the Streets," and class was in session. The city briefly considered requiring all schools to get permits, until the Arthur Murray people growled, and the idea was shelved. In the end, the Straight Theater never did get a permit.

It was a busy pair of gigs. On the second night, Kreutzmann had a guest, a drummer he'd met named Mickey Hart. At intermission Bill approached his guest, who was thrilled by the cacophony, and said, "You wanna sit in?" "Sure, but I don't have any drums." They jumped into Kreutzmann's Mustang, went somewhere and rustled up a kit, and were ready for the second set. Hart took a seat next to Kreutzmann, the band went into "Alligator," and sometime later—Mickey would recall it as two hours—they finished the song, and the band included six people. They hadn't particularly realized they were one piece shy, but they were certainly smart enough to know when it had arrived. Few more concentrated lives are recorded in the annals of music.

Michael Steven Hartman, who had followed his father's lead and changed his name when he got out of the service, because "Hartman" was "too German; 'Hart' was American," was born to two drummers. His father, Lenny, had been world senior solo rudimental (marching band style) drum champion at the 1939 New York World's Fair, and Mickey's mother, Leah, had been sufficiently skilled a drummer to join with Lenny as part of their courting process to win the newly created world mixed-doubles championship there. Their son would devote his very soul to the art.

Born in Flatbush, Brooklyn, in 1943, Mickey was raised by his mother, a gown maker and bookkeeper, after his father deserted them. Leah would wait until Mickey was eleven to remarry, but none of his stepfathers would ever please him. A hyperactive child, he was bright but had great trouble focusing at school and demanded that his grandmother wait for him in the street, where he could see her. Ethel Tessel was sufficiently doting to do just that. At age ten he saw a picture of his father in a movie theater newsreel item about the 1939 world's fair, and at home he discovered his legacy, a drum pad and a pair of snakewood sticks. Leah would hide them and he'd find them, retreating to a closet to practice. When she realized he was serious, she began to give him lessons. "From the age of ten," he wrote, "all I did was drum. Obsessively. Passionately. Painfully." He did not read for pleasure, and rarely socialized. Once a year, he would go with his beloved grandparents on a two-week summer vacation. Sam Tessel was a cabbie, but he enjoyed taking mobile holidays, and they would drive around the United States, young Mickey standing between the two front seats behind the meter, seeing Yellowstone, Mount Rushmore, and other American holy places.

When he began high school, the family moved to Cedarhurst, on Long Island, and he kept drumming. After all, "Only the drum gave me the feeling of power and uniqueness that is so important to teenagers. When I had my drum, I was the prince of noise, the loudest thing in the room." That feeling would never change. He found an encouraging teacher, Arthur Jones, and eventually won the first chair in the All State Band. Leaving high school in his senior year, he joined the air force, " 'cause that's where the great drummers were." While in the service, he came across a brochure for Remo Drumheads, and in the ad was a picture of his father. Transferred to a base in Southern California, he went to see the owner of the company, Remo Belli, who observed, "I haven't seen you since you were a baby." Remo went on to tell him that Lenny Hart was now an executive of a savings and loan in the San Fernando Valley. Mickey was overjoyed at finding his father but was soon assigned to a base in Spain, whereupon Lenny vanished again. In Europe, Mickey competed at a high level in judo, drove rally races, and drummed, in small combos, a marching band, and what-have-you.

On his release from the air force, he once again found his father through Remo Belli. When they met, Lenny invited him to join in the running of a drum store, Hart Music, in San Carlos, a suburb south of

San Francisco. Soon after, Mickey experienced LSD for the first time, sitting in the store watching all the drums around him come alive. His visions inspired in him the idea of painting psychedelic designs on the heads of bass drums. Somehow, Lenny claimed the creation as his own, and there was trouble between them. Just about this time, Mickey went to see the Count Basie Orchestra at the Fillmore, and a stranger remarked to him, "See that guy? He's the drummer for the Dead. You gotta meet him." Having performed his introduction, the anonymous benefactor vanished. Billy suggested a visit to the Matrix to see Big Brother, where Mickey was fascinated when Jim Gurley wrapped his arms around his amp, squeezed it, shook it, and finally dropped it. Sonny Payne, Count Basie's drummer and Mickey's friend, had followed them over to the club, but the volume was too much for him, and he left the scene to the two young men. "Too loud" had never entered Mickey Hart's vocabulary, and he was enraptured. That night he and Kreutzmann wandered around the city in Bill's Mustang, playing on cars, garbage cans, and light posts, literally "playing the city." Billy invited him to drop by the Dead's rehearsal room, but Mickey couldn't find it. A month later Kreutzmann called again to tell him of the Straight Theater gig, and this time Mickey made it.

The first set fascinated him, not least by its loudness, and playing in the second set was heaven, like being "whipped into a jet stream," he said. Afterward he felt clean, as though he'd had a long hot shower. Once invited to join the band, Mickey went back to San Carlos and threw the store keys into the street out front, not even going in to say good-bye to Lenny. He moved into a closet at Billy and Phil's place on Belvedere Street, and the drummers began to study together. Mickey used self-hypnosis, which he'd learned from a book, as part of his regimen, and he shared this technique with Kreutzmann. "We are going to become one, to synchronize our beats. We'll be able to play fast. We're not going to become tired." They would drum with one arm around the other, each contributing one arm. They would check each other's pulse, so that they could lock into their heartbeats as a rhythm yoga. Hart was, and would remain, obsessive, intense, and verbally dominant, and this made Kreutzmann's lover, Susila, very uncomfortable. Billy pushed Mickey to make the hypnosis a parlor trick by hypnotizing Pigpen, and it worked, which convinced Susila that Hart was a Svengali, out to control Kreutzmann's mind. Mickey's motives were undoubtedly pure, but it was easy to be spooked by his driven methods. Garcia and Lesh were enthusiastic about his impact on the band, and it had been Kreutzmann's idea in the first place. Pigpen said little. Weir didn't think they needed another drummer, and wasn't sure a new guy could catch on, or whether there was room on the stage or in the music for more, but given everyone else's enthusiasm, felt "I didn't have a vote." It took him perhaps two weeks to understand his error.

Their ensuing musical ferment was briefly interrupted. There was a man who was a habitué of Kesey's scene at La Honda and a friend of the band's. He was also, it developed, a child molester, and the police threatened him with a long stay at the hospital for the criminally insane in Napa unless he rolled over and helped them make some showy marijuana arrests. Roll he did, and in the course of the afternoon of October 2, 1967, he led the police to four homes in the Haight-Ashbury. One of them was 710. He'd stopped by and asked if he could roll a joint, and made sure that Jerry and M.G., of whom he was especially fond, were on their way out. Shortly thereafter, as Weir meditated in the attic, the chief of the State Narcotics Bureau, Matthew O'Connor, state agent Jerry Van Ramm, and the head of the SFPD Narcotics Squad, Norbert "the Nark" Currie, led a detachment of police into the house while reporters and TV crews watched from the street. "That's what ya get for dealing the killer weed," snickered Van Ramm, and off to jail went nonsmokers Pigpen and Bobby, plus Bob Matthews, Rock, Danny, Sue Swanson, Florence, Vee, Toni Kaufman (the daughter of Beat poet Bob Kaufman, there to work for HALO), and Christine Bennett, by now Dan Healy's lover.

Danny arrived in the middle of the proceedings and was greeted with "Oh, so you're Rifkin." He sat on his desk and called Brian Rohan, who would almost beat the arrestees to the Hall of Justice. Florence was a little behind Danny and got halfway up the stairs when she saw Weir trying to wave her off as a stranger came toward her, but it was a bit too late. Told to sit in the kitchen, she dug a three-gram ball of hash out of her purse, threw it on some ice cream, and downed it. At the Hall of Justice, Jerry Van Ramm was dancing what the prisoners thought of as a little Hitlerite victory jig as he crowed, "I got 'em, I got 'em." The denizens of 710 were certainly not alone. It seemed that day as though half of the Haight-Ashbury was in jail. Claiming that "an investigation kept turning up the address of 710 Ashbury as a supply source," O'Connor went on to say that police had found a pound of pot and some hashish. They also confiscated Pigpen's entirely legal .32 Beretta. Bail was set at $550 each, and they were all processed out quickly, except for the minors, Christine Bennett and Sue Swanson. Florence, who kept sliding off the bench in the fingerprint room, was so stoned that she couldn't speak for four days, but was otherwise fine. After his release, Danny went to the cupboard where the stash had been, and discovered a virtually intact kilo brick (2.2 pounds) that the police had managed to overlook. Someone hadn't missed a hundred-dollar bill in the office desk, however.

The best part of the day was the quick thinking of their neighbor Marilyn Harris, who saved Jerry and M.G. from arrest. Marilyn had been confined to her bed for the previous two weeks by a bout of hepatitis, and the family at 710 had pitched in to care for her during her recovery, complete with a sign-up sheet in the kitchen to cover every chore, from meals to chamber pot. Pig would turn off her lights at the end of the day. Sitting in a chair by the window, Marilyn watched the bust go down, and kept her eyes open, realizing that there were still officers in the house even after the paddy wagon departed. When Jerry and M.G. showed up, she shouted down, "I never thought you'd get here. Bring the groceries up, I'm starving. Just do what I say!" They listened, and escaped detention.

The *Chronicle*'s coverage described the Dead's "way out 13 room pad" and mentioned the Straight Theater School of Dance gigs, which may well have had something to do with the timing of the bust. The Dead responded with a press conference on October 5. They tried to address the issue soberly, though the media could hardly accept the notion, as the release put it, that the law against the killer weed was "a lie," that hippies were "a myth," and that the bust was "annoying." "I think they're just harassing people with long hair," observed Rifkin, while serving coffee with whipped cream and homemade cookies. Because Danny had difficulties with writing, their statement was drafted by his college buddy Harry Shearer (who many years later, would be part of the comedic rock band Spinal Tap). With the other HALO attorney, Michael Stepanian, at his side, Rifkin argued that "almost anyone who has ever studied marijuana seriously and objectively has agreed that, physically and psychologically, marijuana is the least harmful chemical used for pleasure and life-enhancement . . . The president of a company that makes defective automobiles which leads to thousands of deaths . . . [gets] a minor fine . . . A person convicted for possession of marijuana can be sentenced to up to 30 years in jail . . . the law is so seriously out of touch with reality . . . The law creates a mythical danger and calls it a felony. The people who enforce the law use it almost exclusively against individuals who threaten their ideas of the way people should look and act."

"How long did it take to grow your hair that long, Danny?" came one media question.

"We've always figured," replied Danny, "that if we ever held a press conference, the first reporter who asked a stupid question would get a cream pie in his face, and you're him." The other reporters cheered, but then Rifkin's compassion took over, and they spared the lunkhead.

The police then ratcheted up the pressure. In the two weeks after the bust at 710, the police leaned on the Matrix for noise complaints, swept Haight Street for truants and arrested thirty-two, and then arrested adults at a conference on runaways at the Straight Theater because there was a nude dance. All charges were dropped a few weeks later. *San Francisco Chronicle* columnist Herb Caen spoke for many San Franciscans when he wrote, "But if [hippiedom] needed a raison d'etre . . . it has been provided, ironically, by its unbelievably foamy-mouthed critics. In the face of the hippies' implied disdain, a truly well-established society would not have lost its poise . . . in such lamentable fashion."

The rose that was the Haight-Ashbury was shriveling fast. The Psychedelic Shop closed on October 4, staying open all night to give away whatever was left on the shelves. Two days later, one year after the first Haight ceremony, the Diggers, now called the Free City Collective, threw a Death of Hippie Ceremony. "The media cast nets," they announced, "create bags for the identity-hungry to climb in . . . the FREE MAN vomits his images and laughs in the clouds." The "funeral notice" read: "HIPPIE. In the Haight-Ashbury district of this city, Hippie, devoted son of Mass Media. Friends are invited to attend services." The ceremony began in Buena Vista Park with the playing of taps while the participants surrounded a coffin filled with the ashes of hippie detritus and emblazoned with a sign, "Try our friendly lay-away plan." Marilyn Harris knew someone who worked in a funeral parlor, and acquired the "Funeral" signs that mark cars in such a procession. Having cut off the parlor's name to protect the guilty, they handed the signs out to passing cars. Led by women mourners in black singing "Get out of my life, why don't you, babe" and three hooded figures hoisting a silver dollar sign on a stick, a half dozen pallbearers carried the coffin, followed by a hippie on a stretcher with flowers on his chest. They looped through the Haight and ended up back at the Panhandle, where the coffin was burned, drawing the attention of the fire department.

Three literal deaths that month made the news: Woody Guthrie, Che Guevara, and Groovy, a hippie on the Lower East Side of Manhattan who was gruesomely murdered. On October 21, the antiwar movement brought together 100,000 people at the Lincoln Memorial in Washington, D.C., and at least 5,000 of those people then marched on the Pentagon, which was encircled by 5,000 troops. The marchers included such "respectable" activists as Dr. Benjamin Spock, John Lewis of SNCC,

Noam Chomsky, and Paul Goodman, and somewhat more creative anti-war workers like Jerry Rubin and Michael Bowen, the artist and Be-In sponsor. Financed by Peggy Hitchcock, Bowen planned to dive-bomb the Pentagon with hundreds of pounds of daisies, but when he and his co-horts placed an ad in the *East Village Other* seeking a pilot, the FBI answered it, and they were forced to cancel the airdrop. Instead, the nation saw pictures of young demonstrators placing the flowers in the barrels of the rifles held by the men who blocked their way to the Pentagon. It was an authentic evocation of the cliché "flower power," though its impact was uncertain. One very real result of the march was that it accelerated the doubts of a man named Daniel Ellsberg, a Rand Corporation researcher who was supposed to be figuring out how to win the war. Eventually, he would resolve his doubts by releasing the internal record of war-making decisions called *The Pentagon Papers,* documenting the government's various lies.

On November 9 the first edition of *Rolling Stone* magazine hit the newsstands, and rock and roll grew up a little. *Crawdaddy!* would always be important, but its appeal was to an intellectual elite. The *Stone* would have a general appeal, and for a long while, it would matter. Jann Wenner, the U.C. Berkeley student who had so disliked Bill Graham, shared with him a driven, workaholic personality that was destined for achievement. He assembled rock critics like Jon Landau and Jonathan Cott, the San Francisco *Newsweek* writer Michael Lydon, his mentor Ralph Gleason, and the photographer Baron Wolman. Later, Lydon would snipe that Wenner began the magazine so he could meet the Beatles, and certainly there was more than a modicum of hero worship and the cult of celebrity in it. But his faith and commitment to rock were unquestioned. "This is not a counterculture paper," he told Baron Wolman, "this is an industry paper." Cover the industry it did. The first issue led with a picture of John Lennon from the film *How I Won the War,* a Lydon piece on what happened to the money from the Monterey Pop Festival, and a centerfold article on the bust of 710. An interview with Donovan, a Jon Landau piece on Hendrix and Clapton, and some major record company advertising marked the publication as serious.

That fall the synagogue next door to the Fillmore closed, and the Dead rented it as a rehearsal hall. Stimulated by their new drummer, they settled down to work on material for a second album. The new guy encountered—and passed—his first acid test at his first rehearsal. Hart was drumming away when suddenly a guy began talking to him, "right up in my ear," a speed rap that, remarkably, could cut through the extremely high volume of the band. He just kept playing, and then asked at a break, "Who's that?" "Oh, that's Neal Cassady." Neal's practice with Kreutzmann was to shake his arm vigorously and ask, "Are you loose, Bill?" In September they'd recorded at the RCA studio in Los Angeles, but now, in October, the Dead began again. Along with "Alligator," they were working on another new tune. One day back in April, Weir had heard a Yardbirds song on the radio on his way to a rehearsal, and it pushed some button in the back of his brain. Over the summer, he and Kreutzmann had worked at it. Now, with a second drummer, the song really began to take shape. It remained nameless, but since it was the other new piece in addition to "Alligator," they kept referring to it as "the other one."

One of the fundamental rhythms of world music is the clave, the shave-and-a-haircut-two-bits rhythm that came to be identified in rock and roll with the songs "Bo Diddley" and "Not Fade Away," what Bo Diddley, whose drummer Clifton James had perfected it, called "the sanctified rhythm." Now the Dead would take it to another level. Two drummers made for two rhythms, and Bo Diddley's 1-2-3-4 became fours and sixes. "That was the first time that six was ever really swung in rock, was made into a rock and roll groove," said Hart. "Because I was adding the triple while Billy was playing the shuffle, the backbeat to a sort-ofakinda shuffle, and I was on the tom-toms, which suggested more of a primitive, primal . . . you had the backbeat, and you also had the rolling 1-2-3-4-5-6 . . . then Bill would stay in fours, and I would play eight in six, or six in eight, and time would be broken and we'd go off . . . So 'The Other One' was more than a six, or more than an eight. It was the interlocking parts, and how they went together . . . the phrase was very often never completed. Remember, we were doing a lot of acid then, so linear progression was distorted. So we would just drop the one, we would get lost, we would call it the pulse. We would go on the pulse, so all of a sudden the pulse would lead us to a place, and we were completely lost, we didn't know where the original one was, so instead of struggling with the one, we would establish a new one, and that was the telepathy that me and Billy had. And they would catch on to our telepathic one, and they would latch on. When the third person went to it, it became legitimate. It would stay illegitimate for a certain amount of time, and we would be able to fly or float on the pulse, and there was no need to sound the one or recognize the one. Sometimes the one was known, and we'd let it go untouched. Other times we all pounced on it and sounded it and made it into a one. Sometimes we would hint at the one and come off it and never do it twice. A new language was being born, a new rhythmic language was

being born in the Grateful Dead. That's the magic of 'The Other One.' "
Free of the basic 4/4 box of almost all rock and roll, the now polyrhythmic
Dead now had what Hart called a "license to travel."

Weir began to write lyrics for "The Other One," which focused on his
scuffle with the police that spring. He'd spotted the police searching a car
in front of 710, and from the third floor, he put a water balloon in the
cop's ear, "a prettier shot you never saw," said Lesh later. It had come from
nowhere, and the cops were at a loss. But Weir being Weir, he just *had* to
go downstairs, walk across the street, and grin, and the cop knew instantly.
Due process vanished, and Weir went off to jail, where he absorbed a few
punches. "When I woke up this morning, my head was not attached . . .
The heat came 'round and busted me for smiling on a cloudy day." Good,
good, but not quite there. The tension between the rhythms in "The
Other One" made clear why Lesh would call it "a scary song of fun," and
Weir's lyrics did not yet touch its ominous, powerful potential. Time
would reveal more possibilities. October also saw them work on Garcia's
new tune, "Cryptical Envelopment," an extension of his fuzzily Christian
take on "Man of Constant Sorrow." It was a very long way from Corpus
Christi Church for Garcia, but the phrase "He had to die" came from the
same eschatological neighborhood.

In November they went to Los Angeles, first to play some shows at
the Shrine Auditorium and then to record at American Studios in North
Hollywood. They weren't rookies anymore, and this album would be different, one they would make sure would sound good. The worst thing
about the first album had been that they'd learned little about recording,
and that was no longer acceptable. They would seize control of the new
album's recording process in order to experiment and learn. Peggy Hitchcock's family bank owned a castle in L.A. across the street from Bela Lu-
gosi's house, and though it was devoid of furniture, the band moved in. It
was a fairly bizarre environment—which was not inappropriate. M.G.
cooked for everyone. Hart and Kreutzmann were at their most intense,
taking over one of the many empty rooms as a drum room, using hypnotic
techniques and just plain working. Between November 8 and 10 they
recorded a mix of material, including Pigpen's stem-winding show-closer,
Bobby "Blue" Bland's "Turn on Your Lovelight," "Death Don't Have
No Mercy," "The Other One," "New Potato Caboose," and "Alligator-
Caution." On the second night of their run at the Shrine, they brought
out "Cryptical Envelopment" and "The Other One" in their first live performances. Uniting these two songs created, as Lesh would say, "a universe" of music. They were growing as a band beyond anything they had

ever imagined, and the new material showed it. Their lyrics had been their biggest weakness, but these efforts stayed simple enough to endure, while the music was infinitely more interesting than what they'd written only a year before.

They had the material, and they had a fundamental approach, which mixed the implicit access to polyrhythms created by having two drummers with a unique musical foundation propounded by a bass player who contributed not a simple tonic bottom end but was instead, through counterpoint, a harmonic coleader. Over the next year, in the playing of "The Other One" and "Dark Star," Lesh and Garcia would lead the band through explorations that rock and roll had never imagined, a four-handed guitar-and-bass-as-one-instrument that was something altogether new. In the course of the fall's shows, the six of them took their new material and became the Grateful Dead. Playing together night after night while high as could be, they quite often found themselves in a state of grace, and they discovered that they were on a mission from God, serving the universe and evolution. They came to realize that the Dead was far bigger than the sum of six souls, and in fact had become a beast quite separate from them as individuals. As one of their best critics, Michael Lydon, noted somewhat later, "Certainly they are the weirdest [band], black satanic weird and white archangel weird. As weird as anything you can imagine, like some horror comic monster who, besides being green and slimy, happens also to have seven different heads, a 190 IQ, countless decibels of liquid fire noise communication, and is coming right down to where you are to gobble you up." And in playing they found faith. They were still painfully human, often inept, and certainly torn by their human frailty. But in the background, always, there was a shining faith. Six charmingly demented loons had been touched by the divine. Clearly, God has a sense of humor.

Their visit to Los Angeles contained one splendidly goofy moment. They joined members of the Jefferson Airplane and met the Beatles' own guru, the Maharishi Mahesh Yogi. He remarked in passing that they should be called the Eternal Lives, but the band just smiled. After he spoke on transcendental meditation for a while, Rifkin remarked, "That sounds like what we're doing anyway." "No, not *any* way," chirped the Maharishi. "Only through transcendental meditation." Touché, thought Danny, a fairly quick response. But he and the band lost all respect when the time came for them to be given the secret mantra and the Maharishi spoke only to the band, relegating the rest of the entourage to an assistant.

In mid-December they played again at the Shrine, performing "Dark Star" in public for the first time, and then headed east to New York, in part to gig, but primarily to record. They had purchased a Dodge Metro van for the equipment, along with Rakow's International Harvester, and Healy wired the vehicles with CB radios, which would help when the brand-new Metro ground to a halt—in the Sierras, then in Salt Lake City—and when one vehicle was pulled over in Nebraska and the other vehicle pulled up behind the cop car. They were psychedelic guerrillas sneaking through mid-America, and it was good to have a link to friends—that very week, Jim Morrison was arrested in New Haven after bad-mouthing the police from the stage, and Otis Redding's plane went down over Wisconsin the next day, killing all aboard. Rifkin had asked Zonker, a Prankster, to drive the truck cross-country, as he had in June, but Zonk canceled with a promise to send a substitute. Early in December, a short, muscular hippie showed up at 710 and said, "I hear you're looking for a good man." He introduced himself to Rifkin as Larry and asked if he could bring his old lady, Patticake, and that was fine. How about my friend Hagen? Sure. The three of them moved into the attic and made preparations for the trip to New York.

Larry Shurtliff was the last essential piece in the early Dead's evolution. Born in Montana and the product of eastern Oregon ranch country, he'd already passed through a variety of lives, winning a blue ribbon in beef judging as a sixteen-year-old and spending time as a Mormon practitioner, then ending up as the proprietor of a midnight auto supply company in Hermiston, Oregon. His buddy John Hagen brought him to hang out with John's brother Mike's friends, who happened to be called the Merry Pranksters, and in the summer of 1966 Larry and John had gone to Mexico, where among other things he first experienced LSD in the cozy confines of a Mexican jail. Another day, the Pranksters were faced with the chore of fitting seven people into a VW Bug. When Kesey asked for somebody to ramrod the process, Larry proclaimed, "I am Ramon Rodriguez Rodriguez, famous Mexican guide." Ramon Rodriguez Rodriguez instantly became "Ram Rod," because that's what he was. He'd spent enough time riding shotgun with Neal—"More bennies, Rod"—to be far from straight, but he was still a rock, the quiet, honest man who over the next years would become an internal balance for the band.

After a brief stay at New York's Chelsea Hotel, where Kreutzmann came back to his room to find thieves rifling through his belongings, they moved out to another "pink house," this time the Englewood, New Jersey, home of Weir's friend Mark Dronge, the son of the owner of Guild Guitars. Phil's lover, Florence, would cherish one memory of the house in particular: Pigpen in a black leather fleece-lined coat and boots—and nothing else—going happily bananas over his first sight of snow about three o'clock one morning. Mostly, they worked hard. In the evening they recorded at Olmstead Studios on 48th Street, the home of the Lovin' Spoonful, and from midnight to 6 A.M. at Century Studios on 52nd. They were still approaching the recording process in a fairly conventional manner, but these were eight-track studios, and they had a great deal to learn. Their producer, Dave Hassinger, smoked his cigars and tried to stay patient, but it was clear that this album was not coming together in any "normal" way. Just the opposite. The Dead dismissed as irrelevant the received notions of music and how to record it that the record companies and their engineers had developed. It was the band's job, thought Weir, to ignore that.

The end came when they were working on "Born Cross-Eyed." The song was intrinsically odd, because it began on the second beat; although there was a "one," they disregarded it. Consequently, everything was off. As Hassinger told the story, he got along well with everyone in the band except Phil, who was difficult and demanding. Dave wanted the band to sing as a group to cover individual weaknesses, a notion the band apparently rejected. After the recording sessions in New York, Hassinger went back to Los Angeles and talked with Joe Smith, and they agreed that he'd had enough. The Dead would recall their separation differently. At one point in the session, Weir asked what it would be like to record with "thick air." Years later he would understand exactly what he meant and how to produce it—namely, the feel of a hot, humid summer night, created with an audio compressor, which literally thickened the sound. But Weir wasn't all that great at explaining. "Thick air? He wants thick air?" groaned Hassinger, throwing up his hands and leaving in frustration.

Whatever the precise scenario, Hassinger absented himself from the sessions, and the band was set free—and momentarily adrift. As usual, there was simultaneously plenty of other drama going on in their lives. Weir, having promised for weeks the imminent delivery of the lyrics to "Born Cross-Eyed," was now forced to confess that he still hadn't written them. Then Bob Matthews, the crew chief, decided that he did not like the intense new drummer, Mickey Hart, and refused to work for him. One day in New York, Sue Swanson came to Ram Rod and said, "Matthews is fired. You're our new equipment manager." "What?" New

York City itself was a considerable challenge to the San Franciscans. Kreutzmann and Healy went to return some rented equipment, and their long hair triggered a distinctly unpleasant reaction from the shop manager, who refused to let them unload. Bill began dumping equipment into the snow at the rear of the building, with Dan holding the enraged manager off with his feet. The gentleman left, then returned with a fire ax. They split, circled the block, returned, kicked out the remainder of the gear, and fled.

Between recording sessions, they worked some shows, to varying success, in New York and for one weekend in Boston. Warner Bros. had sent them to their first agent, a man at Universal Attractions named Marty Otelsberg, and he had booked them their first shows in Boston, at the Psychedelic Supermarket, on the parking level of an office building on Boylston Street. Though he'd gotten them a new, higher rate of $2,500 (minus 10 percent), the concrete venue was an acoustic nightmare. The band organized a couple of shows on their own just before Christmas at New York City's Palm Gardens with the Group Image, and it was fun to be back with hippies. In fact, it was the most successful Group Image show ever. After Christmas the Dead did another do-it-yourself show at the Village Theater, the old Loew's Commodore, on 2nd Avenue. The building was essentially a wreck, and snow actually came through a hole in the roof while they were playing. It was so ungodly cold that the drummers played in gloves and people built a bonfire on the floor in front of the stage. Paul Kantner stopped by with a stash of Ice Bag, excellent pot so called because of its packaging. The weed helped, but it was still an odd little gig.

They flew home, and as the year ended, most of them wolfed down some pot pound cake and fell asleep. Mickey and Bobby went to Winterland that night, and as midnight approached, Weir took the pack of Pall Malls out of his drummer buddy's pocket, looked at him with tears in his eyes, said, "You're killing yourself," and crushed the pack under his heel. Moved by his friend's sincerity, Hart never smoked another cigarette. Despite his generally healthy regimen, Weir was a smoker and, ironically, remained one. Kreutzmann, Ram Rod, and Matthews were still driving the equipment truck back across the country, and December 31 found them in a motel in Omaha, where they celebrated the new year by splitting a pint of bourbon.

Sitting on Rifkin and Scully's desk was a letter from Joe Smith, dated December 27. Joe noted that the New York tapes were being sent and that the album was planned for a February release, which meant that art was needed "almost immediately." There was "no time for delays or indecision as we must have the package on the market as quickly as possible." The recording in New York had been "very difficult. Lack of preparation, direction and cooperation . . . have made this album the most unreasonable project with which we have ever involved ourselves . . . Your group has many problems . . . It's apparent that nobody in your organization has enough influence over Phil Lesh to evoke anything resembling normal behavior." They were "branded as an undesireable *[sic]*" group in the L.A. studios, and in New York they'd run through engineers "like a steamroller." It was all due to a "lack of professionalism." Joe harumphed in closing, "Now let's get the album out on the streets without anymore *[sic]* fun and games."

As the new year 1968 dawned, the Dead copyedited Joe's grammar and punctuation, graded the letter, and sent him an edited copy with corrections, but did not worry too much about his deadline. Warner Bros. thought it had experienced the ultimate in abuse from an artist after their treatment at the hands of Albert Grossman and Peter, Paul and Mary, but this was something new. It was true that Lesh was impatient, sometimes much more intelligent than those around him for comfort, and sometimes difficult. Garcia would say of Phil and Bill Graham's relationship, "Oh, boy. Phil used to just jump all over Bill and Bill would scream at him and I mean they would get into some *shit*. Because Phil has a little of that beatnik attitude. 'Fuck *you*, man!' You know? *Fuck you!* He's got a little of that edge . . . And when he was younger, he was a short-fuser. It didn't really matter what it was about. Usually, it was just personalities."

But the delays and changes in the recording of the new album were neither wanton nor willful. They were the consequence of experimentation and self-education. School was in session, and the students had taken over the classroom. Real education was in progress, and Joe Smith was paying for it—after all, their contract allowed them unlimited studio time, and they would take the contract, like so many other things, to the limit. In New York, the band had met and agreed that Dan Healy could handle the job of replacing Hassinger, and they all began to talk. The first thing they'd recorded was "Cryptical Envelopment," which sounded unusual because they'd run Garcia's voice through a Leslie, a rotating speaker made for Hammond organs. By the time Hassinger had left, they had perhaps a third of an album recorded, including "New Potato Caboose," part of "The Other One," "Born Cross-Eyed," and "Alligator." Now Phil suggested overlaying tapes of live Grateful Dead music with the studio versions to create many Grateful Deads, with the music opening up, poetically speaking, into waves of energy like a lotus coming out of the void. By the end of the meeting, they had at least a dim notion of where they were going.

It was good for Joe Smith's nerves that he remained ignorant of their plans.

19

Interlude: Purifying the Elements

(SETTING THE STAGE)

ichael "Fish" Fischer is hauling ass. He is herding the Dead's own white Peterbilt tractor, and storms have made him a little late, although the 425 horses of Caterpillar motor under the hood and fifteen-speed overdrive at his touch mean that he can do 100 mph, and he'll soon make up the time. The forty-eight-foot Great Dane trailer behind him is packed with the tools of the Dead's trade, and they are, with office and studio equipment, pretty much all the band collectively owns. The tape deck is turned up to ten with the truckers' national anthem, "The Bandit's Tune," as he reaches for the last gear.

Along with gaffer's tape, guitar strings, and batteries, trucks are a fundamental element in the structure of rock and roll. Somehow, in all their years of touring the United States, the Dead never lost a show to a lack of equipment, and it was not always easy. On one occasion in Virginia, Paul Roehlk, Fish's predecessor, was seriously late, and in a scene stolen from the movie *Smokey and the Bandit*, Dead Heads on the interstate recognized the truck and formed a convoy that allowed him to cruise past the police and make it to Richmond on time. Before a

Boston show in 1973, the truck foundered in snow out on the Massachusetts Turnpike, and it took a Sikorsky Sky Crane helicopter to pull it out. The truck arrived at the theater at 5 P.M., and the band and crew managed to put on a show that night, though it began around midnight. Then there was the time that a rookie driver burned out his truck's brakes in the Sierra Nevada and had his life and his load saved by Bill "Kidd" Candelario, who was driving the truck behind him. Candelario managed to get his own rig in front of the first one and gradually slowed down until they both could come to a halt. No equipment, no show.

The setup of the equipment is a combination of engineering and art. It is a ballet, a construction project, and a feat of diplomacy. And it is usually a very long day.

7 A.M.   The smell of frying bacon drifts through the backstage area as the guys in the catering crew begin their *very* long day. First in to work, they'll be the last out, finishing around 2 A.M. Nicknamed the Binky Boys by production manager Robbie Taylor, John Markward, David Miller, and chef Jim Voss prove that Napoleon was right: this army travels on its collective stomach.

8 A.M.   Load-in, the setup of the stage equipment, sound system, and lighting, is a drama all its own. Every venue and the resulting access to the stage are slightly different, and the way things go into (and thus come out of) the truck vary. The various crews' workday consists of putting a puzzle together, and it's a new puzzle at each load-in. As the trucks open, the riggers clamber around the ceiling like monkeys, setting the points, the hooks from which the sound and lights will hang. At one venue, refrigeration units in the ceiling make a normal hang impossible, and they work around them, offsetting the points with a bridle. Another theater has a Bauhaus pressed-wood roof, all swoops and arcs, and there are no points at all; the speakers must be stacked on the floor.

Access to the stage is frequently problematic. In Edinburgh, Scotland, the crew had to load equipment into a gondola, to be hoisted six floors up to the stage. Red Rocks, the marvelous natural amphitheater above Denver on the edge of the Rocky Mountains, is deeply flawed from the production point of view because a normal truck can't negotiate the road. So every piece of equipment is pulled out of the trailers and put into smaller "bobtail" trucks, which then go to the stage. In the trade, this is known as a fucked load-in.

9 A.M. With the points set, the lighting crew hauls out the elements of the truss, assembles it, and winches it up to the ceiling. Through the 1980s, the Dead's lighting setup is fairly minimal. The Dead use around ten points for sound and lights. Van Halen, by contrast, uses as many as forty-five points, mostly for lights. The Dead's rented setup has 180 lamps and eighteen Panaspots, which not only change colors but move in almost any imaginable way, sending the ever-changing shape of the beam in every direction, including out into the audience. The lighting crew, or "squints" (sound crew members are "squeaks"), will work through the day, first checking each lamp—on one tour a minimum of four per night were fried by a short circuit in the truss—and then, when Candace Brightman, the lighting director (L.D.) arrives, focusing them.

Since 1980, the Dead have used a sound system based on Meyer Sound Lab (MSL) speakers owned by Ultra Sound, the company run by Don Pearson and Howard Danchik, who began their career with the Jefferson Airplane, along with trucker Mike Fischer. The speakers are hung from the ceiling in two large arrays. The sound team uses Auto CAD (computer-aided design), an architectural drafting system, to determine rigging points before they even get to the hall, and the points are set from a stake on the front lip of the stage, with surveyor's tools to get it right. This is not the only area in which attention to detail is carried to extreme lengths. Every rock band has laminates to identify those with backstage access, but only Robbie Taylor and the Dead change them four times a year, spending tens of thousands of dollars on elaborate new original artwork rather than recycle some obvious logo. No other production manager would care so much; no other band would spend the money.

12:30 P.M. On the bus out to the venue, the Dead's crew observes the day and harasses Crazy Eddie the bus driver, because he's gotten lost. Stage manager and dominant crew personality Steve Parish is annoyed today—this is not unusual—with Harry Popick, the monitor mixer, because last night Popick skipped out on helping to load the truck. Ram Rod naps and Billy Grillo sits quietly. Candelario listens to Tina Turner.

1 P.M. The lights and speakers are now hanging from the ceiling, and the stage is empty. The crew arrives, Fish's truck opens, and under the direction of Taylor and Parish, encouraged by a stream of obscene, hilarious, and occasionally downright idiotic sounding instructions, local stage-hands begin pushing boxes up the ramp to the stage. Popick takes a worn Persian-style carpet, which is synthetic, not because the Dead are cheap, but because an organic carpet would hold static electricity, and centers it on the stage. "I lay that rug down and I stand where I know Bobby will stand and look at the P.A. cabinet and how many speakers I can see the fronts of or how far away it is or how high up or close or whatever. Every-thing you do and anything you do affects the other things." It takes about half an hour to empty the truck.

1:25 P.M. Because the crew has been coming to these halls for many years, every show is a reunion of the Dead's crew and local stagehands. Steve Parish is something of a legend to them, and they surround him as he jokes with the local tough-guy IA (International Alliance of Theatrical and Stagecraft Employees) members while hauling out cables to connect up Garcia's stage setup. Kidd is cranky, and rags on John Markward be-cause he didn't get tartar sauce with his fried clams. Scrib sets down a cup in the wrong place, and Kidd barks, "Not only are you a spy, but you're do-ing things wrong."

1:41 P.M. The stage is filled with equipment. Behind it, the Baryshnikov of forklift operators is now taking empty cases down off the stage and stacking them to the side with balletic grace.

2 P.M. Out of their cases, the drums sit lonely on the riser, waiting for their hardware and microphones. Lines snake everywhere. Kidd straps Lesh's personal control board on top of a speaker. Parish selects the smartest local stagehand and tells Robbie to assign him to the stage for the night.

2:12 P.M. Rolling cabinets fly open and hardware pours out. One cabi-net breaks open to reveal what looks like a telephone switchboard—plugs, hundreds of them. Scrib walks past Ram Rod, who is assembling the drums, and asks, "Can I help?" With a small smile, Rod replies, "Just don't laugh."

2:26 P.M. Plugs and wires begin to connect up. A forest of microphone stands sprouts in a corner, awaiting placement. Steve waves a bullhorn be-hind a cabinet, producing feedback.

3 P.M.   Ken Viola is the head of security for the band's tour coordinator, Metropolitan Entertainment, and he travels with the Dead. He is not a bodyguard—the Dead have never felt the need—but a teacher/diplomat, trying to educate and lead the locals. Since every police force and security organization thinks it knows how to handle things, his impossible job is to pressure them into approximating Dead standards. Viola orders the parking lot opened, and immediately he or his assistants have to make sure that it gets done right. There was the time at Star Lake near Pittsburgh in which the parking supervisor lined up all the cars against the outside fence, considerately, if not very intelligently, providing a ladder for gate-crashers to climb on. They didn't stop to thank him, but they certainly used them, denting hundreds of hoods. Evidently not good at learning from his mistakes, he parked the cars the same way the next day.

Minutes after the first cars enter the lot, and despite security's best efforts to herd them together, the vendors have established turf. Tailgates drop, grills come out, and pretty soon, Dead Heads have their choice of basic burritos, grilled cheese with tomato on honey whole wheat, tofu dogs, or Psychedelic Fruit Bobs spiked with Everclear and rum. One food vendor has a van with two deep fryers, a two-door commercial refrigerator, and professional workspace. Others make do with a hibachi. For many Dead Heads, vendors or not, the vehicle of choice is the VW microbus, which a writer for *Car and Driver* called the ultimate "negative status symbol." "Plain as a brick, simple as a lawnmower, slow as glue, cheap to buy, cheap to run, and cheap to fix." Supposedly, sales of the bus peaked in 1969 at 65,000, but at times it seems that there are that many in any given Dead parking lot.

Dead Heads begin to line up at the doors of the arena. "Old hippies never die," reads one bumper sticker, "they just wait in line to see the Dead." Local cops eye them suspiciously, much as Roman soldiers did the barbarians of fifteen hundred years before. The Romans/cops are clean-shaven, their hair cut. The hippies' hair, as historian Thomas Cahill wrote of the barbarians, is "uncut, vilely dressed with oil, braided into abhorrent shapes. Their bodies are distorted by ornament and discolored by paint . . . There is no discipline among them: they bellow at each other and race about in chaos. They are dirty, and they stink."

The hippies talk, smoke, trade tapes, tell stories. They see old friends and jump up for hugs, scream with joy when they recognize someone, catch up on the latest doings. The combined impact of a love for the powerful shows and psychedelics makes relationships blossom quickly and then endure. The line has become a party, a religious pilgrimage on its way to a Dionysian orgy.

3:10 P.M.   Heading to the dressing rooms to take a leak, Ram Rod runs into the house electrician, an elderly gentleman with the smile of a saint. There is an almost palpable glow about the man, and even the most cynical crew member says hello.

Candace Brightman stands at center stage and begins to focus the lights. Kidd clangs on the keyboard, picking the exact high chord that will shatter her ears as she stands in line with the Leslies, the Hammond organ speakers. One of life's mysteries is her capacity to ignore the crew's abuse, but for more than twenty years she's been the only every-time woman on the production scene. Perhaps it was the way she started that makes anything possible. She'd gone to the Anderson Theater in New York City to apply for a job as cashier, met Chip Monck, mentioned her still-limited theatrical background, and was invited to assist him in lighting. On her first night, still wearing a white blouse and panty hose from her day job at Bloomingdale's, she arrived at the booth to find Monck among the missing and the show about to begin. Not entirely sure of the difference between a circuit breaker and a dimmer switch, she grabbed one in panic, and exactly on the first note, the stage flooded in red. She looked like a genius. Things got both easier and harder after that.

As the microphones are plugged in, Harry Popick talks to Dan Healy and Howard Danchik at the soundboard. "I just turned off the woofers to hear what the room sounds like—it sounds like it carries a lot of flows." Howard: "You're all over the place today, man, a third higher." Harry frets, "There's really terrible stuff going on here. Can you punch up Don's twelve-pack?"

3:30 P.M.   Billy Grillo sits in his cubicle behind Kreutzmann's setup weighing drumsticks on an Ohaus triple-beam scale. They vary remarkably, and he and Ram Rod have to make sure they weigh true. He's already checked all the drumheads for wear. One set has endured around eighty shows, but most heads are changed every four to five shows.

As he does every day, Parish changes Weir's and Garcia's guitar strings, the delicacy of his motions contrasting with his huge size and verbal thunder. Afterward he wipes the guitars down with denatured alcohol. At the same time, Robbie Taylor brings Brent's Hammond B-3 organ to a fine gloss with furniture polish.

Out by the truck ramp at the rear of the arena, Marion and George, the Dead's merchandising crew, unload cartons of T-shirts for sale that night.

3:45 P.M.   In the audience, a fire marshal approves the setup of the folding chairs on the arena floor. Fire marshals are God; they can stop a show with impunity, although they have been known to be reasonable. In London Dan Healy once had to prove the safety and groundedness of a cable. He did so by grabbing both ends with his hands, putting his life on the line. The show went on. At other times, money might change hands. One night in Philadelphia, Scrib went out and discovered aisles two feet six inches wide, with nine inches between rows, and decided this could be one of those other times.

3:52 P.M.   Steve is at work on Weir's amp. The stage looks ready, with only a few boxes littering it. Harry creates feedback at Garcia's vocal mike, then tech-speaks to the soundboard. "Sweep this till it goes away." Howard replies, "A little edgy at one thousand but it'll cut through and that's what we want."

3:58 P.M.   Sitting on Brent's piano bench, Harry mumbles, "Lots of low-end reflecting, so try some bass roll-off." From Jerry's microphone, he adds, "This sounds all jangly, kinda nasally and stuff." As Danchik fools with the board, he adds, "A taste too much."

4 P.M.   The first band van arrives, bringing Healy and Lesh. Phil is jovial as he fiddles with his bass. He has a gifted abstract mind, and as a boy listened to a crystal radio set under the blankets. As an adult, his antidote to the blues is to watch a videotape of the final Apollo launch. His light reading is science fiction, and his more serious taste is for what Jung called geomancy, the science of earth magnetism and energy. Along with Lesh, the van brings the guest-list manager, Cassidy Law, the publicist, Scrib, and the tour coordinator from Metropolitan, Amy Clarke. Cassidy's mother, Eileen, has been dealing with the Dead's guest list at home for many years, and Cassidy seems born to the box office. The Dead's list is without a doubt the largest in the history of rock and roll, which is why Cassidy is probably the only person ever to go out on a tour just to handle the guest list—and she does it impeccably. She settles to work in a corner of the production office. Meanwhile, in the management office, Amy Clarke, a frustrated interior designer, rearranges all the furniture, resulting in lots more space. Scrib goes out to the stage, gets white tape from Harry, and marks off where the photographers may stand in the "pit," the area between the stage and the barricade.

4:15 P.M.   A colossal hissing roar fills the arena as Healy "noises" the room. "White noise"—sound at all frequencies—is pumped through the system and then evaluated on the B&K harmonic analyzer. It reveals on the computer screen which frequencies bounce, which linger, which disperse. Ideally, the final result will be a flat, harmonically correct room that is an acoustic *tabula rasa* for the night's show. Of course, the room's profile will change dramatically once it is filled with eighteen thousand sweaty customers, but this is a start.

This schedule applies only to indoor shows. The ante is severely raised for outdoor shows, where the size and risks go up. Everyone in the crew remembers the 1973 concert in Iowa, where the stage roof had been designed by a company from St. Louis and involved wires staked down to create a framework upon which innumerable pieces of fiberglass were screwed together. It was elaborate and beautiful, and the designer was proud. At sunset of the day before the show, to the sound of a choir rehearsing next door, the Dead's crew arrived on the scene to check things out. As they got there, so did a serious plains thunderstorm, and ten thousand pieces of half-pound fiberglass went whirling into the sky, giant plastic snowflakes that sent the choir and everyone else running for cover. The production people cobbled something together, it didn't rain the next day, and the show came off.

4:45 P.M.   Outside in the parking lot, in between the Dead Heads without tickets or money who have their fingers in the air hoping for a free "miracle" ticket, and the scalpers, who are balefully regarded but whom the flush will turn to at times of need, a bearded joker wanders about shouting, "Tibetan Army knives for sale, special mind opening blade." Scrib smiles, recognizing the Gary Snyder poem being quoted.

The stage is set and the band is not sound-checking today, so the crew sits talking. Robbie Taylor rode in the truck last night and reports that it was "uncomfortable, but I dug it." Parish smiles. "You gotta suffer a little pain." Since he has just won $200 on lottery tickets, he feels none. Then he announces his "first poem." "Everyone in the world but me is crazy / And I started to feel crazy today." The air turns blue with smoke from the fattest joints in America. The Binky Boys bring coolers onto the stage, filled with beers, ginger ale, and water. Garcia gets two packs of Camel straights and a lighter. Everyone gets towels.

5:30 P.M.   As usual, the show is sold out, and the energy around the backstage door has started to amplify toward frenzy. One night there was a woman who claimed to be Garcia's long-deceased mother, and hers wasn't even the most ridiculous of stories. Depending on his highly variable mood, Taylor may hand out a ticket or scream.

6 P.M.   The rest of the band arrives in two vans. Phil sits down to his supper, while Garcia goes to his corner to stretch the new strings and commune with his setup. Afflicted by stage fright until the music starts, he is touchy, and doesn't really want to talk with anyone except the band and Parish. Kreutzmann isn't feeling great, and he and Weir go to see the local doctor; one is on call at every show.

Ram Rod leans over the stage railing and asks tour manager Jon McIntire where Healy is. "Lying down, he's got stomach cramps."

"Oh, he's having his period," Ram Rod responds.

"Yes, and I'll bet you're glad," says McIntire.

6:30 P.M.   By now, the security guards and ushers have taken their positions, someone at the soundboard has put on some house music, Cassidy has gone to the box office, and everything is ready. Taylor turns to Viola, who is standing in his usual position at the top of the stage stairs, and tells him to open the doors. He radios the local head of security, and the doors swing open. The process usually works well, even when it doesn't work at all. The first time that the Dead played at the brand-new Knickerbocker Arena, in Albany, New York, they discovered what it would be like to have a show with no security. Though the house was managed by an experienced company, the building's brand-new security guards took one look at the Dead Heads, gulped, and simply disappeared for the night. There wasn't an aisle to be seen. Fortunately, the fire marshals weren't around either, and nothing happened except a good time.

The band warms up quietly most times, although there was the Halloween night in South Carolina when Kreutzmann stopped Scrib and said, "Tell Garcia I won't play tonight if he doesn't open with [Warren Zevon's] 'Werewolves of London.' " Scrib went to Garcia's dressing room and called the message through the closed door. Garcia chuckled. "Sure, but I don't know the words." Weir volunteered that he did, and with a little help, they wrote them down, went out, and performed a well-received if ragged version of the song. Much the same thing happened in Salt Lake City, when it occurred to the band fifteen minutes before showtime to play Weir's song named after the city. One very brief rehearsal backstage later, they did it.

Most nights, though, the time passes, somehow, in the comfort of routine. Eventually, either shepherded by the road manager or more likely in an individual straggle, the musicians make their way to the stage.

Independence
and Its Price

(1/1/68–6/30/68)

Evading label pressure in order to make a record on their own terms was only one of the Dead's ambitions. Though they had never actually toured, they decided to supplant the entire emerging structure of agents and promoters and organize a tour of their own. Even at home, they had played for Bill Graham only once since the Hollywood Bowl in September, and only once for the Family Dog since the previous March. Just as they were beginning to perceive their musical direction, they sought independent control of the music's live presentation. Rock Scully, Brian Rohan, and Ron Rakow were deputized to organize a run north to be called the Tour of the Great Northwest. Rakow had been looking for a niche in the Dead's scene, and it appeared that he'd found it. Rohan would feel that Rakow maneuvered him out, and certainly Brian's presence with the band would start to diminish at this time. Rakow looked to Weir like the Batman character the Joker, and Bobby was certain that he had introduced the word "scam" into the Dead's vocabulary.

Healy and Matthews were investigating the rental of a tape machine at a studio one day when they met a man who told them about the Carousel Ballroom, an Irish dance hall above an auto salesroom on the corner of Market and Van Ness in San Francisco. They rented it from the owner, Bill Fuller, for a show on January 17, Ben Franklin's birthday, and it served as a successful prototype for their run to the Northwest, a self-contained package of the Dead, Quicksilver, and Jerry Abrams's Head Lights. On January 20, the musicians flew to Eureka to begin the tour, exited the plane, and found what appeared to be half the cops in the county there to greet them. Eureka and San Francisco are both in California, but they most assuredly do not share the same state of mind. The Quick and the Dead proceeded to the hall, put on a show that blew minds, and headed on to Seattle. Unfortunately, their cleanup was not perfect, and after the gig, police found roaches and rolling papers, leading the local press to call the show a "pot orgy." This news dogged their tracks through the next weeks. Still, the tour was mostly fun, financially at least modestly successful, and aesthetically a smash. In a significant victory for their self-esteem, they showed that they could go into a college gym and within a few hours create a scene quite as entertaining as the Fillmore, without any of the trappings of conventional show business.

The Dead and Quicksilver were well matched. Their two lead guitarists both wanted to get stoned and play, and their management enjoyed mutual respect and goals. The bands shared equipment, which pleased the two crews. The cowboy and Indians game of the summer of 1966 had now evolved into blank pistol shoot-'em-ups, which occasionally caused a stir. In Portland, Cipollina leaped out from behind a tree and shot Pigpen, who obediently lay down for a few seconds, as the rules demanded, then got back in the car with Rifkin and Scully and drove away. In the meantime, observant locals had called the police, and Cipollina was fortunate to escape arrest. Weir was quite taken by Cipollina, with whom, he said, he shared "the same sort of black, ghoulish sense of humor." Of course, a sense of humor was a tour job requirement. One night eight giant bikers appeared at the door where Quicksilver's manager, Ron Polte, was standing. When asked what he intended to do, he replied, "Move over."

The tour was musically significant to the Dead because they were now performing their new material as a suite, and though they initially did so at extraordinarily fast tempi, it worked. They had found the material that would define their first persona. It began with "Dark Star" and continued with what would become side one of their new album ("Cryptical Envelopment" played into "The Other One" back into "Cryptical Envelopment" into "New Potato Caboose" into "Born Cross-Eyed"). Along with three old songs ("Alligator" into "Caution" or "Lovelight" as a show closer) and three new songs they would add in the course of the spring—"China Cat Sunflower," "The Eleven," and "St. Stephen"—their early repertoire was set. It had taken them three years, but the elements of talent and material had welded themselves into a powerful whole. Before, Garcia's licks and Pigpen's presence had carried them, but now they were a solid ensemble that could swing, playing material that in some cases would endure throughout their career.

Rock Scully was the tour's front man, and no one could better fill the job of bullshittin' nervous locals. "The Dead never played psychedelic music," he told one paper. "We don't take drugs anymore." After Eureka they played Seattle, then Portland State College, where, despite a giant snowstorm, the students got a show their critic defined as "phenomenal." "Flash after flash, skyrockets, bombs . . . I've never seen anything like the Grateful Dead and Jefferson Airplane lightshow." The music "was loud, loud enough that we didn't need ears. We could see and feel the music, it saturated the ballroom . . . [the Dead] kept hitting climaxes, bursting, sense-tearing climaxes, until on some magic cue they relaxed, dropped back to reality, stringing us along," only to finish with "another chain reaction of exploding box cars full of nitroglycerin." For Rohan, the proof of their effort came in Eugene, where a good crowd somehow plowed its way through a major snowstorm to get to the EMU Ballroom.

On a roll, the band returned to Portland to play two nights at the Crystal Ballroom, the local version of the Fillmore or Avalon. The Crystal was an old-time dance hall with a sprung floor built on ball bearings, and it, too, had been booked in the early sixties by the Fillmore's Charles Sullivan with soul artists like James Brown and Marvin Gaye. Open as a "hippie" scene only from January 1967 to July 1968, the Crystal's two Quick/Dead shows were among the high points in the room's history. The Dead enjoyed themselves, too; Garcia left the box office lady a joint, which she thought was her best tip ever, even though she didn't smoke. After a tour-ending show on February 4 in Ashland, Oregon, the musicians grabbed an early flight home. They were just in time. The police stopped the truck outside Ashland, forcing the crew to unload every piece of equipment. Finding nothing, the police then tried to reload the truck, which turned out to be the real joke.

Something very interesting happened to Weir toward the end of the tour. One night in Portland, he began to tinker once more with the lyrics to "The Other One." He'd already settled on the first verse:

> *Spanish lady come to me*
> *she lays on me this rose*

It rainbow spirals round and round
It trembles and explodes
It left a smoking crater of my mind
I like to blow away
But the heat came round
and busted me
for smiling on a cloudy day
Comin', comin', comin' around
Comin' around in a circle

This was neither so romantic nor so psychedelic as one might think. The Spanish lady was in fact a Balinese dancer Weir had met in Seattle the previous year, a lovely who left him with a social disease sometimes called the Spanish sickness. He didn't like his other verses, and now in Oregon, he thought of the Pranksters, and of course of Neal Cassady. Neal had spent some ten days that January sleeping in the attic of 710, generally hanging out with Weir, who slept on a couch on the second floor, most of his belongings in a paper bag. The room with the couch also had the stereo, and Weir would lie there, still silenced by the effects of his past use of LSD, as Neal gobbled speed, juggled his sledgehammer, and raved. John Barlow later speculated that Weir was somehow "dreaming" Cassady. In their polarities, there was a powerful bond. In Portland, Weir reviewed what he had written about meeting Neal:

Escaping through the lily fields
I came across an empty space
It trembled and exploded
Left a bus stop in its place
The bus came by and I got on
that's when it all began
There was cowboy Neal at the wheel
of the bus to never-ever land
Comin', comin', comin' around
Comin' around in a circle

That works, he thought to himself as he finally went off to sleep. A couple of thousand miles south, Neal Cassady lay dying of exposure on railroad tracks near San Miguel de Allende, Mexico. Found and brought to the hospital, he died later that day, February 4, 1968. The band learned of his death when they got home to 710 from the tour.

As they returned to San Francisco, the mainstream news was focused on Vietnam, where the North Vietnamese had begun a gigantic offensive that coincided with the lunar holiday called Tet. It was a savage irony that, in military terms, the North lost. U.S. forces wiped out half of the Viet Cong and perhaps sixty thousand North Vietnamese, against losses of four thousand of their own and five thousand South Vietnamese. But the very fact that the enemy could think of such an offensive with more than half a million U.S. troops in the field shattered the American public's perception of U.S. superiority. The U.S. war machine was suddenly a very naked emperor. A March 10 Gallup poll revealed that 49 percent of the population thought the war was a mistake. The next day Walter Cronkite, the CBS broadcaster widely viewed as the most trustworthy man in the country, announced his doubts about the war.

By this time an alternative press structure had blossomed across the country. The *New York Times* estimated that there were somewhere between 150 and 200 underground newspapers with a nationwide circulation of around 2 million, and while their journalistic standards sometimes took rumor for fact, their distrust of conventional authority was a healthy antidote to the old consensus. For the first time, an alternative point of view cost just fifty cents and could be found in every city and college town. Stoned humor, characterized by irreverent spontaneity, cartoon ideas, surreal wordplay, graffiti, and sexual looseness, reached the mass media in 1968 with the television debut of *Rowan and Martin's Laugh-In*. Film, too, had changed, most brilliantly in that year's *Bonnie and Clyde*. European filmmaking had invaded Hollywood, said one film historian, bringing a "disregard for time-honored pieties of plot, chronology, and motivation; a promiscuous jumbling together of comedy and tragedy; ditto heroes and villains; sexual boldness, and a new, ironic distance that withholds obvious moral judgments."

The Dead stayed independent, playing again at the Carousel Ballroom on Valentine's Day, this time with Country Joe and the Fish, broadcasting the show to those at home on both Tom Donahue's KMPX and on the public station KPFA, which made it the first-ever live FM stereo broadcast. Then came one of their grandest capers ever. On Sunday, February 18, the rainy gray San Francisco winter parted for one balmy day, and the residents of the Haight-Ashbury thronged Haight Street. All was peaceful, but around 4:30 a car narrowly missed a dog, words were exchanged, the police were called, and what the *Examiner* described as six hundred bottle-tossing hippies faced tear gas and riot batons, leading to seventy-five arrests. In an effort to promote domestic tranquillity, the city announced that on March 3, Haight Street would be closed to traffic, and that "a number of musical events are planned." Little did they know. Whatever the city had in mind would be forgotten, but the Dead decided to stage a coup.

The band loaded its gear on two flatbed trucks, one coming down Haight from Stanyan, the other down Cole, which dead-ended at Haight in front of the Straight Theater. As they approached the police blockades, Rock Scully leaned off the running board and saw Sergeant Sunshine, the legendarily pleasant cop on the beat. Rock said, "Hey, here we are, it's okay, we're the music for the afternoon." "Oh, great," the sergeant replied, and pushed aside the barricade. The two trucks met tail-to-tail in front of the Straight Theater, and with commando precision, cohorts tossed down power lines from the Straight, Hell's Angels came in to guard them, and the Dead began to play, smack in the middle of the street. People came from everywhere within earshot, and before long, Haight Street was full as far as the eye could see, with every window, every rooftop, and every square inch of standing space holding an ecstatic crowd. John Warnecke threw joints into the audience, and Jim Marshall crawled around the band's feet taking incredible pictures. For Lesh, it may have been the "highest performance—the highest relationship between us and the audience—but it wasn't anything like an audience, man, it was like an outdoors acid test with more people." Garcia agreed. At heart, this was a farewell, and over the ensuing months the band members would move out of a neighborhood now riddled with doomed speed freaks and lost heroin addicts. M.G. and Garcia had left 710 shortly after the bust, moving to an apartment near the ocean in the Richmond District. Toward summer they would all begin shifting to Marin County, Mickey impatiently first, to a home on Ridge Road in Novato that he would soon share with Weir.

Even as they began to move their homes, they committed to the city as their workplace. Under Rakow's leadership, they formed Triad, which was an essentially fictitious partnership of the Dead, the Airplane, and Quicksilver, to run the Carousel Ballroom. Under it, each band was to play for free and receive 10 percent of the profits. Big Brother was managed by the dark god Albert Grossman and consequently wasn't a formal partner, but in the end would participate as much as the other bands. That January, the Airplane had replaced Bill Graham as their manager with their friend and road manager Bill Thompson, and Thompson and Ron Polte of Quicksilver joined Rock in committing the bands to play often

enough to keep the Carousel going. The Airplane's participation was significant, since they were then the top draw in the country, earning $7,500
a night. But that summer the Airplane was to take its first European tour,
so Thompson became too busy to have much to do with the Carousel. Because Danny Rifkin was traveling in Europe, Rock was now the sole manager, which meant that Rock, too, had little time for the Carousel. In the
end it would be run by Ron Rakow.

The Carousel was not Rakow's only operation at this time. Just for
practice, or perhaps as a display of his talents, Rakow created the All Our
Own Equipment Company, which purchased thirteen Ford Cortinas for
the band members and associates, using as collateral what various people
at various times claimed to be a very rubbery check for $5,000, or future
music publishing rights. Or something. After a number of tries, Rakow
found dupes at S&C Ford and the United California Bank on Haight
Street. Using a check signed by Rock Scully from the fictitious Headstone
Productions, their friend Jon McIntire walked in all blond charm, signed
loan papers, and walked out owning thirteen cars. By the time the bank
foreclosed on the individual owners, the vehicles were sufficiently dispersed to prove a major challenge to even the very best repo men. Rakow
gave his to the Hell's Angels (or was it the Black Panthers?), then told the
bank where to find it. Weir totaled his by running it into a bus, and Bear's
fell victim to a red-light runner. Pigpen loved his, and kept up the payments. The rest were repossessed, mostly on the next New Year's Eve
when everyone was at work, or turned in, as Lesh's was. Possibly due to
karma, his had never worked well anyway.

Having demonstrated his skill at creating something out of nothing,
Rakow proceeded to establish their new home at the Carousel. At one of
their earliest shows there, they invited the owner, Bill Fuller, and a local
real estate attorney, Rubin Glickman, to come and see. Glickman would
recall Janis Joplin cheerleading the evening, "waving her arms and
yelling." Glickman thought that they wanted to buy the Carousel, and being in the real estate syndication business, he suggested that the bands
syndicate themselves and hire an outside businessperson to run the ballroom. He did not recall drawing up a lease, nor did Rohan, who was not a
real estate lawyer. It would appear that Rakow did so on his own, although
he later blamed the lease on "my lawyer." Rakow certainly signed it,
and that was a mistake, as he also later conceded. It was an untenable
lease, based on a flat rate *plus* a percentage of capacity. Familiar with
Rakow's business style, Bert Kanegson, who would later become one of
the house managers, later theorized that Rakow planned to make money

by exceeding the legal capacity set by the fire marshals. This would normally be a reasonable plan, since the limit was usually conservative and permitted tolerable overselling. Unfortunately, the capacity turned out to be solidly realistic, which led Bert to further theorize that Fuller might already have had a conversation with the marshals. "I think Rakow did it all," Bert said. "He kept it all pretty much in his pocket." Once they got into the building, Rakow ensured they could stay for a while by immediately beginning construction to move the stage and make various other changes.

The lease guaranteed that the Carousel could not succeed for long as a business. Given the Dead's utter lack of financial resources, perhaps a bad lease was the only way to bring off the adventure at all. Certainly the wobbly business structure meant nothing to the band, which didn't know or care. But as a sanctuary and an experiment in community, the Carousel was a roaring success, Olompali in the city, a clubhouse for the city's freak community. As Jorma recalled, "I could get in free all the time, and something was always happening there." The Dead were tired of Bill Graham's manner, and working with Chet Helms meant listening to lots of "I have to feed my family, I don't have any money" stories. The Family Dog had made a terrible mistake in opening a branch in Denver. A local cop decided to run them out of business, and effectively did so, bleeding them with legal costs until they closed.

With himself as the booker and chief manager and with his lover, Lydia d'Fonsecca, as chief bookkeeper and secretary, Rakow went about creating a team to run the Carousel. The previous year he had met a man named Jonathan Riester, who was then building a laboratory for some chemists near Cloverdale, north of San Francisco. Born in Indiana, a horseman and handy guy, Riester was a member of the Psychedelic Rangers of Big Sur, one link in the LSD distribution network. Rock and Rakow went down to Big Sur, found Riester, and drafted him to help with the renovation and running of the Carousel. Annie Corson, who had been cooking at 710, was naturally tapped to run the Carousel's food service, which in itself would make it one of the better restaurants in the city. The Carousel had an impressive professional kitchen, with giant stoves and refrigerators, but it was abysmally filthy, and Annie was just beginning to clean it when her friend and regular assistant at 710, Jon McIntire, walked in with news. He had been due to return to St. Louis to deal with a civil trial that had arisen from a car accident, but that morning he'd received a telegram setting him free. Enlivened, he took the bus to the Carousel to help her clean, and in so doing considerably changed his life.

McIntire was an actor and student from an upper-middle-class family in Belleville, Illinois, a few miles across the river from St. Louis. A charter member of the Early Music Society of St. Louis, he had graduated from Washington University and wound up at S.F. State, where he made a specialty of the history of ideas, especially the work of the heavier Germans, like Robert Musil's *The Man Without Qualities*, Hermann Broch's *The Death of Virgil*, Heidegger, and Hegel, as well as the Comte de Lautreamont's *Les Chants de Maldoror*. But he took what he thought of as a Taoist view of his life, going where the wind blew him, and that day it took him to the kitchen. He had just filled up a sink with hot water and was unscrewing a fry grill when Riester, whom he'd met at 710 and instantly liked, came in.

"McIntire! What are you doing?"

"Well, Jonathan, I'm going to take this fry grill and I'm going to put it in that water, and I'm going to scrub the fuck out of it."

"No no no no no no, you can't do that. That's not a job for you."

"Why?"

"Because you're going to manage this ballroom with me."

"Jonathan, I'm an actor. What do I know about managing a ballroom?"

"McIntire, I'm a cowboy. What do you think I know?"

"I don't know."

"Besides, what do you have to do for the rest of your life?"

"Well, as of a few hours ago, nothing," Jon admitted.

"My point exactly."

By now, Annie was staring at both men with daggers in her eyes, certain that she was about to be stuck with a lot of grease. But McIntire made Riester promise that she would get helpers, and Jonathan kept his word. Before long, McIntire ran the ballroom's concessions along with other duties.

After being fired from the Dead's equipment crew in December, Bob Matthews had flown home to San Francisco, where his flight was met by Betty Cantor, a lissome young woman who'd been working at the Family Dog. As the Carousel evolved, she began by selling hot dogs for McIntire, then apprenticed herself to Matthews, who was working on the sound system with Bear. Matthews had ulterior motives, but their subsequent romance did not obscure the fact that she turned into a good engineer as well as an ace hot-dog salesperson. Bear had been busted in December and had decided to retire from the chemistry business, so he returned to the world of sound, hot-rodding amps and designing the sound system.

At one of the earliest shows, Bert Kanegson came to Rock and asked if the Diggers could be admitted free. Rock was happy to say yes, but replied that it was up to Bert to identify them. Before long, that qualified Bert as a house manager, dealing with security and a variety of other issues. Sue Swanson and Connie Bonner sold tickets at the box office. Laird Grant returned from wherever he'd been to be stage manager. Lydia's brother Johnny, a superb carpenter, took care of the rebuilding of the stage. In the crowd of Alameda kids that tagged after Johnny and Lydia was a boy named Bill Candelario, who hung around doing odd jobs and gradually came to be a fixture. What really happened at the Carousel was a latter-day revival of the early Haight, in which people who cared about each other and loved what they were doing came together. The staff practically lived in the place, hanging out night and day. Generally speaking, such pay as there was came to living expenses, which meant rent money on good days, Annie's cooking, and all the dope you could smoke. Their labors paid off, and they created a warm and comfortable environment. Bert was especially proud of the dance floor, which he kept in a state of high gloss with powdered dance wax.

Once the remodeling was completed, the Carousel had its official opening on March 15, with the Dead and the Airplane sharing the weekend. Kelley's poster of a bandaged thumb was entirely apt. Though tickets went on sale at the last possible second, they did extremely well. Unfortunately, the venue was dark the second weekend and lost momentum. For their next shows, they went to the Haight and gave away tickets and then gave away ice cream at the shows. As Rakow put it, "If we're going to lose money, let's make sure that everybody in the place is going to have such a gas that they're going to tell everybody else about it." On other nights, admission took the form of even more provocative social theater. One night the door charge came as a choice: burn a dollar bill or pay five dollars. Ken Goldfinger, a well-known acid dealer, refused to burn money. He could certainly afford the five dollars, but others who couldn't still found themselves unable to torch a bill. Another time, Garcia recalled, someone paid with a piece of butchered sheep, the bloody stump sticking out of the cash register, covered by a bunch of dollar bills gummed together with lamb's blood.

Life at the Carousel was an ongoing example of social deconstruction, and lots of people found it scary—and they didn't even know about the occasional rooftop orgies. The musicians loved it. It was a hangout, always good for a jam, and they were treated as family. One East Coast band manager, Ted Gehrke, recalled coming out to San Francisco about this time on a scouting mission and visiting with Rakow to see about possible gigs. After all his experience with New York diamondringbastard agents, Ted watched awestruck as Rakow fired up a joint and handed it to him. Fifteen minutes later he was on the phone to his band proclaiming the glories of San Francisco and the Carousel.

At 3 A.M. on the Monday after the Carousel opened, the staff of KMPX went out on strike, walking out of the warehouse at Green and Battery Streets that housed the station to gather around a flatbed truck parked in the street. There, members of the Dead, whose gig had ended only a couple of hours before, Stevie Winwood, and others began to play. The strike became a party. In May the strikers would march to 211 Sutter Street and begin a new station, KSAN, which would, with WNEW in New York, define "free-form radio." Influenced by Donahue, a man named Ray Riepen began a similar station in Boston in March, called WBCN, and the trend was on.

With their new home opened, the Dead went off on a logistically ridiculous and not entirely atypical road trip, flying all the way to Detroit for two shows with Eric Burdon and the Animals at the State Fair Coliseum. Their schedule then called for them to play a benefit in Grand Rapids, where the organizer was Rock's brother Dicken's girlfriend's mother, and then go home. In Detroit it snowed fourteen inches, and the benefit was canceled. The lovely poster, which was a drawing of Pigpen with angel's wings, was the only evidence of the dream.

On their return, they went back to the Carousel for a weekend with Chuck Berry, and something quite unusual happened. The Dead's music was new, and utterly challenging. They had broken into an entirely new plane, and it was sometimes incredibly difficult to get any perspective on it from the inside. In the middle of a particularly brutal show, Lesh simply took his hands off his bass, defeated. It was "the first time I discovered that there were realms of music that we could play into that I couldn't even imagine what was going on . . . it got more and more incomprehensible to me as the night wore on." It was the first time he had ever wanted to leave a gig because he felt so bad about his playing. "So I'm walking around the sunken area and I'm just at the door when Jerry comes up the stairs, and I try to just go past him because I know if I said anything it would be the wrong thing. He was so pissed, he just grabbed me and said, 'You play, motherfucker,' and sort of threw me down the stairs. [Others recalled it was a weak punch that was effectively a shove.] I didn't fall down, I just stumbled." Shocked, Lesh reacted first with the usual manly posturing—"You ever touch me again, man"—and then with shame that the two partners could possibly come to such a pass. What really put the cherry on the sundae for both men was realizing, sometime later, that their performance that night had been so good they would include it in their new album. Of course, the album's working title hinted at their musico-emotional difficulties—"No Left Turn Unstoned," a sign Paul Foster had put at Kesey's driveway at La Honda, which did require a left turn.

Two major currents flowed through their musical lives that spring. One was their integration of live and studio music on the album, which went on apace from December, when Hassinger departed, to the weekend of March 29 at the Carousel. The other was something that Mickey Hart had brought in. Shortly after Mickey joined, Lesh had given him an album called *Drums of North and South India*, featuring Ravi Shankar's tabla partner, Ustad Allarakha. In December, after the band's very cold night at the Village Theater, Mickey had gone out to Mineola, Long Island, and met the Indian master drummer, taking with him sticks, a pad, and a trinome, a metronome that could count three rhythms. After gently informing Mickey that the trinome was not entirely accurate, Allarakha taught Mickey a counting game in which one hand counted tens, and over that he would call out numbers that had to be fitted into the tens. It was a game Mickey Hart was born for, and he went bananas. Later, Allarakha would say of him, "What a strange boy. He liked the difficult things."

There was something richly appropriate about the Dead learning about time from Indian music. As the philosopher Art Kleps once wrote, Indian music "in no way encourages you to notice the passage of time—or better, to notice that time has stopped passing and instead is sort of loitering around shooting the shit with space." By then, the band was rehearsing at the Potrero Theater, an abandoned movie theater on Potrero Hill in San Francisco. It was a rat-infested dump and the neighbors complained about the sound volume, but it was a hothouse for creative work, and one of their exercises became playing in time signatures that no one in rock and roll had ever imagined actually using. Two bars of seven, three bars of seven, four of eleven, and so on. They had patience, desire, and nothing in their way. Day after day they ate rogue time signatures until they were as familiar as their teeth to their tongues, and the result was the song "The Eleven," which they debuted in January, a blues shortened by a beat with lyrics from the poetry stash Hunter had sent them with "Alligator." "St. Stephen" was another piece that they put together from Hunter's work but without his direct participation. The song was elaborate, complex, and difficult, but with the amount of labor they put in at the Potrero, it was frequently stupendous.

Now they settled down to making the album. Warner Bros. was alternately aghast and apoplectic. It had been more than a year since the band had recorded its first album, and six months since they'd begun recording this one. They had a tall pile of recording tape in varying formats made at differing speeds on different machines, different versions of the same songs played at basically the same tempo and in more or less the same tuning, but each flawed by the vagaries of live performance, so that one would be interrupted by the power going off, or another by a broken string, or perhaps by a cable that had chosen a moment of ecstasy in which to disconnect. Fortunately, the Dead also had Healy. Garcia and Lesh had a fair idea of what they wanted to hear, but barely any knowledge of recording techniques. Healy not only knew the studio, he had a special gift that made everything possible: he was fearless, completely ready to think of ways to do things that simply were not done. Some of their tape, for instance, came from an old Viking deck that someone (Healy thought it was Bear, who denied it) had made by putting together two quarter-inch stereo tape machines to create a four-track machine. It was idiosyncratic. "You had to set it down," said Healy, "and have a talk with it, warm it up, and if you got it just in the right mood, then it would record for you and cease to stop and warble."

Much—but not all—of the mixdown was done at Columbus Recording in San Francisco, which had three two-tracks, a mono machine, a three-track, and the hot eight-track machine. First they had to convert what they had into the format appropriate to the studio where they were working, eventually getting it all in eight-track. Then, in a collage approach more commonly (and easily!) applied to *musique concrète*, where the music is arrhythmic and atonal, they began to assemble two- and three-bar chunks of music in bits and pieces to create what Garcia would call "an enhanced nonrealistic representation." "How can we make it sound purple?" he once asked. All of this anticipated things that wouldn't exist for years, variable-speed gizmos, uninvented electronic widgets. So Healy, who had a hot soldering iron on hand at all times, did it the hard way. He would put fiddler's rosin on his thumb, rub it against the flywheel of the capstan motor of one tape deck, and, listening to two versions of the same song, slow one down until they synchronized. The hand-done result was something premodern and consequently unique. In the background the band would be cheering him on, rooting for him to find the moment. "Yeah, there it is, you got it, you got it." By now, there was no one around except the band; the adults had all given up. Decades later physicists would describe in chaos theory what the Dead were living as they mixed; different versions would (sometimes) come out at the same musical place (though at different times). At the end "The Other One" dissolved into an ocean of sound, out of which came "New Potato Caboose," so that, in effect, it never did end. (Perhaps it's playing still.) Garcia would recall once being fascinated by phase distortion after hearing a stereo tape in which one side bled through to the other. As he said, "We really mixed [the album] for the hallucinations, you know?"

Phil's friend Tom Constanten worked with them on prepared piano, in which he produced curious sounds by wedging coins (Dutch dimes were preferred), combs, or clothespins in the strings. They used colored noise he'd recorded with Pousseur in Belgium, and the ringing sound in the "We Leave the Castle" section of "The Other One" was from a tape that was cut. In Los Angeles he'd dropped a gyroscope on the piano's sounding board and almost destroyed Hassinger's hearing and sanity. Part of their inspiration was Charles Ives, who composed to reflect the way music would fade in and out as bands marched past each other in a park. And that winter, on a trip to New York, most of the band went to Carnegie Hall to see Ives's Fourth Symphony—twice.

Borrowing heavily from Miles Davis's *Sketches of Spain,* Lesh threw in a little trumpet on "Born Cross-Eyed." Many of the editing techniques they used were, he thought, basically cinematic—jump cuts from the drummers to four Grateful Deads, cross-fades, and so forth. In the end, the album became a performance of mixes, or different performances of the same song. What was most important was not what they did, but the level they did it at. And it was great. Despite all the edits and copies, the sound of the album was superb. Garcia's voice was mournful and in control, the songs sketched infinite possibilities, the cosmic coda after "Cryptical"—"He had to die"—echoed John Donne's bell that tolls for us all, and Pigpen put down so much greasy funk in "Alligator" that it was a miracle the vinyl didn't squirt off the turntable. They were on the edge, over the edge, beyond sight of the edge. They were reinventing themselves and their music on the fly, at a wonderful level of creativity.

On March 31, 1968, President Lyndon Johnson bowed to political reality and announced that he would not seek a second term. Two days later, Eugene McCarthy won the Wisconsin primary. Two days later, on April 4, Martin Luther King Jr. was assassinated, triggering riots in 125 U.S. cities that left 46 dead and 20,000 arrested, and put 55,000 federal troops on the putatively civilian streets of America. Two days later, Eldridge Cleaver of the Black Panther Party was wounded in a gun battle with Oakland police that killed seventeen-year-old Panther Bobby Hutton.

Against a backdrop of social and political chaos and crisis, the Dead played on, in a fifty-fifty balance of benefits, paid gigs, and . . . other. On March 7, the Dead performed for the Diggers on a truck outside San Quentin prison. On March 11, they opened for Cream at an auditorium in Sacramento. After a brilliant Dead set, Cream came out to top them and attacked their instruments so hard they blew out their speakers; the Dead had to lend them equipment to get through the show. On April 3, the Dead played at a KMPX strike benefit. In mid-April they left for some paying gigs—their pay rate was by now up to a barely respectable $2,500—which began in Miami Beach, where they also worked on the album at Criteria Studios. Unfortunately, their work at Criteria was interrupted by half a pound of black African Daga pot, and they accomplished less than they might have.

After a stop in Philadelphia, they passed through New York in early May in a visit that would cover much ground and become an essential part of their legend. On April 30, police had entered the strikebound Columbia University campus, arresting dozens at the occupied administration building. The campus was shut down, each entrance guarded by a gaggle of New York's finest. Enter Rock Scully, with a brilliant idea. He called the *Village Voice,* got connected with the student strikers, and offered them a treat, a Grateful Dead concert on the steps of the student union in the middle of the campus. The band had no political investment in the strike, but an adventure was an adventure, and facing the prospect of a caper pulled off by a desperado gang . . . it was like offering drugs to an addict. The strikers started salivating at the idea of a powerful P.A. system, and said sure, though they were told that the P.A. would be used only for music. Cramming themselves and their equipment into a Wonder bread truck, the Dead pulled up at the student union loading dock, swept in, and were playing before the police or administration could object. For Weir, who was intellectually a small-*c* communist, the strike leaders were dogmatic egotists, drawn to the microphones like "moths to lightbulbs—it felt so good to have your voice get biiiig." Several times, leaders would cut off a song with the statement "Quiet down, we have an important announcement," which would be followed by unfocused rant. At length, Weir booted one strike leader in the ass just to get enough room on the stage to see the other band members, and realized that his audience liked it. From then on, there was a wonderful feeling of generational, if not precisely political, solidarity, and everyone there knew it was an exceptionally cool moment.

Two days later the Dead played free in Central Park, this time with the Airplane and Butterfield Blues Band, and the *Village Voice* writer loved it. "No tricks, just music, hard, lyric, joyous—pure and together, dense and warm as a dark summer country night. There's the Dead and then there's everybody else . . . Then the audience not in rows, but en masse, was up, dancing, screaming frenzied . . ." For Don McNeill, the young critic who covered the emerging youth culture for the *Voice,* it felt as though Central Park had become the Panhandle. "The coasts linked . . . total release, surrender, exhilaration, a new ritual of energy spent that I'd only seen before at the first Easter Be-In." The *New York Times* noted that the Dead "are extremely driving, amplified, and hirsute, even by San Francisco standards." After their free show, the band played three nights at the Electric Circus. The visit ended, at least for Mickey, in a jam with Jack Casady, Steve Winwood, and Jimi Hendrix at Electric Ladyland studios.

On their return home, most of the band completed their moves to Marin County. Pigpen remained on Belvedere Street, but Phil found a cabin in Fairfax that had been a gatekeeper's lodge for Golden Gate Park architect John McLaren and was reportedly still visited by the spirits of some of McLaren's guests, like Jack London and Luther Burbank. Jerry and M.G. moved to a small home in the redwoods in Larkspur, Kreutzmann to Lucas Valley Road, with Weir and Hart in Novato. In addition to their individual homes, they still had a connection to Olompali, which had been taken over the previous December by their Ashbury Street neighbor, Don McCoy, who had inherited money and set up a commune at Olompali that taught children in the manner of the British experimental school Summerhill. Nicknamed by the students the Not School, it served eleven kids and included twenty-five people. Spiritual but not formally religious, it was a good place that summer, with the Dead visiting at times to play music by the pool. Mickey boarded a horse there and Lydia d'Fonsecca's kids were residents, so it felt like an extension of the band's scene. At the same time, the Airplane, rather more flush, purchased 2400 Fulton Street in San Francisco, a four-story mansion with mahogany paneling and crystal chandeliers. For a while, until 710 was completely shut down, the Airplane even shared the services of the Corsons and their friends Eddie and Suzie Washington, who'd formed GUSS (Grand Ultimate Steward Service) to clean and cater and so forth.

By May it was clear that the Carousel had increasingly hard times ahead. The assassination of Martin Luther King Jr. had hurt the music business everywhere, and even when the Dead or the Airplane played, only Friday and Saturday would sell out. Rakow's booking policy was not particularly commercial. Having Thelonious Monk play was certifiably hip, but not profitable. The show with Johnny Cash was his only nonsellout in years, simply because it was at the wrong venue. On May 1, the Diggers threw the Free City Convention.

Philosophically, the Diggers had remained consistent. Among other things, they advocated

> 1. free identity, the ownership ethic of identity in terms of possession is a prison wall built by money, burn money and find your free identity, you are beautiful. . . . 3. free families, the ethic of ownership defines family responsibilities and the education of children. break out of prison / burn money / evolve free families. . . . 5. free myths, the myth of gold, while mystically interesting, is unsatisfying because it requires the ethic of identity in material possession to sustain its power, break out of prison, burn money, you are the myth.

When the Diggers put their philosophy into action at the Carousel, all hell broke loose. At one point someone started a fire in a giant seashell, and Rakow demonstrated his objections to the idea by pissing on it. No less dismayed, Kanegson contributed water. Led by Jefferson Poland, the founder of the Sexual Freedom League, the evening dissolved into a large-scale sexual encounter, or at least that was the way many remembered it. There was something more public in store. That night someone snuck up and changed the marquee to read "Free Cunt," with predictable reactions from the city, local citizens, and the police.

On May 15 the Hell's Angels presented, as the poster read, "In Tear-Ass Sound and Color," Big Brother and the Holding Company, which left so much beer on the floor that it shorted out the lights of the car dealer below. Theoretically in charge of security, Bert Kanegson arrived, took one look at his cherished floor, realized he wasn't in charge, and went home. Members of the SFPD's Tactical Squad came to the top of the stairs, where Riester said, "If you come in here, you're going to start a riot." Agreeing, they left. Three weeks later the police were less cooperative, refusing to allow the Dead and the Airplane to play in Golden Gate Park for three thousand people as a wake for Senator Robert F. Kennedy, assassinated the night before after winning the California presidential primary.

As the Carousel teetered, so did the equilibrium of the Dead, who were experiencing great internal dissension even as they unknowingly found their second home, the place where their playing career would truly be launched. Their two engagements away from the Carousel during this period clearly defined their boundaries. Late in May, they flew to St. Louis for two nights, traveling two thousand miles to sell fewer than four hundred tickets. The promoter, of course, lost his shirt. Their salvation and their future came at the other gig.

In mid-June, the Dead went to New York City to make their first appearance at Bill Graham's Fillmore East, the former Village Theater, on Second Avenue in the East Village. The hole in the roof that had been there in December was now fixed. In fact, the Fillmore East would come to be the premier rock venue in the United States, and no band would play there more often or more successfully than the Dead. Graham had finessed Albert Grossman and local promoter Ron Delsener for the site and spent large sums to make the room work. It was not a ballroom but an old movie palace, with ornate murals and a gilt chandelier, and it became a theater with style. As the house manager remarked, the audience "got up when I wanted them to get up, and they sat down when I wanted them to sit down." Except that "the controlled environment thing always slipped at a Grateful Dead show. You just really couldn't do anything with it, you know?"

At 2,600 seats, it was far larger than most of the other rooms in the country, and more important, it was a short cab ride from the head offices of most of the music business. The most important person in rock in 1968 was not Bill Graham or Clive Davis of Columbia Records, but a man named Frank Barsalona, who'd formed Premier Talent, the most influential booking agency in the business. The most important room in the business of rock was, however, Graham's office at Fillmore East. Barsalona, Warner's Mo Ostin and Joe Smith when they were in town, Atlantic's Ahmet Ertegun—Bill's outer room was their hangout, where they would talk with the ushers and the stagehands to see who was hot and who was not, and with each other, further developing a business. Around now, the Psychedelic Supermarket was replaced by the Boston Tea Party, and a young man named Don Law began to manage it. There was the Electric Factory in Philadelphia, the Aragon in Chicago, and so forth. A new rock vaudeville circuit opened, and the bands became part of a new network.

The Dead returned to San Francisco, where the Carousel was in deep financial trouble. One night the police chained the front doors shut. Rakow and Riester were the only ones with keys, and Ron called Jonathan and warned him. Riester went in the back door, got to the safe, and hid what money was left on the catwalk above the stage. Then he went out and talked with the police. Riester was not aware of it, but Rakow had slipped in after him. As Riester stood considering the situation with the police, he thought of what Rakow had said: "It's real estate, a civil matter. They can't do this, they won't do this." "Of course," Riester added, "I was used to Rakow by this time." His ruminations were interrupted when Rakow ran down the stairs from the inside, a heavy metal table in his hands, and threw it through the glass doors in an act of incredible theater. And at New York levels of rapid-fire delivery, he refused to come out. "I'm on my own property, you can't make me. This is a civil matter and it's in the Constitution." And by all that is remarkable, the police unchained the door!

The Carousel had become a community center as much as a ball-room—the Black Panthers had a room, the Chicanos had an office—and so, inevitably, there was a community meeting. One issue concerned Big Brother and the Holding Company, which had played three shows. John Cooke, the Big Brother road manager, worked for Albert Grossman, and no matter what the band felt, he couldn't not take the money. On the street, this translated to "Janis just ripped off the Carousel." At the community meeting Janis came in, so busy that she'd not been able to eat, and sat chomping on a baguette and sausage, before asking simply, "What do you want?" And no one, not Rakow, not the other managers, no one, had any idea of how to answer. "Do you want music or money? Do you want me to do a benefit or just give you some bread?" And since no one really had a long-range plan, they never did take her up on the offer. McIntire felt that "everyone just wanted to bellyache because we were losing the place." As Airplane manager Bill Thompson recalled it, Garcia was "the one guy who was like a philosopher, a guy who was higher than everybody else mentally, and he could bring everybody into the same circle, all the fucking nutcakes who were around." It had worked for a while, but the problems had come to outweigh the energy. Thompson had never bought Rakow's act, and thought he was a "rotten manager."

On June 24 the charges from the bust of 710 were resolved. Rock Scully and Bob Matthews were fined $200 and Pigpen and Weir, the nonsmokers, were fined $100. At the courthouse Rock used the opportunity to plug the new album, which would be released the following month. "It's beautiful. Wow, it's great." The next day, Tuesday, June 25, the managers and musicians met once again to discuss the future of the Carousel. "Like every meeting anybody ever had like that," said photographer Bob Seidemann, "we all went home and nothing really happened." One of Bill Graham's favorite stories for many years would recount his flight to Ireland, complete with a planeful of nuns, to meet with Bill Fuller, the owner of the Carousel, and arrange a deal to take it over. However, one of the people who worked with him claimed that he never left San Francisco. In any case, Graham's Fillmore Auditorium closed on July 4, and on July 5, the ballroom at Market and Van Ness opened as the Fillmore West, with former "owners" Jerry Garcia and Jorma Kaukonen backstage as the Butterfield Blues Band played.

"It served its purpose," said McIntire. "Four months of the greatest loosest thing that ever, to my knowledge, happened anywhere . . . I don't know that anything that outrageous can really sustain itself."

Or, as the marquee read on June 25: "Nothing Lasts."

21

Interlude:
The Promoters

The Dead ordinarily utilized a tour coordinator (John Scher's Monarch and later Metropolitan Entertainment on the East Coast, Bill Graham Presents on the West Coast) and a local promoter to arrange the hall, deal with insurance and unions, supply the security, supervise the advertising, and make sure the house was ready. It could be maddening. By Grateful Dead standards, some promoters were barely awake. At one gig in the deep South late in the eighties, the audience entrance process congealed because there weren't enough doors open. When a Dead staff person suggested to the local promoter that opening more doors would be nice, the promoter remarked that it was all the fault of the hall manager, who'd never dealt with a sold-out house before. The staff member diplomatically refrained from pointing out that supervising the house was how the promoter earned his share of the proceeds.

That minor mess was trivial compared to the worst sin in rock history, when the promoter and road manager were having dinner together while the Who was going through its sound check. The crowd outside the hall was not organized or properly supervised, and when the people heard the sound check and concluded that the show had started, they tried to force their way into the hall, trampling eleven people to death. By contrast, one night in 1973 before a Dead concert at Long Island's Nassau Coliseum, thousands of kids started pushing and shoving toward the doors. Bill Graham grabbed a bullhorn and went out to face the crowd alone. A boy mockingly called out, "Hey capitalist," and Graham went into one of his truly great performances. Enraged, he dug a twenty-dollar bill from his sock and threw it at the kid's feet before shredding his ticket. It quieted the crowd at least for a while, and very possibly prevented major problems.

The distrust for promoters was epitomized in a 1973 incident between crew member Ben Haller and Philadelphia promoter Allen Spivak. Miffed because the crew had been served spaghetti—the Dead's contract called for high-protein dishes like steak and lobster—Haller collected leftovers from his, Lesh's, and Ram Rod's plates, and proceeded to dump them on Spivak's head. Larry Magid, Spivak's partner, wrote to road manager Sam Cutler to complain:

> We had the set-up you wanted perfect. There couldn't have been a complaint. In fact, the crew commented that it was the best set-up to date and that we finally had it together. The crew was given as many extra considerations as we could muster. Yet when Ben the light man didn't like his dinner, that wasn't even specified in the contract or ever asked for (The crew didn't even work that day), he threw it at Allen Spivak . . . I didn't hear him thank anyone for the filet for Thursday lunch or for the prime rib dinner at night . . . Even though we knew we were losing a lot of money, we still did it. We've had quite a few problems with your crew in the past. You say that the band knows that they're animals but that they can't do anything about the situation. All well and good, but they do represent you.

Cutler replied,

> In the years to come, no doubt, we'll all be able to laugh about it, but until we can laugh together, then I guess it will be hard for the Dead to work with you and Allen . . . allow me to finish with the conclusion that the Dead make their own bed, and thereafter they lie in it.

That they did; for the next three years they worked with another Philadelphia promoter at a much smaller venue, costing themselves a considerable amount of money.

In the final analysis, the most important promoter in Dead—and rock—history was Bill Graham, a brilliant showman who knew that what the Dead did musically was something he adored and coveted, even as he felt in his heart of hearts that the show was his and that the acts were subordinate to that. Moreover, for the two minutes that he was Father Time each New Year's Eve, it really was his show. It was no wonder that the fights over the midnight moment would go so deep—in a bizarre switch, the Dead would become the promoter, since it was their stage, and Bill the artist. The critical difference was, the Dead paid for the moment. Now, heaven for any Dead Head was a Bill Graham–produced Dead show. Instead of cold hot dogs, they got vegetarian goodies. The security was gentler, the ambience more pleasant. But Graham's gnawing, neurotic need to do a better job included the need to prove he was better by pinching off not a pound but at least an ounce of flesh. In his autobiography he blamed the bands. "People forcing me to lie about what food cost for the act in order to make my two cents from the dollar. Being forced to not work straight. I always *wanted* to deal straight. Even though people would say, 'Well, aren't you one of the masters of the game?' Defensively, yeah. I had to get real good at it or go down the drain as a businessman." "It's not the money," went the eternal BGP catchphrase, "it's the money." Once, Scrib grumbled about Bill to a Dead Head visiting from New York, and she grew scandalized. She happened to be a stagecraft professional, and Scrib asked her what she would have charged to build the float that had carried Bill as Father Time on the previous night. "It would cost $3,000," she said, "and I'd bid $5,000." "Bill tried to charge us $30,000—and it was built by his own company."

Early in the 1990s a federal grand jury indicted members of Philadelphia's Electric Factory Concerts (EFC) for fraud in a scheme that involved kickbacks from the local stagehand union. The Dead were among the victimized, yet they continued to patronize EFC. Another promoter once asked Scrib why the Dead did so. "We assume that every promoter steals from us," he answered. "What else can we do?" There are two ways to cheat a band. In a general admission show the promoter can sell tickets that are not accounted for. The other method is to pad the expenses. "I looked at the settlement," said Danny Rifkin of an early-eighties Bill Graham Presents show at the Greek Theater at U.C. Berkeley, "and I noticed that the statement was in two typefaces. It was a Xerox of the bill from Cal for some expenses, but obviously [someone at Bill Graham Presents] had cut it in half and pasted in a new set of numbers, but the typeface was different than the first one. So I called Cal, I forget the guy's name . . . And he couldn't lie, you know. He didn't want to implicate anybody, but the university—they're so strict. He said, 'Well, our rent is dahdahdahdah.' And then I started really detectiving and checking out every expense, and calling people, looking at bills, and going back year after year after year. And that's kind of it. Then I confronted . . . Bill, I guess. He actually paid us some of the money back, in twenty-dollar bills under the table. Like about $150,000 . . . Then I also found him cheating at Oakland Auditorium—also on the rent."

The other promoters were a varied bunch, ranging from the patrician Bostonian Don Law, whose father had helped record Robert Johnson, to former football player Frank Russo in Providence, to Dave Williams, of Cellar Door Concerts in Washington, D.C. For all his many shows with the Dead, Williams spoke to Garcia exactly once. When the road manager told him that he couldn't use a video screen at a show at the Capitol Centre he went to Garcia, who said, "You want to use it, use it, I don't fuckin' care. You can't see anything. The stage is too dark." Garcia was right, and Williams didn't repeat the process. Too big to intimidate—a former bouncer, Dave rather preferred to give than to receive any intimidation—Williams found the Dead's staff professional, noting that where other bands spent thousands on the finest wines and liquors, the Dead spent freely on toys, gadgets, stuff. For the Dead, the important thing was stability. Year after year they used the same promoters, valuing loyalty and responsible competence above all. Even as their status rose, their percentages did not.

The only promoter to become friendly with the band was John Scher. Lacking Graham's genius and flair—and also his anxiety-producing *Sturm und Drang*—Scher was the reliable, trusted friend who took care of business. Younger than the band members, he was born in 1950 in New Jersey, booked the entertainment for his high school junior prom, and was a promoter ever after. In college at LIU Brooklyn in the late sixties, he became part of the network of agents and promoters who would enter the New York arena after Graham closed the Fillmore East in 1971, a group that included Jim Koplik and Shelley Finkel in Connecticut and Howard Stein at the Capital in Port Chester. Over the years he would advise the band in its dealings on many levels, from negotiations with the record company to touring Europe. Once, they even asked him to replace Bill Graham.

After years of frustration with Graham, Dead booker/manager Richard Loren threw in the towel and asked John Scher to act as the Dead's agent in putting on the April 22, 1979, show at Spartan Stadium, in San Jose, California. But the rock world was divided into territories, and Scher, who worked in New Jersey, assumed Graham would object. John had always accepted Graham's preeminence in the field, and would not get involved without his blessing. To John, Bill said, "It's true, I can't deal with those crazy people anymore. I welcome your participation." With Phil Lesh's words in his ears—"We're not paying for the fucking set"—John went ahead, setting up basic parameters—ticket price, on-sale date, etc.—with Danny Scher (no relation to John), one of Bill's associates, but not the expenses, which was the rub. What Lesh had referred to was that each different stadium show paid for the construction of a set, but since large parts of the set tended to be reused, it became a significant source of profit for Bill Graham Presents. About the third time a band paid for a set, the band members, if they were paying attention at all, began to complain to their management. (Of course, few bands had the clout to play three major outdoor shows.)

Weeks passed and tickets went on sale, but no list of expenses came to John. Finally, he called Bill. "Bill, I'm having a real problem. Your guy Danny Scher is just a liar. Three weeks now, he's never sent me the expenses." And Bill Graham went well and truly off. For John, "it was my first experience with a Bill roar. He was berserk. 'I have to deal with fuckin' Jersey? To book my band. You motherfucking ingrate scumbag . . .' It was a nonstop lunatic binge for twenty minutes, and then a hang-up. I called Loren and said, 'I quit.' They did the gig, and they paid for the set, and from then on, my relationship with Bill was acrimonious."

In the end, it was Bill they borrowed money from, Bill they relied on. In the 1970s, he was their bank, lending them the funds to get through dry spells. At a 1987 interview Graham spent several hours speaking of how painful he found the Dead's refusal to let him get too close. It just *killed* Bill that these children would not embrace him fully, and he never ever let up trying to get them to do so. At the time of the interview, he was feeling good about the band, because they'd recently had a meeting with him and asked him to consider a Dead tour of China. At the same time, he'd brought up the idea of the Dead playing at the Golden Gate Bridge's fiftieth anniversary. Graham chortled, "Jerry stood up and said 'I like this idea, and I don't want to get paid for it.'" Graham was sooo happy. "Trust at a very special level, that gives me hope." The trust was that the band had met with him without management. "It was the first [one-to-one] meeting I've ever had with the Grateful Dead. Evah! Evah!"

And alongside the ongoing, eternally stalemated war between the Dead and Bill, there was a succession of endearing moments, from the time he tried to fix Garcia's guitar at the Trips Festival to Bill's theatrical introduction to the band's first performance in San Francisco after a two-year break in the middle 1970s. As the lights went down, a Gregorian chant played over the sound system and a white organ rose from the orchestra pit played by a hooded figure who resembled the fiddling skeleton-monk on the cover of the recent album *Blues for Allah*. Three monks with candles walked down the aisle toward the stage. Each person with a seat on the aisle had been given a lighter, so that the monks walked through a wall of flame. The curtain rose and Bob Weir began to sing "The Music Never Stopped." *That's* showbiz.

22

Forward
into the Fog

(7/68–2/15/69)

On July 18, 1968, Warner Bros. released the Dead's second album, *Anthem of the Sun,* and what should have been a triumph was effectively a disaster. *Rolling Stone* would call it "an extraordinary event," comparing the blend of electronic and electric music to Edgard Varèse. England's *New Musical Express* was quite accurate: "It's so completely unlike anything you ever heard before that it's practically a new concept in music. It's haunting, it's pretty, it's infinite . . . a complete mindblower." So much for the satisfaction of getting good reviews. The band was in catastrophic disarray. This was not an uncommon state of affairs, but a month after the release they would hold a meeting in which they would at least theoretically fire Weir and Pigpen, and that was unique. The new album was much too strange to be commercially viable, so Warner Bros. was less than enthused. None of the band members were all that thrilled with the final result, declaring that they had "lost it in the mix." Weir was particularly dissatisfied with the version of his song, and the cold stream of criticism that he was getting from Lesh, and to a lesser extent Garcia, would shut down his compositional creativity for some years.

The album title had come from one of the strange books that always floated around 710, James Churchward's *The Lost Continent of Mu,* a piece of automatic writing that traced the influence of the mythical Mu on, among other things, Egyptian musical instruments, about which no one actually knew anything. One instrument Churchward imagined, the dead throat, was made of a skull and was used to perform the mythical "Anthem of the Sun."

The album cover's origins were almost as esoteric as its name. On the previous New Year's Eve, Phil's friend Bill Walker had undergone a psychedelic experience in the Valley of Fire, an eerily beautiful patch of desert near Las Vegas, and from his visions he began a portrait of the Dead as a hydra-headed Buddha springing from the muse. Early in the spring, Walker stopped by the Potrero Theater to tell Lesh about his painting, walking in on a particularly acrimonious argument over money, management, or something else, and was greeted by Lesh, who came over and shrugged, "Well, I guess that's it," indicating to Walker that the band was breaking up. Perhaps not. Instead, a few weeks later Phil told Bill that the partially completed portrait, which had been painted on a window shade glued onto wood, would be the cover. Walker continued to work on it, using layer after layer of paint, creating images of the band members that were not portraits but ritual masks. Eventually, the Warner Bros. art director approved it, still unfinished.

Possibly the oddest thing about this most unusual of albums was the single. Released in May, two months before the album, it was "Dark Star," backed with "Born Cross-Eyed." Years later Paul Williams would cite it as a "perfect two-and-a-half-minute distillation," with "originality, power, and enduring appeal," but few people ever heard that version of the song. Of the sixteen hundred copies Warner Bros. shipped, only five hundred were sold.

Early in August the band went to Southern California for dates in San Diego and the Newport Pop Festival, at the Orange County fairgrounds. It was a crummy gig on a flat, dusty field, with insufficient facilities for the 100,000 who had gathered there, and the primary amusement of the day came when the Dead assaulted the Jefferson Airplane with cream pies. As the bands gathered just a few miles from his hometown, Richard Nixon was enjoying the convention that would lead four days later to his nomination for president. Every young American, however, knew that the real show would come three weeks later, at the Democratic convention in Chicago. In New York, Emmett Grogan and Peter Coyote had ensconced themselves in Albert Grossman's office to work telephones in an effort to dissuade young Americans from going to Chicago, having correctly anticipated that a bloodbath was in store for protesters. In January, Jerry Rubin, Abbie Hoffman, and Paul Krassner had created the essentially mythical Youth International Party, the Yippies, and shortly afterward issued a call for a Festival of Life to take place in Chicago during the convention. The Yippie party had no members, but its leaders were certainly shrewd media manipulators, and their prime dupe was the old-school mayor of Chicago, Richard Daley, and his police department, which came to believe every Yippie fantasy.

As the election of 1968 approached, America had broken in half over the Vietnam War. On one side was the World War II generation, people in their forties and older, veterans for whom the pivot of their lives had been service to their country, and for whom opposition to the war was unthinkable. On the other side were the young, who had lost faith in the military and the war. Eighty percent of the votes in the Democratic primaries that year were antiwar. As the convention approached, Daley's mind was captured by the Yippies, and he fell into rampant paranoia: LSD in the water supply, Yippie girls as hookers who would give LSD to delegates, Yippie studs to seduce delegates' wives and daughters. The Yippies proclaimed in a press release, "We are dirty, smelly, grimy, foul . . . we will piss and shit and fuck in public . . . we will be constantly stoned or tripping on every drug known to man."

In the days before the convention, the Soviet Union invaded Czechoslovakia, inducing further tension worldwide. Just three months before, an honest-to-God, in-the-streets revolution had seemed possible in France. As Americans huddled around their television sets, watching the war in Vietnam and the Chicago convention, the divisions grew ever deeper. Barbed wire surrounded the convention hall. Daley's police goons beat reporters, packed the galleries to shout down opposition and roar support for his candidate, Hubert Humphrey, then cheered when Daley responded to Senator Abraham Ribicoff's denunciation of the violence by calling him a "Jew son-of-a-bitch." In the end, ten thousand people came to Chicago to demonstrate, of whom perhaps one-sixth were undercover police and army intelligence agents. On August 28, the demonstrators massed in front of the Hilton Hotel and chanted, "The whole world is watching," as the Chicago police used rifle butts, clubs, tear gas, and Mace to beat them into the pavement. The world did watch, and a majority of Americans, terrified by the images the Yippies had promoted, supported the police.

The Dead spent the month playing music at home, and while their sympathies were with the demonstrators, they were too apolitical and also far too streetwise to ever dream of tangling with the Chicago Police Department. Apart from that, they were stumbling about in a mental fog, the aftermath of the closing of their home, the Carousel. Healy had left the band to work with Quicksilver in Hawaii, and Owsley had returned to his role as the Dead's soundman. Jonathan Riester was now the road manager, and he'd brought with him Jon McIntire, who was given the job of creating some sort of order in the Dead's business files. Jon began by going to the attic at 710, where he found shopping bags choked with nearly three years of receipts. Neither Rifkin nor Scully had cared about details like bookkeeping, and the band's finances were a ludicrous mess. Rock remained as manager, but his strength was always longer on inspiration than organization. In August Jon found some office space above a liquor store on the corner of Union and Fillmore, and they moved in. At the same time, Rock, McIntire, Riester, and Kanegson rented what became known as the Manager's House, on Hermit Lane, in Kentfield, Marin County. By now, their use of 710 was pretty well at an end, and their rehearsal time at the Potrero Theater was severely limited due to noise complaints. As working musicians, they were torn with dissension about who should be in the band, and they had no place to prepare for shows to come.

The August band meeting where Pigpen and Weir were fired was effective, if not in the way that it might at first have appeared. The catalyst for the event was far more in their personalities than in the specifics of performance. The band's dynamics started from Garcia, whose presence was dominant, both emotionally and musically, but who refused to lead. Next came Lesh, because the two of them had bonded as musicians in a way that held primacy among all the other links. They were thunder and lightning, and though they needed the rest of the band quite as much as each other—and knew it—they were, realistically, musical leaders. Lesh was impatient and demanding, and the previous fall the band had "sat me down in a circle and asked me to back off a little, from being so intense during rehearsals." That August it was again Lesh who tried to make things happen. Owsley recorded the meeting, and it was revealing. Weir's obliviousness was simply too much. Two years after he'd quit taking LSD, he was still wide-eyed, and it showed in his music. Instead of nailing a solid chopping rhythm, he played what Hart called "little waterfalls" that were "all over the map." Pigpen's blues had little to do, musically, with what the rest of the band was doing, and his drinking kept him from effectively working to make a larger contribution.

In the meeting, Rock Scully took the lead: ". . . the situation as it exists right now, [as it] is musically, depends on four guys. The weight is on four cats in this band, not six as the band is now formed. It seems like the music is being carried to a certain level, then staying there. I notice it mostly from the way you guys respond to your own music, and you guys tire of music that has much more potential, many more possibilities, too soon . . . it never gets any better. Matter of fact, it begins to get worse. Very fast, too fast for the material, because the material is complex and groovy and much further out than most music is these days . . ."

Garcia agreed. "All you gotta do is listen to the tapes there and test them," and Lesh chorused, "You can't really get but two or three of them *on,* man, even those are with reservation; I mean I only like them with reservation . . . So after this weekend, we decided that's the end of that. No more."

And there was silence. Weir's reaction to Phil's criticism was a stubborn refusal to respond, and his quietude was typical. Rock continued, "[Bob] had no words then, and you see, it's a week later and you still have no words. It doesn't matter, that happens to be where you're at."

Garcia remarked, "Asking him for explanations is like not where it's at . . . Just the whole conflict is not where it's at under any circumstances."

At last, Weir spoke. "The idea of faction is not where it's at . . . I'm losing control of words here . . . they are falling apart in my mouth. I've said all I can say for now. That's more or less why I say I have no words."

Rock replied, "You'd never have to say a word if it were in your music," and Weir riposted, obscurely, "I'd never have to say a word if it was in the way I tied my shoes."

In the classic avoid-confrontation-at-all-costs Dead manner, Mickey hurriedly called for an adjournment. "I think it's time for me to make a motion. Unless anybody else wants to talk about anything."

"A motion? What's that?" asked Weir.

"Split," said Hart. ". . . not unless anybody wants to talk about anything. Not unless there is anything else on the agenda?"

Scully herded the conversation back on track. "Well, we haven't talked about anything more immediate than an EP and this record, really, in terms of Bob and Pig and I think that you guys oughta make your intentions clear—you haven't to them so far. You were planning to, Mickey, but you are now making a motion to adjourn something that was started and not finished."

"I thought it was just all said."

"No," said Rock. "You can't just think those things, man, you have to say them when it's this kind of scene."

Garcia once more tried to sum up. "Well, here's where it's at, man.

You guys know that the gigs haven't been any fun, it hasn't been no good playing it, it's because we're at different levels of playing, we're thinking different thoughts and we just aren't playing together . . ."

Lesh again tried to push the issue. "I really don't want to work in that form [six-man band], man. Really . . . All four of us don't want to work that way."

In a last attempt to focus, Rock pushed Garcia to respond. "Listen, man, why did you not correct him? Why did I have to correct him? . . . he's speaking for all four musicians. Jerry . . ."

And the leader who wouldn't lead murmured, "Oh, yeah, right."

As Owsley later observed, "You can't fire your left hand because it doesn't write as nicely as your right." Though Weir and Pigpen were theoretically fired, they continued to perform at gigs.

On the last day of August, Jon McIntire got a phone call from friends in the band It's a Beautiful Day, telling him that the scene at the Sky River Rock Festival was a groove, and the Dead should come on up. Rural, local, and aesthetically hip, Sky River had a small audience of no more than twenty thousand, and acts that were far more diverse than just rock bands. The festival management made them welcome, so off they went the next day. It was a delightful jaunt, and the festival's closing jam, which featured Big Mama Thornton, James Cotton, and, at various times, Mickey Hart, Pigpen, Kreutzmann, and Garcia, was proof of the upside of spontaneity. Nine days later a gig in San Jose with Frank Zappa was canceled due to poor ticket sales, even though such audience as there was had already entered.

Undaunted, they began recording their third album early in September at Pacific Recording, south of San Francisco in San Mateo, where Bob Matthews had landed a job. They began with "St. Stephen," which they'd been playing for three months. Along with "China Cat" and "Alligator," it had been written as a lyric but with Hunter's own melody, and Hunter felt the "radiance" of it over the two nights it took him. The band had given it a magnificent setting, with Lesh creating the bridge. It was complex to sing and difficult to play, but absolutely gorgeous, a medieval vision set inside a psychedelic ambience. Shortly after, they began work on "Cosmic Charley," which Garcia later dismissed as overdone and clumsy, but which Hunter argued was difficult to play because of its tuning. It was the first time Hunter and Garcia had actually written together, and it was not yet a smooth process—the effortless matchup of lyric and music in "Dark Star" was so far an anomaly. Garcia had a melody and changes for "Charley," and he would play them to Hunter, who'd write something that Garcia, he recalled, would usually reject. Eventually, they settled on a song that Garcia always had reservations about.

Early in October they experimented with the "Barbed Wire Whipping Party In the Razor Blade Forest," which Garcia called "one of our better atrocities," a "little exercise in audio brutality" that was much "too weird to use." Sitting around a tank or two of nitrous oxide one day at Pacific Recording, they all donned earphones and inserted hoses from the tank into their mouths. All sound was fed through a multichannel delay, so whatever was said would come back many times. Betty Cantor gave them each a mike, and Hunter read, "Last week I went to Mars and talked to God and he told me to tell you to hang tight and don't worry, the solution to everything is death!" Behind that, everybody else was chanting "push it and pull it," "meat, meat, gimme my meat," and so on, to the sixteenth power.

Also in early October the band discovered, probably unconsciously, how they would be able to fire Weir and Pigpen—and it would not involve firing. Instead, they would start an additional band, in which the other four musicians, plus occasional guests, would play free-form, instrumental-only music. On October 8, Mickey Hart and the Hartbeats—Hart, Kreutzmann, Garcia, and Lesh—began a three-night run at the Matrix. The audience was tiny, and those few brave souls were about to get a shock. The stage at the Matrix was in the middle of a narrow, not terribly long room, so that the distance from amplifiers to brick wall was less than twenty feet. "We were just scalping them," Hart said. "We were giving them a lobotomy, and they couldn't believe it. They couldn't get up, and they thought they'd die." On the third night the Hartbeats were joined by Jack Casady and Elvin "Pigboy" Bishop, who played the blues in the middle of musical madness. It was satisfying, and Hartbeats gigs would continue to alternate with Grateful Dead shows throughout the fall of 1968, but it was musically inchoate and never did find a center.

Establishing the Hartbeats was a major step toward rebalancing the good ship Grateful Dead, and there were others. After the closing of the Carousel, Bert Kanegson had gone to Hawaii, where he'd gotten a call from Vee telling him that the band was breaking up and to come home. Upon his arrival in late August, he found 710 deserted. Danny was traveling, Rakow had gone off to find a more successful hustle, and the Grateful Dead "office," the giant desk, was stored in Brian Rohan's basement. The Potrero Theater was not only a dump, it was a silly location for a band that now mostly lived in Marin County, and Bert went in search of a replacement. Early in September he found a building renting for $600 a month near Hamilton Air Force Base in Marin, just south of Novato, roughly seven miles from their old refuge at Olompali. The band, crew, equipment, and Bear moved in, with Bert around, as he put it, to "keep an eye on Bear." Rock and McIntire operated out of the office on Union Street. The Dead owed Bill Graham $12,000 for a bailout loan, and they worked off their debt in a couple of ways. That month Bill opened the Millard booking agency, and the Dead joined Santana, Cold Blood, and It's a Beautiful Day on the roster. The agency itself moved into the offices at Union and Fillmore, and for the first time, the Dead were formally connected with Graham, just seven months after being his prime competitor.

Graham's putative other rival, the Avalon, was going out of business. Between 1966 and 1967 the Family Dog had made and spent a million dollars, but by 1968 sales were off. Chet Helms was not a businessman but the de facto director of an environmental theater, and there was no doubt that some employees took advantage of his utter lack of financial controls. The Avalon had always had an ungodly number of guests, and probably 30 percent of the audience never paid. At the end of September the Dog lost its dance permit due to some clearly fabricated noise complaints, and the venue would close at the end of the year. In mid-October the Dead played their first shows there in a year and a half as a kind gesture to Chet, and as a good-bye.

Bob Weir's twenty-first birthday, October 16, 1968, followed the last Avalon run by three days, and he would not forget it. As the day dawned, he was unemployed, without transportation, and living in Bill Kreutzmann's garage on Lucas Valley Road, between San Rafael and Novato. Worse, Bill was preparing to move, so Weir was about to be homeless. Pigpen called and invited him to come into San Francisco for his first legal drink. He hitched to Highway 101 and began walking backward down the shoulder, thumb out, guitar over his shoulder. The oncoming headlights were in his eyes and he could see very little, and nothing at all of the construction ditch that he proceeded to tumble into, nor the foot of water that recent rains had left at the bottom of the hole. It might have been the bottom of his life, and he reacted characteristically. He managed a rueful laugh, crawled out of the hole, made it to the bar by closing, and got through his awful day. When Kreutzmann moved, Weir took a room at the Hamilton Air Force Base warehouse, where he spent most of his time practicing hard and "trying to stay out of the way." He briefly entertained vague plans to move to New Mexico, but they stayed vague.

Pigpen, the other firee, had other things to occupy his time. That month Vee had experienced a blinding headache that turned out to be a stroke. After her surgery the band gathered around in support, and Jerry and Bobby came to her hospital room with guitars and encouraged her with a duo performance. Pig was her therapist through her recovery, and a good one, firmly making her do necessary things rather than doing what was easy. "You can do it, babe, you can do it." At first she wore a wig to conceal her scalp, which had been shaved for surgery, but Pig took her to Fillmore Street, showed her women with short hair, and convinced her to put it away.

Late in November the Grateful Dead, six strong, set off on a tour of the Midwest that began at Veterans Hall in Columbus, Ohio. Only a couple of hundred people attended, and most seemed to be from Ohio University, in Athens. Since the next night was open, the Dead spontaneously went to Athens to play. It was incredibly gratifying to pull off a show in one day, find a ripe audience, and leave them "hanging from the walls," as Lesh put it.

The evening's other interesting aspect was the arrival of a new band member, Phil's pal Tom "T.C." Constanten, who had completed his service in the air force, leaving behind a buried computer program timed to run six weeks after his departure that would type out a rising middle finger followed by the abbreviation USAF. Later, T.C. would ruminate that his presence in the band would be "unwitting glue to divert attention to allow [Weir and Pigpen] to solidify their positions." It was understood that Pig and Weir were out, and T.C. fit the new structure better, but nothing else seemed terribly clear. "It amazed everybody," T.C. recalled, "that anything happened, because there was so much sniping going on. There was always some sort of simmer." With T.C. on keyboards, Pig was "relegated," in Jon McIntire's words, to conga drums. From Mickey Hart's corner, this was all one of Phil's "intellectual trips." Lesh had discussed adding T.C. with Garcia, but neither Mickey nor Weir recalled knowing of it in advance. For Mickey, T.C. "never fit in. He couldn't let go. He thought too much . . . everybody else was strange, but I knew their strangeness. I couldn't connect" with T.C.'s particularly intellectual strangeness. Weir more or less agreed. "He, like I, had to invent his own style—but he didn't. He had no roots in African American music. I couldn't quote the popular modes either, but I ultimately invented something." T.C.'s problem, as T.C. saw it, would largely be one of amplification. Onstage he had two Leslie speakers, and he wanted four, because Garcia's guitar could be louder in his microphones than he was.

Shortly before Christmas, Rock and Riester and a gang of friends took off on one of the greater Dead scene's more bizarre adventures, the London Run, a jaunt to London that became a mission—although a mission to *what* was never entirely clear. There was some razzmatazz about turning on the Beatles, and a further tap dance about dealing with the Dead's European publishing business, but that, obviously, did not require an entourage. Ken Kesey, who came along, called it "a kind of cultural lend-lease, heads across the water and all that."

The genesis of the London Run was the free show in Central Park the previous summer, when a woman named Cookie Eisenberg came, listened, and soon became Mickey Hart's lover. Cookie had connections to Billy Hitchcock and the world of Millbrook, but to this point her life was sufficiently conventional that she was part owner of a travel agency. One of the other actors in this piece of theater was Bob Borden, of all things an assistant district attorney in Philadelphia who had fallen under the Dead's spell. Borden didn't handle being high very well, and eventually broke down entirely. For the London Run, he contributed his American Express card, which ran through Cookie's agency and yielded three first-class tickets to London. According to Rifkin, who was already in London, the tickets were intended to take himself, Borden, and Rock to Switzerland to purchase LSD, to Morocco to put it into capsules, and then home.

Somewhere in there, in the nature of a highly elaborate Grateful Dead plot, the three first-class became five coach tickets, to take Rock, two Hell's Angels, and two Diggers to London. "I was a bit of a rake in those days," Rock said later. Somehow they wheedled more funds out of Bill Graham, and at the end of the very complicated day, thirteen of the oddest people in San Francisco left for London. The two Angels were Frisco Pete Knell and Billy "Sweet William" Fritsch, a former sailor and at one time a San Francisco criminal nicknamed the Panama Hat Bandit. The Diggers were Peter Coyote and Paula McCoy, ex-wife of Don and the doyenne of the Digger salon at 715 Ashbury Street, who liked to wear boots with a mink coat and nothing else. There was Peter "Monk" Zimmels, a former nuclear weapons officer in the U.S. Navy who'd deserted the service and adopted monk's garb as a disguise—and then became a real monk. Minutes before their flight was to leave New York, two more partners in crime came aboard: Ken Kesey and Frankie Azzara, a go-go dancer who'd formerly dated Hart, and would later be Weir's lover for some years, but who on this trip would briefly go to work for George Harrison. Hitchhiking along somehow, because members of the Grateful Dead family simply could not consort with the Beatles without her, was Beatlemaniac Sue Swanson, along with her infant son, Josh.

At length, the group arrived at Apple, the Beatles' headquarters, a white Georgian town house on Savile Row that resembled an embassy except for the young women, "apple scruffs," who patrolled the sidewalk hoping for a Beatle sighting. Derek Taylor had returned from Monterey to work for the Beatles, and he was a charming and tolerant man. "Derek, Adolf Hitler is in reception." "Oh, Christ, not that asshole again. Okay, send him up." After Adolf the San Francisco contingent, which would shortly end up with tattoos reading "Pleasure Crew," was tolerably easy to handle. Derek gave them a room where some of them stayed, while others joined Mouse and Bob Seidemann, who were living in London and had an apartment. The most commonly told tale of their trip was of the ill-fated Apple Christmas party, at which John Lennon made his entrance as Santa Claus at the precise moment that an Apple publicist reproved Frisco Pete for his premature raid on the buffet and earned himself a fat lip. But there was a much better story. That week the Rolling Stones filmed the *Rock and Roll Circus,* a TV show that involved them and most of the top stars of English rock. Jagger didn't like the results, and it was not then released. Sue Swanson and her baby attended, and during a pause in recording late in the night, she asked a cameraman where she might change Josh's diaper. "Go through that door and ask the guy in the brown jacket." A paragon of courtesy, brown-jacketed Mick Jagger walked her into the dressing room and made a space for Josh on a table.

As 1968 neared its end, *Rolling Stone* printed a nude picture of John Lennon and Yoko Ono on its back cover. Columbia Records ran an ad that depicted seven men in jail with the truly stupid caption "But the Man Can't Bust Our Music." Riven by internal dissension, Cream disbanded. The top album was the Beatles' *White Album,* with the Stones' *Beggar's Banquet* moving up. At a free show at the Fillmore East on the day after Christmas, a local gang of rabble-rousers called Up Against the Wall Motherfuckers (UAWMF) attacked Bill Graham, breaking his nose. In Paris, an ongoing argument over the shape of the table stalled peace talks between the United States and North Vietnam. The previous month had seen the election of Richard Nixon as president. The year 1969 was about to arrive with a harsh momentum. The ugliness of the year would drive the Dead ever more inward, and their music-making would benefit.

Over the course of the fall, the recording of the Dead's third album had gone so remarkably well that it could almost be described as efficient. Since the songs were primarily by Garcia, the minimal participation of Weir and particularly Pigpen in the recording process was not disastrous. Then, around Christmas, Ampex installed Prototype #2 at the studio, one of the first two sixteen-track recording machines in the world. The company had built the first successful videotape recorder in the mid-fifties, and now it had combined audio heads with the videotape transport to produce true multitrack recording. The band came in, fooled with it for a couple of hours, and said, "Fuck it, we're redoing the album." Poor Joe Smith.

Two days after Christmas, the band hit the road. "The road is life," some rocker said, some swing musician said, some minstrel show performer, some troubador. Making a living in the performing arts requires travel. The Dead hadn't exactly resolved their membership crisis, and as late as December there was talk of David Nelson replacing Weir, but it was far too late for any personnel changes. The Hartbeats "never really worked right," thought Lesh. "It wasn't working right with [Pig and Weir], and it wasn't without them." Though no one ever openly said a word, they rescinded the firing and backed into the right decision as usual. They had their band, and they had material to play, and now they went on the road, playing more than one hundred shows a year for the next several years.

The circumstances varied dramatically. Texas, for instance, wasn't ready for the San Francisco sound, and there was often trouble. One night Quicksilver opened, playing very well. This challenged the Dead, who responded with a fine set that was abbreviated when the police pulled the plug, a not-uncommon event in those days. Furious, Ron Polte shouted at the promoter, "Those guys earned that fucking encore," and found himself being tackled by a police officer. The ever-volatile Mickey Hart grabbed a mallet and was about to give his gong a whack when he noticed two things in quick succession. One was that he'd get an inconveniently located cop on the backswing, which would further ignite an angry audience. The second thing he saw was that Garcia had managed to interpose himself between the officer and his percussionist. The gong went unwhacked, the cop's skull remained intact, and after an *a cappella* "We Bid You Goodnight," the Dead escaped the Lone Star State.

Sometimes the rub came from the other bands. The Dead once opened for Country Joe and the Fish at Fillmore East, where there were always two shows nightly. As Melton recalled it, his band went on first for the first show, and he went to Phil and insisted that the Dead open the second show so that Country Joe and the Fish could close. As Melton sleepily went onstage to plug in around 3 A.M., he concluded that there were about five people left in the audience. Another time, again in Texas, he was approached by Ram Rod, who announced that the police had been following them—there seemed to be some marijuana issues—over the past few shows, and could the Dead please open? "Are you foxing us? Are you gonna play another three-hour set?" Ram Rod didn't know how to lie, so Barry and Joe agreed that "Hey, they're our brothers, we gotta be nice." The Dead went on, played forty minutes, packed, and split. Just as Country Joe and the Fish went on, police blanketed the entire backstage, thinking that C.J. and the Fish were the Dead. Eventually, Joe and Barry got the confusion cleared up, but they learned a lesson: Ram Rod was always truthful, but "never trust a Prankster" was always good advice.

Bands the Dead didn't know were even more likely to catch it. Early in January 1969 the new band Led Zeppelin put out its first album and toured the United States. Zep guitarist Jimmy Page said, "It was the Fillmore West in San Francisco when we knew we'd really broken through. It was just *bang*!" In the long run, Zep would be known as the most decadent, demonic, and brutal band of all, satyrs whose arrival produced the sound of "garter belts sliding up young thighs all over [town]," as their chief groupie gushed before going on to enumerate the whips in Page's suitcase. While in San Francisco for their Fillmore West show, Zep went over to Herb Greene's studio on Laguna Street for a photo session. During the shoot, Greene heard from the Dead that they, too, needed a new picture. Zep said sure, let them come over, and lived to regret it. Pig came in wearing Mickey's .22 Ruger pistol, and when the wait bored him, he began to fire it off. He was, Weir recalled, "using it as punctuation. A shot through the ceiling was a period on a sentence. He wasn't particularly impassioned by it. He was just fuckin' around. He wasn't trying to get on anyone's nerves, he wasn't trying to scare anybody . . . He was quoting *Pogo* at the time, he was big on doing that, his favorite comic strip. I'm thinking, Herbie's gotta be loving this. We didn't even see [Led Zeppelin] leave. 'Hey, what happened to those guys?' " Herb never did get paid for Zep's session.

A week later the Dead found themselves in an even more bizarre place, on the set of the television show *Playboy After Dark,* joining Sid Caesar, astrologer Sidney Omarr, and Hugh Hefner. The Dead were not impressed. Even the set's bookshelves were "filled with mindless books not even worth stealing," thought T.C., and Garcia found Hefner "wooden." The premise of the show was that the TV audience was invited to see a party at Hef's house, complete with attractive male and female models standing around in the background while Hef chatted with the special guests. What no one at the show knew was that it was widely considered to be a poor idea to eat or drink anything around the Grateful Dead. There was a coffee urn, with cups lined up, and Hagen and Riester went by with eyedroppers, also making sure to acknowledge Hefner's personal mug of Pepsi. The routine delays of any show combined on this one with the built-in time lag incurred by having Bear as soundman. Then the coffee kicked in. Gradually, it became obvious that there was a new glow in the air. Things began to get odder and odder. Technicians began to stare up into the lights. The male extras began to loosen their ties, and the women started to loosen their tops, their makeup melting along with their inhibitions. The Dead played "Mountains of the Moon" splendidly, and as Phil and Kreutzmann left, Hefner stopped them and said, eyes bright, "I want to thank you for your special gift."

Not everyone found the Dead's presence so amusing. Airline clerks, for example. "Ten minutes after takeoff time," wrote journalist Michael Lydon, "and the passengers wait in two clumps. Clump one, the big one, is ordinary human beings . . . Clump two is the Dead, manic, dirty, hairy, noisy, a bunch of drunken Visigoths in cowboy hats . . . Pigpen has just lit Bob Weir's paper on fire, and the cinders blow around their feet. Phil is at his twitchiest . . . Jerry discards cigarette butts as if the world was his ashtray . . . Over on the left in the cargo area, a huge rented truck pulls up with the Dead's equipment, 90 pieces of extra luggage. Like clowns from a car, amp after amp after drum case is loaded onto dollies and wheeled to the jet's belly. It dawns on Clump One all at once that it is those arrogant heathens with all their outrageous gear that are making the plane late . . . It dawns on the heathens too, but they dig it, shouting to the quippies to tote that amp, lift that organ."

On another occasion, Dan Healy and his girlfriend could not sit together on a sold-out flight, and she cursed the stewardess. Lesh laughed. "I wonder how long it'll take to get us off this plane," he said. About two and a half seconds. A police officer arrived and said, "Grateful Dead. Up." Danny Rifkin approached the cop and said, "Can I talk to you man-to-man?" "You stand over there," came the reply, "and get away from me." Poor Riester—road managing Visigoths was no joke. On the most benign level, he had Weir, the youngster, the prank-loving pain in the ass. "At LAX once," Riester said, "I'm at the counter, Weir waltzed up and said, 'You're high on marijuana, aren't you? Got any dope on you?' I got rid of him and charmed the lady at the counter, but it was stuff like that. He had a very realistic Luger squirt gun that once got him surrounded by cops. Going down the jetway, he'd be mooing, then the rest of the band would pick it up." There were countless on-board pillow fights, which Weir usually started, and he was also known, without provocation, to moan as the plane descended for landing, "We're not gonna make it, we're all gonna die."

Phil, Riester thought, was demanding about food and accommodations, but usually legitimately so. "He could always understand that the onion skin, no matter how thin, had two sides." Kreutzmann, depending on mood, might not, and he was always suspicious of outsiders trying to burn them. Garcia was easy, thought Riester, who felt "privileged to have known him." Pig's heavy Hammond organ caused Riester extra work, but "Garcia liked Pig, and that was enough for me." T.C. he dismissed as too intellectual. What made Riester's job possible was Ram Rod, "the sixth musician. The Dead would not have survived without him. He did the impossible all the time, twenty-four seven." Hart had a toy cannon that fired a blank shotgun shell that at least once went off in Rod's face, leaving him with singed hair and blackened cheeks. To Weir's amazement, Ram Rod "never stopped working. It didn't faze him at all." When Hart realized that the injured Ram Rod had never stopped loading in order to be ready for the cue, he concluded, "No more cannons."

Riester hung in there, too. He did have one major weakness, and that was what Weir would call a "bump of misdirection," not a good thing when one left the airport in a rental car on a tight schedule. Of course, Weir found their explorations of the back alleys of American cities not only diverting, but "it sure taught us how to pull together to play a show with no time to spare." And at airports, Riester was a champ. "I was allowed to take guitars directly to the plane for hand loading, and in the process figured out who was the guy who actually released the plane from the gate." Once, the equipment truck had a flat tire and was terrifically late. "I got the guy who released the plane aside, gave him $100, plus promised him albums and such, to hold the plane. He called the gate and told them to let the truck drive directly to the plane. As a result, everyone on the plane missed their connections. We got kicked off the airlines for a minute."

A letter from United Airlines to the band's travel agent sometime after this incident noted that the Dead had "caused so much confusion arriving at the airport with all their equipment just a few minutes before flight departure, shouting obscenities at employees and passengers, drawn and fired a revolver (fortunately loaded only with blanks) at the check-in area" that United was no longer accepting reservations from the band. In January 1969, with Bill Graham booking them, and provided "that en route they conduct themselves in a manner that will not disturb other passengers," United granted them another chance.

For this tour, Graham had an ace in the hole, and his name was Bill

Belmont. Riester was honest, but he did not always return home with the money, having been shaken down either by the band, usually the drummers, or by Rock Scully. So Graham sent Belmont out to protect the cash. It was not an easy job, and Belmont's efforts earned him Garcia's label as "the most paranoid person" he'd ever met because of his acute sense of business propriety. The Dead had met Belmont two years before when they played at the Rendezvous Inn and Belmont had managed the opening act, the Wildflower. He'd been raised in Mexico and spoke three languages, and after passing through the U.S. Navy, he'd gone to San Francisco State. After working with the Youngbloods as a road manager, he'd become involved with Country Joe and the Fish.

Belmont's winter 1969 tour with the Dead lasted two weeks and eleven shows, from Chicago to New York, and it was a vivid experience. For starters, he was stoned for the duration, and didn't really like it. "It's not possible to do efficient things," he reported, "because there's this committee, or rather a couple of committees—the drummers' committee, the . . ." Though Phil and Jerry made a lot of decisions, Kreutzmann, he thought, "had a lot of say" due to a close, largely unspoken relationship with Garcia. Decisions were never exactly made, but only put off. "At some point, they had decided that if they were in enough debt, no one could really mess with them—they would have to let them work, or the creditors would never be paid." By now in debt around $100,000 to Warner Bros., they got by on the road with an American Express card that Riester needed to pay in town A so he could get the band to town B. Belmont's tour was primarily in the Midwest, and the band had little clout there. There were few FM stations at that place and time, and very few Dead Heads in Omaha. Audiences would frequently be bored by forty-five-minute jams, and promoters would futilely request "songs." At every show there would be arguments with the promoter over the guest list, "a war council/game every night," said Belmont.

Adopting conventional business attitudes would challenge their image of being unique, Belmont thought, so that "if they were to start worrying about nickels and dimes, it would become a business or a job." The Grateful Dead at this point was, Belmont thought, "a cocoon of chaos and habit" that didn't like change. For Garcia and the rest, chaos was far more comfortable than smooth efficiency. Just leaving a hotel was a bore. Instead, more than once, Jackson, Hagen, and Ram Rod rigged firecrackers in the elevator shaft just as Riester was checking the band out. They passed through the lobby, said, "See ya later, Riester," and headed to the waiting van, just as all hell broke loose in the elevator. Knowing what he was hearing, Riester signed the credit card slip, mumbled, "Got an airplane to catch," and vanished.

The band also had extra expenses that were hard to anticipate. At the first gig, in Chicago, Bear went off in a rental car and was stopped for weaving. When the police ran his name through the files, the telex machine reacted as though it were the cosmic bingo payoff, squirting out five feet of telex paper to describe his distinguished career. Belmont called their promoter, Aaron Russo, who was extremely sophisticated about Chicago politics. Late that night a limousine pulled up at their gig and a man in pajamas, slippers, a camel-hair overcoat, and a homburg, with an enormous cigar and accompanied by a bodyguard, got out. "I hear you have a problem. I think I'd like to take care of this." Two thousand dollars later, Bear was on their doorstep. The gig went well enough to just about cover the cost of doing business, but they refused to let Bear drive anymore. Another tour expense in Belmont's files was the tip money paid to various maids at a hotel in Omaha, where Weir and Pigpen were entertaining some rather young female Nebraskans. Thanks to the maids, Belmont and Riester had a few minutes' warning when the parents arrived, and the Dead were able to record one more narrow escape. By contrast, Garcia usually went to bed after the show, got up early, and spent the morning in the road manager's room, running scales and watching *Captain Kangaroo* with the sound turned down.

They ended the tour with shows in New York and Philadelphia. They'd headlined at the Fillmore East the previous year, and the reviewers had written that Jeff Beck had topped them. This time they opened for Janis Joplin and her new, post–Big Brother band. Riester had rented a truck, which turned out to be a great idea when Manhattan was smothered by a blizzard. They awoke to a silent city, eighteen inches of snow and no cars, just kids, dogs, and the subway. That night's backstage guests included Mike Wallace and the crew of *60 Minutes*, and Janis was anxious. She later remarked, "Jerry Garcia told me that I made him cry . . . the Dead have been so good to me, man. They're so warm and everything. I really needed that because of the pressure." After the show, when she performed only adequately, she became too drunk to descend the steep spiral staircase from her dressing room, and it was Riester who carried her out to the truck, so both bands could return to the hotel.

For Belmont, New York was trouble because that's when Rock came and the money went. "Always slightly left of dubious" in Belmont's opinion, there was a "shiftiness about him that was always off-putting." Oh, well. *Most* of the money got back to San Francisco.

The tour ended with two shows in Philadelphia. For a band in ruins only months before, a note on one of the tape boxes told of musicians having a creatively good time: "Show actually ended 5:38 A.M." East Coast audiences, especially back at the Fillmore East, would come to expect the Dead to play all night.

23

Interlude:
The Circus Is in Town

(THE FIRST SET BEGINS)

February, Oakland Coliseum Arena

At production manager Robbie Taylor's command, the house lights dim and the band strolls out onto the stage. It is the first show of the year, part of a three-day stay that will climax with Chinese New Year. They are absurdly rusty. Grateful Dead rehearsals in the eighties and nineties are rare and spotty, frequently consisting of one or two band members smoking dope with the crew in the lobby of the warehouse on Front Street, as other band members call in to the pay phone there and talk to crew member Steve Parish, who commands the room from his chair in front of the phone. Weir says he's running late. Kreutzmann wants to know who's there. Lesh says call him when everybody's there. Brent and studio engineer John Cutler work on his monitor setup, and Jerry schmoozes about his dive trip to Hawaii. When the Dead hit the stage in Oakland, they've played no more than a couple of hours together since the New Year's Eve show six weeks before, if that. And, of course, there is no song list prepared—this is an improvisational band not only in how it plays but in how it selects. If at times they are unable to remember lyrics or even the key of songs, the two lead vocalists, Weir and Garcia, can always remem-

ber who started the last show and, if it was a recent one, a fair proportion
of what they played. After agreeing on which of the two will take the first
song, and acceding to their choice—drummers get to complain, if not always vote—the only job that faces them is, as Ezra Pound said, to "make
it new."

The inevitable happens: Weir's amp blows. Parish hurries out, and
with Kidd on the other side of the amp with a flashlight, they confront
the problem. Weir loves toys, both at home and in his equipment rack,
and he has a very complex setup. It is so very complicated that Garcia,
who has much less actual electrical power, is actually much louder. Weir
would attribute this to Healy, the mixer, whom he has always suspected of
coveting his job, but this does not presently concern Parish, who is on his
knees in front of the setup. Weir is his despair. The band noodles, and as
the minutes pass, the noodles grow into fragments of a song, sometimes
the "Beer Barrel Polka," or perhaps Miles Davis's "So What." Parish
leaves, Weir shakes his head, Garcia keeps playing, Lesh screams, and
Parish returns. Finally he's done, and Weir rises from his knees and approaches his microphone.

"Ladies and gentlemen, boys and girls, the circus is in town." He gives
a piercing blast on a whistle, Brent runs a little circus calliope run down
the keyboard, the drummers rat-a-tat-tat, and at the board, Candace
whispers into her headset, " 'Truckin' '—trust them to start the year
with something weird. Preset 707." The computerized Panaspots whirl
red to white from the sides and flare out, the initial guitar riffs roar, and
Weir begins the year: "Arrows of neon and flashing marquees out on main
street / Chicago, New York, Detroit and it's all on the same street / . . .
Together—more or less in line / Just keep truckin' on." He gets in only a
verse before he fluffs the first lyric, par for the course. In fact, he rarely if
ever gets through this song perfectly. The audience loves the errors, correctly perceiving themselves all the more a part of the process for recognizing the mistake, and cherishing the utter normality of the band in its
capacity for error. After all, this is not theater or a performance in any
remotely conventional sense. This is the Dead sharing their lives with
them and that means the whole package. Critics frequently find it
lazy, but a fair judge will acknowledge that the usual rules do not entirely
apply here.

"Truckin' " is their autobiography, the summation of a life spent performing, where there are only three places: home; New York, which is
palpably distinguishable from anywhere else in the world by the amphetamine rush of Manhattan; and the road, which is everydamnwhereelse.

Truckin' was hippie slang for traveling, taken from twenties and thirties black dance slang, like Blind Boy Fuller's "Truckin' My Blues Away." The song was almost a hit for the Dead when they put it out in 1970, and it is still one of their most popular tunes. Behind it is an entire world, a composite of sixties motel rooms that Garcia called as "interchangeable as Dixie cups," and also more recent experiences, like the world's finest hotel bathrooms, which happen to be located in the Four Seasons Hotel in New York, their home in the nineties. It is about the time that Rex Jackson hitched for help after the truck ran off the road in a Wyoming blizzard, and as his beard slowly froze, barely made it into town. It is about Brent Mydland going down the wrong jetway at San Francisco Airport and damn near starting a tour by flying to Hong Kong. It is about Healy, Lesh, and Steve Brown passing a baggie of pot behind their backs at a customs barricade in Switzerland, and getting away with it. It is about Weir, the most civil man around, melting down in Berlin and wrestling with a really rude fan.

Scrib stands behind Harry at the monitor console, watching the crowd surge ecstatically. Harry probably has the worst job in the Dead, because he is responsible for what the band will hear, and that is too painfully important. Someone always has to be at the board, Harry once told Scrib. "Yeah, you gotta cover the board," Scrib agreed. Harry smiled. "Fuck no. The board's fine. Somebody's got to pay attention to the band." But this time it's the equipment that's wrong, and the yellow light flashes on the communication headset connected to the soundboard. There's a buzz in the system, and it's going to plague them all night. "We are at the corner," groans Healy, "of pain and burn." Sound can form a wall and block other sounds, which will then be inaudible or come in funny in terms of direction or strength. Sound is tactile and three-dimensional, and just turning it up to the mythical 11 (dials generally run 1 to 10) doesn't work here. There is a hum coming from Weir's microphone, and Fuzzy, one of the Ultra Sound guys, disappears, digs up a new microphone cable, and replaces it. "We got no signal, we got no signal," says Harry, and as Fuzzy rushes off, he grabs him and says, "See if you can cross the wires at the source." They muddle through, but it will be several shows before they discover that their problem is in a snake, one of the heavy-duty cables that connect the soundboard to the stage. It has been crushed.

Sometimes there are people problems. Once the lighting crew spotted Allen Gross, a Dead Head who happened to be a union stagehand, watching the show from the front rail, and pulled him out of the audience. One of the spotlight operators had been dosed with LSD and had barricaded himself in the booth just below the ceiling. His work was not entirely reliable, and Candace was going crazy. "You know how to get through the ceiling and go through the trapdoor, and we don't have any-body else to do that." Allen went up, the dosee was led to a calm and quiet place, and Allen had to work that night.

Mid-March, Capitol Centre, Landover, Maryland

Back on the road: colds, labor troubles, fucked load-in and a down crew, snits, troubled logistics, power fluctuations that mess with the lighting system, weird sound in the hall or on the stage, police, lame local pro-moter (not usually more than once). The earliest road gigs were often pro-moted by hippies, and it was common for the band to be met by a VW van at the airport and to stay at someone's home. One time in Cin-cinnati the entire band supposedly ended up in the same room at a college dormitory.

The band kicks off "Sugaree," a Hunter-Garcia take on Elizabeth Cotten's "Shake It Sugaree," and tonight it's soggy. There is the thinnest of margins between the rambling shuffle that this song demands and too damn slow, and tonight this song of love and betrayal goes nowhere for the first half. At the board, Healy is still building the sound in the mix. He starts with the rhythm section. He can hear the drums acoustically, and from there, "I sort of have to build the whole band on how I hear Phil." And Phil is not convinced of anything tonight. He paces the length of his cord, from near Harry at the monitor board to his right. "Sugaree" is one of Garcia's favorites, an early-in-the-show warm-up that usually ends with guitar fireworks. The singer is an outlaw, but he retains a fragment of faith: "Shake it up now, Sugaree / I'll meet you at the Jubilee / If that Ju-bilee don't come / Maybe I'll meet you on the run."

They try, and it's still a shitty night. As Phil said, "Or there's the one where nothing you can do makes any difference . . . I'll try to play more, I'll try to play less, I'll try to spread out my registers, I'll try playing one note." Of course, anything that one tries consciously to do will almost cer-tainly fail.

Late March, Knickerbocker Arena, Albany, New York

One of the last things any road warrior ever wants to hear is a limo/van driver saying, "I think the exit's . . ." The classic version of the lost limo

driver actually took place on a spring tour early in the 1990s. A run in
D.C. ended, the band got onto the plane and landed in Detroit around
1 A.M. Two vans awaited, and the lead driver told the second driver to
"follow me." Scrib fell asleep on the back row and awoke dimly sensing
that all was not right. He was in a van with Garcia, Weir, and Candace
Brightman. Trying to be polite, he inquired of the driver, "Do you know
where you're going?" "Obviously not," snapped Weir, who was stiff with
fear—because they were in Ann Arbor, whose University of Michigan
basketball team had, hours before, won the NCAA "March Madness"
basketball tournament, and the driver had managed to drive to precisely
the worst place in the world—the main drag of downtown Ann Arbor,
where thousands of fans were whooping it up. Fortunately, the van had
dark windows. Scrib looked at his itinerary, hopped carefully out of the
van, handed a twenty to a cabdriver, and said, "Lead us, very slowly, to this
address, please."

Weir kicks off Merle Haggard's "Mama Tried," and tonight it feels
good. Though he's a guy who spent exactly one summer on a ranch, Weir
often affects a drawl, and he loves cowboy tunes sufficiently that there is
one in almost every first set. The band's treatment of them is extremely respectful, and they were mightily pleased when word filtered to them that
Haggard likes their work. He is part of the America that they come from,
the unglossy, authentic part. The audience joyfully kicks up its heels, while
the "spinners"—a Dead Head subgroup who dance in a permanent neo-
Sufi spin—pick up their pace. Ever since the Dead began to install speakers in the concourse area of shows, the spinners and other dancers haven't
seen the stage, happy just to hear and . . . spin.

Late March, the Omni, Atlanta

It's late in the tour, and the mood has an edge. "I'm so horny," Kreutzmann said yesterday, "I felt like I was playing with three drumsticks
tonight." Which inevitably recalls the stripper who managed to get onstage at a 1972 concert at American University and began talking with
Kreutzmann. "Play a slow number so I can dance." "You're gonna dance?"
"I'm gonna take my clothes off and dance." "You can't do that, they'll bust
you." "That's what I want." She kept her clothes on, but the show proved
no less exciting for that.

It's highly appropriate that Weir follows this night's "Mama Tried"
with his own "Mexicali Blues." It is a superb border town wastrel's confes-
sion, and Weir has spent enough time charming sweet young things to

make it authentic. "Laid back in an old saloon with a peso in my hand / Just watchin' flies and children on the street . . . / And It's three days' ride from Bakersfield / And I don't know why I came / I guess I came to keep from payin' dues / So, instead, I've got a bottle and a girl who's just fourteen / And a damned good case of the Mexicali Blues." Naturally, the song changed a little in the leap from lyricist Barlow to Weir's recording. In John's head it was a slow and stately hangover ballad. He handed off the lyrics to Weir, who stuffed them in his pocket without comment. A year later, as Weir prepared for his first solo album, *Ace,* he took out the lyrics again, but what he heard was a Tex-Mex polka. The band plays it beautifully tonight, with the requisite bounce.

May, Shoreline Amphitheater

Garcia swings into "Ramble on Rose," a bit of whimsy from Hunter that melds icons and a lover over a slow shuffle.

> *Just like Crazy Otto*
> *Just like Wolfman Jack*
> *Sitting plush with a royal flush*
> *Aces back to back*
> *Just like Mary Shelley*
> *Just like Frankenstein*
> *Clank your chains and count your change*
> *Try to walk the line*
> *Did you say your name was*
> *Ramblin Rose?*
> *Ramble on baby*
> *Settle down easy*
> *Ramble on Rose*

Hunter stands at the side of the stage in one of his rare appearances at a show, smiling at the performance. He is a private and mysterious man, a regular drop-in at the office, but now in the late eighties and the nineties, a poet who has somewhat separated himself from the day-to-day life of the band. He is genuinely respected, if slightly aloof, and there is pleasure in Ram Rod's demeanor, for instance, on seeing him.

Late May, Cal Expo Amphitheater, Sacramento

One of the year's annual rites is the Dead's Rex Foundation charity run, three late-spring shows in Sacramento. Although Dead Heads would gladly pay extra for charity, the band sees the donation as coming from themselves, not the audience, and the ticket price is standard. Actually, the shows do come with a bonus, because in the late eighties and after, the ten-thousand-capacity grass field is probably the band's smallest venue. Benefits are one of the complications of every musician's life. The nuns probably asked troubadours to work for free in 1210, and certainly every good cause of the sixties had the Dead playing. This was not always fun. There were various benefit concerts that dissolved into internecine war-fare within the recipient organization, up to and including lawsuits and/or violence, most memorably at a couple of Native American events in the seventies. Finally, the Dead took over the process and created the Rex Foundation. The band plays, puts the profits in a pot, and gives it away in $5,000 or $10,000 increments.

It's wretchedly hot here in Sacramento, and Weir kicks into "Cassidy," one of his best songs. Weir likes to write fairly complex stuff, and this one works brilliantly. It was one of the songs that led to his split from Hunter, since Weir didn't like Hunter's original lyrics, which concerned gambling. In the summer of 1970 Weir's housemate, Eileen Law, was giving birth to her daughter. She had already chosen the name "Cassidy" for her child, from the film *Butch Cassidy and the Sundance Kid*, because it worked equally well for a boy or a girl. The homonym made Barlow think of Neal Cassady, gone two years, and the result was remarkable, "the *only* one that I am proud of," said Barlow. He was not thinking of reincarnation, but rather the cycle of life. "I can tell by the mark he left you were in his dream / Ah, child of countless trees / Ah, child of boundless seas / What you are, what you're meant to be / Speaks his name, though you were born to me / Born to me / Cassidy." The royalties are dedicated to her educa-tion expenses.

Garcia snaps the lead ferociously behind the voices, the drums push, Lesh fills in, and the music accelerates. Harry pushes Brent's voice up in Garcia's monitor, and Jerry glances at Mydland, smiling. Kidd, with a pencil and a clipboard, comes to the back of Phil's amp and begins taking notes, a fat roach in his mouth. Candace calls for an odd shade of green, and a union spotlight guy grumbles, "Lady, I'm not gonna argue, but I don't wanna make that guy green." There is an opening in the middle of "Cassidy" for a jam, and every time the path up the hill is new. There's the same general curvature, but the details are always different. Anything that really works perfectly, Garcia will remind you, is immediately trite and therefore must be instantly discarded. And so the band thumbs through an infinite deck of cards, Lesh playing bass as though he invented it, Weir's approach to rhythm guitar unique.

Behind them, Parish beams. After three days of trying to find an elusive hum in Weir's stack, they've figured it out, a combination of a low battery, a particular sound effect, and a certain setting.

No Turn Left
Unstoned

(2/19/69–6/20/69)

Late in January 1969, Ram Rod and John Hagen and their new cohorts, Rex Jackson and Bill Candelario, loaded up Ampex's Prototype #2 recording machine at Pacific Recording in San Mateo, drove to San Francisco, and hauled it up the stairs at the Avalon Ballroom, where the Dead would make the first live sixteen-track recordings in history. They did it again in late February at the Fillmore West, and in a total of seven nights, they caught lightning in the bottle. What would be called *Live Dead* was not only the first such recording, it would be among the great live albums in the history of popular music. Four years after they'd begun, and only months after being completely riven by musical and personal dissension, they had reached an apotheosis. Though *Anthem* had been a remarkable technical triumph, the inherently fussy, minutiae-oriented nature of studio recording was not the Dead's métier. They had found their souls onstage, and *Live Dead* was the proof.

While at Pacific Recording, they had met an Ampex employee named Ron Wickersham, a brilliant problem-solving engineer who could help translate Bear's ideas into reality. Wickersham's philosophy of recording— "a minimum intrusion into the performance process"—was identical to

Bear's and the band's, and derived from his radio broadcast background. Ron's prime contribution to the making of *Live Dead* was a "mike splitter," which sent one channel of sound into the P.A., the other into the recording setup. Supported by Bear and Wickersham, Bob Matthews and his assistant Betty Cantor captured the Fillmore West run and some subsequent shows on tape, and the Dead laid down their musical identity: "Dark Star" into "St. Stephen" into "The Eleven" into "Lovelight," with "Death Don't Have No Mercy" and "Feedback," and the *a cappella* blessing "We Bid You Goodnight" for dessert. The breakneck gallop they'd employed when first playing "Dark Star" and the rest had been replaced by an elegant canter. Lesh would later say that playing fast was the habit of the young because it "felt so good." Perhaps because of all the pain of the preceding year, by now they had tasted the wisdom of Mozart, who reflected that it is much more difficult to play slowly. It was certainly better for the material, which had become magnificent. "We were after," Garcia said, "a serious, long composition, musically, and then a recording of it." Done.

In effect, it was two bands. There was the elite jazz fusion ensemble that could play "Dark Star" for half an hour with hardly a vocal, bouncing off planets in space, dodging or causing cosmic storms in the heavenly spheres of "St. Stephen," going back out past Pluto for a lengthy foray into eleven-beat vibrations in "The Eleven," then gracefully bringing the gleaming titanium spaceship in for a landing. And out of the hatch would step Mr. Funk himself, Pigpen. Having pounded conga drums for an hour, Pig could now bring everyone onto solid ground with the Bobby "Blue" Bland hit, "(Turn on Your) Lovelight." A sympathetic critic once remarked that it was generosity of spirit that made the Dead unable to throw him out, that the band was more ineffably magical without him. But this era of Grateful Dead music was at a profound peak in its evolution in part because Pigpen could close a show like nobody's business. Soul is always in order. Pig, wrote Ralph Gleason one night, took "Lovelight" and "made it into a one-man blues project. He sang for almost twenty minutes, stabbing the phrases out into the crowd like a preacher, using the words to riff like a big band, building to climax after climax, coming down in a release and soaring up again." He was "not a lesson but a course in outrage," said Weir, and had been known to go into mid"Lovelight" raves so twisted, so insane, that he once sold the Brooklyn Bridge to a guy in the audience for $1.25. Show after show in 1969 closed that way, and a very high proportion of them were brilliant.

Which was more than one could say of the new, third studio album in progress. The possibilities opened by sixteen tracks had become some-thing of a quagmire for a bunch of very stoned musicians. As Mickey re-called it, they spent much of their time loaded on a psychedelic drug called STP, using pinhead-size portions to produce an effect like speed. The musical result was "real fuzzy. You couldn't find a real center," he thought, and *then* they started sucking down nitrous oxide. Later, Mickey would speculate that their particular stonedness during this period was in fact an unconscious attempt to "camouflage" what was actually going on with the band, which was an essential musical transition. Even as they were playing the finest free-form ecstatic instrumental—psychedelic—music on the planet, they had turned a corner as musicians and were adding a new dimension to their repertoire: songs. Not just excuses to jam, but well-crafted songs meant to be sung.

More than a year after he'd written "Dark Star," Robert Hunter would spend 1969 becoming a primary member of the Grateful Dead. Having pursued the experimental as deeply as any rock band ever would, they were now rather brilliantly expanding sideways into the more conven-tional. The transition was demanding and at times confusing. So they got stoned. "I don't think it was an intellectual choice," said Hart, "but I think there was a gray area that we were passing through. All those psychedelics clouded the lens in a certain kind of way. They'd give you great detail, but then you'd hear the most obscure aspect in the mix." As they bogged down at the mixing board at Pacific Recording, their debt to Warner Bros. as-sumed truly impressive proportions, peaking at about $180,000. They had autonomy over the music and artwork, but they needed money for studio time, and finally even Joe Smith cracked. Early in 1969 Rock and Rohan went down to Los Angeles to hit Joe up for more money, and this time he literally chased them down the stairs, out the front door, and down the street, screaming that they were making him look bad. *Live Dead* was not only brilliant, it would save them at Warner Bros. Though it would not come out until the end of the year, the fact that it was in the can helped them finance the third studio album.

The burgeoning creative partnership between Hunter and Garcia was in part a matter of simple propinquity. At the beginning of the year, Hunter and his lover, Christie, moved in with Jerry, Mountain Girl, and Sunshine in a house on Madrone Canyon Road in Larkspur, a road that wriggles delightfully through a redwood grove—the builders shifted the road rather than cut trees. The atmosphere was a good one. Garcia sat downstairs, running scales up and down the guitar in front of the (usually silent) TV, while Hunter worked upstairs. One night during his first week there, Hunter stayed in when everyone else went out, got a little sloshed, turned on a tape recorder and laid down "Dupree's Diamond Blues," beginning the final cycle in his personal transition from novelist to poet to lyricist. (Interestingly, "Dupree's" was the only song the band would ever use that he'd written while inebriated; once was enough.) The real-life Frank DuPre killed an Atlanta Pinkerton detective in 1921 after robbing a jewelry store, and the incident spawned many songs, including Josh White's "Betty and Dupree." Hunter adapted freely, changing the victim and the guilty party, while reflecting that "many a man's done a terrible thing / Just to get baby her shiny diamond ring." Garcia's music had a friendly, almost cartoonish feel, and T.C.'s circus-style organ carried the album version beautifully. The band would be playing it within a few days, along with "Doin' That Rag" and "Mountains of the Moon." "Doin' That Rag" had a good-timey bounce that communicated a certain similarity to "Dupree's," but from a much less literal point of view: "Sitting in Mangrove Valley chasing lightbeams / Everything wanders from baby to Z." But this baby is no ring-seeking puppet. She is a player, and the aces "are crawling up and down [her] sleeve . . . Come back here, Baby Louise / and tell me the name / of the game that you play."

Each song showed Hunter growing, and the third one, "Mountains of the Moon," was a masterwork. "Jerry," he remarked later, "had written a minuet." And Hunter responded to the stately, elegant tune with a labyrinthine tale of romance peopled by the fragments of a thousand dreams. He began with a first-line nod to Gary Snyder's "Cold Mountain Poems":

> *Cold Mountain water*
> *the Jade merchant's daughter*
> *Mountains of the Moon, Electra*
> *Bow and bend to me*
>
> *Hi Ho the Carrion Crow*
> *Folderolderiddle*
> *Hi Ho the Carrion Crow*
> *Bow and bend to me*
>
> *Hey Tom Banjo*
> *Hey a laurel*
> *More than laurel*
> *You may sow . . .*

It is a symbolic tale set in a magical land. Tom Banjo is a suitor who pursues the jade merchant's daughter, jade being the symbol of long life. Electra is one of the eighty-seven daughters of Atlas, who was pursued by Orion, and saved only by being changed into a star, the dark, so-called lost star of the Pleiades. Laurel, or the laurel tree, is another symbol of long life and of success, the laurel crown or wreath. The carrion crows suggest heroes, who feed the crows by killing their enemies in Celtic and Nordic poetry. Having touched on sources from much of Western mythology, Hunter saluted his hero: "Hey Tom Banjo / It's time to matter / The Earth will see you / on through this time." At the song's bridge, Hunter introduced a toad demon, the Marsh King's Daughter, from Hans Christian Andersen, and the listener is left to ponder the result, which is quite properly left wildly open to question. Utterly distinctive, "Mountains of the Moon" was an incredible mix of mystery, intellectual content, gentle musical swing, and chivalrous romance. It had nothing at all to do with rock and roll, but everything to do with the development of a great songwriting relationship, a partnership that was about to create a postmodern dreamworld based on its own terms and vision. T.C.'s exquisite harpsichord locked it perfectly into vinyl.

Stoned, stoned . . . on top of everything else, they brought nitrous oxide tanks into the studio, and *truly* lost themselves in the mix. Nitrous triggers an " 'I'm dying' mechanism," said Garcia, and creates a fast, synchronous, "telepathic thing that's fantastic," as when Huey, Dewey, and Louie finish one another's sentences. They were still new to production in general, and sixteen-track in particular, so while much of the material on this album was purest gold—"St. Stephen," "China Cat Sunflower," "Mountains of the Moon"—much was also confusing and not successful, such as "What's Become of the Baby." In "Baby," Garcia wanted the sound of the entire band to come out of one voice, which required voltage-controlled amplifiers, filters, and pitch followers, which had not yet been invented. Once again, their ambitions had overshot their skill. And the descent into total lunacy initiated by mixing while inhaling nitrous oxide majestically confused everything. By April they were mixing it by committee, always a bad idea. The one firm thing they had was a title. The album had begun as *Earthquake Country*, but Rick Griffin, their cover artist, had a better idea. Fascinated with palindromes, he suggested *Aoxomoxoa*, which has no literal meaning, and it was accepted. Not only did it have a pseudo-Egyptian, "vaguely cabalistic ring" to it, thought Rock, but the palindrome also had a geometric symmetry, so that it could stack vertically as a/oxo/moxoa.

As the *Aoxomoxoa* sessions wobbled their way to a conclusion, they were punctuated by live gigs. In the course of one week in March, the Dead played a benefit for striking San Francisco State students at Fillmore West, and three days later for the beautiful people of San Francisco high society at the Black and White Ball, the San Francisco Symphony's social event of the season. The job had, of course, come through Weir's mother, chair of the entertainment committee, and it was an imposing gig. They were playing at the Hilton Hotel's Grand Ballroom, and admission was $17.50 at a time that $4 was rock's absolute maximum. The situation being what it was, they naturally screwed it up royally, and it became one of their very finest professional disasters. The band and equipment arrived on time, but Bear announced that he needed a missing item back in Novato, and vanished. While the musicians prepared themselves in a room upstairs, Bear actually went to sleep in an equipment case under the stage. When the lateness of the hour dawned on the band, they rousted him from his refuge, scourged him into setting up the stage, and at long last began to play. McIntire had induced them to echo the evening's theme and wear black and white costumes: Pigpen and Jerry were pirates, Mickey was Zorro, T.C. was an eighteenth-century bell ringer, Kreutzmann a French sailor, and McIntire himself came in a clown costume of white satin with black buttons. Rock's girlfriend, Suzie Gottlieb, was there as a belly dancer, Rakow's wife, Lydia, and their friends the Jensen girls from Marin were angels, and their friend Ken Goldfinger, hook hand and all, came as a bishop.

The Dead played for an hour, and McIntire told them to stay put while he pinned down the night's schedule. It took him quite a while to find the right person, too long in fact, and when Mayor Joe Alioto arrived around midnight for the grand ceremonial, there was no band left. McIntire and Weir's sister, Wendy, were standing at the door as the mayor entered, and Jon coped by telling Bear to put on some recorded music, then taking Wendy for a spin around the floor. The *Chronicle's* social columnist, Frances Moffat, referred to them as the "Ungrateful Dead," although Herb Caen was much nicer, calling M.G. "the most beautiful girl" at the ball. Caen continued, "As Garcia walked away, a society matron followed him with her eyes and said, 'Oh, it talks, does it?' Yeah, it talks. 'What in the world do you find to SAY to people like that?' she asked. I couldn't find anything to say to her, so I left." Perhaps not solely because of the Grateful Dead, this would be the last Black and White Ball for nearly twenty years.

The society lady's hostile attitude bespoke the era. On March 18, the

Dead were informed that their upcoming show in Miami had been canceled, because earlier in the month Jim Morrison had been accused of exposing himself onstage there. That there was little reliable evidence that
he had actually done so was irrelevant to the building management. They
were also blind to the cultural chasm between the Dead and what Morrison called the "erotic politicians" of the Doors. "They're the same type
people and the same type music as the Doors," said the man who ran the
auditorium. "It's this underground pop music." A confidential newsletter
put out for the use of the Concert Hall Managers' Association created a
highly effective blacklist that blocked Morrison's performing career and
with it that of the Doors for the better part of a year. The Doors and the
Dead were not alone in sensing a repressive new atmosphere. Richard
Nixon had been inaugurated two months before, and a grand jury that
had met since the previous fall on the subject of the Chicago Democratic
convention riots, now under the guidance of his attorney general, John
Mitchell, had swiftly returned indictments on Abbie Hoffman, Jerry
Rubin, Tom Hayden, and five others—the Chicago Eight. The White
House had already proposed two frightening pieces of legislation, one of
which would effectively eliminate the Fourth Amendment, the "no
knock" bill, and "preventive detention," which potentially eliminated bail.
CBS-TV canceled the Smothers Brothers program over censorship issues.
Rock and roll felt the same cold totalitarian breeze. Columbia Records
stopped advertising in the underground press that April; there was reputable evidence that it did so in part because it was pressured by the FBI.

As the month of March progressed, the Grateful Dead's business affairs
were in a colossal mess. That was, of course, entirely normal, but this time
the band actually did something about it. Earlier in the year, Bill Graham
had theoretically managed them, but his administration had been short-
lived. Briefcase in hand, Graham had arrived at the Novato warehouse,
and by the middle of the meeting had come to verbal blows with Bear. As
their voices reached critical mass, Bill finally roared, "It's him or me."
"Bye, Bill." Art trumped good business every time. He slammed his briefcase shut and stormed out.

Early in April they held another band meeting, and Mickey made a
suggestion. The one businessman he knew of was his father, Lenny.
Mickey hadn't seen his father since joining the Dead, and had somehow
forgotten how Lenny had magically taken over his son's idea for psychedelic drumheads. In the interval, Lenny had become a self-ordained

fundamentalist minister, which lent a gloss to the persuasive persona he'd always had. Mickey called him, and he came to meet with the band. Mickey introduced him, saying, "All right, we have a problem, and we need someone to help us solve it. Enter Lenny Hart, my father."

At first Lenny assumed a modest profile and listened. But as the weeks passed, he began to preach an ongoing sermon that various band members recalled as: "I am the Reverend Lenny Hart, and I am here to save the Grateful Dead. You've been fucked around. Now, I don't ask you to believe in Jesus, but believe in me. Fill the vessel. We're talking about the spirit. Talkin' about the spirit of God, talkin' about the spirit of the devil. It's all the same thing, we're talking about the spirit."

At this time, the band's day-to-day management was Rock Scully and Jon McIntire. Jon had little experience, and Rock was handicapped by extreme personal disorganization. Worse still, he was a brother. The fundamental need in the Grateful Dead was for someone to control spending, and Rock couldn't say no. "I had no control on them. I mean, if they wanted the money for their gear I gave it to them. I couldn't keep the money from them—I couldn't scare them." The band was sufficiently cynical about money to be open to any "solution." Phil Lesh later remarked that he "didn't really care. If [Lenny] could help us out with our management, that was okay with me." Weir figured Lenny was a hustler, but a hustler for the Dead. Mickey was ecstatic, thinking, "This is great. I've got my dad here, I've got my dad back. I'll be able to get some more drumming lessons and the band will be able to make enough money to go on. Yahoo, this is really great."

Not everyone bought Lenny's line. McIntire had seen Southern preachers before and had reservations, as did Bear. At an early meeting at Phil's house, Bear inquired, "We're doing the devil's work. Are you sure you want to do this?" Lenny was sure. He asked the band, "Do you want to take the money and run, or is it a lifetime commitment?" They affirmed their commitment. One person soon came to object aloud. Jonathan Riester had gone over to the Fillmore West to pick up a check from Graham, but was told by Bill that Lenny had said only he, Lenny, could handle money. Graham, who knew from con artists, remarked that Lenny was "not right," and Riester grew doubtful. On the road Lenny showed other flaws, like being unable to count money quickly and efficiently, and Riester's doubts increased. Feeling displaced by Lenny, he called a band meeting at Lesh's house and quit. As usual, the band went limp in the face of problems. Jackson and Ram Rod said they were going to quit, too, and Jerry joined them. Riester told Garcia not to be ridiculous and then appealed to the crew's pride. "You can't quit. Their show is never any better than how sharp we are at getting it together." Then Riester left, making the saddest mistake of his life. With his departure, McIntire became road manager, and he had much to learn. Fortunately, his first gig was with Quicksilver, and Ron Polte once more came to the rescue. Having completed his own settlement, he went over Jon's figures and remarked pointedly, "You'd rather have cash [than a check], wouldn't you, Jon?"

One of the first fruits of Lenny's administration was the band's near-participation in the film *Zachariah,* a bizarre Western with electric guitar-slinging cowboys. Arguing that it would provide good exposure, Lenny briefly convinced them that the idea could fly. In the end, they didn't trust Hollywood and opted out of the movie, to be replaced by the great jazz drummer Elvin Jones, but before that, Mickey began practicing the art of rolling a cigarette one-handed. They toured the MGM back lot and were fitted for costumes, and then Mickey, the experienced rider, took the band out for lessons at his ranch. At a later lesson, the cinch on Jerry's horse was insufficiently tight, and when he put his weight on the stirrup, the saddle slooowwwly twisted around, dumping him on his shoulder, which ended his interest in the project. Before that, though, they had a number of wonderful group rides, crossing the road in front of Hart's and going out behind Burdell Mountain, an outlaw gang hell-bent for leather.

Horses and Mickey's ranch were a considerable part of their lives that year, and for a good while after. Having grown up in Brooklyn, Mickey had spent time each summer with an aunt who lived in the country. For a kid from Flatbush, it was heaven, and he kept a taste for the outdoors. While selling drums for Lenny, he'd met three young female Beatlemaniacs who wanted drum lessons and who were from the horsey town of Woodside. He became a serious student of riding, eventually competing in show jumping. When he left San Francisco for Marin, he moved first to a home on Ridge Road in Novato. He owned horses, stabling them at Olompali, but it was not terribly convenient and he got a friend, Rhonda Jensen, to seek a better place to rent. The place she discovered, though nicknamed by some the Pondariester after Jonathan, an expert horseman, was instantly Hart's domain. As far as Mickey was concerned, Riester was his foreman, and it wasn't long before Mickey was right. Riester soon left.

The ranch—it never did acquire a name—consisted of thirty-two acres off Novato Boulevard, and Mickey was officially a caretaker for the owner, the City of Novato. The rent was $250 a month, and the spread included a house, a barn, and various sheds. Many people lived there over the next few years, but the first wave included Mickey, Riester, and

Mickey's informally adopted "daughters," the Jensen girls, Rhonda, Sherry, and Vickie. The Jensens had been living at Olompali, part of Don McCoy's child-based commune. Their mother was Opa Willy, a pot smuggler, and when she failed to return from a business trip to Mexico, Mickey became a substitute parent.

Of course, this was not a conventional ranch. Mickey's favorite pastime in those days was to return from a gig, dose his horse Snorter and dog Glups with a proportionate quantity of LSD, and go out riding in the hills around home. "[Snorter] was so *there,* he put down so beautifully," Hart said. "The only thing you'd notice was his hair used to stand up on end. And when you stopped, sometimes he'd roll, like a pussycat." Other ranch activities included firing guns, which almost everyone owned. As a side effect, Garcia became an adept gunsmith, puttering at home between shows just like his grandfather. On one ceremonial occasion, a friend dropped by with $1,000 worth of ammunition, and the band put a television on a long, long extension cord out by the creekside firing range, waited until the most atrocious possible commercial came on, and executed the offender with an extra-lengthy fusillade. They made so much noise that the police came around—but because of the volume, the officers declined to enter the ranch's grounds, and after things quieted down, they discreetly left.

The ranch attracted a wide range of souls. In addition to the Dead family, Mickey was particularly close to Sweet William and other Hell's Angels, who were frequently around. In fact, Angelo, the Richmond Chapter president, would marry Sherry Jensen. Mickey had by now taken up with Cookie Eisenberg, the New York travel agency owner, and through Cookie the Dead had met a new circle of people, extremely wealthy New Yorkers like Roger Lewis, who owned a seat on the New York Stock Exchange, and Marina Maguire, the heir to the Thompson submachine gun fortune. Marina owned an apartment in Manhattan so large that she used a small golf cart to get around. She was a hard-core devotee of what can only be described as decadence, and the parties at her place following New York shows were nothing short of drug orgies. The New York scene also introduced them to Loose Bruce Baxter, a Texas heir who would live at the ranch for some time. Periodically, Hart recalled, they'd clean him up and send him to a meeting with his mother so that he could continue getting his $10,000 monthly allowance. On the more sober side, Lydia's brother Johnny d'Fonsecca, who had been the carpenter at the Carousel, moved himself and his family to the ranch and, working with Dan Healy's designs, remodeled the barn into a studio and took care of everything else that needed fixing. And there was Rolling Thunder, a Native American from Nevada also known as John Pope, who had come to San Francisco in 1967 guided by a vision that colorfully dressed young white people might prove to be allies to Indians. Rolling Thunder was an authentic healer and a fascinating character, whose flagrant lechery made him all the more interesting. Rock and his new lover, Nicki, were there. So was Kreutzmann, who lived in a fixed-up hay barn out back for a while.

That April the warehouse at Hamilton Air Force Base acquired a new tenant and a name. Bear wanted to build a room that was ideal for studying and making music, and when he described his notion to his friend Bob Thomas, who was there acting as caretaker, Bob remarked, "That's an alembic," the place in alchemy where the magical transformation happens. The band wanted to simplify things and separate the sound system and instrument repair functions from their rehearsal space. In his usual catalytic role, Bear brought together Ron Wickersham, who'd left Ampex, and a luthier (maker of stringed instruments) named Rick Turner, and the two of them formed Alembic. They began by dealing with the bass, always a problem in mixing sound—low end gets lost, while the high notes always cut through. Alembic's home was only a tin-roofed shed at the back of the Dead's warehouse, but presently it began to produce magic.

In April 1969 the apolitical Dead took off on a tour of colleges, just as the very act of being on campus became a political statement. They played for the University of Arizona Student Peace Association, at the University of Colorado, and outdoors at Washington University in St. Louis, where the issue was not politics but their volume, which generated complaint calls from blocks away. As the band members flew on to the next show, at Purdue, they read of a student strike at Harvard. Anti-ROTC protesters had seized the administration building, and riot police had violently torn through hundreds of students to enter the building and arrest those inside. At Purdue, students were riled over raises in the student fee structure. The campus newspaper reported, "A capacity crowd in the Union Ballroom for a dance featuring the Grateful Dead was informed of [the president's decision to pass the fee increase on to the students], but leaders averted any disturbances which might have ensued by keeping the band playing."

Late in May the Dead briefly acquired a special witness, reporter Michael Lydon, whom the band members so trusted that they granted him a remarkable level of access. He rewarded that faith with what Garcia would consider the best journalism ever devoted to the Dead, a major

Rolling Stone cover story. Lydon's timing was superb, and he was able to sit in on a band meeting that was a duel of wills between Lenny, whose "Southern preacher thing" disturbed him, and Bear, who was to Lydon "a strange guy," and in Jerry's words, "Satan in our midst." His article detailed inept travel arrangements that had the band driving in two rental cars down to Santa Barbara for a rotten show where the promoter wouldn't let them use their own sound system. Bear was "flat on his back" out of it, and after playing awhile, Garcia quit. "Sorry," he shouted, "but we're gonna split for a while and set up our own P.A. so we can hear what the fuck is happening." Backstage there was a raging argument. "We should give the money back if we don't do it righteous." Jerry was shouting. "Where's Bear? . . . Listen, man, are you in this group, are you one of us?" Jerry screamed. "Are you gonna set up that P.A.? Their monitors suck. I can't hear a goddam thing . . . How can I play if I can't hear the drums?" . . .

"Let's just go ahead," said Pigpen. "I can fake it."

"I can't," said Jerry.

"It's your decision," said Pig.

"Yeah," said Phil. "If you and nobody else gives a good goddamn."

One of the shows Lydon witnessed was a benefit for People's Park at Winterland. The putatively apolitical Dead were once again in the activist soup, because it was hard to imagine being young and in the Bay Area that month and not having a positive feeling about People's Park. In April, hundreds of local people had, "in the name of the people," taken over a vacant lot on Telegraph Avenue owned by the university, cleaned it up, and built a playground. Early on May 15, rifle-carrying California Highway Patrol and Berkeley Police Department officers in flak jackets entered the park, tore down the playground, and put up an eight-foot steel mesh fence. That day six thousand Berkeleyites marched down Telegraph Avenue from campus, and when they approached the park, the police fired on them with double-ought buckshot. For the next three days, demonstrators would gather, then be dispersed and arrested by the National Guard. Late the night of the nineteenth, one of the men shot on the fifteenth, James Rector, died. A rally the next day on campus ended when troops trapped three thousand people and strafed them with tear gas from helicopters. Across the country that same week, New Haven was under siege, as the local African American community demanded attention from the town's primary industry, Yale. The war had come home.

What music could do in those circumstances seemed difficult to say. That week John Lennon and Yoko Ono were holding a "Bed-In for peace" in Montreal. When asked about Berkeley, Lennon replied, "There's no cause worth losing your life for . . . Christ you know it ain't easy, you know how hard it can be man, so what? Everything's hard—it's better to have it hard than to not have it at all." What musicians could do best was play, and the Dead, as always, were there to raise bail money. The People's Park show itself was awful. The next day Garcia told Lydon, "But, y'know, I dug it, man. I can get behind falling to pieces before an audience some-times. We're not *performers;* we are who we are for those moments we're before the public . . . and that's not always at the peak." The times were extreme, and ripe for philosophy. As Lydon listened, Garcia considered good and evil. "They exist together in their little game, each with its spe-cial place and special humors. I dig 'em both. What is life but being con-scious? And good and evil are manifestations of consciousness. If you reject one, you're not getting the whole thing that's there to be had."

That sort of philosophical overview would confer on him a mantle of sage wisdom that would eventually be crippling, but for the present it got him through strange times—and the times kept getting stranger. Early in June they played three nights at the Fillmore West with Junior Walker, and someone, as usual, dosed the apple juice. This was not just any dose, it was the biggest dose ever. Most say it was several people, but one in-formed source argued that only the big-time smuggler/dealer Ken Gold-finger, a friend of the band's, could have had such a quantity at hand, for there was probably a full gram of crystal LSD in the juice, worth perhaps $50,000. In Hart's memory, "the bottle was *glowing."* Lesh said later that one could taste the LSD in the juice. When it came time to play, he was so ecstatically zonked that he politely declined when Mickey told him it was time to go to work. "I don't really care to play right now, thank you." Hart was, as Lesh put it, "so sweet about it. He didn't guilt-trip me." Mickey helped him up, walked him to the stage, propped him against an amp, draped his bass over his shoulders, plugged it in, and turned the amp to maximum volume. To Lesh, "It felt like some sort of fabulous artifact that I'd never seen before. The strings were all snaky, but beautiful colors, kind of fish or reptile scales." They began to play, and it was, Lesh contin-ued, "the strangest polyphonic blues ever, literally in that sense, many-voiced," because there was no first chord, no downbeat, just utterly strange music utterly in flux. And in the middle, they invited poor Elvin Bishop, who'd just walked in, to join them. Lesh played a thirteen-bar blues, someone else a sixteen, and Elvin had a look of "Where am I? What uni-verse is this?" Lesh called it "snake music," and he was right.

Not everyone had such a good time. Snooky Flowers, who was in

Janis Joplin's band, was severely dosed, and Janis went ballistic, verbally assaulting Bear, whom she accused of the deed. Hunter's lady friend, Christie, ended up walking down Market Street, where she was picked up by a sleazeball with bad ideas. His worst notions weren't consummated, but he did dump her out somewhere in Daly City. Distraught over the disappearance of his friend, Hunter hallucinated blood spurting from Janis's mouth, then mentally experienced every assassination he knew of, dying with JFK and with Lincoln, among many other deaths. At one point he was lying on the sidewalk near the Fillmore West stage door seeing giant lobsters from the ninth dimension devour Market Street. When Bear approached him, he swung from the ground, socking him and uttering one word: "Owsleystein." Bear absorbed the punch, and they set off for Goldfinger's, since Bear wanted to ask Ken what, precisely, was in the apple juice. Goldfinger was elsewhere, and they were taken in by Ken's lover, Nicki. Eventually, they sent for Garcia, who would play calming guitar to Hunter until dawn.

Goldfinger got his reward, in any case. Jon McIntire was too high to drive, and Ken and his friend Peter Monk bundled him behind the gearshift in Ken's Porsche to give him a ride home. When Ken hit the defrost button, the resulting blast of hot air had a negative effect on Jon's digestive tract, and he tossed his cookies all over Ken, Peter, and the Porsche. It took Ken two days with a toothbrush to get his car clean again. Frankie Azzara had just returned from working for George Harrison and moved in with Bobby, and would be his live-in companion for the next several years. As people melted down into various puddles, she caught Phil's eyes, and he muttered, "Nero burning Rome." "It was really flames," she said, meaning psychic flames. "There were people screwing on the floor, people being sick." The game was truly thick that night, good and evil manifesting as fully as even Garcia could ever want.

25

Interlude:
"When the Music
Plays the Band"

(THE DEAD TALK ABOUT PLAYING MUSIC)

It is highly unlikely that Tony Bennett ever played a show after "I Left My Heart in San Francisco" became a hit without singing it. Contrarily, observed San Francisco musician David Freiberg, "I like the idea of jumping off a cliff whenever you feel like it just to see what's there. If it works, it's wonderful. If it doesn't, so what? At least you tried. That's what I like about the Grateful Dead." Out in the breezes above the abyss, there is still form, still the opportunity for communication, symmetry, and beauty; "deep form" as Jack Kerouac put it. It is a desperate struggle. Said B. B. King, "But I know this, I've never made it. I've never played what I hear inside. I get close but not there. If I did, I'd play the melody so you'd know what it was saying even if you didn't know the words. You wouldn't know when Lucille stopped and my voice began."

These moments take place in quiet times, too. One night, Scrib stood behind Garcia's amp during a Garcia Band sound check. Parish was fussing with John Kahn's amp, and a relaxed Garcia began to noodle on "If I Only Had a Heart," from *The Wizard of Oz*. It was a perfect jewel, tossed off for his ears and his fingers and no audience at all. Scrib listened raptly. At length, Garcia looked up and caught his eyes, smiled, chirped, "Great song, man," and continued. It was a perfect moment.

WEIR: "Every night when we walk onstage, our first solemn duty is to abandon reason. We do that with remarkable aplomb and from there unexpected stuff is easier to discover."

GARCIA: "[Playing is] like being strapped to the back of a horse in the middle of a stampede . . . like being on the brink of collapse . . . I like to be as close to the brink as possible."

WEIR: "The jams are an exercise in group direction. There isn't a whole lot of leading or being led done. Actually, the least flexible guy at a given moment is the leader."

GARCIA: "For me, a real important model is Golden Gate Park . . . you can go from one kind of reality to another . . . prehistoric looking, giant ferns, everything is weird . . . a little further, all of a sudden you're in this little pasture—sheep . . .

"Eventually, if I have a place to go, I can make it and make it pretty seamless. Because, for me, the [musical] relationship between one thing and another is always obvious . . . I like that invisible thing, that sort of sleight-of-hand approach, but I'm learning to be able to appreciate the thing of just clumsily blundering into it . . . the existential reality . . . is note to note.

"For me, that idea is not one note; an idea is like a sentence, or a paragraph sometimes. Know what I mean? The nature of it is rubbery . . . I'm doing this thing and it has a certain kind of curvature . . . and it's going to last four bars, say. I tend to think in even number of bars generally . . . So there'll be a sentence, it'll be X long, like four bars, and then there'll be like the answer to that, four bars long, then there'll be like a summing-up of it that'll be like eight bars, and then there'll be an argument from the other direction, that'll be eight bars, it's kind of like that.

"But, as it's going along, there's also things coming in from the other band members, which sometimes say, like on bar three, 'No no no, *this* is now number one' . . . Then I say, okay, so my sentence went that way, so what I'm going to do, to make it syntactically correct, to make it so it goes four bars to include the third bar beginning, then it's only going to go two more bars for a three-bar sentence but it'll still maintain the symmetry that I want it to have because it overlaps . . .

"It's kind of like that. These things are not so conscious, but they are conversational like that. They tend to be sentences. That part of it has to do with just melody . . . for me, melodies have the kind of sense that poetry has, they have meter . . . So a melody will start composing itself while I'm playing. We start off with a simple A melody. I'll say, that's working, that's something that has a certain gesture to it that's nice at this moment, so I'll say, 'Here's expression A.' Okay, A again. Now here's B. And B again. Then another A to bring us back to that moment, and now C, and it's like a new discussion . . . Really, there are hunks of stuff like that, like language . . . I don't really have that much control over it . . . it's not me being logical on purpose by any means."

In speaking with Phil Lesh, radio host David Gans once remarked that "[The Dead is] America's longest-running musical argument."

LESH: "A musical argument makes the two sides one thing, like counterpoint . . . that's really a good description, in sort of an abstract verbal sense."

"So I like to play it more in the sense of the continuo bass of the baroque period . . . polyphonic counterpoint."

GARCIA: "I've gone through so many [things], all the way up to and including perversely trying to make it be as miserable as I can. But I wouldn't want it to have less range than that. [I want it to have its] full capacity as an experience."

WEIR: "Intimacy, by the way, is a musical dynamic."

KREUZTMANN: "They don't have a note value for the endless whole note."

GARCIA: "[A transcendent moment in playing] occurs in a mediumistic way, something involuntary. I trust it because I know it's *not* me. If it was me, I wouldn't trust it because . . . I know myself too well."

LESH: "We used to believe that every place we played was church. But the core of followers is not the reason it feels like church; it's that other thing, 'it' [inspiration, grace, transcendence]."

GARCIA: "We've chosen to go with the thing of we don't care whether they have expectations or not. We do what we want to do anyway, because that's—what's in it for us otherwise? We don't want to be entertainers. We want to play music."

26

If My Words
Were Gold

(6/20/69–8/15/69)

oxomoxoa hit the stores on June 20, accompanied by Warner Bros.'—specifically Stan Cornyn's—best ad campaign ever, a spoof of teen magazines called the "Pigpen Look Alike Contest." Reviews were generally befuddled, but they scarcely mattered, because the band was climbing an arc of change that would consume it for the next year and a half. Late in the spring, Robert Hunter had brought three new songs downstairs to Garcia, who was, as usual, running scales in front of the TV. Jerry said he'd look at them later. "Garcia," Hunter snorted, "if you think I'm living here for the pleasure of your mythical sunny personality—I'm here to write songs. Do you want to write songs or not?" "Oh!" Garcia picked up the songs, and had the first of them, "Dire Wolf," worked out soon after.

One night Hunter and M.G. had sat up and watched *The Hound of the Baskervilles,* and she'd remarked that the hound was "a dire wolf." It made for a picturesque night in Hunter's personal dream theater, and in the morning he transcribed his visions, unaltered. Later, Hunter would acknowledge, "I can touch that dreamspace. The stuff you dream is kind of close to consciousness for me, which is a bit of a talent and in normal life it's a bit of a disability. I've got a little tunnel into my subconscious." In part because Garcia gave it a countryish lilt, the song was clearly a bench-mark in the trail they would follow over the next several years.

> *In the timbers of Fennario*
> *the wolves are running round*
> *The winter was so hard and cold*
> *froze ten feet neath the ground*
>
> *Don't murder me*
> *I beg of you don't murder me*
> *Please*
> *don't murder me*

"Dire Wolf" begins in a stripped, barren white setting, spiritually and in-tellectually related to Melville's white whale, the wolf coming out of the white void. Fennario is no place in particular; it is the no-place, where hu-mans confront their doom. It is about fear. The narrator in "Dire Wolf" is what would eventually come to be perceived as the fundamental Grateful Dead character, a workingman, an underdog without pretense or slick-ness, part of the old gritty America. And the narrator is Garcia himself, exposed and vulnerable onstage, and even in the street. Just at this time, the San Francisco area was beset by a random serial murderer, the Zodiac Killer. Driving around late at night, Garcia's adrenaline would flash as another car pulled up next to his at a traffic light.

> *The wolf came in, I got my cards*
> *We sat down for a game*
> *I cut my deck to the Queen of Spades*
> *but the cards were all the same*

Our character is brave, even if that seems futile. The wolf comes, he's in-vited in for a game, but our man gets the death card, the queen—the game is stacked. In fact, our narrator is *really* a member of the Grateful Dead; he is a ghost, and this card game is like Bergman's chess game in *The Seventh Seal.* The Dead's music had gone far beyond pop. Yet there's much more. The wolf, "600 pounds of sin," is also the devil, and the fact that our guy invites him in speaks volumes. By and large, the Dead stood for moral goodness, but later they would also write a song called "Friend of the Devil." The pivotal moment in American blues history had taken place some forty years before, when, as Son House told the story, Robert

Johnson made a Faustian compact and sold his soul to the devil for the ability to play his guitar, leaving the church and setting out on the blues road. The Dead's postmodern, post-Christian cosmology didn't demand that choice. They made a friend of the devil. They didn't fight the wolf; they invited him in for a game, stuck a joint in his mouth, and had as good a time as they could manage. Intellectually, they embraced black as well as white, and death was part of their game from the beginning. Rather than be impaled on the dichotomy, they celebrated it and embraced it. Like Walt Whitman, Hunter and the Dead's new literary world contained multitudes. A friend of the devil, sure—after all, you should never trust a prankster, even junior ones. And like Whitman, their constructed musical universe became a road, a "road for wandering souls," a road that contains everything and everybody; the American road.

The primary reason that Garcia had given "Dire Wolf" a country feel was that he had recently taken up the pedal steel guitar. Someone had given him one in 1966, but it wasn't tuned and he couldn't play it. In April he'd visited a music store in Boulder, sat down at a pedal steel, and "played with the pedals a little bit. I dug the tuning, and I said, 'Oh, I see!' Suddenly, I finally started to understand a little of the sense of it . . . I said I want to buy this fucking thing, but can you send it to me in tune? I'll never remember this tuning." As always, it was the experiential and not the abstract that inspired him. Remarkably, the partially strung instrument made it to Marin County in tune, and he began to practice it fiercely.

In May, he reconnected with an old Palo Alto friend, John "Marmaduke" Dawson, who had been writing some country songs. For a few Wednesday nights beginning in mid-May, Garcia began to drive his midget school bus down to a tiny coffeehouse in Menlo Park called the Underground. There he'd back up Marmaduke, more commonly called McDuke, on such tunes as "Wildwood Flower," "Six Days on the Road," "Lay Lady Lay," "Long Black Veil," "Tiger by the Tail," and McDuke's own "Last Lonely Eagle." It was fun, and in the way of the Grateful Dead, it evolved into a group activity. Their rehearsal space progressed from Weir's living room (where Frankie was, as she later put it, gently displacing Weir's "little honeys and Mama was setting up house") to the barn at Mickey's ranch, where Garcia and McDuke began to concoct a bar band. Before long, they would mutate a page from Zane Grey and call the band the New Riders of the Purple Sage.

There were many reasons that the Dead expanded their approach to include acoustic and country music. Not the least of them was that the

Dead's hour-long space jams were, in Lesh's words, "too explosive. It took too much out of us, for one thing." They had gone far, far out on an edge, and the pendulum was swinging back. In Rock Scully's words, "After all these years of mind-gumming psychedelics we are all actually beginning to *crave* the normal. We need something to ground us—our hair is talking to us, our shoes have just presented a set of demands, the walls are alive with the sound of intergalactic static. Please remind us whereof we come? Our home planet is what?" As well, the Hunter-Garcia material was the most ripely creative thing happening with the band. "I remember how warm and fuzzy it made me feel," said Mickey. "The electric side was so fun and so stimulating and so rewarding and so energetic, and then all of a sudden we were starting to explore the soft side of the G.D. And I thought, what a beautiful thing—acoustic guitars. It was cold out there in the feedback, electric G.D. world. It was a great cold, a wonderful freeze, full of exploratory moments and great vision, but here we were exploring the soft side . . . I thought it was really cool." This was especially true for Mickey, because he played in the New Riders, in a new-for-him straight-ahead way that included brushes.

Having gone through acid and war and the upheavals of the 1960s, the Dead had turned to their musical roots to see what was left of the American dream and what of those roots might still be viable. They did not simply replace psychedelia with country; they added new dimensions to an established oeuvre. They did not particularly want to pursue the American dream of financial success; rather, they wanted to invent a new dream, and a new mythology. The original American dream—that anything is possible, and that the frontier must be sought and then left behind—remained real for them. After psychedelics, everything *is* new, is possible; the frontier is shown to be within. And so the Dead took traditional song stylings and mixed them with a postmodern self-created mythology to create a new American frontier. Only one band influenced them, and not in any explicit stylistic way, but only as an inspiration. David Crosby from the Byrds, Stephen Stills from Buffalo Springfield, and Graham Nash from the Hollies had formed Crosby, Stills and Nash in late 1968, recording their eponymous first album in February 1969 and releasing it in June. Stephen Stills liked horses, and that summer he fell into the low company of Mickey Hart, living at the ranch for several months, learning to ride by going out with Mickey for jaunts in the hills, telling intricate tales of Civil War battles as they trotted along. Stephen's presence there brought Crosby and Nash around as well, and as they hung out at the barn, their magical vocal blend made singing seem the most natural possible thing. Crosby, of course, had been a friend since the earliest part of the decade, and had spent time at 710. As big an acidhead as anyone in the Dead, he also shared a caustic iconoclasm with Lesh and Garcia that made them close.

Horses and good weed made the days at the ranch seem sunnier, and in the process the Dead's singers, thought Hart, discovered the voice as "the holy instrument." "Hey," said the Dead's vocalists, "is that what a voice can do?" Naturally, the Dead's singers did it their own way. CS&N sang in systematic parallels, while, typically, the Dead were idiosyncratic, all over the place, with harmonies that worked but often made no sense. In other words, they sang as they played. As they worked out the harmonies to the song, they might well agree that a note had to be hit. "Well, you do it." "But I'm on top," Phil might protest. "So what," replied Weir. "If you want that note, sing it." "We weren't methodical," noted Weir. "Well, we were methodical, but it was our own method."

Later comparisons of the Dead's work in this era to that of the Band seem off the mark, except for a nearness in time, because the ethos of the Band's material was explicitly southern and Appalachian. However similar the Dead's material might have sounded, it was thematically much, much weirder, and appropriately so. After all, the Dead were from San Francisco, while Levon Helm, the Band's drummer and lead vocalist, had grown up on a cotton farm in Turkey Scratch, Arkansas, listening to Sonny Boy Williamson's *King Biscuit Flour Hour* while sitting in a corner of the studio of origin, only a few miles from his home. He and his bandmates, Canadians Robbie Robertson, Richard Manuel, Rick Danko, and Garth Hudson, played rockabilly with Ronnie Hawkins, went out on their own, and eventually became Bob Dylan's backup band from 1965 to 1966. In the summer of 1967 Dylan and the Band jammed on a variety of traditional and new songs, making what would eventually be called the Basement Tapes. "We didn't know if he wrote them or if he remembered them," said Robbie Robertson. "When he sang them, you couldn't tell." Their own album *Music from Big Pink*, released in the summer of 1968, along with Dylan's *Nashville Skyline*, the countrified Flying Burrito Brothers, and the Dead's next album, made music journalists quick to spot a trend. Whatever the new material was, the Dead's use of it was not trendy. Nor even always easy. Tapes of shows at this time reveal an audience struggling to assimilate the new material, with assurances coming from the band: "We'll get into all that heavy stuff [like "Dark Star"] eventually," said Garcia.

Shortly after Garcia completed the music to "Dire Wolf," Hunter had another dream. In it, Bobby Petersen was writing a song, and Hunter was able to look over his shoulder and read the lyrics. He awoke, wrote them down, and handed them to Garcia, who proceeded immediately to pick up a guitar and have a tune fall out. It was called "Casey Jones," a modern take on the legend of John Luther Jones, from Cayce, Kentucky, who did indeed leave Memphis's Central Station at a quarter to nine, ignored a signal to stop, and died. This "Casey Jones" was different, however, because it also dipped into the folk tradition of cocaine songs, making it a warning to Casey and the world to "watch your speed." As Garcia said, it was a "pretty good musical picture of what cocaine is like. A little bit evil. And hard-edged. That singsongy thing." "Casey Jones" was an immediate hit with the audience. At the same time, Hunter wrote what he thought of as a straightforwardly romantic country-western song, "High Time," so Jerry had something on which to play pedal steel.

The country bar band, the New Riders of the Purple Sage to be, began to grow up. Garcia on pedal steel, Marmaduke on guitar and vocals, Mickey on drums, Phil on bass. There was at least one embryonic concert at the Peninsula School, where Bob and Jerry had played in 1961, and then on June 11, Bobby Ace and the Cards from the Bottom of the Deck played at California Hall. It was a quasi-benefit for Scientology, because Weir had listened to T.C. over the winter and studied L. Ron Hubbard's ideas as a way of strengthening his position in the band. After a few months he decided that he neither felt nor played better, and was tired of paying money for nothing, so he quit. The benefit was actually his good-bye to Scientology, and featured Garcia, McDuke, David Nelson, Phil, Mickey, Peter Grant on banjo, and T.C. on piano.

Late in June the Dead returned to the road, going first to their home away from home, Fillmore East, and then to Central Park, where they played for free, "with a spirit," wrote the *Voice*, "that can only be likened to missionary or religious zeal . . . Ask no favors of the crowd; rather let the[ir] musical, physical, and spiritual presence . . . fill the atmosphere." Even *Variety* thought they had "proceeded to turn New York into a Dionysian festival of love. Orgy might be a better word." They went home, returned to New York, and this time played at the old world's fair site in Flushing, where a couple of interesting things happened. The promoter, Howard Stein, employed a young lady to give pieces of candy to the audience. As legend had it, she spent the night with a member of the Grateful Dead's scene, and while she slept, someone went through the candy and dosed each piece. The audience atmosphere at the second show in Flushing was a winner. And the crew found a new friend, a tall young

man from Queens named Steve Parish, who worked the show as a security guard. They'd see him again.

On the band's return home in July, they found that the central topic of
conversation in San Francisco music circles was the planned Wild West
Festival. Festivals were the keynote and overriding trend of the rock music
business that summer, although most of them were less than successful.
Newport '69 in Los Angeles in June, Denver Pop the next week, the
Newport Jazz Festival (which included rock acts) in early July, and the Atlantic City Pop Festival in early August were all marred by violence and
gate-crashing. The generation gap between youth and any sort of authority was deeper than ever. The Wild West Festival had been Ron Polte's
idea, in conversation with Kingston Trio producer Frank Werber. In
March the two of them brought together Tom Donahue, Bill Graham,
Ralph Gleason, Bert Kanegson, Barry Olivier of the Berkeley Folk Festival, Rock Scully, Bill Thompson, Jann Wenner, and David Rubinson, a
producer then working with Bill Graham, and formed the San Francisco
Music Council. The idea was to celebrate the city and the scene, "a party
and a spiritual statement" in the words of the minutes of their first meeting, with shows over several days, some for money, some free, some big
rock shows at Kezar Stadium in Golden Gate Park, with smaller shows
involving theater groups or ethnic musicians like Ali Akbar Khan. The
Airplane and Jann Wenner kicked in some money for start-up costs, and
the council, trying to prevent it from turning into a Bill Graham event,
chose Barry Olivier as director and began to lay plans. "No one's talking
hope—except those who are singing and dancing," said Rock. "This *is* the
revolution," added Werber.

On July 20, most of the Dead gathered at Garcia's house, because he
had a TV, and watched the most amazing television program of their
lives, the first human steps on the moon. It was an extraordinary moment,
but it came at a time of gross dissension back on planet earth. Four days
before, *Easy Rider,* the film that would for many define the essence of the
sixties, had premiered, and Jack Nicholson's character, a well-meaning liberal attorney driven to drink, slurred, "This used to be a helluva good
country. I don't know what happened to it . . . people talk about freedom,
but when they see a really free individual it scares them." A few minutes
later his character is beaten to death. The rebellious heroes, Peter Fonda
and Dennis Hopper, are murdered as well.

At the planning sessions for the Wild West Festival, the fault lines
among interest groups began to appear, as well as a vivid fantasy life. At a
meeting at Tom Donahue's house in Marin, someone suggested having

horses and covered wagons transport people within the park, and even the always-visionary Mickey Hart had to explain gently that teams of horses required expert handlers, not volunteers. Then the light-show artists began to brainstorm. On June 23 they imagined a special building for a 360-degree light show that would be 150 feet in diameter with a 30-foot ceiling. At the next week's meeting they decided that a screen 240 feet long and 20 feet high would do. Glenn McKay, whose Head Lights traveled with the Jefferson Airplane and received 10 percent of the Airplane's gross, then around $30,000 a show, appeared at this meeting and casually told the light artists that they deserved more. He showed off his fancy boots, and said, "I see a new projector, I buy it. Get together and organize." And he left. The light artists, who generally earned $100 a show from Graham and around $300 from Chet Helms, ran with the idea. On July 14 they proclaimed, "There must be good publicity for light shows," and if they were not allowed to do daytime shows in the park, which required a building, "doing shows at Kezar at night for money would run contrary to the spirit."

Festival plans began to solidify, and the July 18 *Festival News* newsletter revealed that there would be three paid nights at Kezar, and otherwise everything would be free. By July 28, the incipient discontent of street radicals focused on the imaginary wealth that was about to be made by the festival, and at a community meeting at Glide Memorial Church, a black community activist and S.F. State student striker named Arnold Townsend verbally squared off with Bill Graham. A murky, never-defined group called the Haight Commune, joined by the Mime Troupe and various interlocking combinations of vaguely politicized street people, had all decided the festival was going to be a rip-off. By now, the city fathers had begun to wonder if the festival idea was such a good one.

In the last days of July, promoters Bill Graham and Chet Helms received a letter from the Light Artists Guild (LAG) signed with the pseudonym "Ma." It announced the existence of the guild, demanded equal billing for light shows with the bands and a fee of $900 for a two-show weekend. "Nobody talked to me, I just got this letter," roared Bill. "Who is this 'Ma' who signed the letter? Nobody knows! . . . But what they will not accept is that they are not a draw . . . Their only negotiating point is 'art' . . . You know what demanding is? Demanding means WEIGHT! Where's their weight?" Graham was right—the LAG had none. They did have chutzpah. They would not confront Graham, and instead chose Chet Helms, who had reopened the Family Dog that June at a building left over from Playland, an old amusement park at Ocean Beach, on the

Great Highway. The Dead were booked to play three shows there beginning August 1, Garcia's twenty-seventh birthday. It would not be a happy one.

When the band arrived, they found the guild picketing the building and, with power supplied by Helms, staging a light show on the outside walls of the Dog. Years later, Jerry Abrams, the LAG leader, would defend their actions: "As long as light shows were being hired and we were a certified art form . . . we felt we should be compensated and publicized . . . we struck the Family Dog first because it just turned out that that was the first weekend we were going to do it. The Dead were playing and we figured we could reach the most people . . . I had assurances from Jerry Garcia . . . that he would honor our line. Chet knew [about it in advance]. Everybody knew." Both Chet and Jerry said they did not know in advance, and Garcia certainly felt that, as he later put it, "The whole thing was stupid."

There were around four hundred people inside and perhaps a thousand outside at the Family Dog when Garcia and Hart arrived. Whether Jerry Abrams knew it or not, he had a perfect victim in Garcia. His grandmother Tillie was alive, and although she was quite senile, she would have come across the park like a tornado if her grandson had crossed a picket line, and Garcia couldn't. Whatever he thought about the merits of the strike, he felt a sense of responsibility to his greater musical community, an obligation to try to mediate if nothing else. Chet, Jerry, Mickey, Rock, and a representative of the LAG, Bob Ellison, crowded into Ram Rod's equipment truck and began to talk. As Hart recalled it, Garcia said, "It's not about the fuckin' lights, it's about the fuckin' music . . . Yeah, there should be more equity and lights should be treated with respect, but this is not the way to go about doing it." Mickey, being Mickey, was ready to fight his way out, but calmed down. And instead of a negotiating session—there was nothing, really, to negotiate—it became a catharsis, each of them singing the same tune. No one was making money, and they were all emotionally stretched to the limit. By the time they exited the truck, it was too late to play; in their absence, the band had thrown together a jam, but the full Dead did not perform.

On August 5, there was a Wild West/LAG/music community meeting at the Family Dog, and Ralph Gleason turned to Bill Belmont and said, "You guys have lost it. You gave it away to Bill Graham—why?" Belmont shrugged. "He screams louder than the rest of us, I guess." Though Graham had actually been assisting Chet financially, the meeting began to focus on Graham as a monopolist. "I'm fucking sick and tired of four years of POINTING," he said. "I'm sorry, world, for being a success? I'm sorry for making a good living? For bringing good music to this town? Apologize for what? Feel guilty about what?" Dramatic as always, he announced that he was closing the Fillmore West at the end of the year and concluded, "I leave here very sad. I may be copping out, but your attitudes have driven me to my choice." Stephen Gaskin, a power in the freak community, replied, "Bill, we've heard that rap many times before. You took the choice between love and money. You got the money—don't come looking for the love." Graham went off. "I apologize, motherfucker, that I am a human being. I fully apologize. Emotional—you're fucking right . . . you're full of shit, and I have more fucking balls than you'll ever see. You want to challenge me about emotions, you slimy little man, fuck you. *Fuck you.* Don't get peaceful with me. Don't you *touch* me." Unfortunately for Bill, Gaskin immediately recognized the line "Don't get peaceful with me" as being from the play *The Connection* and responded, "I saw the play, it was better." Exit Bill Graham.

Minutes later, a brick came sailing through a window, hurled by some wandering stranger. Suddenly, there was barely a Family Dog, Friday's canceled show having all but bankrupted Chet, and hardly a music community, either. That night, still planning a Wild West Festival, Ron Polte and Tom Donahue attended a meeting of the Haight Commune, where a member named John the Motherfucker told them that the "pimp merchants of bread and circuses" were going to pay $150,000 rent (the actual figure was $12,000) for Kezar Stadium, and that the festival was part of the establishment, and not of the freak community. At a press conference the next day, Donahue speculated that psychedelics, in addition to opening people's minds, might encourage paranoia. "I find it difficult to understand the motivation of people who want to bring a halt to the getting together of their brothers in a celebration. I want to know who sent them up or set them up." He announced that the governing council of the festival would triple the number of seats on the board in an attempt to include and conciliate the various factions.

Eleven days before the festival was to begin, the city's Recreation and Parks Department limited the number of places in the park that could be used, and the handwriting was clearly visible on the wall. There were ongoing threats of violence, and Barry Olivier finally canceled the event. As Ralph Gleason wrote, "Apparently there is no place for dreams anymore." The San Francisco music community lay in ruins.

27

Interlude:
"Eastbound and Down"
(END OF SET ONE)

June, Miami Arena

God, Florida is a weird place. The band has taken a cross-country commercial flight to begin the tour, although from here on, they'll use charters, and the flight is filled with guys who are apparently extras on *Miami Vice*, every damn one of them dressed in gold-chain, open-to-the-navel, coke dealer/pimp shirts. Airplanes and airports are a Dead field of expertise. Most of our party can tell you more than you want to know about anything taxiing by, and some of them can pilot small planes. It is a life spent in airports, "tunneling from one vacuum to another," as the rock journalist David Dalton once wrote. Submitting to other people's schedules is not the Dead's favorite thing. As road manager, Rock Scully developed a technique for when Weir was, as usual, late. He would dump his briefcase out on the jetway and then oh-so-slowly gather his things up, to gain a delay. Pity the poor Grateful Dead travel agent. In the seventies it was a man named Randy Sarti, who recalled standing at the S.F. Airport curb with then road manager Danny Rifkin, waiting—what else?—for Weir. Bob finally arrived, they grabbed his stuff and ran to the gate, and Sarti ended up with a Halliburton briefcase full of pot. Security wouldn't put the metal case through X rays without opening it, so Randy was stuck with the case—until he happened to see a luggage handler he knew, and the man threw it in the belly of the plane. At the other end, the band and crew spotted it on the luggage carousel and gave Sarti a standing ovation in absentia.

The Dead also know hotels. On first arriving, the experienced tour participant checks his rooming list to see who might be on either side. There's at least one crew member who is a semiprofessional eavesdropper, and Scrib, for instance, has a very penetrating voice. The rooming list contains various pseudonyms, an interesting reflection of personality. Garcia won't use one, arguing that it would be giving in to fame. This might be noble, but it also means that he frequently shuts off the phone, so that those who work for him must go and knock on the door whenever they need to speak with him. Weir is Hugo Fuguzev ("You go fuck yourself"), Hart is Dr. Kronos (time), and Phil has been known to be Buck Mulligan (from James Joyce) or Chester the Molester. Brent is Clifton Hanger.

It's an amazingly good night for the opening of a tour, and Jerry is smiling as he kicks off "Bird Song," from his first solo album. Hunter dedicated it to Janis Joplin in his book of lyrics, and that feels right: "All I know is something / like a bird within her sang." It's a wide-open vehicle for jamming, and done right, it is exquisite. Tonight it's right. "Tell me all that you know / I'll show you / snow and rain." The jam ignites, and they play music like an endlessly variable Lego set, Garcia betraying the romantic's ultimate love of form, in that he unceasingly tests any shape with yet another possibility. It is a statement of unswerving faith in the creative moment. The song is a jigsaw puzzle, in which the first chorus is a picture with missing parts, and with each repetition they fill in the musical open spaces until the final chorus coalesces into the full, richly detailed picture. Playing like this is really all about bonding and breaking, blasting and dissolving. They regroup, regenerate, and push on. It is remarkably formal playing, but composed on the fly; not least of Garcia's gifts as a player is a clear sense of underlying architecture, of a precise shapeliness to even the most extended solo.

A kid in the front row gets a little out of it, hops up and down in front of the rail pointing at his face and talking at Garcia. "It's all right," says one crew member. "It's a message from Jerry's dentist. He owes for the kid's braces."

Backstage, Robbie Taylor's production assistant, Eric Colby, has gathered up a shopping list. Over the tour, his runners, two in each city, will gather this and much, much more.

MICKEY HART: all available CDs and cassettes of Argentinian tango
　　accordionist Astor Piazzola
　　　　1 pair AIWA mini speakers—sample pictured in Sharper Image
　　　　catalog
　　　　1 AIWA remote controller RC-8R ditto
　　　　1 pr Kolodny headphones
　　　　2 pr New Balance running shoes, #996 size 8
KIDD CANDELARIO: repair oxygen tank
　　　　CDs: John Mayall's Bluesbreakers, Charlie Musselwhite, Norton
　　　　Buffalo
　　　　10 small toggle switches: 7201 CNK with 6 poles. 10 nuts
　　　　12 lamp bulbs: halogen OSRAM 5.2V .85A w865
　　　　small bag assorted rubber bands
　　　　2 red road cases with 1" thick foam rubber insulation
MORPHEUS [the lighting company] request—1 cheap wooden stool, drum
　　throne height
DAN HEALY: one baby bottle warmer for travel—looks like shower cap
ROBBIE TAYLOR: 12 lanyards [for laminates]
　　　　4 boxes (total 96 pieces) DURACELL pro cell or copper top only
　　　　batteries
RAM ROD: book—*Jane's*—pictures of military aircraft
　　　　5 rolls 400 ASA Kodak black and white film 36 prints
HARRY POPICK: 1 travel water pik
CREW: 4 ICOM radios $273, 6 ICOM bp-20 battery packs . . .

June, Silver Stadium, Las Vegas (Second Night of Three)

Dead Heads in Vegas; what a hoot. "Thousands of tie-dyed, braided,
wiggy, happy kids," wrote Rip Rense in the *L.A. Herald Examiner,* "swirling and twirling among the roulette wheels and crap tables, staring with
electric eyes into the spinning faces of slot machines and hoping to influence the outcome . . . You can look at it as poetic: the Dead's gentle philosophy and open heart energy descending on the city of cheapness and
cutthroat chance like (as one observer put it), 'a rose dropping on
Formica' . . . And you can look at it as wholly appropriate: The Dead—
whose lyrics are rife with tales of luck and fate, cards and dice."

　　In fact, the Dead's annual visits to Las Vegas in the 1990s were a show
business phenomenon. Three 40,000-capacity stadium shows, all sold out,
and of those 120,000 tickets, at least 105,000 were sold to people from
somewhere else—Los Angeles, Phoenix, Denver, San Francisco. Danny

Zelesko, the promoter, has a piece of the show from Bill Graham Presents because they owed him for a money-losing show. In the long run, he is a lucky boy. Vegas is a pleasure city, and as long as the promoters schedule the weekend carefully, the Dead are welcome. Up the street from the band's hotel is the Mirage—what a perfect name for the American consumer culture. Across the desert, 30,000 New Bedouins cruise, freak flags high, in buses with greenhouses in the back, a Sphinx above the driver's seat, a bus that is a wooden chapel, with stained-glass windows, pews, and altar. And inside the buses, all hair and stoned eyeballs, are Dead Heads laughing at Vegas.

The band is rocking, and Weir toasts the Vegas vibe with his tribute to the decadent eighties, "Hell in a Bucket." "You imagine me sipping champagne from your boot / For a taste of your elegant pride / I may be going to Hell In A Bucket, babe / But at least I'm enjoying the ride." It is a hot, up-tempo rocker, and the dancers are in a languid frenzy. Up front, the audience presses ever forward against the rail, creating the frog people, they of the flat faces and bulging eyes. Eventually, the band will have to play the "Take a Step Back" chorus to parcel out some breathing room. In the parking lot, license plates read 10ACJED, ANY WNDO, BTWIND, DRKSTAR, DRUMZZ, GR8FUL, JK STRAW, OTH ONE, RUKIND. In the back of the stadium, a man in his sixties, balding, with glasses, begins to dance and snap his fingers, and his wife edges away, embarrassed. The song ends, and Weir steps to the mike: "Billy broke a snare, and you can't beat that." Actually, the drummer is sneaking off to take a leak. In the brief pause, Scrib thinks of Garcia, who was grievously disappointed with yesterday's show. "A shoe store. I should open a fuckin' shoe store. I could fuckin' sell shoes."

June, Giants Stadium, East Rutherford, New Jersey

Hot and steamy tonight. Jerry begins the riff that signals "China Cat Sunflower," one of the most enduring of Dead songs, and parallel beams like yellow tendrils stab out into the audience as though from the spaceship in *Close Encounters of the Third Kind*.

> *Look for awhile at the China Cat Sunflower*
> *proudwalking jingle in the midnight sun*
> *Copperdome Bodhi drip a silver kimono*
> *like a crazyquilt stargown*
> *through a dream night wind*

Krazy Kat peeking through a lace bandana
like a one eyed Cheshire
like a diamond eye Jack

The queer, neo-Carrollian doggerel rolls to the beat of a slightly unbalanced drive wheel, a whirring hypnotic rhythm that is entrancing—and entraining: it sucks you into it. The lyrics were written long before Hunter thought of himself as a lyricist, and they show it in their opaque abstraction and the odd way they break rhythmically. "I had a cat sitting on my belly at one point," he said once, "and followed the cat out to—I believe it was Neptune, but I'm not sure—and there were rainbows across Neptune, and cats marching across this rainbow." Thematically, it has an almost Zen-like feel to it. Properly approached, its imagery induces a dream state, and it is psychedelic in exactly the same way as is *Alice in Wonderland.* The final line, a reference to the "Queen Chinee," is a tribute to the Edith Sitwell poem "Trio for Two Cats and a Trombone." As the lyrics end, Garcia's quicksilver notes haul the band into a new tempo, the energy pulses, and they *rip*—

Early July, RFK Stadium, Washington, D.C.

—into "I Know You Rider," a traditional folk tune that they've played since 1965. They glued it onto "China Cat" soon after they had the song, and jacked up the tempo to make it a most worthy set-closer. Dead Heads dance, the sweat flying. God, it's miserably oppressive here, hot and disgustingly humid. This is where Jerry became terribly ill in 1986. It's not as bad tonight as the 120 degrees he once faced in Las Vegas, or the 113 in Kansas City when he refused to come out of his trailer for a while, but it's damn nasty. In the nineties, the band got air-conditioning onstage, giant tubes that snake under the deck and blow cold air on them through grates. D.C. is the home of Gallaudet College, so there are many deaf Dead Heads here, holding balloons to pick up the vibrations in the air as signers give them the words. "I can almost see the music" from the way the audience moves, said one Deaf Head. "Here they don't stare when I sign," says one Head, as a man wearing a ten-inch Pinocchio nose strolls by.

Hail today the size of golf balls landed eight miles away, so big it smashed car windows, and there was heavy rain all night. Watching a new storm approach, Scrib turns to Ram Rod and says, "Keep the faith." "Faith helps," he says, "but always have a Plan B." Putting on entertainment in the outdoors gets complicated. Once at Giants Stadium a tornado touched down three miles away from the show. Lightning danced all around the facility. The audience members refused to leave their seats to take cover, and as the rain poured down, Scrib could not stop looking at the guy who was up on the roof of the stage with a broom, pushing off water as it collected, right in the middle of the biggest lightning rod in Bergen County, New Jersey.

The music shrieks and roars, and Harry goes over to talk to Brent. After a long colloquy, he returns to his board, and Scrib asks what Brent said. "I don't know. I think he said he's okay, but not singing very well." Harry kicks his monitor speaker in and out in a nervous gesture and tells a joke. "What's the difference between a monitor mixer and a toilet? A toilet only has to deal with one asshole at a time." The only time Scrib ever saw Garcia actually yelling in anger was at Popick. Playing when you can't hear yourself is not a fun thing. Working for a band one cares about isn't always easy either. Candace bleeds internally when she fails to meet her own standards. Healy, too. Scrib fucks up by giving an adult rather than a facile made-for-TV answer to a TV newsman, and spends the night lacerating himself. Being a front man for magicians has its complications, but being part of a group of people committed to the Muse is very fine.

> *I wish I was a headlight on a northbound train*
> *I wish I was a headlight on a northbound train*
> *I'd shine my light through the cool Colorado rain*

And at the word "headlight," one Panaspot onstage stabs wildly into the audience and the audience melts into a gently frenzied puddle. The band sweeps to the end of the song, stacking up the harmony until it hits the tonic and the set comes to an end. Weir mumbles, "We'll be right back," and everyone sits down.

28

Bethel to Sears Point

(8/16/69–12/4/69)

Sometime near midnight on Saturday, August 16, 1969, the Grateful Dead made their way onstage to play to about 400,000 people in Max Yasgur's back pasture in Bethel, New York. Their performance at the Woodstock Music and Art Fair would rank in their memory as one of their worst ever. The circumstances were not ideal; to begin with, their set began late, for two reasons. One was that the stage design was based on a rotating turntable, so that the upcoming act could set up on the concealed rear half of the turntable during the current group's performance. In Bear's account, he and Ram Rod warned the stage manager that their equipment was too heavy for the staging, but they were ignored. So the turntable turned a few degrees—and squished to a stop. Second, there was a major problem with the electrical grounding of the stage, and Bear insisted on fixing it before the Dead went on, which created a substantial delay. His efforts were not entirely successful. When the vocalists approached their mikes, they received shocks, and not small ones. Weir's lover, Frankie, saw him start to sing, "and I saw a blue arc go from the mike to his top lip and—you know how he gets on one leg and he jumps back— he did that except *he* didn't do it—he just got his ass knocked back there. He had a huge blister, awful, when the song was over."

It was pouring rain, and the wind was blowing hard enough that it turned the light show screen into a sail, threatening to take the stage off its foundations until people hauled out knives and slashed holes in the screen. In the process, the Dead could hear people from behind their amps passing pleasantries like, "The stage is collapsing."

There were other distractions. The Dead were scared spitless. They still saw themselves, Mickey said later, as a fairly "humble, small-time band," happy lunatics playing music as well as possible, and surely not stars. They never had nor would operate well under stress, and the 400,000 invisible people out there on the other side of the blinding, nightmarish lights made for an incredible amount of pressure, as did the continuous stream of helicopters, the knowledge that the show had become a national event, and the imposing lineup of other bands. Yet the event was "a sort of culmination of our trip," thought Mickey, "free in the park. So we felt on one hand it was our party." Perhaps they were a tad excessively ripped on whatever LSD was around, which Phil recalled as being speckled tablets from Czechoslovakia. Finally, the festival structure, which allocated only an hour or so to any given band, guaranteed problems for the Dead. They were not showmen, and they rarely had a show that launched itself with all thrusters roaring. They built from a start, and after a while . . . *boom*.

So they made a big mistake. Knowing all this, they went for a knock-out punch and threw "St. Stephen" at the audience as an opener. Hart looked over at Garcia as they were about to begin, and saw fear in his eyes. Mickey thought to himself, " 'Oh, man, we're in trouble.' His eyes were *wide* open." Mickey was right. They hadn't warmed up enough to play it brilliantly, and in fact barely played it at all, going to another song after the first verse. Over the years, they would "train a generation of audiences," said Jorma Kaukonen, "how to respond to their music." But that time was not yet here, and this mass audience did not really get off on the free-form aspects of "Dark Star." It was not the "total disaster" that Garcia and the rest of the band would claim, but in context, it was not surprising that Garcia turned to Jon McIntire as he left the stage and said, "It's nice to know that you can blow the most important gig of your career and it doesn't really matter." As usual, he was right.

Woodstock would come to signify an entire generation, and up until the time they went onstage, the Dead had as good a time there as anyone. It began as the vision of Michael Lang, a Florida head-shop owner, and Artie Kornfeld, a low-level music business wheeler-dealer and associate of the Cowsills, a successful, fluffy pop recording group. The two of them found John Roberts, a reporter and heir, and Joel Rosenman, an attorney, who'd run an ad reading, "Young men with unlimited capital looking for interesting and legitimate business enterprises." There gradually evolved the notion of a three-day music festival at Woodstock, an Avalonesque town that had symbolized hip separation from conventional mores at least since the American Communist Party had been founded there in 1919, and even more so since Bob Dylan had moved there to be part of its art-colony ambience in the 1960s. When the town rejected the idea, the festival moved to Max Yasgur's farm.

From the time the organizers got to Max Yasgur, dozens of details worked out instead of failing, and it became clear that the Woodstock festival was somehow meant to be. Yasgur was an important fellow in Bethel, and the town went along with him. The underground press was suspicious, but Wes Pomeroy, former San Mateo County sheriff and head of security, met with them late in June at the Village Gate in New York City and charmed their socks off. The festival began with one helicopter pad marked with Christmas tree lights; it ended with fifteen choppers coming in and out. It took a remarkable maneuver to get sufficient telephones put in, but it happened. John Roberts could and should have backed out of his financial commitments, but instead bankrupted himself by staying in. New York City police officers were told by their superiors that they could not work security, but they showed up anyway, incognito, and there was no significant violence. The Fillmore East was closed for the summer, and most of the critical details of staging and ticketing were handled by vacationing professionals Chip Monck and John Morris. Early on, the producers decided they needed the Who, but Pete Townshend was dead set against playing. Lang and Pete's agent, Frank Barsalona, worked on him all night, and by dawn he cracked and agreed to do the gig. Frequent and considerable advertising gave the show massive impetus. That Bethel was within a hundred miles of an enormous population had something to do with it, but there was more at work. Woodstock became a pilgrimage.

By Thursday the fourteenth, there were already 20,000 people on the field. A "cash register guy" turned to the Dead's friend, Prankster and Hog Farmer Hugh Romney, and said it was time to clear the field. Said Hugh, "You wanna good movie or a bad movie?" As Hugh added later, the promoters were neither stupid nor piggish, and so it became a free concert. By 7 A.M. on Friday, 175,000 people had arrived on-site, the roads had congealed, and people began to desert their cars, first at the side of the road, then in the road, and walk. Among them were Mickey Hart and Sue Swanson, who had come early to visit Mickey's mother, Leah, and grandmother Ethel Tessel, staying at Leah's summer place eight miles from Yasgur's farm. Rock Scully tried to get to the show in a limo, got stuck in traffic, and wound up trying to direct it, the rain melting the LSD in his pocket into an orange streak. The police estimated that 1 million people tried to get to Bethel on Friday. "No one honks," wrote Gail Sheehy. "No one shouts. No one shoves. It's unnatural."

The world of rock gathered at the Holiday Inn in the town of Liberty, New York, near Grossinger's Resort, which made for odd juxtapositions. T.C. took a walk and found himself being stared at by ultra-orthodox Hasid youth, who thought he was from the moon. Bill Thompson, the Airplane's road manager, got room 1. Dale Franklin, then Graham's secretary at the Fillmore East, ran the motel lobby. Joan Baez, Sly Stone, Ravi Shankar, and Janis Joplin joined the Grateful Dead in the waiting line for room keys. In the bar, as the day passed, Spencer Dryden, Thompson's assistant Jacky Watts, Keith Moon, and Janis Joplin played poker. Bear prowled around giving out samples of the finest LSD. At various times, Garcia would share his room with Rock Scully's new lover, Ken Goldfinger's ex-wife, Nicki Rudolph, Bert Kanegson and his girlfriend, and Paul Williams of the rock magazine *Crawdaddy!* With the scheduled first act stuck in traffic, stage manager John Morris smooth-talked Richie Havens into a solo spot, then John Sebastian, then Country Joe. Then came the rain. But at Woodstock the rain turned out to be a good thing, a mild test that bonded 400,000 youth in good-natured loving joy. They were the chosen children, and they seemingly knew it.

On Saturday the Airplane's Bill Thompson ran into Lang and Kornfeld backstage, barefoot and loaded, babbling about love and beauty and peace. Being a road manager, he had other worries, and he proceeded to gather up the road manager of the Who, and Rock Scully and Jon McIntire from the Dead, among others. They sat down with the money guy, Joel Rosenman. Once again, signing the movie release became an issue, and neither the Dead nor the Airplane did so (although the Airplane would like their footage and later change their mind). Then the road managers demanded their money up front. Rosenman moaned, but found the cash.

As Saturday passed, Woodstock entered American history, dodging disasters and justifying everyone's faith in the special joy of rock and roll. "You could feel," Garcia said, "the presence of invisible time travelers from the future who had come back to see it, a swollen historicity—a truly pregnant moment . . . as a human being, I had a wonderful time." The new San Francisco band Santana was there only because Bill Graham had played hardball with the bookers, and Carlos jump-started a lifetime career with an electrifying set. Backstage, Garcia poked his head into a tent where John Sebastian, Stephen Stills, Graham Nash, and CS&N's drummer, Dallas Taylor, sat with a comatose fourteen-year-old, commenting, "Wow, man! Hippie rock stars! Will you autograph my butt?" Stills grumbled, "Fucking Canned Heat is making more than we are." For Taylor, the show was the highlight of what would be a fifteen-year nightmare of depression, drug addiction, and the full-blown screaming horrors. Out in the medical tent, William Abruzzi handled things brilliantly. A veteran of demonstrations and civil rights marches, he had eighteen doctors, thirty-six nurses, twenty-seven EMTs, and what he called the "superb paraprofessionals" of the Hog Farm, who would gather up someone coming unglued and tell him or her softly, "Guess what—it's going to wear off." When people came down, the Hog Farmer would point to the newest casualty and say, "That was you four hours ago. Now you're the doctor. Take over." They got by. Paul Krassner and Abbie Hoffman arrived with political leaflets, were duly ignored, and ended up working hard at the hospital tent. As Abbie later put it, "Hog Farm politics" was stronger than left-wing politics, because the Hog Farm was about survival.

As the night passed, the festival management confronted problem after problem, and managed to solve them. The most significant came when they realized that the rain had washed away the dirt covering the power cables. There was a real potential for mass electrocution if they didn't turn off the power, but to do so would leave half a million people in dark silence. Rosenman told his chief electrician to shift power to other cables without turning anything off—and it worked. After that, minor ego problems were easy. Bill Belmont, once the Dead's road manager, was helping with various aspects of the show, and reported to stage manager John Morris, "Sly is not ready to go on. Sly doesn't feel the vibes." Morris and Belmont looked at each other and said in unison, "Do a Bill Graham." It worked, and Sly went out and shredded the crowd with a galvanic performance, probably the peak of his entire career. As the Who played, Abbie Hoffman decided that this would be a good time to interrupt the music for a lecture on John Sinclair's legal problems. Townshend batted him away with a swipe from his guitar.

Then it was dawn and Hugh Romney went onstage to announce, "What we have in mind is breakfast in bed for 400,000." The *New York Times* would initially be hostile, writing in a Monday editorial headlined "Nightmare in the Catskills" that the crowd had "little more sanity than the impulses that drive the lemmings . . . [a] nightmare of mud and stagnation . . . What kind of culture is it that can produce so colossal a mess?" Yet even the *Times* had to concede, "the great bulk of the freakish-looking intruders behaved astonishingly well." Or, as Max Yasgur pointed out from the stage, "I think you people have proven something to the world— that a half a million kids can get together and have three days of fun and music and have nothing but fun and music [applause]! And I God bless you for it."

Three died: one Viet vet with malaria, one person run over by a water truck, one of a burst appendix. Four hundred drug bummers, all of whom walked away. No violence. As the Dead choppered out on Sunday morning, thunderheads were lining up once again. They landed in Liberty, changed to cars, and were driving to Kennedy Airport when all around them exploded the wrath of God, a lightning bolt and thunderclap in perfect timing that stunned them. T.C. cracked, "Now that's the P.A. we need." For their labors, the Dead received $2,250. Jimi Hendrix topped the payment list at $18,000. Santana got $750.

There was one other thing the Dead got from Woodstock and the other festivals, though its worth was hard to measure in dollars. With all of the bands using more or less identical road cases, Bear had concluded that a simple, easily identified logo would be useful. He had envisioned a simple symbol that was a bolt of lightning in a red and blue circle with a white border, but his artist friend Bob Thomas delivered a more refined rendering in which a skull, the forehead cleaved by a lightning bolt, would fill a circle. The bolt had thirteen points, as in the number of stripes in the U.S. flag, and its colors were red, white, and blue. They may have been stoned, but they were still patriots. Variously called the Laughing Jap— the Dead were not ordinarily racist, but the skull's eyes are vaguely Asiatic, and its expression is mirthful—the Cosmic Charley, or the Steal Your Face (from the later album of that name, the cover of which it graces), it would become one of the most recognizable logos in the world.

The Dead continued to play festivals, ranging from Oregon's tiny Bullfrog Festival to the international Vancouver Pop Festival and then the heavyweight New Orleans Pop Festival, which included Janis Joplin, the Who, and the Jefferson Airplane. At the time, Louisiana law mandated a fifty-year maximum sentence for selling pot, and the parish sheriff had 116 undercover officers on-site. The local underground newspaper was in a fight with the promoter, and ran a front-page item describing a mythical "People's Park Annex Hardware Department Wire Cutting Sale." It was not surprising that there was trouble. In Bear's recollection the promoter refused to supply a truck to transport the band's gear from the airport, and when their stage equipment was late, he told the promoter, "It's your problem, mate." In addition, Bear and the Dead wanted to use their own P.A., a naive thought in a festival.

It was a portentous fall. The leader of North Vietnam, Ho Chi Minh, died on September 3. Radical scholar Angela Davis was fired from a teaching job at UCLA on the nineteenth, part of a nationwide effort by the FBI to destroy the Black Panther Party and its supporters. On September 25 the federal government began to prosecute the Chicago Eight, not for what they had done in Chicago—this group could not have unanimously organized a serious tea party—but because they were prominent radical social critics, and the government was out to intimidate. "I wish we had done what they said we did," wrote Jerry Rubin. "Our myths were on trial." The cover of the September 10 *Life* was a red flag, and the subject was "Revolution." The *Life* article on the Chicago trial concluded, "It seems less a trial than an act of vengeance." Early in October the Weatherman faction of SDS committed political suicide, dashing about Chicago breaking windows and hurling itself facedown into the dustbin of megalomaniacal political irrelevance. Later that month Jack Kerouac died, fat and lonely, in St. Petersburg, Florida. And in some cosmic balancing act, one marvelous, magical thing also happened that fall: the once stunningly inept New York Mets won the World Series.

The Dead passed through New York in September, doing shows at the Fillmore East for good money—$5,000 a night—and shows at the Cafe au Go Go and in Boston for closer to $2,000. Of course, not all their pay came in a check; sometimes there were less formal compensations, like their guest list. At the Cafe au Go Go, a long line waited outside penniless, and Pigpen let them all in and then remarked, "I think we just got fired." Lenny Hart had not yet effected a noticeable improvement in their business affairs. That fall in San Francisco, sheriffs repossessed Pigpen's organ from the stage as the show was about to begin, settling a $1,200 unpaid bill from the previous year. What the band did not know was that Lenny had just negotiated an extension on their contract with Warner Bros., since their original three-album deal had run its course. The new deal included an advance of $75,000, and Lenny flew to Los Angeles, met Joe Smith at an airline counter, got the check, and returned home. Not only was the band ignorant of the new deal and the money, they did not know about a counteroffer from Clive Davis at Columbia Records. If Lenny was successful at anything, it was at keeping the band in the dark.

At the same time, Rock Scully was out of action, wherein lay a tale. Around Labor Day, Ralph Gleason reported that three San Francisco bands—the Dead, the Airplane, and the newly arrived Crosby, Stills and Nash—were planning a free show in London's Hyde Park. Early in September Rock went to London to advance the show, but at customs he was called aside and busted for possession of a modest amount of LSD (thirty hits). He attributed the arrest to a Machiavellian plot of Lenny's, so that in Rock's absence, the Dead would re-sign with Warner Bros. He told no one of his suspicions at the time, which casts doubt on the theory. In any case, Rock called an old pal, Chesley Millikin, who'd known the band in San Francisco but was now an executive for Epic Records in London. Along with Chesley came his friend Sam Cutler, who worked for Blackhill Productions, and had therefore stage-managed the Rolling Stones' giant Hyde Park concert on July 5. They bailed him out, and Rock and Sam became fast friends; there was a bond between London and San Francisco, and Rock and Sam were kindred spirits.

Back home, Mickey Hart and Rock's new lover, Nicki, made candles embedded with the finest pot, and Nicki filled up her brassiere with LSD, then flew off to London to sell the acid to pay the lawyers to get Rock home. The pot they smoked with the Stones. Rock seemed exotic to Sam, who was, he said of himself, "receptive of the West Coast bit, very enamored," and very much charmed by "the chemicals which coincided with that sort of consciousness." Part of the West Coast bit was talk of free concerts, and Rock planted the idea early with Sam and the Stones. As the Stones began to prepare for an American tour that fall, they "didn't have anyone to look after them personally," said Cutler, and Sam became that person.

As the fall progressed, America shuddered with conflict. Late in October *Life* magazine's cover asked if marijuana should be legalized. The same week, in the Chicago Eight trial, Judge Julius "the Just" Hoffman ordered Black Panther Bobby Seale gagged and chained to his chair. It was no wonder that the Airplane's new album, *Volunteers,* would include the line, "Up against the wall, motherfuckers / Tear down the wall." San Francisco's musical influence was at a peak; Janis Joplin, Santana, and Creedence Clearwater Revival were all in the Top Ten on November 10, when Warner Bros. released *Live Dead. Rolling Stone* would rave that the album "explains why the Dead are one of the best performing bands in America, why their music touches on ground that most other groups don't even know exists . . . But if you'd like to visit a place where rock is likely to be in about five years, you might think of giving *Live Dead* a listen or two."

But only one music story really mattered that fall: the Rolling Stones were touring the United States again. In many ways, it was the first great rock tour. When the Beatles and Stones had toured from 1964 to 1966, hardly anyone had listened or been able to hear the music through the screaming. In the ballroom era the ambience was nearly as important as the act. At Woodstock the audience had been the star. Now, with the Beatles off the road and Dylan vanished underground, the Stones were certifiably what Cutler called the "world's greatest rock and roll band." Having resolved their legal problems, they were coming to the States to prove it. Brian Jones had left the band in June and died by drowning a month later. *Let It Bleed,* their new album, was demonically brilliant and fit the edgy tenor of the times perfectly. But some things had changed.

On their way to the first show, Jagger told the ubiquitous Bill Belmont, on the tour as one of the road managers, that he planned a half-hour set. Bill warned him that in 1969 an hour was a bare minimum, and so Mick and Keith added some acoustic tunes. Their ticket prices were significantly higher than normal, and the very arrogance that they had used to take them to the top was now interpreted as contempt. In 1969, their press conferences included not only "straight" (conventional) press, who asked stupid questions about hair length, but underground reporters, who asked about ticket prices and the band's responsibility to the freak community. During rehearsals in Los Angeles in October, Rock, Danny Rifkin, and Emmett Grogan met with Jagger and Sam Cutler to urge again the idea of a free Bay Area concert, with the proviso that it be kept secret until the last possible moment. There was yet another Stones connection with the Dead. Ram Rod and Rex Jackson found themselves with a bit of time off in November, and via Bill Belmont, hired on with the Stones. They would end up working most of the tour.

Writer Stanley Booth accompanied the Stones, and as the tour arrived in Oakland in early November, he noted Rock Scully's arrival backstage. "Scully was wearing Levi's and a plaid cowboy shirt, and with his beard and his bright eyes, he appeared a pleasant open-faced charming western guy." They resumed considering the notion of doing a free show, presumably in Golden Gate Park, using the Hell's Angels as security. "The Angels are really some righteous dudes," Booth quoted Scully. "They carry themselves with honor and dignity." Booth added, "He was so blue-eyed and open about it, it seemed really convincing." The Stones' show in Oakland did not go smoothly. Bill Graham did not like Sam Cutler, whom he dismissed as "an opportunist without much talent," or the Stones' demands, and he catered the show from a local burger joint.

When the Stones took the stage forty-five minutes late, he ended up wrestling with Cutler onstage.

At home, Grateful Dead life only got weirder. Gail Turner was a friend of the band's who in October had gone to work for Lenny, just as the band closed the Shady Management office on Union Street and moved operations to the Novato warehouse. Lenny was proving to be a peculiar manager. He wouldn't allow Gail to put stamps on their mail, making everyone pay postage due at the other end. He'd never let Gail or anyone else see the books, and would issue the payroll in the oddest way. But he was a straight family man dropping out and becoming part of the counterculture, and his mantra was, "I love the Grateful Dead, I love this happening to me." She accepted his foibles and forced herself to believe.

On November 15, 500,000 antiwar activists marched on Washington in an event called Moratorium Day. U.S. military leaders suggested ringing the White House with concertina wire to stop the marchers, though in the end city transit buses proved sufficient. The Dead played for Moratorium Day at a small theater in Crockett, California. Eight days later, on November 23, CBS broadcast a Mike Wallace interview of a soldier who had been at a place called My Lai in Vietnam, and the young man began his story with, "We landed and we began shooting." The December 5 issue of *Life* led with "The Massacre at My Lai." The growing realization that American soldiers had butchered civilians would be devastating to support for the war. At the same time, President Nixon began Operation Intercept to slow the influx of pot into the United States from Mexico. Shortly thereafter, any connection admittedly uncertain, heroin began flowing into the United States from Southeast Asia in body bags returning from the war, courtesy of the CIA.

Late in November the Stones performed two blistering concerts at Madison Square Garden, after which Mick Jagger announced that they would end the tour with a thank-you to "the people" with a free show in Golden Gate Park on December 6. Not only would this make up for high ticket prices and late shows, but it would also provide a fabulous climax to the movie that the Stones had hired the Maysles Brothers to film. If they rushed, they could get their movie out before the Woodstock film, once again proving that the Stones *were* the world's greatest rock and roll band, superior to even a magical three-day event. The free show assumed an inexorable momentum, even as the original site, Golden Gate Park, was automatically eliminated by the public announcement—the city's Board of Supervisors was allergic to the idea of hundreds of thousands of people streaming into the park due to advance publicity, and refused to approve a permit. The Stones ended the regular part of their tour on November 30 in West Palm Beach, Florida, and then headed to Muscle Shoals, Alabama, to record. Free-show headquarters were established at the Dead's Novato warehouse. Cutler, Scully, and Chip Monck chose Sears Point Raceway as the new site for the show. Only ten miles from Novato and thirty-five or so from San Francisco, Sears Point offered good access and plenty of room. They decided to put the stage halfway up the side of a natural bowl, so that while the stage would be low—scaffolding cost money, and it was a free show after all—it would be safe. Sears Point asked for $6,000 rental, plus $5,000 to be held in escrow against possible damages, and all seemed under control.

On December 4, a certain morbid current in the national news began to thicken. In Muscle Shoals, the Stones (and everyone else) opened their newspapers and discovered pictures of hippie and ex–Haight Streeter Charles Manson, now considered responsible for the horrific Tate-LaBianca murders in Los Angeles the past summer. In Chicago, the police department quite simply murdered two Black Panthers, Fred Hampton and Mark Clark. Closer to home, the Stones' brutal business tactics finally blew up in their faces. Concert Associates had at one time thought they had the right to promote the Stones' L.A. shows, but in the end these had gone to Bill Graham. Concert Associates was aggrieved. Filmways owned both Concert Associates and Sears Point Raceway. Suddenly, Sears Point wanted a very sizable insurance policy for the event, to be paid for by the Stones, and perhaps a percentage of the movie—the stories varied tremendously. Neither option was acceptable to Mick Jagger, and so just a few days before the scheduled concert, Sears Point was eliminated as a site, and the scramble to find a replacement began. The flamboyant San Francisco attorney Melvin Belli became involved, and his offices replaced the Novato warehouse as control central. Worse, the two Top 40 rock stations, KFRC and KYA, began to run hourly bulletins, each trying to be the unofficial "Stones station," while Tom Donahue's more responsible KSAN was edged out. Belli came up with a site in Corte Madera, but it lacked road access and was impractical.

On the afternoon of the fourth, Mel Belli got a phone call from a man named Dick Carter, owner of the Altamont Raceway in Livermore, forty miles or so east of San Francisco. Thinking that it would be great publicity, he offered his raceway as a site for the big free concert.

29

Trouble
All Around

(12/5/69–3/70)

am Cutler was in Alabama when he learned that the Sears Point location was out, and when he heard about the Altamont offer, he sent Rock Scully and Woodstock promoter Michael Lang, who had somehow materialized in San Francisco, in a helicopter to look at it. They came back and said, "Yeah, it's possible." They also sketched out a location for the stage, at the bottom of a hill. Later, Jon McIntire would recall that Rock expressed doubts even then, but the dream of the Dead playing with the Stones was too much for Scully's judgment, and he wouldn't let go of the idea. "California's driven by wonderful dreams," said Cutler. But when he saw Altamont, he saw a "shithole in a desert."

The San Francisco Bay Area is surrounded by an arc of hills, and one of the major breaks in the arc is the Altamont Pass, which links the greater Bay Area with California's Central Valley. The gap is meteorologically critical, generating such tremendous air pressure between the cold ocean and warm inner valley that the crest of the pass is lined with hundreds of shiny steel windmills. On the other side of the range, as the road flattens out, there is a demolition derby track on the right. It is cheap and sleazy-looking, an ugly desolation of crushed auto bodies. In December the hills are sere and yellow. The farmers in the Sacramento Delta fifty miles north burn off their rice stubble, and the air is bitter and smoky. From the Altamont Raceway, there is nothing else in sight but the hills and the freeway.

Early in the process of preparing for the concert, Sam Cutler had attended a meeting at Mickey's barn. Dressed in a fur-collared suede jacket, dripping in turquoise, he must have looked, he later thought, "like a demented rock-glam version of a manager to the assembled denim-clad Frisco people, a visitor from another planet." After spending the night, he was taken for a ride on Snorter, "frantically galloping alongside up and down the hills of the ranch . . . basically hanging on for dear life." Having passed this first test, he met with some Hell's Angels, including Mickey's close friend Sweet William and Frisco Pete Knell. Every free show in the Bay Area since 1966 had included the Angels, who would assume pride of place with their motorized steeds near the stage and generally behave with equanimity, taking care of lost children, guarding power lines, and so forth. The Angels were elementals in the alchemical sense, not governable, physically intimidating, but usually safe enough. Since they'd be at the free Stones show in any case, it seemed reasonable to have them sit on the front edge of the stage. "[Pete] was absolutely adamant," said Cutler later, "that nobody hires the Hell's Angels to do fuck all. The only agreement there ever was, basically, was the Angels, if they were going to do anything, would make sure nobody fucked with the generators, but that was the extent of it. And it was $500 worth of beer that we got together for them . . . But there was no 'They're going to be the police force' or anything like that. That's all bollocks, media-generated bullshit. 'The Rolling Stones hired the Hell's Angels' is one of the great rock and roll canards."

Bert Kanegson was also at the meeting and recalled it somewhat differently. "I'm storming that this is insane, 'How can these guys do security? Those guys on top of the Rolling Stones? This is absolute disaster' . . . They were clearly security; there was no question . . . We discussed it in this meeting . . . And I remember it coming from Emmett [Grogan], and I never forgave Emmett for that." Sweet William told his friend Peter Coyote that Cutler had asked them to do security, and they had refused—sort of. "We don't police things," Sweet William said. "We're not a security force. We go to concerts to enjoy ourselves and have fun." "Well, what about helping people out—you know, giving directions and things?" asked Cutler. "Sure, we can do that." When Sam asked how they might be paid, William replied, "We like beer." The deal was for one hundred cases.

With around thirty-six hours to move the show from Sears Point to Altamont, a whirlwind descended on the Novato warehouse. The sound system for the day would come from the Dead/Alembic and the Family Dog's Bob Cohen. Renting cars was passé—now they were renting helicopters, and Alembic got stuck with lots of the bills. In the frenzy, Emmett Grogan wrote on a blackboard, "Charlie Manson Memorial Hippie Love Death Cult Festival." Point taken. Yet there had never been a big problem with a Northern California free show before, and "the show must go on." The various problems were simply obstacles to be overcome, and the feat of moving a show in so short a time was a logistical triumph. The omens, if omens they were, were ignored until it was too late. Bear and Dan Healy drove out to the site early on the morning of the fifth, and just as they crossed over the crest of Altamont Pass, they saw a fantastic explosion in the sky from an aborted weather rocket. They wondered if it was a sign. Then they saw Altamont Raceway, and their doubts grew. The stage was only three feet high, and setting up the P.A. largely consisted of trying to meld different sound systems—Healy's from Quicksilver, the Dead's, the Family Dog's—into a unit. With the help of some Orange Sunshine LSD, they worked through the day and night to get things ready. The women of the Grateful Dead scene spent the day tie-dyeing banners for stage decorations. Mick and Keith Richards flew out to look at the site, but when Mick flew back to get some rest, Keith stayed, sleeping in the back of the Hog Farm's cook tent, so grungy that hardly anyone recognized him. People began to gather and the roads thickened with cars from Friday night on, and for most, it was a pleasant time. Tim Leary's drive to Altamont was a treasured memory of "passing joints, fruit, wine and beer from car to car as we inched along."

As December 6 dawned, Peter Monk and Bert Kanegson sat onstage, planning a morning mantra that would chant in the sun's rays and bring good vibrations onto the scene. As they were about to begin, the audience kicked over the low perimeter fence and came storming down the hill to get in front of the stage. By late afternoon there were about 300,000 people on the site. As showtime approached, the Angels arrived, driving their bikes through the audience to park them in front of and to the side of the stage. The situation was set: 299,000 people had come to see a show and were comfortably arrayed; and then there were the 1,000 desperate to be up front, some of whom were not acting sanely. Some of them were "the weirdos too," wrote one witness, "speed freaks with hollow eyes and missing teeth, dead faced acid heads . . . Is this [Hieronymus] Bosch or Cecil B. De Mille; biblical, medieval, or millennial?" Perhaps they'd had nasty brushes with Angels in the past. Some of them were temporarily demented on whatever drug was their choice. Between the beer and their favorite amphetamines and/or barbiturates, the Angels were ripped as well. The ultimate job requirement for a good security person is a detached, intelligent sense of humor. The Angels did not qualify. They were also in a completely untenable tactical position, one hundred of them (at most) standing at the bottom of a hill in front of a low stage.

A couple of days after the concert, Sonny Barger, president of the Angels' Oakland Chapter, would comment, "I didn't go there to police nothin', man. I ain't no cop. I ain't never gonna ever pretend to be a cop, and this Mick Jagger like put it all on the Angels, man. Like he used us for dupes, man. And as far as I'm concerned, we were the biggest suckers for that idiot that I can ever see. You know what, they told me that if I would sit on the edge of the stage so nobody would climb over me, I could drink beer until the show was over. And that's what I went there to do. But you know what? When they started messing over our bikes, they started it. I don't know if you think we pay fifty dollars for them things or steal 'em . . . ain't nobody gonna kick my motorcycle. And they might think because they're in a crowd of 300,000 people that they can do it and get away with it, but when you're standin' there lookin' at something that's your life, and everything you got is invested in that thing and you love that thing better than you love anything in the world and you see a guy kick it, you know who he is, you're gonna get him. And you know what? They got got. I am not no peace creep by any sense of the word."

Around noon, Santana took the stage, and trouble broke out immediately. "During our set," said Carlos, "I could see [an Angel] from the stage who had a knife and just wanted to stab somebody. I mean, he really wanted a fight. There were kids being stabbed and heads cracking the whole time." The Flying Burrito Brothers played next, and then the Jefferson Airplane. Marty Balin was neither large nor strong, but he lacked for nothing in the *cojones* department. Seeing a group of Angels beating a young man with pool cues, he dove off the stage and was beaten unconscious by an Angel named Animal. Friends dragged Marty backstage, where he came awake, saw Animal, and piped up, "Fuck you," whereupon he was knocked out a second time. Marty was the only man onstage to resist the Angels. Paul Kantner, always feisty, did remark to the audience, "I'd like to mention that the Hell's Angels just smashed Marty Balin in the face and knocked him out for a bit. I'd like to thank them for that." In response, an Angel walked across the stage and challenged him. "You talkin' to me, man?" Grace Slick kept on singing, she later said, because she'd forgotten to put in her contacts that morning and was thus unable to see the madness going on around her. In the melee in front of the stage, Bert Kanegson, a pacifist who had gotten to know the Angels at the Carousel Ballroom, managed to talk them out of beating one kid. As the kid walked away, he cursed the Angels, who shrugged and then beat Bert senseless.

The Airplane played on, and the members of the Dead arrived via helicopter. On the way from the landing pad to backstage, Phil and Jerry were walking through the audience, and Phil stopped short, smacking Garcia in the head with his instrument case, which felt to Lesh like a "weird start." Backstage they found chaos. The Dead's truck was stage left, and the Dead, their family, and various friendly Oakland Angels were there. The stage-right side was seemingly controlled by strangers, Angels from San Jose, and they were coming unglued. At one point an Angel wouldn't let the Dead out of their truck. He was preparing to rearrange Lesh's facial features when their friend, San Francisco Angel Terry the Tramp, intervened. Between the beatings of Marty and Bert and this action, the Dead decided they were not playing. Crosby, Stills and Nash went on, and Angels took to poking at audience members and musicians with long bicycle spokes. Stephen Stills was one victim, and though he was bleeding, he decided to keep playing.

Things got worse. For nearly two hours, as the wind picked up and people shivered, there was no music. Later, Cutler would say that Bill Wyman had been missing, shopping in San Francisco. If so, it was a nice coincidence that he turned up just in time for the sun to set. The Stones were escorted from a trailer to the tuning tent, Angels punching at faces that peeked through holes in the canvas, and then to the stage. The lights bled red, the Stones came out to the tune of "Jumpin' Jack Flash," and Jagger realized "there's no control." Four Angels jumped off the stage, and a pool cue slashed down, hitting an unseen target with a "burst of water as if it had crushed a jellyfish," wrote Michael Lydon. Stanley Booth described the scene: "Many in the audience nearest the stage are demanding to be made victims . . . stripping nude despite the cold, [they] climb onto the stage only to be thrown off and beaten on the ground below. They raise themselves, hair and faces matted with blood, and climb up again. To be beaten again. Collaborating in the violence." At "Sympathy for the Devil," the scuffles between audience members and Angels picked up in intensity, and the Stones stopped. Mick Jagger, cockgod of rock and roll, was terrified. He pleaded, "Sisters, brothers and sisters, brothers and sisters, come on now. That means everybody just cool out." They began the song again and somehow managed to get through it. Keith Richards shouted, "Kee' it cool. Hey, if you don't cool it you ain't gonna hear no mu-sic!" Years later, Sonny Barger wrote that he responded to Richards's threat by sticking a revolver in his side. The Stones began to play "Under My Thumb," and a black man named Meredith Hunter wearing a "black hat, black shirt, [and an] iridescent blue-green suit" became visible in the crowd, waving a revolver. Suddenly, Angels swarmed over him, and one, Alan Pasaro, pulled out a knife and stabbed him repeatedly. No one on-stage realized immediately that things had come to the ultimate pass, and Jagger called out, "If you move back we can continue and we will con-tinue." They did so, and the Rolling Stones began to play for their lives.

Many in the audience knew only that they had seen a fantastic con-cert and were unaware of the horrors. The Grateful Dead family was sickeningly well informed. Dazed and confused, they headed for the heli-copter pad, "just trying not to see what was happening to the sides of us," said Frankie Azzara. They crowded into a helicopter, the door closed, "and it was like a Vietnam sound." The chopper lifted off. "Then all of a sud-den it was stone silence, we were up in the air, everyone is thinking . . . and M.G., out of nowhere, yells, 'Does anybody know where the constel-lation Cancer is?' And we all just sort of automatically looked up at the stars . . . and started bullshitting, 'Oh yeah, it's probably that.' It got real quiet and she gave us a scenic tour of the heavens . . . an M.G. psycholog-ical workshop and 'the project today is look up and we are not going to think about the real world until we land.' "

The insane truth was that the Dead still had a show to do that night, at Fillmore West. McIntire did his best to soothe everyone's nerves with food and drink, taking them to Grison's, a fancy San Francisco steak house. Toward the end of the meal, Kreutzmann arose and announced that he wasn't playing, and he and Susila left. "If Billy's not playing, neither am I," added Mickey. Poor McIntire was left to journey down Van Ness Avenue to the hall to tell Graham's manager, Paul Barratta, that the Dead were a no-show. Frantic, Barratta offered the audience free tickets to other shows.

As Scully told the story, later that night Graham accused him of mur-der for his part in the show. It was true that without Rock's support for the move to Altamont, his refusal to stop the train when it had been twice derailed, Altamont would probably not have happened. Scully was surely not alone in making abysmal decisions. "We believed—however naively—that this show could be organized by those San Francisco people who'd had experience with this sort of thing," said Mick Jagger much later. "It was just an established ritual, this concert-giving thing in the Bay Area.

And just because it got out of hand, we got the blame . . . *we did not organize it."* Partly true; Sam Cutler was on their payroll and okayed the arrangements, but he was dependent on Rock. Of course, Jagger established the tone of the event by ignoring advice and announcing it well in advance, by sanctioning business practices that resulted in being blown out of Sears Point, and by delaying coming onstage until dark so that he and the Stones could have their movie. Garcia quoted the San Francisco hippie thinker Stephen Gaskin: "Altamont was the little bit of sadism in your sex life, that the Rolling Stones put out in their music, coming back." There was truth in that. The Angels were placed in an untenable situation—but they should never have been placed there at all. Meredith Hunter *was* armed, and Alan Pasaro was later found not guilty of murder on the grounds of self-defense.

Stung by Ralph Gleason's criticism of their role in Altamont, the Dead responded by producing, in just two weeks, one of their few topical songs, "New Speedway Boogie." In Hunter's words:

> *Who can deny? Who can deny?*
> *it's not just a change in style*
> *One step done and another begun*
> *in I wonder how many miles?*
>
> *Spent a little time on the mountain*
> *Spent a little time on the hill*
> *Things went down we don't understand*
> *but I think in time we will . . .*
>
> *One way or another*
> *One way or another*
> *this darkness got to give*

Hunter, who had decided in advance that Altamont would be a mess and had instead gone to see the film *Easy Rider*, was profoundly antiviolence, and had been greatly disturbed, for instance, by the tone of the Airplane's song "Volunteers." Later, Hunter would say, "I wanted to stand back . . . There's a better way. There has to be education, and the education has to come from the poets and musicians, because it has to touch the heart rather than the intellect, it has to get in there deeply. That was a decision. That was a conscious decision."

Hopeful resignation was not chic in America in late '69. Even Garcia found "New Speedway Boogie" "an overreaction" and "a little bit dire," although he was firmly aware that a responsibility for the audience's well-being was essential to performing. He had always been dubious about politics, but Altamont was the capper. "If a musical experience is forcibly transferred to a political plane," he argued somewhat later, "it no longer has the thing that made it attractive . . . a musical experience [is] its own beginning and its own end. It threatens no one." The critic Robert Christgau was fascinated by the Dead's philosophical approach to the disaster. "I recognized how smoothly the Dead Americanized volatile intellectual imports like karma and eternal recurrence. Only within a culture as benign and abundant as that of Northern California could anything real and humane accompany such vast cosmic notions, but it did, and the Dead were its highest manifestation. They were not uncomplicated men, but within the controlled environment of the concert hall they generated a joyful noise that went beyond complications." At Altamont, the Dead were "naive," and Jagger was "probably something nastier. I would call it criminally ironic. Jerry Garcia's serenity is religious, and smug; Jagger's detachment is aesthetic, and jaded."

"New Speedway Boogie" also spoke of running with the weight of gold, but that was not yet a Grateful Dead problem. Each member of the Rolling Stones earned approximately $425,000 for the tour, and while Jagger kept up with events from the largest suite at the elegant Huntington Hotel on San Francisco's Nob Hill, the band's ever-loyal pianist and road manager, Ian "Stu" Stewart, flew to Switzerland with the cash.

Not long before Altamont, Garcia had given Robert Hunter a cassette. It was forty-five minutes of sizzling repetition, the band working through endless variations of what were clearly the changes to a major new song. Hunter set to work, and though it came along very well, it still took him the relatively lengthy time of two weeks to complete it. From the beginning it felt important and anthemic. For the first time, Hunter would write about the band itself, calling the song "Uncle John's Band." They first performed the song on December 4. It was very much a part of the dark atmosphere—even before Altamont—of 1969. It begins with a caution, and then an invitation set as a question:

> Well, the first days are the hardest days,
> don't you worry anymore
> When life looks like Easy Street

there is danger at your door
Think this through with me
Let me know your mind
Wo-oah, what I want to know
is are you kind?

Hunter would hate the rhyme of "kind" with "mind," even though it was exactly right for the situation. The fragmented images of "Uncle John's Band" are a storehouse of the American consciousness, ranging from a "buckdancer's choice," the buck-and-wing of the street performer, to a nod to Robert Frost in "fire and ice," to the entire American Revolution and heroic dedication to freedom in the lines "Their walls are built of cannonballs / their motto is *Don't Tread on Me,*" to the reference to the Bible and/or Woody Guthrie's "Pastures of Plenty" in "like the morning sun you come / like the wind you go." It was a masterpiece for both Hunter and Garcia. On the same night the Dead premiered "Uncle John's Band," they also first played "Black Peter," the fruits of Hunter's multiple imagined deaths during the Big Dose that spring. A month before, they'd begun performing "Cumberland Blues," an archetypal miner's lament. "Cumberland" was so good, and so patently true, that a miner assumed that it was a traditional song stolen by these loathsome hippies, and rhetorically asked Hunter what the man who'd written the song would have thought at such a theft. It might have been the greatest compliment Hunter ever got.

Following a journey East to play New Year's Eve in Boston, the last time they would celebrate the holiday away from home, and gigs in New York and the West Coast, the band flew to Hawaii early in the new year 1970 for dates in Honolulu. Hawaii was, of course, paradise, but they also had some old friends there, including Healy, who with Laird Grant had built a studio for Quicksilver on Oahu in an old World War II bunker, Opaelua Lodge. The Dead rented a house on the beach, Ken Goldfinger threw a serious party, and their visit was thoroughly pleasant. After the shows, McIntire, Ram Rod, Lesh, and Bear stayed on for a few days in Maui, then flew to San Francisco and on to New Orleans for the next gigs, with McIntire stopping only to go the office for some business files, and to the Airplane House on Fulton Street to get some weed. The Airplane had recently been busted in New Orleans, and Bill Thompson warned McIntire to be careful in the Big Easy. The afternoon the Dead arrived there, Pigpen came to McIntire to report a warning he'd gotten from a hotel security cop. Since Pigpen was paranoid about drugs in general and the police in particular, McIntire dismissed it with the comment "Pig, this guy just wants his hotel clean. Thanks, but don't worry."

That night, before their first show in New Orleans, they had a meeting that ended Tom Constanten's membership in the band. It was, in T.C.'s words, "cordial" and a "mutual" decision, utterly without recriminations. T.C. was not enjoying himself and felt underamplified, so that "I never felt I had a secure platform to work from." Because of his low volume, the drummers couldn't hear him, and he felt that he at times became a pawn in the run-of-the-mill bickering wherein a complaint about T.C. could mean a complaint about his sponsors Phil and Jerry. Hunter found him "holier than thou" because of his devotion to Scientology, and his resulting refusal to take LSD alienated him from Owsley, among others. In any case, he was not fully a part of the Dead ethos. From the band's point of view, he simply didn't swing. His best contributions had come in studio situations, but in performance his classical background constantly betrayed itself. In the end, T.C. got an interesting offer to be composer and music director of *Tarot*, a play that was opening in New York, and he was happy to move on.

Their first show in New Orleans was a disappointment, and at least one observer thought that the opening act, Fleetwood Mac, had bested them. Afterward they gathered in McIntire and Weir's room, where a young man had shown up with a pound of pot and a goodly quantity of hashish. As usual, there were plenty of strangers around, kids from the show who'd managed to get invited to the party. Kreutzmann and Hart visited a girlie show across the street, and on their way back to their rooms, Kreutzmann saw some men in the lobby and said, "Those guys are plainclothes cops." Hart laughed the idea off, and they both went to the party room. McIntire began to clean the pot in a bureau drawer when he heard a key in the door and looked in shock at his roommate, Weir, as what appeared to be the entire New Orleans Police Department Narcotics Squad, led by Captain Clarence Girrusso, came through the door. Garcia had been out raving with some locals, and when he returned to the hotel, he saw two cops in his room going through his suitcase. He kept on walking and got nearly to the end of the corridor before one of them figured out who he was and said, "Hey, you—buddy." Roommates T.C. and Pigpen had been out looking at antique weapons on Royal Street and were contemplating going to hear Earl "Fatha" Hines, who was the lounge act of their hotel, when the cops arrived at their room. Not only was their room clean, but the cop who came to their room was ex–air force, and he and T.C. began to chat about their times in the military. Pig and T.C. were not arrested.

1/30/70

CRIMINAL DISTRICT COURT FOR THE PARISH OF ORLEANS

STATE OF LOUISIANA

Case NO._____   Item No._____

S E A R C H   W A R R A N T

ORDER OF SEARCH

TO: THE SUPERINTENDENT OF THE NEW ORLEANS DEPARTMENT OF POLICE
and/or HIS DESIGNATED REPRESENTATIVE(S).

AFFIDAVIT(S) HAVING BEEN MADE BEFORE ME BY_____

DET. LOUIS DABDOUB, NARCOTIC DIVISION

That he has good reason to believe that on or in the

(premises) (~~person~~) (~~vehicle~~) located at __300 BourbOon Street__

I Room 2134
within the Parish of Orleans, State of Louisiana as more fully described in the application for this warrant, there is now being
concealed certain property, namely, __Opium derivatives, amphetamines,__

__barbiturates, marijuana, synthetic drugs, and narctoic paraphernalia__

WHICH said property constitutes evidence of the commission of a crime or offense against the Laws of the State of Louisiana
set forth in the Louisiana Revised Statutes, and as I am satisfied
from the affidavit(s) submitted in support of the application for
this warrant that there is probable cause to believe that the aforesaid property is being concealed on the (premises) (~~person~~) (~~vehicle~~)
above described, and that the aforesaid grounds for the issuance of
this search warrant exist;

YOU ARE HEREBY ORDERED to search forthwith the aforesaid (premises)
(~~person~~) (~~vehicle~~) for the property specified, serving this search
warrant and making the search, and if the property be found there, to
seize it, leaving a copy of this warrant and a receipt for the property seized, to make your written return on this warrant including a
written inventory of the property seized, and to bring the said
seized property before me within ten (10) days of this date as required by law.

YOU ARE (~~NOT~~) AUTHORIZED to execute this warrant and to make this
search during the daytime or the nighttime and if the the property
herein described be found on the (premises) (~~person~~)(~~vehicle~~) herein
described to seize said property in accordance with law.

YOU ARE (~~NOT~~) AUTHORIZED to execute this warrant and to make this
search on a Sunday and if the property herein described be found on
the (premises) (~~person~~) (~~vehicle~~) herein described to seize said
property in accordance with law.

NEW ORLEANS, LOUISIANA, THIS _3 1_ DAY OF _January_ , 19_7 0_ .

_____
JUDGE, SECTION " J "
CRIMINAL DISTRICT COURT

/i5Da.m

COPIES:
1-Person Upon Whom Warrant is served
1-Judge Signing Warrant
1-District Attorney
1-Record Room
1-2nd Copy (When Making Return) to Judge
Who Signed the Warrant

FORM 117 A
Revised December 1966

The *New Orleans Times-Picayune* would report on those not so lucky: "Rock Musicians, 'King of Acid' Arrested." Handcuffed to Bear during the paddy wagon ride to jail, Mickey Hart discovered that he had two pieces of ID in his coat, and one of them was for Summer Wind, "spiritual adviser to the Grateful Dead." It cost him his peacoat, since the garment had his real name in the collar, but Mickey Hart was not officially arrested in New Orleans. The scene at the station was ludicrous. The cops were enjoying their high-profile bust, and especially liked staging a "walk of shame" for newspaper photographers. The Dead responded in kind. Few would have the temerity to play a practical joke on a cop, but Bob Weir was that man. While others distracted one cop, he slid behind him and handcuffed the officer to his desk with his own cuffs. After all, Weir reasoned, the cop did have the keys.

Bailed out, they played superbly at the show on Saturday night, February 1, and then on a rainy Sunday afternoon played a get-out-of-jail benefit for themselves with Fleetwood Mac opening. As the Dead edged into "Lovelight," they were joined by various members of Fleetwood Mac, a relatively young band quite excited to be playing with veterans. Everyone from both bands had munched and sipped various electric cakes and beers, and the show assumed a certain jovial tone. Being the Dead, they'd invited the police who'd arrested them to come to the benefit, and being from New Orleans, the cops had taken them up on the offer. But the most elegantly apt visual of the night was Mick Fleetwood, all six feet nine inches of him, flying higher than anyone. He'd found an Out of Order sign on a broken soda machine and hung it around his neck as he looned about the stage.

Their bust on Bourbon Street had one major effect on the Dead, and that was the imminent loss of Bear as their sound mixer. Coming on top of his 1967 LSD arrest, he would find his ability to travel severely restricted, and eventually prohibited. The band had a somewhat easier time of it. Word of their plight reached Joe Smith, who put in a call to Jim Garrison, the district attorney of New Orleans who was already an American legend for his advocacy of a conspiracy theory in the assassination of President Kennedy. Joe let Jim know how much he admired Jim's style, and mentioned that he wanted to contribute $50,000 to Jim's reelection campaign. And oh, by the way, we have some friends in jail in New Orleans . . . Garrison took note, and mentioned that his police labs had analyzed the confiscated materials, "and we have some things we don't even know what it is." "Well," said Joe, "I can promise you that the Dead won't be back in New Orleans anytime soon."

Although Ram Rod, Mickey Hart, and Rex Jackson had to return to have their charges dismissed, the price of the Dead's Delta misadventure was mostly financial. The person who got the biggest shock was M.G. On February 1 she called the hotel to tell Jerry that she was going into labor with their first child, who would be born the next day and be named Annabelle. The hotel operator was extremely kind and sympathetic as she informed M.G. that her husband was down in the city jail at the moment, but promised that he'd call as soon as possible.

After a show in St. Louis, the Dead returned home to Chet Helms's Family Dog on the Great Highway venue near the ocean to join Santana and the Airplane in filming one of their best early TV appearances, for the local public television station KQED. It was a high-quality show, even though the visuals of the jam were dominated by slow-motion shots of a woman's breasts moving unfettered under her loose blouse as she danced.

If the bust or the loss of T.C. bothered anyone, it was hard to tell. Early in February they returned to New York for their sixth appearance at Fillmore East. Their opening act, the Allman Brothers Band, was extremely simpatico. The Allmans' long jams were more concretely blues-based than the Dead's music, but their explorations were consonant. The Dead's show on February 13 would swiftly pass into legend, not least because the Fillmore East soundman made a secret basement tape of the performance that would come to serve as a keystone for all Dead tape collectors. It was utterly worthy. The brand-new material was rounding rapidly into exquisite shape, and "Dark Star" and the other extended material that night were loose, fluid, and magnificent. Serve the music, Garcia kept saying. Serve the music. Now the quality of the music was serving them.

30

Interlude/Intermission: "Waits Backstage While I Sing to You"

(1980s)

August, Greek Theater, Berkeley

As the first set ends, the crowd noise registers 110 decibels on the meter at the monitor mixing board onstage. Cranky, Garcia stomps muttering down the stairs to his dressing room, only to discover that he has been locked out. Weir passes by, and Garcia barks, "Where are those drummers? I want to kill both of them." Weir turns to Lesh and says something inaudible, and gets the reply "So I'll turn down my bass, but I can hardly hear myself onstage as it is. I'll have to stand right next to the speakers." A stream of friends and family members trails in their wake down the stairs.

The Dead have always had more people backstage than any other band. In the nineties the band gave away on the order of $600,000 a year in free tickets to their guests. Some of those tickets went to the usual sycophantic gaggle that surrounds each successful musical group. But if there was one element other than sustained musical genius that nurtured the band for so long, it was the cocoon of good and decent friends, the family, that accompanied them. Everything that happens to a family has happened to the Grateful Dead. Marriages and divorces, car accidents, deaths, arrests, graduations, pregnancies, lawsuits, mortgage payments, wayward children, braces, glasses, new cars, high school athletics. "My relationship with the Grateful Dead family," said Garcia, "is way closer than with any of my blood relatives. I only see my brother because he works in the Grateful Dead community. You know? Otherwise I would never see him."

For Weir, it is a family modeled after an old-style multigenerational extremely nonnuclear family, with Neal Cassady as the original and forever paterfamilias. "We're all siblings," said Weir, "we're all underlings to this guy Neal Cassady. He had a guiding hand, though it was . . . good and strange." For good and bad, the message of the Dead's experience in making music is that magic can't happen by intention, that what Weir called "noninterference . . . dynamic benign neglect" is the method they learned from it all. That benign neglect often applied as well to the band members' nuclear families, the children who grew up seeing not so much of their fathers, and the wives ditto. "GD music has been a cruel and jealous mistress," said Weir, "for most of us, *period.*"

Taking a look backstage in the middle eighties, for instance, one might see M.G., then amicably separated from Garcia. She spends most of her time with her daughters near Eugene, Oregon. Jill Lesh had been a waitress at the Station Cafe in San Rafael, only a few blocks from the Dead's office, and after a long period of friendly chatter, Lesh had asked her for her phone number. He had to work for her attention; she'd given him the number at the café. Eventually, they married, and now she sits backstage reading the libretto to the opera *Lulu,* which they'll be seeing soon. Kreutzmann lives with his wife, Shelly, on a ranch 150 miles north of San Francisco, raising horses and dogs. On their first date, she asked him if he had any eyedrops for her contact lenses. He went to his bathroom cabinet, took out a Murine bottle with LSD, took some, and asked, "Is this going to be okay?" A voice came back, "Everything's going to be fine, don't worry." "That voice," Bill said, "was not coming from me, I was just receiving it," and he said to himself, "You were allowed to see the future this time, Billy. Don't distrust it." Then he handed Shelly the bottle.

Also backstage is Florence Nathan, now known as Rosie McGee. Romantically coupled with Phil Lesh for several years in the late sixties, she decided by the early seventies that her name had become "Florence, Phil's Old Lady," and changed it to Rosie McGee, in tribute to the Dead's iconic flower and Kris Kristofferson's song "Me and Bobby McGee." It would be ridiculous to suggest that the Dead is a bastion of feminist liberation, but it is also relevant to remember that Rosie was quite comfortable working for Alembic and later the Dead's travel agency long after her separation from Lesh. "I dug that there was more between me and the Grateful Dead than just me and Phil Lesh."

Asked once about his personal highest take on women, Garcia remarked that "it's a kind of angelic archetype. Those girls always have sort of a golden, giving aura, which is representative of safety and nurturing. Not a Mother Earth type of thing. It's like inspiration to an artist." This contrasts sharply with the band trucker who once said, quite sincerely, "I love the sight of spandex in the morning," or of the woman who once sent a band member a picture of herself engaged in intimacies with a German shepherd.

A certain form of trickery between the sexes is deemed acceptable. Ron Rakow observed a young hotel coffee shop waitress smile at Garcia one day, and the next day Ron handed her a note that read, "Rakow— Take Dolores [her name tag; her real name was Emily Craig] to dinner— Garcia." It was, of course, forged, but by the time all was said and done, Emily had married Rakow. Later she worked on film projects with Garcia. Sue Klein was a Dead fan who sent Garcia a funny card, "a lunar passport," and ended up sitting between him and Weir in a hotel hospitality suite. Hospitality suites are commonly referred to as hostility suites, since they are (a) prowling grounds for flesh and/or (b) a place to find a cold beer at three in the morning. She found Garcia "gentlemanly," and after a while stopped thinking of him as anything but an exceptionally humorous guy. But the atmosphere of the party room, in which everyone else was watching Garcia, weighed upon her, and she came to realize how brave it was of him to even be there. If he leaned forward to talk to her, the room leaned forward. Parish came in to ask Garcia about something, and the audience's heads followed the two of them, swiveling as though at a tennis match. Even the rather well-known women members of *Saturday Night Live*, Gilda Radner and Laraine Newman, acted awestruck around him, and when a particularly spaced-out young lady gave him a cake, he was especially kind to her. "Being around people like that," he said, "is like being around antique furniture. Imagine how much energy it must take to be that vulnerable."

But Frankie Weir's story—though they never married, she adopted the name—might well be the archetype, for at the end it has much more to do with her and the Grateful Dead than sex or romance. Frankie was the woman Weir had in mind when singing "Sugar Magnolia," and when their relationship ended, it would be twenty years before he committed himself to another woman. Funny, bawdy, a high-energy dancer, Frankie had been a finalist on *American Bandstand* and worked at the Peppermint

Lounge in New York, then on the TV shows *Hullaballoo* and *Shindig*. Following her first Grateful Dead show in 1968, she ended the night at a jam with Mickey. Afterward, she and Hart walked around Washington Square, and Hart persuaded her to run away with the Grateful Dead. They had not kissed or even touched, but something made her say yes. She went home to bed, and was awakened the next morning by Ram Rod, Jackson, and Hagen, who were there to pick her up and give her a ride in the truck to the next show, in Virginia. "I wasn't packed, I didn't have anything ready, not even my fake eyelashes were on and I wore two pair—I was naked without them—and was told abruptly that they really didn't have time to wait for Hart's honey, weekend honey, because you know, here today, gone tomorrow. 'Hey look, lady, you're either coming or you're not.' All of a sudden there was some sort of adventure that just went hohohoho—I left my clothes, false eyelashes, I might have grabbed a toothbrush, a coat and what I had on, not even a change of clothes. I got into the truck and we drove away."

31

Might as Well
Work

(3/70–7/70)

The Hunter-Garcia songs that had been gestating over the past few months, most popularly "Uncle John's Band" and "Casey Jones," had evolved beautifully, and the band set to work recording them. Though *Live Dead* had lessened their debt to Warner Bros., the stakes were desperately high, and they were in no financial position to be elaborate in the making of the album. Nor did the material call for it. Garcia thought of this version of the Dead as a wing of the Buck Owens/Merle Haggard/Bakersfield school of country-western. With Bob Matthews and Betty Cantor producing, they went into Pacific High Recording, a tiny room half a block behind Fillmore West, and rehearsed for a week. Then Matthews took the best song versions and spliced them into an album sequence. The band rehearsed for another week, and they prepared to go back to the studio to lay down final versions.

Their work was briefly interrupted by a spot of unpleasant internal business when the frayed ends of Lenny Hart's reign as manager finally unraveled. As the Dead had been busted in New Orleans, he'd been in the process of moving their office from Novato to the Family Dog on the Great Highway (FDGH), with Lenny to become manager of the FDGH

as well as the Dead, and with Gail Turner to be the FDGH secretary as
well as Lenny's. The idea of sharing space with the Dead appealed to
Chet Helms, but it became evident to him and Gail that the numbers
weren't adding up and that there had to be at least two sets of books. Before anyone in the band even knew, Lenny moved the office back to Novato. But early in March, Chet and Gail sat down with Ram Rod,
McIntire, and Rock to talk things over. All of this only served to confirm
the deep suspicions that had been generated by the repossession of Pigpen's organ the previous fall.

As the band settled down to recording its new album, which with its
stripped-down approach would appropriately be called *Workingman's
Dead* (driving back from a session one night, Garcia had remarked that
the songs seemed to be about working people, "kind of the Workingman's
Dead"), the dime finally dropped on Lenny. Earlier in the year Garcia had
worked on the sound track of a film by Michelangelo Antonioni,
Zabriskie Point, and the check for his contribution was due—in fact, over-
due. M.G., as Gail Turner would put it, was "beside herself" waiting for it,
because the Garcias' much-loved home in Madrone Canyon was up for
sale, and they hoped to buy it and avoid being forced to move. Every day
she would call Gail, and finally in mid-March there came the day when
Gail replied that yes, it had arrived. But when M.G. got to the office,
Lenny said there was no check. The two women did the natural thing,
and called Ram Rod. There was a meeting, and Rod finally said of Lenny,
"It's him or me." Garcia responded with the obvious: "Lenny, Ram Rod
says it's you or him, and we know we can't do without him." As a sop to
the honor of a band member's father, Mickey and Phil told McIntire that
Lenny could have a week to get the books in order, then went off to talk
with Lenny. When he refused to show them the books, Mickey was taken
aback, realizing instantly that Lenny was guilty. His own father . . . They
left, and within an hour Lenny and the files were gone to Mexico,
along with his lover, who'd worked in a local bank and helped his depre-
dations.

Lenny's treason mostly affected Mickey, who was completely devastated. "Everything turned black for me. It was more than I could bear. I
was almost suicidal." Mickey got nothing but support from his band
brothers, but he had been dishonored and unmanned. Garcia asked Sam
Cutler, who'd been staying with him while recovering from Altamont, to
look into things, and with the help of the well-known San Francisco detective Hal Lipset, they learned that Lenny had been stealing from the
beginning. He'd opened an account in Lake Tahoe called the Sunshine

Account, which was supposed to contain money for tax payments. Pigpen was a frugal soul, and would always have some of his pay set aside in savings. Lenny loved giving advances on pay—the band member would sign, and when he paid back his advance, it would be diverted into the Sunshine Account. In the end Lenny made off with about $155,000, leaving the band essentially penniless, so broke that Kreutzmann briefly resumed poaching deer for the pot to feed his family. Except for Mickey's agony, it scarcely mattered. It was, after all, only money. There was plenty of loose talk about sending the Hell's Angels after Lenny or perhaps arranging for a psychedelic assassination, but in the end they would not even press charges. "Karma'll get him," said Garcia, and everyone came to agree. They were as tightly knit a band of brother musicians as one could imagine, and they pressed forward. Their reaction to treachery was to close ranks and get serious about their work, and with the help of cocaine, then just entering the band's life, they worked very hard indeed. Loose Bruce Baxter, their wealthy friend, had showed up with a large baggie full of the powder. At first it seemed a benign stimulant, a luxurious assistant that provoked conversation or the energy for hard work. As the years went by, it would prove to have other, less pleasant facets, and they would experience all of them.

However lunatic events might appear, the music was utterly sane. They went into Pacific High to record *Workingman's Dead,* and in about three weeks they had an album made up of "Uncle John's Band," "High Time," "Dire Wolf," "New Speedway Boogie," "Cumberland Blues," "Black Peter," "Easy Wind," and "Casey Jones." The combination of great material and minimalism in the recording process produced a stunningly good series of tracks. In the absence of experimentation, the band could work together and record nearly live. There was a great joy, said Garcia, in just being "a good old band," without pretension or self-indulgence. Hunter sat glowing in the corner as he watched them at work. The absence of a primary keyboard player mattered not at all. Always an ensemble player, Kreutzmann was more than happy for the drums to be more supportive and less up-front. Garcia's voice suited the material perfectly, and Lesh and Weir served admirably as harmonists.

Joe Smith was in for a pleasant shock. Down in Los Angeles he got the first tape and put it on, expecting "Psychedelic Opus #6." At first he was confused, half thinking that it was a joke. Then he broke into an ecstatic smile, running into the corridor to grab people—"We got a single! We got a single!" The same thing would happen somewhat later in the spring when Jerry and Bobby went down to the *Rolling Stone* offices.

Everyone gathered in Jann Wenner's office, and the new album blew the staff away with its effortless accessibility.

The business response to Lenny's financial piracy was a considerable restructuring of the band's management. A sometime source of inspiration but a man lacking in day-to-day reliability, Rock Scully found his impact considerably trimmed. Although he continued to serve the band, he was not only not the manager but also not on the payroll, instead slipping into a promotional role paid for by the record company, a pattern he would follow for the next decade. At Garcia's suggestion the band established a tripartite management. Jon McIntire was the band manager, which primarily meant he dealt with the record company, the office, and individual needs. Sam Cutler became the road manager and dealt with their booking agent. And Dave Parker, once the washboard player in Mother McCree's, came in with his wife, Bonnie, on a two-workers-on-one-salary deal to take care of the books. It was an effective, though by no means perfect, setup. David and Bonnie were honest and competent employees, but they were family, which meant that they were no more able than Rock to say no to the random demand for a new piece of equipment or almost anything else.

Sam Cutler would prove to be a superb road manager, but he was divisive. There was a wheeler-dealer bad-boy feeling to him that appealed to Garcia in much the same way that Rakow had. Cutler didn't care for McIntire and undermined him with the crew, which was not difficult. Jon was intellectual, arty, occasionally pretentious, inclined toward hypochondria, utterly nonathletic, and gay. These were distinctly not the crew's preferences, and as de facto band members, their feelings would always have a major impact. Also, Jon was not a trained businessman or a deal-maker. Sam got them the deals and the money. But as a diplomat and mediator within the band, and in dealing with the record company, Jon was brilliant. It would help that *Workingman's Dead* was a more accessible album than its predecessors, but McIntire brought the right style to the process. Tall, slender, blond, and regal-featured—"I'm a direct descendant of King John," he'd been known to proclaim—he was also a psychedelic brother, philosophically and morally committed to the Grateful Dead quest, but in more control than most in their scene. Cutler would snipe that John was charming but "shallow," and depict himself as not charming—though he had certainly charmed Garcia—but an effective leader. He likened the job of road managing to leading a wagon train through hostile territory, where someone must lead, "in the face of pleasure, danger, whatever it is. That's not necessarily the most popular position to be in."

Late in March David Parker found a brown shingle house on the southeast corner of Fifth Avenue and Lincoln Street in San Rafael, a small city about fifteen miles north of San Francisco. They picked Jon as the most presentable, sent him to woo the owners, and on April 1, 1970, the Dead's management signed a lease. Fifth and Lincoln, as it customarily was called, was a house, not an office building, and it became and remained their business home, with a kitchen, which had its own entrance, and a kitchen table for a "conference room." Anyone who came to the front door was a newcomer. They acquired some stationery, which initially featured a skull with a Viking helmet, and a post office box, 1073, that they would keep for decades. After considerable effort, McIntire enticed the fabulously competent Dale Franklin away from the Fillmore East, and she joined them at 5th and Lincoln as his assistant. One of his other early actions was to put Hunter on the regular payroll, at forty dollars a week.

Early spring 1970 was a mélange of shows and new songs. In mid-March the Dead set off on tour, accompanied for the first time by Hunter, who had concluded that the band needed a road song, and that he needed to see the road to write the song. His first stop was a hilarious one. On St. Patrick's Day the band played a benefit for the Buffalo Philharmonic, which was directed by Phil's acquaintance, a colleague of Luciano Berio's, Lukas Foss. The Dead, a local rock band, and members of the orchestra played an improvisational piece that involved having the orchestra members stand up, flap their arms, and make strange noises. Since the snow in Buffalo was "up to our shoulders," as Hunter recalled it, it was a place where you had to "mellow slow," and so began his road song. Later in the tour they reached Florida, and Hunter sprang the verses of "Truckin'" on the band. Pigpen was elsewhere, doubtless romancing a fair maiden, and the drummers were up to something. But Weir, Lesh, and Garcia joined Hunter, and the four of them sat around the swimming pool with acoustic guitars and worked up the song.

The week before, at the Chelsea Hotel in New York, Hunter had written the lyrics to "Stella Blue," a song that would not be completed for a couple of years. Around this time he also wrote "No Place Here," which would never be recorded but would instead serve as his lyric bank, being cannibalized for elements to at least four songs in the next couple of years. He was also partway into a major song cycle to be called "Eagle Mall" when Garcia reminded him, "Look, Hunter, we're a goddamn dance band, for Christ's sake! At least write something with a beat!" Songs were called for, and songs came forth. In late February they first performed "Friend of the Devil," which Hunter had written during early New Riders sessions—he was the New Riders' bass player for about twenty minutes—with John Dawson and David Nelson. Garcia added the bridge, and a staple of the repertoire was born, an up-tempo fugitive's tale of the American West with a bluegrass feel. "Candyman" followed in short order, an even less specific tale of gamblers and the ladies who love them—and candy, in all its metaphorical forms: drugs, booze, jewelry, all the objects of desire.

In the middle of April they played a weekend at the Fillmore West that would be memorable for a feeling of utter silliness induced by following their opening act. Going on after hearing Miles Davis and the Bitches Brew band was, as Garcia put it, "ridiculous." "I don't ever want to hear anyone snivel about following *anyone*," said Lesh. "Because I got the *one* man, right there. Made me feel so dumb. I thought, 'What the fuck am I doing here, why aren't I at home digesting what I just heard?' " Stimulated by Jimi Hendrix, Sly Stone, and James Brown, Miles had recorded *Bitches Brew,* a landmark statement of jazz-rock fusion. Miles's record company president, Columbia's Clive Davis, then suggested that he expand his audience and play some rock venues, and introduced Miles to Bill Graham. In March Miles opened for Steve Miller at the Fillmore East, but Miles's low opinion of Miller created complications. Miller "didn't have shit going for him," wrote Miles, "so I'm pissed because I got to open for this non-playing motherfucker just because he had one or two sorry-ass records out. So I would come late and *he* would have to go on first, and then when we got there, we just smoked the motherfucking place and everybody dug it, including Bill [Graham]!"

Miles enjoyed his shows with the Dead at Fillmore West much more. The Dead had asked for the privilege of playing with Miles. Being a Dead audience, it was a stoned audience. "The place was packed with these real spacy, high white people," Miles continued, "and when we first started playing, people were walking around and talking. But after a while, they all got quiet and really got into the music. I played a little of something like *Sketches of Spain* and then we went into the *Bitches Brew* shit and that really blew them out." The Dead stood on the side of the stage, slack-jawed, watching Miles and Dave Holland, Jack DeJohnette, Chick Corea, Stephen Grossman, and Airto Moreira make magic. As Ralph Gleason wrote, "it was sorcery and it worked." "Totally embarrassed" to be asked to follow, Kreutzmann recalled that "we played really free, loose," afterward, "but I couldn't get Miles out of my ears." Mickey, naturally, would primarily recall his fellow percussionist Airto "crawling around on the floor foraging for instruments. I was really high, and he turned into some kind of animal, foraging for percussion sounds. I'd never seen percussion played like that. He was playing the floor."

Altogether, it was an interesting experience for Miles, who actually preferred the larger halls of rock to smoky jazz nightclubs, but who'd discovered the technical ignorance of most rock musicians: "They didn't study it, couldn't play different styles—and don't even talk about reading music." Then he met Jerry Garcia. They "hit it off great, talking about music—what they liked and what I liked—and I think we all learned something, grew some. Jerry Garcia liked jazz, and I found out that he loved my music and had been listening to it for a long time. He loved other jazz musicians, too, like Ornette Coleman and Bill Evans." It was a wonderful experience for Garcia as well. After all, Miles was a hero and true teacher. Years later Garcia would say he learned from Davis's music the concept of "open playing. I got part of that from Miles, especially the silences. The holes. Nobody plays better holes than Miles, from a musician's point of view, anyway. In Indian music they have what you call 'the unstruck,' which is the note you don't play. That has as much value as the stuff you do play."

On May 1, 1970, in the appropriately obscure college town of Alfred, New York, the Dead began a new phase of their touring career, a series of shows called "An Evening with the Grateful Dead." With variations over the next year or so, the show would include an opening set from the New Riders of the Purple Sage, an acoustic Dead set, and two electric Dead sets. Garcia and Hart would play through all of it, sometimes more than five hours of music. Along with *Workingman's Dead* and the next album, this presentation of the Dead as a full-bore experience would fully establish them, after five years, as a commercially viable band. The ticket buyer certainly got value for money. In fact, the "Evening with" setup proved its worth almost instantly. The second show, on May 2 at Harpur College, was simply staggering, a concert with so much quality in so many different styles that it became deservedly legendary. Their psychedelic explorations continued; the Dead had simply added other options to their playing. They had become what Garcia liked to term a full-range band. Over the next two decades they would play nearly 500 different songs, of which roughly 150 were originals. Those 350 cover tunes would span a large portion of American music, to a level unmatched by any other band.

And so their repertoire would include basic rock and roll (Chuck Berry, Rolling Stones), blues (Pigpen's entire repertoire), jug band music ("Beat It on Down the Line," "Viola Lee Blues"), folk ("Peggy-O," "Cold Rain and Snow"), Stax-Volt ("Midnight Hour"), rhythm and blues

("Lovelight"), rockabilly ("Big River"), country-western ("Mama Tried"), gospel ("Samson and Delilah," "We Bid You Goodnight"), sixties garage rock ("Gloria"), calypso ("Man Smart, Woman Smarter"), western swing ("Don't Ease Me In"), and New Orleans ("Iko Iko"). A bystander once remarked to Garcia that the one major missing element from the Dead's song repertoire was formal jazz, and that they should do at least one Duke Ellington song, just to know they'd done it. Garcia agreed, and said that he actually wanted to do Billy Strayhorn's "Lush Life," and someday he'd get around to working it up. It was one of those good ideas that he never quite got to.

The band's playing levels stayed high, but the atmosphere of the world around them grew very dark. On May 3 they played a free show at the alma mater of Weir's prep school friend John Barlow, Wesleyan College in Middletown, Connecticut. Forty miles down the road in New Haven, various Black Panthers were on trial. One of the prime leaders of the Black Panther Party, Bobby Seale, had last been seen shackled and gagged in the trial of the Chicago Eight. His refusal to cooperate with what could only be termed a Kafkaesque trial had resulted in his case being severed from the other seven. In February 1970 the Chicago verdicts came in, with the jury finding no evidence of conspiracy, although five of the seven were found guilty of intending to create a riot. The draconian contempt citations meted out to the lawyers caused an uproar. Most of this uproar was taking place on college campuses, which in the sixties had moved to a central place in American culture—in 1960, 27 million Americans were young (fourteen to twenty-four), and of them a fifth went to college. In 1970, there were 40 million young Americans, and half of them were in college. That May college students and Black Panthers had essentially shut down New Haven. The protests centered on Seale's continued incarceration, but his former codefendants from the Chicago conspiracy trial came to New Haven in May to take part. It was an extraordinary time, and the effects were felt up the road in Middletown. At Wesleyan the stage and the gig were controlled by the African American student community in consort with various Panthers. Roadie Sonny Heard, not known for his liberal racial views, objected, but reconsidered the situation at the point of a .38 being shoved into his stomach. As one bystander recalled, Kreutzmann was hassled by some of the students, and Cutler, after telling them not to turn on the sound system, gave in. America was a rough place in May 1970, and it was about to get even rougher.

The next day, May 4, began as an ordinary spring day. President Nixon had ordered American troops to invade the putatively neutral country of Cambodia, and students across the nation protested. In the afternoon, members of Troop G, the 107th Armored Cavalry Regiment of the National Guard, were on duty at Kent State University in Kent, Ohio. James Rhodes, the state's law-and-order governor, had ordered them onto the campus based on "intelligence" that there were "outside agitators" at Kent. Kent's president, who knew that there were no outside agitators, but who had already authorized the guard to disperse demonstrations, sat down to his second martini. One of the men in Troop G was injured, and his colleagues responded by opening fire on the demonstrators, killing four. Two of the dead were a hundred yards away; two were passersby, about four hundred feet away. Nine more people were injured, including a man 240 yards away, shot in the back of the neck. Mary Vecchio, a fourteen-year-old runaway, knelt over one man's body and was photographed in the act of screaming, an image that would win a Pulitzer Prize and define the day. Within three days 437 colleges were out on strike. On May 14, two more students were killed as a result of protests—they were black, so there was little public notice—at Jackson State in Mississippi. On May 8, conservative construction workers, dubbed "hard hats," beat young people demonstrating against the war on Wall Street, earning verbal applause from the president of the United States. Fifty-eight percent of the American people supported the National Guard's actions.

The Dead were as appalled as most young Americans, and while they continued to avoid the question of direct politics, they made their feelings plain when Bob Weir silk-screened the idealized red fist logo that symbolized that spring onto Mickey's and Billy's bass-drum heads. The Dead's job was to play music, and so on the sixth, still in shock, they played a free show outdoors on a plaza for the striking students at MIT, followed by a regular gig at the Dupont Gymnasium there the next night. During their visit to Cambridge they also encountered Ned Lagin, an MIT student studying hard science on that side of the Charles, and jazz piano at Berklee College on the Boston side of the river. He'd been fascinated by a gig of the Dead's the previous fall, and had written a letter to Garcia. He'd never gotten a reply, but members of the band sought him out during their visit and struck up a friendship that would blossom in the future. A few nights later the Dead got to Atlanta, where they shared a stage with the Hampton Grease Band and the Allman Brothers in what the local underground paper called "one of the great musical/sensual experiences the Atlanta hip community has ever had."

Late in May Warner Bros. sent the Dead off on a promotional visit to England, a one-shot gig that would establish their legend and build future demand. The single performance was at the Hollywood Festival, at a farm in Newcastle-Under-Lyme. It was "cold as a whore's good-bye," said Weir, a stereotypically rainy English day. The band spent most of its performance fussed by amplifier problems, but late in the show, Lesh said, "all of a sudden this jet plane bifurcates the sky at the high point of 'Dark Star,' this vapor trail," and everything mutated in an instant. By the end of the show, wrote an English critic, "the hillside of people was on its feet, the more insatiable begging for more . . . Even the pop weeklies . . . had to admit . . . [the Dead] commanded respect simply through their style, their approach and the nature of their music." They charmed the Brits, too. Pigpen reassured them, "Oh, we've got past the stage of thoughts of breaking up. What usually happens is that we go into town, to a saloon, shoot some pool or play cards. Then we accuse one another of cheating and start fighting."

Workingman's Dead came out on June 26, and from music to packaging, it was just right. Alton Kelley had taken them down to a corner in San Francisco's working-class Mission District. It was a blisteringly hot day, and the band was in its usual awful humor when required to pose for pictures. Kreutzmann grew so irritated that he refused to cooperate any longer and went and sat in the doorway, ready to hop the next bus out of there. Miraculously, Kelley's little Brownie camera captured the moment, and it worked. On the back of the album were Mouse's romantic airbrush drawings of the six players. Naturally, there were complications. *Workingman's* was Robert Hunter's coming-out party, and so he was included on the cover. But he was typically ambivalent. "I was a little frightened about what had been wrought there, and I wasn't sure how soon it might turn nasty. And I very much kept myself out of the public eye." On the other hand, he was highly irritated that he "didn't get a *glamour shot* on the back like everybody else," he recalled with a laugh. "And I said, 'Right, that's the last picture you're going to get of me!' It was simple spite."

A far more important complication in the album's release stemmed from the fact that the single "Uncle John's Band" contained the dreaded word "goddamn," which had to be excised for radio play, or "hacked to ribbons," from the Dead's point of view. Promotion was difficult, since Garcia and Weir refused to do a radio promo tour for no particular reason other than they didn't feel like it. Hunter and McIntire substituted, which was effective only to a point. McIntire recalled how much he believed in the music, that it was the Dead's chance to "become big in a way that was consistent with the G.D. way of living. It would be our music that carried us." Hunter also toured radio stations, and naturally fell into a classic bit of Grateful Dead synchronicity. Arriving at WBCN, the hip Boston FM station, he did his interview and then was arm-twisted to play "Uncle John's Band." This particular visit preceded the official album release day, and he'd been firmly instructed not to offend all the other stations by playing anything, but after all, it couldn't be that big a deal . . . Just as they were about to play the tune, WBCN's antenna was struck by lightning and the station went off the air. With that sort of a cosmic message, it was easy for Hunter to refuse to play the song when the station resumed broadcasting.

In the long run, *Workingman's Dead* was going to have a profoundly positive effect on the band's touring fortunes, but it would take a while. Their gig in Memphis the week before the album came out was more typical of their middle-American shows at that time. A local underground newspaper reporter sat with Garcia backstage talking about the local police, about whom Garcia said, "When we first came here, we thought there was something horrible happening, or that somebody was getting beaten up or something . . . And then we suddenly realized that's just the way they are." Surly and generally uncooperative because of the atmosphere, Garcia dismissed the reporter's questions about the acid tests ("We're just waiting for everybody else to get high"), the Woodstock movie, and what he expected to play that night: "We don't have any plans. We'll do anything that we like. There's no reason to restrict yourself. A plan is only something to deviate from and none of us have the kind of minds that are capable of planning, anyway."

Their opening act that night was Country Joe and the Fish, who had been warned that if the kids left their chairs to dance, they'd be arrested. After playing a deliberately lethargic set, they were still called back for an encore, and despite a glacial pace, they watched in horror as a kid started dancing. They exited the stage briskly, leaving it to the Dead. Sam Cutler approached Garcia and warned him of the night's policy, and the interviewer interjected, "They do it. Sly came here and there was one section of people dancing. The police cut their power." The band played, the kids stayed mostly in their seats, and they struggled to a generally unsatisfactory conclusion, confirming what Garcia had told a fan earlier. The young man had remarked that it was too bad there was such a small audience that night. "We're used to it," Garcia replied. "We've played a lot of flops . . . That's where it's at in the South."

The entire continent, however, was not like Memphis, and a grand adventure awaited them. Thor Eaton was an heir to a Canadian mercantile fortune, and he'd concocted a marvelous scheme—a mobile, trans-Canadian festival with the musicians traveling by private train. Faint echoes of *Murder on the Orient Express* reverberated, and the idea was an instant hit with the musicians, who came to include the Dead, Janis Joplin, Delaney and Bonnie Bramlett, the Band, Mountain, and Buddy Guy. The tour was to begin on June 25 in Montreal and end ten days later in Vancouver. It was a fabulous idea, but it was cursed with endless snarls. The first show, in Montreal, was canceled when city officials feared a possible disruption of the locally important celebration of St. Jean Baptiste Day.

As the festival arrived in Toronto, it became enmeshed in local countercultural politics. Tickets were eight dollars, which although relatively high for the era, covered ten major acts; the Dead for eighty cents seemed reasonable. To the students of Rochdale College, an eighteen-story government-subsidized student housing project, this was a rip-off. In the wake of Kent State, they had formed the May Fourth Movement, or M4M, and they issued a statement: "We demand that Transcontinental (Rip-off) Express be free for everyone and all tickets be refunded; there be free food, dope and music . . . with no cops. Failing these totally reasonable and just demands, we demand that twenty per cent of the gate receipts be returned to the community."

When festival organizers rejected the demands, the June 27 show at CNE Stadium, Toronto, became a magnet for gate-crashers, and at least 2,500 showed up, chanting "Make it free, rip it off. Save the trouble, let us in." By the end of the afternoon, perhaps one hundred had broken in. The Toronto police were represented by John Sagar, a member of the force's so-called Mod Squad, and despite ten injured police, there were only twenty-seven arrests for breaking in, and only four drug arrests. The crowd's violence, however, so appalled Garcia that when he implored them to calm down, he almost, against all his personal inclinations, slid sideways into making a value judgment and criticizing the M4M protesters. After a day consumed by negotiations, he and a police inspector arranged a free concert the next day as a way of defusing the situation. The Dead, the New Riders, Ian and Sylvia, and James and the Good Brothers played for about two thousand in Coronation Park.

With a first show like that, the festival seemed doomed. But the party was about to start. On the twenty-ninth, 140 musicians and associates boarded the Festival Express, which included twelve cars, two bar cars, and a formal, elegant dining car complete with nine waiters, white linen, and old silver. The sleeping cars had names like Etoile and Valparaiso, and each compartment had a picture window, bed, couch, toilet, washbasin, jump seat, clothes closet, air conditioner, and cupboard, all in tiny but perfect proportion. The compartments were so small, in fact, that one had to get into bed from the corridor, not always easy when drunk at 4 A.M. As they boarded, the atmosphere was "cautious, almost morosely quiet," said one observer, with "overtones of the first day of summer camp." One non–summer camp problem was that they'd anticipated marijuana from the promoter in order to make their border crossings smooth, and he had reneged. The Dead looked like cowboys, with boots, sheath knives, and shirts from Miller's Western Store in Denver. Then Leslie West and Felix Pappalardi of Mountain pulled out guitars, Garcia, Delaney, and Delaney's bass player Kenny Gradney followed suit, and the party began, presided over by the queen spirit, Janis. Hunter, of course, got a song—"Might as Well"—out of it: "Great north special were you on board? / Can't find a ride like that no more . . . Never had such a good time / In my life before . . . One long party from start to end I'd like to / take that ride again."

They set out from Toronto and passed English-sounding towns like Islington, Tottenham, Bayswater, and Bethnal, then French trapper posts like Foleyet, Lainaune, Girouxville, La Broquerie, Paqwa, Penequani, Ophir, Snakesbreath, Decimal, and Malachi. They rolled through what *Rolling Stone* writer David Dalton saw as an "infinity of lakes and river cut into a wilderness of birch trees," singing all the way. At one point Garcia looked out from his berth and gaped at a large black bear scratching its back on one of those birch trees. The party picked up steam, and the Dead blew off a scheduled gig in Chicago—Garcia said it was the only time they ever did such a thing—and then invited various family members from home to join them toward the end of the ride. It got wilder. Lesh looked out of his room once to see Garcia and the Band's Rick Danko on their knees in the corridor, crawling drunkenly back to their compartments. Garcia was not really a drinker, so this was a grand exception, especially unforgettable because he looked up through a whiskey haze at the sky that night and saw the northern lights for the first time. Janis Joplin had chosen young Marmaduke Dawson as her companion for the ride, and late of an evening, her pre-orgasmic yowl of "Daddy, daddy, daddy" would ring through the train. Country-western replaced the blues, and Hank Williams, Merle Haggard, and Kris Kristofferson songs, especially "Me and Bobby McGee," drifted mournfully through the cars, Janis singing with Garcia picking out steel guitar behind her. Delaney taught Garcia "Going Down the Road Feelin' Bad," a traditional tune that Woody Guthrie had recorded, and a few months later it would enter the Dead's repertoire.

They played in Winnipeg, where a hundred demonstrators showed up to chant "Make it free" and were largely ignored. Unfortunately for the festival organizers, only about four thousand ticket buyers appeared as well. By Saskatoon they'd nearly run out of booze, which would have been dire, so they passed the hat, and Janis's road manager, John Cooke, the son of the distinguished writer Alistair Cooke, bought out the town liquor store, including a gallon bottle of Canadian Club whiskey that would be a dead soldier by dawn. At the drunkest moments, the Beatles' "I've Just Seen a Face" became the theme song, and its chorus of "Fah-ling, yes I'm faaaah-lll-iing" would circulate endlessly, like a musical Möbius band. "If I could remember how it began," said Weir, "maybe we could find an ending or we could just go on singing this all night."

The Vancouver gig was canceled, so they knew that Calgary was the end, and the last party was a winner. "I got the Dead drunk," cackled Janis, and Garcia wobbled out onto the tracks, groaning, "I promise never to drink again, Your Honor!" The Dead got their revenge, dosing Janis's birthday cake, a treat shared by a good part of the Calgary Police Department, occasioning an early shift change.

Five days later the Dead were back at the Fillmore East, the one place at that point where they could reliably make enough money to continue recovering from Lenny. It was the fourth of their six visits there that year.

An American
Beauty

(8/4/70–12/31/70)

oodstock, the movie, had opened on May 1, and it was extraordinary. The rock and roll hippies led by Michael Wadleigh had used a new level of technology that started with special cameras and the cinema verité style to document the creation, for one blissful weekend, of a separate nation, a pilgrimage, in Joni Mitchell's words, "back to the Garden." Just as important, they had protected their artistic vision from their corporate sponsors at Warner's, and what was on the screen would touch the hearts of more young Americans than could ever have actually found Yasgur's farm. The film won an Oscar and became the highest-grossing documentary of all time. The Dead were absent. Given their low opinion of their performance, they would never have signed the release, but that never even became an issue. *Woodstock*'s editors, including the Dead fan Martin Scorsese, couldn't find any footage sufficiently well lit to be usable. The Dead were quite literally in the dark.

The film had various side effects, one of which was giving Tom Donahue an idea for a documentary film on the music/youth scene. He convinced the film end of Warner Bros., then enjoying the cash flow of *Woodstock,* to finance it. To be called the *Medicine Ball Caravan,* the movie would follow a band across the United States, stopping four or five times for concert encampments. No doubt someone at Warner Bros. called it "Woodstock on wheels." With Donahue in charge and able to call in old favors with band members who couldn't say no, it briefly seemed like a scheme that was crazy enough to be feasible. There were, however, several negatives. The caravan would live in tepees, and as McIntire noted, "I had Phil Lesh and Bill Kreutzmann, who were not guys who would be willing to rough it." Donahue was always longer on inspiration than detail, and the event seemed "appallingly organized" to Cutler, who recalled, "The energy that was supposed to be developing behind it never came into fruition." In the end it was somebody else's movie, and the Dead didn't really feel comfortable. As the August 4 departure date closed in, McIntire began to discern mixed messages from the different Warner representatives with whom he was negotiating. Finally, late on the night of August 3, he pulled the plug. Alembic, which had been hired to provide the sound system, remained involved, so mixers Bob Matthews and Betty Cantor and the sound crew went off with the Caravan.

For Weir, the cancellation was a special blessing. He was living at 2200 Nicasio Valley Road in western Marin County at a putative horse ranch called Rukka Rukka, after a crew joke referring to women's derrieres. It was a striking location, with a hill rising steeply behind the house to provide a wonderful setting, but the ranch was, said Weir, a "rich man's hobby for folks who weren't rich," and although they had as many as a dozen horses, it was not a galloping success as a ranch. This was a particular concern for the neighbors, who raised fine Arabians and did not welcome the advances of such horses as Rukka Rukka's Apache Chipper, a less than well bred animal that would periodically escape. Along with his lover, Frankie, and crew members Rex Jackson and Sonny Heard, Weir shared Rukka Rukka with a young woman in their scene named Eileen Law, now nine months pregnant. She had already had one false alarm, and instead of going into San Francisco a second time at the onset of labor pains, she moved from her tent in the back to Weir and Frankie's bed to give birth. Weir's compositional dry spell had ended, and he had already written two new songs that year, "Truckin' " and "Sugar Magnolia." As Eileen's long day passed, he sat on the couch strumming his guitar and worked on another new song, which would share the name Eileen had chosen for her baby, Cassidy, the daughter of Rex Jackson.

Two weeks later the Dead played a weekend at Fillmore West, and once again they had a flock of new songs to introduce. Flush with the success of *Workingman's Dead,* Hunter had visited England in June, staying at his old friend Alan Trist's flat on Devonshire Terrace near Hyde Park. Ecstatic to be in the land of Shakespeare, Robin Hood, and Peter Pan, and fueled by the sight and taste of a full case of retsina (a resinate Greek wine) in a corner of the flat, he took in the sunny, lovely day and sat down to write, producing the lyrics to three songs in an hour and a half, including "Ripple" and "Brokedown Palace." That same month, on the train ride somewhere near Saskatoon, Garcia had fooled around with Weir's new, custom-made guitar, and a song had fallen out. The next time he saw Hunter, Robert had said, "Here, I have a couple of songs I'd like you to look at." One was "Ripple," and lyric met tune with a perfect flow. It was a marvelous and an unlikely song, a hymn that was almost too spiritual for Garcia to be able to sing. "One more word and I couldn't sing it," he said. "When I sing that song there's a moment when I say to myself, 'Am I really a Presbyterian minister?' "

> *If my words did glow*
> *with the gold of sunshine*
> *and my tunes were played*
> *on the harp unstrung*
> *would you hear my voice*
> *come through the music*
> *would you hold it near*
> *as it were your own?*

The words do glow with sunshine; the song is positively lambent with grace. There is faith—"there is a fountain / that was not made / by the hands of man"—but it is not sappy. "There is a road, no simple highway," but it is solitary. There are no promises except for the haiku that makes up the bridge:

> *Ripple in still water*
> *when there is no pebble tossed*
> *nor wind to blow*

"Brokedown Palace" is a death song, but a death that is part of the peace that passeth all understanding. It is the death of the old and accomplished, an ending of dignity and serenity. These songs joined "Attics of My Life," a cantata set by Lesh that had Hunter at his best, although the band simply could not sing it consistently enough onstage to make it work.

In the attics of my life
Full of cloudy dreams unreal
Full of tastes no tongue can know
And lights no eye can see
  When there was no ear to hear
  You sang to me

Garcia was twenty-eight, and Lesh was thirty. They had reached both the fullness of their talent and the age of the inevitable deaths that accompany adulthood, the rituals of succeeding generations. Late in August Jerry's mother, Bobbie, put her little dog in her car and set off from her home on Twin Peaks, the mountain at the center of the city, to take it for a walk. On the way it became entangled between the gas and brake pedals, causing the car to go off the road and down the nearly vertical hillside, where it finally impaled itself on a cypress tree. When he learned of the accident, Jerry went to get his brother, Tiff, who was living in the mountains near Santa Cruz. They returned to visit Bobbie at San Francisco General Hospital, where she had resumed working as a nurse a couple of years before. It was in the Mission District, only a couple of miles from Harrington Street. Bobbie was conscious, but on a respirator and unable to talk, although she could communicate by writing. She would survive for a month after the accident, and day after day, the Garcia boys and their wives came to visit. Jerry was no more emotionally open at twenty-eight than he had been as a teen, and the fact that he had never properly reconciled with her would gnaw at him for the rest of his life. Because of Bobbie's remarriages, the Garcias would not permit her to be buried with Jose. Jerry hadn't liked Wally Matusiewicz in life, and he didn't like seeing his mother next to him in death. There would be no peace or closure for him when Bobbie died, only a change in his pain.

At exactly the same time, Phil's father, Frank, was diagnosed with terminal cancer. Phil had been working on a song, and he handed Hunter a tape that Robert recalled had "every vocal nuance" except the words. Hunter listened to the tape, and before he was through it the first time he was writing words. He "heated the lyrics up" on the second listen, and "Box of Rain" was complete. Mr. Lesh was in a nursing home on the other side of the Berkeley hills, in Livermore, and as Phil drove out each day to visit him, he would sing "Box of Rain" and cry the sweet tears that come when you truly cherish someone you must lose.

The time that had opened up for the Dead because of their withdrawal from the Medicine Ball Caravan sent them to the studio. They'd made a stab at working at Pacific Recording in San Mateo, but that had washed out, and without their regular engineers, Bob Matthews and Betty Cantor, who were off with the Caravan, they went to take a look at Wally Heider's, the first high-quality studio in San Francisco. Heider's had opened in April 1969 and had already been the birthplace of the Airplane album *Volunteers,* Crosby, Stills, Nash and Young's *Déjà Vu,* and the many hits of Creedence Clearwater Revival. The combination of the studio and Steve Barncard, the engineer who came with it, was irresistible. Between August 6 and September 16 the Dead recorded yet another album, which they would call *American Beauty;* after his lover, Christie, suggested "big full fat American Beauty rose," Hunter wisely edited it down. It was another masterpiece, perhaps their best studio album ever. The songs were not only exquisite, their performances were illuminated by an inner light born of sorrow, as well as the light born of psilocybin mushrooms, which Rock's lover, Nicki, was doling out to the band during the recording process. They all set up in the same room, without baffles, so the album was essentially recorded live. Since a good portion of the greater scene was away, distractions were few and the studio's atmosphere was quiet and industrious.

As with *Workingman's,* there was little experimentation; they were there to support the text. The only difficulty, in Weir's memory, was Hunter's nerves, which came to be called Hunteritis. "You can't do it that way! What are you trying to do to my song?" Eventually, Weir asked him to step out so he could finish "Sugar Magnolia." In his polite, aw-shucks decent way, Bob Weir was at least as stubborn as Hunter, and completely unwilling to follow the Hunter system of "one man writes the words, one man sings them." They were destined to lock horns, and so they did. The line about "jumps like a Willys in four-wheel drive" was in fact written by Weir, and Hunter didn't appreciate the assistance. Nonetheless, he supplied the "Sunshine Daydream" coda on demand, and it put the perfect finishing touch on a superb song.

Barncard did a lovely job of making their harmony singing sound great. With three microphones and two passes each, there were six vocal tracks on each tune. This required a mix team, with two mixers and a person behind each of them to lean over their shoulder to push mute buttons, EQ (equalization), or whatever. It had a more human sound than later, all-automated mixing, and it was gorgeous in its simplicity. Everything worked.

On a day off that month, the Dead played softball with the Airplane in Fairfax, and whom should Garcia spot down the first base line but his old pal David Grisman, newly arrived in the Bay Area. "Hey, man, I got a recording gig for you." The next day, Grisman limbered up his mandolin at Heider's, listened to "Ripple" once or twice, took two or three takes, and, in Barncard's words, "ripped our heart out." He also contributed to "Friend of the Devil." Ned Lagin got off a Greyhound bus from Boston and went to Heider's, where he and Garcia were the first ones in. "Good," Jerry said. "You can play on our record." For a finale they brought in office staff, friends, and neighbors and conducted a candlelit chorus of about thirty sitting on the floor, some in tune and some not, just like a church service almost anywhere, to finish off "Ripple."

On September 16, the Dead flew to New York for gigs at the Fillmore East, and it turned out to be a thoroughly wonderful plane flight. Their fellow passengers included Ray Charles, who played chess with Sam Cutler and beat him, and a gaggle of Greek people on their way to visit their homeland. As the Greeks began dancing up and down the aisle, the Dead focused on yet another passenger, Huey Newton, the charismatic head of the Black Panther Party. Natural-born skeptics, the Dead knew that the media image of the Panthers was not to be trusted, and they were delighted to sit and rave with an intelligent and personable man. Six miles in the air, the conversation was good and the vibes even better. Interestingly, their encounter was documented in their FBI file just twelve days later.

The shows at the Fillmore East were not only successful, with *Cashbox* reporting that their "impact on the audience was absolutely phenomenal, and their popularity continues to grow with every performance," but also made musically exceptional by the presence of David Grisman. The run's good mood was interrupted on September 18, when word reached them of Jimi Hendrix's death in London. They dedicated a set to him, but it was not satisfying. "I never saw him," Garcia said, "without a half-dozen weird people hanging around him—vampires and shit." The Dead's own profound relationship with "the family" of crew, staff, and friends was their proof against rock angst, and they knew it. But it was still sad to see those who couldn't survive the vampires. Hendrix's loss was all the more poignant because they'd never jammed with him; on the one occasion that he'd come to a show, ax in hand, the Dead had gotten so high on LSD and so deep in their music that when Mickey Hart finally remembered to signal for him to join them, it was hours later and he'd departed.

Returning home, they joined Quicksilver and Jefferson Airplane for two shows on October 4 and 5 at Winterland, working not for Bill

Graham but for his former house manager, Paul Barratta. Barratta's challenge to Graham failed in short order, but this run was distinctive. In addition to putting the old "big three" of San Francisco bands together, the
shows had Jorma Kaukonen and Jack Casady's blues band, Hot Tuna, a
live TV broadcast on the public station KQED, and the first quadraphonic radio broadcast in history, combining two stereo FM stations,
KQED and KSAN. Winterland was packed, and thousands were turned
away. Hot Tuna opened. Quicksilver's sets included a five-piece horn section, and they were such a mess that they were John Cipollina's last with
the band he'd helped begin.

Just before the Dead's first set on October 4, a horrible rumor spread
through the backstage, a rumor that proved to be sadly true. Three hundred miles south, alone with some heroin, Janis Joplin had died. Mickey
suggested to Garcia that they dedicate the set to Janis, but Garcia demurred. "Let's not bum 'em out. They'll know soon enough." Backstage
there was a dead silence for about thirty seconds, and then the futile talk
of denial, and when the truth was established, a grim attempt to party past
various metaphorical graveyards. The Dead had last seen her in July, when
she'd come onstage at a show in San Rafael to share a lewd and lascivious
"Lovelight" with Pigpen. McIntire found it a peculiar performance, and
felt she was drunkenly trying to upstage Garcia rather than show exuberance. Chet Helms, the man who'd brought Janis to San Francisco and Big
Brother only four years before, had been profoundly disturbed by her behavior that night. She seemed cadaverous to him, like some reptilian
William S. Burroughs character, and her death did not surprise him.
"Comfort is made of compromises, and Janis would have no part of its
nasty cycle," wrote one of her biographers. "The paralysis of Kozmical despair seemed to be at the very center of her everyday life."

On October 10, the Dead were back in New York, this time to start a
college tour that would be chaotic, insanely long, and critical in establishing them commercially outside San Francisco and Fillmore East. Ron
Rainey was a young man who'd progressed from setting up college shows
to working at the booking agency Ashley Famous (later International Famous, IF) and had become the Dead's new agent. Sent to a New York
Dead gig to get Garcia to sign some contracts, he was happy to take the
beer he was handed, and later found himself being allowed to play tambourine with the New Riders. "They took care of business and had great
fun at my expense," he said. Having passed the test, and being the
youngest guy at IF, he entered training on how to be an agent for the
Dead. "Get the money" was the agent's credo, but the Dead were

"concerned with things I hadn't come to yet." "How can you give me a contract," asked McIntire, "without the promoter's home phone number?" "I got trained to cover every detail. He was patient with me, but strict. He trained me how to do this, but his way." In the fall of 1970 the action in rock was shifting from the ballrooms to colleges, because "colleges had budgets," and Ron took the Dead to campus.

The fall tour began at an auditorium at Queens College, Flushing. From the beginning, crowd control was a problem at colleges. At Queens, there were break-ins, people outside calling for a free concert, and people inside blowing police whistles. The college paper quoted the head of campus security as saying the band left early, because "they were afraid of the audience." A subsequent interview with Garcia disposed of that notion, but the growth in the band's popularity was inescapable. "Yeah," said Garcia, "it's too weird after all this time." When told of the frenzy that was producing all-night ticket-buying vigils in front of the Fillmore East, Garcia would reply, not for the last time, "that doesn't mean I oughta carry around the responsibility of being that guy that dispenses our music."

"Are the Grateful Dead devils or angels?" asked the Queens College paper, which attributed to the band "the ability to drive people to peculiar heights of ecstatic frenzy . . . their whole beings absorbed, taken over." "Last night was a free zone," said the University of Pennsylvania paper, "reality suspended, the law flagrantly violated. The Grateful Dead was the cause of it all." They toured out into the Midwest, and for Halloween came back to where they'd started on the East Coast three years before, at Stony Brook, a totally chaotic show which included a bomb threat. The gym was cleared, the audience exited, and two thousand additional people reentered. Scheduled for two shows, they played until midnight for the first show, and the turnover was anything but graceful. As well, the sound was mixed by students—it was a low-budget tour, without the Dead's own sound system—and they were not ready for the Grateful Dead. Even that most civil of rhythm guitarists could bark, "Hey, man, turn the microphones up, leave 'em right there. Don't touch the fuckin' things. Don't touch the fuckin' things, man, 'cause you don't know what you're doing." Pigpen was even more pithy. "Mister Soundman, sir, can I have a little more main in the monitor if it's at all possible? If I don't get it the way I want it, I'm going to rip off your head and shit in it."

The sound guy wasn't the only person intimidated by the Dead. As Sam Cutler wrote later, "the people who lead bands from relative obscurity to 'mega popularity' . . . are NOT usually very nice people!! . . . Nowadays managers are diplomats, in my day they were aggressive bastards who got what they needed for their band, come what may." At least twice on this tour, students on the concert committee would report that the aggression included the sight of a gun, something Cutler flatly denied. "They're mad. I have NEVER carried a weapon in my life other than a sharp and incisive mind." He was contradicted by a band insider who recalled comparing his own pistol, which Sam had noticed, with Sam's. The business was a rough one at times. For instance, a show scheduled for November 15 in Albany, New York, produced a headline in the local underground paper, "Ungrateful Dead Rip Off Tri-Cities," and an article that asserted that the Dead "walked out of the Washington Avenue Armory Sunday night with $7,500 cash in their pockets without ever appearing onstage." Of course, the reporter's only basis for this notion was that Cutler had carried a satchel when he left. The local promoter, George Freije, had booked the Dead at the last second after Delaney and Bonnie had canceled. It was the Dead's eleventh night of gigs in a row, but work was work. When a bomb threat cleared the hall, the band left. Twenty years later the same reporter concluded that the threat was in fact an excuse for the promoter to end the show early, and since the Dead never saw any money, their departure was in order.

It was the tour that wouldn't end. The next night, a Monday, they joined what was left of Jefferson Airplane—Grace Slick was pregnant and a no-show, Marty Balin had essentially left the band—for a night of jams at Fillmore East that included members of Traffic. A few nights later Jorma Kaukonen stopped on his way to visit his family at the U.S. embassy in Ottawa and jammed with the Dead in Rochester. Because they liked Boston, Weir and Garcia demonstrated their appreciation by joining Duane Allman at the WBCN studios after their show there and jammed with him. At too long last, the Dead finished the tour on November 29 at a club in Ohio.

That week *American Beauty* landed in the record stores. "Truckin'" was the single, and actually reached no. 64 on the charts, although Warner Bros.' editing job was singularly inept. Kelley's cover, on the other hand, was superb. On being told the title, he'd naturally thought of a rose, and then etched the rose into a mirror backward. The flame lettering could be read as "American Reality" as well as "Beauty," an unexpected but entirely welcome double message. Originally, there was to have been a photo of the band on the back cover that would have included some members holding guns, but Hunter protested. One loud no was a veto, so they used a picture of Kelley's cluttered bedroom table.

As the year wound down, their tour schedule eased slightly, although they performed 120 shows in 1970, their most active year ever documented. What few shows they played late in the year were in the Bay Area. Mostly, they relaxed. Of course, relaxation for Garcia meant hanging out and playing. And he could partake of a unique situation that was then conveniently at hand. From the time of recording *American Beauty* until the following March, the Dead, the Airplane, Santana, and CS&N were more or less continuously in residence at Heider's, and for more than six months some of the best music in America was being made there. It was a three-room musical circus, and when one take was done, there was always the possibility of something fun happening next door. The previous year, Garcia had played pedal steel on "Teach Your Children," the lead song on CSNY's *Déjà Vu.* Santana's epic *Abraxas* had been released in October 1970, and in December RCA put out *Blows Against the Empire,* Paul Kantner's science-fiction fantasy project, featuring Grace Slick, Jack Casady, Jerry Garcia, Mickey Hart, David Crosby, and Graham Nash. In the course of the fall and winter, David Crosby's *If I Could Only Remember My Name,* released in March 1971, and Graham Nash's *Songs for Beginners,* released in June, drew on the same group of musicians. It could only have happened in San Francisco, said Crosby, for nowhere else did you have the "degree of talent that was willing to be that free with itself, that willing to be that unself-conscious or that undefensive." Only at Heider's could you find so many fearless musicians, "especially Garcia." Because "the weirder you got," said Crosby, "the happier he got."

One consequence of *American Beauty* was the return of Alan Trist, Garcia and Hunter's buddy from 1961 Palo Alto. When he'd left California, he'd attended Cambridge, eventually marrying Robert Hunter's friend from the same Palo Alto circle, Christie Bourne. Through the sixties, Christie maintained a close friendship with both men, which kept the connection alive. After the Hollywood Festival show in 1970, Alan had gotten together with Hunter and McIntire, and eventually Jon had offered him the job of running Ice Nine, the Dead's music publishing firm. Alan faced an interesting quandary. He was then working with the Tavistock Institute, which studied social change, and now he had the opportunity to live it. McIntire had impressed him deeply with an energy that was clearly and consciously oriented toward positiveness and the pursuit of quality, and so his decision was not terribly difficult. The Dead won, and late in November, as *American Beauty* was released, he moved to the Bay Area and joined the office staff at 5th and Lincoln.

McIntire's motivations for the job offer were complex and significant. Jon felt that as a social anthropologist, Alan might be able to help the band look at its internal processes, become more conscious of them, and learn from them. The Tavistock was anti-ideological; the Dead were anti-dogmatic. McIntire thought Alan might help make the Dead "more wholesome in our dealings with ourselves. I was trying to harken the scene back to the heart and roots of 710, the kind of care that everyone took for each other, the kind of openness that everyone had for each other." Hunter's fundamental question in "Uncle John's Band" was "Are you kind?" McIntire's job, with Trist's help, was to try to make that attitude live outside the song.

At Christmas Columbia released the eponymously titled first New Riders of the Purple Sage album, so that wing was prospering. The Dead ended the year at Winterland, where each of the balloons that dropped from the ceiling at midnight had a beautifully engraved card with an attached barrel of Orange Sunshine LSD. That the band had even survived through 1970 was, on reflection, a little miraculous. That they had prevailed was just good old Grateful Dead dumbshit synchronicity. For once, the joke was theirs.

33

Interlude/Intermission II:
Uncle John's Children

As the house lights come up, the tapers change batteries, flip tapes or insert fresh blanks, and tend to their housekeeping. They are an interesting bunch, one of a number of self-created subgroups within the larger Dead Head culture, of particular importance because their labors produce the sacred talismans that unite the tribe as a whole. Their dean is Barry Glassberg, who attended 352 shows, made 310 tapes, and—when it was an unsanctioned activity—was caught fewer than twenty times, because he wore a suit, carried a briefcase, and put his tape deck in a hollowed-out medical journal. The tapers are extremely serious. The Dead, wrote taper Dan Hupert, "is a compilation, every night, of every show that went before . . . without a tape, what they played in Laguna in '68 is nothing more than past history. With it, however, it becomes a part of my present . . . If you see two shows a year, or five, or seven, they are individual concert experiences. If you see twenty-five and listen to tapes of most of the others, it is no longer an individual experience or a set of them. It is a continuing process. Each tour has its own momentum, its own inner logic and cohesiveness. And each is quite clearly, if you look at it at all closely, the result of the time and place and of all the shows and tours in all the years that went before it."

The band's decision to allow taping, said John Barlow, was "one of the most enlightened, practical, smart things that anybody ever did. I think it is probably the single most important reason that we have the popularity that we have . . . [Tapes are the] article of currency for this economy, our psychic economy to say the least . . . And by the proliferation of tapes, that formed the basis of a culture and something weirdly like a religion . . . A lot of what we are selling is community. That is our main product, it's not music." That community was actually a collection of families, for Dead Heads almost invariably find themselves a member of a small group as a practical response to the various logistical requirements of touring. The solitary Dead Head is a rarity.

The community was a collaboration between the fans and the Dead, who gave the Dead Heads their name, symbols and motifs to share such as the various logos, and a commitment demonstrated by constant performing, outstanding sound, and the lowest possible ticket prices. Because the band dressed and acted like the audience, because there was no "show," the audience correctly perceived them as people like themselves who happened to be able to play—equal partners in a psychic quest. The Dead then displayed music and values that were just strange enough to invite a stigma that the Heads could share. It was not a coincidence that the subculture exploded in size during the Reagan administration, when anything odd or liberal was swept away in a sea of greed.

Indeed, by the eighties and nineties the Dead Head subculture, a community, tribe, family, and traveling circus, was, as Garcia put it, the "last adventure." Like the Dead, the Dead Heads were quintessentially American, heirs to Daniel Boone and Huck Finn, who lit out for the frontier when things got too "sivilized." The Dead Heads' frontier is within as well as on the road, but they were no less pioneers for that. The Dead Heads had only one thing absolutely in common: each one had experienced some inner click of affinity, some overwhelming sense of "here I belong," when confronted by the Dead, its music and scene. It was the recognition of an essentially spiritual experience that bound them together. They found a faith in the pursuit of transcendence, as initiated by psychedelics and music, and shared antiauthoritarian values that placed a premium on tolerance. After that, each person's role within the culture was improvised, in the same way as the music was played. The parking lot denizens who attended every show and dressed solely in tie-dye were extreme and attracted the media attention, though they were a tiny fraction of the whole. But all Dead Heads shared the faith of the pilgrim. In a cynical age, that made them highly vulnerable to mockery: "How many Dead

Heads does it take to screw in a lightbulb? One to change it, fifty to tape it, fifty thousand to follow it around after it burns out." They were white, slightly more likely to be male, and mostly middle-class, although large outposts of Dead Heads were to be found at upper-class prep schools.

Dead Heads ranged from the young and unformed to Owen Chamberlain, a Nobel laureate in physics who enjoyed sitting between the two drummers, he said, "because it gives me interesting ideas." One of the great athletes of his era, Bill Walton, recognized the profound affinity of improvisation on the basketball court and the concert stage, and became one of the band's favorite Dead Heads. The artist Keith Haring recognized the invigorating energy of the concerts. So did Senator Patrick Leahy of Vermont, who exchanged his normal pinstripes for tie-dye and shorts at shows and then danced up a storm. Unfortunately, he could not fully escape his role, which led to one of the more surreal conversations ever held onstage. As the opening act performed at a 1993 RFK Stadium concert in Washington, a runner brought Scrib a message for Senator Leahy which had been called into the stadium offices from the White House. The senator requested a phone, which Robbie Taylor provided, and returned the call, to Secretary of State Warren Christopher. Christopher informed the senator, who was chairman of a Foreign Operations Subcommittee, that reprisals were about to go forward against Saddam Hussein, and then went on to remark that the radio was on rather loud where the senator was. "No, that's Sting." There was silence. "Sting, the musician." Silence. "He's opening for the Grateful Dead." A very deep silence ensued, until Christopher replied, "Would you have time for the president?"

Undoubtedly, the Dead Head who got "it" at the most profoundly scholarly level was the great mythologist Joseph Campbell. Campbell had no interest in or contact with popular culture, having seen two movies. He didn't read a newspaper and hadn't been to a pop concert in decades. The head of the Bay Area Jungian Institute lived next door to Weir, and Bobby was delighted to have Campbell as a dinner guest. Garcia had been a Campbell fan since reading *A Skeleton Key to Finnegans Wake*, Mickey since encountering *The Way of the Animal Powers*, and they were delighted to join in. Soon after, Campbell came to a Dead show and was enthralled. "I just didn't know anything like that existed," he told his associate Sam Keane. "This was a real Dionysian Festival." He'd always argued that the great mythic patterns endured in contemporary life, but the evidence before him was thrilling. After the concert he wrote to the band members, whom he identified as "magicians," that he felt "in immediate accord" with their art. To Campbell, a Dead concert was "25,000 people tied at the heart," and the "antidote for the atom bomb." Given Campbell's right-wing political views, Keane found it doubly surprising that the Dead "got through his barriers . . . The spirit of the thing, a community, a celebrating community, and it was a pretty orderly community, it was really pretty sweet—whether he liked the music or not wasn't quite the issue—it produced a kind of benevolent frenzy I guess you would say . . . It was very important to him . . . he mentioned it frequently." Such validation from a wise elder of the race was a very rich reward for the musicians.

Phil Lesh had often remarked that "everywhere we play is church," in the sense that the act of playing was a form of devotion. It is difficult in America for the average person to associate celebration and religion, but Dead Heads have no such problem. "The great thing about the Dead," explained one disciple, "is . . . like, you can have these wicked cosmic thoughts and dance at the same time. Really spiritual and really sensual." There were also the social bonds of ritual, the waiting in line, choosing where in a general-admission show one customarily sits, the rolling of joints, and so forth. "There is something religious about our thing," remarked Garcia. "The desire on our fans' part is to have some high moments in your life, some mystery."

Dead Heads were not paragons. Like all fans, a word derived from the same root as "fanatic," they could become tediously obsessed with the object of their joy, and while there were far worse forms of competition than being "Deader than thou," it still led at times to what one person called "obnoxious religious bliss." Their frequent unwillingness to listen to fine opening musicians indicated a self-limiting deliberate cultivation of ignorance. An even more annoying example of obliviousness came with every performance of "Black Muddy River." Night after night, Garcia would depict the agonizing "dark night of the soul" as he sang, "When it seems like the night will last forever," and some Dead Heads would choose to cheer it as a reference to an unending party. More, the Dead Heads' adoption of a uniform—tie-dye in all its manifestations—invited, demanded, stereotyping.

At its worst, the faith could slide into rank superstition, as when rumors of the band's imminent demise swept the Dead world after they began playing the Rolling Stones' song "The Last Time." Watching a stoned zombie ignore his/her own child while under the influence of drugs was a depressing sight. There was also the pathology that Barlow and Weir depicted in "Estimated Prophet," or in the following letter to Garcia:

Dear Jerry:

... Please read my letter to you. I think you will find it very inter-esting, if not the truth ... I am the young man who helped turn some very confused and potentially destructive psychic energy around at two of your recent concerts ... In both incidences there was a great deal of weirdness emating [sic] from Bob Weir and the entire Bill Graham production of your concert ... I am positive that you personally were acknowledging my presence in the audience this past December.

Thankfully, this sort of lost-in-the-ozone stasis was not terribly common. More often, they would agree with the fan who wrote,

The Grateful Dead represents the high water mark of civilization, as far as humanity has come towards establishing universal conscious-ness. Like unravelling the DNA helix or hearing the echoes of the big bang, their work pushes back the frontiers of knowledge; the shining resonance of the music of the spheres is clearly heard, the voice of a higher consciousness.

The band recognized the bond, and within human limits, respected it mightily. As Garcia said, he'd "never experienced the click of great music without an audience ... We exist by their grace." "What I'm talking about," said Kreutzmann, "is, when it's really happening, the audience is as much the band as the band is the audience. There is no difference. The audience should be paid—they contribute as much."

The band definitely paid attention to its audience, both in the whole and in the particular. Early in the 1980s there was a string of three or four shows in which an extremely large fellow occupied the same seat in the front row. Since the seats were reserved, the question arose as to how he'd acquired such fine tickets. About the third night, at the break, Scrib ran into Mickey, Billy, and Bobby, who were discussing the guy. Kreutzmann had briefly observed a bright blue flame around him and concluded that the guy was smoking freebase, which enraged him. Mickey was in agree-ment with his brother drummer. Weir went along. When he found him-self in Parish's corner a little later getting Garcia to sign some things, Scrib asked Jerry if he'd noticed the man. Garcia had indeed noticed him, had noticed details of his dancing style and how it connected with the flow of the music. Parish commented that the hostility to the guy had to do with his size—both men liked the guy's vibe. They had also some-how discovered that he was a ticket broker, which explained his source of tickets. Out of pure curiosity, Scrib polled Lesh, who remarked that he had no attitude on the guy personally, but tended to grow sick of always seeing the same people night after night.

Just as the band has its ultimate bumper sticker ("There Is Nothing Like a Grateful Dead Concert"), so do the Dead Heads: "We Are Everywhere." There was the pilot who saved Mickey Hart from arrest after a scuffle with a flight attendant by pulling one of Bear's gold Dead logo necklaces from his shirt and saying, "Mickey, you're responsible for getting me kicked out of my house when I was sixteen years old. Thank you so much." In 1973 one of the pilots of "Looking Glass," the permanently circling airplane that is the alternative headquarters for the U.S. military in case of all-out war, was a Dead Head named John Babuini. As he flew quadrants around the United States, he would call a Dead Head buddy, who would patch him into his home stereo over the phone lines. When the Strategic Air Command saw Babuini's phone bills, they ran a security check. Both Babuini and his friend passed, and John served his nation with "Dark Star" in his ears.

Being a Dead Head is about faith: faith in synchronicity, faith in joy. On the first (Friday) night of a three-show run at Shoreline Amphitheatre, a few miles south of San Francisco, an extremely pregnant lady named Robin Kraft sat in the front row making jokes about how one good sonic boom from Lesh might cause her to give birth to her child, already named Stella Blue Kraft. Robin was not in her seat on Saturday, having gone into labor. It was a long, long birth process, but finally, on Sunday, her baby was born—just as the band began to play "Stella Blue." Of such events is faith derived.

Dreams
and All

(1/71–7/71)

n the night of February 19, 1971, a man named Malcolm
Bessent, a great-nephew of theosophist Annie Besant, lay sleeping in the Dream Laboratory at Maimonides Medical Center in
Brooklyn. The Dead were playing at the Capitol Theater in
Port Chester, New York, about forty-five miles away. Out in the audience
at the Capitol, a young man named Ronnie Mastrion, assisting Dr. Stanley Krippner, a noted researcher in the realm of ESP, flipped a coin to determine which of two envelopes holding images he would select. Upon
opening one, he put a sequence of slides in a projector, and the audience
began to read. "1. You are about to participate in an ESP experiment. 2. In
a few seconds you will see a picture. 3. Try using your ESP to 'send' this
picture to Malcolm Bessent." In addition to the instruction slides, the
band occasionally spoke about the experiment between songs. One of the
six pictures that night, called *Seven Spinal Chakras,* showed a man meditating in lotus position, with his chakras vividly illuminated. When awakened, Bessent reported dreaming, "I was very interested in . . . using
natural energy . . . thinking about rocket ships . . . an energy box," and a
"spinal column."

The next night, the audience saw Magritte's *Philosophy in the Boudoir,* a portrait of a headless woman in a gown, and Bessent dreamed of "a little girl's doll" and "a stop watch on a cord around my neck." Dr. Krippner reported that academic peers who evaluated Bessent's responses gave him high scores four out of six times, a level Krippner found statistically significant. Stanley Krippner was yet another of the fascinating people the Dead had attracted, a distinguished psychologist who was comfortable with the notion of a rational study of "fuzzy" things like ESP, or psychedelics, or both together. Already familiar with the Dead, he had hit it off with Mickey Hart at a birthday party for the distinguished Indian musician Ustad Allarakha. Eventually, Krippner found himself in conversation with Garcia, who wondered about the potential interaction of various altered states of consciousness, for instance sleep and the psychedelic state, and whether or not that could aid sensitivity to ESP. Their conversation yielded the Dream Experiment, which was deemed worthy of publication in a formal, academically refereed journal of psychology.

Life at the Capitol was extremely eventful. In the course of a week's residence, the Dead helped with a scientific experiment, lost a drummer, added a lyricist, and introduced eight new songs, seven of them original. Mickey Hart had been in a pit of mortal anguish since Lenny's departure. Self-medication had not helped, and although the band was supportive, his insecurities were exacerbated by what he perceived as Susila Kreutzmann's suspicion of him. He had never been fond of the road, either. It had been a long time since he'd been able to sleep decently, and by the time the band arrived in Port Chester, he was a complete wreck, plagued by suicidal thoughts and essentially in the middle of a breakdown. Dr. Krippner hypnotized Mickey on the first night so that he could perform, then took Hart to his mother's place on Long Island. He still couldn't sleep. At length, Mickey took some medication that would drop an elephant in its tracks, and slept for the better part of three days. When he awoke, he went back to the ranch, where he would essentially take root for the next three years.

Weir and Hunter had been destined not to have a long-term relationship as songwriting partners. Hunter, as Weir's friend John Perry Barlow put it, was "not just magisterial, he's irascible, and Weir's inscrutable." At Port Chester the band debuted the best of the Weir-Hunter lyric collaborations (although Mickey Hart had written much of the music), "Playing in the Band," a wonderful vehicle for improvisational jamming that somehow can also rock the house down. Not bad for a song in 10/4 time. "If a man among you / Got no sin upon his hand / Let him cast a stone at me / For playing in the band."

Weir had survived years of being the Kid with a stubbornness masked in decency and politeness, and if Phil Lesh couldn't tell him what to do, neither could Hunter. For some reason, the process of writing "Playing in the Band" had gone reasonably well. This was not true for another song that debuted in Port Chester, "Greatest Story Ever Told." "Story" was an unlikely song from its inception, which happened to be the rhythm of a pump at Mickey's ranch. Being Mickey, he made a tape of the sound, and convinced Weir that there was a song to be found. Somewhere in the process of creation, the tempo of "Froggy Went A-Courtin' " came into play, and the tune came to Hunter for lyrics, which he duly produced. Trouble broke out when Weir began to mess with the words. "I had no more disregard for Hunter's first drafts than Garcia did," he said. "It was just simply that Hunter couldn't put up with another one [i.e., another collaborator]." In Hunter's view, Weir wanted lyrics that were "a wash . . . atmospheric . . . leaving only Bobby." They clashed again over "One More Saturday Night." Having gotten Hunter's lyrics, Weir rewrote them— badly, in Hunter's opinion—and then asked to call the resulting song "U.S. Blues," which Hunter refused to permit. In the end he declined any association with the song and it was credited to Weir alone. The final straw came over the song that Weir had been working on the previous summer as Eileen Law had given birth. Hunter had produced a piece about gambling he called "Blood Red Diamonds," and Weir didn't think it worked for the tune. When he rejected it, Hunter concluded that it was time to move on.

Conveniently, it was just at this time that Weir's prep school friend Barlow turned up. He was not in good spirits, which made him part of the prevailing atmosphere. Cocaine had become an essential part of the Grateful Dead's scene. What had once been an occasional lark was now pretty much a daily requirement, and the problem with cocaine is that there is no such thing as "enough," at least until one has ingested far, far too much. The noted connoisseur of drugs William Burroughs theorized that cocaine acted directly upon the pleasure centers of the brain; whatever its mechanism, its effect on the Dead would be generally negative. Cocaine would erode the band and crew's senses of humor and good judgment for many years. Barlow had completed college, written half a novel and sold it to Farrar, Straus & Giroux, then taken the advance and gone to India. Now he was living in New York, dealing cocaine, and carrying a gun.

In the course of the week in Port Chester, Rex Jackson, as Barlow put it, "a fundamentally good man, held me upside down and shook me by my boot heels, to try to see if any cocaine would fall out . . . Kreutzmann told me he was going to kill me if I didn't quit fucking their groupies." Crew member Sonny Heard dubbed him "Bum Barlow," which seemed to John to put him as low as he could possibly get. At one point during that week, Barlow and others, said Barlow, went "bopping around shooting cocaine and hanging out at Vassar, the weirdest thing we could think to do . . . Darkness, darkness." So dark an era, in fact, that six weeks later Marina Maguire, their decadent queen of darkness, the heiress and hostess to so many postshow parties, died in jail in Porterville, California, under mysterious circumstances. She had been arrested, ostensibly because her credit card had expired and the motel she was staying at was suspicious, but more likely because in the process of demanding payment, a motel employee saw a syringe in her possession. Once in jail, she died, supposedly of a ruptured gallbladder incurred during a paroxysm generated by barbiturate withdrawal. Whether her injuries were accidental or deliberately inflicted by the police, Marina died as a consequence of her drug abuse.

Backstage at the Capitol, Hunter and Weir got into an argument about "Sugar Magnolia," which had evolved in the playing from a sweet country tune to a ripping, show-closing rocker. Furious, Hunter turned to Barlow and said, "Barlow, you wrote poetry in college, right?"

"Well, yeah."

"So you could write songs, probably, huh?"

"Well, maybe. I know they're different."

"Take him, he's yours."

Hunter even took Barlow aside and gave him a bit of avuncular advice about songwriting: "Remember, every song is a story." "It was actually," said Barlow, "the last clear view of Hunter I had, because after that it got so complicated." The month before, in January 1971, Barlow, Weir, and McIntire had driven around Mexico for a couple of weeks in an elderly Saab that broke down every day about the same time. They visited, among other things, both of the tequila distilleries of Guadalajara on their way to see some old smuggler friends in Michoacan. One morning, his ears full of Mexican radio, Barlow sat in the car while his companions were in a store, and heard Kris Kristofferson's "Sunday Morning Coming Down." Barlow was in the grip of an awesome, truly psychedelic tequila hangover, and the song resonated mightily. He began to write something in that vein. Then, after Hunter's blessing at the Capitol, Barlow got out the Wild Turkey and that week completed the tale, which he called "Mexicali Blues."

Realizing that he needed to escape New York, Barlow headed for the West Coast in March, not sure whether he'd join Weir in San Francisco or go to Los Angeles to work for Warner Bros. He stopped to visit his family at their Wyoming ranch and found a turbulent situation. His father had suffered a stroke, and his mother was trying to run things from the office, while the foreman was trying to run the ranch "without going into the office." He was the prodigal son, "hair down to here," as he put it, and he had no intention of returning to ranch life. But he couldn't leave his family, already a million dollars in debt in mortgages, in the hole, so he planned to stay a few months to get things in shape. A note above his mother's desk read, "Life is what happens to you when you're making other plans." A few months became seventeen years.

The early 1971 songs at the Capitol reflected a modest pendulum swing back to rock and roll in contrast to the tranquil elegance of *American Beauty*. "Sugar Magnolia" had acquired a rock drive, "Playing in the Band" was played at a brisk tempo, Garcia's new tunes "Bertha" and "Deal" kicked along smartly, and their one new cover song was *the* rock song, "Johnny B. Goode." With only one drummer and a minimalist keyboard player in Pigpen, the music had simplified, and they laid plans for another live album, to be recorded in April.

In the meantime the band returned home to play some benefits. Their conversation with Huey Newton on the airplane the previous fall had led to a March show at the Oakland Auditorium for the Black Panther's Free Breakfast Program, which was a very mixed experience. Huey as a person was one thing, and the personal ruled in the world of Grateful Dead. But Panther notions of security led to pat-down searches of everyone in the band and crew, and the evening's effective boss, Panther Elaine Brown, failed to charm the Dead. Later in the month the Dead played at Winterland for a local Sufi organization, whose leader, Phil Davenport, did work for Ice Nine. But the spring of 1971 would mostly be recalled as the sad period in which both of Weir's parents died—within weeks of each other, and each on the other's birthday. Weir would never be terribly adept at acknowledging his pain, and the symmetry of the two deaths moved them, in his mind, from the tragic into the protocosmic, but it was still a painful season.

Using local sound systems had caused many unacceptable problems the previous fall, so early in 1971 the band purchased the Alembic P.A. Consequently, a number of new faces joined the touring party. One of them was a lanky young New Yorker named Steve Parish. He'd read William Burroughs's *Naked Lunch* at sixteen, run away at seventeen, and gotten into considerable trouble at eighteen over a spot of illegal business. While dealing with legal exigencies, he answered a summer 1969 advertisement seeking people over six feet tall—he was six five—to work as ushers at the New York State Pavilion in Queens. The Dead were the first band to play at the Pavilion, and Parish quickly became friends with Rex and Ram Rod. After working at the Capitol in Port Chester, he migrated to San Francisco late in the year and was metaphorically adopted by Ram Rod, who among other things taught the New Yorker how to drive and gave him work carrying equipment for some of Jerry's earliest solo projects. He was living at Rukka Rukka when Cassidy Law was born, and working with Dan Healy for Quicksilver Messenger Service. With the new P.A., the Dead needed more hands, and Parish joined the tour in April.

The crew had always been an essential part of the Grateful Dead, but now it grew considerably in numbers. Bob Matthews mixed the sound and was boss of the P.A. crew, which included Parish, Kidd Candelario, and Sparky Raizene, a burly fellow from Chicago who'd seen the Dead at a show in Wisconsin, talked to the crew, and arrived in San Francisco a week later. Jackson, Heard, and Ram Rod were the Dead's crew. John Hagen covered the New Riders. Another Oregonian, Joe Winslow, joined the P.A. crew with Parish. The new crew members' first big tour would hit colleges across Pennsylvania in April. For the first time, the band used buses, which suited Garcia just fine. Anything that kept him out of airports seemed "more like travel and less like matter transmission." The crew mostly rode the trucks. It was still a time in which most of the band and crew consumed LSD each night, and they saw themselves as part of a group mind. Within the crew in particular, this also translated into sexual sharing of the various willing female followers.

The tour opened in New York City at a new-to-the-Dead venue, the Manhattan Center, and the shows were so oversold that Joe Winslow spent his first night on the road pulling suffocation victims out of the squirming mass of bodies mashed together in front of the stage. The house was obviously oversold to begin with, but there were also dark suspicions that members of the house security force were going around the corner and reselling tickets rather than tearing them up. A visiting reporter from the *New Yorker* remarked that "there was room in some parts of the room for rhythmic breathing [but] dancing was rarely a possibility." The "balconies looked like the decks of a huge foundering hippie cruise ship." Despite the crush, the audience was calm, and there was "a pleasant low-key trust around. People lay on the floor, for instance, and were not trampled, and the coat checkroom had no coat checker and was run on sound anarchistic principles."

After busing around Pennsylvania, the tour stopped at Wallace Wade Stadium at Duke University in North Carolina, one of their first shows in the South since New Orleans. Eric Greenspan was the student responsible for booking the show, which included the Dead, the Beach Boys, and the Butterfield Blues Band. It was his first large outdoor event, and he was ill prepared. The stage was low and had no roof, the security barricade was a rope, and there were no trailers for dressing rooms. The weather forecast was for rain. Having just seen the Rolling Stones' Altamont movie, *Gimme Shelter*, Greenspan met with Sam Cutler the day before the show. Thinking to propitiate this legend, Greenspan offered Cutler a gram of hashish. When Sam simply tossed it back like an aspirin tablet, Eric realized that he was in deeply over his head, and then listened as Sam pointed out the requirements outlined in the contract, which are called riders, and the various ways in which he had failed to deliver. "We knew nothing from riders," Eric recalled.

The sun was bright as the gig day dawned, and Eric stood on his little stage as Cutler and Garcia drove up and Cutler revved up for some more ass chewing. Finally, Jerry cut him off with a grin. "Sam, give it a rest. We'll play." Among other chores that day, Eric took Candelario to the store, where he bought fifteen pairs of Converse sneakers, and swapped them around so that everyone had two colors. Eric also sampled Kidd's electric Visine bottle, and although there were only seven thousand kids in a fifty-thousand-seat stadium—there had been no advertising or off-campus sales—or perhaps because there were only seven thousand kids, it was a blissful day that established the Dead in North Carolina forever.

From Carolina they returned to New York for five nights at Fillmore East. On their arrival they learned what Bill Graham would only announce on the morning of the last show: that he was closing the building in June. His resignation, reported *Rolling Stone,* was "a great document, a brilliant combination of bitterness, bullshit, self-pity, candid revelations and his coach-like brand of big ball pontification. He attacked greedy artists, greedy agents, greedy fans, rock festivals and mediocre talent. And of course, the abusive press."

Graham's announcement lent the Dead's last stand a special poignancy and power. This was where they had established themselves as a functioning commercial act. In just six years of existence, they had traveled far, and already they were leaving things behind. Duane Allman dropped by one night and T.C. sat in for a dosed Pigpen on another. Having met the Beach Boys at Duke, the Dead had invited them to join the party, and partway into a set, Garcia announced that "another famous California group" would join them. As the Boys sang "Help Me, Rhonda," members of the crew called John Hagen's pregnant wife, Rhonda, back home, and discovered that she was giving birth to their son, all alone.

Back in San Francisco, the band's rising popularity and Cutler's more systematic booking policies had resulted in something no one had ever expected—free time. The years when they would take any gig were behind them, which pleased everyone except Garcia, the music addict. He wanted to play five nights a week, and with the Dead easing back, he had to find other ways to stay busy. In the summer of 1970, he had taken up with an eccentric, gifted keyboardist named Howard Wales and effectively began a career outside the Grateful Dead. Wales was a midwesterner who had played piano since the age of four, and in the sixties he had gone from playing in Mafia joints on Chicago's Rush Street, to backing Jerry's old hero Freddie King, to a band that dyed its hair green and wore space suits, to the band Sugarloaf, which had a big hit with "Green-Eyed Lady." After emigrating to San Francisco, he landed a gig at the Matrix organizing a regular jam on Monday nights. Late in the spring of 1970 Garcia began to sit in regularly, soon joined by John Kahn, a bass player then working with Mike Bloomfield. There was almost no audience, and they didn't have songs, either. "We didn't play anything very basic at all," said Kahn. "It didn't sound like any music you would be used to." "Howard would just play through tremendously extended changes," said Garcia. "It developed my ear . . . so outside and totally unpredictable." Later, Garcia would add, "John and I played for a year before we even really talked to each other. 'Hey what's doing man?' and then plug in and spend all night muttering to each other, 'What key are we in?' " Even Wales would describe their music as musical adventures, "free-form jams . . . I generally induced certain phrasings and stuff that basically would incorporate sort of a composition of a song, but the thing is, it started at one place and ended up in other places."

"What happened was," said Kahn, "we went there one night, and really out of nowhere the place was packed . . . Howard freaked. It got to be too much of a scene. Since it was fun, we decided to get another keyboard guy, and I knew Merl [Saunders]. Vince Guaraldi played for a while. With Merl, we started to learn songs, and developed." By May

1971 the quartet was Jerry, John, Bill Vitt on drums, and Merl. Merl Washington (Saunders was an adopted stage name) was a San Franciscan raised in the fifties just four blocks from 710 at the corner of Ashbury and Page. A classmate of Johnny Mathis at Polytechnic High School, he had grown up listening to Erroll Garner and Jimmy Smith, and after serving in the army from 1953 to 1957, he had worked with Oscar Brown on the play *Big Time Buck White*, backed Dinah Washington, and jammed with Miles Davis.

Having explored music from Wales's completely "outside" perspective, Garcia now began to learn standards and structure from Merl. Early in 1971 Jerry and Merl ran across a man named Freddie Herrera, who in 1969 had opened a club in North Beach called the Keystone Korner (as in Keystone Kops, because it was next door to the police station). One day early on, Nick Gravenites wandered in and remarked that the place needed music and he had some friends. They turned out to be the bulk of the recently disbanded Electric Flag, including Mike Bloomfield, and they kept the club going for a while. Garcia and Saunders followed them, and Freddie Herrera became a permanent part of Jerry's musical family. The Korner made little money, and in the beginning the quartet's take was no more than $180 a night. A year or two later Herrera moved his operation to Berkeley and changed the club's name to the Keystone Berkeley. Both clubs were small and funky, just the way Garcia liked it. He would arrive at the club around three in the afternoon. From the start, Parish was his roadie for club gigs, since Ram Rod, like the rest of the Dead, was grateful for a little downtime, and was glad to bring Parish into the mix. Parish's original salary was five dollars per show, plus pot. Garcia would sit and run scales as the afternoon passed, stories would be told and joints rolled and smoked, and he and Parish bonded. Occasionally, Jerry would say, "Go out and bring me somebody weird," and Parish would find a street crazy who would be suitably entertaining. So was the music. "I played big fat chords and did a lot of that walking-style chord shifting," Garcia told a friend. "My style is much more conventional, in a way, with [Merl], and it's very satisfying for me to play and hear myself as a conventional player."

After taking most of May 1971 off, the Dead played two Memorial Day weekend shows at Winterland. Perhaps they should have stayed on vacation. Too many people had spiked the garbage cans full of Kool-Aid that went out into the audience. It was a hot, hot night, and too many people drank too much; thirty people ended up at the Mount Zion Hospital emergency room, although none were hospitalized overnight.

Graham's new stage manager, Patrick Stansfield, a theater professional who'd recently worked at the Tyrone Guthrie Center in Minneapolis, later said that when he pulled out of Winterland around six the next morning, he saw kids still plastered against the walls across the street like "starfish," some bleeding at the ears and nose. Some bigwig's daughter was injured, and city police chief Al Nelder suggested to the press that Bill's permit be revoked for his "failure to protect his patrons." Bitter over the flap, Graham responded by declaring that he was closing Fillmore West as well as Fillmore East, with a final show to come on July 4.

June passed quietly, and around the middle of the month Weir stopped by 5th and Lincoln, where Jerry sat talking with Jon McIntire. Garcia and McIntire looked at him with an odd expression until he asked, "What?" Garcia asked him, "You bored? You bored yet? How'd you like to go to France this weekend?" Well, sure. There was no money to be made, but their expenses would be paid to fly to France and play for a festival on the outskirts of Paris. Why not? Jean Bouquin was a fashion designer with a chic boutique that sold overpriced blue jeans in the exclusive St. Germain district of Paris, and he wanted to be France's minister of youth. Part of his campaign was to throw a rock festival, which translated as "Free Freedom Three Days," at a movie set, Strawberry Studios, in the town of Hérouville, near Auvers, the burial place of Vincent van Gogh. The studio was in a chateau owned by Michel Magne.

Upon their arrival, the Dead discovered that the festival had been rained out, and after a couple of days of killing time with fine wine and games of tennis at the 450-year-old chateau—the doors were noticeably lower than contemporary people required—they decided to throw a party, and invited the townspeople of Hérouville. On the solstice, June 21, the weather cleared and they set up in back of the chateau near the pool, which the children of Hérouville had encircled with hundreds of candles. As Lesh recalled it, their guests included "the police chief, the fire chief, and the mayor . . . Magne was pointing out all this little kinky shit in the locals, man . . . *No* Dead Heads—it was just boogie down . . . a little acid being passed around, not too much, just right, and of course, the Light Sound Dimension [light show] was there, Bill Ham . . . they played too. We did our set, and they did their set. And they were great—we were all getting real high by that time," Lesh said, laughing. "It was outdoors at the chateau, right around the swimming pool . . . the classic garden party with the G.D. and the LSD. Talk about a piece of San Francisco transplanted into the heart of France . . ." Topped off with a round of dunkings in the pool begun by the police chief—Weir exacted the Dead's revenge, of course, dunking him back—it was among the best parties the Dead had ever enjoyed.

They loaded out in a false dawn, then went to Orly Airport and checked the equipment. But their tickets were held hostage while they awaited a freight document. Rosie McGee, who was working as McIntire's interpreter, was dealing with supervisors who represented two airlines, the airport, and the French government, all of them shouting at once. Winding down from the fun, the band stood a few yards away. Finally, Rosie had an inspiration. "Monsieur, *look* at those guys over there. I can't say WHAT they'll do if they don't get on SOME airplane *immediately*. Do YOU want to be PERSONALLY responsible for an international incident, right here, and right now?" The band members responded suitably to their cue, flipping middle digits and growling audibly, and the boarding passes materialized. They flew to New York, waited, flew to San Francisco and got to Marin, and Bob Matthews suddenly realized that he'd been in daylight for about twenty-five hours. When Rosie awoke on the morning after their return, it was one week exactly since McIntire's first call to her about the jaunt, and she wondered if she'd dreamed it all.

One very real dream died that month as well. The Haight-Ashbury was a ruin, and the notion of a counterculture was essentially dead, but there were holdouts here and there, and ideas don't die even when they don't flourish. In June Peter Coyote visited Gary Snyder, who was part of a healthy alternative community in the San Juan Ridge area of Northern California. Peter had the notion of such places serving as way stations for countercultural caravans, since much of what seemed to be hippie life at this point was mobile. More interested in protecting his own community than promoting an abstraction, Gary rejected the notion. "He told us that the people in their area were committing themselves to articulating a sense of place and understanding its species diversity," wrote Coyote later. "They planned to be there for the long haul, to serve as its guardians. They had reservations about travelers. Furthermore, he added, they didn't need much." Freeman House commented, "We Diggers were building a culture, we weren't building a life."

On July 2, the Dead played their last show at the Fillmore West, and although they played so poorly they asked not to be in Graham's film *Last Days of the Fillmore* (their resistance drove Graham crazy, until eventually they relented and allowed him to have one song), they did realize one ambition, which was to get Bill Graham high on LSD. It was fun for him, too. When he realized the source of his giddiness, he looked at the band and cracked up. Someone handed him a stick, Bill hit the gong, and in "one of the dozen great nights of my life," he conducted the Dead "and probably lovingly made an ass of myself."

Everything changed, and nothing changed. In the ensuing years Bill Graham produced more shows than ever before, using various halls instead of just one. The Dead stopped breaking out the garbage cans of dosed Kool-Aid, but the audience members remained as bright-eyed as ever, their faith in the dream unbroken.

Jerry Garcia and Mickey Hart, 1971.

The band photo for the *Skullfuck* album, Spring 1971.

Sound technician Betty Cantor lugs cable at Hérouville, June 1971.

The Dead onstage in Europe, 1972.

Sam Cutler and Chesley Millikin onstage at the Bickershaw Festival, 1972.

A bozo on the bus named Lesh, 1972.

PHOTO BY MARY ANN MAYER

Keith Godchaux at the keys, Europe, 1972.

Bob Weir and Dickey Betts at Watkins Glen, July 1973.

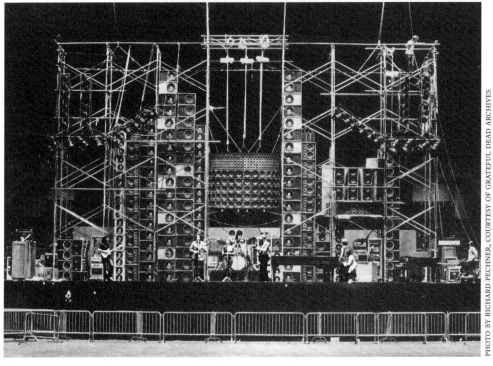

The Wall of Sound, 1974.

The band onstage at Winterland, June 1977.

A pregnant and pensive
Donna Jean Godchaux
onstage, 1973.

The stage and the pyramids, Egypt, September 1978.

Band onstage, Egypt.

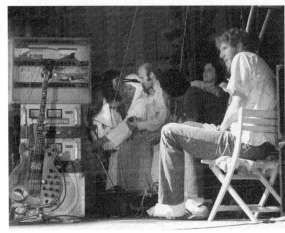

Bill Walton, Ken and Chuck
Kesey backstage, Egypt.

The Rhythm Devils,
Mickey Hart and Bill
Kreutzmann, Oakland
Auditorium, 1979.

Ram Rod prepares a tar (drum), 1981.

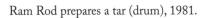

Sweaty and rejuvenated at the Melk Weg (Milky Way) Club, Amsterdam, October 1981.

Bob Weir, Bob Dylan, Jerry Garcia, summer 1987.

Bob Weir, Jerry Garcia, Clive Davis, Roy Lott, and Don Ienner of Arista, Mickey Hart, and promoter John Scher, celebrating *In the Dark,* Madison Square Garden, fall 1987.

Mickey Hart, Frost Amphitheatre, 1988.

Brent Mydland onstage, 1989.

Mike Brady of Ultra Sound and Bill
Kreutzmann, Phoenix, 1992.

Mickey Hart and Bill Graham, 1990.

Jerry Garcia, benign, 1993.

Bob Weir at the Waldorf-Astoria,
New York, 1994.

Vince Welnick onstage in Seattle, June 1994.

Jerry Garcia and Bruce Hornsby, Paris, 1990.

Robert Hunter, smiling.

Bob Weir and
John Barlow.

Crew and Staff

John Cutler at the mix-
ing board, Highgate,
Vermont, 1995.

Monitor mixer Harry Popick and lighting designer Candace Brightman, 1986.

The crew—Steve Parish, Ram Rod Shurtliff, Bill Candelario, Robbie Taylor, Bill Grillo—1985.

Howard Danchik of Ultra Sound and Dan Healy, Las Vegas, 1993.

Cameron Sears and Ram Rod,
Fenway Park, 1991.

Dick Latvala in the vault, 1993.

The office staff and family take part in the *Hell in a Bucket* video shoot, fall 1987. Front seat: Nancy Mallonee, Maruska Nelson, Jon McIntire. Back seat, front row: Mary Jo Meinolf, Eileen Law, Sue Stephens, Janet Soto-Knudsen. Back row: Trixie Garcia, Diane Geoppo, Frances Shurtliff, Basia Raizene.

Dead Heads, Friends, and Family

Taper heaven: mike stands reach to the sky, Pittsburgh, 1990.

Two happy cops, Buckeye Lake, Ohio, 1993.

Dancer, Pittsburgh, 1990.

Branford Marsalis on-stage with the Dead, Los Angeles, 1993.

Scrib, Carolyn Garcia, Jerry Garcia, Mickey Hart, Caryl Orbach Hart, Vice President Al Gore, Phil and Jill Lesh, and Cassidy Law, at the White House, 1993.

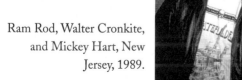

Ram Rod, Walter Cronkite, and Mickey Hart, New Jersey, 1989.

Bill Graham as Father Time
(1979–80), as a butterfly, Nicki
and Rock Scully as skeletons.

Jerry Garcia
teaches Taro
Hart to play,
1995.

The last happy moment: Grateful Dead encounter the University of Michigan
women's gymnastic team in the lobby of their Salt Lake City hotel, February 1995.

35

Dealing Solo Aces and the New Guy

(7/71–3/72)

he first town on the Pacific coast north of San Francisco is called Stinson Beach. It is only twenty miles from the city, but they are hard ones, a dizzying succession of hairpin turns, and the town is tiny. Five miles farther north is the hippie enclave of Bolinas, where the sign on Highway 1 that identifies the town is routinely stolen by locals in the hope that tourists will miss the turn. Stinson was less polarized than Bolinas and had more connection with the outside world, but only slightly. There were no police in Stinson in 1971, although its fire marshal, Collen White, had once been involved with the CIA's LSD program. There was a water tower on the road to Stinson someone had decorated with the word "Seek," and Garcia felt good about that. He and M.G. had been happy with their home in Madrone Canyon in Larkspur, but it had been sold out from under them, and the same thing happened to them with another house.

Late in June M.G. found a place in Stinson called Sans Souci, "Without Care." It was isolated at the top of the hill and backed by county reserve land, which made it a fine place for a neighboring pot patch, and it had a swimming pool. The panoramic ocean view was beyond spectacular.

The price was $60,000, and the deal called for a $20,000 down payment. That was roughly Jerry's annual income at the time, and the Garcias certainly didn't have any significant savings. The only way to get that kind of money was for him to do a solo album, with the added bonus that he could cut in Kreutzmann and Ram Rod toward the same end. "Being able to move in and get solid," he told an interviewer, "that's what that record was about for me, really, to be respectable and so forth, which is laughable but . . . that's why it ends with 'Wheel' and starts with 'Deal'—it's wheeling and dealing to get a house. Basically that's the truth of it." He went on to dismiss the project as "idiosyncratic." "I don't intend to follow it with a career as a solo performer or anything like that."

There were other elements operating in these decisions. Part of coming to Stinson Beach and of making the solo album was to clear a modest space, both socially and musically, between himself and the Grateful Dead. The distance from 5th and Lincoln cut down the mental as well as physical traffic, and there were musical directions he wanted to follow in the studio that didn't seem appropriate for the Dead. On the twenty-eighth of the thirty days they were allowed to produce the down payment, M.G. flew to Los Angeles, got the advance check from Warner Bros., and delivered it to the rather shocked owners. Sans Souci was theirs.

They were not exactly isolated. Jon McIntire and Alan Trist lived in Bolinas, and Jerry's old buddy David Grisman was down the hill in Stinson. Laird Grant and Willy Legate were around. Before long, Parish and Ron Rakow would move over the hill into Stinson. And of course, there were new people.

Sue Stephens was a sometime X-ray technician who would, for a time, supplement her unemployment checks by cleaning house for Jerry and M.G., among others. The pay was sometimes M.G.'s excellent home-grown, and life was good. "Keep my mouth shut, clean, and leave" was Sue's motto, and she became a trusted friend. Goldie Rush was another Stinsonite. She was baby-sitting for some of the Garcias' neighbors and had to visit Sans Souci to report that five-year-old Sunshine was stealing from her charges. She, M.G., and Jerry ended up in a long, hilarious conversation on various offenses from their respective childhoods, and she fell into their scene. In the long run, she grew especially close to M.G., and later to McIntire. "There was always a good meal, a good joint, good music, and a great conversation going on up there."

David Grisman's business partner was a man named Richard Loren. Together they managed a group called the Rowan Brothers, and David also produced them. One day in the summer of 1971 soon after moving to Stinson, Jerry went down to the Rowans's studio to check them out, and the gardener, Sue Stephens's boyfriend Fred, frostily told him it was a closed session. Later, Fred explained that he'd assumed Jerry was a local pot dealer, since he seemed to have fine weed. Garcia genially allowed that he'd be happy to wait, and Grisman eventually came out and made introductions. Over time, Loren and Garcia became particularly friendly.

Richard had been a theater manager and then a booking agent with the Agency for the Performing Arts (APA). He was one of the APA's earliest rock agents, and soon he was working with the Jefferson Airplane and the Doors, which gave him the dubious honor of being the man to bail out Jim Morrison when he was arrested in New Haven after a scuffle with police. In 1968 he quit the agency and moved to Europe for a time, and on his return to New York in 1970 he and Grisman formed Hieronymous Music to manage the Rowans. One night that year Grisman went to Fillmore East to hang out with Garcia, bringing along Richard to introduce him to Jerry. Loren got to talking about the book *Morning of the Magicians,* a study of the occult and other forms of strangeness. Since this was one of both his and Jerry's favorite subjects, they connected. Jerry asked what he and Grisman were up to, and suggested that San Francisco had a healthy club scene for the Rowans. That fall of 1970 the Hieronymous bunch moved out to the Bay Area, and by the summer of 1971 the Rowans had signed with Columbia. Over the course of the year, as Garcia came to play more and more regularly with Merl Saunders, he asked Richard to manage his non–Grateful Dead business affairs, which, of course, made waves at 5th and Lincoln, all outsiders being viewed with some doubt.

Early in July Garcia went to Wally Heider's to begin recording an album that would be called, with impeccable accuracy and zero flair, *Garcia.* His first decision was to play all the instruments except the drums himself, which made it an exceptionally efficient process. The origins of that decision lay in his two previous experiences in recording away from the Grateful Dead. Early in 1970 he had been hired to record solo for Michelangelo Antonioni's film about youthful resistance to the mainstream culture, *Zabriskie Point.* It had been a frustrating experience. Still very much a cinephile, Garcia had admired Antonioni's *Eclipse* and had studied him. He was flattered to be asked and found the director a pleasure to work with. The experience of sitting alone on a soundstage at MGM where Gene Kelly had danced and *The Wizard of Oz* had been shot gave him the shivers. Antonioni described to him in a strange stammer the emotions he wanted communicated, ranging from sad to cheerful to scary, and as the film splashed across a giant screen, Garcia played. The frustration entered in after a few takes, when Antonioni pronounced himself delighted, but Garcia felt that he was just beginning to understand what he was there for. Antonioni might well have been right about Garcia's "Love Theme"—it was achingly beautiful and worked incredibly well in the film—but it left Jerry forlorn. This would happen again, later that spring of 1970, when he played pedal steel on Crosby, Stills, Nash and Young's "Teach Your Children." After the second take, just as he was warming up, Crosby told Jerry, "That was great. Have a snort." And that was the end of the session.

With *Garcia,* Jerry was in control. The only people in the studio were the recording team of Bob and Betty, Ram Rod the guitar roadie, Kreutzmann the drummer, and Hunter the lyricist. They put a sign on the door that read "Anita Bryant sessions" and became effectively invisible, the reverse of the Kantner/Crosby/Nash hangout albums. What would become side one of the album was made up of relatively conventional songs: "Deal," "Bird Song," "Sugaree," and "Loser." "Deal" mixes romance and good card-playing advice: "Goes to show you don't ever know / Watch each card you play / and play it slow / Wait until your deal come round / Don't you let that deal go down." "Loser" is also about a gambler, but a deluded one, the quintessential victim of his own optimism. "Bird Song" is an exquisite meditation on a woman, and in "Sugaree" a ne'er-do-well denies an old love. The songs were lyrically and musically strong, and would be standards in Garcia's repertoire from that time on.

Side two of the album was more experimental. Garcia began by laying out the entire side musically, although one section, "To Lay Me Down," was already a fully formed song. "To Lay Me Down" was the first song he'd composed at a piano, and it has a certain gospel feel. It is a love song, but tinged with sorrow, for it is a lost love. "to lie with you / with our dreams / entwined together / To lie beside you / my love still sleeping / to tell sweet lies / one last time / and say goodnight." In the actual recording of the album, he played piano throughout side two, and then went back and overdubbed. The side two closer, "The Wheel," had a wonderful birth. Garcia and Kreutzmann were jamming, and out of an inchoate sea of notes, a pattern emerged, a chord, then a set of changes, then a chorus, and then a song. Hunter was sitting in the corner listening very carefully. By the end of the night he had a rough set of lyrics, and by the next day they were polished. It is a gospel hymn as much as anything—"Small wheel turn by the fire and rod / Big wheel turn by the grace of God / Every time that wheel turn round / Bound to cover just a little more ground"—and it turned into a gracefully effective rock song in performance.

Garcia's work pleased almost everyone but Rock Scully, who had to sell the album. As Scully pointed out, the most radio-friendly cuts, like "The Wheel" and "To Lay Me Down," were surrounded by what he called "Insect Fear craziness" like "Eep Hour," bizarro *musique concrète* sound collages that the average citizen was not going to grasp, with razor-thin gaps in between, breaks so thin that a disc jockey in a hurry couldn't cue up the song, which meant he wouldn't play it. Garcia didn't care about sales, so Rock could only groan.

Having recorded and mixed the album in three weeks, Garcia returned to the Grateful Dead in August. As usual, there was plenty to keep everyone occupied. On July 26 Lenny Hart had been found by a private detective and arrested in San Diego. He claimed to be studying to be a minister in the Assembly of God, although the local pastor denied that he was even a parishioner. Portraying himself as a naif dazzled by rock and roll, Lenny claimed to be a financial virgin in a new world where everyone was ripping off each other, and "I just succumbed to the temptation to take my share." The Dead did not press charges, although they did sue for the return of their money, and recovered $55,000. The district attorney pursued criminal embezzlement charges, and Lenny was convicted and sentenced to six months in jail. Joe Smith attended the trial, and Lenny told him, "The Lord has forgiven me. I hope the boys do." "Lenny," Joe replied, "the Lord didn't lose seventy-five big ones." Busy building a studio at the ranch, Mickey found out about Lenny's arrest only by reading the *Chronicle*.

His was not the only building plan in the works, although it would be the only successful one. That summer an idea circulated around the office for a project called Deadpatch, a home for the Grateful Dead. In a charming blend of Cantabrigian social science and stoned hippie rave, Alan Trist drew up some notes, beginning from the "100 percent level of concept/bossness/fantasy, in terms of facilities, materials, and equipment, and then work backwards to the immediately pragmatic." He postulated needs that began with a rehearsal hall, led to a recording studio, then an office, then perhaps living space, and ended with a rocket launchpad. His report noted that "we all like to work and hangout together, there may (or not) be conflict between making music, doing business and hanging out. Personally I see them as inseparable . . . difficulties can be avoided by the right . . . design." John Cipollina's father had found them a bit of land on

Lucas Valley Road in West Marin, and they managed to put a hold on it for a while, but since they had no financial resources, the idea was, in Alan's English slang, "a definite nonstarter." If a real desire had been there, such a handicap might have been overcome. But Garcia—and to a man the band agreed with him—did not want to have to deal with much beyond the tuning of his guitar. A home for his family, fine. But to the end of his days, he held a consistent Thoreauvian view that perceived possessions as a weight.

That summer Jann Wenner and Yale law professor Charles Reich came to talk with Garcia for a two-part cover story in *Rolling Stone* that would eventually be published in book form as *Garcia: Signpost to New Space*. Reich, the author of *The Greening of America*, was a good-hearted romantic who idolized the youth culture, but was not terribly sophisticated. A repressed and closeted gay man, Reich seized on the freedom of the San Francisco scene, and his visits to Sans Souci were heavenly for him. In person, he was bumbling and innocent. Wenner asked the historical questions, and Garcia ran down the lore. Philosophy was Charles's angle, especially the social philosophy of making life more satisfying. Garcia obliged. "The question is, can we do it and stay high?" Charming, thoughtful, and a man who authentically enjoyed conversation, Garcia tried to educate the overly respectful Reich.

In part two of the book, "A Stoned Sunday Rap," Jerry brought out one of his favorite esoteric works, *The Book of Urantia*, and chatted about "the twelve principles of information, that's the whole basis of alchemy, and one of the things is polarity . . . gender, that's another one." He had to be careful with Reich's feelings. He pinched his nose after a snort of cocaine and Reich thought he was miming a bad smell in reference to Charles's remarks. Mostly, Jerry tried to be encouraging. "It's cool with me for life or death, either one is okay . . . but I've made my pitch, I've put my stand in for the life cycle, that's the thing . . . Look man, here we are, we're on the edge, and we can make it. So can you, give it a try." Charles went home dazzled. Jerry went off to the Keystone to play.

By the end of summer, the live recordings the Dead had made in April were ready for release, and they were good ones, reflecting a lean sound born of a single drummer and virtually no keyboards, although on three songs, Jerry brought in his club partner Merl Saunders to overdub organ parts. It was an energy-packed double album filled with first-rate, vital, accessible rock: "Bertha," Noah Lewis's "Big Railroad Blues," Kris Kristofferson's "Me and Bobby McGee," a new original called "Wharf Rat," and a smoking jam of Buddy Holly's "Not Fade Away" combined with the tune Jerry had learned from Delaney Bramlett on the trans-Canadian train, "Going Down the Road Feeling Bad."

In the past year the Dead had given Warner Bros. two classic, commercially viable studio albums, so now it was time to give Joe Smith a hotfoot. During a so-called band meeting, which was in fact an all-employee meeting, Phil Lesh suggested calling the album *Skullfuck*. Lesh didn't particularly like Warner Bros. "I didn't like anybody who told us we couldn't put *Anthem* out and sell two million copies," he said with a laugh. "*Skullfuck* was an attitude." Rex Jackson and Sonny Heard became vociferous proponents of the title. They were, Weir recalled, "adamant about it. And to the extent that all decisions were made in general meetings, and they were loud . . . basically, the meetings were shout-outs." But Jackson and Heard had also tapped a common vein.

The Dead had artistic control, and Jon McIntire duly informed Joe Smith that the album would be called *Skullfuck*. "You can't do this to me!" "It's not me, Joe," said Jon. "It's *all* of us. We're *all* doing this to you." At first Joe thought Jon was joking, and then he spoke with Jerry, who assured Joe that he'd settle for very small sales to keep the name. At length, Joe asked for a meeting, which became a Grateful Dead classic. "But any decision that concerned them had to involve everybody," Joe said, "and their families were involved . . . and the other people . . . it was necessary to hold a meeting with all of them."

Fifty-five people flew from San Francisco to Los Angeles, too many for the Warner Bros. conference room, so the meeting was moved to the Continental Hyatt House. "We've set up the tables," wrote Rock Scully, "with the Warner people on one side and us on the other. It's the North and South Korea Unilateral Treaty Conference. Release all prisoners!" Poor Joe Smith. He had polyps on his vocal cords and could barely speak at all, and certainly not loudly. In Stan Cornyn's opinion, Joe handled the situation masterfully, making the chain-store buyers the bad guys rather than himself. "Do you want to sell ten thousand copies?" In the end the band gave in and agreed to change the name to the dull and accurate *Grateful Dead*. To Stan, this was evidence of nascent careerism, proof that the Dead really did have a commercial sense. The fact that the Dead were, after all, Merry Pranksters—and you never trust a Prankster—did not seem to have occurred to anybody. "Oh, we wanted to use it so badly," Garcia said, chuckling. "We had a big meeting with Warners. They were horrified! They were shocked! They sat there so seriously . . . They fully believed we were going to do something awful if they didn't . . . it was more a joke on our part."

For Dead Heads, *Skullfuck* it was and *Skullfuck* it remained. Kelley did the cover, the familiar skeleton crowned in roses from the Avalon poster and *The Rubáiyát of Omar Khayyám,* and on the inside there was a lovely picture of the band taken by Bob Seidemann in the yard at 5th and Lincoln. Far more significantly for the future, the back cover invited fans of the Grateful Dead to write in: "Dead Freaks Unite (Who are you? Where are you? How are you? Send us your name and address and we'll keep you informed.)" A second piece of fallout from the meeting at the Hyatt House was a hefty promotional budget for the album, including about $100,000 for radio broadcasts of fourteen shows that fall, which would help make *Skullfuck* the Dead's first gold album. The broadcasts were direct and effective, which was fortunate, because their other efforts would be less useful. The members of the band were supposed to go out on radio promotion visits in an event that involved seven people going seven different places with seven plane tickets. According to Joe, not one person made his flight. "I think that was a Rock Scully production."

The tight, mobile sound also got them some interesting reviews. Lester Bangs, not normally a fan, wrote that it was "not only great American music but a total personification of the American west both as musical genre and, more importantly, state of mind . . . And even if I still think they're Tom Hippies and probably never will learn to love them for their own smug selves, I've at least stopped worrying because now I know at last that they can and do when, great galloping gogamooga, the Karmic Vibes are Right, play some mighty rock and roll. In spite of everything, and I can hardly believe it myself, I'm a Grateful Dead fan."

The Dead played few shows in the summer of 1971, and it served as something of an interlude. Mid-September brought a harsh reality check. On September 17 Pigpen went into Novato General Hospital with a perforated ulcer and hepatitis. Ironically, his drinking had already slackened considerably, after he had reached the point of sweats, faintness, and incipient D.T.'s. He had lost an enormous amount of weight, and the *Skullfuck* portrait revealed the small, gentle bluesman who lived behind the biker persona. The band lined up to give blood, and Pig started to heal. Around that time, they finally confronted their need for a new keyboard player. They auditioned Howard Wales, but as Weir said, "we spurred him towards new heights of weirdness and he spurred us towards new heights of weirdness . . . much too weird much too quick . . . everybody backed off, scratched their head and said, 'Well, maybe, uh, next incarnation.'"

Which was where the issue remained until early September, when a beautiful woman named Donna Jean Godchaux grabbed Garcia by the arm as he was walking to the dressing room at the Keystone Korner and said, "My husband and I have something very important to talk to you about." "Okay," Garcia said. "Come on backstage." But the Godchaux were both extremely shy, especially Donna's husband, Keith, and they couldn't force themselves to go back. Garcia returned and sat down at their table, but Keith avoided his gaze. "Honey," Donna said, "I think Garcia's hinting he wants to talk to you." Keith put his head on the table and said, "You'll have to talk to my old lady, I can't talk to you right now." Donna Jean was sweetly blunt: "Well, Keith is your new piano player, so I'm gonna need your home number so we can keep in touch." Since the Godchaux were not aware that Pigpen was sick, it was a particularly exquisite bit of synchronicity. Jerry smiled, and gave Donna Jean his number and the number at 5th and Lincoln. She called the office and left several messages, but was ignored. Finally, she got him at home, and he said to come to a rehearsal, which at that time was in a warehouse off Francisco Boulevard in San Rafael. It was a Sunday afternoon, and it developed that no one had mentioned to Jerry that the rehearsal had been canceled. Jerry and Keith began to jam, and then Keith and Donna played Garcia a song they'd written, "Every Song I Sing." Eventually, Garcia picked up the phone and called Kreutzmann. "Why don't you come down? There's this guy . . ." They played and played and played some more, and on Monday the whole band joined them. Even though he'd never practiced Dead tunes, Keith was instantly right. They'd throw him musical curves, Kreutzmann said, and he never missed—he was just a great jazz and free music player. By Monday night Keith Godchaux was on the payroll. They invited Donna Jean to sing as well, but she wanted to give her husband pride of position, and she waited.

The notion that things are meant to be is frequently hard to shake around the Grateful Dead. Just when the Dead needed to enrich their sound, a perfect contributor showed up. "It had to happen," said Keith. "I knew it had to happen because I had a vision." Donna Jean added, "I had a dream that it was supposed to happen. It was the direction our lives had to go in. The only direction." Unfortunately, it was a direction that would eventually kill Keith Godchaux.

He was born in 1948 and grew up in suburban Concord, California. He had classical training and played in a country club band, then cocktail jazz in piano bar trios. He was small, gentle, spaced-out, depressive, and extremely vulnerable. Given some stimulation, he was happy to stay up all night discussing Heidegger, Nietzsche, and dualism, but he read little, and his personal presence was so modest that Lesh would think of him as a "cipher," although he greatly admired him as a player. He was definitely graced with what Jon McIntire would call "psychic knowledge." Jon recalled Keith telling him, "You have gone up to the gates of heaven many times and have refused to walk through because you think that heaven is not big enough to contain your individuality. And I would like to tell you that it is. And the next time those gates open for you, walk through." Once he had joined the Dead tour, Keith made it an absolute policy never to get on a small plane unless Jon was on it, too. When asked why, he said, "You have that air of permanence about you."

Donna Jean had been born and raised in Muscle Shoals, Alabama, where at age fifteen she was already a regular harmony singer at Fame Studios, the renowned home of the Muscle Shoals sound, on tunes like Percy Sledge's "When a Man Loves a Woman" and Elvis Presley's "Suspicious Minds." After a while, it seemed a one-dimensional life to her, and she moved to San Francisco, going to work at Union Oil processing credit cards. Many of her friends at Union Oil were Dead Heads, and she went along with them one night in October 1970 to Winterland. The New Riders she recalled as "a little different" to her, Quicksilver was "really different," Jefferson Airplane was *"realllly* different," and after the Dead finished, she went home and sat in her apartment saying, " 'How did they do that, how did they do that? That's what I want' . . . it was spiritual."

Keith was part of her social circle, and although she had her eyes on him, they'd never really spoken. One night he came over, they listened to the Grateful Dead, and, still not having really spoken, they looked at each other. They began walking toward each other, and he said, "I love you." She responded in kind, and they sat down and began figuring out when they were going to get married. It was only on the following weekend that she discovered Keith played piano in a bar band. Later a friend suggested listening to the Dead on the record player, and Keith replied, "I don't want to listen to it, I want to play it." And Donna Jean knew. Spotting an ad for a Saunders-Garcia gig at the Keystone Korner, she took their destiny in her hands and Garcia by the arm.

After a few weeks of rehearsal, the Dead took off for Minneapolis, where they would open the tour with a first show that introduced the new band member and six new songs on a live radio broadcast. It was typical of the Dead that the process of integrating both the songs and the player would take place not only onstage but on the air, because one result of Keith's joining the band was that they would fail to record a new studio album with the new material—they were simply too busy absorbing Keith to make time for the studio. Hunter was bitterly disappointed, but that was the way of it. His new work included Garcia songs "Tennessee Jed," "Ramble on Rose," "Brown Eyed Women," and "Comes a Time," along with his last Weir song, "Jack Straw." Weir also introduced "Mexicali Blues," his first song with Barlow.

"Jed" was the result of a vinous night in Barcelona. Hunter and his lady, Christie, were on their way back to their hotel and found themselves in a little alley with high church buildings on each side. Into this resonant space came the sound of a man playing Jew's harp, an odd thing in the Spanish night, and when they got back to their room, he began to jot down verses. "Jed" is the musical equivalent of a tall tale, the legend of an eternally resilient displaced wanderer so buffeted by outrageous slings and arrows that even his dog tells him, "Let's get back to Tennessee, Jed." "Ramble on Rose" was inspired, so whimsical that it was at times hard to distinguish the mythical from the literal, which was, of course, just the way Hunter liked it. The song's "Crazy Otto," for instance, was a real piano player who had cut six honky-tonk albums, including a song about a crazy giraffe, "Oodley Oom Bah."

"Brown Eyed Women" was a nostalgic look at rural America, an anthem of generations and the passing of fathers. "Sound of the thunder with the rain pourin' down / and it looks like the old man's gettin' on." "Jack Straw" was dogged by feminist objections to the opening line, "We can share the women / we can share the wine." As Hunter would plaintively remind the critics, it was this very sexism that would generate the tale of betrayal and murder, but few seemed to take notice. It was a terrific cowboy song: "Leaving Texas / fourth day of July / Sun so hot, clouds so low / The eagles filled the sky / Catch the Detroit Lightning out of Santa Fe / Great Northern out of Cheyenne / From sea to shining sea." It is mythic America, superbly rendered. "Bertha," "Sugaree," and "Wharf Rat," a haunting depiction of a waterfront alcoholic who dreams of redemption, had already been introduced earlier in the year. It was an extraordinary collection of songs, and any other band would have gotten a studio album out of it.

The fall's tour went remarkably well, given the presence of a new player. In November Garcia gave up his seat with the New Riders of the Purple Sage to Buddy Cage, and after that month the Riders were on their own. In early December Pigpen returned to the band, although he was wobbly and frail, and for a little while they had two keyboard players. For his review of shows that month at New York City's Felt Forum,

Robert Christgau became one of the first of hundreds of writers to write primarily about the audience. Though Dead Heads were swarming over the front rows, he noted the ease with each he claimed his seats, and how when his date lost her wallet it was swiftly returned to her. "Regulars greeted other regulars, remembered from previous boogies, and compared this event with a downer in Boston or a fabulous night in Arizona." The sixties were gone, the seventies were less than inspiring, and none of it mattered to the Dead. They were on the planet to play music, and they were in it for the long haul. The band ended the year at Winterland as usual, with Donna Jean coming out to sing on "One More Saturday Night," Weir commenting, "I know you're not used to seeing a girl up here, but . . ." They earned $8,000 for the two nights. For the new year 1972, they planned their first real no-fooling vacation, with no shows scheduled until March. Of course, this would be followed by three continuous months of work.

In conventional rock and roll practice, songwriting is an object of sometimes vicious competition, since the songwriter makes more money, and in many ways artistically controls the band. As usual, the Dead were different; there was a certain amount of gentle pressure on Weir to write songs. The band, said John Barlow, "wanted to see Bobby get some creative expression. Garcia, for instance, had always been really enthusiastic about Weir's taking a major role in all that." Late in 1971, with studio time for his first solo album reserved for late January, Weir took stock. He had three and a half songs—"One More Saturday Night," "Playing in the Band," "Mexicali Blues," and the rhythm guitar part to "Cassidy." There being a considerable gap between songs completed and songs necessary, he called Barlow and said, "We gotta do something."

Early in January 1972, Weir and his malamute, Moondog, drove to Wyoming, and once at Barlow's ranch, settled in at a cabin which was isolated even by Bar Cross standards. On his first night, he discovered that he had a non-rent-paying co-tenant, namely a ghost. Moondog was quite literally scared "shitless" by the ghost, and Weir was not too crazy about it, either. This was the Grateful Dead cowboy period, and Weir was a manly man, but . . . The ghost manifested itself at the bottom of his bed in the middle of the night, and it was impossible for Weir to open his eyes. He quickly turned to a spiritual expert. Late in the night, Weir called Rolling Thunder, his Native American shaman friend, for advice. After he explained his situation, Rolling Thunder said gather this herb and that—no, no, replied Weir, I need *immediate* help. In that case, Rolling Thunder advised, smear charcoal on your face. So Weir burned kitchen matches, ground them up, applied them to his face, and went to sleep. He forgot about his "makeup," which drew an interesting reaction from Barlow the next morning.

The ghost abated, although the snows did not. Over their three weeks of writing, Barlow had to keep about eight hundred cows fed, hitching up four huge Belgian horses to a sled containing ten tons of hay. They set to work on the songs with what Barlow thought was a random approach but the zeal of newcomers. "I wrote a lot of words," said Weir. "He wrote a lot of words and I wrote a lot of melody," rejoined Barlow. "Oftentimes it was like the lost-wax treatment. You can't write lyrics without a melody. And since what he would give me was a rhythm guitar part, then I had to come up with some kind of melody. And sometimes that stayed and sometimes that didn't." Weir: "It almost never stayed because melodies never stay." Barlow: "In Grateful Dead songs they're a moving target." They began with "Black-Throated Wind," for which Barlow had actually written a line—"Ah mother American night I'm lost in the light, I'm drowning in you"—in Nepal two years before. Weir took the rhythm from New Orleans songwriter Allen Toussaint, and by the time he left the Bar Cross, he had two verses and the chorus, which seemed enough. When he got home he became entirely stuck, until Alan Trist took him home and told him he couldn't leave until the song was done.

One of the decorations at the cabin was a Wyeth engraving of an Indian on a horse with his hands out. Well lubricated on Wild Turkey one night, Weir looked at it and said to Barlow, "You know what he's saying, don't you?" "What?" "Looks like rain." When it finally came together, "Cassidy" came together perfectly. Having rejected Hunter's "Blood Red Diamonds," Weir also rejected Barlow's first take, written the previous fall. Barlow had been in a dark mood, born of, among other things, the war in Vietnam, and an experience he'd had in a café in Rawlins, Wyoming, where as a longhair he'd asked for lamb chops and been served a skinned lamb's head, eyes intact, in a pool of blood. His first version of "Cassidy" included lines like "ten pound rat in a trashcan, nuclear war neanderthal man." "I thought it was a little heavy-handed for the melody," observed Weir. At the Bar Cross, Barlow connected the now toddling Cassidy with Neal Cassady and produced a gem.

Weir returned to San Francisco and began recording at Heider's, at first with Kreutzmann and Dave Torbert of the New Riders. Then Rock Scully showed up, and suavely convinced him that the simple solution for his musical needs and the Dead's relationship with Warner Bros. was to let the Dead back him on his solo album. Since Phil and Jerry were working with Crosby in the room next door at Heider's, it really was simple. And the truth was that Weir had no time. He had only two and a half weeks to record and mix the album, and, recalled Barlow, "many of the songs had not yet been written. A certain amount of very limited studio time had been bought and not all the songs had been written and those that had been were so incomplete that, for example, I mean there was one song, I can't remember which one it was, where I'd written twice as much in the way of lyrics than there should have been, and they just slashed half the lyrics, on the spot. I mean, they were just gone. And I remember Garcia saying, 'Hey listen, we're in a hurry here.'" It was Weir's first session as boss, and it worked remarkably well, considering the radical change in roles. As the songwriter, etiquette demanded that everyone defer to him, and they did. But as Barlow pointed out, it was also "one of those moments where Garcia was really at his best. He was being a paterfamilias, he was being the Dutch uncle, he was being the guy who understood how it all went down really and he really was being wonderful. He was being incredibly facilitative . . . he understood something important, which was that if it was just gonna be him and Hunter, it was going to be a monoculture. As juvenile or puerile or whatever that I could be, the whole deal was going to be a lot more interesting if we were part of the mix."

By late in February they had one song left to write, but John had a big problem. "I had to leave because my father had died and I had one song to write, which ended up being 'Walk in the Sunshine,' probably the worst song we ever wrote. Frankie Weir kept me up all night making me take drugs and just write anything, so I came up with 'Walk in the Sunshine.'" Convinced that Weir would never accept it, Barlow decided that the only way he could get out of town was to write an even worse song, and he did so. Having just read Pär Lagerkvist's *The Dwarf*, he began, "I'm just a small man / I'm not a tall man." Sometimes, just finishing is a triumph.

Late in March the Dead set out on tour again, beginning in New York with seven shows at the Academy of Music. The week before they arrived, Francis Coppola's masterpiece *The Godfather* had opened in New York City in the middle of a blizzard, and Garcia and most of the band would see it repeatedly. In six months, it would be the biggest-grossing film of its time. The Dead would get to know Coppola, their fellow San Franciscan, better in the future. One of their nights at the Academy was a benefit for the Hell's Angels of New York, in which they backed up Bo Diddley and watched besotted Hell's Angels, as M.G. put it, stack up in the doorway like "rhinos."

When the Dead were done in New York, they boarded a plane and headed east for their first tour of Europe.

36

Interlude:
The Home Front:
Money and Management

(1980s AND BEYOND)

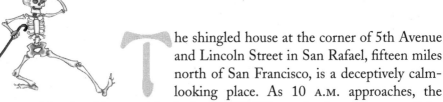he shingled house at the corner of 5th Avenue and Lincoln Street in San Rafael, fifteen miles north of San Francisco, is a deceptively calm-looking place. As 10 A.M. approaches, the parking lot fills up with the band's BMWs or the Japanese cars of the women who staff the office. The crew members drive American cars, but don't usually stray from the studio, a mile away in an industrial neighborhood. A sign tacked up on the side of the individual mail slots asks, "Do you want to talk to the man in charge, or the woman who knows what's going on?" 'Twas ever thus. The Dead are sexist, but they trust women to guard their money, and that is the primary function of 5th and Lincoln. Except for the occasional meeting, the band generally gathers at the studio. Phil comes in daily for his mail, but only Garcia spends any time in the office, although less and less as the years go by. He sits at the kitchen table sipping coffee and bullshitting with studio engineer John Cutler or whoever walks by. Those with business to transact line up and hand him things—contracts to sign, mail or music or videotapes to consider. Most of it he forgets and leaves behind on the kitchen table when he departs. Fifth and Lincoln has a pleasant atmosphere, not because of the

decorations—aside from the originals of the *Workingman's Dead* back cover portraits and a wonderful cartoon of Goofy with a dose in his hand, there aren't any—but because of the women who work there, Eileen Law and Janet Soto in particular.

Janet is a bookkeeper and has worked for the Dead off and on since 1969, when she began at the Shady Management office on Union Street. A beautiful Mexican Native American Italian, she was raised in a large family in the town of Cambria, south of Big Sur next to Hearst Castle, before attending S.F. State and falling into the Dead's scene. She jokes that she and Eileen must have been sisters in a previous lifetime, and though Janet can be gruff, her relationship with Eileen is sweet, and sets a tone for the whole office. Eileen runs the Dead Head mailing list—she is the spiritual mother of all Dead Heads, their most direct link to the band—opens the mail, deals with the guest list at home shows, does fifty other things, and generally occupies the same essential moral position as Ram Rod does on the crew. She is a genuinely lovely human being. She grew up on the Russian River in a town called Guerneville, worked at an insurance company in San Francisco after graduating from high school in 1964, and first came around 710 Ashbury Street with her friend Vee. After living with a sometime Dead crew member named Slade at the Digger commune in Olema, she moved to Mickey's ranch in Novato, one of many people who lived there in every available space. "It took seniority to get a room," she said. Eventually, she lived at Rukka Rukka ranch in Marin with Weir and others, where she gave birth to her daughter Cassidy, who is also part of the 5th and Lincoln staff. In 1972 Eileen came by the office to help work on the Dead Head mailing list, and except during the mid-seventies hiatus in touring, she's been at it ever since.

Janet's in the right-front ground-floor office. Eileen and Cassidy are at the top of the stairs. Bonnie Parker, the senior number cruncher, is next to Janet. In 1986 Bonnie was succeeded by Nancy Mallonee, a CPA who is the first office employee with formal credentials. Scrib comes in once or twice a week and works in the "interview room" off the kitchen. Between the kitchen and Nancy's and Janet's offices are a couple of rooms occupied at various times by Annette Flowers, who worked with the Dead's music publishing business, Ice Nine, and Basia Raizene (ex-wife of crew member Sparky), Suzanne Gottlieb, and Mary Jo Meinolf, all of whom deal with money and numbers.

Past Eileen's second-floor office is a middle room where Alan Trist runs Ice Nine—the name was taken from Kurt Vonnegut's *Cat's Cradle*—and then comes the last room, where the headaches are. It's the large room where first Richard Loren, then Danny Rifkin, then Jon McIntire, and eventually Cameron Sears worked as manager. Actually, the band manages itself. Except for Loren, who received a percentage as a booking agent, these men were salaried employees rather than managers, who receive a percentage. The truth is, the band is quite unmanageable. Once in the 1990s there was a calm, sober band meeting in which everyone agreed that the band should never travel on gig days, because staying that extra night, say, in New York, and then flying down to Atlanta or Carolina on the morning of the show inevitably resulted in a bad show. On the very next tour, this rule was violated twice.

Consider the beginning of Cameron Sears's career. In 1987, Jon McIntire was manager and decided that he needed an assistant. Jon had met Cameron, an environmental lobbyist and white-water rafting river guide, in the course of some river outings Cameron had put together for office staff, and concluded that anyone who could shepherd people down a river could do the same for a band. Jon got the band's approval for the hire just before a jaunt to Ventura, where Jon fell sick. Cameron met the various band members for the first time when he gave them the half-hour time call onstage. This worked until he got to Kreutzmann, whose nicest comment was "Don't talk to me." When Brent Mydland trashed his room after the show, Sears had more work to do. It is one of the twists of the Dead's karma that Sears went on to have a fruitful career with the band, despite, as he put it, a management situation in which "there are always twenty burners going, they're all boiling over, and no one wants to turn any of them down."

Willy Legate once meditated on the business aspects of the Dead: "Having been born into a world of rather curious values, values apparently unrelated to the direct experience of human truths, [the Dead] pursue a direction of self-determination in as many ways as interestingly possible, believing that this course will best aid a continuation of integrity and meaning in their music and other life spaces. This has meant that their business activity seeks to be in control of as many areas as become possible, employing their own people to do the work that would otherwise be farmed out to straight business. Thus there is the possibility that the message in the music can be reflected in the manner and purpose of conducting the business necessary to get the music heard."

In a sour moment, Rock Scully reviewed his career and composed "Rock Scully's Ground Rules for Conducting Bad Business, Progressive Rock Category." Some of the rules included "1. Make no move to copyright or otherwise own your band's name . . . 3. Do not include your name in any contracts with the record co. . . . 7. Whenever poss. get record co. to pay your salary (and for your sec. too). 8. Never take any % of any gig monies . . . 10. Always allow the band unltd. spending of co. monies for equipt., engineers, research and development, deployment of expensive gear to bands homes and to equipt. men's living rms." His plaint concluded that when the money vanished, the poor manager would take the blame, and a band member, usually a drummer, "will want to know what it is you do for them anyway?"

What Rock called bad business was really just the band managing itself, paying a salary to the "manager." By the 1980s Rock was a "manager" who wore sunglasses to the breakfast table. Setting up an interview with him involved, wrote one reporter, "almost-daily telephone calls that went like this: / Hi Rock / Hi, how ya doing? / Fine. Can we get together today? / Sure, call me in an hour at the office. Bye. / Two hours later he wouldn't have made it to the office yet. Three hours later: / Hi Rock / Hi, how ya doing? / Fine, can we get together? / Hey, yeah, we'll get it together. Check in with me tonight. / And so on for weeks at a time." In sharp contrast is the more mainstream attitude of the manager of Styx, a highly successful, utterly faceless band that had hugely effective advertising and promotion. He saw himself "not merely as the manager of a rock band, but as executive vice president of a large-volume retail operation."

In the long run, Danny Rifkin's moral authority had a longer influence on the Dead than Rock's rakish inspiration, but the man who would best define the band's management in terms of quality and understanding of the band's mission was Jon McIntire. Clive Davis, with whom Jon dealt as the New Riders manager in the early seventies, and then with the Dead in the eighties, found him "very organized, very professional, copious notes, focused." Lyricist John Barlow said of McIntire that he "recognized that it took a gentleman to manage barbarism." Jon represented the pursuit of excellence as against the piratical quest for size, glamour, and cash advocated by his rival, the road manager, Sam Cutler. Sam was a gloriously good pirate, who was convinced that the Dead would succeed, as Barlow put it, once it put away "sentiment." Though different, Jon's ego was not terribly smaller than Sam's; as promoter Dave Williams once put it, Jon could be difficult because "he had an ego like he was one of the artists." When security would not permit him to enter the front door of a show without a ticket, he grew so angry that the building manager finally asked what it would take to fix the situation. "Pheasant under glass and a good bottle of wine" was the answer, and they served him.

The hidden ace of Grateful Dead management was a man few

outside the business had ever heard of, the band's attorney from 1971 on, Hal Kant. A world champion poker player—he won with $1 million on the table for the last hand—a collector of Joseph Conrad first editions, a Ring Cycle enthusiast, a painter, and a former clinical psychologist, Kant was a complex, gifted, and highly civilized man who was a fundamental stabilizing force within the band because, as he put it, his ultimate role with the band was that of ombudsman. Because he saw his work for the Dead as something of a lark, a hobby that he didn't worry about terribly much, he supplied a detachment that worked very well. In contrast, wrote record industry critic Frederic Dannen, "There is scarcely one music lawyer of prominence who does not also do legal work for the label, often on retainer. Conflicts of interest that would scandalize most businesses are commonplace in the music field." The Dead were Kant's only music business clients.

He was born in Queens in 1931 and raised in the Bronx, and after two years at CCNY, he got as far from New York as possible—"I'd heard of America, but I'd never seen it"—by finishing college at the University of Washington. Afterward he got a master's degree in psychology from Penn State, which doubtless stood him in good stead in dealing with the Dead, and after serving time in the army, decided to get his career going by attending law school. After graduating from Harvard, he joined a small Beverly Hills law firm that happened to be next door to the William Morris Agency, and eventually began to add entertainment clients to his list. One day late in the 1960s, a "charming psychopath" friend of his from graduate school brought to Hal's home another charming rogue, Chesley Millikin. Chesley was quite taken by Hal, and was a close friend of Rock Scully's, so when the band sought an attorney in 1971, Hal's name came up. "Jon [McIntire] asked me," Kant said, "not to represent any other band if I represented them. Since I was doing TV and film and corporate work at the time and not representing other bands, music didn't matter to me," so it was easy to agree to McIntire's request. He settled into his relationship with the Dead.

In 1975, Kant decided to give up his law practice and write, having already been one of the authors of the report produced by the U.S. Commission on Pornography and Obscenity, but he decided to keep the Dead as clients, because "they were entertaining." Having no career aspirations for himself, "it was easy to help the Dead not have theirs." He had established a number of precedents that would be important in the long run. He charged a rate commensurate with top-class lawyers, but never took a percentage, and in fact, "I kept them from paying anybody percentages the whole time," whether it was the conventional 5 percent to the attorney, 10 percent to the agent, 15 to 25 percent to the manager, or 3 percent to the accountant. Kant didn't even get a serious retainer until the 1980s. First he got the band to reorganize as a corporation, which would help over the years, and then he tried to get his clients what they wanted. He generally succeeded.

He saw the often-rowdy band meetings as effective democracy. "The insanity of those meetings had a certain beneficial effect, because you heard every point of view . . . Once [Jerry] made up his mind, that pretty well decided it—so you did get a decision . . . I don't remember a vote—if they can't turn around a dissenter, they don't do it—and therefore, when they do do something, they have everybody behind it. It means they don't do anything reluctantly . . . One of the lucky things for the band was they had me for their lawyer because I didn't live in San Francisco, I didn't hang out with them, they were not an important client to me financially, so I could be very independent . . . I didn't know I was supposed to be intimidated by Garcia, I didn't know the mythology around him, or anything."

The Dead's last contract with Arista, in 1988, earned them a higher royalty rate than Madonna or Michael Jackson, but Hal was proudest of its brevity: it came in at under five pages. But that wasn't what made him important to the Dead. They actually listened to him, even when they wouldn't listen to each other or anybody else. Even Garcia, who could imitate stone walls in his ability not to listen, usually responded to Kant. Early in the 1990s Ben & Jerry's ice cream produced a new flavor, Cherry Garcia. Despite a well-deserved reputation for ethical behavior, they did so without even discussing the idea with Garcia, then went so far as to approach the Dead's publicist to discuss promotion. Scrib went bananas, berating a marketing person who, of course, had no notion of what he was talking about. "You're stealing the man's name," he raved. When asked about it, Garcia replied, "At least they're not naming a motor oil after me, man," and refused to lift a finger. "Besides, it's good ice cream." Garcia's personal manager, Steve Parish, was equally unconcerned. "If Jerry doesn't care, I don't care." Finally, Scrib thought to call Kant, who told Garcia, "They *will* name a motor oil after you if you don't confront this, Jerry. You'll have no control over your name at all." Finally, Garcia shrugged, "If it bothers you, go ahead." In the next few years, Jerry would have no problems in spending the large sum of money he'd earn thanks to the letter Kant wrote. Sometimes it's smart to listen to your attorney.

Bozos Abroad

(3/72–12/72)

The Dead would return from their first tour of Europe with the tapes of what would be their third live album, and in designing the cover, Kelley and Mouse at first suggested calling it *Over There*, using a military patch with a lightning bolt. When that didn't fly, they came up with a takeoff on *National Geographic*, wrapping the familiar yellow border around a picture of the band debarking from an airplane. The staid publication's lawyers proved underwhelmed by the idea, so Kelley went to Plan C. The final back cover was the "Rainbow Foot," a logo he'd already done for the Dead's and Sam Cutler's new booking agency, Out of Town Tours, which showed a hippie's colorfully clad foot stepping across the ocean. For the front cover, he thought of a story he'd once told at a party, in which a spastic child wins the prize, an ice cream cone, and proudly brings it to the middle of his forehead. Since Kelley was in approximately that condition at the time of the telling, it seemed screamingly funny. And since the band members thought of themselves as precisely that sort of doofus half the time anyway, especially when encountering Europe, the parent of our crude American civilization, the "Ice Cream Kid" became their cover.

The band's two previous forays to Europe had been so brief as to barely count; this was the real deal. Early in 1971, *Billboard* had reported a fantasy Alan Trist had conjured up in the wake of the great train ride, in which the Dead and family would travel England and Holland on barges, using one as the stage. In 1972, Sam Cutler used a more conventional approach to organize a two-month tour. Once the basics were set, he tackled the final and thorniest question at one of the usual giant family meetings: who gets to go? After the usual emotional storm of personal needs and desires versus business capability, Garcia said the only thing possible: "Fuck it. Everybody goes." The family cheered. Europe, here we come. As Rock later put it, "Look out, Ye Ancient Fingernails, the barbarians are coming. Open the gates! Saracens with 5,000-watt amps will soon be storming the Bastille. Not that the Dead are *just* another band of uncouth rowdies, motel-demolishing loons, or shark-copulating deviates on the road (boorish *Schweineri* like Grand Funk or satanic deviates like Led Zeppelin). Our crusade is basically, uh . . . molecular!"

On April 1, the Day of Fools, forty-nine people, among them seven musicians, ten crew, five staff, seventeen assorted friends, wives, girl-friends, and children—Garcia, Weir, Kreutzmann, and the Godchaux had partners, Lesh and Pigpen were single—flew to London, landing on April 2, Easter Sunday. They brought themselves and fifteen tons of instruments, a sound system, and a sixteen-track recording system which they would install in a truck as a mobile studio. There was also lighting gear and their first traveling lighting designer, a woman named Candace Brightman whom they'd met at the Capitol in Port Chester. She'd gone to work a show in Buffalo because she wanted to see John McLaughlin's Mahavishnu Orchestra, and the opening act was Jerry Garcia and Howard Wales. Impressed with her work, Garcia asked her to join them for the tour of Europe. He also hinted, "Y'know, a lot of people work for us for free." Candace drawled, *"That's* interesting." The Dead's 1972 extravaganza in Europe was—but of course!—not your average tour, and was really as much vacation as work. What would be astonishing was that the Dead would maintain a phenomenally high level of performance quality while doing only twenty-two gigs in two months.

They were scheduled to open at the Rainbow Theater in London with the New Riders, who were also in Europe although traveling separately, when, shortly before the Dead left San Francisco, the Rainbow went bankrupt. They tried to book another theater, but it didn't work out, and with ten days to go to the first show, Rock flew ahead to London to evaluate a venue called the Wembley Empire Pool, where a badminton match was in progress. Despite the last-second argle-bargle, they pulled off the Wembley gig and pretty much all the rest of the tour. Though they didn't always sell out, they did reasonably well, and there were no economic disasters. Wembley was a hard place to start, though. The building was godawful cold, and London has a species of bureaucrat that at times made even their Parisian brethren look generous. Preparing the "carnet," a list of every item of equipment that was required for them to pass through the customs of a then distinctly ununified Europe, was less than fun.

The body heat from the audience helped, and their first show was tolerable; the second was superb. The local press noted the emergence of Weir as a co–front man and the decline of Pigpen's presence. Though Pig had rejoined the band, it was probably a bad decision, medically speaking. He was still frail, and the long, inspired raves of the sixties were pretty much gone. Before the tour, he'd come to 5th and Lincoln and helped the staff staple the tour itineraries, and in Europe he frequently baby-sat Ram Rod and Frances's son, Rudson. Jim Furman, an Alembic technical assistant, had breakfast with Pigpen several times, since few others made it up that early, and was pleased he did. Furman found him much more intelligent than his image. He had quit drinking, and now "my only vices are smoking cigarettes and pestering the wenches."

Another new member of the tour was Dennis Leonard, an Alembic employee more commonly called Wizard. In the fall of 1971 Wizard had walked into Alembic, and though he had only a minimal background in electronics, he soon became so proficient that Alembic found it easy to send him out to assist with recording. Bob Matthews would mix the house sound, Betty Cantor would make an initial rough two-track mix in the truck from the sixteen tracks they were recording and make sure it sounded okay, Furman would fix things, and Wizard would watch the recording console for red lights. They had a black-and-white TV monitor that displayed the stage, which made them pretty advanced, but at least one of their pieces of equipment was quite useless. In front of Garcia's monitor were three lights that went green-yellow-red to warn him of an impending tape reel change, when he would presumably stop playing. In twenty-two shows he never paid the slightest attention to it.

The tour's first days in London involved a great deal of talking with the press, and much of it was tedious. Stereotypes don't improve when they cross the ocean, and as a foreigner, Garcia didn't feel that he could goof on the press with quite the ease he could manage at home. The one relief in the ink-stained sea was a French hippie who asked him to draw a picture of an elephant in his book, "the neatest thing anybody ever asked me to do." Otherwise, he kept it straight. Discussing the band's material,

Garcia told one reporter, "There's a sort of peak optimum, and right now we're at one of those peaks. We've got a lot of brand new material . . . that we've never recorded, in fact that's why we're recording these tours." He discussed the Dead method of playing: "We remember how to play, each time, by starting with simple things, moving into more complex things, and then finally after having built a kind of platform, then we sort of jump off it . . . a kind of continuity—from off the street to outer space, so to speak." And back again? asked the reporter. "Sometimes, but then sometimes we just hang out there."

And he discoursed on the notion of having their own record company, already the subject of much talk. It wasn't "going to be a record company in the standard sense in that it's not going to be designed for profit, it's going to be designed to sell our records in a way compatible with the way we run our scene." "It would be like families here and there, who would be like distributing our records, selling them . . . they might be sold [only] in health food stores and head shops . . . We're looking to totally break away from that thing, we're not interested in competing with the rest of the record world, we're not interested in playing that game at all."

In London they stayed at the Kensington Hotel, which, said Alan Trist, "held their madness in its middle-class velvet glove," and the reporters who descended on them had to cope with the cross-fire raps of band members, managers, equipment crew ("quippies"), and whoever else was around. There was time for manifold pleasant pursuits aside from music, including softball and baseball in Kensington Gardens, a stoned afternoon in the country gardens of a stately house in Kent, or even more esoteric inquiries. Alan Trist had begun one line of interest by reading and sharing a book by Francis Yates called *The Art of Memory*, which described using visualization of medieval buildings as a mnemonic aid. This had led to RILKO (Research into Lost Knowledge Organization), which Alan and Phil had joined. RILKO led to Robert Fludd, a fifteenth-century alchemist, and Fludd to Fulcanelli, his intellectual heir in the twentieth century and author of *Mystery of the Cathedrals*. But their main teacher was Jean Michel, also known as John Michell, who was the contemporary father of geomancy, the study of ley lines, lines of magnetism and power on earth. Ley lines form a grid on the earth that connects megalithic power spots like the ancient stone circles. It was upon these sites that old English churches were frequently built, which was how early Christianity co-opted the ancient Druidic/goddess religion. There was a store connected to one of Michell's major sources in Soho, and Alan, Phil, and Jerry went there after visiting him. Their next step was to rent a car and go to the most important of all English power spots, Stonehenge, and the surrounding Salisbury Plain, the legendary home of Avalon, the burial place of King Arthur. Stonehenge overwhelmed Lesh, and instilled in him a lifelong intellectual curiosity about geomancy. It "clarified my whole idea of trying to put our music into a place, how it would change. How it could be different. And the whole concept of places of power . . . so much consciousness poured into it, that it still vibrates."

The tour truly began when they left London. Two buses pulled up to the Kensington Hotel, driven by a Brit named Mick and Sven, a Swede. Sven smoked a pipe, was bald and very stolid and quiet, and spoke almost no English, but somehow he and Mick managed to get on delightfully. They had radios, and flashing quartz beacons on top of the buses to find each other, and their expertise made the journey work. On April 10, the tour left London for the next gig, at a venue called City Hall in Newcastle, and something funny, philosophical, creative, and Grateful Dead happened. Their buses were open to the world outside, and as they went along, people in the street would see longhairs inside and point. Naturally, the Dead's response, said Trist, was to give them "a real freak show, a circus, with clowns." Anticipating just such an eventuality, roadies Steve Parish and Sparky Raizene had gone to the joke shop on 42nd Street in New York before leaving for Europe and purchased an enormous bag full of masks—Bozo masks and fright wigs, an old man, a Martian, a dog's head. That was step one. Step two: Their traveling party consisted of two buses and a considerable number of intermittently bored people. By and large, bus one had the band, and bus two the crew—except that Steve and Kidd came over to bus one, where, M.G. recalled, they "made it a point to sit directly behind me and Jer for the rest of the tour. Those guys tortured me to death. Kidd would say this horrible stuff in my ear . . . how this one had cut his throat . . . the two of them would just get off on this hysterical kid stuff, very funny at the same time."

As the buses pushed north into Britain, Hunter ruminated on the Bozo masks, and on the Firesign Theater's classic comedy album title, *I Think We're All Bozos on This Bus.* And in the long quiet spaces of small English roads he gave birth to "hypnocracy," the classic Grateful Dead joke. Willy Legate would describe it later: ". . . buses which came to be known as the Bolo Bus and the Bozo Bus. The Bolo Bus had a john in it and its seats faced forward. The Bozo had a refrigerator and some of its seats were installed facing back, to accommodate four tables. And to look back. The subtle difference in character and import and atmosphere between the two omnibuses was so profoundly hidden and enigmatic that you could never possibly understand it. The Bozos wore masks, and the Bolos showed their faces . . . One St. Dilbert defected from the Bozos and lived for a season with the Bolos . . . it came to be said that he was a true hypnocratic missionary to Bololand. And to look back, it appears evident that Bozo and Bolo knew themselves each the other's raison d'être."

In fact, the Bozo bus was generally occupied by band members and was the more active bus, with people raving in conversation, while the Bolo bus was largely crew, plus Phil and those who were more inclined to nap. Hypnocracy was a Bozo enterprise, "the hoi polloi," sniffed Kidd. It was essentially a language joke, "surrealism as metaphor." It began with the word "technocracy," which entered their lives because one of the odder people in Garcia's acquaintance had been a member of this political fringe group from the 1930s, moved through philosophy, and ended up in humor. "In the sea of hypnocracy the shore is just another wave." Like technocracy, hypnocracy was, Trist explained, "a utopian philosophy that almost could have been," but didn't quite complete itself, and died when the tour ended and the buses went back to their garage.

"Is hypnocracy not the aspiration to know what it is?" asked Willy Legate. Yet, wrote Charles Perry of *Rolling Stone,* who investigated hypnocracy in depth, "it's considered bad form to ask. 'It's for me to know and you to find out,' said Garcia. 'I used to know,' said Frankie Weir, adding that it depended on whether you asked a Bolo or a Bozo. When asked the meaning of Hypnocracy, St. Dilbert replied, 'Is not Hypnocracy no other than the aspiration to discover the meaning of Hypnocracy? Say, have you heard the one about the yellow dog yet?' " "Perhaps—one must be tentative when speculating about deep matters," wrote Perry, "it has something to do with the Acid Test legacy of psychedelic faith, the sense that the unexpected and inexplicable are truth on the hoof and when it comes down to it all you can do is run along. And philosophic meditation on the doofo may be inevitable when you're in a scene that runs on the karass principle rather than on some narrow-minded program of eliminating fuck ups."

Armed with a philosophy, they pushed on. Copenhagen—a gig at the Tivoli and then a ferry to a castle in Sweden. Aarhus University in Denmark, where the show was in a low-ceilinged cafeteria, people hanging off wooden trusses all over the place. Back to Copenhagen to play a one-hour television show, *TV from the Tivoli,* which was surprisingly good. The fact that everyone in the audience was openly smoking hashish might have added to the grace of the gig. In Amsterdam, however, they also had an encounter with authority. Dan Healy, who was possessed of a mercurial nature and a volcanic temper, got into an altercation with a conductor on the train, and the entourage went into action, shielding him from arrest. "We were the underground," said Wizard, "saving someone from the Gestapo." The police came, three stolid Dutchmen who seemed to the family members like something out of *The Third Man*. It was almost disappointing when an interpreter arrived and everything was smoothed over.

And so to Germany, through a border, where "clouds of hash would go up as everybody scarfed down what they had on them before the check," recalled Dave Parker. "We'd pull up, windows wide open, we had Ozium air fresheners for a while till we ran out, customs guys would hardly get on the bus, or just walk in and out—we were too weird for them." Germany would always be problematic for the Dead. As M.G. put it, "Germans really hated us. Course it was the baseball in the hotel lobby . . . Kidd and Ram Rod and Johnny [Hagen] and Parish were on big baseball kicks . . . Sonny Heard was priceless with the ball and bat . . . practice swings in the lobby, samurai stuff, like Toshiro Mifune walking out and slicing flies in the lobby when his room service was late, not saying a word, just a few swings of the bat. The point got across that they really loathed us. Ice cream kid. Such Americans. We were bad. We were ugly, too." For some reason, Kreutzmann always reacted badly to Germany, and an incident involving smashed antiques required Cutler's financial attention.

Bremen, Dusseldorf, Frankfurt. Every morning they would get their road money from Sam Cutler. Jim Furman would testify in amazement that this arrangement covered even his wife, Mary, who was along as his guest—the Furmans only had to pay for her plane ticket. A Phi Beta Kappa graduate student in oriental art history, she did not exactly fit in with the crew's sense of humor, especially because she was fluent in French and German and was not afraid of the surroundings. The tour as a whole was "something like an invasion," Furman thought, "because there were so many of us, we could just take over a hotel or a restaurant. Most of the people had never been to Europe before, and it was also the longest Dead tour ever, so a group consciousness developed that tended to exclude the surroundings . . . We were the All-American Kid in Europe, in a sense a little spastic about relating to people." Instead of being touched by European culture, they all too often became a "self-contained bubble," mused Wizard, and "turned it into our trip." Which was not to say that Donna Jean would not recall for the rest of her life the "heavenly" bus ride looking up at Mad King Ludwig's castle on the Rhine.

The Nazis had built Frankfurt's Jahrhundert Halle entirely of plastic, though it looked like wood and velvet and sounded good. There were the usual clashes—Wizard went up on the roof to take pictures, and "some Nazi bastard wanted me dealt with by the authorities because I was in the wrong place . . . we put him in his place." Hamburg was *really* Germany, on two counts. Wizard went to find the local crew to get the snake (main power cable) in, and in the basement of the Musikhalle discovered that someone in the local crew had been in the Luftwaffe, with the battle flags, photographs, and crossed swords to prove it. "Wow," he thought to himself. "These guys would have thrown me right in the oven, Dennis Leonard from the Bronx." But when he asked them for help, "they were totally cool."

The day before the gig, Lesh had a somewhat different experience. He'd gone down to the hall to check it out, looking at busts of famous composers in the foyer, and a symphony orchestra was rehearsing. Someone with him said, "You've got to see this, man." From the balcony, they looked down on the orchestra, which was rehearsing an excerpt from *Carmen*. "See anything unusual down there?" "No." "Look at the solo cellist." And Lesh realized, "The solo cellist is my double. He has my same hair, he has my build, my eyes, my movements. He looks like a clone of me. I went and looked for him, couldn't—I'm in Pendleton, jeans, all but the hat—and they're all looking at me like I'm . . . it turns out that in every German city there's fifty Leshes in the phone book."

A month on the road, a month to go, and on May Day they ended a long bus ride in Paris, at the Grand Hotel. M.G. was delighted. "Our room looked out on the gilded angels, with their big trumpets, that graced the top of this place. We had this little balcony, you open the thing and there is this beautiful gilt angel." The Paris Opera House, home of the Phantom, was visible half a block down the street. The next night Warner Bros. sponsored a dinner at La Grande Cascade in the Bois de Boulogne, and after three hours of food, wine, champagne, liqueurs, and a little hashish, it was the waiters who ended up with the happiest, stonedest grins. "Here ya are, *mon-sore*, do yer head some good."

Their visit came only four years after Paris's youth-led near-revolution, and clumps of machine-gun-toting *flics* still covered the Left Bank in those days, including the area around their gigs. Walking through lines of police, thought Kreutzmann, "was the coldest feeling ever," although the 180 cops on the first night shrank to 30 on the second. Keith and Donna were not handling the tour all that well, either, having been "thrown into this huge, monumental, exorbitant scene, you know, and I think that we were both a little freaked-out," said Donna. "I stayed in my room. In Paris, stoned on acid, I found myself lying under the piano, digging the Grateful Dead—and then realized, 'Oh, no. I sing with this band! How am I possibly going to be able to get it together to do that?' " Ice cream kid or no, she managed.

It was during their second and last night in Paris that the most hilarious adventure of the tour began. A young Frenchman approached the band at the theater and began arguing about their lack of political consciousness. To Kreutzmann, it seemed "obvious he wanted free tickets." They put him off, and he moved his harangue to Cutler and Rex Jackson, getting no satisfaction. When everyone returned to the hotel, he took up a position in front, bracing every member of the tour party as they came in or out. He was wearing a velvet jacket, which caught their eye, and when they eventually concluded he'd become a bore, Rex dumped ice cream on the jacket he was so proud of, and the Dead all had a good laugh and went to bed. While they slept, Monsieur la Politique had his revenge, introducing a foreign substance into the equipment truck's gas tank.

The next day they were scheduled to play Lille, a very political college town. The buses and one truck arrived, their equipment truck did not. No amps, no show. The promoter was not able to offer instant refunds—according to some memories, he was unable to offer refunds at all. Sensing trouble, the streetwise Garcia decided that honor did not require going to the hall, and along with Kreutzmann, elected to stay at the hotel. "You guys are nuts" was his analysis. Phil and Bobby went out on the stage and talked to the audience, but *"Pas de musique"* was about the best they could muster, even after Weir's five years of high school French. "It quickly became my job to explain to a crowd of irate Frenchmen just exactly this— no show tonight, sorry about that. I got three or four sentences off before the crowd became very surly."

Ushered offstage into the dressing room, Lesh, Weir, Rosie, and a few others suddenly realized they were in deep shit. The audience was furious, convinced of American perfidy, and though no one was thinking in terms of death, Weir thought "they woulda thumped us good and proper." The door to the dressing room had a window, and they covered it with newspapers and considered their options. Other than being thumped, there was only one: climb down the drainpipe to the top of the truck, jump down on the hood, then to the ground, and run run run for the bus, which was waiting with the engine idling. The furious Frenchmen began to pound on the door, and as the hinges started to creak, Dead family members began going out the window. A gentleman to the end, Weir's main worry, as he thought about it later, was getting the interpreter, Rosie McGee, and photographer, Mary Ann Mayer, down the drainpipe. That accomplished, he turned to the promoter, promised they'd make up the show, dropped a rose on the sill, and scooted down the pipe like the part monkey he was. He was on the roof of the truck when he heard the door give way, and he hit the ground running for "what physicists called the absolute elsewhere, in a big hurry." A couple of hours later, after wrapping themselves around some good Bordeaux, it was all pretty funny, but it had been a near thing.

The time it took to replace the damaged truck complicated travel to the *next* gig, the Bickershaw Festival, near Manchester, which they absolutely could not afford to miss, since it was one of their largest paydays on the entire tour. The truckers changed trucks and hauled ass for Manchester, driving like demented bats to make the last possible ferry. Winslow and Wizard were in the recording truck, behind a professional driver who had the main equipment truck. Time was flying, and so was the front truck driver, who began to take insane chances to beat the clock, running cars off the road in the process. They made the ferry, got through London, and then went really nuts, scraping off the side of at least one car before arriving in Manchester with aplomb.

Not surprisingly, in the wake of the Lille debacle no one felt like separating, and the band and family bused back to Paris and then flew to Manchester and the cold gray ooze of northern England. This was no Woodstock-warm shower puddle. This was nasty, primordial stuff that felt as though bones were going to rise to the surface, with a horrific wind to boot. It was sufficiently frigid that the crew put a space heater on the stage to keep the band's fingers from turning blue. Once again the Dead worked magic. They came on around 7 P.M., and the skies lightened, then cleared. First "Truckin'," then "Mr. Charlie," got the audience up. The crowd had built bonfires around the perimeter of the field to keep warm, but now they piled on the fuel and Bickershaw became a pagan festival, dancers circling the flames, and, in the words of a local writer, the "Dead had offered safe passage through weird terrain."

Amsterdam, where the Concertgebouw was a jewel of a theater, the cocaine was far too good—Rock and Jerry were particularly self-indulgent, and the spouses were not pleased—and the draft Heineken tasted fabulous. Having visited Amsterdam before with the Medicine Ball Caravan, Kidd Candelario knew the ropes, and took Lesh to a pub, where Phil discovered the difference between mere beer and draft Heineken. Lesh had never been a big drinker before, but the combination of cocaine and Heineken would become a big favorite of his, leading to what he would later call "the Heineken years."

Rotterdam, and then back through Belgium to France, with a middle-of-the-night delay. The customs inspectors were in bed and wouldn't get up to let the truck in, and Pig, who'd ridden the truck thinking he'd get some extra snooze time—"Ol' sly Pig, you know," chortled Kreutzmann, " 'Figure I'm gonna get me some extra z's,' you know?"—spent the night in the cab. Winslow, too, was totally wiped out with pneumonia, but he insisted on doing his job, upholding the crew tradition.

Once in France, they returned to Lille to keep their word to the promoter and the students. Stunned by their honesty, the promoter was in tears as they set up in the town's fairgrounds, which was a little park, "an old fort, with gun emplacements and every age of stonework and masonry," said M.G. There they played for workers eating their sausages and baguettes, mothers with children in prams, and some of the students. It was a cold day, and threatened to rain, and at one point it did rain, so they took cover for a while. It stopped, the sun came out, they returned to the stage, and Lille looked like an impressionist painting, cows in the distance, poplar trees in rows; with a little LSD, it wasn't hard to see why Monet and company liked the light in their native country. For Phil especially, it was one of the truly spectacular experiences of a lifetime, as though for an hour or two he lived inside a Seurat or a Cézanne. They finished as the sun was setting and the rain was starting up again, and Cutler drove up in a car and handed the keys to Kreutzmann and Lesh and said, "Hey, you guys, you said you wanted to go to the Monaco Grand Prix. Here's the tickets, here's the car. All you guys got to do is get to Orly Airport." "B.K. got us there, man," cackled Lesh. "I was the navigator from the backseat, Susila rode shotgun. He drove, and he got us through Paris in record time. You can't believe what he did to those Frenchmen— he left them laying in the road. You can imagine the Gang of One hits Paris in a little Fiat rental car!"

The Dead played on Radio Luxembourg, which was enlivened when the queen spoke and the show cut to the announcer, who was standing on a garbage can onstage. Just as he began to speak, he was knocked off the can by Parish, standing on things onstage being a no-no. The bonus of the performance was getting to see the actual broadcast station, where three or four diesel locomotive engines were on standby in case of a power failure. Healy, Furman, and Wizard were in technical hog heaven, and everyone else was merely fascinated. "Those things run? You keep them running?" Their host walked over, hit a button, and one of the diesels started up. They had vacuum tubes the size of small garbage cans behind inches-thick glass walls.

Then to Heidelberg, where switchblades were legal and everyone stocked up. Since the crew already looked rowdy and tough, and since they would stand around and play with their blades—why else have one?—they got a bad rap, looking even more sinister than they really were. Munich. Hal Kant, their attorney, had joined them at the Munich Hilton, and one morning he got a call from Bonnie Parker. "Hal, we have a problem. We have fifty people checking out of the hotel, and they won't take my credit card." "One of the most valuable things I've had in my life," remarked Hal later, "is a Hilton Preferential Card. In Germany, heels clicked when I handed them that card. Then they forgot to bill me, and a year later I got the bill for $15,000."

On their way from Munich back to London they looped through Switzerland, where Cutler performed a prank on the management of the Grand Hotel in Lucerne. The hotel was a five-star, triple-fancy, utterly formal establishment, and Sam paid cash in advance so that the reservations were airtight. Expecting an appropriately garbed orchestra, the hotel's management took one look at Dan Healy's neon shirt and the tie-dyes lounging in the lobby and gulped. Garcia matched Cutler with another joke. On the way into Switzerland the safety valve on the bus stove's propane bottle blew off because of the altitude. "All of a sudden *whooosssssh* and the whole bus starts filling with propane," said M.G. " 'Stop the bus, stop the bus.' We whip the bus over to the side of the road. We've got those little gray flannel airplane blankets, you know, and everybody is coming out from underneath [them] . . . Jerry says, 'I'll strike a match and see where it is' and he lights a match. I was out the front door as soon as he said 'light a match.' Think, Jerry? He doesn't think. He acts. I was mad at him for a week. It was like 'I dare you.' " "Kidd was my main henchman on that," snickered Garcia. "I knew it wasn't really going to blow, it was a small flame, and we took it out and smothered it—a dumb thing to do, but an opportunity. I can't resist a setup like that."

And so to London to end the tour with four nights at a small place called the Lyceum with the New Riders opening. The Visine bottles came out, and the levels of LSD consumption went up; they were heading home. On one night, Candace could barely see the stage and thought everyone there was wearing an animal mask. And then there was Wizard's tale. Wizard was an enthusiastic psychedelicist, but on the final night, May 26, he realized that while he'd taken LSD on the tour, his commitment to work had been such that he had never let go his self-control and gotten really high. He dropped, and before the show he went to the lobby to see the booths set up by Warner Bros. and the New Riders' record company, Columbia. They seemed rather lame, and he split. Betty had added some Punch and Judy masks to the costume stash, and Wizard wore Punch, with the ringlets of his hair around the edges of the mask so that the edges were invisible. When he returned to the lobby, he inspected the booths a second time and discovered that the staff had been dosed and were considerably startled over his mask. "No no no, it's only a mask," and he pulled it off—and they freaked harder.

The Dead began to play, and this time Wizard was feeling his LSD. The VU meters were melting, and seeing them clearly was difficult. Still, he managed. Since it was the last night, Betty was a little anxious and asked Wizard if it sounded okay. He soloed up each channel and said, "Yeah, it sounds great." Forlorn, she asked for reassurance. Falling back on the basic checklist, she asked, "Are we recording?" Just to be a psychedelic wiseass, Wizard replied, "In fact, everything we're hearing now happened a few milliseconds ago, because we're listening off the playback head." Betty had come to the end of her tour. She looked at him, eyes pinwheeling, and said, "Wowwwwwwww." Wizard smiled. " 'Betty, go inside and have a good time.' Now I'm alone. The truck is sitting there vibrating. All is great. Late in 'Truckin',' I had put a fresh pack of tape on, so that's smooth. And then I hear a microphone fucking up and realize I have to leave—which you never, ever do. Close and lock the truck, go inside, fix the mike, and then I let go [of control]—and they went into 'Morning Dew,' and I can't leave. J.G. looks up and sees me and realizes the truck is empty. I nod, and he smiles! He's playing with his back to the audience, tears streaming down his face, the music playing the band, and the music recording itself. Ecstasy on every level."

During the production of the album, Garcia ran into Wizard and said, "Hey, man, guess what? 'Morning Dew' is definitely on." Lowering his voice, "And no one was in the truck!" "We all took a step over the cliff," said Wizard. "We were all being guided by the muse."

Going in the opposite direction in every way—geographically, socially, psychologically, aesthetically—were the Rolling Stones. Shortly after the Dead got home, the Stones began their 1972 tour of the United States on June 3. Anxious to dispel the memories of Altamont, they mounted a businesslike invasion, "trying to pass themselves off," wrote one critic, "as a bunch of middle-class Balzacian businessmen, possibly even with ties to the *ancien régime*." Their tour included about sixty stagehands and other crew, a traveling sideshow with a cast that included Truman Capote, Terry

Southern, Princess Lee Radziwill, bodyguards, and a security chief. And there were orgies—the unofficial tour theme song was "Cocksucker Blues." Both the Stones and the Dead tours were connected to great albums *(Exile on Main Street, Europe '72)* and lots of cocaine. The Stones, unlike the Dead, made lots of money. The Dead, unlike the Stones, performed a free concert. It was a juggernaut versus the Toonerville Trolley with Bozo masks, yet both tours delivered highly professional rock.

The Rolling Stones' former and the Grateful Dead's current road manager was busy upon his return from Europe. Sam Cutler's natural inclinations made him an empire builder, and he wanted to be more than a road manager. In May he founded Out of Town Tours (OOT), a booking agency that would handle the Dead and several other bands, bringing in Gail Turner as office manager and Chesley Millikin as vice president. Chesley was an interesting character in the Dead's scene. A little older than the band members, he'd fled his native Ireland to become a martini-guzzling businessman in Berkeley before going to a 1966 Dead concert on campus, where he fell in with Danny, Rock, and Pigpen. After taking LSD for his alcoholism, he dropped out, eventually becoming the manager of a band called Kaleidoscope (which featured David Lindley), then the in-house hippie at CBS in 1968, and then Epic Records' European manager in 1969. He'd tour-managed the New Riders for a spell, and now he and OOT began to book Doug Sahm, the Sons of Champlin, Big Brother, and the New Riders, as well as the Dead. Chesley was fond of Rock, but felt that Scully's lack of a work ethic made him hard to take seriously. "The people who were supposed to be in charge," thought Chesley, "were not in charge." Garcia, in fact, spent more time at the office than Rock, out of sheer curiosity. Sam was "megalomaniacal," smart, and hardworking, and in Chesley's opinion, wanted the band to be more successful but only in a righteous sense. For Chesley, McIntire was "too smooth," the "flimflam man." Sam's creation of an alternative power base to the band itself would, in the end, spell disaster for him. Yet his aggressive improvement of their moneymaking ability over the previous two and next two years would make some dreams possible.

May saw the release of two solo albums on Warner Bros., Mickey Hart's *Rolling Thunder* and Weir's *Ace.* Building a studio and coming to ground had been beneficial for Hart. His then lover, Nancy Getz-Evans, recalled him as a wonderful teacher and a compulsively generous man, giving away what money he had to the point of shorting himself. He shared everything, including his studio. One day a guy showed up who'd walked over the hills to the ranch—he looked to Nancy "as though he'd been in the hills forever"—and asked Mickey if he could record. Sure. "One of the most creative, far-out people I've ever met," Nancy said of Hart. "A patient, slow teacher." She would become a distinguished studio professional in her own right.

Rolling Thunder was a very good album that comprised, wrote a dubious Robert Christgau, "Alla Rakha, Shoshone chants, a water pump, big-band jazz, and electronic music, not to mention Paul and Gracie and Jerry," but it was actually a great deal more conventional than such a combination might suggest. Mickey had gotten a three record deal from Joe Smith, and *Rolling Thunder* gave him the means to improve the barn's equipment. Warner Bros. even released a single, "Blind John," backed with "Pump Song," the earliest version of "Greatest Story Ever Told." This gave Mickey a chance to step much, much further out on the edge. His next album, *Fire on the Mountain,* began with the song of that name, and then moved into Hartian (as in Martian) percussion/electronica space. One piece, "Marshmallow Road," was written by Mickey and Barry Melton in Hart's mother's home in Sunrise City, Florida. Their means of inspiration was to take lots of acid and lock themselves in a room with eight or ten cartons of marshmallows. After two days the LSD, the Florida heat, and the marshmallows combined into a nasty goo, and they fled the room and jumped into the nearest swimming pool. In Joe Smith's opinion the album was as gooey as the Marshmallow Road, and he rejected it.

Mickey responded by making a sound track to a martial arts film script called *The Silent Flute,* written by, among others, Bruce Lee. Martial arts was a Hartian specialty and brought out his greatest intensity. For two weeks he did not change his clothing and had his food left at the barn door. Since he did not even have a copy of the script, he relied solely on his memory of one reading. "Piano. Low frequencies. It was my best work." This, too, was rejected. "They actually walked out on me while I was playing it for them."

Ace found an only slightly better response than *Rolling Thunder. Rolling Stone,* by now into its seventies dish-the-Dead policy, dismissed the album as "half good." Weir did get one bonus, however. Shortly after returning from Europe, he was sent out with Warner's head of promo, former Beatles publicist Derek Taylor, to visit radio stations around the country. "Derek was wonderful," Weir recalled. "He was civilized, but he was also incredibly funny. Like, you know, this old lady would get on the airplane—[wobbly old-lady voice] 'What will I do with my umbrella?' and Derek, in this impenetrable English accent, 'May I suggest you stuff it up your bum, miss?' 'Oh, thank you very much.' She couldn't understand it, of course, the way he said it [and she'd reply] 'Oh thank you, but I think I'll just put it here.' "

The Dead returned to work, but very quickly lost Pigpen, who played a little at a Hollywood Bowl concert on June 17, but sang only one song, "Rockin' Pneumonia." They sent him home and pressed on. At two that morning, a security guard at the Watergate apartment complex in Washington, D.C., Frank Wills, caught four men working for the Committee to Re-Elect the President in the act of burglarizing the headquarters of the Democratic Party. The ensuing scandal would have a considerable impact. For the Dead, the specific day was memorable for a song, one of the finest ballads Garcia and Hunter would ever produce. Hunter had written the lyrics years before at the Chelsea—"a blue-light cheap hotel"—and in the spring, in Germany, Garcia had picked up a guitar and the melody had fallen out. It was called "Stella Blue," and it was lovely. "All the years combine / they melt into a dream / A broken angel sings / from a guitar . . ."

As the summer progressed, the Dead toured the East Coast, and the shows continued to grow in size, ranging now from four-thousand-seat theaters to small stadiums. In the wake of the closing of the Fillmore East, a number of young men had emerged as New York City area promoters, including Jim Koplik and Shelley Finkel in suburban Connecticut and John Scher, who was still a college student, in New Jersey. Ron Rainey, the Dead's booking agent, had discovered Roosevelt Stadium, a minor-league ballpark in a rat-hole neighborhood of Jersey City, and suggested it as a site to Scher. The fall before, the Dead had played at Gaelic Park in the Bronx for Koplik and Finkel, selling out twenty thousand tickets. The July 18 Roosevelt Stadium deal of $20,000 against 60 percent of the gate—whichever was higher—would mean (20,000 $5 tickets = $100,000 gross × 60% = $60,000 pay) a very fat payday for a band that was not yet averaging $5,000 per show. The Dead had become a stable, economically functioning band at Fillmore East. With John Scher as their promoter, they would become a giant band at Roosevelt Stadium.

Back home in August, they passed one particularly odd interlude, working a recording session as a backup band for folksinger David Bromberg. Garcia had met his manager, Al Aronowitz, and they'd become good friends. In the late 1950s Aronowitz had been a *New York Post* feature writer who'd drawn the assignment of skewering the Beat Generation, because the *Post*'s editor's son was smoking pot and falling under its influence. What the editor got, however, was the best journalistic coverage of the Beats ever. Aronowitz had gone to the extent of interviewing Neal Cassady in prison, and that alone would explain his attractiveness to Garcia. Now Al managed Bromberg, among other things an extraordinary acoustic guitarist, and one day in August he asked Garcia for help. "Hey, Keith," Garcia said, turning to Godchaux, "d'ya feel like playing some rock and roll?" The result of their day at Wally Heider's was side one of *Wanted: Dead or Alive*, a good album that would have been better if Bromberg had been more comfortable with the Dead or the Dead had spent more time with Bromberg.

A few days later the Dead played at Berkeley Community Theater, with a new/old face at the mixing board. After serving two years in federal prison for manufacturing LSD, Bear had been released, to begin two years of what proved to be intense frustration in his relationship with the Dead. In his absence the social structure of the touring Dead had changed dramatically. To Bear's mind, tasks—except for mixing—had been shared in his day, but since then Matthews had defined "compartmentalized" roles. Worse still, from Bear's point of view, was the addition of cocaine and beer to the social mix. Foul language offended him, and at one point he gathered the crew together to say, "I'm used to working with my friends. I don't want to work with people who use language like you guys do." That fall there was a college gig at which Matthews disappeared and Bear grabbed some local kids to lift and carry. In the process the mixing board ended up in a college dormitory room. When the crew arrived at the next gig and discovered the loss, they blamed Bear. During the self-criticism session that followed, Sparky Raizene picked up Bear and threw him across the room. Simply put, the crew did not acknowledge Bear's self-perceived status as a core member of the scene, a near-member of the band. He went to the musicians and said, "Put me in charge of the crew. Let me have the power over the crew, tell them they're working for me, that I have the hire/fire, whatever." The band declined to challenge the status quo, leaving Bear in a limbo he described as "Here's a piece of your job back, just a taste—and stand over there."

Toward Labor Day the band reached out to other old friends. Just as Garcia had settled into a home the previous year, some of their Eugene, Oregon, friends like Ken Kesey's brother Chuck and his wife, Sue, were doing the same. In a nod to the past, the Dead chose to do a benefit for the Kesey scene, a show often called Kesey's Farm, but actually the Springfield Creamery Benefit at a field outside Eugene in Veneta. Oregon shows still had a touch of the old acid test flavor. The first of the band's visits to Oregon that year, in June at the Paramount Theater in

Portland, was remembered by the promoter, David Leiken, as the craziest of his life. The show was insanely sold out, "and then Kesey showed up with two buses full of guests . . . The fire marshal tried to close us down—with guests, we had three thousand people easily. A guy fell out of the balcony, rolled to the orchestra wall with a bang, got up, and returned to his seat. They were screwing in the balcony." The Creamery Benefit would be dominated by one fact: it was, Weir recalled, the hottest day in Oregon's history, and since the stage faced the setting sun, they were unable to keep their instruments in tune. For all of that, the band played wonderfully.

The day was also a major episode in one of the subplots in the band's history, its relationship with film. Phil DeGuere was an apprentice filmmaker and Stanford film school graduate—one of his fellow students was Jerry's first wife, Sara—who in 1972 had hooked up with a man named Sam Field and the Merry Pranksters' movie team, FWAPS (Far West Action Picture Services). Early that year he approached Garcia, who was standing outside the Keystone waiting for Freddie the owner to get there and open up, and asked him about filming the band. "Why?" Garcia replied. "We just stand there. We don't do anything." After a further pitch, Garcia shrugged, "Well, I guess somebody's going to do it sooner or later." In the mysterious, informal way of the Dead, Field and DeGuere's group became the band's film team, at least to the extent that they were used to run interference with Charlotte Zwerin, representing the Maysles Brothers, who also approached the Dead at this time. Her New York manner put off the band, so Field and DeGuere seemed to have an opportunity. DeGuere had settled in Eugene, and the Veneta show seemed the right time, so they shot it without a deal, "on spec." As loaded on LSD as everyone else, they managed a decent amateur job of documentary shooting, staying generally in focus, although they unintentionally excluded Keith from the shoot, except for one song. Then they settled down to edit, a process that would take them a considerable time.

The Dead began their fall tour after Eugene with an outdoor show in Boulder, Colorado, where their ability to alter the weather was at least apocryphally established. As a dealer threw hundreds of free baggies of pot into the crowd, the Dead played magnificently. After hours of rain, one shaft of light appeared from the black clouds, and within a few moments the entire cloud cover peeled back like magic. Down the road, they had another show at Roosevelt Stadium. Another sellout, more rain.

Late in October the Dead arrived in Milwaukee, where they shared their hotel with the Democratic presidential candidate, George McGovern.

It was a hilarious conjunction in the middle of a terrifying election. Richard Nixon was seeking a second term, and he was doing it by blaming the previous four years' social change on the Democrats. "Amnesty [for draft resisters], Abortion, and Marijuana," wrote Hunter Thompson. "Not just four more years of Nixon, but Nixon's *last four years in politics*—completely unshackled, for the first time in his life, from any need to worry about who might or might not vote for him the next time around." Even to the apolitical Dead, it was a scary thought. Not that they were in love with McGovern. Earlier in the year the Dead had met him on an airplane flight. When he said, "I'll get elected and you guys can come play the White House," they replied, "We won't play till you legalize marijuana." There was a silence. So when Garcia got a call in October from the McGovern campaign asking for him to help, he was not excited. "To hear that somebody who might be president even knew my name—I put the phone under the pillow for the rest of the weekend."

In Milwaukee the strangeness began on the first of two nights with a postshow argument between Weir and Kreutzmann on the profound question "Which freezes first, cement or metal?" Kreutzmann held for the latter, in a debate that started on the ride home, then spilled out onto the sidewalk in front of the hotel. They began to wrestle, to the point of fury. The burly Kreutzmann had Weir's head and was about to bring it down on the sidewalk when Ram Rod inserted the toe of his shoe where Weir's head would land, catching Kreutzmann's attention in a way no other action would have. Very subtle, very Ram Rod. They stopped wrestling, and much later Weir would concede intellectually as well as physically.

On the next night, their last in Milwaukee, Weir was in the final van load back from the gig to the hotel. Some of the local union stagehands had sold a considerable stack of fireworks, legal in Wisconsin, to the always enthusiastic crew. Just as Weir was halfway across the lobby, the first fusillade went off. All the men with sunglasses, tiny radios in their ears, and bulges in their armpits dove to the floor, guns out. Weir kept moving. Upstairs, he got on the phone, found out where the fireworks were stashed and got his share. The hotel was horseshoe-shaped, and so with a little care and the rooming list it was possible to figure out who was where and take aim. At first everyone fired at everyone else, but when the incoming got too thick, the procedure was to go to another room, make an alliance, and start firing at someone else. Coalitions emerged, then defectors. Garcia picked up his phone to hear "terribly distorted popping sounds," which turned out to be Kreutzmann playing with fireworks in the bathtub. Events assumed their own momentum.

Candace Brightman had been something of a teenage vandal and was an enthusiastic participant in the proceedings. Now Ben Haller, who had the room above hers, upped the ante. He slit a pillow and had someone knock on her door. Opening it created a draft that sucked in the feathers, leaving her cohort Weir to emerge looking like the abominable snowman. Eventually, the warriors turned their attention to the Ramada Inn across the parking lot, and slowly their ammunition ran low. By now, of course, local police and the Secret Service were furiously trying to find the source of the artillery. Weir had landed in Keith's room, and fortunately, all that was left of their armory was blue smoke. When the police entered and demanded identification, Keith, who looked to Weir like the archetypal wavy-lipped cartoon drunk, snarled and slurred, "Fuck you, pig, I'm not showing you no fucking ID." Remarkably, he was the only person arrested that night, although Kreutzmann was ejected from the hotel after getting rude at the front desk. Weir got Keith bailed out and stashed him at the Ramada, along with Kreutzmann, who in typically cyclical fashion had achieved a temporary nirvana. Once in his new room, he had turned on the radio and gotten a jazz station that was the best he'd ever heard. He lay down, blissed out, and listened to music for hours.

In November they released *Europe '72*. For a number of reasons, it was an exceptional live album. One reason was the elegant overdubbing, which polished their harmonies and allowed Merl to drop in some B-3 organ. Their work was so meticulous that they re-created the stage setup of the instruments in the studio to approximate the original ambience. Willy Legate's liner notes were also superb, and quite unlike anything else in rock:

> Anguish and despair are only the sugar-coating on the bitter pill of understanding. And what is self and what is not are only learned learnings who stand without the gate while imaginations glance off the innocent one.
>
> Silence speaks to silence when one who has consciously renounced the interior dialog of wishful astrological gossip and the exterior array of false stimuli which engineer it, continues to experience the music of the Grateful Dead across wider bands of life . . . You know that anything you seek, you've known already. Find = recognize . . . Why are the dead grateful? Because their presence is invoked. Acknowledgment of the dead is new life. All the living who have entered the mystery of the name of the Dead have begun to die. The gratitude of the dead is music.

The album received an especially accurate review from Patrick Carr in the *New York Times:*

> In the realms of hip legend, astral pleasure, rock and roll and business as usual, the Grateful Dead stand higher than any other veteran American rock band . . . a music which often induced something closely akin to the psychedelic experience . . . It sounds pseudomystical . . . but the fact is that it happens, and it is intentional . . . [the album] demonstrates a widening of perspective—or perhaps an addition of several narrower perspectives . . . perhaps the most technically proficient and musically integrated band in the world . . . They will still be playing together when their contemporaries have long gone their separate ways . . .

Another important aspect of *Europe '72* was that it was de facto their last Warner Bros. album. (They would actually complete their contract by having Bear compile an album, *Bear's Choice,* from old tapes.) On July 4, 1972, Ron Rakow had presented to them a plan for their own record company, and they'd gone for the challenge. Late in 1972 they'd met with Clive Davis, the head of Columbia Records, who had tried to sign them. Accompanying Clive was his head of FM promo, a serious Dead Head named Michael Klenfner, who'd been a security guard at Fillmore East only two years before. A joint came out and went around the table—Clive declined—and someone asked, "Clive, are you sure that you're going to make sure that our pressings are right?" Klenfner interjected, "If he doesn't, I'll be there because I want to hear it right." "It was an incredible cross-examination, exhausting and exhilarating at the same time," wrote Davis. As impressed as they were with Clive, the band would say, "Thanks, but no thanks," to his offer; they were going out on their own.

One other aspect of *Europe '72,* something that also came from Willy, would leave a special mark. It was a slogan in the liner notes, and it would spread via bumper-sticker through the next couple of decades, as truthful and self-evident as anything in rock:

"There is nothing like a Grateful Dead concert."

Megadead

(1973)

After a busy January of songwriting and rehearsal, the Grateful Dead began its 1973 tour year early in February at Maples Pavilion, the Stanford University basketball facility, introducing seven new songs and a special sound system. Healy, Bear, and Matthews had taken Electro-Voice tweeters, rebuilt them, "pinked" the room—pink noise is the sound of a specific frequency, generated to equalize the sound in the room so that no one frequency dominates—and spent perhaps $20,000 on amplifiers and other new equipment. In the first two seconds of the first song, the band wiped out every brand-new tweeter. The sound crew managed to fake its way through that little disaster, but it was an aptly dramatic beginning.

Over the next two years the sound system would be the overwhelming focus of the band's attention, and Dan Healy would be the motivating force. After years away, Healy had come to a show in New York late in 1971 and declared that the sound was only average. This outraged him, and after the show he went backstage to see the band and said so. "I want back in. We'll talk when you guys get home." The band agreed, and though Matthews would mix through much of 1972, and Bear would have a major role after his release from prison that August, Healy began to exert a significant influence. Unlike Bear, who did not have the crew's confidence, and Matthews, who was easily distracted, Healy was an effective leader, able to take some of Bear's inspirations, as run through the design minds at Alembic, and make them work on the road. His passion for quality extended to the very buildings the band was now working in. He and Ron Wickersham rendered architectural drawings and plots of room acoustics, then offered them to the halls, which in the case of the Springfield, Massachusetts, Civic Center, resulted in vastly improved acoustics.

The new songs at Maples Pavilion, all of them by Hunter and Garcia, withstood the test of time considerably better than the tweeters. "Loose Lucy" celebrated a ribald and tempestuous romp—"Singing thank you / for a real good time." Another up-tempo rock shuffle, an early version of a song that would become "U.S. Blues," mixed pop icons, cynicism, and patriotism: "I'm Uncle Sam, that's who I am / been hidin' out / in a rock 'n' roll band / Shake the hand / that shook the hand / Of P. T. Barnum / and Charlie Chan . . . I'll drink your health / share your wealth / run your life / steal your wife." "China Doll," originally known as "The Suicide Song," was a fascinating writer's exercise in that it was sung by a person who has committed suicide, a ghost. It would be one of Garcia's great ballads. But the new song that would be played over and over was "Eyes of the World." Its Whitmanesque, mystical celebration of compassion and the organic— "There comes a redeemer / and he slowly too fades away / There follows a wagon behind him / that's loaded with clay / and the seeds that were silent / all burst into bloom and decay / The night comes so quiet / and it's close on the heels of the day"—was to some ears a hippie song of enlightenment that dated itself quickly. But the tune, an incredibly seductive rhythm when done correctly, was entrancing, and the band would come back to it again and again.

Early in March they were rehearsing at the Stinson Beach Community Center when an old friend, photographer Bob Seidemann, stopped by with Pigpen. Pig was extremely sick with a damaged liver, and he had asked Bob for a ride so that he could have his picture taken with the band. In Seidemann's view, "They coldly put him down, turned him away. They pecked him and pecked him and pecked him." As far as Weir knew, Pig wasn't going to be able to play with them for a while, but he had stopped drinking and was working on a solo album. They all expected him to recover. Garcia had asked McIntire to investigate any possible help for Pigpen, and Jon had found someone at the U.C. Medical Center, but it was too late. In any case, on the day of Pig and Seidemann's visit, the band didn't want to be distracted, and Pig went on home. He was living alone, because in November he had sent Vee away, telling her, "I don't want you around when I die." Their relationship had even degenerated into a horrible squabble over the division of furniture that required the intervention of Hal Kant and another attorney.

After a couple months of recuperation with his family in Palo Alto, Pig had returned to Marin in January. He was lonely, and a number of times he called Girl Freiberg, who had moved into his and Weir's old Novato home, and invited her over to his place to play chess. His solo album included the following lyrics:

> *Seems like there's no tomorrow*
> *Seems like all my yesterdays were filled with pain*
> *There's nothing but darkness tomorrow*
> *If you gonna do like you say you do*
> *If you gonna change your mind and walk away . . .*
> *Don't make me live in this pain no longer*
> *You know I'm gettin' weaker, not stronger*

On March 7, a friend of Healy's named Monterey Mabel called Dan with a premonition of trouble, but he was unaware of any bad news and their call ended inconsequentially. The next morning Dave Parker got a call from Pig's landlady, who said that she hadn't seen him around lately. Parker went over, and through the window he could see Pig lying on the floor. He had died of internal bleeding from the esophageal vein, a result of prolonged drinking, the same thing that had taken Jack Kerouac four years before. Ron was twenty-seven.

Two days later, Hunter and Weir turned to each other. There had been only one possible response to Pig's death, and that was a righteous wake, to be held at Weir's new digs, a lovely glass-and-wood hillside home in Mill Valley. As the gathering was about to begin, Hunter said, "If there's one thing I learned from Pigpen, I think I'm going to get drunk and have a real good time." They did so, with enthusiasm. There was, said Weir, "substantial collateral damage." It was raining to beat hell, and there were five hundred—someone actually counted—people there, which meant there were hundreds on the hillside next to the house, which could not possibly accommodate more than a few dozen. Inside, there was an "informal wake/riot," said Weir. "Outside, it was an orgy." People no one had ever seen before had wound up on the hillside, there being no fence or yard, and they'd responded to death by trying to create life—or something like that. There was another response. Alana Wyn-Ellis was a friend of

Julie Christie's who'd met Marmaduke Dawson at the Bickershaw Festival the year before and shortly after had married him. She found herself standing at the wake with a cream pie in her hand, but no one was eating, and "I didn't know what to do with it till [Sam Cutler] turned the corner." Sam struck her as a pretentious fraud, and without thought, the pie left her hand and intersected with Sam's face with perfect timing. For one-tenth of a horrible second, she realized that she was relatively new to the scene and this was rather unlikely behavior for her—and then the crew roared, and so did everyone else.

The traditional Roman Catholic funeral was attended by the band, Kesey and Babbs, Hell's Angel Sandy Alexander, KSAN disc jockey Dusty Street, and Jason McGee, the boy who'd been informally adopted and raised at 710. At the wake Pigpen was dressed in a leather jacket and a brown shirt, his cowboy hat on a pillow beside him. He was buried at Alta Mesa Memorial Park in Palo Alto under a stone that read, "Once and for-ever a member of the Grateful Dead." His books—Kerouac, Ginsberg, science fiction, Pogo—and his records—Sam and Dave, Little Richard, Jimmy Reed, Lonnie Mack, Flip Wilson, Sonny Boy Williamson, Light-nin' Hopkins, the Four Tops, Bessie Smith, Ray Charles—went to his sis-ter, Carol. The loss left Garcia despondent, and he considered folding the band. Finally, he and Hunter wrote some tunes "so weird," recalled M.G., that he was able to recover his balance. But in his heart, the Grateful Dead would never be quite the same again.

In the course of the preceding winter, Garcia had spent considerable time playing music and hanging out with David Grisman in Stinson Beach. Born in Passaic, New Jersey, Grisman shared with Garcia the loss of a musician father at an early age. First from the radio and then from a Mike Seeger album, he'd developed an interest in bluegrass. His tenth-grade English teacher, Elsie Rinzler, sent him to her cousin Ralph, a member of the Greenbriar Boys, who introduced him to the music of the New Lost City Ramblers and to the regular Sunday afternoon Washington Square Park folk jam sessions. A natural-born nonconformist, David chose the mandolin instead of the more popular guitar. Then he saw Bill Monroe, and his interest in bluegrass was set in concrete. He spent four years at NYU, but got his real education while working for Israel Young at the Folklore Center. His first recording credit was an album with the Even Dozen Jug Band, with John Sebastian and Maria D'Amato (later Maria Muldaur). He met Garcia during the summer of 1964, and they stayed in touch, with Grisman visiting the Warlocks in 1965 in Palo Alto and then seeing the Dead at the Cafe au Go Go in 1967 on their first New York visit.

Once David settled in Stinson Beach, the inevitable happened. One day he brought Peter Rowan, who'd played guitar for Bill Monroe, up to Sans Souci, and the instruments came out. "We need a bass player," said Garcia, and they went to John Kahn's house; the music started, and kept on rolling. Jerry had come a long way since 1964. His obsessive need to be great on banjo had diminished with the satisfaction derived from other music forms, so he could enjoy playing bluegrass once again. Grisman was far and away the best mandolin player he'd ever known, and Kahn played a satisfactorily spritely bass. Rowan was erratic, thought Grisman, as when he "tends to forget that he's a rhythm guitar player in becoming the Mick Jagger of bluegrass," but he contributed plenty. Before they had even played outside Kahn's home, they were a band. "Jerry directed it," said Grisman, "but he never wanted to be the leader. Nobody did. Maybe Pete, but we wouldn't let him." As usual, other egos tended to defer, pleasantly and for the best musical reasons, to Garcia. They hung out, played, and gave each other nicknames. Rowan had written "Panama Red," so he was "Red." Garcia dubbed Grisman "Dawg," for no particular reason. Kahn was "Mule," and Garcia, again for no good reason, became "Spud."

And while playing at home is fun, an audience adds adrenaline to the enjoyment. "Shit," said Garcia, "why don't we play a few bars and see what happens?" In March they played the first of their eighteen club dates, which, along with four concerts, three school performances, a radio show, and a bluegrass festival, constituted the complete history of their new band, Old and in the Way (OAIW). It was a tightly knit group. There were the musicians, but no roadies, since acoustic instruments required none. Garcia's manager, Richard Loren, booked the gigs and became road manager. Bear was looking for something to do, and eventually, despite Garcia's complete lack of enthusiasm, he and his girlfriend, Victoria, became part of the scene, setting up recording gear at each show. The Lion's Share, a club in San Anselmo, was tiny, which made it a fine place for the band to make its debut.

At his first show Garcia had to remember that he wasn't plugged in, and remarked afterward, "I'd forgot how physical it is. But it sure is fun." Later he would concede, "At this point, I'm like super primitive . . . This is the group I wanted to play with when I was first real deep into bluegrass, but they weren't around then." Garcia was approaching musical saturation—which for him was merely full satisfaction. In one week he could play with the Dead, with Merl Saunders, and with OAIW. Bluegrass was especially fine, because there was no pressure at all. They'd begin by warming up for three or four hours, play three hours onstage, and very possibly cool down for another two. Life was good. In fact, it was so good that Garcia reached out to share it. One of his favorite bands was the then-unknown group from Ireland, the Chieftains. Hearing that they were in San Francisco on a promotional tour, he arranged for them to open for Old and in the Way, set up an interview for them at KSAN, got them a limo, and then went with Chieftains front man Paddy Moloney to the station, where he joined Tom Donahue as co-interviewer. Never having heard of the Grateful Dead, Moloney was at first bemused by Jerry's enthusiasm, though he found him utterly charming and knowledgeable. "A few jars [drinks]" later, said Paddy, they were pals, and would stay that way for life.

Back on the road with the Dead, Garcia found himself one day in March in Baltimore with a day off, the next show in Springfield, Massachusetts, and Robert Hunter at his side. Hunter suggested a walk, and most uncharacteristically, Garcia accepted. Back at the hotel, they didn't want their good mood to end, and they decided to avoid the airplane scene, rent a car, and drive to Springfield. A couple of hours into their jaunt, New Jersey State Trooper Richard Procachino pulled Garcia over for doing 71 in a 60-mph zone in Mount Holly, and Garcia went to the trunk to get his driver's license out of his attaché case. Alas, there was a highly visible bag of pot in the case. "You know I can't let you get away with this," said Procachino. "Yeah," shrugged Garcia.

They went to the local lockup, and after a while Hunter followed Garcia into the bathroom. There on the toilet seat were the scattered remains of the other drug, cocaine, that Garcia had been carrying—fortunately, he had never been searched. Hunter called Sam Cutler, who called John Scher. Later, Scher would muse that if Cutler had been a little more cognizant of American geography, he'd have called the Philadelphia promoter, who was many miles closer. But as it was, New Jersey meant Scher. John raided his safe at the Capitol Theater in Passaic for the $1,000 bail, got to Mount Holly, and rescued Garcia. Ten minutes out of town, Garcia relaxed, and for the next couple of hours he and Scher would rave and bond on the ride to New York City. The primary result of Garcia's misadventure—in the end, he received probation, and briefly had to visit a psychiatrist—would be the close relationship he'd enjoy with Scher for the rest of his career.

The Dead returned home and got on with the real business of the day, creating their own record company. Wrote Hunter years later in a blank-verse memoir, "tired of working for Bugs Bunny anyway, / put together a record company of our own / and d-d-do it the way we want it d-d-done / and have only ourselves to answer to? / It might work. It should work. It *will* work."

On March 18, 1972, Ron Rakow had been driving between Bolinas and Olema when he conceived an idea for a Dead record company. He researched the notion in SEC files, copying the financial statements of the big record companies, and that Fourth of July he submitted to the band a ninety-three-page report with supporting bibliography called the So What Papers. Whether or not anyone in the band ever really read the So What Papers is unclear. Rakow had Garcia's ear. It was not hard in any case to convince Garcia to look for an alternative to conventional record companies, so Jerry was, as Rakow later expressed it, "maximally enthused. That was something I could do to him at any time." "To him" was the relevant phrase. Rakow fulfilled Garcia's need to travel the dark side, where lived the hustlers and weasels. Through him, Garcia could vicariously enjoy a con game. Intellectually, Garcia really was an outlaw. If they could somehow subvert the entire American music industry, terrific. Rakow's machinations with the All Our Own car company and his inept management of the Carousel had damaged no one whom Garcia knew, and generated a huge amount of good trips, high times, and a marvelous challenge to the status quo. It seemed that it could happen again, shaking the Dead out of the torpor of their success. "Jerry was my ally in this," said Rakow. "Every morning I would go to Jerry's house in Stinson Beach. He liked my desire to have a lot of random events going on."

The plan Rakow initially presented had two aspects that were memorably foolish. One involved bypassing the entire world of music distribution to sell records from ice cream trucks. Another involved financing the deal through the federal government's Minority Enterprise Small Business Investment Company (MESBIC). Somehow, they would get themselves declared a minority, and $1,350 would become $300,000. Rakow had an impressive chart on an easel set up in front of everyone, and it all seemed real. When Bonnie Parker remarked that she'd worked in a job that dealt with the Small Business Administration and that the feds were unlikely to lay down dead, Rakow merely took out a sharp Puma knife and sliced the MESBIC section out of the chart. The main person who might have been expected to challenge Rakow, band attorney Hal Kant, did not take him terribly seriously. "I'd listen to their crazy raves; it meant nothing to me because first of all I wasn't involved in the music business except for them at the time, and second of all, it was hobby time, it wasn't a major thing. It was amusing, that was all . . . Rakow is supposed to be a serious businessman? He doesn't have a clue."

Later, Rakow would create a second company to produce side projects called Round Records, which was co-owned by him and Garcia. This Kant took seriously, pointing out that it was a major conflict of interest, since it commingled the band's finances with a side project. Garcia blew up, telling Hal that he represented the band, not the record company, and replaced him at the record company with a San Rafael attorney named David Hellman, who also represented Rakow personally. This conflict of interest escaped criticism at the time, but it would have major long-term side effects. A week later, Hal recalled, Garcia apologized to him for his outburst. "Ron is such a weak guy," Garcia said. "If we confronted him with this, he'd fall apart. I knew you could handle it but I didn't think he could." "Garcia," Kant said, "just wanted people who would do what he wanted them to do, but frequently he had trouble deciding what that was." And in fact, when it came time for the ultimate meeting to decide on the project, Donna Jean would remember that Garcia was a no-show, since he didn't really want to deal with business anyway. Lesh was no big fan of Rakow's, but his attitude was the one that held sway: "I thought it was worth trying."

In the end, they compromised. No ice cream trucks. Rakow came up with financing derived from two sources: a revolving line of credit from the Bank of Boston and a lump-sum advance from Atlantic Records for foreign rights to their releases. With that in hand, they had their own company. "It's the most exciting option to me," said Garcia, "just in terms of 'What are we gonna do now that we're enjoying this amazing success?' The nice thing would be not to sell out at this point and instead come up with something far out and different which would be sort of traditional with us."

The Grateful Dead was now a megabusiness. Fifth and Lincoln remained headquarters, home to manager McIntire and also record company president Rakow. One of the first new people to join Grateful Dead Records was Steve Brown, a fan who'd coincidentally submitted a proposal for a record company to the Dead in January. Brown's proposal was a book that included a picture of Garcia walking to work at the Haight Street show in March 1968, a show Brown had also taped. His job interview ended up being a raving conversation with Garcia about growing up in San Francisco and working for Don Sherwood, a well-known local disc jockey. Brown was hired to be the album production coordinator, but he would also man a booth at Dead shows for the next two years, giving away postcards, signing up Heads to the mailing list, and so forth. Emily Craig, the Boston waitress Rakow had inveigled into the scene, knew a photographer in Massachusetts named Andy Leonard, who was put in charge of manufacturing and advertising. Bob Seidemann, who'd been one of the band's photographers off and on forever, was made the art director. He got the job, a desk, and a phone, but for him the trouble started immediately, because he had nothing to do. "Essentially, Ron wanted all the power, that's it. He didn't want anyone around who had any influence other than himself." There were two other obvious candidates for employment at the record company, Rock Scully and Chesley Millikin, but despite their qualifications, they were never hired.

About three blocks down Lincoln Street, there was a small modern office building at 1333. There, the tie-dyed second floor was the fiefdom of Out of Town Tours, Cutler's booking agency. It had expanded mightily, adding clients and employees, including Mustang Sally Dryden, wife of Spencer; Cutler's lover, Frances Carr (sister of Loose Bruce Baxter); Frances's sister Libby; Gail Turner; and Rita Gentry, who later became a fixture working for Bill Graham. Rita would remember OOT as a place where Peter "Craze" Sheridan and Bear would come on to her and Hell's Angels would stop by to see Sam and pop wheelies in the parking lot. It was a scene tinged by an aura of madness, and she loved it. Sam had style. That Christmas, OOT employees received solid-gold skull necklaces. Sam was equally skillful in making sure the crew responded to him. Danny Rifkin had returned from his travels and by now had joined the stage crew. He once had an accident, and Sam took him to the hospital. When the nurse said wait, Sam waxed eloquent: "Don't you understand, we're touring. This man has to be onstage." "McIntire never got in the truck with the crew," said Danny. "McIntire never got drunk with the crew. Cutler would fight promoters, and McIntire would have them take him to an expensive dinner and schmooze them."

Downstairs from OOT was the office of Fly by Night Travel, a travel agency run by "Melon in Charge" Frankie Weir, with Rosie McGee booking travel for the bands. It was probably the only travel agency in the world where the decor failed to include a single travel poster. With the Dead, the New Riders, Jerry and Merl, and many other bands as clients, they had plenty of business. The Fan Club had rebegun with the "Dead Freaks Unite" note on *Skullfuck*, and Mary Ann Mayer had kept a list of names, starting with the initial group of 350 respondents. Eileen Law had succeeded her in early 1972, and she would stick with it for many years.

By September 1973 the number stood at 25,731 and rising. Thanks to the record company, there was now a budget for regular mailings, and two or three times a year they'd go out. The newsletters were low-key and astonishingly intimate. A stoned Hunter would spin a hypnocracy yarn, Alan Trist would add some tour information, and Garcia might be persuaded to contribute a little sketch. After a year, there was a postcard from Rakow that Hunter deemed too commercial, and Bob stopped participating.

There were even more spin-off enterprises. Susila Kreutzmann and Christine Bennett started a store in San Anselmo called Kumquat Mae, which sold Dead T-shirts (made by Kelley and Mouse's Monster Company), records, tie-dyes, crochet work, and so forth. It was both store and hangout. Next door, Rex Jackson had a garage where he would work on his candy-apple-red '55 Chevy. Later, Kumquat Mae would move to Mill Valley and become Rainbow Arbor, and soon after, Susila began selling T-shirts at Winterland, the genesis of a mighty business.

June brought Old and in the Way's first and only tour, hitting theaters and a bluegrass festival back East. On the day before the tour began they added the legendary fiddler Vassar Clements—one night's rehearsal was entirely adequate—and with that further ingredient of consummate bluegrass professionalism, they went out smokin'. To Kahn at least, the festival turned out to be a disappointment. "It was kind of rough, and kind of a letdown, really, to see how tacky the whole thing was. It was like *Hee Haw* . . . Not esoteric at all . . . all the bands played ten or fifteen minutes; they had a comedian as emcee, a terrible sound system, we couldn't hear . . . We were the only band like us; every other band was straight bluegrass. I remember that we were real nervous about playing and only got to play about three songs and the mikes didn't work and things kept breaking . . . The coolest things were stuff that didn't have to do with the actual show itself. Jamming. There was this fiddle player that became tight with us and we did a couple of fiddle songs with Vassar, real fast, I could barely keep up—Tex something or other [Logan]—he was a physics prof in college and played bluegrass on vacation . . . bluegrass people play all the time in hotel rooms. During Old and in the Way, we always played. Every second. We'd get up in the morning and go in somebody's room and start playing. All the instruments are portable . . . the best tapes were dressing room tapes. It was one band that was never late, except when Bear recorded—that was always late. We'd get there early and we all needed to warm up, because playing acoustic instruments is hard work."

The Dead's summer of '73 was dominated by two things: the Watergate hearings on television, which fascinated everyone but especially Garcia, who would spend mornings at Stinson watching Senate Judiciary Chairman Sam Ervin and a colorful cast of characters, and dealing with technical/sound system/equipment matters. A May letter from Ron Wickersham of Alembic to David Parker, the Dead's moneyman, detailed seven different current projects, including a new type of microphone, a preamp for such a microphone, a new P.A. array, and new instruments.

By now, Garcia was playing a reworked Fender Stratocaster guitar, using a Fender Twin Reverb amp as a preamp and McIntosh 2300s as his amp, powering three Alembic B-12 speaker cabinets stacked eight feet high. Weir had a Les Paul, and Phil . . . Phil was in tech heaven. He had a quadraphonic bass, the first ever made; each string had a separate access to the sound system. On the first fret two lightning bolts leaped out of a block of lapis lazuli; on the third fret, a cosmic serpent ate its tail. A crescent moon perched on the fifth fret, on the twelfth there was a salamander and an infinity symbol in mother-of-pearl, and on the back of the neck was Osiris, Judge of the Dead, pointing his divine flail at whoever held the instrument.

Intended or not, all of the technical developments, especially as they applied to the P.A., were making it possible for them to put on the prime gig of the summer, an extravaganza that would turn out to be the largest gathering of people in the history of rock and roll. Multiday festivals were generally out. Towns didn't want them, and state laws that set rigorous logistic requirements for gatherings were now on the books. Promoters turned to one-day events as an alternative, sacrificing ambience for practicality. The one big show in 1972, the one-day Mount Pocono Festival, sold 125,000 tickets, although 50,000 people crashed the gates. That summer, when the Dead had played at Dillon Stadium in Hartford, Connecticut, the Allman Brothers Band's Berry Oakley, Dickey Betts, and Jai Johanny Johanson had sat in, inspiring promoter Jim Koplik to conceive a one-day concert uniting the Dead and the Allman Brothers. When he came upon the Grand Prix racetrack at Watkins Glen, New York, he knew that it was the perfect location. He brought the idea to the Dead, and Sam Cutler loved it. McIntire thought a show so large—surely at least 100,000 would come—was "playing with fire." Its size lent it a grand potential for disaster, and guaranteed that instead of being a good opportunity to hear music, it would only be a party. But *what* a party.

In 1973, Jim Koplik was a twenty-three-year-old Westchester kid who'd turned to rock promotion to fill his time after the devastating assassination of Robert Kennedy. Financing his first show with his bar mitzvah money, he'd wound up in Connecticut with a partner named Shelley Finkel, and at one of his first Dead shows, at the Waterbury Palace Theater, he sat down next to Kidd Candelario, who handed him a Pepsi. Soon finding himself on a "down elevator moving a hundred miles an hour," he appealed to agent Ron Rainey, sitting next to him, to "Stop the elevator, it's going too fast." "You've been dosed," said Ron. "Don't worry about it, we'll run the show. I've got a good way for you to enjoy this. Go onstage, lean on Jerry's amp, put your chin on your hand, and watch his fingers." "I had the best time in the world," Jim said. "The next time they played the Palace, Sparky brings a Visine bottle for me. 'Hold out your finger.' This was no dose, it was welcome."

Koplik and Finkel were kids, but they were in the right place at the right time. They offered the Dead and the Allmans $110,000 each, and at the insistence of Sam Cutler, brought in Bill Graham to do the staging and set up the backstage area. Since neither band wanted to open, they needed a third band. At first they considered Leon Russell, but at the last second, the Dead suggested the Band. In the end the promoters had to pay Leon not to play. With a solid lineup, they figured on between 100,000 and 150,000 people, and the combination of heavy advertising and a clever poster, which combined the Dead's skull, the Allmans' mushroom, and the Band's pipe, ensured that sales were brisk. Logistically, they were ready; New York State's Mass Gathering Law required that. They had dug twelve wells, they had one thousand portable toilets, two hundred acres of parking, five hundred state cops, three choppers, $30,000 worth of fencing, 135 drug abuse control people, food for 150,000, and 100,000 gallons of water. Two weeks before the show, they had sold 100,000 tickets at ten dollars each.

The audience began to gather a week before the show, and by Wednesday there were already 50,000 people on-site. On Thursday, P.A. crew member Jim Furman was sent on the "best errand I ever ran." Healy decided they needed six or eight more McIntosh 2300 power amps, and it just so happened that they were built in Binghamton, New York, about fifty miles away. Sam peeled $8,000 from his roll and handed the wad to Furman, who couldn't fit it in the pockets of his shorts and ended up rolling it in his T-shirt. The roads had already turned to sludge, so Jim hopped onto a chopper and flew to Binghamton. The factory was closed for summer vacation, but the local dealer had pulled strings for them. Jim landed at Binghamton airport and took a cab to the dealer's store. The president of McIntosh pulled up with his wife and three children in their loaded station wagon, on their way out of town for vacation. They went to the factory and pulled six amps off the line, forever identifiable because they lacked the number plate, which was the last step in assembly. They took them back to the store and Jim paid the local store owner, who then topped himself. "I know the chief of police," he said, and arranged for the chopper to land in a park across the street from the store. Jim persuaded the pilot—"Are you *sure* you've got permission?"—and the police swarmed in and blocked traffic. By now, downtown Binghamton was enjoying itself. Reporters were interviewing Jim, and the streets were buzzing. However briefly, the circus had come to town. The chopper landed, they loaded the Macs and Jim, and slooowwwly—McIntosh amps weigh 125 pounds each—lifted off, barely clearing one building, before returning to Watkins Glen and a hero's welcome.

By Friday afternoon there were at least 200,000 people on-site, and Koplik experienced his worst moment of the weekend when he got a call from the New York State Thruway Authority telling him that the highway had closed. This meant that he'd have to refund everybody's money, because people wouldn't be able to get in. He turned to his partner. "It's been fun, Shell, but we're about to go broke." An hour later the highway reopened. Because of the number of people already there, there was no alternative but to make the sound check a public affair. The Band came on and did about forty minutes, and the Allmans followed with an hour and forty. Cocaine had lent a competitive edge to the scene, from trailer sizes to backstage amenities, and so the Dead one-upped them and did an entire show.

Early that day, Koplik found out what a Dead concert could be like. He went onstage to introduce himself.

Parish growled, "Who are you?"

"I'm the promoter."

"You're not the promoter. Shelley Finkel's the promoter."

"I'm his partner."

"He never told me he had a partner."

With that, Parish picked up all five foot six of Koplik, walked to the edge of the stage, and dropped him fourteen feet to the ground. On his way down, Koplik wondered, "Is this what it's going to be like to work with the Grateful Dead?" There was more to come.

Saturday, July 27, was stinkin' hot. An audience of about 600,000 stretched for two miles from the stage, but the county sheriff said, "We have four or five times as many people here as we have at our [auto] races, and we are getting less than half the trouble. These kids are great." Two sets of sound delay towers made it an experience that most could hear.

Graham's FM Productions had built the stage, which had been a full-time job for two people for six months. The Dead, who had had to walk the last mile back to their beds the night before after the sound check, awoke on Saturday in a modest 1950s bungalow motel that lacked phones and sufficient hot water, got up, stepped out of their rooms, and got into a helicopter to go to work. Rifkin shrugged, "It was just a big business deal, a promotion—not a gathering."

As the Dead went on, Koplik said, Sam Cutler shook him down for another $25,000 (the Dead earned either $100,000, $110,000, or $117,500—memories vary) in view of the large audience (though it was largely nonpaying—the ticket-taking system had been overwhelmed), and Jim had to send a chopper to another one of his venues to get the cash. The one dangerous moment of the day came when thousands began to press on the fence surrounding the backstage compound. As McIntire stood there, momentarily uncertain of what to do, Bill Graham zoomed past, got a water truck, and began to hose down the audience, quite literally cooling the fans out. The Dead opened the show and played listlessly in the heat, perhaps fearing what might happen if they encouraged the crowd to do more than sway. As Weir saw it, they were "rattled" by the sheer size of everything. Joe Winslow had done his fair share of LSD that day, and he felt trapped, as though the stage was "our only reality." Behind the stage was a huge mass of trees, and there were people in all the trees and everywhere else. Too damn many people. The Band, already enervated by heroin and internal politics, had not played together in a year. The Allmans were superb, and the night ended with a jam that Butch Trucks recalled as edgy. "I remember that Jerry Garcia came out onstage with us and took over. There was no *doubt* he was going to dominate. He'd step right on top of Dickey's playing. Then he made the mistake of playing 'Johnny B. Goode,' and Dickey just *fried* his ass, and we left."

Watkins Glen would prove to be the largest rock concert ever, and the last of its era. Twenty-five years later, John Scher would try twice to revive Woodstock, with less than joyous results. The risks of bringing such a large group of people together overwhelmed the potential for fun—or even profit.

Back home, the Dead returned to the studio for the first time in three years, putting in 289 working hours at the Record Plant in Sausalito to create *Wake of the Flood*. It was to be the first album on their own label, the first that was truly *theirs*, and they worked very hard. In the end they didn't quite pull it off. The material was largely first-rate and interestingly consonant. The organic cycle in "Eyes of the World" extended throughout the album, from Weir's "Weather Report Suite" to Rick Griffin's cover. Rick had taken his theme from the Book of Revelation, the next line after the one used in *Europe '72,* about the dead being judged. "And the sea gave up the dead which were in it; and death and hell delivered up the dead which were in them: and they were judged every man according to their works." That gave them the flood, and thus the ocean that is part of the cover, while the prime visual is a smiling reaper and a sheaf of wheat. Weir's major contribution, "Weather Report Suite," began with an instrumental solo, which he'd worked out with Eric Andersen, a Guthriesque folksinger he'd met on the Great Train Ride who had settled in Mill Valley. "Part II," Weir said, amalgamated licks copped from Villa Lobos and Miles Davis, with a little mariachi seasoning. However much Weir later deprecated it, it was fine work, as were the lyrics. Weir and Barlow—who was not even sure he was still Weir's lyricist—had met in John's mother Mim's apartment in Salt Lake City in the spring. The other 363 days of the year, Barlow was a rancher, but the Dead were passing through Salt Lake City, so he was taking a very short vacation. The result of their work was beautiful, and as organically authentic as one could ever hope:

> *Round and round,*
> *the cut of the plow in the furrowed field*
> *Seasons round,*
> *the bushels of corn in the barley meal*
> *Broken ground,*
> *open and beckoning*
> *To the spring,*
> *Black dirt live again!*

For the first time, the band recorded without a record company to blame, so they were organized, efficient—and perhaps just a little lacking in fire. The result was a lovely, pastoral album that came close to excellence. Released October 15, it would sell 400,000 copies, and with their vastly increased profits, it would contribute to the ongoing task of paying for their 1972 European vacation. Their business was accelerating wildly upward; Cutler was having an impact. Their September 1973 operating statement, in rounded figures, placed income from eleven gigs at $250,000, with travel expenses of $55,000, equipment costs of $20,000, office expenses around $6,000, salaries of $18,000, legal $9,000, and payroll taxes $3,000. Profit before partner draws, $110,000. The partners drew $33,000, leaving $77,000. Their positive bank balance wouldn't last terribly long.

They were a very large act by now, but still capable of whims. On September 11, they played at the College of William and Mary in Virginia, and at the end of the show they announced a second show the next day for three dollars. Five thousand fans came. Garcia told *Rolling Stone* at the time, "Right now, somehow, we've ended up successes. But this ain't exactly what we had in mind, 12,000-seat halls and big bucks. We're trying to redefine. We've played every conceivable venue, and it hasn't been it. What can we do that's more fun, more interesting?" That October a writer visited their show in Oklahoma City and noted that there were 163 speakers on each side of the stage, plus 133 for monitor purposes. They were powered by a military surplus ship's connector designed to plug ships into shore power. It conducted six hundred amperes of electricity in three phases, an amount sufficient to serve ten modern homes. They had started, Healy remarked to a reporter, with two extension cords.

Two moments defined the end of 1973. One was the phone call they placed to the FBI, asking for help in fighting the counterfeiting of *Wake of the Flood.* They also sent a message to Dead Heads:

> Our record is being counterfeited, the authorities move too slowly not recognizing that our survival is at stake. We need your diligent efforts. The counterfeit has square (not round) corners on the stickers and a white (not orange) 0598 on the spine. Check all stores and immediately report phonies to us. Thanks, GDR.

Even with the FBI's help, the culprits remained uncaught.

The second moment came backstage at UCLA in November, when Bob Matthews, now working as an advance man for the tours, addressed the band. He'd just evaluated the Boston Music Hall stage, and at the trainer's room blackboard he showed them that the Boston stage was fifty-seven feet wide, and their present setup was eighty-five feet wide. Their amp line—the minimum for their instruments and stage amps— was only fifty-four feet wide, but that left out sound towers. But that fall they had installed phase-canceling vocal microphones, which permitted a solution. Such microphones come in pairs; the singer sings into the top one, and the sounds that hit both microphones (from other amps or speakers onstage) cancel each other out, leaving only the vocal. With this equipment, they could move the towers behind the amp line and put the sound behind the band, like an enormous wall.

Like a wall.

39

Interlude: Into the Zone

(SECOND SET BEGINS)

September, Madison Square Garden

Garcia is back onstage twenty minutes before the end of the break, infected by the sheer nervous energy that is the Grateful Dead at the corner of 7th Avenue and 33rd Street, the innermost circle of performance rock and roll, the Dead's home away from home even though it is an antipodal mirror for this bunch of San Franciscans. It is a Monday night in late September, and Ram Rod has a TV perched on his road case with the 49ers game on. Garcia stops to watch. He's not really a sports fan, and once said that he's serious about the 49ers only when they're winning because "I don't need the additional heartache, you know what I mean?" The band gathers attentively as Joe Montana takes the team down the field until a bomb to Jerry Rice seals the game. This is the city Garcia fled immediately on his first visit, the place where Weir was mugged on *his,* where the animal energy of youth is most obvious, and where the band responds.

It is the place where Garcia has preserved his sanity by locking himself in his room for twenty years of visits, and it is where Scrib, along with everyone else who works for the band, goes craziest. As in the fall of 1987, when the Dead had a Top Ten single, "Touch of Grey," and a hit album,

In the Dark, and were premiering an hour-long video, *So Far,* that would also be a hit. Much later, Scrib realized that for those few days he was at the vibrating center of the American myth machine, and he'd been so busy that he'd been unable to exploit it personally or professionally; he'd just tried to stay upright. New York is media central for every entertainment group, the electronic cortex of the nation, where the Dead, like every band, performs the bulk of its media activities. "What's the dumbest question you've been asked?" queried New York disc jockey Alex Bennett of Bob Weir in 1970. "That." The band's best efforts, of course, are collaborative. In 1982 Weir and Garcia treated David Letterman to a latter-day Abbott and Costello routine that Weir finished by comparing the Dead playing experience to "gestalt linkage." Garcia added, "Yeah, a Jungian might say that."

Media and comedy routines be damned, it is time to do a show. Lights down and the crowd's visceral roar snaps everything into focus as the band launches into "Cold Rain and Snow," the tune Ken Frankel had taught Garcia in 1962, plaintive banjo picking transformed into powerful rock chords. Out front at the sound mixer Healy is bopping; the Garden rings like chimes as Garcia mournfully declaims, "Well I married me a wife, she's been trouble all my life, run me out in the cold rain and snow." The music is thick, rich. "Cold Rain" ends with a satisfying final chord that falls gently into a transition, something akin to watching a ten-ton truck turn on a dime.

September, Richfield Coliseum, Cleveland, Ohio

Cars roll into Richfield, with bumper stickers that read "The Fat Man Rocks," "Question Reality," "You've Been Selected for Jerry Duty," "Who Are the GD and Why Do They Keep Following Me Around?," "Fukengruven." A sign on the front window of a VW: "If you ask us for drugs, you owe us a nickel. P.S. We don't have any drugs."

The first song is not yet over as a new up-tempo rhythm is established, and Garcia begins to sing Hunter's lullaby to the child in all of us, "Franklin's Tower." "In another time's forgotten space / your eyes looked through your mother's face." They dig in, reach deep. Garcia and Weir knit gentle riffs together while Lesh plays a counterlead over the quiet moments. Garcia's lead picks up the stage and shakes it, kicking the moment from 70 to 120 decibels, then goes berserk, playing the melody backward, down in descending scale, strumming it up and then strumming it down, till all six musicians fuse in perfect proportion, all responsive and individual. It is still the melody and yet so much more, molten creation, conversation and dance. The tune levels off to a quiet shuffle, the cymbals whisper *dippity dippity shush shush shush,* the twelve-armed being picks gently into the sweet refrain yet again, slowly, exploring the figures to the point of hypnosis. The pulse is so right that it almost seems the music is perpetual, always out there somewhere, wanting only the right catalyst to be audible.

"When I'm really getting off," said Garcia once, the music "has the effect of surprising me with a flow of its own." It's not me, each musician will say, but the muse. Parish leans over to Scrib at his perch and says, "Man, sometimes [the music]'s like being on a bike dropping into third and cruising." At its prime level it is something very like a state of grace, when one is not playing but being played. Lesh goes ape, his face contorted, almost duckwalking across the stage toward Garcia, then backing up, his head bobbing. Weir gets a particularly dopey ecstatic grin, and inspiration moves brightly across the stage. The drums burst into double time, the band erupts as one in a focused line that reaches crescendo one more time, then focuses down into the *boingboingboing* thrum of Lesh's bass line; Weir plays thick slide chords that smear a background for Garcia, who picks a mountain high. Lesh holds it to one note, they build a final peak—"In Franklin's Tower the four winds sleep . . . May the four winds blow you home again"—and they explode out in solid chords and chorused harmony, thick and crunching, "Roll away the dew, roll away . . ."

September, Boston Garden

Down the road a week to Boston, and it is celebrity time. As the band prepares to cast into the improvisational void, the essential purpose of the second set, the stage holds the tallest Dead Head, former NBA star Bill Walton, and his friends from the Boston Celtics, Larry Bird and Kevin McHale, Vic Firth, the first tympanist of the Boston Symphony Orchestra, and Richard Alpert, aka Baba Ram Dass. It is an interesting range of fans.

Even as the band settles out of the preceding tune, Weir flashes ten fingers (the song is in 10/4 time) at the drummers and strums down the scale while Garcia picks the melody and Mydland's Hammond B-3 organ wails the beautiful chords of "Playing in the Band." Candace whispers into her headset, "Stand by, everybody, for—oh, never mind." Lesh beats out a march-hard tempo and Kreutzmann's rhythm floats, liquid yet crisp at the same time, a subtle wrist-flip that generates an utterly relentless polyrhythm perfectly captured in the images of the video *So Far,* where dancers boogie six ways at once. Lesh touches his hand to his mouth and then lowers a flattened palm at Popick, requesting lower vocals in his monitor mix. As Weir steps to his microphone, Candace hits him with a stunning crisscrossed array of white lights. On the charter flight the night before, she and Garcia had talked about the lights, and though he recalled days when they had actually burned his skin, he'd also said, "It doesn't bother me anymore. If you have any residual reluctance [to crank up], erase it from your mind."

Weir sings.

> *Some folks trust to reason*
> *Others trust to might*
> *I don't trust to nothin'*
> *But I know it come out right . . .*
> *When it's done and over*
> *Lord, a man is just a man . . .*
> *Some folks look for answers*
> *Others look for fights*
> *Some folks up in treetops*
> *Just to look to see the sights . . .*

The second verse ends and they go into their first instrumental break. Gracefully focused, Mydland shifts ninety degrees on his bench and elegantly reaches to the synthesizer. He is such an addition to the band, in so difficult a role, still the new kid after nine years, and sometimes it hurts. Once Scrib had remarked to him on a flight between gigs, "Pretty moon," and he replied, "It looks nicer at home." Now Garcia focuses on Mydland, stroking him with his eyes, and the music lifts. Lesh's face vibrates in different planes of joy.

Garcia reaches down and twice fiddles with a pedal as lights wrap the band in purple haze with green pools all over the stage behind them. The melody line wanders, builds, becomes thunder, an atonal storm diversion, then pulses faster, thicker, a musical Möbius strip, a line that twists, shimmers, dances around six separate lines within it, musical DNA chains with color and texture, chains that harmonize and clash, unite and scatter. Images, ideas, entire worlds appear, collapse, return to a fused, perfect unity. This is the very definition of an ensemble sound. The room is full of music to the point of absolute density, a Jackson Pollock painting in notes.

"When the Dead are playing their best," wrote Hunter, "blood drips from the ceiling in great, rich drops. Together we do a kind of suicide in music which requires from each of us just enough information short of dropping the body to inquire into those spaces from which come our questions . . . about how living might occur in the shadow of certain death; and that death is satisfactory or unsatisfactory according to how we've lived and what we yield . . . Satisfaction in itself is nothing to be sought, it's simply an excretion of the acceptance of responsibility." Swept by the trance state of free improvisation over a never-lost pulse, one actually thinks in those terms. The future is here.

"Suddenly the music is not notes or a tune," wrote Michael Lydon in 1969, "but what those seven people are exactly: . . . an aural holograph of the GD. All their fibres, nuances, histories, desires, beings are clear." It is, in T. S. Eliot's words, "Music heard so deeply / That it is not heard at all, but you are / the music / While the music lasts." This is Dionysus in the late twentieth century, kin to William Blake, a transcendental art better experienced than described. Bent notes are scattered and tossed, all seems aimless, drums crash, Lesh sinks into lower and lower rumbling chords, the music slows, becomes giant boulders, high on the arid arm of a mountain . . .

October, the Spectrum, Philadelphia

Playing to audiences means the road, means a peculiar combination of motion and boredom. On the bus coming up, Parish had looked out and smiled. "Hey, there goes a '59 . . . nothing." The road is a stream of jokes, sexism, sarcastic testing, the improbable, and the obscene. Even when it is focused comfortably in four three-and-a-half-week bouts over the course of the year, the isolation of touring and the resultant group identity of the odyssey is inescapable. The road is a way of life. Ram Rod: "Did you ever kick over an anthill and feel bad about it?" Parish: "Yeah." Ram Rod: "Thanks. I needed that."

. . . and Garcia hits two notes; a beat, and a musical spring erupts from the mountain rocks, the lyric anthem that is "Uncle John's Band." All is sweetness, the audience clapping in perfect rhythm. Garcia, Weir, and Mydland lean to the mikes and the cautionary first verse proceeds, the band astonishingly direct to its audience, "When life looks like Easy Street / there is danger at your door." Each verse ends with a question, a test: "Are you kind?" The second verse speaks of life as a "buckdancer's choice," an adventurer's chance, because in the end life offers you motion, risk, and death, to embrace as you will. The verse ends with hope, with an invitation: "Will you come with me?" The third verse grounds itself in the intelligent, conscious Americanness that is this group: "Their walls are built of cannonballs / their motto is Don't Tread on Me / Come hear Uncle John's Band." This is the American voice as Whitman and Kerouac and Ginsberg and William Carlos Williams dreamed it, but wrapped in dance trance. It is their invocation, an authentic American folk tune that began as a hard-edged electric jam. When Hunter heard their rehearsal tape, he turned it into a masterpiece of reflection, an account of evanescent lives striving for authenticity, pondering the third question: "Where does the time go?"

Scrib has gone up behind the drums and stands talking with Ram Rod, who has his back to Hart. Scrib vaguely notices a sound that is not quite right, but by the time he opens his mouth to remark on it, Ram Rod has turned, checked, and gone to recover a stick Hart has dropped—an exquisite awareness, normal for the crew. As Ram Rod goes around him on the way back, Scrib murmurs, "Sorry." "Why?" " 'Cause I'm in the way." Smirking, Rod replies, "That might be your opinion." It is one of the good nights. Kidd goes up and takes over the monitor board from Harry, and the elevated group mood is clear.

Comes the fourth verse, where a silver mine becomes a beggar's tomb, and the musicians can only wonder, self-deprecatory to the last, "How does the song go?" And off the precipice, the drums tap fast on high hats and Lesh, Weir, and Mydland take a three-note riff out of the main chord and begin to repeat it endlessly, each instrument's notes varying yet blending flawlessly into the main melody line, while Garcia's lead races up and down mountains, the driving woof against a luxuriant warp. Deep in the last break his guitar makes an ancient, hollow sound, somehow medieval . . . then broadens to rock and roll strums. Scowling in concentration, Garcia peers over his glasses at a point approximately six inches in front of his nose. "He looks like an Old Testament prophet," says Scrib to Mountain Girl. "More like Geppetto to me," she responds.

"Wo-oah what I want to know, how does the song go? / Come hear Uncle John's Band / by the riverside . . . Come hear Uncle John's Band / playing to the tide / Come on along or go alone / he's come to take his children home." And Garcia's guitar simply *weeps* out the final chorus, and at each note, each phrase, the balances change, each testing, feeding, mocking, and finally driving each other on, further and further on. As Lydon wrote, first quoting Lucretius, " 'The barriers on the world / Dissolve before me, and I see things happen / All thru the void in empty space . . .

I feel a more than mortal pleasure in all this' . . . the whole goddamn place begins to scream. And Jerry, melodies flowing from him in endless arabesques, leads it away again, the crowd and himself ecstatic rats to some Pied Piper."

Anything can happen. On another night, perhaps they could stage one of their famous musical arguments about which song to play and change their (group) mind three times in as many bars of music. But tonight their decision-making, as well as their playing, is in perfect unity, with perfect rhythm, so that every riff has an overwhelming power, chords stacked like mighty walls, energy exactly expressed, synchronization, not synchronicity, although they can be contiguous. The jam out of the song trails quietly away, and the guitarists and Mydland leave the stage to the drummers.

The Wall

(1/74–10/20/74)

The new year began explosively. The minutes of a mid-January band meeting noted that Out of Town Tours was "taking a vacation until May," a fudging of the truth that only served to emphasize the importance of what had happened: Sam Cutler had been fired. His efficient harnessing of the energy from *Workingman's Dead* and *American Beauty* had increased the band's draw enormously, but he had made few friends. There was always the impression that he regarded the Dead as a squirming puppy that needed to be dragged up by the scruff of its neck to purebred levels, that it needed improving and change, that it needed to make lots more money. His associate, Chesley Millikin, felt that Cutler had been sabotaged, that he had "tremendous energy, and should have been left to do his job if he hadn't been stabbed in the back by Miss *[sic]* McIntire and Richard Loren and those fuckers . . . and Jerry was nonconfrontational and wouldn't stand up for him."

Sam, on the other hand, pointed at Rakow and the record company, which he said he opposed. "I thought it was a dumb move, a Rakow scam. And I said so. It was a fantasy that wasn't worth pursuing." Rakow and Loren, whom Lesh would call the "Stinson Beach Mafia," had moved to West Marin, and there were dark suspicions as to their influence. "Cutler's getting far too much money for what he's doing." Sam's reply was that "OOT was charging 10 percent, I wasn't getting 10 percent, I was getting a salary of $200 a week." Loren suggested later that Cutler's downfall was the sound system, which by now had grown so large and costly that it required huge gigs to pay for itself. Richard said that he respected Sam, "not necessarily his character, 'cause he was kinda shady . . . but he really understood the business of booking, like nobody else that had worked for the Grateful Dead." What also crippled Cutler was the feeling that money earned by the Dead was being spent on offices, secretaries, and a big scene at OOT, a competition for economic power guaranteed to raise band eyebrows.

Came January 14, and Cutler knew what was about to happen; he was to be the sacrificial lamb, and he pointed the finger at the reluctant leader, Garcia. "If I'd had a gun," he wrote, "I would have shot the miserable sod and put him out of his misery then and there! I said ONE word, 'okay' and left . . . To have that spineless and easily influenced man tell me what he told me (in public!) when I was effectively 'fired' was the most humiliating thing that has EVER happened to me in my life, and I said not a word in reply. BUT, I never forgave him, and I never will. It was the act of a moral coward."

Shortly after the meeting, Rita Gentry received an ominous visit from a Hell's Angel who told her that it would be inadvisable for her to attempt to work for the Dead—any other band, but not the Dead. Taking the message quite seriously, she went to work for the New Riders.

It must have been a considerable relief for Garcia to turn from internal politics to music, specifically the recording of his second solo album. Again called *Garcia*, it was nicknamed *Compliments* when a sampler entitled "Compliments of Garcia" was mailed to Dead Heads. Motivated largely because Grateful Dead Records needed product in the pipeline, Garcia went into the project thinking of himself as a studio vocalist, letting his producer, John Kahn, choose much of the material, none of which was original. Instead, Garcia covered Chuck Berry, Smokey Robinson, Van Morrison, Mac Rebennack, aka Dr. John, Jagger-Richards, and even Irving Berlin. It was not a bad album, but it lacked the punch of his first solo work and the style of its immediate inspiration, thirties jazz guitarist Oscar Alemán, a musician whose work absorbed Garcia at the time.

Except for some band meetings, January had become a time for personal projects. Weir was away writing, Lesh was in Hawaii, and Garcia was working on his album. The meetings covered a lot of ground. Deadpatch, Alan Trist's vision of a homesite for the band, which at this time would have required an additional $100,000 to finance, was given the coup de grâce. The next gigs, in February, would generate funds for a down payment for Keith and Donna's new home, a computer for musical experiments Phil Lesh and Ned Lagin were conducting, and a donation to old KSAN friend Milan Melvin's program for Napa schools. The band made one other decision, and it determined the best part of their next year. They approved building a modular unit, a cluster of speakers at the center of the system, that would replace the individual cabinets. It was the final element in building the Wall of Sound.

Late in February they played three nights at Winterland, among other things debuting "Ship of Fools" and "U.S. Blues" in its final form. Both reflected the political atmosphere of 1974, in which the specter of a modern-day presidential impeachment was no longer a fantasy, but an emerging reality.

Saw your first ship sink and drown
from rocking of the boat
and all that could not sink or swim
was just left there to float
I won't leave you drifting down
but woah *it makes me wild*
with thirty years upon my head
to have you call me child

Of course, "Ship of Fools"—the title, at least—could easily represent the Grateful Dead without Pigpen.

On March 22 the crew went into the Cow Palace in San Francisco and set up the Wall for the next day's "Sound Test." The Wall of Sound was not merely a sound system, it was an electronic sculpture. To walk into a facility for a Dead concert that year was to see something like the pylon on the moon in Stanley Kubrick's *2001*, something so grand, so elegant, so utterly preposterous, that words simply failed. The Wall was 604 speakers (88 JBL fifteen-inch, 174 JBL twelve-inch, 288 JBL five-inch, and fifty-four ElectroVoice tweeters), using 26,400 watts of power from fifty-five McIntosh 2300s. The music came through nine separate channels, through a differential summing amp, to a four-way crossover network, then to the power amps, the speakers, and out into the hall. There is a standard joke in rock and roll about turning an amp up to 11, given that all amp dials are calibrated to 10. With the Wall, there was so much power available that the musicians generally turned things up to 2. It was, in Lesh's words, "Like piloting a flying saucer. Or riding your own sound-wave." Because they were only turned up to 2, there was no distortion. In fact, Healy said, no two sounds went through any one speaker, so that it was "the ultimate derivation of IM [intermodulation] cleanliness." Alembic's notes modestly stated that it had "quite an acceptable sound at a quarter of a mile without wind and an extremely fine sound up to 500 to 600 feet, where it begins to be injured by wind." Healy estimated that the system had cost $350,000 and was the product of eight years of experimentation. Later, Garcia pointed out that the Wall in fact represented a "physical model of the *size* of the sound" they were creating. The bottom note of a bass was thirty-two feet tall, and that was what the Wall produced. It was brilliant, but not terribly efficient. It required too much power, both electrical and logistical, to function in the real world.

The band took a day off, and on March 25 went into CBS studios on Folsom Street in San Francisco to record a new album. It would be called *Grateful Dead From the Mars Hotel,* in tribute to the shabby building of that name that had thus far escaped an urban-renewal holocaust in the studio's neighborhood. Though no one in the band realized it at the time, it was interestingly synchronistic that the Mars Hotel had been one of Jack Kerouac's favorite wino flophouses. The album was another exercise in Grateful Dead reactionism, the pendulum swinging yet again. *Wake* had been in-house and conceptual, a fine whole that lacked the final soupçon of energy and drive to make it great. *Mars* would be a slick-sounding album of stand-alone songs, recorded by Roy Seigel, an outstanding CBS producer. It was highly professional, but not inspired Grateful Dead. Lesh and Lagin's electronics research had produced the gorgeous synthesizer sounds in "Unbroken Chain," a terrific song that Lesh would not perform until twenty-one years later, both because he was dissatisfied with the recorded version and because his voice was shot. He also contributed a country rocker, "Pride of Cucamonga." Garcia and Hunter brought in "China Doll," "U.S. Blues," "Ship of Fools," and "Loose Lucy," but the jewel of the album was "Scarlet Begonias," a masterpiece. "Scarlet" had a Caribbean feel that Garcia would later relate to Paul Simon's "Me and Julio Down by the Schoolyard." It was an acoustic song done electrically, and it invited opening up in the classic Dead manner. Hunter was then living in England, and his lyrics echoed the British nursery rhyme "Ride a Cock Horse to Banbury Cross": "To see a fine lady upon a white horse / With rings on her fingers and bells on her toes / She shall have music wherever she goes." Whether it was Queen Elizabeth or Lady Godiva, the lady with the flowers was one of Hunter's most exquisitely romantic objects of desire, a quest destined to fail.

Well there ain't nothing wrong
with the way she moves
Scarlet begonias or a
touch of the blues
And there's nothing wrong with
the love that's in her eye
I had to learn the hard way
to let her pass by—
let her pass by

Weir's contribution was not well received. Barlow had written a take on Mose Allison he called "Finance Blues" and Weir called "Money Money," which both of them thought of as a humorous wink on the ancient grumble of men and the price of their ladies' tastes. Weir thought of it as a joke, but the rest of the band and most Dead Heads saw it as hard-edged, and borderline mean. It would not stay in the repertoire for very long.

In May the band set out on the road, and it was like an invasion force. "The bigger we got," reflected Joe Winslow later, "the more powerful, but the more headaches. I was really rude a lot." It had been possible to be stoned and be one with the audience in a small theater, but in a big show ten feet above the audience, the stage became an island. The Wall required two stages, which leapfrogged each other, alternating shows, so that as one was being set up, the other was traveling to the next show. Inside stages were 76 feet wide by 30 deep, and outside they were 104 feet by 40. Ten feet above the ground was a floor of one-inch plywood, bolted, nailed, and tied to the scaffolding, because it could rise and fall as much as a foot from the sound pressure. Typically, the caravan included six band members, ten crew/sound guys, four people for lights, seven for staging and trucking, and three for road management. There were up to four trucks, which hauled around seventy-five tons of equipment.

The setup was so elaborate that the contract rider for that year was simply called "The Book," and included eleven realms of information, including 1. Stage and related structures. 2. Electrical requirements (600 amperes at 120 volts minimum for sound, 600 amps for lights). Grounding: "When in doubt, assure a supply of large wire and wait for us." There was also a lecture on quality of electricity, complete with Ohm's law. Security: "[Guards] should not confuse exuberance with malice, and . . . should realize that taking a certain amount of shit from an occasional wise guy is precisely what they're paid for . . . GD audiences, as a rule, react well to reason and requests, and badly to arbitrary authority." Their first show, outdoors on May 12 in Reno, was scary. A heavy wind, known locally as the Washoe zephyr, blew off the Sierra Nevada, swinging the twelve-hundred-pound center sound cluster like a child's balloon above Kreutzmann's head. The zephyr pushed hundred-pound McIntosh 2300 cases around like toys. Wheeled instrument cases wouldn't stay still. Somehow they managed to get through it.

The record company released *Mars Hotel* on June 10, with superb packaging by Kelley and Mouse. The front cover was a photo of the hotel at sunrise taken with an architectural camera, then manipulated by the artists. The back cover was also heavily embellished, beginning as a photograph of the band sitting in another seedy establishment, the Cadillac Hotel, where Garcia had lived for a few weeks some thirteen years before. They wanted to subtitle the album "Ugly Roomers," referring to the band, but it occurred to them that this might reflect poorly on the actual last residents of the Mars Hotel, so the slogan became "Ugly Rumours." This was shortly to be a self-fulfilling prophecy of the finest kind.

By now the record company had found its way, and the mailing list would get considerable use that spring and summer. A letter from Rakow, under the nom de guerre Anton Round, went out to the list in May along with many different samplers of upcoming albums:

Dear Guerrilla:
    . . . The question for us is, can you joyously and systematically make sure, by repeated gentle mentions and phone calls, that every record dealer knows that our records have to be in plain view.

The letter noted that the record company would have a booth at upcoming gigs

to give info and stuff away, get our minds blown, and blow some . . . Remember you gorillas are our guerrillas and we love ya, but we only want you to do stuff if you dig it. Dig it? . . . P.S. There'll be an ugly rumour in your life soon . . . WHAT TO DO: 1. Nothing unless it's fun. 2. Call stores, see stuff is there, neatly arranged. 4. Put up the posters, stickers, and handbills. 5. Call radio stations, etc. 6. Whatever you can think up that's fun for you and fun for other folks, too.

It was never clear how many Dead Heads got involved, although their response to various requests for information was substantial. By mid-

August the album had sold 258,000 copies, but reviews were generally mediocre. *Rolling Stone* dismissed it as "moribund."

It would be a peculiar summer. Late in June the Dead played at the Miami Jai-Alai Fronton. Lesh had been working with Ned Lagin on what would eventually be called *Seastones,* an entirely abstract album of electronic music that combined white or pink noise with bleepborp sounds. Lagin had degrees in both molecular biology and music from MIT, and they intimidated Lesh. Their collaboration had almost nothing to do with music, but rather the physiological effects of sound. "The way they describe it," said Garcia, "is 'recorded drugs, electronic drugs' . . . When they play it live and it's real loud, you hear these incredible things—subharmonic thumpings below fourteen, fifteen cycles, below what the ear can register as pitch, and it starts to turn into a physical thing . . . And they have super high-frequency things that sound as if they're originating inside your head." For Lesh, Lagin's synthesizer presented Ned with "a virtually infinite range of sounds and music that he can play, and I've got a very limited range . . . there's no possible way that one guy with two pedals and a ring modulator can possibly compete with an entire computer/synthesizer system."

Consequently, Lesh did not want to try out the Seastones—Mickey Hart had also dubbed it "Warp 10"—music live. However, on the first night in Miami he underwent various private adventures that rendered him somewhat malleable, and on the second night he and Ned filled the intermission with something radically new. Later, Lesh would dismiss the Seastones interludes as jive improvisation which only occasionally hit a height. Interestingly, the set that followed the first Seastones set was truly remarkable, a sample of group mind in which the band elegantly played two or three different songs simultaneously and then sequentially, and yet made perfect sense, which was not always the case that year. As Weir conceded, the Dead were "so musically inbred that we were playing some fairly amazing stuff, but almost nobody could hear it or relate to it except for us."

By August they'd run out of creative gas. Coincidentally, so had Richard Nixon. His efforts to block Congress's various investigations had gone for naught, and it was clear that he was about to be impeached. On August 9, he resigned the presidency. The Dead weren't in much better shape. On the full-moon night of August 2, they had endured one of the worst moments of their history. They were at Roosevelt Stadium, and in front of them were thirty thousand rabid New York fans who wanted a show, and who had in their pockets tickets that read "rain or shine." The band would insist that they were not aware of this, but in any case, after a sunny day, storm clouds rolled in just as the gig was about to start. The heavens opened, and going on was impossible. When Weir stepped out to explain that they would have to postpone the concert, he was hit by a bottle thrown from the crowd. Rifkin, then a crew member, would recall hiding behind equipment while waiting for the assault to die down. It was the only time he was ever afraid of a Dead audience. They looped back a few days later to play the show and end the tour, but it left a bitter taste.

On the band's return home, there was yet another company meeting. Rifkin stood up and said, "I'm not having any fun anymore. I'm thinking I'd like to take some time off and give it a rest, and see what it feels like." As Weir saw it, their main problems at this point were (a) cocaine and (b) the crew, which seemed to him to be "drowning in mountains of blow." "We had a crew that was being paid like executives for doing blue-collar work, and they were abusing our generosity." The crew chimed in with Rifkin, and the band made plans to take time off. To Weir, the hiatus was never meant to be permanent, but the decision was phrased so that certain crew members would be forced to find other jobs and not hang around waiting for work. Late in August a *Chronicle* headline read, "Is the Dead Going to Die?"

It was in this frame of mind that the band arrived in London in September for a short European tour. It was a very different scene from 1972, without family or any sense of adventure or vacation, and the run began with Rex Jackson briefly quitting as they arrived at Heathrow. What it did have was drugs. The London gigs were at the Alexandra Palace ("Ally-Pally") with a promoter named Tom Salter, who was better known as a man about Carnaby Street. It was Rock Scully's gig, said Richard Loren. "I fought it. Rock was always trying to get in with promoters who weren't promoters, who had money and drugs. I wanted to work with Harvey Goldsmith, of course. Salter had the drugs." Rock didn't dispute Loren, and later wrote of that time, "I am as coked up as a Taiwan freighter, and the vibes are getting just as quaky. When your brain crackles and your eyeballs burst out of their sockets, it's usually a sign that you're overdoing it just a wee bit. I have to do something, but what?" He certainly didn't figure it out on this tour. Things were so bad that near the end of their stay in London, Ram Rod dared the band members to destroy their drug stashes, and they met his challenge. Unfortunately, stashes can be replenished. As a matter of business, the London run was a fiasco. Salter could not account for a large part of the ticket stock, the shows lacked security, and getting paid required the band's attorney, Hal Kant, to sit "in

[Salter's] house three days after the tour was over . . . I eventually got about 40 or 50 percent of the money we were due. Chesley was there most of the time with me. But I just wouldn't go. Otherwise, we never would have seen any of it."

Garcia's interviews with *Melody Maker* and other English music magazines made his mood quite clear. "The most rewarding experience for me these days is to play in bars and not be Jerry Garcia of the Grateful Dead. I enjoy playing to fifty people. The bigger the audience gets the harder it is to be light and spontaneous." Thoughtful as always, he went on to consider the realities of owning a record company, from the environmental consequences of vinyl—"Records are such an ecological disaster . . . It's time somebody considered other ways of storing music that don't involve the use of polyvinyl chloride"—to the Dickensian nature of work in a record pressing plant. Having visited one, Garcia thought, "Do we really want to be putting these people through this?" He might well have been thinking of himself and his band at the time. Even though some of the music at the AllyPally was superb, it was coming at a profound cost.

From London they went to Munich, and things grew even darker. They hadn't been in Europe in two years, and now they had a sound system that required successful gigs to feed it. Plus, Germany had an odd effect on some people on the tour. As Chesley Millikin recalled it, "the attitude of people changes, almost like—some people become like fascists." One night in Munich there was a confrontation between Lesh and Kreutzmann on the one hand and the management—McIntire, Loren, and Scully—on the other, "a knock-down-drag-out," as Millikin put it. Kreutzmann was at this time part of what John Barlow called the "neo-cocaine cowboy aesthetic" that characterized one chunk of the crew, and this aesthetic had no affinity for an intellectual like McIntire. After plenty of abuse, McIntire had had enough and quit.

The next morning Chesley met Hal Kant in the hotel lobby and asked him, "What are you looking so forlorn for?"

"Don't you know? Didn't you hear?"

"No, what?" said Chesley.

"The band fired their management last night."

"No kidding. Who's management now?" asked Chesley.

"You are," said Hal.

With only three shows to go, one in Dijon and two in Paris, Chesley and Hal took over the tour. "I'm in the lobby," said Chesley, "thinking I've got to get them all together, buses out in front, we're all riding together, if ever we need to ride together, this is it, right. Oh, wrong." Hal came out of the hotel and said, "By the way, Chesley, Phil and Bobby and Garcia and Kreutzmann are [each] driving cars. Mercedes-Benzes." Hal had been driving a car, which had generated complaints within the crew although he was paying for it himself, and so he gave it to Parish and Ram Rod. Hal and Chesley went to the train station. "There was a bench between the tracks," said Hal, "and who's sitting there but Keith and Donna. 'What are you doing there, guys?' 'We thought someone was going to pick us up. We thought this was where we were supposed to be.' Everyone else had long gone, by different methods of transportation, and they're sitting there not knowing where they're going or how they're supposed to get there."

Everyone made it to Dijon, where the arrangements continued to be rough. At the Dijon gig, Chesley went to the box office to settle with the promoter, who started to renege on the deal. Joined after the show by Ram Rod and Kreutzmann, Chesley explained to the promoter how inadvisable changing the deal after the fact would be, though in truth the gig had been a total flop, with only a few hundred in attendance. The promoter was the proud owner of a lovely leather attaché case. Having just come from Germany, almost everyone in the Dead had a shiny new knife. Without saying a word, Kreutzmann began to strop his blade on the fine leather, and their payment was forthcoming.

Paris was only marginally better. Someone dosed the backstage catering, and the lobsters for dinner grew psychedelic claws, but the group continued to experience social problems. One night, twisted on wine and LSD, Kreutzmann found himself deserted by his hosts because he was, he confessed, acting like a "problem child." Barely able to stand up, he took to the street and began gulping fresh air. He sobered up enough to realize that he couldn't remember the name of his hotel, and then further realized that he had no idea how to find the speakeasy/disco he'd just left. Freaking, he tried to hot-wire a moped and failed. Finally, he threw it through a window just to get a reaction—nothing. A Mercedes passed by, and Kreutzmann kicked it. When the driver emerged, he proved even larger than Kreutzmann, who seized a car antenna and persuaded the giant to leave a crazed drummer alone. At long, long last, Bill flagged down a car and somehow got back to his hotel. The next day, students rioted all over the Left Bank, and he theorized that the absence of police in that neighborhood that night had been part of the preparations—the fix had been in. Phil went to the impressionist centenary at the Louvre.

When the band returned home, the esteemed *Chronicle* columnist Herb Caen confirmed that the Dead were about to retire, "to rest, recuperate, rethink, and one hopes, regroup," he wrote. That might happen eventually, but first the members of the Dead would have to endure among the hardest five nights of their lives, October 16 to 20, 1974. Since the future was so uncertain, one planned benefit of the run was to secure house down payments for some members of the family, including Ram Rod, Kreutzmann, and Rock. Then, just to make sure that things were revved up enough, Rakow and Garcia added a twist. Who knew? Since these might actually be the band's final performances, Rakow and Garcia decided that they should be documented, although they lacked the money to do so. Garcia's secret dream was to be an auteur filmmaker, and he was going to get his chance, although it would exact a terrible price. There had been talk about a movie since spring, but it was only late in September that Rakow asked Eddie Washington, their old friend from Palo Alto and a Stanford film school student, to prepare a budget. Hal Kant, who knew something about the costs associated with a movie, had resisted the idea and thought it had gone away. Then he walked into Winterland, where four different crews were shooting for four days. The movie was by no means a unanimously popular idea. "The kids [audience] are walking into a film studio," roared Bill Graham. "And never leaving a film studio! And that's wrong! Five fuckin' nights in a row! . . . And the kids are bugged by it! One night, two nights, five fuckin' nights, *no!* Of all the groups, the *Grateful Dead!* Of all the groups!"

On the last night, the missing band member finally showed up, three and a half years after he'd retired from the road. Early in the week, the crew had begun to call Mickey Hart. As far as anyone could be certain, October 20 might be, as the ticket read, "The Last One." Mickey demurred. "I'm recording," he said. Gently harassed, first by Rex Jackson, then by Jim McPherson, the man he was recording, and finally by his lover, Jerilyn, Hart finally cracked on the afternoon of the twentieth. After all, as Hart later put it, with the Dead, "you don't sign up and you don't sign out." If the band was truly over, it required a proper burial—and that required Mickey. "Well," Hart mumbled, "we'll put some drums in the car, but they have to ask me. Don't tell anyone I have them." They arrived at Winterland at the break, and met Rex and Kreutzmann, who were standing at the top of the stairs. Kreutzmann was ambivalent. "I don't know if he can," said Bill. "He doesn't know our arrangements." Hart was about to storm off, with Kreutzmann following, when Jackson grabbed them both, jammed their heads together, and said, "You guys are gonna play together, you got that?" It was settled.

No one was allowed onstage without taking psychedelic communion from Father Rex Jackson or one of his associates, and it showed in the playing. Hart didn't play particularly well, nor did the rest of the band, but it didn't matter; in some peculiar way, the night was a new beginning. Afterward Keith told him, "This is the first time I heard the Grateful Dead." It was the first time they'd met. Then Keith and Donna went home to do an interview with the film crew. Since it largely consisted of them staring at the coffee table, it would not be used. Lesh went up into the space behind the center cluster, smoked some DMT, and spaced out. As he left the stage, Garcia ruffled Rifkin's halo of curls in a genuine gesture of affection.

The *Village Voice* quoted Ron Rakow: "Listen, if there's one thing we learned in ten years on the road, it's that celebration is a valid form of revolution." The paper replied, "He's wrong. There are any number of reasons why the Dead are going into hibernation, and one of them is that they tried to run their revolution as though it were a celebration. It didn't work." In May, Hunter had written, "We falter and fall away, nothing holds. Political action is impossible. All we are left with are our arts . . . It is time to retreat. It is time to advance backwards. No longer are there any choices. What a relief."

The Hialus

(10/21/74–6/76)

After a quick dash to Vancouver with Hal Kant to resolve a pot bust from earlier in the year, Garcia found himself back onstage just five days after the "last show," this time with Merl Saunders, John Kahn, Martín Fierro, and Paul Humphrey. As the rest of the Dead gladly embraced some downtime, Garcia & Saunders, later called Legion of Mary, would work steadily throughout the hiatus. At a much less concentrated level, Weir would dabble with the band Kingfish.

The first effect of the hiatus was the consolidation of the Dead office. The record company retained the premises at 5th and Lincoln, and since their booker/manager, Richard Loren, maintained a separate setup, this boiled down to having Bonnie and David Parker move into the lobby of the band's new rehearsal hall and storage space. Formally called Le Club Fronte and more commonly Front Street, the new space was located at 20 Front Street in the Canal District of San Rafael, perhaps a mile away from 5th and Lincoln. It was a small, soon-to-be-congested warehouse that looked on the rear windows of the town's magnificently sleazy Bermuda Palms Motel, and the raffish atmosphere seemed entirely suitable.

The newly unemployed members of the crew went in a variety of directions. Danny Rifkin, joined by Sue Swanson, Alan Trist, and the movie producer Eddie Washington, went to live at Slide Ranch, a natural-history field trip site for children near Stinson Beach. Crew member Joe Winslow, his wife, Sandy, and some other former crew members began Hard Truckers, which manufactured speaker and instrument cases and cabinets. Their work was excellent and they prospered, at least until they overexpanded. Jim Furman, who'd run the errand at Watkins Glen, had better luck. He invented a preamp equalizer, which was basically a studio-level tone control for stage equipment. Jim built twenty himself, sold them to friends, and eventually developed a thriving business. But he did not forget where he had started, and his first "sale" was actually a gift to Garcia.

Over the course of the hiatus, there were other adjustments. While he had never been the most faithful of husbands, Garcia was patently drifting away from Mountain Girl by 1974, first with a young woman named Deborah Jahnke, but primarily with a young woman from Ohio named Deborah Koons. It was a very old paradigm. M.G. was at home in Stinson Beach with what was now three children—Sunshine Kesey, Annabelle, and Theresa ("Trixie"), born in 1974. Day after day, Garcia would go over the hill, and although he came home almost every night, it wasn't always gigs or rehearsals that kept him late. Also in this era, in 1975, Weir's longtime romance with Frankie collapsed, the victim of too many years on the road for Weir and insufficient rewards for Frankie. Always dramatic, she would in the end shoot herself—not fatally—during a particularly tempestuous scene, and shortly afterward they separated. Weir's scars ran deep. For the next twenty years he would live out what one of his lyrics described as "this tomcat heart with which I'm blessed." On the road he would require a suite, and the living room became a party room, the "hospitality suite," commonly referred to as the "hostility suite." Weir was also known to have young women friends in three or four different rooms at once, circulating like a honeybee among flowers, before settling on a winner for the night.

The record company generated sufficient income to give the band time off the road, but there was naturally a price: they owed an album to United Artists, which Rakow had brought in to save the Grateful Dead Record Company from bankruptcy. Coincidentally, Weir was in the process of building a studio, Ace's, over the garage of his Mill Valley home. Having the Dead help him finance construction appealed to him, and early in 1975 the Dead began to move in to Ace's to record. One of the new guys around was Robbie Taylor, a jeweler who'd met Frankie and been recruited for the construction project. Taylor was still on his back wiring things under the console when they began to roll tape for the first time, on a stormy full-moon shakedown night with a local band called Heroes. The studio still lacked alternating current, but Healy had a converter in his car, and they were able to run in an extension cord to power the board, tape machine, and amps. The lighting may have come from candles, but Ace's was off to a good start.

For the first time, the Grateful Dead went into a studio with no material and no notion of the next gig, a creative tabula rasa that would be unique in their recording history. Rock Scully later theorized that Garcia set it up that way to end the Garcia-Hunter domination of songwriting by ensuring that the whole band participated in the creative process from the beginning. Without economic pressure, at least for the first five months of their sojourn, they laughed, got crazy, and thoroughly enjoyed themselves. Every day they would convene in midafternoon, their cars choking the tiny amount of hillside space, and begin to rattle the canyon with their playing. Garcia made a point of inviting Mickey to join them, and Hart made a point of not bringing a full drum set—"I knew I had to come back the right way," which was to say gradually and modestly. They were making music just for themselves, and a slowed, contemplative, almost monastic feel emerged, a cool, blue-green tranquillity. Bit by bit, songs seeped out and evolved, and they were generally first-rate. Garcia said that he "wasn't listening to things" at the time. "I was really in an internal, interior kind of space, and I was really involved with a certain level of theoretical relationships. My point at that time was constructing scales and creating scales that generated their own harmony in ways that weren't symmetrical in regular, classical major-minor relationships. A whole different sensibility." And the different sensibility was exactly expressed in Hunter's lyrics, even though he was in England for a considerable part of the recording. His spare, reflective words could not have been further removed stylistically from the tall tales of earlier days, and they were just right.

The album began with "Help on the Way," a cosmic love song—

> *Paradise waits*
> *on the crest of a wave*
> *her angels in flame*
> *She has no pain*

Like a child, she is pure
She is not to blame

Poised for flight
Wings spread bright
Spring from night
into sun

—and then fell into a rhythm riff, "Slipknot," that Robbie Taylor would hear so many times in rehearsal he would feel it engraving itself on his DNA: it was, after all, his first time in a recording studio. "Franklin's Tower" followed, a bouncy rocker that would become a tour de force for Garcia over the years. Lyrically, it is fascinating, a lullabye birthday wish from Hunter for both his one-year-old son, Leroy, and the United States, then approaching its bicentennial. For it is Benjamin Franklin's tower and the bell of liberty that he addresses. "Wildflower seed on the sand and stone / may the four winds blow you safely home / Roll away . . . the dew." And it is the atomic morning dew of modern America that he would like to see roll away, like the stone at Gethsemane. Later, Hunter would say that the lyrics were labored over and then rushed when the recording frenzy came upon them. It did not sound that way.

"Crazy Fingers," which began side two of the album, was unusual in that Garcia wrote the tune after seeing a series of haiku in Hunter's notebook. The song had started out, he said, as a "power-rock raver," but the loveliness of the haiku called for a more graceful sprung rhythm. "Midnight on a carousel ride / Reaching for the gold ring down inside / Never could reach / It just slips away but I try."

A theme began to emerge from their deliberative state of mind and creativity. Their manager, Richard Loren, had visited Egypt the year before, as had Ken Kesey. Since his visit to Stonehenge in 1972, Phil Lesh had pursued an interest in geomancy, the study of power spots on the globe—and what more powerful spot could there be than the Great Pyramid? The previous two years had seen a major Israeli-Arab war and a gasoline crisis within the United States, which kept the desert fresh in their consciousness. And so they began to consider naming the album after the current leader of Saudi Arabia, Prince Faisal. They had a feeling, Lesh recalled, that perhaps Faisal was a bit "more of a humanist than any of his predecessors," that he was "trapped by history, by religion," by fate. His death by assassination on March 25 changed things, and the album title became *Blues for Allah*. The title song occupied most of the second side, and it was among the Dead's most remarkable compositions, with a structure that created openness by definition. Each player could play a note or an interval for as long as he wanted, until at a certain harmonic structure, they would have to change. Three-chord rock and roll it wasn't—it wasn't in a given key, or even in a particular time signature. And Hunter's lyrics were majestic, a cultural transfer that was respectful, non-exploitative, and apt.

> *Arabian wind*
> *The Needle's Eye is thin*
> *The Ships of State sail on mirage*
> *but drown in sand*
> *in No-Man's Land*
> *where ALLAH does command*
>
> *What good is spilling*
> *blood? It will not*
> *grow a thing*

One of Hunter's best friends and drinking buddies in this period was Barry Melton. One day Hunter showed Melton the lyrics to "Blues for Allah" and said to his highly left-wing friend, "Look, I'm political now. Are you happy?" "That doesn't sound political to me, Bob. That sounds abstruse." "Let's meet as friends / The flower of Islam / The fruit of Abraham"—perhaps not overt, but clearly political. Beneath the Middle Eastern drone of instruments and oblique lyrics, "Blues for Allah" also featured some remarkable sound sculpting, including the chirping of crickets—naturally, some escaped their cage and were just at hand when the engineer reached for something on the mixing board—and Garcia's voice, highly manipulated through a voltage-controlled amplifier. "He'd be saying 'Allah,'" recalled Mickey, "it's the envelope, and within the envelope is his voice, and delicate sounds like the paintbrushed glass, chimes, wood, and metal I was playing, and the crickets, which were slowed down three times and played backwards at half-speed, the sounds of the desert."

As usual, the Dead managed to shoot themselves in their collective foot. They'd put together a wonderful set of material under ideal and relaxed circumstances. Now Rakow and United Artists were screeching for product, so they slammed through the final recording process in two or three weeks. In the middle of this, Weir called Barlow. "Listen, I need a song tomorrow." He then played some riffs over the phone, and Barlow set to work. Fortunately, the melody that he imagined turned out to approximate the one Weir had in mind, and over the course of a day's ranching, he came up with words. At sunset he called Weir and dictated the lyrics to "The Music Never Stopped," which went essentially unchanged. Weir's other contribution, a Bach-inspired étude, "Sage and Spirit," came harder. Weir had worked himself into a complete corner in the studio, and nothing seemed to work. It was time, in the words of Monty Python, for something completely different. Down the road in Lagunitas lived a well-known flute player named Steve Schuster, and one night at midnight he got a phone call. He arrived at Ace's at 1 A.M., and by daylight they had a version of "Sage and Spirit" that made Bobby and the band happy.

The *Blues for Allah* sessions were briefly interrupted by one of the Dead's oddest live performances, the genesis of which was Bill Graham's fury. Graham had read in the newspaper that the City of San Francisco had reacted to a fiscal crisis by eliminating all extracurricular activities from its school budget, including all music and sports. He'd gone ballistic, and put on the SNACK (Students Need Athletics, Culture and Kicks) benefit concert at Kezar Stadium on March 23, 1975. In one of his finest moments, Bill assembled the Doobie Brothers, Graham Central Station, the Jefferson Starship, Joan Baez, Santana, Neil Young, Bob Dylan, and Marlon Brando among others to raise $250,000 for the school board. Since their old buddy David Crosby was around and interested, the Dead created "David and the Dorks" and worked up "Blues for Allah." But on the morning of the show, David's son was born, and the Dead went on without him, although with Ned Lagin and Merl Saunders. In front of an audience of fifty thousand that wasn't their own, and a radio audience of much more and ditto, and after being off the scene for six months, they chose, as always, to play what they liked—forty minutes of atonal majesty, followed by an encore of "Johnny B. Goode." What a sense of humor.

It was a year for goofiness. In late January Grateful Dead Records sent out the following letter:

Dear Guerrilla:

You, along with the Dead Heads, will be getting within a few weeks a major communication from us. Since you are our advance guard, a little advance word . . . We want you to organize and communicate with each other so that you can help us take this trip to a dramatically higher level . . . but further it's a possibility, if remote, that the Dead may play in spots with advance notice to you guys as the only announcement (organization is, therefore, essential). "Big Steve" Parrish *[sic]*, one of our most energetic brothers, has volunteered to be the main guerrilla contact point. He can be reached at Box 548 Stinson Beach, California 94970. We realize that this message is vague but this is heavy water we're treading in strange times and we've learned "loose lips sink ships." God Love Ya!—Grateful Dead Records.

More directly, the mailer also mentioned the impending release of Robert Hunter's new solo album, *Tiger Rose;* Keith and Donna's eponymous solo album; *Pistol Packin' Mama,* a Garcia bluegrass production adventure at Mickey's barn with Chubby Wise, Don Reno, and Frank Wakefield; *Old and in the Way,* a live album recorded by Bear; and Phil Lesh and Ned Lagin's *Seastones.* Each would have its moments, but *Old and in the Way* would document the good and the bad of Grateful Dead Records. Round Records paid David Grisman $1,000 to assemble the album, and despite significant sales, he never saw another dime. Garcia was aware of the sloppiness of the business, but hid rather than confront the situation. As a result, although Jerry and David would play a number of gigs in 1974 and 1975 with a varying cast of people, including Taj Mahal and Richard Greene (the Great American String Band), their relationship lapsed into nothingness after a final jam session at David's house, and they did not speak for the next fifteen years. On the other hand, the album itself had a phenomenal impact on bluegrass, and in David's opinion "kind of turned bluegrass around," turning on thousands of people to the music form and kick-starting a new and larger audience. "It's one of the pillars that's holding up bluegrass now," he said in the nineties.

Seastones would also have a depressing economic history. Lesh would call it "a horrible bummer for Ned both aesthetically and financially—it was a rip-off. It was the lowest priority project for Round Records." Musicians rarely respect their record company, even (or especially) when it's their own record company.

One other bit of their past resolved itself that winter. On February 12, 1975, Lenny Hart died of natural causes. Since his release from jail, he'd been teaching music in Mill Valley. Mickey went to the funeral home, cleared the room, took out the snakewood sticks that had been his inheritance, played a traditional rudimental drum piece, "The Downfall of Paris," on Lenny's coffin, and split.

The Dead's suspension of touring had its intended effect, and every band member found something of interest to pursue. Kreutzmann retreated to Mendocino County, where he began developing a horse ranch. Mickey joined up with the young tabla master Zakir Hussain and created the Diga Rhythm Band, a percussion group—he called it a "twenty-first-century rhythm machine"—which opened for the Jefferson Starship in May at Winterland. Keith and Donna put together a band under their own name and began to gig around the Bay Area. Weir fell in with King-fish. And Lesh joined with Ned Lagin to perform a couple of live versions of *Seastones,* the first in June at a small college in San Rafael, a few blocks from 5th and Lincoln. It included Hart, Garcia, and David Crosby, who had a ball. "[Garcia] and I talked back and forth," said Crosby. "Garcia with his guitar, me with my voice. It sounded like a couple of Martians talking. Very weird, but great, man."

The Dead celebrated the August release of *Blues for Allah* with a private party at the Great American Music Hall in San Francisco, inviting members of the Billboard Radio Programmers Forum to hear the new music. They used McCune Audio's P.A., and Mort Feld, an industry pro who'd been setting up P.A.s since well before Monterey Pop, found himself challenged. He'd never worked with crickets before—they were caged and miked in the basement—but once convinced, he enjoyed himself thoroughly. Fortunately for cricketmaster Hart, this bunch did not escape. Always a fount of ideas, Mickey was coming back strong. As they set up at the Great American, he told Ram Rod to go to the beach and get a truckload of sand so that everyone entering the hall could feel like they were at the desert. The building management was not thrilled, and the idea went away. They played splendidly, and the show was taped for radio broadcast.

Philip Garris's album cover of a skeleton fiddler was brilliant, reminiscent of Mahler's Fourth Symphony, subtitled "Death Takes a Fiddle," wherein the metaphorical boatman on the Styx plays a violin. No one liked the painting at first, because the skeleton had green-lensed sunglasses and looked repulsively insectoid. Then the record company's Steve Brown suggested to Garris that he change the lenses to red, and that made all the difference. With the release came another missive from the band.

Dear Dead Heads:
 After going collectively insane about two years ago from pressures of traveling and devastating internal and external intrigue . . . What was known as "The Grateful Dead" was dismantled and the parts sent off for repairs . . . This is an operation a monster can sustain, which distinguishes him from an individual body . . . If this seems a fanciful

account, I remind you that no two stories agree, only that something happened and it was kind of like that . . . A new kind of tour "hit and run" consisting of unannounced concerts is being considered.

There were two such gigs in 1975. In June, the members of the Dead came together onstage—the evening's bill was listed as the Jerry Garcia and Friends, Kingfish, Keith and Donna Band, and The Mirrors—in a benefit for the family of the late Bob Fried, a much-loved poster artist. Although no one mentioned or probably even thought very much of it, it was the Dead's tenth anniversary as a band. In September they joined the Starship—then on top of the world with the no. 1 album, *Red Octopus*—at Lindley Meadow in Golden Gate Park.

But they were in no hurry to hit the road. In August, Garcia's bar band made a major shift. His projects the past three years had always had Merl as a covocalist, mostly doing covers or standards, with Garcia as a partner. Now the band's keyboard player was the brilliant, though sadly alcoholic, Nicky Hopkins, and the band became Garcia's own, playing originals like the Hunter-Garcia song "Mission in the Rain." Hopkins's disability made him a player who couldn't last, and early in 1976 Garcia recruited Keith and Donna to replace him. Friends speculated that part of Garcia's motivation in recruiting Keith was as a therapeutic gesture for the troubled pianist. But Godchaux was a game player who could follow Garcia up—or down—any musical avenue, and their rehearsals were as much fun as shows. What they called the Front Street Sheiks might spend a day doing all Dylan tunes or all Beatles tunes, most of which were never performed. They spent weeks on gospel material, or piano jazz, the Swan Silvertones or Art Tatum, drenching themselves in music for no reason other than personal pleasure.

Early in 1976, the future of the Dead was revealed. A Dead Head mailing that announced several releases, including *Diga,* and included animation stills from the movie that Garcia was slowly pulling together from the October 1974 Winterland shows, also said, "and a decision that vacationing is too exhausting to continue, meaning the Grateful Dead has decided to get back into touring." Lesh added, "We're all horny to play . . . If you're as hot to hear us as we are to do it, we can get the mother rollin' one more time, for sure." Late in January Garcia visited Bonnie Simmons at KSAN and opined that the movie—*The Grateful Dead Movie* was as clever a title as they could come up with—might be out in July, "if we get lucky." He was only a year off. And in April he told an interviewer that the most important thing to him is "the survival of the Grateful Dead. I think that's my main trip now . . . Well, I feel like I've had both trips [the Dead and his individual efforts] . . . And, really, I'm not that taken with my own ideas. I don't really have that much to say, and I'm more interested in being involved in something that's larger than me. And I really can't talk to anybody else either," he said, laughing.

As spring wore on, the shaky economics of the record company, exacerbated by the financial drain of the movie, ran up against reality. It had been financed by a line of credit from the Bank of Boston, and from all accounts one of the reasons for the bank's interest was the Dead Headedness of the chairman's daughter. As Rakow later related it, he brought Garcia to Boston to meet the board, where after some light schmooze— "Should my daughter study clarinet or violin?" "What she wants, man." "Are EPI speakers any good?" "Yeah, we like them"—Garcia leaned over to Rakow and snickered, "We're gonna own this place. This is fuckin' backstage, man." The thrill of marching into the Bank of Boston in blue jeans, of being treated like somebody by stuffy bankers, tickled the pirate in Garcia, even as he knew that it was a mirage. He owned little—in fact, in November 1975 he had signed away the Stinson Beach house to M.G. in settlement of their separation—and yet here he was swashbuckling. It was fun for a while, although he could hardly take it seriously, and didn't. That Christmas, Rakow asked him to put together a musical Christmas card for the chairman's daughter. Nothing loath, he and Mickey went into the studio, goofed around like crazy, and produced a mess, screeching carols like soused reindeer, complete with sonic effects. Shortly afterward in early 1976, the Bank of Boston began to call in the Dead's debt. No doubt Mickey and Jerry's cavalier attitude didn't help, although it was surely the record company's hopeless finances that caused the bank's change in position.

Years before, on their first visit to New York City, Rakow had turned to Laird Grant and said, "I'll show you New York." He bought two ice creams from a cart and then began screaming that they weren't worth the price. A crowd gathered, and eventually he walked away without paying. "See, if you look up, everybody looks up." On a grander scale, he was still stealing ice cream. Rakow later claimed that he'd gone to United Artists and demanded another million dollars to finish the movie, in return for delivering four Dead albums and solo albums from Garcia and Weir. Since UA already had a contract for the Dead albums, they inquired as to their motivation. Rakow responded that if they didn't come up with the money, he would deliberately bankrupt the Grateful Dead and then make a deal with Warner Bros., since bankruptcy trustees would nullify existing contracts. Rakow recalled Garcia's response as "he fucking loved it. He was jumping up and down." Perhaps, for Rakow's benefit, that was so. But while Garcia cared nothing for his own finances, he had respect for his brothers and the Grateful Dead as a separate entity. As Rakow was fond of saying, "I was the family barracuda. You don't ever want to fuck with your barracuda because the barracuda will do what barracudas do. He will fucking eat you. What happened was that the Grateful Dead became convinced that it was in their best interests to fuck me. Garcia and I had a meeting on it and Garcia looked me right in the eye and said, 'It's clear that this is going to happen.' Because I went across a really entrenched interest in the Grateful Dead and that was Hal Kant." True, Kant was an entrenched interest socially, but not economically—he was a retained attorney giving legal advice, but he had no financial interest. Bob Seidemann's thought was that Rakow "would drive this economic train into the wall just to watch the parts fly all over the room."

Two other events crashed down on Rakow and the record company late that spring. One of the items promised to United Artists was a live album from the final week at Winterland in 1974. Lesh and Owsley were given the tapes and told to have it mixed in nine days. But the tapes were disastrously bad. "We had sixteen tracks," said Lesh, "and the bass drum was reading over at +3 in the red on the VU meter and everything else was reading -20, down into tape noise." Donna's tracks were entirely missing, Ned Lagin hadn't been recorded, and there were weird noises all over. Rakow dismissed Lesh's complaints as "ethereal bullshit." Lesh replied, "Rakow wouldn't know good material if it came up and pissed on his shoes." After eighteen days of work, using delays, filters, and tricks, they had what was still the worst Grateful Dead album to date, *Steal Your Face.*

It was not possible to mortally offend Phil Lesh and continue to work with the Grateful Dead, but there was more. At the same time, Mickey Hart was in the throes of mixing *Diga.* Rakow was on Mickey's back demanding the album, and in fact, he would blame Hart's endless remixing and delays for crippling the company. Hart had finally gone to work at Wally Heider's studio, sharing time with Maria Muldaur. He only had five or six days available, and it took his crew a full day to set up his highly elaborate gear. As he left on the first night, he warned everyone to leave his stuff alone, but when he returned, the cables had been disconnected to make way for another job. And so unto the second day. On the third day he melted down. "We are taking this studio in the name of the people," he announced, and called (a) Rakow and (b) Sweet William, his old Hell's Angel buddy. Rakow wouldn't respond to the call, which was a demand for defense. Sweet William, carrying a sword cane and with some compatriots, soon arrived and took up a position at the top of the stairs in front of the door. Grace Slick was recording downstairs and became confused when she had to ask permission to come in. She asked her old friend Mickey what was happening. "What's going on," Mickey replied, "is that we're trying to make a record. It's okay—you're the safest now you've ever been." When Heider threatened to cut off some equipment from outside the room, Hart counterthreatened, "For every missing line, I'll throw a piece of equipment out the window." Heider decided not to call the police, Maria Muldaur took some time off, and Mickey and his engineer, who was by now demanding $500 an hour hazardous duty pay—Hart agreed, then reneged—settled down to work. About four days later they stumbled out, tapes in hand, and Heider and his employees shook Mickey's hand in tribute to genuine rock and roll madness.

A couple of weeks later, in Los Angeles in June, Mickey saw Rakow for the first time and began to berate him for desertion. When Rakow responded by telling him to wait in the car, Mickey jumped up and choked him. "He wouldn't say uncle," recalled Hart, "so I put him out. He walked with a cane for a year behind that." A day or two later Rakow got a call from the Grateful Dead Record Company attorney, David Hellman, who told him that he'd been fired. He considered the possibility of just going away, but that wasn't his style. "Or do I make sure everyone feels as fucked as I do?" He wrote himself checks for $225,000, effectively disemboweling Grateful Dead Records. He went to visit his ex-wife, Lydia, then living in Bolinas, and told her that "he had done something with the Grateful Dead, that they were going to be looking for him, and I should beware or something." He also told Lydia that the real reason he wanted to fuck the Dead was that he'd been subjected to racist jokes about being a "New York Jew." He had a final meeting with Lesh and Garcia, where he said, "I'm cutting out. I already cut the check. So, fuck you." Lesh got up and walked out, "because I wanted to strangle Jerry," since Rakow had always been Garcia's protégé within the Dead.

Rakow, and a few others, argued that the money was due him based on separate negotiations, although taking it at that time was clearly a vindictive act. It was Hal Kant's professional opinion that the $225,000 was out-and-out embezzlement, but that Garcia did not want Rakow prosecuted. In the end they negotiated a settlement in which he kept the money but retained no interest in the record company. Steve Brown and others tried to keep the company going, but without Rakow's tap dance—and the money he'd taken—their efforts were futile. As the summer came in, the company folded.

Other than Mickey, who'd poured his soul into *Diga,* the last of the Round Records releases, and watched it go unnoticed in the wreckage of the record company, the most disappointed person in the whole mess was possibly Chesley Millikin, who'd had actual record company experience and who was a true believer in the Dead. He felt that Rakow "seriously took advantage of the mojo that was the Grateful Dead, that was Jerry Garcia, that was this whole thing that we all were . . . There was one brief shining moment when a truly independent record company could be a 'Camelot,' could have the same feeling as 1967—and that sonofabitch killed it."

The Monster
Revives

(6/76–8/78)

he dragon breathed once more, and the Dead returned to the
stage on June 3, 1976, at the Paramount Theater in Portland,
Oregon. Appropriately enough, they began with a new song,
"Might as Well," Hunter's tribute to the Great Train Ride of
1970. With two drummers again, they had actually given some conscious
thought to what they should be up to musically, and it boiled down to
simplicity. Though they would play "Cosmic Charley" and "St. Stephen"
for some time, their general pattern was to play relatively simple material
with authority rather than their most complex work, because their rehearsal time would be minimal. Lesh had preferred to stop singing rather
than accept throat surgery, and so a number of tunes were put away for a
while, including "Jack Straw," "Candyman," and "He's Gone." Garcia
heard a tape of Kenny Loggins doing "Friend of the Devil" as a slow ballad, and transformed his own version into a dirge. Weir brought in the
Reverend Gary Davis's "Samson and Delilah" and a new tune he'd come
up with during his Kingfish sojourn, "Lazy Lightning," which combined
7/4 time, an R&B rhythm, and jazz chords.

Their first tour was in small theaters, with tickets sold directly to
the Dead Head mailing list. Richard Loren and Bill Graham had never

gotten along very well, not least because Bill continued to think of Loren as his former employee, and during the hiatus Richard and John Scher had developed a self-contained touring setup for the Jerry Garcia Band that included in-house catering courtesy of chef Sy Kosis, a solid production manager in Mo Morrison, good security, and a generally smooth style. Early in 1976, Scher came to Marin and sat on Weir's floor for a four-hour band meeting. Garcia said, "John, explain to people how we tour," and John outlined the virtues of keeping almost everything, especially catering, in-house. For the next nineteen years, Scher would handle Dead concerts east of the Rockies, with Bill Graham Presents continuing to work along the west coast. The first tour was a thundering success, even if it did take two squads of tactical police to keep the peace in front of Manhattan's Beacon Theater. The legend of Heads trying to break in through a next-door basement by digging through the walls with knives was definitely apocryphal. The tour was marred only by an exceptionally egregious *People* magazine article, which the band had agreed to as a vehicle to promote *Diga*. What came out, thanks to an overly helpful record company source, focused almost exclusively on Garcia's divorce from M.G. Simultaneously, the magazine covered rock and roll's ascent into national politics. The gonzo drug king himself, Hunter Thompson, and Phil Walden, the head of Capricorn Records, were to be significant players in the nomination of Jimmy Carter as Democratic candidate for president, while the social event of the Democratic convention in Manhattan that bicentennial summer was the *Rolling Stone* party. Rock had come of age.

Two weeks after the small-theater tour ended in San Francisco, the Dead returned to the East Coast for two large outdoor dates, and it appeared that they had returned to business as usual. The summer ended in tragedy. Early in September, Rex Jackson was in the grip of a cocaine-fueled bender, and after several days of being tended by Mickey at the ranch, he'd worn out the drummer, who turned him over to Bear. On September 5, 1976, Rex was driving back to his home in Mill Valley from West Marin when his car went over the edge of the road, killing him in the crash. Rex was a special personality, the first crew member to accept a promotion to road manager. It was a considerable loss to the scene, robbing Cole, his son by Betty Cantor, and Cassidy, his daughter by Eileen Law, of their father, and the Dead family of a brother. Forty members of his extended family flew to Oregon for the funeral. Donna Jean Godchaux would write the song "Sunrise" for him.

The performance year peaked at Oakland Coliseum with two shows in mid-October with the Who. Hanging with the Who was fun. Garcia,

Weir, and Keith Moon sat backstage together, and Garcia told Moon, "Congratulations on your fabulous record of trashing hotel rooms, man, it's truly part of the tradition." Weir interjected, "Is it true that you drove a rented car into a swimming pool?" Moon smirked, *"Rented?* That was my own bloody Rolls-Royce Silver Corniche," then turned to Garcia and winked: "If you've got it, sink it."

On the first day, the Dead choked, ultraconscious that the audience was not exclusively their own, and tried too hard. On the second day, they loosened up and it was a triumph, so much so that the Who dedicated their encore, "Shakin' All Over," to the Dead and their fans.

Having put the circus back on the road, the band's other great need was to find a new record company. Even though their orientation, both aesthetically and economically, was to live performance, they shared the universal belief of American musical entertainers that a record company contract was essential. In a very few years, they would be able to challenge that assumption, but not yet. For the present, they were warily cynical. In an atypically cranky interview in 1970, Garcia had been asked his opinion of Warner Bros. and had griped, "Shitty. They have terrible distribution and they don't sell records. That's the only thing a record company is good for . . . They like to think they're far out, but they're not . . . A record company is a vampire. It's really no fucking good. It's an evil trip. It's like bleeding musicians." Later he calmed down and admitted, "I'm not really that far down on Warner Bros. because they've been OK to us. We've been a pretty weird band of fellows as far as relationships with artists and record companies. Warner Bros. has got some good people but I really don't think that they know how to do it."

Their search in 1976 would turn out to be pretty simple. "It wasn't like a whole lot of people wanted us," said Hart. Joe Smith had exited Warner Bros., and there was no inclination to return there. That left Clive Davis, who had signed the New Riders while at Columbia Records and made an offer for the Dead. In 1973 he had been ousted from Columbia in a pseudoscandal about petty cash that actually masked a corporate power struggle, and his breakfast date the next morning was with Jon McIntire, to whom he reflected, "There are people more powerful than me." Davis had assumed leadership of Bell Records and changed the name to Arista, after a New York City high school honorary that he (and the Dead's attorney, Hal Kant) had belonged to. It was a relatively small company in 1976, and the Dead gave it visibility. He attributed the Dead's interest in Arista to a meeting he'd had with the band while they were planning for Grateful Dead Records. "I came up to San Francisco . . . [1 said] I think you're being naive—they were asking me questions about virginal [vinyl] discs, Good Humor trucks, offbeat, nontraditional, and it sounded good, but they were not aware of credit—so I, in a very, very factual way, not in any scoffing way, but treating them with respect that intelligent but misguided people deserve, I really made a very factual case for the warning signals they must consider and solve. The feedback was very positive over the next years." Davis said that he was "touched" when the Dead called him in 1976, displaying a "faith and belief in a year-old company."

At first sight, it was a relationship loaded with potential for disaster. Davis was hands-on, and the Dead were anything but open to guidance. A few years earlier, Jon McIntire had mused that if he'd driven his rental car through the front doors of Warner Bros., no one would have been surprised, since he represented a gang of lunatics and such behavior was almost expected. Later he'd used the word "apocalypse" in a conversation with Elliot Goldman at CBS, and Goldman had asked him what he meant. ". . . and I say I don't think you really want to hear this right now." "Yes, I do," said Goldman. "So I started going on about the image of the apocalypse in visual art and literature . . . the crisis leading to the transformation." In 1976, Hal Kant and Goldman, who had come to Arista with Davis, were able to go straight to business, and it was a fairly easy negotiation. It was a good deal for the Dead, though as Hal Kant recalled, "we were desperate, so the deal could have been better. It was supposed to be a five-year contract, and ended up as a twelve-year one [because of extensions on delivery of albums]." But it ended their relationship with United Artists and gave the band a fresh start with a record company.

Arista's first hit was Barry Manilow's song "Mandy," and over the next twenty years, the company's greatest triumphs would come in the pop world. Yet its relationship with the Dead turned out to be largely positive, in part because after their experience with running their own record company, they wanted someone, as then company treasurer Alan Trist put it, to "take all those headaches away." Initially, Davis tried to make the kinds of specific musical suggestions he offered his other acts. In 1978 he wrote Richard Loren, "This might be an off-the-wall suggestion but I've come across a song that if restructured a little, could be a possible hit. Perhaps it's too pop for The Dead but I thought I would submit it in any event to you for the group's consideration . . . The song really would require strings, so once again I present this to you with some hesitancy. Since a hit single could add a million units to any Dead album, here's the tape. If you feel it's not in the Dead image, I understand." Though it must have frustrated him when the Dead ignored his input, Davis concluded at length that the Dead, like their label mate Patti Smith, were visionaries that could not—and should not—be controlled. So even though Garcia sat at one of the meetings drawing a picture of a shark with Clive's head on it, its teeth dripping blood, he kept his sketch pad to himself.

Davis's primary demand was that the band use producers, and they did so for the next three albums, willing enough to get what Garcia called "fresh ears." The first suggestion was Keith Olsen, who'd recently done a Fleetwood Mac album. It had a unified band sound and wasn't overloaded with extras, so Phil pronounced himself willing. Weir liked Olsen's style and was enthusiastically in favor. The rest of the band went along. As usual, the group had zero energy for the exhausting business of interviewing applicants. Olsen flew up to Marin and spent six hours talking with band members. At a second meeting the next day, he spent seven hours with Weir waiting for the rest of the band to show up. "Garcia never made it." Olsen finally met Jerry the following week at the Burbank Studios, where he was working on *The Grateful Dead Movie.* The energy Garcia displayed at work excited both of them. Olsen was the first guy they talked to, and they grabbed him.

Early in 1977 they began work on the album that would be called *Terrapin Station,* and it would prove to be yet another Grateful Dead flawed masterpiece. Much of the material was brilliant. Weir's main tune, "Estimated Prophet," was one of his finest. Jamming in the studio, he came up with a 7/4 "carpet," and "it freaked me," he said. "I loved it." Barlow was conveniently at hand, and they swiftly hammered a song into shape. Though not technically reggae, it had that feel. But no reggae band has a rhythm section that changed 7/4 into 14/8 to make it, as Kreutzmann put it, more "subtle." The song's subject, the prophet, was a takeoff on the crazed man-with-a-message who hangs out near every backstage door, what Barlow would call "a gonzo psychedelic derelict . . . but every once in a while, he's standing in a shaft of light. It's *God's* shaft of light, it's not just his; he's not just brain-damaged." There was a certain tension between Barlow and Weir, Barlow thinking Weir enjoyed complexity for complexity's sake, Weir denying it. "I was just writing it because I wanted to hear it. I wasn't trying to prove anything. I was just following my fingers." But as Barlow remarked, "The tension [between himself and Weir] was perfectly attuned to the character we're talking about, the utter madness."

"Terrapin Station," which would occupy side two of the album, was simply stupendous, and an eerily amazing example of simultaneous inspiration. One day that winter, Hunter had looked out on San Francisco Bay from his home on the shore at China Camp and seen a storm. The lightning flash on the water sent him to his table, where he began to write. His tale was universal and mythic, something he could have told a thousand years before around a fire pit. Derived from the English ballad "Lady of Carlisle," which Hunter would also record in a solo project, "Terrapin" began with an invocation to the muse—"Let my inspiration flow / in token lines suggesting rhythm"—and went on to tell the story of the lady and the fan, and the two men who pursued her, a soldier and a sailor. He wrote for three days, producing one thousand words on eight pages.

As Hunter was madly scribbling away, Garcia was driving home from the East Bay to Marin, and halfway across the Richmond Bridge, within sight of Hunter's home, he began to hear a song in his head. He raced home and got the chord changes down before he forgot them, and the next day went over to China Camp, where Hunter showed him his work. Of Hunter's work, Garcia took the first page, half of the second page, and the last page. He fit the words to the music, showed it to the band, and had them work out their own parts. Very quickly, they had a new tune, if a majestic, rolling, near-symphony can be called a tune. Late in February they went to Southern California to try out some of the material and opened the first show with "Terrapin," a version so good that Hunter got "about as close as I ever expect to get to feeling certain that we were doing what we were put here to do." By April they were finished with the major recording. Thanks to higher percussion levels than usual and Olsen's habit of selecting extremely unflattering takes for playback, the album sounded quite decent. With the Dead's work done, Olsen flew to London, where he brought in Paul Buckmaster for an orchestral score that would complete the piece.

Meanwhile, and at very long last, Garcia was finishing *The Grateful Dead Movie.* What had begun almost as a lark in 1974 was, in May 1977, approaching its end. It came at an extreme cost, both for Garcia personally and for the Dead as a whole. Eleven days before the "last shows," he and Rakow had hired forty-six people to document them, including Leon Gast, Al Maysles, and Don Lenzer, who'd helped shoot *Woodstock.* There was no director. Occasionally, Gast would tell the cameramen who were shooting handheld to get off the stage so that the boom camera could get some shots that didn't have cameras in them, but other than that, they were on their own. By the third night, the band had stopped noticing the lenses and the cameramen had synced into the rhythm of the Dead. Rakow informed an appalled Hal Kant that the movie budget was

$125,000. Hal replied, "Ron, the amount of film you're shooting here, four days and four crews, you will not be able to process the film—not editing, just processing—for $125,000. I don't know what you're paying your crews, but whatever you're paying them, and then the whole postproduction—you have no budget here."

Ultimately, the film would cost more than $600,000, at a time when, because of the hiatus, the band had no extra money. As Kant put it, "We had to find every way in the world to get money for that film, which got us into big problems with banks . . . we screwed a bank out of a lot of money." Actually, Hal got the Bank of Boston to settle for one-third on the dollar for what they'd fronted the Dead's record and film companies. Making the movie was, Garcia said, more than "two years of incredible doubt, crisis after crisis, as [it] was endlessly eating bucks. Every time I thought about something, my mind would come back to the film and I'd get depressed." Meantime, other band members—Phil in particular— thought of it as "Jerry's jerkoff," and pondered the fact that the band as a whole was financing one man's obsessive vision.

After the shows, Garcia had sat down in a house in Mill Valley they called Round Reels with 125 hours of raw footage, which he and assistants would watch, match to the sound track, and catalog. "I wanted elegantly framed, seamless photography," he told an interviewer. "And I wanted a sort of roughness to the general quality of everything else. That was the only original conception." Originally, he'd thought of the film as a canned concert, but as he watched film, he began to see a real movie. Garcia had the type of photography he wanted, and his years of movie-watching had given him the gift of seeing rhythm and flow in film. What he did not anticipate was the sheer tedium of the filmmaking process at that time, before videotape and computers. Early on, someone came up with the idea of using Dead posters as the background for the titles, and then of animating some of that. Susan Crutcher, one of the editors, knew an animator named Gary Gutierrez, with whom she'd worked on the children's television program *The Electric Company,* and he joined them. Since the bicentennial was fast approaching, they chose "U.S. Blues" as the music for the animation sequence and budgeted $8,000 for it. Guided by what Gutierrez would come to realize was the most encouraging boss he'd ever know, Gary's ideas for the animation flourished, and the budget grew, eventually reaching $25,000. Gary worked away, manipulating images under a camera in real time, eighty times for eighty frames, which was a mere three seconds of film. The artistic results were glorious. To the accountants, band management, and other band members, the animation was a black hole that inhaled dollars.

By late 1976 Garcia was purchasing books of airline commuter tickets to fly daily to Burbank Studios to mix the sound track. Now his partner in crime became Dan Healy, who would be an essential part of transferring the aural part of the vision to film. Together they invented new technologies like "phase panning," so that the sound on the film would subtly follow the camera. Though they'd gone in with negative expectations, the freedom they gave the union filmmakers at Burbank paid off. "Our willingness to be totally crazy," thought Garcia, "inspired them." They earned one of his favorite compliments: "They were game." So game, the studio used *The Grateful Dead Movie* to demonstrate dubbing room techniques during the 1977 Oscar week festivities. Ironically, the film that followed them into Burbank Studios, and would open just a few weeks before them, was *Star Wars,* economically the precise opposite of Garcia's "little movie." Made for about $10 million, it grossed more than $300 million, and with its sequels and succeeding merchandising would, over the next two decades, generate more than $4 billion in business. George Lucas and the Dead would cross paths regularly, the Dead working at his Skywalker Ranch, both sharing an interest in and a relationship with Joseph Campbell.

By spring 1977, Garcia and company were nearing completion. In the meantime, something very sad had happened: Jerry Garcia had discovered heroin. There were any number of reasons why he reached for a psychic painkiller. Rakow, his comrade-in-conspiracy, had betrayed him, and although Garcia would never permit a bad word to be said about Ron, the pain Rakow had caused him was evident. (Contrarily, Richard Loren would argue that the loss of the record company mattered relatively little. "They were musicians, not record company people. They could still make music, so, so what?") The grinding stress of film editing was a considerable shock to Garcia. He'd long daydreamed about his cinephile talents, but this tedious reality was not fun. Rex Jackson's death was painful.

The adulation of being "Jerry Garcia" with a capital *J* and *G,* combined with the required role of being a leader who didn't want to lead, clearly contributed. Fame, thought his old friend Bob Seidemann, had turned him into a "Flying Dutchman" of loneliness, condemned to wander without intimacy. In particular, intimacy with a lover had always been a problem for him, dating back to his shattered and never-healed relationship with his mother. Later, Garcia would say of women that "I like 'em weird, the weirder the better," which suggested, among other things, a certain lack of self-esteem. For that, he was in the right company. None of the band members had showed to this point in time any gift for enduring intimacy with women, and their day-to-day relationships with each other took place in the Dead world, where the permitted range of emotion, said John Barlow, "ran the gamut from irony to spite." The only place things really worked was in what John called the "sacred space" of playing. As Kreutzmann put it, "Words would make us enemies, but music makes us lovers."

All of the realities of Garcia's life added up to extreme external pressures on his personal sphere. And that personal realm was being shredded by the messy end of his relationship with Deborah Koons. Late in 1976 Sue Stephens, Richard Loren's assistant, was at work at their Mill Valley office when a breathless Garcia burst in, ran upstairs to the loft, and said, "Hide me, hide me." Locked out, Deborah stood outside shouting, then picked up a full Alhambra water bottle and heaved it through the kitchen window. Climbing in over the shards, she was met by a couple of visiting crew members, who dragged her back out. She literally left "claw marks on the wooden paneling down both sides of the hallway walls," said Stephens.

It had been a tumultuous relationship for a very long time, as Deborah apparently had an inclination for physical violence, at least as directed against glass and furniture. Weir later recalled coming home and finding Garcia on his couch. "What's up?" "Deborah broke up the house." "Oh, your old lady mad at you?" "Well, yeah, but it's more than that. She broke up everything—I mean everything—in the house." Deborah's cook would recall a more or less permanent sign in the kitchen that read, "Be careful of broken glass." The incident at the office marked the end of the relationship, and various friends speculated that one of the subconsciously desired results of Garcia's heroin use was a decrease of sexual desire. With heroin, all you need is heroin—and maybe cigarettes. In any case, around this time a man showed up at the Dead office with what was called Persian Opium, though it was actually a smokable brown heroin. Jerry and Richard Loren sampled it. After all the cocaine, the "first taste of heroin," Loren said, "was so ecstatic—a balm for frazzled nerves." Garcia took to it with sad enthusiasm. In the long run, it would have predictably horrific effects, including the destruction of his unquestioned moral authority within the band, but in the short term, his pain went away, his doubts were stilled, and he was able to finish the movie.

On June 1, *The Grateful Dead Movie* made its debut at New York City's Ziegfeld Theater. It was a Monarch/Noteworthy Release, which told a tale. Hal Kant had wanted to take the film to a normal distributor and get an advance that would cover the costs. Garcia, however, wanted to treat it as a concert experience, and so at a meeting at Hal's home in the spring he brought out John Scher and told him in front of Kant, "You're going to distribute the film." John sputtered, "Excuse me? The only thing I know about movies is that I go to them. I don't know anything about the movie business." Garcia replied, "That may be true, but you know more about promoting the Grateful Dead than anybody. And this is the Grateful Dead." As a result, John (Monarch) and Richard Loren (Noteworthy) were given the assignment of "four-walling" the movie, which meant renting the movie theaters from scratch. There being only ten prints, they chose the nicest old movie houses in the biggest Dead Head cities, brought in the best possible sound system, and tried to involve the local promoter. They did not make the band's money back.

Critical opinion varied. The *New York Times* pronounced, "Aural excitement is pitted against visual monotony. Monotony wins." At home, the *Chronicle*'s John Wasserman acclaimed the opening animation "which, as a short, would merit an Academy Award," and announced that no rock and roll film "has ever as faithfully represented the feeling, the vibes, the essence of the relationship between a band, its music and its audience." In the *Village Voice*, Robert Christgau wrote that the film "justifies itself visually by catching the hesitations and second thoughts that go into Jerry Garcia's improvisation." And in classic criticspeak, he noted how the ordinary faces of the audience were such a significant part of the movie. "Jerry no doubt considers each beautiful in its own way. Such soft-headedness is his fatal flaw, and such equanimity is the secret of his magic."

With the movie now off their collective back, the Dead resumed the road on June 4, with a show in Los Angeles and then three brilliant nights at Winterland. They were gearing up for the release of *Terrapin* and a busy summer when a giant monkey wrench came swirling out of the cosmos. Some weeks before, Bear had given Mickey Hart a damaru, a Tibetan drum made of a human skull. It did not produce a great tone, and Mickey put it away. In the weeks after, he found himself out of sorts, getting sick, bumping into things, injuring himself in minor ways. Finally, he remembered the drum and decided to get rid of it. At length, Phil Lesh suggested, "Why don't we give it back to the Tibetans?" A lama named Tarthang Tulku was in Berkeley, and they went to visit him. He accepted the drum and said, "I hope you have been most careful, Mickey Hart. This is a drum of great, great power. It wakes the dead, you know." Maybe Mickey hadn't been so careful. On June 20, he was returning from a Norton Buffalo gig at the Miramar Beach Inn to his friend Valerie Hawes's nearby ranch in Half Moon Bay, some thirty-odd miles south of San Francisco on the coast. Somewhat the worse for wear from drink, he rolled the car over the edge of the road and down about twenty feet, where it caught in the branches of a conveniently located tree. The next stop was three hundred feet down. His passenger, Rhonda Jensen, had been helping Mickey since the ranch's earliest days, and she saved him again, crawling out of the car to get help. He needed it. He had a broken arm, a broken collarbone, several cracked ribs, and a punctured lung, and his left ear was nearly ripped off his head. His Hell's Angels friends moved into the hospital and kept an eye on him during his early convalescence, which made smoking pot at the hospital somewhat easier. It was instantly clear that his full recovery would take some months, and so the other band members looked for something to occupy them for the summer.

His peculiar sense of humor working overtime, Weir consciously decided to "go L.A." and work again with Keith Olsen to create a truly slick solo album. McIntire booked studio time, the date approached, and Weir and Barlow looked at each other and wondered where the songs were going to come from. Shortly before they were due to start at the studio, their work was interrupted by John Barlow's wedding to Elaine Parker, a celebration that very nearly cost them Weir. Around 4:30 A.M. of the wedding day, after a party where they decided that Wild Turkey was kid stuff and Everclear was the drink of choice, Weir decided a little sleep was in order, and headed for his bunk in the refurbished chicken coop.

"Now this was in a period in my life," Barlow recalled, "when I felt like the best way to make a certain kind of point was to shoot a gun off indoors. It will get everyone's attention, even if they're sort of used to it . . . So I ask around, everyone says Weir went to bed. 'He did *what?*' This is not permissible. So I went out to the bunkhouse to reinvigorate him, and I figured I could whang off a round into the floor and get his attention . . . what I didn't realize was that it would ricochet off the concrete floor, unlike every other domicile that I inhabited, so this .357 slug turned into shrapnel and sprayed the wall behind him. It was a miracle that I didn't kill him."

Somewhat disconcerted, Barlow departed the ranch on his motorcycle. The gathered guests dug the fragment out of Weir's shoulder and then entertained the question of following Barlow. The first question seemed to be "Is he still armed?" On further consideration, it became much easier to go to bed. Somehow the wedding itself went off fairly smoothly, and conventional thinking called for a honeymoon. So Barlow went to Los Angeles with Weir to work on the record.

They actually began to make progress when they moved to L'Hermitage, a suitably L.A. hotel, where they wrote "Heaven Help the Fool," "Bombs Away," and "Shade of Grey." At length, they moved on to the Hotel Utah in Salt Lake City, where they stayed up for two or three days and very nearly finished the songwriting for the record. They had one song left to do, and after a long night of cocaine and Jack Daniel's, they decided to catch some fresh air and strolled across the square to listen to the Mormon Tabernacle Choir. Barlow was a jack (lapsed) Mormon, but even he had never entered the Tabernacle stinkin' drunk. They wobbled back to the hotel and wrote a song about Salt Lake City that, Weir claimed, "was meant to be as laudatory as [possible]." Of course, Weir's sense of humor is by no means standard issue, especially for Utah. Weir went into a studio with the cream of L.A.'s session players and made an album for himself. The material on *Heaven Help the Fool* was uneven but frequently good, though true to its L.A. origins, it was considerably overproduced.

Unsurprisingly, Garcia took a different tack. Poking through an old trunk, he'd come across a fragment of Hunter's lyrics on an old piece of yellow paper from 1969 or so, a scrap of paper so dry, the lyrics so "sparse," that he cracked up. They became the song "Gomorrah," and generated a theme for the album, which would be called *Cats Under the Stars:* don't look back. Perhaps as a consequence of his sojourn with Healy in Burbank, *Cats* was possibly the best-sounding album of his career, even though it was recorded at Front Street, a warehouse that didn't even have a control room. Working with John Kahn, Keith and Donna, Ron Tutt, and Merl Saunders, Garcia went into his soul for the album, at one point mixing for fifty hours straight until he could no longer see the mixing board for hallucinations. "Rubin & Cherise" was something he'd been working on for seven or eight years, a retelling of the legend of Orpheus, who went to hell to recover his love Eurydice, a tale told by Homer, Virgil, Dante, and now Hunter. "Rubin was playing his painted mandolin / when Ruby froze and turned to stone / for the strings played all alone / The voice of Cherise / from the face of the mandolin / singing Rubin, Rubin tell me true / for I have no one but you." It was a magnificent, utterly noncommercial piece of work, and Garcia was deservedly proud.

Late in July Arista released its first Dead album, *Terrapin Station,* complete with a full-page ad in *Rolling Stone:* "A NEW DEAD ERA IS UPON US." The Kelley-Mouse cover mixed turtles by Heinrich Klee with a hobby shop model railroad station to general Dead Head approval. Olsen's mix met a more varied response. He had deleted Mickey Hart and

Garcia's timbales-guitar duet, "Terrapin Flyer," and replaced it with strings; in fact, he had erased the passage, presumably so that the band would have no choice but to accept his decision. Hart's reaction was predictably explosive, but Garcia agreed. Olsen had crossed the line, and Hart and Garcia redid the passage. The strings by Paul Buckmaster with the Martyn Ford Orchestra were certainly unique, and on the whole they worked, although Garcia did remark that Olsen had "put the Grateful Dead in a dress." The use of the London Chorale, thought Lesh, was "incongruous." Olsen also had Tom Scott play saxophone on "Estimated Prophet," and Weir liked it. Lesh's "Passenger," a take on the Fleetwood Mac tune "Station Man," came out without the funk it demanded, and the shameful responsibility for the disco version of "Dancing in the Streets" was the band's. The critical reaction to the album was generally tepid. And if Dead Heads thought that strings meant the band was selling out? "Fuck 'em," said Garcia, "if they can't take a joke."

One of the Dead's dumber decisions that year was to resume touring in front of what they knew would be an audience of at least 100,000, which turned out to be more than 150,000. John Scher had created a September gig at the Englishtown Raceway in New Jersey that would make up for their missed summer in a hurry, but it was the height of chutzpah to make it the first show after three months. Just a few weeks before, Mickey had proudly shown Garcia he could lift his arm about halfway to his shoulder, and Garcia cried, distressed at the weakness rather than pleased at the progress. Recovering from surgery, Donna Jean would sing sitting down. The performance site was surrounded by a barrier made of railroad boxcars, and although traffic backed up about eight miles, there were no crowd control problems. It was a hot day with leaden skies, but no rain, and the performance went well. For a change at a large-scale outdoor concert, everyone could hear. Healy had brought in three sound companies to construct twelve delay towers, and they were effective. Scher had told the civic authorities that he expected 50,000, and his deception would win him no local friends, but it was a production success. As promotion, it was instantly legendary. After a nearly two-year hiatus and an album that would sell decently but was no hit, the Dead had pulled off the largest East Coast concert by any band in years. They were indeed back, and Arista ran a second ad in *Rolling Stone* proclaiming "A NEW DEAD ERA" over a picture of the crowd.

Theirs was a peculiar popularity. At the beginning of 1978 the Dead were capable of selling many tickets, but only in certain places. Critically, they had sunk below the waterline. The focus of the music industry, if not always the record-buying audience, was punk music, which had begun in 1975 at a New York City club called CBGB & OMFUG with Patti Smith, Richard Hell, and the Ramones. And then from England came a band called the Sex Pistols, "so rude, so outrageous, so vile to their audiences," wrote one critic, "that they literally begged to be despised. Of course, they were loved by the press and public alike." Their tour brought them to Winterland on January 14, 1978, for what would prove to be their final concert. That night the Dead played Bakersfield, and Dan Healy got caught up defending some Dead Heads from the police and was hauled off to the pokey. Bob Barsotti, from Bill Graham Presents, called Winterland to report on events and could hear the Sex Pistols, clearly more exciting than life in Bakersfield.

The Dead's—and the Dead Heads'—sense of what was exciting was perhaps a little more subtle than that of Sid Vicious, Johnny Rotten, et al. Their tour continued up the coast, and on January 22 they played at MacArthur Court, on the University of Oregon campus in Eugene. Toward the end of the space segment, Garcia slipped in a fragment of ambient music, the tocsin five-note signature of the film *Close Encounters of the Third Kind,* and his choice of riffs came at the end of what some might call a series of coincidences but that he chose to call synchronicity. The previous November Garcia had seen *Close Encounters* "about six times." After all, he thought, weird events like close encounters with aliens were far more interesting than so-called normalcy. Though he was interested in esoteric lore, he retained a solid skepticism about UFOs, thinking them most likely of local origin. What fascinated him was the struggle of an ordinary person to communicate an extraordinary experience, epitomized by Richard Dreyfuss and his mashed potato sculpture. Between viewings, Garcia read an article on coincidence by Jacques Vallee, the real-life model for François Truffaut's role in the film, in which Vallee spoke of studying a biblical character named Melchizedek. That month Garcia flew to Los Angeles and got into a cab, and when he looked at his receipt the next day, discovered that his cabbie was named . . . Melchizedek. Vallee had also written about the coneheads of *Saturday Night Live,* comic alien characters who claimed to be from France, Vallee's own home. While in New York, one of Garcia's business decisions was to okay a conehead poster because one of them wore a Dead T-shirt. He'd not heard of them before the article.

As the year wore on, much of the memorable news was bad. *Cats*

Under the Stars was released in March and disappeared without a trace, perhaps permanently destroying any desire in Garcia to ever work in a studio again. In April his old friend Emmett Grogan was found dead on a New York City subway train, the victim of a heroin overdose. In May, the Dead canceled the last show of their tour, at the Uptown Theater in Chicago, because Kreutzmann had gotten into a squabble with Keith Godchaux that had so upset Bill he'd flown home. In June, the Dead played at U.C. Santa Barbara in a show opened by Warren Zevon, whose "Werewolves of London" was a current hit that so intrigued Garcia he'd taken to performing it, the first contemporary song the Dead had covered in many years. Unfortunately, Zevon chose to perform drunk, was treated rudely by the audience—opening for the Dead is a miserable lot at best—and responded in kind, earning some of the most enthusiastic boos in Dead Head history. At that, he escaped the fate of the Dead's friends at Jefferson Starship, who that month in Germany lost all their gear when fans reacted to a canceled show by rioting. In July, at Arrowhead Stadium in Kansas City, it was so hot that for half an hour Garcia refused to leave his trailer.

It was time for another vacation, or better still, an adventure. Something cosmic, something special. Shows ran into shows, some good, some not. But if they were to have a life that wasn't a stoned version of nine-to-five, they needed something more. On September 2, before a concert with Willie Nelson at Giants Stadium, New Jersey, they had their first formal press conference since the bust at 710 Ashbury Street, and announced what "something more" was going to be: they were going to Egypt in mid-September to play three concerts in front of the Great Pyramid of Cheops. It seemed to qualify as an adventure.

43

Dark Moon
over Gizeh

(9/78)

Dr. Saad Ed-Din, Egypt's minister of culture, was an impressive man. A poet, a friend of Lawrence Durrell's, the former head of the secret police, he was the most important Egyptian that Phil Lesh, Alan Trist, and Richard Loren would meet in their advance scouting trip to Cairo. Dubbing themselves the MIBS, the Men in Black Suits, the trio had come to Egypt early in 1978 to clear the way for a Dead visit to the pyramids.

"Have you ever played anyplace outside the U.S.?" asked Dr. Ed-Din.

"Yes, we've played in Europe," said Lesh.

"Have you found that your music changes when you play in different places?"

"Precisely," replied Phil, "and that's why we want to play at the pyramids."

"I thought so."

"And that was it," recalled Lesh. "That was the fulcrum, right there."

The notion of taking the Dead's circus to an exotic place had been around for a long time, and had picked up considerable momentum in 1972, after Lesh and Garcia visited Stonehenge and grew acquainted with John Michell and geomancy. In the course of shooting *The Grateful Dead*

Movie, Garcia and Bobby Petersen were filmed speaking of Kesey, who was then doing a story on the pyramids for *Rolling Stone.* But the real impetus came during the hiatus, when their booker/manager Richard Loren, his wife, Elaine, and a Stinson Beach friend, Goldie Rush, had vacationed in Egypt. Loren came to feel that the consciousness of the Egyptians, a river people very different from their nomadic brethren to the east, had a fabulous looseness that reminded him of the hippies of Marin. He became convinced that "we'd all get along well there." As Goldie put it, the Egyptians, like hippies, had a "nonlinear concept of time." Both groups of people were also frequently stoned. Richard, Elaine, and Goldie's trip had been a smashing success, and included meeting Ati, a Nile boatman, during a search for hashish. He had not only taken them up the river, he and Goldie had enjoyed a romantic interlude that would bless them with their son Ali. As they floated on the Nile, the trio thought, said Goldie, "wouldn't it be nice to have some more friends here, wouldn't it be nice to play some music, and then pretty soon, the fantasy became the Grateful Dead at the pyramid." On a return visit, Richard Loren took a horseback ride in the area of the pyramids and discovered a small stage for sound and light shows at the base of the Great Pyramid, and the idea gestated. It became Loren's mission.

Phil Lesh and Alan Trist became Richard's partners in the mission, and they began to make connections. One of Alan's English journalist friends, Jonathan Wallace, was the editor of a respected Middle Eastern journal, and he sent them to Joe and Lois Malone, former government employees—Joe was also a distinguished former professor of history at the American University of Beirut—who now advised Americans doing business in the area. At considerable length, the MIBS went off to Cairo to meet with Dr. Ed-Din. Before they left, they asked Bill Graham if he wanted to be involved. Of course, their method of asking was to have Mickey and Phil picket Bill's house in the middle of the night with flashlights and placards that read, "Better Gigs, Better P.A." and "Egypt or Bust." Bill came out and they raved all night, telling him that he should take the Dead to Egypt. He thought they were crazy—after all, the most recent war was only five years past. When Loren followed up, Bill briefly became involved, but then suggested bringing Santana. "No, Bill, it's not that sort of trip." Since it wasn't his trip, Bill dropped out. They'd do it themselves.

In March 1978 the MIBS went to Washington, D.C., where they met with Joe and Lois and created the strategy that would seal the deal: all funds generated would go to charity, half to the Waf Wal Amal (Faith and

Hope Society), the president of Egypt's wife's favorite charity, half to the Egyptian Department of Antiquities. In Cairo the next week, the Malones proved equally charming at the American embassy, and after their meeting with Ed-Din, the game was on. On March 21, they sent a telegram home: "Two count them Two open air concerts [in fact, they would be allowed to play three] at the great pyramid sphinx theater in lower egypt confirmed repeat confirmed for September 14 and 15. Steering committee landing sfo Thursday with signed repeat signed agreement."

It would have been a thin party if only the band went, and in April their travel agent, Randy Sarti, was told in secrecy to work on a charter. At first the price was astronomical, but Randy lucked out and found a charter that fit their dates at a cost of $999 a head, twelve nights at the Mena House included. The family began to gather, and by the time they set out, Randy had 65 on the band's charter and 109 on the family charter, which didn't count the Texas and Bill Walton contingents, who came independently. In September they were off. It was not your average flight. As M.G. would recall it, "all of us, a huge Prankster contingent . . . two telescopes, a shovel, fishing pole, broad net, screens for screening artifacts out of the sand, three or four tape recorders, the video equipment, endless amounts of stuff . . . There were Pakistani stewardesses and they freaked out completely about halfway to New York because we were having so much fun on the plane. They took all the liquor off the plane in New York, which really upset some people seriously as I'm sure you can imagine." Even if a few people might have had too much fun, the cacophony that results from having a tape deck in every third row, each with a different tape, was distressing to the airplane crew. "Then you hit Africa," M.G. continued. "It's like flying over the moon . . . made Nevada look like the Garden of Eden . . . [At the airport] the first thing you see out on the runway are these army guys with machine guns, standing there. They have no shoes, their trousers are in total shreds . . . the machine guns are old and patched."

They staggered off the airplane, and were as much confused as reassured when not one bag was opened; the proper arrangements had been made. Then they plunged into Cairo, unlike anything they'd ever experienced. "Mix in your mind," wrote Kesey, "the deep surging roar of a petroleum riptide with the strident squealing of a teenage basketball playoff; fold in air conditioners and sprinkle with vendors' bells and police whistles; pour this into narrow streets greased liberally with people noisily eating sesame cakes fried in olive oil, bubbling huge hookahs, slurping Turkish coffees, playing backgammon as loud as the little markers can be slapped down . . . thousands of people, coughing, spitting, muttering in the shadowy debris next to the buildings, singing, standing, sweeping along in dirty damask gellabias, arguing in the traffic—millions! and all jacked up loud on caffeine. Simmer this recipe at 80 degrees at two in the morning and you have a taste of the Cairo Cacophony." Noise and traffic. Oh my, yes, traffic. They drove to the Mena House down what Kesey described as "an unlit boulevard teeming from curb to curb with bicycles, tricycles, motorcycles, sidehackers, motorscooters, motorbikes, buses dribbling passengers from every hole and handhold, rigs, gigs, wheelchairs, biers, wheelbarrows, wagons, pushcarts, army trucks . . . rickshaws, buckboards, hacks both horse- and human-drawn, donkey-riders and -pullers and -drivers, oxcarts, fruitcars, legless beggers in thighcarts."

Mena House, a Victorian relic in the shadow of the pyramids, was a tranquil colonial refuge, and the hotel's guards, packing Armalite automatic weapons, made sure it stayed that way. The sudden appearance of longhairs in jeans and Dead T-shirts didn't seem to bother anyone at the hotel, and except for Bear, who spent mealtimes sending back his meat, which he wanted raw—"Burned! Burned!"—and grousing at the waiters, everyone enjoyed his/her stay. At any rate, few stayed in their rooms for long. Outside the hotel gates was Mena Village, home to the guardians of the pyramids and hustlers of tourists since—Marc Antony? Napoleon? "Everyone seemed to be yelling at me all at once," wrote one of the party, a friend of Bear's and sometime crew member and truck driver named Bob Nichols. " 'Mister! Mister! Ride my camel!' 'Hire my horse!' 'I will run up the pyramid with you!' 'Let me guide you!' Hands clutched at me, and hungry-looking children yelled, 'Baksheesh! Baksheesh!' " Goldie had been concerned that her friends might embarrass her in Egypt, but she was swiftly reassured. Instead, an authentic cultural exchange took place. Even the constant harassment of sellers was fun. "It's not like they were pissed if you didn't buy," said Sunshine Kesey, "it was more of an argument about the value of something, rather than bringing down the price . . . I was walking back to the hotel and this guy followed me trying to sell his bracelets, I'm going 'No, leave me alone,' he kept following me. Finally, he ended up giving these bracelets to me, for a present. I go, 'Thank you, thank you.' He goes, 'One piastre' . . . hahahahahah."

The exchange transcended barter. All over Mena Village there were plenty of willing Egyptians licking LSD from Dead Visine bottles off their fingers, with no complaints. As Garcia would say, Egypt was "no cops, no parents." "It's so much of another world," said M.G., "and it's so ancient, wonderful, everywhere you'd look there would be little outcroppings of bizarre culture. Like the pyramid goats . . . On all the pyramids, you hear their little hooves going boing boing . . . The thing about the pyramids is, go off behind them and there is nothing, vast nothingness . . . rubble, rubble, everywhere. They will be working on it forever." George Walker planted a Grateful Dead flag on the peak of the Great Pyramid, and it stayed there for days. Everyone climbed the Great Pyramid at least once, even Bill Walton in his cast—he was then on leave from the Portland Trailblazers following surgery.

If international relations were run by Dead Heads . . . M.G., Paul Krassner, and Goldie went off to the Medina, the oldest part of Cairo, to buy hashish, which came in slabs the size of a large, heavy Hershey bar. That their party included two tall women, one of them blond, attracted a certain attention, but they did their business and then lit up without incident. But Krassner was a purist and would not mix hash with tobacco, as local custom dictated. The Egyptians thought this "profligate," but it would set things off in a charming way. "These other Egyptians," said M.G., "decided they were going to try their hash without tobacco . . . to be polite you hit everybody in the place, it's like buying a round, so we sent around one with no tobacco in it. [One of the Egyptians] got a big hit going on that and started to cough. It was just like the Grateful Dead crew, once again, they razzed this guy to death. It was a real bad one he had going, they put their foot behind him and shoved him off the bench, laughing. He gets up, brushes himself off, he's still coughing and coughing, and laughing and coughing . . . the next guy says, 'I can do it,' he starts coughing, the third guy, he's going 'Okay, I have to stay cool,' that's enough with coughing, and he just takes a tiny, tiny hit, right, and doing all the horrible facial contortions that you do—he didn't cough. It made it around those guys without any of the rest of them blowing it. Then we were okay. So we sent that around a few more times and got out of there."

They did have shows to do, however, and there things were a trifle more complicated. Cairo in 1978 was a city of 10 million with a sewage system fit for 3 million. There was no telephone book. It was basically a pretechnical society, a place where everything was falling apart all the time, saved only by fix-it men. "Malesh"—"Never mind"—was the standard response to almost everything. The chief of the local stage crew was Abdul, who announced, "I have the heart of a camel! I have outlived eight of my wives, and even now I must have a young woman!" They needed Abdul, since trucks could get no closer than thirty yards to the stage, which resulted in Anvil equipment cases being flipped end over end across the sands. Creativity was the order of the day: Candace Brightman wanted to light the stage with flaming torches, but was overruled. Dan Healy wanted to "play the pyramids" by using the King's Chamber as an echo chamber, broadcasting from the stage to a receiver on the side of the pyramid, through wires to a speaker in the chamber, then back to the control board. Made of stones so precisely cut and fitted together that one cannot slide paper between them, the King's Chamber is a box sixty feet by thirty feet by forty feet deep inside the pyramid. It is so solid that it can create "indefinite sustain," said Healy, defying physical laws so that it resonates in tempered Western scale as well as the scale of physics. It was the band's favorite playground.

Garcia, Hart, M.G., Weir, and David Freiberg visited the King's Chamber and enjoyed a small epiphany. Hart brought a tar, a desert drum that resembles a tambourine without jangles. "Going *bitabitabi—tabita,*" said M.G. "Every sound is held and amplified and reverberated . . . so I hmmmmmmed and snap! flashed instantly that here was something . . . So I said, 'Shut up you guys, listen.' They wore down and I got in the box [sarcophagus] and hmmmmmmmed a bit and they all tried it . . . Everyone took their turn in the box, then they started to talk. I told them all to shut up again. Then Freiberg and Jerry and Weir started singing little parts. It sounded incredible . . . You start to sing in there with the lights out, you think you're in the biggest church in the world . . . little teeny square room . . . suddenly it becomes, the walls just fall away, it's this vast amphitheater sound, the world's biggest bathroom . . . We stayed in there till we couldn't sing another note . . . They were playing around with what parts you couldn't sing, anything with any dissonance would just build up into a wave of feedback, terrible, dreadful, instant pain." Trying to wire this magic place was a wonderful idea, but even though soundman John Cutler wore his knees bloody raw trying to make it work, the inferior local phone cable could not stand up to the human tourist traffic over it during the day, and it failed.

Still, the Dead and its crew got to know the pyramid, at the very least one of the most remarkable structures on the planet. In Kesey's words, "It's a multidimensional bureau of standards, omni-lingual and universal, constructed to both incorporate and communicate such absolutes as the bloody inch (a convenient ten million of which equals our polar axis) plus our bloody damned circumference, our weight, the bloody length not only of our solar year and our sidereal year but also our catch-up or leap year . . . not to mention the bloody distance of our swing around our sun, or the error in our spin that produces the wobble at our polar point."

At sundown on September 14, the Dead played their first show.

Garcia told one reporter, "This place has really freed me from something that I am normally quite concerned with, which is just professional competence . . . But this experience is greater than the elements of performance in a normal sense." It was the right attitude to have, because their playing was handicapped by a number of things. That summer Kreutzmann had broken his wrist playing basketball, and he was not able to make his normal contribution, effectively playing one-handed. Lesh spent much of the visit in the Mena House bar: "I was a drunk in 1978," he said. Keith's piano was untuned, as their tuner had taken offense with the crew and not shown up. Overall, the band in 1978 was at a low point in its playing. But the shows were for the experience, and that was rich. On the first night, a local police official took stage guard Jeff Boden aside and asked him and the rest of those onstage not to smoke hash visibly, then took him behind the amps, broke off a fine chunk, gave it to Jeff, and said, "Here it's okay." Sue looked at Garcia and smirked, "I can't believe we're getting away with this." He nodded, grinning. The web of peaceful synchronicity reached beyond the Dead: several thousand miles away outside Washington, D.C., the leaders of Egypt and Israel were concluding a peace agreement known as the Camp David accords. It was a special moment in Middle Eastern history.

Their first show was preceded by a choir and percussion ensemble from the Abu Simbel School of Luxor, whose appearance was arranged by the band's friend from Marin, Hamza el-Din, a master of Nubian music. Then the Dead came out to play. As they began, Weir swatted a bug, and then another. Their stage lights were the brightest thing around, and they weren't far from the Nile. He began to fall into a serious gloom with the realization that he'd come ten thousand miles to be eaten alive, and then something whipped past his head. And something else. Under the stage lived bats, thousands and thousands of them forming a cloud around the musicians. The bats dined royally and all was well. It was as stunning to Weir as the simple fact of playing rock and roll in front of the pyramids. Tickets cost from $1.50 to $7.50 and were purchased by Dead Heads, a few government people, and the occasional American living in Egypt, such as the kids at the American School, as well as local Cairo youth; still the audience was only in the several hundreds. Advance word about the shows was mostly rumor, although it was interesting that bootleg tapes with labels like "Oxomoxo," "American Booty," and "Tearapin Station" had appeared in local music stores. But tickets weren't terribly important. The theater consisted simply of plastic chairs separated from the desert by a rope, and the locals and Bedouins from the desert gathered freely.

Just to take everything to the planetary edge, the third night included a complete eclipse of the moon. This time, instead of opening the show, the choir waited and began the second set. The eclipse began just after moonrise as the wind whipped at the sand. The Bedouins who lined the stage area wailed in a match for anything on the stage. Mena Villagers began to pound pots and pans and shake cans filled with stones to bring the moon back, as the choir sang and played their tars. Then, magically, one by one the members of the choir drifted off the stage, and one by one the members of the Grateful Dead replaced them. Voices and the rhythm of the tars were oh-so-elegantly displaced by the first notes of Hart's "Fire on the Mountain," as the Dead played the moon back from darkness. Healy stood on stage thinking, "If there is a moment and a place to be somewhere, this is it. It's the best fantasy anybody ever had about us, and we did it." Later, Mickey Hart asked Omar, one of the horse and camel purveyors, if the music had moved him. "It makes me feel like that man on TV who leaps tall buildings and breaks bricks," he said. It was Omar's first experience with large-scale amplified music.

Bill Graham had been invited to be a guest on the adventure, and after the third night he threw a party for everyone at Sahara City, a gambling and fornication tent out in the desert. Dozens of camels and horses stood at the side of the stage, and after the show the band mounted up for a moonlit ride to the party. Belly dancing, booze, and fabulous food made for a good night. Kesey and Garcia raved about literature, and a roadie waved a bottle of Jack Daniel's at them and asked, "R'all yew guys sittin' round talking 'bout books?" Mickey and Graham, both ex-waiters, challenged each other to a race around the tent with loaded trays; the winner remained forever in dispute. Sunshine would remember the hundreds of cats that milled around on the roof, waiting for scraps.

After the shows, Mickey took off for Hamza's hometown in Sudan, Kom Ombo, with MERT (mobile engineering and recording team), which included Jerilyn, Bret Cohen, and John Cutler. He pulled out his tar and initiated a rhythmic encounter between cultures that entranced both sides. Meantime, the rest of the band had taken Goldie's friend Ati's boat, the *Sobek* (Crocodile), up the Nile to Luxor, dubbing the vessel and themselves the real "Ship of Fools." After a few more days of bliss, they piled back on airplanes and returned to the real world, where the band had an album to finish and a tour to start. The Egypt visit quickly seemed like a dream, for two reasons. One was that shortly after their return they all visited San Francisco's deYoung Museum, then home to the traveling Treasures of Tut Ankh Amen tour, which, thought David Freiberg, "was everything that wasn't still in the tomb. You say, 'I just left the sarcophagus over there . . .' It wasn't as good as being there, though."

And on the 5th and Lincoln kitchen bulletin board was a note from Ashraf Ghorbal, the Egyptian ambassador to the United States, to Jerry Garcia, noting that all accounts and reports "give me, as they must give you and your colleagues, great satisfaction . . . concerts have become a unique chapter in the story of Egyptian-American friendship . . . My sincere congratulations and best wishes of success to the Grateful Dead."

44

Interlude:
The Rhythm Devils

(DRUM BREAK)

October, The Capital Centre, Washington, D.C.

As the other musicians leave the stage, Bill Kreutzmann and Mickey Hart settle in to one of the Dead's
profound rituals, the drum duet. On the night they
met, the two men drummed on cars, lampposts, the city itself; the conversation has continued. At different times, "drums" has included oil drums,
garbage cans, chains, and the sound of Brent Mydland gargling. Mickey's
first dramatic instrument was the "beast," a giant hoop of iron from which
various drums were suspended. In later years he and Kreutzmann both acquired electronic drums, in which pads are hitched to sampled sounds via
MIDI (Musical Instrument Digital Interface). But tonight their taste
goes to the ancient. Mickey picks up the tar and evokes the dry sound of
the desert in a light *pitapitapitapita*. Kreutzmann picks up the talking
drum, for which he's always had an uncanny facility. Of African origin,
the talking drum is squeezed under the arm to produce differently pitched
tones. A stream of beats courses through the room, first chasing each
other a la Dexter Gordon and Wardell Gray, then circling. It is elegant,
very old, and new as the dawn. It's a monstrous challenge for the sound
guys, who must follow them like kids tracking an escaped pet. Since the

drummers have moved back behind their trap sets into the land of boom-boom, monitor mixer Harry Popick can't see them. At the monitor board, he groans over a random screech, "It can't be the tar mike, which one is he playing?" An Ultra Sound guy runs off, and returns to say, "More tip" (the microphone at the top of the setup). Another trip, "Just a taste more tip."

As the drummers make waves, the audience divides. A large proportion live for the drums, and they surge forward. A sizable portion finds that this is a good time for a bathroom break. At the back of the stage, Garcia and Weir take a breather with their roadie, Steve Parish, and the laughs begin. Fragments of Garcia's rap float out, disturbing the nearby guests trying to listen to the music, until they begin to listen to the humor and finally break up laughing. Tonight, Garcia's on a pirate rant, and in a low, perfect growl, "Shiver me timbers" leaks out of the curtain in front of his space. In between a Hart balaphon riff, one hears "Keelhaul the—" then "bodies—" creeps between the sound of chimes. The duet is exquisite as one of the catering guys brings a load of towels onstage, just doing his job, while the audience sways, rapt.

Though the performance is a partnership of drummers, the energy and motivation to go beyond the conventional has always derived from Mickey Hart. Early sound effects included cannons and frying bacon. In August 1968, in the middle of a performance of "Alligator," the amps were rolled apart, drum risers came forward, and Mickey and Billy welcomed Vince Delgado and Shankar Ghosht into a drum quartet jam. During Hart's retirement from the road, he also received his greatest gift. His teacher, the Indian tabla master Ustad Allarakha, sent Mickey his son, Zakir Hussain, and they began a long-term and blessed partnership in sound. One of the first results was the band Diga, which means "naked" in Sanskrit, and is a specific type of sound in Indian drumming.

But the true flowering of Mickey Hart's abilities as a percussive maestro took place in 1978. One night in October that year, Francis and Eleanor Coppola came to a Dead concert at Winterland at the urging of Bill Graham, who had had a role in Francis's film *Apocalypse Now*, then in postproduction. Francis was looking for someone to do a musical score for the film, having just received a score that he didn't like. They sat onstage behind the drums, and it was, Eleanor wrote, "amazing. It had physical impact." The evening reminded her of a night inside an Ifugao priest's house in the Philippines, where *Apocalypse Now* had been filmed. "The scale was different, but everyone being joined together by rhythms and images was the same." Exactly.

Francis hired Mickey to produce a percussion sound track, and for the first time, Mickey had found an "employer" who was as willing as he was to flirt with insanity in pursuit of the muse. Mickey set up video screens all over his home—the bathroom, the kitchen, next to the fireplace—and began to absorb the odyssey of Captain Willard, the man sent to kill Colonel Kurtz. Over several months he assembled a collection of percussion instruments, some invented on the spot, and then laid them out on the floor of the Front Street warehouse in batteries, according to compatibility. To mime the sound of walking through the jungle underbrush, they created the "scritch," a collection of vertically mounted metal and glass rods played by rubbing them with a rosin-powdered gloved hand. Willard's perusals of Kurtz's dossier had a sound signature, a glass harp. There were wind chimes, devil chasers made from bamboo grown at the ranch, and the Beam, a ten-foot-long piece of aluminum, which produced the sound of a napalm explosion. At length, Mickey took Billy, Phil, and his old students and/or Diga members Michael Hinton, Greg Errico, and Jordan Amarantha "up the river," playing to the film as they moved from place to place within the jungle/garden of instruments. The recording sessions took on not only the obsession of all Hart projects but also an echo of the lunacy that permeated everything to do with the film. Only a little of their work made the final cut of the deeply flawed and utterly brilliant masterpiece that was *Apocalypse Now,* but it was a fantastic stimulant to Hart's imagination. Ever after, he would be, as John Barlow put it, a "sorcerer," assembling the elements to make powerful magic—most especially with his band Planet Drum.

As the eighties passed, Hart began to research the origins of his chosen world—for the drums are not merely his instrument, but his reason for being. Particularly inspired by his encounter with Joseph Campbell, he began to study the lore of percussion, and through it the roots of shamanism and the alteration of consciousness, the very foundation of the Grateful Dead experience. "In the beginning was noise," he wrote in his first book, the memoir *Drumming at the Edge of Magic.* "And noise begat rhythm. And rhythm begat everything else. This is the kind of cosmology a drummer can live with." *Edge* was followed by his visual encyclopedia of drumming, *Planet Drum,* published in 1991. "People play music for different reasons," he said in an interview about the first book. "I go for the spirit side of things; not necessarily to be perfect. What I'm after is changing consciousness."

Onstage tonight with Kreutzmann, drumming in pursuit of magic, they leave aside the ancient tar and talking drum and leap straight into the twenty-first century, walking to the back of the stage and to electronic drum pads which are hooked into computers containing sampled sound—any sampled sound. One whack of a stick and a snarling dog can come out, or the sound of breaking glass, or thunder, or rain. They have always had a variety of different sound possibilities at their command, but now this variety has multiplied to stratospheric levels. Billy stands casually and produces a pulse; Mickey stands rigid, still militarily erect, bouncing off, over, around, and through the pulse. It builds into a roar and they go off. We are whipped with sound until the only possible response from the audience seems a prolonged scream.

Back in Parish's clubhouse, the guitarists are loosely working on a concept for the space jam segment. Sometimes the subject is serious, as on certain nights when the knowledge of some hero's recent death is fresh, sometimes it's a sly take on current events—"Khaddafi Death Squads," an earthquake, Reagan in China—and sometimes it's outré. As they scheme, Mickey finishes with a Beam solo and Billy leaves the stage, it being pretty well impossible to play something at the same time as a Beam solo. Beam sounds are the fullest expression of Mickey's muse, for the Beam produces not just music but noise, and there is one part of Hart that simply wants to make the loudest, most attention-getting noise possible. The Beam is a slab of aluminum strung with piano strings over a magnetic pickup, and is based on the Pythagorean monochord. Robbie Taylor spends considerable amounts of his time tuning it. Mickey Hart uses a piece of pipe, his feet, and you-name-it to wrestle the nastiest sounds he can imagine out of it. It is like nothing any average music listener has ever conceived, a drumming on the very edge of magic—or, as one critic so evocatively misheard it, "drumming at the edge of madness."

45

Shakedown

(10/78−10/80)

he tension was exceedingly thick in the Dead's dressing room on the night of November 11, 1978. They had never before appeared on live national TV, and, as usual in critical moments, their vulnerabilities were exposed. *Saturday Night Live* was, in one critic's words, "the victory party for the sixties on television." Dressed as Elizabeth Taylor for his first skit, John Belushi poked his head into the room and smirked, "You can do it, it's okay, relax. You're only performing in front of"—and his voice dropped into a croon—*"60 million people."* Ulp.

The Dead's appearance on *SNL* was an anomaly, not the result of being chic or successful (that year *SNL*'s musical guests included Mick Jagger, and the show's spin-off comic blues band, the Blues Brothers, had the nation's number one album), but because of something more personal. Even in 1978 everyone, it seemed, knew at least one Dead Head. *SNL* producer Lorne Michael's in-house Dead Head was one of his most creative writers, the author of Belushi's Elizabeth Taylor skit, Tom Davis. Davis had encountered *Live Dead* at a party in high school and staggered onto the bus to stay, attending college in California mostly because of its proximity to Dead shows. In the mid-seventies he had joined an improvi-

sational comedy troupe with his friend Al Franken, and around that time
met Garcia. Davis's and Garcia's senses of humor fit perfectly, and their
initial raves touched on books and movies, especially science-fiction films.
Garcia had a poster of the film *Alien* on his dressing room wall, and the
conversation swiftly turned to Kurt Vonnegut's *The Sirens of Titan,* which
proved to be both Tom and Jerry's favorite novel.

Franken and Davis had gone on to be among the first writers hired at
SNL, and by 1978 Tom was able to go to his boss and beg him to book the
Dead, "just for me." Ever distrustful of television as a performance
medium, Garcia didn't want to do the gig, despite the heavy boost it
would provide the new album, *Shakedown Street,* which would be released
four days later. The drummers, however, were sufficiently in favor to sway
the band. There was an intuitive bond between them and Belushi, the
reigning star, a true sharing of manic energy. In fact, the drummers
wanted to use giant drumsticks to do a samurai drum piece, a takeoff on
one of Belushi's favorite shticks at this time. The idea was scotched, although Kreutzmann had a part in a skit. Though they were the biggest
fans, the drummers had considerable difficulty in actually *doing* comedy.
Bill Murray later told Davis that looking into the "dark, dark pools" of
Kreutzmann's eyes during Murray's "Nick Sands" lounge lizard skit almost bumped him entirely off his stride.

The band asked Davis what he wanted them to play, and he told
them, "You know, I think Jerry should play pedal steel, because it sounds
so good on television." This less-than-practical notion ended Davis's input into the song choice discussion. Ultimately, they chose a reliable old
tune, "Casey Jones," and a Weir medley from the current album, "I Need a
Miracle" and "Good Lovin'." They had rehearsed for several days at a
New York studio prior to the appearance, but they were still quite nervous
when they got to NBC, especially Garcia. When the director, Dave Wilson, asked Jerry to stand in front of the microphone and stay there, he got
a simple "No." "Well, then I'm not going to get you [in the shot]." "I don't
care." Fortunately, Garcia settled down for their performance, which
proved to be respectable. By the postshow party, everyone was in the best
of moods, as well as extremely ripped; *SNL* was one of the very few scenes
on the planet that could compete with the Dead for drug abuse. The
evening ended at the Blues Brothers Bar, a private club Belushi and Dan
Aykroyd owned in the Village, with the "Stink Band"—Belushi played
drums, Hart played bass, Aykroyd blew harp, and after every song, they'd
chorus, "We stink."

Their performance had little effect on the reception of *Shakedown*

Street, which was a hit-or-miss piece of work. The cover was brilliant, a comic depiction of Front Street by Gilbert Shelton, creator of the Fabulous Furry Freak Brothers. The Dead had brought in Little Feat's Lowell George as a producer, at least partly on the premise that he would "understand band mechanics." Unfortunately, Lowell was no more disciplined than the Dead, and contributed very little. Once, he spent the night at Front Street with Mickey Hart, snorting coke and writing a never-recorded song called "The Drum Is My Woman" instead of doing the overdubs they were supposed to be working on. At dawn, as they were leaving, Lowell turned to Hart and said, "You know the conga drum sound on *Diga?* I hated it. It sucked." Always gracious in the face of criticism, Hart tackled him and began to choke him, at which point Lowell began to hyperventilate and have heart palpitations. In any event, the trip to Egypt had interrupted recording, and when they returned, Lowell was on tour, so the band finished it themselves.

There was great material on *Shakedown Street,* especially the title song, which though indifferently recorded on the album would be a performance staple for years to come. "Fire on the Mountain" was another brilliant song, written as the hills near Mickey's ranch were in flame, and the reggae influence was superbly tasteful. The same could not be said of the flimsy pop sound on "Good Lovin' " or the lightweight lyrics of "I Need a Miracle," a portrait of a woman with an unhealthy obsession about Weir who lived next door to Front Street. "If I Had the World to Give" was one of the odder songs Garcia and Hunter ever produced, an extremely sentimental love song weighed down by its somnolent tempo. It was not terribly surprising that the band would play it only three times. At that, they were pleased to have ground out an album, even if they'd padded it with a retread, a second studio recording of "Minglewood Blues."

As usual, any number of dark clouds hovered over the Dead. Garcia's drug abuse was only marginally worse than that of the rest of the band members, but because everyone depended on him to be the emotional center, it got more attention. Studio technician John Cutler had even tried to protest Garcia's condition by organizing a strike that would prevent them from performing on *Saturday Night Live.* By now, Jerry had moved to the downstairs in-law unit of Rock Scully's home on Hepburn Heights in San Rafael, not far from 5th and Lincoln. Garcia's room—it was essentially a studio apartment—was relatively small and plain. Upstairs, Scully conducted his business from a large walk-in closet off his bedroom. In the early eighties, Garcia rarely went to bed, sleeping sitting up in his large lounge chair in front of a TV that was always on, even when he went on tour. Hepburn Heights was a pretty sad place. Somewhat later, Rock and his wife, Nicki, would separate.

The most regular visitor to the house was Nora Sage, a fan who'd been incessantly sending mail and gifts to Garcia since 1976. One day Nicki asked Jerry's assistant Sue Stephens who the new gardener was. Sue was confused, then replied, "Is she short, and does she wear a string of pearls? Oh-ohhhh." Sue told Nicki that she felt that Nora was bad news, because at least once she'd been bodily removed from a Garcia Band show at Jerry's and John Kahn's request. By now, Rock's main function, as perceived by the rest of the band, was as Garcia's partner in drugdom, and it was Sue's belief that Rock used Nora as a diversion in this pursuit. Soon Nora was the housekeeper at Hepburn Heights, bringing receipts to Sue for reimbursement, and she managed to entrench herself.

The rest of the Dead had plenty of their own emotional problems. Keith and Donna, as individuals and as a couple, had deteriorated badly over the eight years they'd been in the Dead. Keith was a once-brilliant player with terribly low self-esteem and a great deal of emotional pain, and the worst possible environment for him was one with lots of stress and myriad opportunities for self-medication. Cocaine had damaged his sense of time in playing, which had always been his weakness, and by now he was drowning in whatever he could find, ranging from prescription drugs to heroin. The ongoing marital battles between Keith and Donna were distressing to everyone.

The band also had major financial troubles. The adventure in Egypt had cost about half a million dollars, and the plan had always been to release a live album to pay for it, making a special package out of photographs and Kelley's marvelous pyramid poster, in which American rattlesnakes and roses took the place of asps and indigenous rushes. But Garcia stunned Loren by refusing to allow the material to be released, attributing his decision to the fact that Keith's electric piano was out of tune. This was true, but if the band had played well, the piano could have been ignored. They hadn't. The Egypt debt combined with the remaining leftovers of the Bank of Boston/Grateful Dead Records mess meant that there was never any extra money, and that led to squabbling over the infamous O/A, office slang for "on account." Band members and employees could get advances on their salaries by taking out money O/A, and they did so with abandon. Phil had his Lotus sports car, Kreutzmann had his ranch, Mickey wanted equipment for his studio, Keith and Jerry bought drugs. Despite their increasingly high ticket revenues, their finances were an oppressive carousel that kept everyone stuck.

Late in November they were struck by two waves of trouble, one from outside and one within. On Thanksgiving Day, the twenty-third, they were in Washington, D.C., and Rock Scully came back to his room to tell the band about true horror, strange news coming from the obscure country of Guyana. The story hit home to any Bay Area resident. A local charismatic preacher by the name of Jim Jones had blended left-wing politics and religious cultism and led hundreds of Bay Area people to establish a new world in Guyana. Now they were all dead, victims of a bizarre mass murder/suicide that also killed an investigating U.S. congressman.

The next day the Dead played for a national FM radio hookup at John Scher's Capitol Theatre in Passaic, New Jersey. Garcia was extremely sick with the flu, and his nerves absorbed further damage after the show. He was sitting on a bus chatting with John Belushi when someone put a brick through the bus window. By the next day, he was too sick to perform. The audience for the show at the New Haven Coliseum was already seated, and Danny Rifkin turned to Jim Koplik and said, "You're the promoter, you gotta tell them." As he started up the stage steps, Koplik was terrified, thinking the audience would turn on him, and it was one of the sweet moments of his life when he found Mickey and Bobby flanking him as he approached the mike. Bobby made the announcement, and in fact, there was only one response. Someone in the audience threw a rose onstage, and then the audience went peacefully home.

Garcia recovered, and they spent a good part of December back on the job. It was a measure of their financial needs that they played that month in such unusual places as Alabama and Mississippi. On December 30, they played in Los Angeles, and on the morning of the thirty-first they prepared to fly up to San Francisco, where they were to play the traditional New Year's Eve concert. It would prove to be a stressful day. Because of a bomb scare, they sat at LAX for four hours before they were able to take off. Winterland was not a great deal calmer.

Winterland had been the "big room" of Bill Graham Presents for twelve years, but it was a crumbling wreck; the previous New Year's Eve, tiles had fallen from the ceiling after the audience had left. Repairing it would cost too much, and the owners decided to tear it down and build condominiums. Graham decided to give it a big send-off, and of course the final night had to be with the Dead. In his initial pitch to Loren he had noted, "The bulk of the space in my musical memory tank is taken up by my memories of my involvement with the GD. I should like very much to add another gem to my collection." The Dead would headline, coming on at midnight. Breakfast would be served after the show. The band said yes, and the circus began. Ticket demand was mind-boggling. At a press conference, Graham estimated that "there is 100 times the demand than there are tickets . . . I would venture it could have been half a million. You may think I've gone off my rocker, but you haven't seen the letters from Tokyo, New York, Boston, Miami." In an effort to ease the ferocious demand, Graham induced KSAN to broadcast the show live, with KQED-TV broadcasting. All over the Bay Area, Dead Heads set up their TVs and stereos.

The show itself was problematic in many ways. It simply meant too much to Graham, and his security created a hostile atmosphere. He blamed the Dead, who "invited too many bikers. When that happens, an element of fear comes in and I couldn't just let it all hang out. I had some problems backstage." Some of the problems included Dead family members like Mountain Girl not being able to get to the stage from backstage. The backstage atmosphere affected only the few, but it poisoned the experience for the band. For the audience, the Dead chose to do something special, playing a third set that included "Dark Star" and "St. Stephen." Unfortunately, the band was in terrible shape and the material was under-rehearsed; the audience went out of its mind listening, but the performances, though exciting because of the song choice, were less than inspiring.

Four days later, the band arrived in Philadelphia to start another tour. It was the sort of schedule that only the healthiest could endure, and the Dead weren't healthy. None of them were really robust, but Keith and Donna were in the most evident bad shape, both personally and musically. Donna Jean had a great studio voice, but singing in a high-noise environment required a stronger instrument than she possessed. As a result she would push herself and go flat. Keith's problems with time had long been evident, and now his habit of parroting Garcia's leads on the piano became seriously irritating. Their personal behavior was worse. Sober, Donna Jean was a lovely woman. Drunk, she was a terror: "I was an alcoholic," she recalled. "Never went a day without getting drunk . . . I punched out limo drivers for not letting [her baby son] Zion sit on the armrest . . . I would never be able to count the hotel rooms that I completely destroyed . . . If they didn't have my cleaning back in time at the hotel, I would just freak out and tear everything up . . . [In one town] all the band came up because they heard that it was the best job that had ever been done on a room." Her violence was not just directed at limo drivers. "Keith was in a sling from where I'd broken a chair over his arm. I would have my eyes black from where he'd hit me. Once I did half of a tour with a tooth missing that he knocked out."

One of their most spectacular tiffs took place in the parking lot of Front Street, where they decided to play bumper cars with their BMWs. "I totaled both of them," she said. Her behavior was more spectacular than Keith's, but the pain was the same. A man of limited emotional resources, he simply drowned his torment in drugs. Too sensitive to handle life on the road, he also became a scapegoat. "People would see him doing things they were doing," said Donna, "and put it all on him." Given the Dead's eternal rule of noninterference, the situation had festered for months. Garcia would simply moan, "Oh fuck, oh fuck," said Loren. "Keith was just strung out, nodding, wrecking hotel rooms, and being really crazed." It was painful to watch them, and it would get worse when they tried to get the rest of the band to take sides. As Hart put it, "The music became secondary to the soap opera that was going on."

Finally, late in January 1979 in Buffalo, reality penetrated the haze. On the day that Sex Pistols member Sid Vicious died of an overdose, Donna Jean looked at her life. "Rock and Keith were doing smack, but everybody was doing something. My marriage was a travesty, Zion had no homelife, the band—after every show, one clique would be getting together to bad-mouth another clique . . . every week somebody was getting fired. It was all exactly the opposite of what it's supposed to be about. I said to myself, 'This is hell.' So I called Robbie Taylor on the phone and said, 'Get me my ticket, I'm leaving. This is it, I can't handle this anymore. This is jive.'" With two days remaining in the tour, Donna Jean flew home. "When Keith got home, we talked and I said, 'How do we get out of this?' And he said, 'I don't know, but it's going to kill us. It's a monster, and it's malignant.'"

Donna Jean concluded, "As a whole, in general, the Grateful Dead is not benign." Certainly not to its band members. It is a full-range experience, as Garcia was wont to say, with the good and the bad in perhaps equal measure. It is a world of theater and illusion, and there's plenty of evil around. Good or bad, it consumes. Keith and Donna had had enough. In February there was a band meeting at their house, and the message from the band was simple: "It's not working out." There was no argument. "You're right, it's not working out." "Everybody agreed perfectly," recalled Donna. "A million pounds lifted off of me."

The previous October Garcia had played some Garcia Band shows with the Bob Weir Band, and he'd listened carefully to Weir's keyboard player, Brent Mydland. As Keith sank deeper into the abyss, Garcia suggested to Weir that he send Dead tapes to Brent to study as a potential replacement. On March 1, Keith resigned from the band's board of directors, and Brent became the new Dead keyboard player. Brent was a solid player and a fine harmony vocalist, and his musical contributions would be excellent. His lead voice bore an aesthetically inappropriate resemblance to that of the Doobie Brothers' Michael McDonald, but a few years of booze and stress would roughen it into something much more suitable to the Dead. Unfortunately, in his lack of self-esteem, emotional blockage, and paucity of resources for coping with stress, Brent bore an eerie resemblance to Keith. Neither he nor Keith read, so neither had access to any sort of intellectual understanding that might help them cope with the hard, dangerous life of the Dead. And just as Keith's bond with Donna ended up satisfying neither of them at the end of their stay in the Dead, Brent's marriage to a lovely but extremely young woman, Lisa Sullivan, would lead to a marriage as raddled with confusion and pain as that of the Godchaux. Born in 1952, Brent had grown up in suburban Contra Costa County. After early classical piano training, he began to absorb rock, including Pigpen, then Jimmy Smith, Herbie Hancock, and Chick Corea. After a stint with a group called Batdorf and Rodney and a spell with an Arista band called Silver, he'd ended up with Weir. It would all prove to be too much too soon for him.

Mydland made his debut on April 22 at Spartan Stadium in San Jose, and as he learned the repertoire, the band began to add new material. "Althea" was a Hunter-Garcia love song that sounded the cautionary note of a man in his thirties, a certain weariness.

> Ain't nobody messin' with you but you
> your friends are getting most concerned—
> loose with the truth
> maybe it's your fire
> but baby . . . don't get burned . . .
> Can't talk to me without talking to you
> We're guilty of the same old thing
> Talking a lot about less and less
> And forgetting the love we bring

Perhaps it is facile to see in this a message from Hunter to Garcia, but it is certainly tempting. At any rate, it was a song that, with all the rest of the material from what would be called *Go to Heaven*, would be considerably overplayed in the early 1980s. The Dead, said Weir, got stuck. His own "Lost Sailor," which Garcia grumbled was simply "Weather Report Suite" run through a blender, was another of the 1979 songs that would be overplayed, partly because integrating the new band member necessitated some repetition, and partly because the band as a whole . . . was stuck. The year's musical highlight was a side effect of technology. In August they played two nights at the new version of Winterland, Oakland Auditorium (later renamed Henry Kaiser Auditorium), a venerable hall that had over the years housed Buffalo Bill's Wild West Show, a Jack Dempsey fight, and an Elvis Presley performance. It was worn, funky, and comfortable, and would be a good home to the band for a number of years.

The shows were the occasion of major new experiments in sound equipment and design by Healy and his new allies, former members of the Airplane/Hot Tuna/Jefferson Starship sound crew who would form a company called Ultra Sound, and a speaker designer named John Meyer. One of Healy's other new associates was monitor mixer Harry Popick, who'd begun working for the Garcia Band during the hiatus. "We tried so many experiments," said Harry, "so much equipment, in so many configurations . . . one night I might have one speaker cabinet in front of each person with everybody's voice, the next night I might have three cabinets, each person in a different cabinet . . . Nobody was chicken. Nobody ever fell into a groove 'cause that wasn't good enough, especially for the performers." That August they began adding the first Meyer gear, the subwoofers, and the result was awesome. The Dead Heads would nickname it Lesh's "Earthquake" feedback, because the sound was so dense—not necessarily all that loud—but so tactile, so palpable, that it was possible to watch it roll through the audience simply by observing the physical reactions of each row.

That New Year's Eve the sound experiments peaked. They combined equipment from several different sound companies with Ultra's crossovers and got a five-way time-corrected stereo image that was perfect, among the best sound systems ever. Alas, it could not travel, and they would spend the next decade and more trying to give it wheels. The five show run in the last week of 1979 also established Oakland Auditorium as the new home for the Dead and especially Dead Heads. On the first night of the run, Bob Barsotti of Bill Graham Presents made a casual but far-reaching decision. There was a small park in front of the auditorium, and he permitted a number of Dead Heads to sleep there. By the end of the week they numbered in the hundreds. Over the next few years, camping at shows would become a tradition, establishing an ever more intimate relationship between Dead Heads and concerts. As Bill Graham welcomed in the new decade by soaring over the audience in a butterfly suit, two things would be retroactively clear: Dan Healy and company's labors with the sound system, and the development of the subculture that was the Dead Heads, would be the most creative aspects of the Dead world in the eighties. The band would play on, the sound track to an evolving world, part of a general phenomenon called California-ization.

By late in the 1970s, the economic energy of the United States had begun to shift from East Coast ("rust belt") cars and steel to California, home of the space industry, and then to the microtechnology and bioengineering of the Bay Area's Silicon Valley. California had what Americans wanted—from hot tubs to food styles. Considered as a separate country, the state was the eighth largest industrial power in the world, with a growth rate during the decade that was four times the national average. It was the rootless social future, where divorce rates were 20 percent higher and affiliation with traditional religions was dramatically lower. It was the home of U.S. music and television, and that made it the center of the American dream—or nightmare, your choice. One fundamental change, the development of the personal computer, originated with the Homebrew Computer Club, whose members included Stephen Wozniak and Steven Jobs, a club with no dues, no rites, no bylaws. It most closely resembled one of the Stephen Gaskin–led discussion groups at the Family Dog on the Great Highway, but its technological focus and open sharing produced Apple computers. And out of the same sixties ambience came an emerging scientific theory, best stated in Fritjof Capra's *Tao of Physics*, which made the psychedelic experience and quantum physics make sense together.

Wierdly enough, the Dead were at the center of that sociointellectual shift to the postmodern. Writing in *New West* around this time, Charlie Haas pinned the Dead phenomenon perfectly. "It is no coincidence that the Dead's repertoire is so threaded with spookadelic images of disaster and treachery, that so many of the songs portray the universe as a tumble-down casino in which all the games are fixed . . . The common ground between the Dead and the young Heads is the belief that the way to meet an impossible circumstance is with voluntary craziness . . . It is the kids' best guess that they have been born into the sudden-death overtime of Western Civ . . . And if the whole situation is irretrievably warped . . . it becomes incumbent upon the human to warp himself *into* shape."

The Dead mostly stayed warped. As 1980 passed, they were in their second year of working on material for *Go to Heaven*. As John Barlow put it, "They came together over a long period of time and they kept seeming like they *were* together and then they *weren't*. And the GD were in the studio for, Jesus, two years, and they had the same amount of material two weeks before they finished as they did two years before . . . doing over-dubs like demented people. And I just lost all faith in it." The lead Hunter-Garcia tune, "Alabama Getaway," was an up-tempo version of "Dupree's Diamond Blues" for the eighties. "Feel Like a Stranger" was one of Weir's superior tunes, but the lyrics caused strife. Weir had visited a Marin County singles bar where Huey Lewis, then just short of becoming famous, was the leader of the house band, and had come away with a meditation on casual sex, early-eighties style. He and Barlow came to disagree over the lyrics. Said Weir, "[Barlow] was trying to throw in highfalutin' concepts and stuff like that, trying to crowbar them into a song which didn't want 'em—and he uttered the line 'If there's one literate man left in America, I'm writing for him,' at which point I bolted, ran upstairs, locked myself in the bathroom. John kicked his way through the door and we went to the mats out in the hall for a little while."

"Saint of Circumstance" was an interesting musical take on Stax-Volt rhythms and changes, although the phrase "I'm gonna go for it for sure" was a cliché on the day it was first uttered. "Far From Me" and "Easy to Love You," Brent's two contributions, with lyrics by Barlow, were fairly commercial love songs, and it was no surprise that Clive Davis was perplexed at hearing them in the context of the Dead. In fact, Brent even changed things in "Easy to Love You" to please Clive. According to Lesh, Davis interfered even more deeply. "Clive Davis actually went round the producer and made edits! . . . I think *[Go to Heaven]* is dogshit, I hate producers, if I ever have to work with one again I'll probably kill myself." Complete with a cover that portrayed them in white disco suits, the album was released late in April and actually enjoyed good sales, spending twenty-one weeks on the charts and going to no. 23. Most reviews were negative, from *Playboy*'s "Mediocrity on the march" to *Rolling Stone*'s "uninspired fluff."

Discounting any motions to the contrary, the Dead were still capable of splendid doofusness. Despite considerable advance promotion of their June 7 and 8 shows in Boulder, Colorado, as a celebration of their fifteenth anniversary, the band was blissfully unaware of the significance of the date, and played an utterly conventional show on the seventh. After a postshow reminder, they managed a special song sequence—"Playing in the Band" into "Uncle John's Band"—to open the next day's show.

They were also still righteously in touch with whatever peculiar ethos it was that made them who they were. On June 12, in Portland, Oregon, they played "Fire on the Mountain" early in the second set, and as they played, Mount St. Helens erupted. "It was like I didn't know it was going to happen," said Kreutzmann, "but I knew it was gonna happen . . . We did 'Fire' and it felt great. I just loved it. After the song, during drums, somebody came onstage and said, 'Hey, the volcano erupted at 9:18, while you were playing 'Fire.' " After the show, Weir "went to my room, opened a window, and it went off again. I ended up in Rifkin's room, listening to calls about trucks and logistics, watching *Alien* on the tube. It was surreal." As one Dead Head put it upon leaving the hall that night, "We do not want to be on the wrong side of a Dead concert under any circumstances," and proceeded to drive through a rain of ash and mud up Interstate 5, using his left hand to clear the windshield, going from a crawl to, at times, a dead stop in zero visibility conditions. He got through.

From there, the band went on another adventure, three shows in a high school in Anchorage, Alaska, which paid for a week in Hawaii using triangle tickets. Thanks to a free supply of bush planes available to the traveling party, at least some of the gang enjoyed exploring Alaska. Mickey Hart seized on the occasion as an opportunity for MERT to go into action, taking three eleven-year-old boys—Justin Kreutzmann, Rudson Shurtliff (Ram Rod and Frances's son), and Creek Hart—as his crew. Each signed the MERT pledge—"Record more than you erase"—and crossed the Arctic Circle to record Inuit music, fish in the Bering Strait, and acquire Eskimo hoop drums, which would become part of Dead percussion in the coming years.

The Dead also still managed to get into trouble. As they were leaving the stage in San Diego a couple of weeks later, several police officers were engaged in beating a young man they'd arrested for drug possession. Hart inquired if it took all six of them to do the job and was immediately arrested and placed in a choke hold, which with his old judo training he turned around before enough additional police arrived to arrest the man they called Bruce Lee. Weir protested and swiftly joined the booking process. Then Danny Rifkin rounded the corner, saying, "No, you don't understand. This is our show." This earned him a charge of participation in a riot, interference with police, and assault on police. In addition to incitement and assault charges for Hart and Weir, Weir and Rifkin were accused of "lynching," trying to remove a prisoner from custody. Not surprisingly, all charges against the band ended up being dismissed, although the SDPD's score versus the audience was somewhat higher.

On August 31, 1980, Bill Graham Presents ran a full-page advertisement in the *San Francisco Chronicle*'s entertainment section that depicted a male and female skeleton crowned with roses, with the caption "They're Not the Best at What They Do, They're the Only Ones Who Do What They Do." It listed twelve dates (three were added later) in late September and October at San Francisco's intimate (2,400 seats) Warfield Theater. It did not mention the name of the band, and of course it didn't need to; all of the shows sold out immediately. Only a few months late, the Dead had decided to celebrate their anniversary, make a live album, and use some of their newfound *SNL* friends and production techniques for a long run at two venues, first at the Warfield and then at Radio City Music Hall, ending on Halloween night with a closed-circuit television broadcast. There would be three sets, an opening acoustic hour plus the normal two electric sequences, and for Halloween, there would be skits written by Franken and Davis that spoofed the Jerry Lewis muscular dystrophy telethon. The Dead's telethon would also feature a "Jerry's kid," but the donations would buy him a dose of LSD and a ticket to the next concert. The Warfield run kicked off on September 25, and it was an extraordinary three weeks, with two people in particular getting the chance to shine: Dan Healy and Bill Graham.

With so many shows, Graham had an opportunity to go wild as a promoter, and he did. The lobby was magnificently decorated with a treasure trove of memorabilia from his own and the Dead's collections. At his suggestion the sound crew placed speakers in the lobby so that those who wanted to dance could do so without standing in front of those who wanted to see from their seats. Every day he would dictate a critique of the previous night's performance—not the Dead's, but BGP's:

> . . . right slide projector did not work for first five minutes of intermission . . . glad to see that no one, not one, stood on their seats . . . food prices seem to be somewhat high, especially sandwiches . . . you see we have sufficient time and opportunity to gradually perfect the environment . . . early Saturday evening I came down the main steps from upstairs lobby, and it felt as if I were the operator of a Mississippi River gambling boat . . . the most important piece of work this company has ever done . . . Also, I want some lobby visual changes to appear after each off date . . . Make a sign for the water fountain in the rear on the main floor. Present sign not acceptable . . . Mr. Lesh has requested

hand towels larger than the ones presently available to him. I must say, simply based on the amicable manner in which the request was put forth, I see no reason when we don't attempt to comply with his simple wish. The only thing to be determined at this point is size, color and whether these are on consignment, a gift, or a sale.

In truth, the band's contribution to the party was at a very good but not superior level. Brent was still being integrated, and their musical tendency was to play relatively safe. The acoustic set, the first in a decade, had been rehearsed only two or three times for half an hour or so, and Garcia's acoustic touch at the beginning of the run was atrocious. But Healy and his (relatively) new henchmen, Don Pearson and John Meyer, overcame that by assembling a sound system and team that took live recording to a new level. Meyer, the man who would supply them with speakers for the next decade and more, was a Berkeley kid who'd worked for Steve Miller and then McCune Audio, the first of the Bay Area's sound companies. In 1974 he'd gone to Switzerland's Institute for Advanced Musical Studies, testing fifteen-ply Finnish birch and other esoterica to take speakers to a new level. By 1980 he had created the Ultramonitor, a quantum advance in the essential problem of high-volume music, that of helping the musicians to hear themselves while playing. Meyer focused on linearity—"what you put in, you get out"—to produce a sound that was as transparent and nondistorting as possible. To that point, loudspeakers like JBL and Marshall had been made for guitars and were nonlinear; they had a sound, which is to say they had a recognizable distortion. Unlike almost everyone else in rock, the Dead cared about dynamic range, playing both very quietly and very loudly. Since most bands simply wanted to turn it up to the mythical 11, the Dead were actually working in a territory that would be occupied by classical musicians.

Meyer built 'em; Pearson and his partner, Howard Danchik, brought them to Healy. Although he'd started as a photographer, Pearson had hooked up with Danchik, a Washington, D.C., high school friend of Jack Casady and Jorma Kaukonen, and they'd all ended up working together for Hot Tuna. At the Warfield, Wizard and Pearson acted as engineers for Bob, Betty, and Healy, and were utterly necessary. There was so much tape being pulled at the Warfield that they needed a database just to keep track of what would turn out to be eight hundred reels. Healy had placed microphones at various layers out from the stage, with the goal of creating an aural hologram. The results were *Dead Reckoning,* an acoustic double album, and *Dead Set,* an electric album.

The fall was an adventure in more ways than one. Though they had sent blueprints of the Neve recording console ahead to Radio City Music Hall, someone at Radio City goofed, and when they arrived, they found that they could not get the console into the allotted room. Mickey Hart, observing, shouted, "Take the doorjamb out," and sledgehammers removed two inches of a national landmark. This was not their last problem with Radio City. Bill Graham's stage manager, Peter Barsotti, and his friend Dennis Larkin, had designed a wonderful poster in San Francisco that had one of the rose-crowned skeletons leaning on a depiction of the Warfield. Then they added a second poster of the skeletons with Radio City. In a remarkable display of noncommunication, Radio City's management became convinced that the poster was in fact a secret insult to the venerable theater that suggested the hall's "impending death," and filed a $1.2-million suit against the band. The suit was dropped when Radio City came to understand that this was not the point and the band agreed not to use the poster at that time.

Two images from the fall's run resonated afterward. One was the Associated Press photograph of the line that sprang up around Radio City Music Hall three days before tickets went on sale, a line that literally encircled NBC's offices at Rockefeller Center. The media coverage of that line and the Dead Head phenomenon was enormous. The second image was provided by Bill Graham. When the Dead left the stage after their last set at the Warfield, they returned for their encore to find a small table with glasses and champagne in a silver bucket. Garcia went over to the table, did a take, cocked his eye, and picked up a glass. As he did so, super trouper spotlights splayed over the audience, revealing each member with a raised glass of his or her own toasting the band, as a garland of roses hung off the balcony along with a sign that read, "Thank You." It was a classic moment.

46

Interlude:
Beyond the Zone

(END OF SECOND SET)

December, McNichols Arena, Denver

Garcia wheezes in the mile-high air as he walks from the van to the stage, and agrees that, on the road, to quote Gilda Radner's Roseanne Roseannadanna character, "It's always something." The definition of boredom for Scrib will, to the day of his death, be one endless hot summer Sunday in Cincinnati, in a cheap hotel with nonfunctioning air-conditioning, where the only two movies in walking distance were *Rambo* and something worse, where his TV got two stations and the radio sucked. By contrast, almost every member of the Dead tour will define terror as the flight to—was it Milwaukee?—where the sky was solid lightning for virtually the length of their journey, and no one was ever quite sure how they survived.

As the last notes of Hart's Beam solo bounce off the back wall, Garcia and Weir contemplate the evening's performance of "Space." It is the direct musical heir to the acid tests, with roots in Ornette Coleman and Charles Ives, a place where something truly original will be played once and only once. There are no rules. On occasion, and usually in the form of a joke, Garcia and Weir will give a name to the upcoming jam, but the mandate is simply to make it new. In Las Vegas once, Healy contributed the sampled sound of slot machines. Another time, they miked a Harley motorcycle, and Parish sat in on throttle. Train whistles have been popular, as was the sound of frying bacon—until a furious Mickey poured the contents of the frying pan, which had been plugged into Garcia's twin reverb amp, all over Garcia's amp when the pan wasn't hot enough to produce a sizzle. Ram Rod cleaned up the mess and then announced, "That's the end of bacon." In Baltimore one year, Lesh honored Poe by improvising a rant on "The Raven."

Tonight, Panaspots sheet the front of the stage, leaving the guitarists in darkness. As Garcia tunes in the shadows, a very straight visiting couple passes behind his amp and gives him a big thumbs-up. He never sees them as he steps out to his spot. His hands flutter like insect wings up the neck of his guitar, but his body never moves. Weir bangs his guitar with his slide, Lesh leaps into a lead, and Garcia follows him in some dissonant progression. His note line flutters and races, darting first like a butterfly, then starts a riff that repeats and rises. Then he doubles the riff with a digital delay that allows him to play harmony with himself. Weir falls in with a second harmony sweeping behind him. Candace blackens Garcia's face, makes it a dark hole, then gives him a halo. They take every musical chance, fall to pieces, and then come back and reassemble. It's not rhythmic, nor really attached to any Western musical norm.

In the midst of chaos, Weir begins a figure, a rhythmic extract of Miles Davis's *Sketches of Spain* that the band has played dozens of times since 1968 and never bothered to name. The Dead Heads call it "Acid Bolero" or "Spanish Jam," and it is stately, classic, and heavy, leading straight into their masterpiece for improvisation, "The Other One." Still in his digital delay, Garcia picks up the beat of "The Other One," their supremely spooky-weird reification of the Bo Diddley beat. Extended and pushed in those weeks of inspiration in the fall of 1967 into a psychedelic musical wavelength that patrols the downside of the psyche, it pauses and shifts, each musician acknowledging the riff in his own way. Garcia leads, defining quest, exploration, and change, the song a demand to find out what's possible in a tune you can dance like crazy to. Brent piles up the synth chords, Garcia charges, Lesh pounds, Kreutzmann and Hart stroke the pulse, it repeats, repeats not incrementally but exponentially, the guitar riding a mountain ridge of screaming upper register notes at the top that unites an entire slabbed mountain of melody that settles into Weir's first verse, then another break, and then the second verse: "The bus came by and I got on / that's when it all began / There was cowboy Neal at the wheel / of the bus to never-ever land."

And the audience sings along, screaming now, for this is what the Dead is all about—a voyage, a search, a quest, perhaps sacrifice and martyrdom. This isn't the entertainment business, pal. "We're in the transportation business," said Hart. "We move minds." Sound is made into something solid and real, tactile as a punch in the face, architectural designs evanescent but no less distinct, cloud-capped peaks and rainbows, human cries and a voice torn by Healy's octave splitter into a triple echoing blast.

December, Compton Terrace, Phoenix

An Ultra guy scoots by, yelling "Tape, tape." Someone throws him a roll of gaffer's tape, and he fixes Brent's microphone control box, which is slipping. The band goes into "Throwing Stones," one of Weir's typically eccentric compositions, one that—most unusual in Western music—begins on a dominant chord, and thus is balanced with a jam in the middle from the Bahamian tune "Bye and Bye." Weir slashes chords on every third beat; they come to fullness, crescendo, then into a slinking, insinuatingly quiet riff. Brent picks up the lead, and Weir steps to the microphone:

> And the current fashion sets the pace
> Lose your step, fall out of grace.
> And the radical, he rant and rage,
> Singing someone's got to turn the page.
> And the rich man in his summer home,
> Singing just leave well enough alone.
> But his pants are down, his cover's blown . . .
>
> And the politicians throwing stones
> So the kids they dance
> And shake their bones,
> And it's all too clear we're on our own.
> Singing ashes, ashes, all fall down.
> Ashes, ashes, all fall down . . .

December, Oakland Coliseum

As the show nears its end, tour manager Cameron Sears paces behind the stage. Settlement is done, and the band has been paid. The vans are moving into position behind the stage. Onstage they have reached the "Garcia weeper" slot. Though open to variation, the drums are generally followed by a Weir rave-up, then a Garcia ballad—"Stella Blue," "Black Peter," various others—and then a Weir rocker to close the show. Because it is a good night, Garcia slides from "Stones" into *the* great closer, "Morning Dew." Written by Bonnie Dobson in 1961 after seeing *On the Beach*, it is a postapocalyptic conversation between the last man and last woman on earth. Laird Grant had come across the song on a Fred Neil album late in 1966 and brought it to Garcia. What the Dead would do with it over the next decades would be an ultimate example of postmodernist deconstruction. The Dead's "Dew" is a simple folk tune exploded into structural bas-relief like a DNA double helix diagram, enlarged, highlighted, colored, texturized, and thrown in the audience's face, equalized, blown up until it rips out brain cells, so slowed down and clarified that you can see every pattern, every possibility, and watch the band choose among them.

"Walk me out in the morning dew, my honey . . ."

The sound seems a little ragged, and Parish, a slight smile of satisfied comprehension on his lips, calls over Ram Rod, picks up a power drill and a new speaker for Garcia's rack, and with Ram Rod behind and himself in front, replaces the blown speaker in about forty-five seconds. The sound is now pure and sweet, and he swaggers slightly as he returns to his cave. "You have to completely surrender," to play a ballad, said Kreutzmann, and they do. It builds and builds, and they play the variations like a waltz of light beams, first Garcia and Lesh playing counterleads with Brent and Bobby on rhythm chords, then Garcia and Brent take the lead, Phil and Bobby support, and then Garcia and Weir . . . like some kind of liquid gear assembly that can move in four directions simultaneously. Garcia's guitar simply squeeezes out the lead, the same sure descent but with overtones of pathos and majesty, repetition for the gods, and then they send it *up* one more time and then speed it up and split it into a shimmering waterfall glissando of grace notes, tears from the goddess muse. And a little shitty feedback, too. There is a death samba at the end of the second verse, slow, Zen playing, the statement of sanity as the one ideal, notes like quicksilver fill every available sonic space, all six at once, existential final statement/question, and Garcia's voice is exactly right as he sings "I thought I heard a baby cry this morning," sings it for the family's dead children, and the ones to be born, and they come to the final jam, his guitar bucks, moans, and dances, the scales start, like tap-dancing up a frozen waterfall, and suddenly Garcia hits a note like a dentist's drill bursting straight down to the nerve, the true note impossibly painful and alive, the audible edge, and six streams of music pour into one, edging into each other, coalescing with each other, a dance of six patterns and all the possibilities of meaning, reflection, refraction, and acceptance, all the way to a love supreme at our hearts.

Garcia croaks out the last line, "I guess it doesn't matter, anyway," and twenty thousand people know that he's right.

After Heaven

(11/80−7/86)

O n December 8, Garcia was at Front Street working on *Dead Set* when he got a call that told him of the assassination of John Lennon. Work was impossible. He sat down at Keith Godchaux's old Steinway (more pain: Keith had died in a car accident that summer) and noodled for many hours, lost in thought. After all, he and Lennon had more than a little in common. Both had emerged from childhoods damaged by deeply flawed relationships with their mothers, and through their losses had found a stunning creativity that had put them in the prison of celebrity. Lennon, of course, had experienced Beatlemania, which made the enthusiasm of Dead Heads look quite demure. And in Marin County Garcia had a home where his celebritydom had a minimal impact; elsewhere, Dead Heads treated him as family, "Uncle Jerry," and (usually) not as God. Still, Garcia felt it. A few years later, he made a very rare direct request of Scrib. "Hey, man, you gotta bail me out." His wedding anniversary was only two days away, and he needed a restaurant reservation; only a terribly au courant place would do, and the date happened to be a prime holiday. Scrib replied, "Sure, but you know I'll need to throw your name around to get it." "That's okay, man. It's just that I could never do that."

Early in 1981 the Dead went to Europe to play a few shows in London and then appear with the Who on the German TV show *Rockpalast*, and while in London Garcia gave one of his most extraordinary interviews. Few patently hostile interviewers get within yards of a star, and rarer still is the star who will tolerate hostility. Garcia found it stimulating. The interviewer, Paul Morley, was a cutting-edge young punk from *New Musical Express*, and Garcia revolted him. "You're just a part of a perpetuation of bland, blanketing myths," said the punk. "Does that disappoint you?" Garcia chuckled. "Naah! I didn't have any expectations . . . If you start out expecting to fail and expecting the worst then anything that happens is an improvement over that . . . we're just starting." Does it upset you that I don't dig you? "No! I don't give a damn. I would be afraid if everybody in the world liked us . . . I don't want to be responsible for leading the march to wherever. Fuck that. It's already been done and the world hates it . . . a combination of music and the psychedelic experience taught me to fear power. I mean fear it and hate it . . . First of all, I don't think of myself as an adult. *An adult is someone who's made up their mind* [italics Morley's]. When I go through airports the people who have their thing together, who are clean, well-groomed, who have tailored clothes, who have their whole material thing together, these people are adults. They've made their decision to follow those routines . . . I would say that I was part of a prolonged adolescence. I think our whole scene is that . . . I feel like someone who is constantly on the verge of losing it, or blowing it. I feel tremendously insecure." "My heated irrationality bumps into Garcia's sheer reasonableness," wrote Morley, and it was true. Garcia's egoless interest in authentic communication, even when it involved mocking him, made for one of the more fascinating encounters in rock journalism.

On May 6, the Dead played at Nassau Coliseum. They began "He's Gone," which Weir dedicated to Bobby Sands, an IRA soldier who had just starved himself to death in prison. "I'm not a supporter of bombers," Lesh would later muse, "but it meant something to me and I played it. Sands was never convicted of any real crime except carrying a weapon— and how the fuck will I know who he was, how he had the balls to go all the way. I don't know what would make me grow the balls to go that far." After the song came a ten-minute blur of improvisation that was as good as anything they'd played in years. Even though, as Garcia noted, the new guy needed to relax and to learn how to keep Bob Weir out of his hair, Brent Mydland had arrived, and the band had achieved a new quantum level.

It was an ironic coincidence that the future of rock and roll would find a new, and largely nonmusical, focus on Garcia's birthday that year, his thirty-ninth. On August 1, 1981, MTV, a partnership of WEA (Warner Bros., Elektra, and Atlantic) and American Express, went on the air, or more precisely the cable system. With techniques taken from advertising, MTV linked music and visuals in a way that contributed to ever-dwindling spans of attention and ever-rising revenues. It took rock straight back to the showbiz values it had once rejected, producing visually conscious stars like Madonna and Michael Jackson who enshrined style as the apogee of the medium. The next year, Jackson would release *Thriller,* selling 40 million copies. MTV was slick, elegant, visual, and commercial, which is to say that it was everything the Grateful Dead was not. By contrast, the band's best moment in 1981 came in a tiny, smoky club in Amsterdam, where they celebrated musical friendship with a spontaneous, financially meaningless gig dubbed the Oops Concert.

The band had gone to Europe for a second time, in September, and it was not a terrific business success. Kreutzmann had fired Richard Loren during the March tour of Europe. After the tour, Kreutzmann had apologized and Loren had been rehired, but with Garcia adrift, the job wasn't much fun anymore, and in September Loren had quit. As a result, the fall tour was run by Rock, and his instincts for drugs and entertaining lunacy were still intact. When a gig in France was canceled, he arranged for Jerry and Bobby to play an acoustic show at the Melk Weg club in Amsterdam, a four-hundred-seat room that had among its features the Markt, which sold comic books, candy, and various kinds of hashish. The police station was directly across the street. The duo so enjoyed themselves that they inveigled the entire band into a little Amsterdamian adventure, and they had a ball. Lesh was already walking on air, because he'd just seen Leonard Bernstein conduct the Vienna Philharmonic in a program of Brahms and Mozart, one of the cherished experiences of his lifetime.

The spontaneity of their jump to Amsterdam had cost them their normal equipment—Lesh somehow managed to finagle his regular bass, but Garcia and Weir played on loaners—so they couldn't rely on their usual bells and whistles, and they reveled in this freedom. In a hot room, so crowded that people were sitting under Brent's piano, they returned to their garage band roots, pulling out "Gloria" and "Hully Gully," as well as Pigpen's "Lovelight," which simply fell out of Lesh's fingers, and which Weir ran away with. It all worked. Clowning around between swigs on a vodka bottle, Lesh realized that he hadn't sweat so hard in ages, and it was a healthy sweat. Somehow, in the middle of their usual sea of troubles, they'd returned to what they were about. The catharsis would mean a great deal down the line. Three days later in Barcelona, after the last show of the tour, Lesh wrote out a note for Garcia and made the rest of the band sign it. Though arch in tone, it was a deadly serious attempt to confront Garcia, their emotional anchor. "Dear sir and brother: You have been accused of certain high crimes and misdemeanors against the art of music. To wit: Playing in your own band; Never playing with any dynamics; Never listening to what anybody else plays . . ." The long party was taking its toll on all of them, but especially on the leader who wouldn't lead.

The year 1981 ended with the usual Grateful Dead mixture of the conventional and the utterly bizarre. Mickey Hart and Joan Baez had taken up romantically. Mickey thought Joan wanted to "get wild." He'd fallen for her voice at first, sound above all, and then he'd fallen fully in love. Although the relationship would come apart when he found himself unable to cope with her bouts of depression, it resulted in the Grateful Dead backing Baez at a mid-December benefit called Dance for Disarmament. The show was an underrehearsed and only partially successful event. Two weeks later, on New Year's Eve, Jerry and M.G. were married by Peter "Monk" Zimmels in Jerry's dressing room, partly for tax reasons and partly out of a fond flickering of a once-bright romance. The new year began with a ferocious, weeklong storm, which brought January to Marin County with such force that few could leave their homes for the duration. Jerry's place at Hepburn Heights was too small for a second person, and he and M.G. soon decided that they could not live together.

Phil Lesh spent early January stuck in the Berkeley Marriott Hotel bar, for his home was inaccessible. Being in limbo further encouraged his ongoing life changes. He'd recently moved to San Rafael to escape his old patterns, which for years had centered on Nave's Bar in Fairfax. For some time he'd breakfasted every day at the Station Cafe in San Rafael, just a few blocks from 5th and Lincoln. In February 1982, he invited Jill Johnson, a Station Cafe waitress, to a Dead show, and the romance of his life began. For the first time since 1965, he would have something essential in his life other than the Dead.

The Dead's "new" *Go to Heaven* material was now three years old, and though the fall of 1982 saw the end of their collective writer's block, it would take a violation of the rules. "No politics" and "no lectures" were the implicit and fundamental rules of the Dead's lyricists as far as Barlow was concerned (Hunter had written political material, but Garcia had tossed it), and with the possible exception of "New Speedway Boogie," those limits had always been observed. But however entertainingly surreal, the era of Ronald Reagan, a figurehead president who was most distinctive in what historian Frances FitzGerald called his "limitless capacity for denial," demanded stern choices, and Weir broke the code. "I didn't like his movies," said Garcia, "and I don't like his politics. I like things wide open, with question marks hanging over it, everything changing—nothing settled."

Weir and Barlow would raise their voices. John Barlow had been active in the movement that fought the installation of "Star Wars" MRVs in Wyoming. One day he pointed out to a judge that there had been no environmental impact report, and the judge replied that since using the missiles was unthinkable, there could therefore be no consequences. Faced with this conundrum, Barlow's mind flashed back to his high school years at Fountain Valley School in the shadow of the Strategic Air Command's headquarters at Cheyenne Mountain, where he heard sirens wailing because of the Cuban missile crisis. He and Weir went to work, beginning with the English nursery rhyme "Ring around the rosey . . . Ashes, ashes, all fall down," a ditty that derived from the plague years. The ring referred to a sore, the ashes to cremated corpses. The result was "Throwing Stones," which Weir called an "anarchistic diatribe" against all manner of evil, and was by far the most overtly political song in the Dead catalog. He wasn't finished. A few days after debuting "Throwing Stones," he began to sing "My Brother Essau," a take on Cain and Abel and the Vietnam War, a superior song marred only by the ungainly refrain "shadowboxing the apocalypse, and wandering the land."

Along with these songs, Garcia and Hunter introduced "West L.A. Fadeaway," a musically simplistic take on the traditional San Francisco disdain for Los Angeles; "Keep Your Day Job," a musically lightweight shuffle with a cautionary message that Dead Heads would dislike; and "A Touch of Grey." "Touch" was interesting on a number of levels. Musically, it was an up-tempo variant of "Bertha." Lyrically, it was a superb rendering of the morning after a cocaine binge—"Must be getting early / Clocks are running late / Paint by number morning sky / Looks so phony," complete with a catalog of middle-age grumbles, from the high cost of rent to a recalcitrant child, but Hunter included an uplifting closing that turned the song into an anthem:

> *Oh well a Touch Of Grey*
> *Kind of suits you anyway.*

That was all I had to say
It's all right.

I will get by / I will get by
I will get by / I will survive
We will get by / We will get by
We will get by / We will survive

As with most Dead tunes, it would take a while for the song to find its soul. It would marinate well over the next few years.

Meantime, as always, there were gigs, some memorable, most not. In March the Garcia Band enjoyed its strangest show ever, at a country-western bar in San Jose called the Saddlerack. Rock Scully had outdone himself with this booking. Complete with a mechanical bucking bull and punching bag, the club was an enormous cavern half filled with wide-eyed Dead Heads. The front row was occupied exclusively by the off-duty waitresses in beehive hairdos and the security force, each man no less than 220 pounds, all dressed in red T-shirts. Clearly amused, Garcia chuckled and smiled throughout the show. For his main band, September 1982 brought them their first gig actually scheduled for 9 A.M., Breakfast in Bed with the Grateful Dead. At the last second, Bill Graham had taken over the booking for the US Festival, a giant outdoor festival sponsored by the computer tycoon Stephen Wozniak. With a respectable chunk of Wozniak's fortune at his discretion, Graham convinced the band to open the second day. As is so often the case with jobs taken exclusively for financial reasons, it was not an aesthetically rewarding morning for the band.

Their other weird morning gig that year was in November at the World Music Festival in Montego Bay, Jamaica. Due to the vagaries of festival scheduling, they hit the stage at about 4:30 A.M., and though they played into a beautiful dawn, various distractions created by armed guards, too much dust, and a strange sound system made for a terribly difficult gig.

The year ended with a New Year's Eve concert that was one of the few in that era not afflicted with burnout, largely because for the final set the Dead became Etta James's backup band on tunes like "Lovelight," "Tell Mama," and "Midnight Hour." At one point, the zaftig James leaned on the rotund Garcia, mugging in a bit of standard R&B showbiz shtick that was utterly unlike Garcia's usual stage demeanor, and he simply beamed. A few days later, Scrib would remark to Garcia that he seemed just as happy as a sideman as he did as a leader. "Y'know," Garcia replied, "I coulda spent my life playin' blues in a Mission Street dump and been just as happy. All my life, man, all my life."

Danny Rifkin had replaced Richard Loren as the band's manager late in 1981, and it denoted a significant return to their roots. A thoroughgoing small-c communist, Rifkin had been nicknamed Danny the Dime by the crew for his parsimonious ways. Loren had received a percentage of the band's guarantees in a deal that gave the band a percentage of the gross, which meant that promoters had little incentive to control expenses. Now, with Rifkin on his relatively modest salary, and with deals based on the band getting a percentage of the net rather than gross, there was a surplus, which led to raises. Early in 1983 Danny took another step, one with enormous ramifications. Buying tickets to Dead concerts had long meant getting in line on a frozen sidewalk in the middle of the night, and although no one on the planet can make waiting in line a more pleasant occupation than a Dead Head, by the eighties there were committed Dead Heads with jobs who could not spare the time. First with movie producer Eddie Washington, and then with Steve Marcus and Frankie Accardi in charge, Rifkin established a Dead mail-order ticket office. Effectively run by four strong women in middle management—Calico, Joanne Wishnoff, Carol Latvala, and Mary Knudsen—it proved to be a marvelous idea, not only because it employed dozens of family members but also because it opened up the demographics of the audience to include people with more or less conventional lives. The hardest core would always find a way, but now the respectable could, too. The first tickets sold were for benefit concerts in March 1983 at the Warfield. Over the next decade in-house ticket sales grew from 24,500 the first year to 115,000 the next to 500,000 annually in the early nineties.

Across the country, the band's venues usually had exclusive contracts with Ticketmaster, a national ticket sales company. Eventually, push came to shove. Fred Rosen, boss of Ticketmaster, and John Pritzker, part of the family that owned the Hyatt chain of hotels as well as Ticketmaster, met with Hal Kant, Danny Rifkin, and others from the Dead. At some point, Hal offhandedly began to ask Fred Rosen, a tough and aggressive businessman, various biographical questions. After the umpteenth question, Fred said, "Why are you asking me these questions?" "Because I want to see what kind of witness you're going to be." "Witness? What?" said Fred, who then sputtered to Hal, "You're claiming [that Ticketmaster violates antitrust laws], but you're interfering with my contractual relations."

"That's interesting," replied Hal, "because we just hired a law firm to handle this litigation, and I told them, 'Forget about antitrust, they're interfering with *our* contractual relations.' When did you go into business, Fred? How long have our contractual relations existed with these venues before you ever came along? Who interfered with whom?" "[Rosen] sort of turned white," recalled Hal, "and then he *really* turned white when he heard the name of the law firm, because it happened to be his law firm. He had the West Coast office, and we had the East Coast office. At that point everything changed, and he agreed to everything we wanted . . . I think at some point I did say, 'I don't think you want five thousand crazed Dead Heads staying at Hyatt Hotels unhappy with you.' " It helps to have a good lawyer.

After the ticket office, the hippest and most consequential of Rifkin's moves came in 1984, when the band founded the Rex Foundation, named after Rex Jackson. Just as every greedhead in America was making buckets of money, the Dead figured out how to give it away more effectively. Too many benefits had proved to be inefficient, requiring huge amounts of energy but yielding small amounts of money for the cause. The 1982 Vietnam Veterans benefit at Moscone Center in San Francisco was a case in point. An enormous trade-show and convention center, the site was a terrible place for music and was selected only as a favor to the mayor. The recipient organization splintered into dueling factions, wasting much of the money raised. With the Rex Foundation the Dead would take over the benefit process entirely, setting up a board that included some band members and friends like Bill Graham, John Scher, Bill Walton, M.G., and an Alabama dentist named Bernie Bildman. Benefits became simple. The band performed, and the profits went into a "pot," which would be emptied in increments of $5,000 and $10,000. Over the next few years the Rex Foundation would give away more than $6 million to organizations for the environment, human services, and arts, groups like Wavy Gravy's Camp Winnarainbow and the San Francisco Mayor's Fund for the Homeless, and direct grants to obscure English avant-garde composers. It was remarkably efficient and direct, because the board did not accept applications—it learned of good causes and gave money away.

Shortly before the first official Rex shows, in February 1984, the band made noises about recording a new album and went into Fantasy Records' Studio D in Berkeley. The sessions were a farcical waste of time. The musicians didn't particularly want to be there, and their ever-increasing popularity as performers—that year at the Saratoga Performing Arts Center they would sell twelve thousand tickets on the day of the show in a pouring rainstorm—removed any economic incentive to record. One night Scrib attended a session. They began with a tentative take of "My Brother Essau," Weir fiddling with his guitar, Garcia off by a full beat at the end. The second version was much better, and a happy Weir called out, *"Uno más."* Mickey chimed in, "Let's do another," then got up from his chair. Garcia stood up, observed, "Well, it's not getting worse," and wandered off to the next-door lounge.

When they resumed, they began working on "Keep Your Day Job." Garcia was playing an odd twangy pattern that made no musical sense. Lesh lost the song again, and Garcia remarked, "None of you seem to remember it tonight." Weir said, "I'm searching for a part." Garcia snapped, "Play a rhythm fuckin' part." At the end of the session, Kreutzmann emerged from the studio furious with Weir, swinging at the air, yelling, and telling himself to calm down. In great good humor, Garcia came out and talked with Billy. "Hey, man, 'Day Job's' a boogie-woogie tune," and began drumming on a tabletop with him. Their talk shifted to Art Tatum, and Jerry gleefully told stories of pianists contemplating suicide after listening to the master. Finally, Kreutzmann grabbed Weir and they went back into the studio to work things out, while Parish took Garcia home.

They no longer had the stomach for life in the studio, and it was no surprise that nothing came of the sessions. On the other hand, their concert sound had gone to levels most bands didn't know existed. That summer a veteran CBS-TV soundman stood in front of the speakers, listening first to the mix in his headphones as beamed from the soundboard, and then to the sound system. He was astounded when he could not distinguish between them. A few years later the snootiest of all sound magazines, *Absolute Sound,* published the following: "The other night I experienced the finest large-scale High End audio system I have ever heard. It shattered my preconceived notions of what the state-of-the-art in High End sound reproduction is capable of . . . Never at any time did I hear distortion . . . stereo imaging was pinpoint and extremely accurate . . . [The] emotional connection between the listener and the music . . . was absolute, total, complete."

Healy was the consummate live engineer, with an ability to identify what was most positive in the music on a given night—or who—and mix to it (him). He had his failures, such as allowing the band to perform in the HHH Metrodome in Minneapolis, very probably the worst-sounding venue in Dead history, as well as an inability—Weir felt it was an unwillingness—to present Weir fully. But his commitment to the band, the music, Dead Heads, and the quest for Better were unparalleled. One of his major goals was to plug the system's "ears," the B&K wave analyzer which was created to evaluate the harmonic strength of metals, directly into a computer so that the system could balance itself. When asked if he was trying to do himself out of a job, he replied, "No, just make it a better job."

Change accelerated through the organization in 1984. The previous fall, Alan Trist had been fired and departed for Oregon to work on his drug problems, leaving Rock without an ally. It was ironic, because it had been Alan's attempt to act as a staff lieutenant and keep Rock functioning during the post-Loren, pre-Rifkin period in 1981 that had sucked Trist's life into the drug haze Rock loved so much. The band's action was in part an attempt to save Trist's health and in part an attempt to isolate Garcia from his most egregious codependents. It proved more useful to Alan, who would, some years later, return to work. Rock's continued employment in the Dead scene was by now a mystery. He was undoubtedly the latest man in the world, and his excuses for his tardiness grew ever more imaginative; apparently, every woman going into labor in Marin County tended to be in a car in front of Rock at just the right time, and he'd assisted with all their deliveries.

In March 1984, Garcia's loyal assistant and bookkeeper, Sue Stephens, had had enough. "I finally threw my hands up and said, 'it's Rock or me.'" Given Rock's inability to cope with schedules, the Garcia band would tend to miss flights, so that Rock would have to buy a new set of tickets. But, Sue pointed out to Jerry, at the end of the tour the unused tickets would have been cashed in. In addition, Rock would "duck out on paying the hotel bill, for God's sakes," said Sue, "which he would have been allowed cash for from the settlement [the night's pay] . . . So at the end of the tour I'd end up with all these airfares I still had to pay, all these hotel bills I still had to pay—that the money had been allotted for and doled out to Rock out on the road . . . And it was blatant, too. He'd apologize and be laughing, too. So we went and told Jerry we couldn't deal with [Rock]. And he just said okay," and agreed to fire Rock. "He was almost gleeful," recalled Sue. "And he thanked us. 'I depend on you guys to deal with this shit because I can't deal with too much of it.'"

One of Danny Rifkin's many virtues was that he was not addicted to the Grateful Dead. In the summer of 1984 he decided to leave the road, and once again the band reached out to its past, asking Jon McIntire to return. After his 1974 departure he'd worked as Weir's personal manager, then returned to St. Louis during his father's terminal illness, where he worked as a domestic violence and substance abuse counselor. He was also, he said, "teaching occasionally in a Methodist church in southern

Illinois, giving talks on things like Joseph Campbell's cosmology of myth, the Book of Job, the sermons of Paul Tillich." He studied religion because he was interested in "the essence of individual transformation . . . we need to be better than we are in order to exist." Phenomenally bright, he was engaging, even to the man who'd fired him, Bill Kreutzmann. Shortly after going on the road with the band, he and Bill found themselves together. "Wanna hear a story?" asked Jon. "I'd love to," said Kreutzmann. Jon proceeded to tell of staying at the edge of the Grand Canyon at a time of great personal confusion. Trying to grasp the meaning of the canyon, he threw the I Ching and realized that he had to surrender, stop trying to grasp. "The word 'can't' doesn't exist, the word 'why' doesn't exist," said Kreutzmann, himself a spiritual seeker who could spin mysto word games with any guru. Conversations like that were the reason McIntire was part of the Dead, and though he was not entirely convinced at the wisdom of his return, he found the scene still remarkably collective, although the band was in greater control than before. Thanks to Rifkin's honesty, the Dead's business was healthy. But the audiences were much, much larger, and there was that much more adrenaline around every night.

A second bit of fallout from Rock's firing took place in June at an all-employee meeting. Mary Jo Meinolf, then the band's receptionist, complained of getting repeated calls from members of the media because Rifkin did not return them, being both too busy and not overfond of journalists in any case. "Get [Scrib] to do it," said Garcia. "He knows that shit." After a fifteen-minute training session in which he was instructed to avoid currying favor with the media, Scrib took over as the new publicist.

As 1984 wore on, Garcia set to work with his old friend Tom Davis on creating a script for a film of Kurt Vonnegut's *The Sirens of Titan*. Davis had come to Hepburn Heights to begin, and was greeted with, "Come in, sit down, and get high, we'll talk about it tomorrow." Both of them were fans of Bob and Ray, and many of their earliest sessions had more to do with laughter and television than work. Jerry and Tom eventually produced a script, based on their mutual understanding of the book as a definition of love, said Davis, "in Kurt Vonnegut's stark, minimalist way—romance with no romance, just kernels of love." Davis managed to arrange a meeting that included the Hollywood superagent Michael Ovitz and *SNL* star Bill Murray, but nothing came of it, and the script languished.

The year ended in awful tragedy. Late on the twenty-eighth of December, Steve Parish's wife, Lorraine, and their young daughter Jennifer died in a car accident. His closest brothers—Angelo and Robert from the Hell's Angels, John Cutler, Kidd Candelario, John Hagen, and Mickey—

wrapped themselves around Parish in a hard protective knot, and he survived, as those left behind must. As the band played New Year's Eve, he sat helpless onstage and grieved, and when Garcia ended the year with Dylan's "It's All Over Now, Baby Blue," *everyone* cried.

A large part of the reason McIntire had returned as manager was to catalyze the band's concern for Garcia's drug use, and in mid-January he arranged a confrontation. This was neither the first nor the last intervention for Garcia, and as usual, he promised to seek help. He almost made it. He planned to enter a facility in Oakland, and on January 18, 1985, he set out for it. Halfway there he stopped in Golden Gate Park, where he sat in his car meditating on his life, and, not coincidentally, finishing off his drug supply. Unfortunately, his BMW, a gift from a disreputable source, was not registered. A passing police officer took notice of the car and ran the plates. When he approached the car, he saw Garcia trying futilely to conceal things. The legal results of the bust were minimal, and a good attorney named Chris Andrian quite properly got Garcia into a diversion program, where he attended counseling meetings with Grace Slick, among others. The sessions had no significant impact on his habit, but something else did. Early in the summer the consequences of almost total physical passivity caught up with him, and he began to experience massive edema, a swelling in his ankles and lower legs that was so bad his trousers needed to be cut. The appearance of his legs was so shocking that Garcia finally had undeniable proof of the damage. Bit by bit, as the year 1985 passed, he began to clean up and exercise at least a little.

For the band, the spring of '85 was dominated by a new experience. Phil DeGuere had come to the Dead's attention with the failed 1972 film project called *Sunshine Daydream*. Since then, he'd moved up the Hollywood TV ladder with a writing stint on *Baretta* before becoming producer of *Simon and Simon*. Now he was the producer of a new version of Rod Serling's classic *The Twilight Zone*. Few shows could possibly have been more appealing to the Dead and Garcia, who remarked, "Man, I *live* in the Twilight Zone." They leaped at the chance to record their own version of the signature three-note motif, *"neenerneenerneener,"* that identified the show. They didn't stop there. DeGuere and his music director, Merl Saunders, came to a board meeting to discuss the band's doing all of the music for the show, the "stings" and "bumpers" that set the atmospheric soundscape. Garcia left the meeting early, announcing that he voted yes. Lesh was "adamantly opposed," recalled DeGuere, and the decision was made to proceed without him.

They set to work, and while their music was appropriate and effective, the deal's business aspects were badly handled, dooming the project to continuous friction among all parties involved. Hal Kant had delegated the negotiation of the arrangement with CBS to an associate, who didn't know the Dead very well and produced a fairly standard contract. The head of the music department at CBS didn't like the deal, since he now had no control, which put Merl in the middle of both an unhappy CBS and the Dead. Very quickly, Mickey Hart took the lead for the Dead in the studio, and proved to have a gift for sound design. Just as they began, he went into the hospital for back surgery, and ordered that all the necessary equipment be set up in his room. At first Ram Rod vetoed this seeming insanity, but Mickey pleaded, "When I wake up, I want to go to work." The Demerol he'd gotten for his surgery proved to be aesthetically stimulating, and he produced music for the first four episodes from bed.

That spring, Hart set out on another sonic and social adventure. On a tour off-day, Mickey and Dan Healy journeyed to Amherst, Massachusetts, to record the Gyuto Monks of Tibet, who were staying with Amherst College professor of religion Robert Thurman, a Tibetan Buddhist monk (and father of the actress Uma). The Dead and its technology met one of the most esoteric of spiritual traditions, and the results were wonderful. Each monk could sing a three-note chord, and the assembled choir sounded like the edge of the universe. The Dalai Lama had explained that the long-term "benefit" of the Chinese occupation of Tibet was the spread of Tibetan Buddhism in the wider world, and he had encouraged the Gyuto Monks to visit America. But their efforts to raise money to build a monastery in India had gone poorly. On hearing that, Mickey volunteered to put on a Bay Area show, which turned out to be a resounding success. Over the next decade, Danny Rifkin and other members of the Dead family would take the reins so that Grateful Dead Productions became the monks' de facto American promoters.

The otherworldly moan of the monks was not the only music in the Dead's ears that late spring. Shortly after tickets for two early-June shows in Sacramento went on sale, the shows were canceled, because band members wanted to attend the San Francisco Opera's production of Wagner's Ring Cycle. "Jesus," said Lesh, the band's main but by no means only Wagnerian, "we couldn't resist it. That's some of the most transcendental music there is." Most of them went. The sound of the "Ride of the Valkyries," as played by Lesh, began to crop up in the rehearsals the band was conducting at the Marin Civic Center. Over three days in April they had shot video for *So Far*, a project that would not be released for two years. They were also lightly preparing for another challenge, their twentieth anniversary, which they would celebrate in mid-June at the Greek Theater in Berkeley. Aside from a superb Rick Griffin backdrop that transformed the Revolutionary War fife and drum bandsmen into a skeleton holding a guitar, they needed to do little except produce a musical surprise. "[Dead Heads] just want something old, right?" asked Garcia, turning to the publicist as the representative Dead Head in a meeting. "Yup." And so they resurrected the long-unperformed "Cryptical Envelopment" segment of "The Other One." Before they played the first of the three shows, they performed for the media, in their third press conference in twenty years.

Q: "How has your music changed in the last twenty years?" [mumbled curses]

JG: "We're involved in something that's in progress, so we don't know." . . .

Q: "Blind devotion doesn't scare you at all?"

JG: "I don't know, I'm too blind to tell!" [he continues, laughing] "My bias is *way* over here, man." . . .

Q: "Do psychedelics still have a large role in the appreciation of your music?"

JG: "What? What?"

PL: "Psyche-what?"

JG: "Well, we have to go now."

BW: "His lips are moving but nothing's coming out."

Q: [much louder, thinks they can't hear] "Do drugs still play . . ."

MH: "I can't hear a word he's saying." . . .

Q: "After twenty years, do you guys ever get tired?"

JG: "No!" [and his head drops to the table] . . .

Q: "What have the last twenty years taught you?"

PL: "It's a good life."

MH: "Never take your eyes off the guy to your right [JG] or your left [PL]."

JG: "Keep your ammunition dry."

BK: "Don't swim with piranhas." . . .

Q: "Are you still having fun?"

PL: "Not *now*."

JG: "Soon. In about an hour."

The young men who'd gigged at Magoo's Pizza Parlor certainly hadn't imagined that they could continue for twenty years, but for all the ongoing madness, it was a tremendously vibrant musical ensemble onstage at the Greek, even though two months later they would play among the worst shows of their lives at a Northern California ski resort called Boreal

Ridge. If they were no longer at the extreme edge of their talent, they were now sophisticated, subtle, and strong. What was even more remarkable was the growth of their audience, which had proceeded apace, slowly but oh so steadily, for twenty years. That summer they set yet another record at Saratoga Performing Arts Center, a pleasant amphitheater only four hours from Manhattan, selling more than forty thousand tickets, including seventeen thousand on the day of the show. That summer was also the last time they could play at Merriweather Post Pavilion, a relatively small facility on the outskirts of Washington, D.C.

The future was visible. At an informal meeting in December in the lobby of Front Street, the band and crew talked about the increase in audience size and conceded, reluctantly, that they had outgrown arenas and amphitheaters and would need to perform in stadiums during the coming summer, when Dead Heads would be out of school. They were perhaps not quite large enough a draw to sell out a stadium on their own, but they were getting there. The talk turned to appropriate cohorts, and the first names were Eric Clapton and Bob Dylan. Planning began. The year ended with a New Year's Eve show, of course, but even at home they had outgrown the 7,800-seat Oakland Auditorium, and moved to the largest possible local room, the Oakland Coliseum Arena. Their show was broadcast live on the USA cable network for visuals with a jury-rigged FM radio network for sound, earning a .8 Nielsen rating, meaning 250,000 homes and at least 500,000 viewers. The size of the show did not eliminate the Dead scene's capacity for random numbskullery. At midnight Bill Walton and Tom Davis were supposed to act as hosts, but when Father Time, Bill Graham, approached the stage on a float, Ken Kesey stole the microphone and began to rave about Rasputin and FDR. His various "fucks" and "shits" had the director in a cold sweat, but the FCC didn't seem to notice.

As 1986 passed, Garcia grew visibly healthier, Lesh quit using cocaine, Kreutzmann began to attend AA meetings, and one of the last seriously druggy employees, Bonnie Parker, was let go. Hard drugs were no longer chic around the Dead. Unfortunately, all Brent needed was booze. His erratic love life bottomed at a bizarre show on April 21, when he bypassed art and turned a solo performance of his song "Maybe You Know" into a shattering revelation of torment, screaming rather than singing. It was bleak reality without a shred of artifice, a frightening nakedness of soul, and so shocking that the band didn't quite know what to do. Ordinarily, the slot would have been followed by drums and then space, but in an act of extraordinary compassion, Garcia came out, helped Brent finish his song, smiled tenderly at him, and launched into "Goin' Down the Road Feeling Bad."

The summer of 1986 was meltingly hot, especially in Washington, D.C., where the tour, which included Bob Dylan backed by Tom Petty and the Heartbreakers, ended at RFK Stadium. It was a standard-issue D.C. summer day, with the temperature over one hundred and the humidity nearly that high. Garcia was only outside his air-conditioned dressing room for three hours, but he was intensely dehydrated when he left the stage. He flew home the next day, July 8, and once there complained of thirst.

He began to slip into a coma. "I started feeling like the vegetable kingdom was speaking to me. It was communicating in comic dialect in iambic pentameter. So there were these Italian accents and German accents and it got to be this vast gabbling. Potatoes and radishes and trees were all speaking to me," he said, laughing. "It was really strange. It finally just reached hysteria and that's when I passed out and woke up in the hospital." On the tenth, his housekeeper, Nora, frantically called Weir to say, "Jerry's in the bathroom, and he's not making a lot of sense." "Call 911," said Weir. She did, and it saved his life. His blood was "thick as mud," he'd later say, but there was worse to come. In a deep coma of initially unknown origin, he resisted the doctors' efforts to give him a CAT scan, so they injected him with liquid Valium. Unfortunately, he was allergic to it, and his heart stopped. The doctors zapped him back to life in a Code Blue response, and placed him on a respirator for forty-eight hours before he was able to breathe on his own. Eventually, they concluded that the coma was the consequence of adult-onset diabetes, and his healing commenced.

"My main experience was one of furious activity and tremendous struggle in a sort of futuristic, space-ship vehicle with insectoid presence. After I came out of my coma, I had this image of myself as these little hunks of protoplasm that were stuck together kind of like stamps with perforations that you could snap off. They were run through with neoprene tubing, and there were these insects that looked like cockroaches which were like message units that were kind of like my bloodstream." As he came awake, one of his first visitors was M.G. First he wrote a note that read, "Be tactful." She chuckled through her tears of anxiety and appreciated it. Then he muttered, "I'm not Beethoven." This was charming, if mysterious. Was he saying he wasn't dead? Or not deaf? When Hunter visited, Garcia began to describe his visions, demons and mechanical monsters that "taunted and derided" him with endless bad jokes and puns, and then asked his partner, "Have I gone insane?"

"No," Hunter replied. "You've been very sick. You've been in a coma for days, right at death's door. They're only hallucinations, they'll go away. You survived."

"Thanks," whispered Garcia. "I needed to hear that."

A Suitable
Touch of Grey

(8/86–12/89)

The weeks following Garcia's collapse were the true hiatus in Grateful Dead history. Trying to maintain that they were in charge of the situation, Lesh and Hart called in the newest employee, Scrib, and laid him off until they might resume touring. The office was very quiet that day, as every other employee sat wondering. But Bonnie Parker's odd notions of compartmentalization had resulted in the bookkeeping staff finding money they didn't anticipate, and as the summer wore into the fall, no one else had to pay the price, although the company attorney, Hal Kant, ceased collecting his retainer for a year. Laird Grant went to Hepburn Heights and cleaned it of leftover stashes, M.G. moved in as nurse, and Garcia slowly began to recover. At first he was wobbly. That summer during a visit to Camp Winnarainbow, where his daughter Theresa was a camper, his halting shuffle was the gait of an elderly man.

As the fall passed, he regained his strength. Mickey stopped by to drag him out for walks, and once brought Carlos Santana by for some guitar talk and good company. Merl Saunders and John Kahn came to visit, running through changes on standards like "My Funny Valentine." The coma had played havoc with Garcia's neural pathways, and he had to start from scratch. "It took a while," he said, "before I really had a sense of how music worked. I had to kind of reconstruct all that." Merl was "kind of like a father figure to me," Garcia told another interviewer. Saunders would sit at the piano and "bring along the chord changes or something to a tune and I'd slowly put it together a little and he'd play through the changes and then things started coming back together for me." Music— and cards and prayers—healed him. His favorite card came from San Francisco's juvenile hall: "Hey, Garcia, get well or we'll mug ya!"

After a while, Merl and John Kahn began to alternate visits with David Nelson and Sandy Rothman, so that Garcia's acoustic side got a workout. Aside from music, he spent considerable time on his art. He'd always sketched or doodled, and in the course of the eighties he'd taken up airbrush and then computer graphics. He didn't take his art terribly seriously, saying that it "doesn't live past the moment for me . . . I can't take it seriously because there's no serious side of me that's a graphic artist. It has no value except for the execution . . . I have never had a graphic idea in my mind visually before the doing—my pen starts going, after a while I recognize it and finish it." Alas, the opportunity to have a piece of Jerry Garcia's mind was something many would be interested in. In years to come, his artwork would generate a great deal of money and lots of contention.

He returned to the stage with the Garcia Band at the Stone nightclub in San Francisco on October 4, then again at Halloween, and while his playing was subdued and his solos were limited in scope, his good health was evident. On October 14, he taped an interview for a San Francisco Dead Head gathering that made it clear he was still Garcia. When his interviewer remarked that both Lesh and Weir had talked about changes in the Dead concert format, he chortled, "Those lyin' sons of bitches! . . . Saying anything about anything we're gonna do, ever, is just bullshitting . . . Whole weeks have gone by when I didn't know what the hell was going on. But you don't have a choice. You can't opt out, y'know . . . The thing to do is stay in there and slug it out . . . Sometimes it's successful when we don't agree." Their conversation ranged over many topics, including the twentieth-anniversary video, now called *So Far*, which he optimistically said would be finished soon, but was in fact not released until a year later. By 1986, compact discs had replaced vinyl albums as the music format of choice, and he talked about releasing old Grateful Dead Records albums like *Wake of the Flood* on CD. This would be an in-house project, and it would grow.

As Thanksgiving approached, there was much to be thankful for, and

Jon McIntire organized a family party. The next Dead concerts had been scheduled for mid-December, recording sessions for the first new studio album in seven years were set, and the traveling party, including Scrib, was once more intact. There was even new material. Late in November, Hunter had stopped by Front Street and given Garcia a stack of seventeen new lyrics. Two of them would end up going to Bob Dylan ("Silvio," "The Ugliest Girl in the World") and three to Hunter's next album. Two went to the Dead—"When Push Comes to Shove" and another. Though he was working hard that day on So Far, Garcia came to the lyrics for a song called "Black Muddy River," stopped what he was doing, and sat down at Keith Godchaux's Steinway. A couple of hours later he had the music down. Strongly gospel-flavored, "River" touched on the Old Testament, Yeats, and Dante, and it was a major addition to the canon. Dark and majestic, narrated by a singer terribly conscious of being no longer young and of the wretched glory of freedom, the song came out of one of Hunter's dreams, of burrowing to a place that was beyond the Styx, where, he said, it was "vast and it's hopeless. It's death . . . with the absence of the soul," and the narrator is "whistling in the dark, saying there's something warm on the other side."

The family gathered for Thanksgiving at a little lodge in a park in Marin County. Entertainment was provided by an acoustic band that included Jerry, Sandy Rothman, David Nelson, and Robert Hunter. It was a genuine and heartfelt celebration, made even better a couple of weeks later when Phil and Jill Lesh celebrated the birth of their firstborn son, Grahame Hamilton.

The Dead resumed playing in mid-December at Oakland Coliseum to the joy of all concerned, beginning the first show with "Touch of Grey," which would swiftly assume anthemic associations to Garcia's resurrection, though it had been part of the repertoire for four years. A more subtle moment came on the third night, when Garcia sang "Black Peter." Absorbing lyrics was for him a mnemonic rather than a conscious act, and when he heard himself singing the line "laying in my bed and dying," he stumbled and almost lost his grip. The audience's cheers helped him.

In January 1987, the band went into Marin Veterans' Auditorium, the comfortable hall where they'd recorded So Far, to lay down a new album. They were in the best mood they'd shared in ages. Best of all, they had good material that was solidly road-tested. A new noise reduction system from Dolby allowed them to record the basic tracks live and still sound good, so they decided to set up onstage at Marin as though for a concert, with the Le Mobile recording truck parked outside; anything to avoid a conventional studio. Produced by Garcia and John Cutler, the new album resembled *Workingman's Dead* in the speed with which it was completed, and work went so well they could even fool around a bit. One day Mickey suggested that they try playing in a completely darkened hall. They turned off the lights, and the song they were working on swiftly mutated into the realm of the bizarre, as drummers couldn't find cymbals and guitarists lost control of their fretboards. It was a fascinating, if not practical, exercise, and gave them a name for the album—*In the Dark*. From that, Herb Greene suggested a cover depicting just their eyes. Coincidentally, Bill Graham had called Weir late one night to complain, "I just want to know one thing. Who the fuck's in charge here?" "I can't really tell you, Bill," sighed Weir. "I don't know what you're talking about, and I've been wondering this myself, lately." Graham came by the studio the next day to discuss his gripes and ran into the cover photo shoot, so his eyes joined the band members' on the cover.

As tickets for the spring tour went on sale in February, Cutler took to wearing a T-shirt that read, "Think Platinum." The overdubs were relatively few and went well. Weir's up-tempo celebration of mild misogyny and singleness in general, "Hell in a Bucket," required a motorcycle blast and the sound of snarling dogs. Mickey supplied pit bulls, which when recorded and slowed down sounded positively satanic. As work tapes found their way to New York, the folks at Arista took notice. Roy Lott had been at Arista since 1979, first as an attorney and then as vice president for operations, but this was the first time he'd dealt with the Dead. One Saturday in late winter he got a tape at home, and when he put it on and heard "Touch of Grey," he "jumped out of [his] skin," yelling, "The Grateful Dead wrote a fuckin' hit," calling up a dozen people at the office to say, "You gotta come in early Monday morning. You're not gonna believe this—the Dead have written a fuckin' hit." What really struck him, he realized later, was that they'd written a first-rate pop song that was nonetheless totally in character.

On February 20, seventeen hundred fans were in line by 6 A.M. to buy tickets in Hartford, and it took just two and a half hours to sell out two shows. Three concerts in Philadelphia sold out in three hours, with fans lining up fifteen hours early at a ticket outlet in distant Harrisburg just on a hope that Philly tickets might be available. The fuel for a cultural bonfire was stacked very high. McIntire had visited Warner Bros. the previous fall to discuss contracts, and found that the Dead's catalog was outselling Jimi Hendrix. In the spring of 1987, the *Grateful Dead Hour* radio show, begun at San Francisco's KFOG by Paul Grushkin and then produced by David Gans, went national, broadcasting selections from the Dead's vault as well as news to Dead Heads across the country. The year saw the publication of *DeadBase*, the Dead taper's guide to shows and song lists. *The Golden Road*, quite possibly the most intelligent and literate rock fan magazine ever—rare is such a publication that puts out serious musicological analyses of the history of cover songs along with interviews of band members—had been started by Blair Jackson and Regan McMahon in 1984, and sales were booming. Perhaps the single most emphatic pointer at the ubiquitousness of Garcia and the Dead was the extraordinarily successful release in February of Ben & Jerry's Cherry Garcia ice cream.

Off the Dead went on the spring tour, to be greeted by headlines like "Another year, another classic concert," "The Dead and Garcia alive and well." Even that bastion of the au courant, the *Village Voice*, joined the chorus. ". . . radder, riskier, rootsier, and ruder than you-name-it's; plus, they swing. Double-plus, the Dead do something no other musicians of their stature or influence can: they suggest the possibility of utopia in *everyday life* . . . indirectly nurture humanity, goodness, joy, truth, and solidarity among their devoted audience in a much less corny manner than you'd suspect . . . [they] do no less through their music than espouse the quaint notion that art can save your life."

When the tour came to New York, Jon McIntire, Garcia, and Scrib sat down with Clive Davis, Roy Lott, Don Ienner, and Sean Coakley (Arista's boss, two vice presidents, and head of FM radio promotion respectively) to get acquainted. After all, this was the first new album in seven years, and on the Arista side only Clive had been there for *Go to Heaven*. They met in a conference room of the Parker Meridien late one morning, and there were the usual refreshments, including coffee and a giant jug of orange juice. Garcia broke the ice by speaking to Coakley, who'd been a Dead Head in high school and seen his first show in 1970. Pleasant as Jerry was, Coakley, the junior representative from Arista, felt real pressure. The company attitude at Arista was that they *had* to do well, not only because this was the last album on the contract but because the Dead were fully capable of never making another record. "Lemme ask you a question," Garcia began. "Have you listened to our CDs since they've come out?" "You mean the ones on Arista?" said Sean. "Yeah, the ones on Arista." Sean confessed, "I think the albums sound better than the CDs do." Smiling like a teacher who gets the right answer from the student, Garcia bounced in his chair. "Yes, yes, that's right. You know, we've got a real problem with the audio on these CDs. The mastering is terrible."

Don Ienner smiled. "You want to remaster them? Tell us who, no problem, done."

The changeover to the CD format would bring vast profit to the record companies, and somewhat less money to the bands, but the lack of aesthetic control was the Dead's real gripe. Arista's positive message about that issue, and its overall message—"We're new, give us a chance"—established the Dead's first positive attitude toward a record company in far more than a decade. As they left the meeting, Don looked at Sean and said, "I wasn't gonna drink out of that jug of orange juice, no way." "Not me," said Sean. Old reputations die hard.

By May the album was finished, and for the first time the band made a video to go with it. Not surprisingly, they chose an approach that would require the least possible commitment of their time. Gary Gutierrez, who had contributed the brilliant animation to *The Grateful Dead Movie,* and since then worked on *The Right Stuff* and other films, had conceived a clever idea that would transmute the band into life-size skeleton puppets for the bulk of the video. The puppeteers came to shows at Frost Amphitheatre in early May to study their subjects, and a week later at Laguna Seca, a racetrack and natural amphitheater near Monterey, they shot for reel. Because the facility permitted camping, many thousand Dead Heads were close at hand. After the day's concert, the campers were welcomed back to watch first the band and then its stand-in puppets be filmed. The fog was a freebie, courtesy of the nearby Pacific Ocean.

Once done with the video, the band began to work on the summer tour. Early in January, Bob Dylan had come to Front Street to hang and play for two days, just to see how things went. Among other things, they played the Beatles' "Nowhere Man" together and discovered a unique chemistry, neither Dylan nor Dead. A month later, he called and said he thought a dual tour might work. Early in March, the Dead played in Oakland for Mardi Gras, and Dylan came by for a photo session to promote the tour. Shortly thereafter, the Foxboro, Massachusetts, selectmen publicly approved a license for a concert, breaking the story of the tour. Dylan and the Dead spent three weeks in May at Front Street, rehearsing upwards of one hundred songs. "[Dylan] didn't know what he wanted to do," thought Weir, but were anyone less adept at simple, direct verbal communication than the Dead, it might well have been Dylan. When the Dead broke up short rehearsals for long sessions with the TV to watch Bill Walton's Boston Celtics in the NBA playoffs, Dylan would sit on a car hood in the parking lot, withdrawn, while the hookers across the street whispered among themselves about him.

The band spent more than the usual amount of time doing advance press for the album, and the first result was a cover story in the "capitalist tool," *Forbes* magazine. Scrib had convinced the band that something so bizarre as the Dead in *Forbes* would generate especially intense talk— "buzz," in the jargon—in the music industry about the coming album. Coincidentally, nine days later, there was another boomlet. Bill Graham owned a vacation home in the resort town of Telluride, Colorado, and wanted to put on a Dead concert there. Some residents objected, and the issue went to a referendum. On May 26 the town voted 384 to 117 to welcome the Dead, and the item flashed around the country.

The "Touch of Grey" video made its debut on MTV on June 19, and it was an instant hit. The bonfire of success had begun to burn. The process had more than a few elements of lucky accident, chance, or fate— call it what you will. At its inception, MTV's taste in videos had run to Michael Jackson/Madonna flash dance, and then moved on to heavy-metal big-boob pieces. It was the Dead's peculiar luck to produce "Touch of Grey" at precisely the time that MTV's hierarchy decreed that some old guys would be nice. The first time that MTV's staff saw the video, they watched not merely the customary first minute but the whole thing, and then ran it again.

That weekend the Dead played at U.C. Berkeley's Greek Theater, and Garcia chatted with journalist Blair Jackson about what seemed to be the band's impending major success. Garcia had no answers. The band was already in stadiums, which were no fun. Video couldn't replace live gigs, and the entire concept of being too successful was foreign to his mind—after all, his idea of success was still the day-to-day reality of not having to work a job. Besides, he had heard the promise "*This* album's gonna be big" too many times to take it seriously. Arista's enthusiasm for the album was extraordinary, he admitted, "almost contagious," but he was not quite convinced. In part, his dubiousness derived from modesty. *In the Dark* and "Touch of Grey" would succeed for many reasons, and his near-death was a major one. It helped that the single was a very good song, excellently recorded, and supported by a record company and an entire industry that had positive feelings about the band, now twenty-two years along. In the *Rolling Stone* cover story, Mikal Gilmore quoted Dead-basher Dave Marsh, who dismissed the band as "nostalgia mongers . . . offering facile reminiscence to an audience with no memory of its own." Robert Hunter responded that yes, the band did appeal to "some sort of idealism in people." In the 1980s, idealism *was* nostalgic. Even the most happily narcissistic yuppie on Wall Street could not fail to see the screaming avarice of the decade. For a brief incongruous moment, the Dead's daffy integrity had a general appeal.

In the Dark was released on July 6, opening at no. 77 on *Billboard*'s chart and the "Hot Shot Debut" of the week. Two weeks later it reached no. 47 in sales and no. 1 in album rock track airplay. *Rolling Stone* gave it its warmest review in years: "[It] bespeaks an effortlessness long absent from their *ouevre* . . . [The songs] hark back to the sprawling, easygoing charm of their hallowed *American Beauty* era. Despite nods to technology . . . this *sounds* more like a Dead record than anything they've done in years." And in the *New York Times,* Jon Pareles gave them an intelligent appreciation: "The best Dead songs do something most rock doesn't even attempt. Like old-time mountain music and blues, they stare death, bad luck and metaphysical demons in the eye, then shrug and keep on truckin' . . . [Songs like "Touch of Grey"] are all obstacle course, realistic and illusive; they insist that with a wink and a grin and a little ingenuity . . . it's possible to make it through . . . They don't spell things out; their music demands an active, cooperative listener . . . The Dead are professional amateurs, happy to stay that way. And even if their music weren't such a pleasure, they'd be something rock always needs: the exception to every rule."

On July 4, the Dead and Dylan began their six-stadium tour together near Boston, on a hot and humid night made steamier by an overcrowded field after fans jumped down out of the stands. By and large, the tour was a disappointment. For once, the Dead were sober and enthusiastic. Unfortunately, Dylan was neither. He forgot his own lyrics, and the keys the songs were played in. "There were plenty of occasions," said Weir, "when he'd start playing a song and I had no idea what he was doing . . . He might play a song that we'd rehearsed but in a completely different way." Only one show seemed inspired, and that was at the New Jersey Meadowlands, where 71,598 people saw songs like "Wicked Messenger" and "Chimes of Freedom" played with passion. In Oakland, the next-to-last show, critic Derk Richardson wrote, "It was easy to suspect that the agin' folk hero was actually capitalizing on the popularity of the Grateful Dead . . . Dylan didn't extend himself to the band or the music." He retained a sense of humor, however. At the last show, in Anaheim, he pulled out "Mr. Tambourine Man," which they'd never rehearsed.

Later, Dylan talked at length about the positive effect the Dead had on him. They "taught me to look inside these songs I was singing that, actually at the time of that tour, I couldn't even sing. There were so many layers and so much water had gone round, that I had a hard time grasping the meaning of them . . . I realized that they understood these songs better than I did at the time."

In the Dark's success had many effects. One of the more positive ones was a noticeable increase in Brent Mydland's self-esteem. For the first time, he had a crew member paying direct attention to him, although Bob Bralove was hardly a conventional Dead roadie. A graduate of Hampshire College and a professional pianist himself, he had worked for a computer company and eventually become Stevie Wonder's synthesizer programmer. After working with Merl Saunders on *The Twilight Zone*, he had helped John Cutler on the *In the Dark* overdubs, and in June he'd joined the organization. His larger mission with the Dead was to introduce them to MIDI (Musical Instrument Digital Interface) technology, and over the next two years they would slowly move into a new level of electronics. A new Kurzweill synthesizer added to Brent's capacities, and he began to sing at least one song in almost every show. In the fall he would add more cover tunes, including the perfect-for-him Neville Brothers' song "Hey Pocky Way." In the healthy era of 1987, everyone got a little more and rather better attention.

Naturally, the impact of *In the Dark* peaked in New York City, where the band had come in September to play five sold-out nights at Madison Square Garden. The band was sitting in a dressing room one night before a show when Scrib came in to tell them that "Touch of Grey" had just hit the Top Ten, topping out at no. 9. "I am appalled," said Garcia, and he mostly meant it. They had their first immediately platinum album (*Workingman's* and *American Beauty* had sold that well, but over years), and that called for a presentation ceremony backstage, a stereotypical "grip and grin" of happy band and smiling record company executives. If the band was especially impressed by their success, it didn't show, and getting them to pose with Clive Davis was one of Scrib's less amusing chores. Later, a paternally proud Davis would feel that the band members were excited by their success, but he was perplexed by one thing. "I could not believe that they could have a set during the life of this single that did not include the single. I knew that's the way it worked, but—"

In the Dark was only part one. That same week, Garcia, Weir, Hart, and Clive Davis hosted the New York media at a premiere screening of *So Far*. It was an excellent piece of work, and codirectors Len Dell'Amico and Garcia had much to be proud of. Video and computers had made editing fun, and let them experiment, to the point that the staff at their editing facility initially thought them crazy. After the sound track was edited down, they began to free-associate visuals, with Garcia clucking, "Too literal, too literal!" Eventually, they found images of 1940s jive dancers, war, and a computer-generated chessboard that fit beautifully with the excellent music, and *So Far* would be worthy of the weeks it spent on top of the video charts. The video also represented an important business move for all parties concerned. *So Far* was Arista's first video project, and the company would do very well by it.

It was also part of a new record deal, though not the one the band at first anticipated. As the band finished *In the Dark,* they had sworn repeatedly that they would avoid multialbum deals in the future, leaving themselves free to do what they wanted. Instead, Hal Kant and Jon McIntire negotiated a three-album deal for the then-highest royalty rate in recording history, at $3.50 per CD. Amazingly, the contract also permitted the Dead to release live recordings from their archival vault, an idea that would gather considerable momentum down the line.

When asked how he was reacting to success, Weir replied, "You know those occasional pistachio nuts that are really tough to open? Now I just throw them out." Prosperity definitely showered down. Hunter was able to buy a new home, and there were new cars aplenty, including Garcia's top-of-the-line sixteen-cylinder BMW 750. A more important change in his life was his new lover, Manasha Matheson, and their daughter, Keelin, born later that year. After years of isolation at Hepburn Heights, Garcia had almost immediately greeted his return to health with a new relationship. He spent most of his time at Manasha's place in Mill Valley, although he bought himself a new home, too. But before he could really enjoy it, he had to go to work.

Back in March, he, Sandy Rothman, John Kahn, and David Nelson had played an acoustic set at a benefit gig in San Francisco, and Bill Graham had come into the dressing room raving. "This is great. I can see the roots of the Grateful Dead here. It's so cool, I've got to take it somewhere." In an effort to find a venue in New York that John Scher had not already used, Parish had earlier suggested to Graham a Broadway theater. *"Broadway!"* said Graham, and acted on the thought: in October 1987, Jerry Garcia played eighteen shows at the Lunt-Fontanne Theater, selling out so fast that he set a Broadway record for ticket sales. It also meant that Garcia was playing in two bands, electric and acoustic, both matinees and evenings. In between, he would nap in a dressing room that had been used by Mary Martin and Vivien Leigh.

It was a good winter for Garcia. He told an interviewer, "I see more light than I do darkness right now. There is a trend towards understanding." More practically, he spoke up at a December all-employee meeting and suggested closing down the office for two weeks in early January. When someone asked, "Can we afford to?" he responded, "Hey, this is looking like work; this is supposed to be fun!" For his own fun, he took his first vacation in years, going to Hawaii, where he completed his scuba training with his old friend Vicki Jensen, one of the gang from Mickey's ranch. He returned tanned and in love with the underwater world, and he would stick with his new hobby.

Late in January 1988, he joined Carlos Santana and Wayne Shorter in a benefit, "Blues for Salvador," and he was so brilliant, playing with such fire, that Carlos Santana stopped playing and saluted him. Just to confirm the sweetness of the moment, the master jazz saxophonist Ornette Coleman invited him to contribute to the album *Virgin Beauty*. It was a lovely experience. At one point Jerry asked for some musical clarification, and Coleman hauled out his saxophone and explained his "harmelodic" theories. "When I hear his playing," Garcia said of Ornette, "I hear something that I always wish would be in mine—a kind of joy and beauty. And it always sounds right."

Nineteen eighty-eight began for real on March 12, when the band attended the Bammies, the Bay Area Music Awards. It was an act of noblesse oblige, and for Garcia in particular, it was very hard. After winning Best Bassist, Best Album, Best Song, Best Guitarist, and Best Group, the Dead joined Huey Lewis and the News in a final jam, where Garcia had to play on a borrowed amp, which was hell for him. But for him the night was intrinsically twisted. The very concept of awards implies winning and losing and competition, and that was foreign to him. Acknowledging the respect of the Bay Area's music scene was the courteous thing to do, but it was a forerunner of the price that a hit record would exact. That month, as part of the preparation for the spring tour, Hunter sent a letter to the Dead Heads.

> Here we are sitting on top of the world . . . which raises the question of who *we* are—the answer is: partly us, partly you . . . The good old days when we were your personal minstrels have been overshadowed by a new reality which *must* be addressed. We are not a political, religious nor a grass roots movement; not a counter culture, drug culture, nor the latest big shakes snatch and run glamor act—we are a symbiotic funmachine designed to get 10,000 or more heads straight at a pop . . . Many doors have been closed to us in the last several months due to the trash and boogie behavior of new fans who have no regard

for the way the Dead do things . . . What began as a spontaneous vagabond marketplace has devolved into a competitive and obnoxious full scale illegal rip off, squeezing out the gypsy Deadheads . . . We intend to step on it—hard! . . . Understand that we are doing what *must* be done to ensure our rights and yours . . . In other words, "when life looks like easy street there is danger at your door."

During a three-night run at Oakland's Henry Kaiser Convention Center in March, press coverage focused on neighborhood gripes about public urination and the Dead Heads' absorption of parking. The day after a spring-tour concert in Hartford, Dead Heads camped in the city's Bushnell Park were rousted at 6 A.M. by cops with bullhorns and a fleet of tow trucks. A check for $2,500 to the park's foundation mollified the local authorities, but the negative press buzz was established. While the band typically refused formal responsibility on the principle that Dead Heads had created themselves, they tried to address the situation by choosing two members of the Hog Farm commune, Calico and Goose, and two other Dead Heads, Lou Tambakos and Barbara Lewit, to go out on the summer tour to establish some form of direct communication with the audience.

What neither these four nor the band could do was cope with the ticketless, since checking for tickets of the people in cars entering parking lots only backed up traffic more. Late in June the Dead created gridlock in a good chunk of southern Wisconsin. Dylan had played the Alpine Valley facility on Saturday night, and the promoter was unable to clear the lots by Sunday. The Dead played Monday and Tuesday, with forty thousand inside and at least twenty thousand in the parking lots, which de facto extended for about five miles in each direction. There was no violence, just lots of trash smelling awful in the 105-degree heat. The summer passed with no great disasters, and while it was true that crowd control issues were primarily management's problem, everyone in the band and crew felt a certain tension at the possibilities. As a Tacoma police sergeant said, "I wouldn't say we've got a tolerance policy. We have just totally lost control. And don't quote me saying, 'It was a zoo out there.' We're doing just enough to maintain safety and propriety."

The tour brought new songs, and they weren't altogether warmly received. Weir's new tune, "Victim or the Crime," included lyrics by a friend, actor Gerrit Graham. If he and Barlow had not had a parting of the ways before this song, they certainly would after Barlow, upset by his desertion by Weir, went on the radio to urge Dead Heads to write Weir their objections to the song, so infuriating Bob that he put his fist through a nearby wall. The song was complicated, morally grim—the opening line is "Patience runs out on the junkie / the dark side hires another soul"— and hard to dance to. In Garcia's opinion, "Well, it's a hideous song. It's very angular and unattractive sounding. It's not an accessible song. It doesn't make itself easy to like. It just doesn't sound good, or rather, it sounds strange. And it *is* strange. It has strange steps in it, but that's part of what makes it interesting to play." Weir, of course, reveled in the opposition. By contrast, Garcia's first new tune, "Foolish Heart," had a snappy hook and was an obvious single. Barlow turned to working with Brent, and their "Blow Away" was a good, if typically tormented, discourse on the end of a romance. "Gentlemen, Start Your Engines" explored the state of mind in which a normal drinker slurs and calls it quits, but an alcoholic—both Brent and Barlow qualified—thinks, "Gentlemen . . ." It was performed a few times but never fully recorded.

The Dead's single most important response to their hit was to do something they'd never done before—put their name behind a cause. They'd been happy to do endless benefits, happier still to fill the Rex moneypot, but that fall of 1988 they threw a concert to raise money for the preservation of earth's rain forest. The last night of their nine-show Madison Square Garden run, the event required their personal involvement and commitment. "We don't want to be the leaders," said Garcia, "and we don't want to serve unconscious fascism. Power is a scary thing . . . But this is, we feel, an issue strong enough and life-threatening enough that inside the world of human games, where people regularly torture each other and overthrow countries and there's a lot of murder and hate, there's the larger question of global survival. We want to see the world survive to play those games, even if they're atrocious." Before they were done, Garcia, Weir, and Hart would appear at the United Nations for a press conference, do every interview they possibly could, and even endure intra-recipient (there were four beneficiaries) bickering and jousting for status as they went along. After a long tour that had ended with the benefit concert, Garcia and Weir dutifully marched off to an after-show reception for the high-end donors and signed autograph after autograph, a harder thing for them to do than writing a check. The next year, they would even visit with politicians, as the three of them addressed the Human Rights Caucus of the U.S. House of Representatives on saving the rain forest. When a congresswoman sniped that Dead Heads didn't vote,

Garcia replied, "It would be nice to think there was something to vote for, you know what I mean? I know this. I know that Dead Heads will chain themselves to a tree."

Despite their success and good works, the Dead were in no danger of being seen as saints or prey to anything resembling conventional behavior. Dead Heads were thrilled to learn that, at the request of a dying young man, the band had played an electric version of "Ripple" for the first time in eighteen years at a show that fall. What they did not know was that the request had come to Weir, who then told Garcia, "I'll bet you ten bucks you can't remember the lyrics." Garcia took and won the bet—and Weir still welshed on it. As part of the rain forest campaign, they had posed for Francesco Scavullo at *Harper's Bazaar,* getting in return the free use of the picture after it was published. When that time came, even though it was a wonderful picture of all of them, Garcia had decided he was fat, and the picture was never used. The year ended with Dead Heads in an uproar over the use of "Eep Hour," a piece of music from Garcia's first solo album, on a television advertisement for Cher's Uninhibited perfume. Drawing an often-overlooked distinction between his own and the Grateful Dead's music, Garcia snorted, "Fuck 'em if they can't take a joke. I can sell anything, even my ass, if I want."

Nineteen eighty-nine kicked off in February at the Kaiser Center in Oakland. The band had been busy in the off time, and the new songs were worthy. Garcia and Hunter had produced "Standing on the Moon," a marvelous image of looking down on earth's strife—"I hear the cries of children / And the other songs of war." "We Can Run" was a righteous if bald environmental proclamation by Mydland and Barlow, and it found a suitable niche when the Audubon Society made it the sound track to a series of natural images as part of a public service announcement. And Weir brought out his last song with Barlow, "Picasso Moon," a more musically angular take on the "Hell in a Bucket" subject matter of loose women, replete with a peculiar (and unpopular) chorus: "Bigger than a drive-in movie, oooo-eeee." The last new song, Mydland-Barlow's "Just a Little Light," was yet another complaint about women, although beautifully done.

Then they went on the road and the troubles began. Before the band had even left San Francisco, neighborhood pressure around Kaiser had forced the cancellation of three gigs scheduled for March. The tour began in the South, and at first things went well. Every day, Brent would come to the venue early to work with Bralove on the music-box sounds for his lullaby, "I Will Take You Home." But the tour had one stop scheduled in the Northeast, in Pittsburgh, and despite repeated warnings to the facility, the police were caught unawares. Thousands without tickets flocked in, and some tried to gate-crash the many glass doors. After the usual scrum, which included twenty-three arrests, eighteen for public intoxication and five for drugs, the evening was over. But TV had caught the melee, and the film ran everywhere. The cameras also caught a cop punching a Dead Head whose arms were restrained by two other cops. The officer was arrested, although the charges were later dropped. The local newspapers defended the Dead and criticized the police and Mayor Sophie Masloff, but the image of a violent audience was established. By now, the simple presence of the Dead in town was a major story, and as such, they made a convenient political football. In Irvine, California, that spring, a candidate for reelection to the local city council, Cameron Cosgrove, described the scene outside the show as a "potential riot." Though both police and press dismissed him, and he failed to be reelected, his phrase circulated widely.

The early summer began with another special effort by the band to support a benefit, this time a major Bay Area fund-raiser for AIDS research. Before leaving on the summer tour, they experimented with a pay-per-view concert from Shoreline Amphitheater, a new facility in Mountain View, only a mile or two from their Palo Alto origins, hoping that it might do well enough to make it possible to cut back on touring. It didn't do that well, but viewers were rewarded with an opening in which Weir, frustrated with his amp, hauled off and gave it a healthy kick.

The greatest change wrought by playing stadiums was in the realm of Candace Brightman, who had to make them work visually. Until late in the 1980s, the lights had been minimal and her budgets small, but now she began to push the envelope. Garcia once remarked of her proposed budget in a band meeting, "Give it to her. God knows why they [the Dead Heads] keep coming to see us. Maybe it's her lights." He paid attention to her work. Once in the middle of a discussion with Candace, Garcia whipped out paper and pen and sketched her light setup in an effort to understand what she was saying. She was intrigued to notice that the sketch was from her and the audience's perspective, not his own, and was an extremely well rendered drawing. "My feeling," she said, "was that it was the band we wanted to see . . . one of the things I like to do is turn off all the lights at a high point in the music, which is really idiotic, but I still approve of it—you only want to hear the music, and in the darkness your sight doesn't get in the way of your listening . . . In general, don't make a statement; let the band carry the show." Under her supervision, a Polish artist named Jan Sawka made the band's first elaborate stage set, a journey from sunrise to sunset with the following moon.

Video reinforcement directed by Len Dell'Amico accompanied each stadium show, and the tour marched down the East Coast like the proverbial eight-hundred-pound gorilla, from Boston to Buffalo to Philadelphia, where they closed the rotting old JFK Stadium, and then Giants Stadium in New Jersey. There was, briefly, trouble in Washington, where another local politician, Nadine Winter, decided to use the Dead in her feud with the mayor, Marion Barry. When the Dead's management and the local promoter were done with their political ploys, she was buying tie-dye T-shirts in the parking lot for a photo op on the day of the show. The gorilla kept stomping, but it was starting to run out of places to stomp. One of the band's favorite venues was Berkeley's Greek Theater, and that summer would mark the Dead's final series there. The environment—the town, the campus—simply couldn't absorb the numbers of ticketless Dead Heads the shows attracted. The last show at the Greek was a Rex benefit, with recipients including Earth First, the Environmental Defense Fund, Heart of America Bone Marrow Donor Registry, New Alchemy Institute, the Oceanic Society, St. Anthony's Dining Room, the Albert Hofmann Foundation, and the Wyoming Outdoor Council.

The rest of the summer and early fall were spent working on the new album, *Built to Last*. Garcia and Cutler produced again, but that was the only resemblance to the methods that had produced *In the Dark*. Instead, in good Dead fashion, they went to the extreme alternative. The songwriters—Garcia, Weir, and Mydland—would each lay down basic tracks, and then the other musicians would work separately on their own parts, using what are called slave reels. It was true that, with Garcia producing, Mickey Hart recorded three hundred sound effects, including the sound of a crushed lightbulb and that of a vacuum cleaner, at his home, "Studio X," of which Garcia would use two notes in the final mix. The musicians almost never spent any time in the studio together, and the songs, in general, had little opportunity to grow onstage. Once again, they had accepted a deadline. They were doing their best to meet Arista's schedule, which had settled on a Halloween release. As Weir put it, "We create a deadline somewhere in the impossible, hazy future but it's a real firm deadline. And then we just ignore it." He laughed. "When the real world's gonna-end deadline comes, we keep ignoring it until panic sufficiently motivates us to get to work. Then we make most of our records in about a month and a half. The last two weeks are particularly hellish." The prevailing theory held that without a deadline, they'd never record anyway.

Fall 1989: Desperate to avoid being "cops," the band found itself dragged into exercising authority anyway. "Overnight parking" (i.e., camping) and vending attracted the ticketless, who absorbed parking spaces and generally made concert logistics come unglued. Getting rid of camping was easy; security simply cleared the parking lots. Dealing with vending was not so easy. The band sent out a message, which read in part, "The music and the dance is important; being able to buy a T-shirt or camp out are not. If you're a Dead Head and believe in us and this scene, you will understand what the priorities are." Of course, Dead Heads are Americans, which means that they feel entitled to whatever it is they want. Many of the vendors dismissed the effort as a ploy for the band to sell more T-shirts. Me? I'm good vibes. The band doesn't mean me! The band also tried another technique to cut down the scene outside, selling tickets to two shows in Hampton, Virginia, under the name "Formerly the Warlocks," and putting them on sale only a week before the concert dates. The plan was a success, and it took three days to sell out. This meant the tickets went to local people, which cut down on travelers. Then the band sabotaged itself perfectly, playing a brilliant set that included such old treasures as "Dark Star," "Death Don't Have No Mercy," and "Attics of My Life," thus ensuring that no Dead Head would ever miss a "Warlocks" show again.

Hampton was not their only superior performance that fall. Even so demanding a critic as the *New York Times*'s Jon Pareles applauded their work at the Meadowlands. "But what the concert lacked in psychedelic explorations, it made up for with focused, resonant performances of songs with the Dead's own amalgam of tall-tale Americana, fatalism and benevolence. And while the Dead did not take many risks tonight, it made well-constructed songs ring with conviction." The shows were remarkably good, considering that the Dead were sharing their hotel with the Rolling Stones, who were playing at Shea Stadium on their "Steel Wheels" tour, and Weir and Ron Wood enjoyed each other's company.

The run of good vibes was not destined to last. Around 10 P.M. on October 14 at the Meadowlands, a ticketless Dead Head gave up trying to get into the show and went home. On his way to his car, he discovered the body of Adam Katz lying in the road. Adam's death from trauma was destined to remain a troubling mystery. Many assumed that this slight, 115-pound boy was unintentionally killed by one of the arena security guards in a scuffle and then dropped in the road. It was certainly true that many of the guards were goons. But despite a considerable reward and severe police pressure, no guard—they worked in pairs—had any information. Katz's parents later filed suit claiming a cover-up, but in truth, the local prosecutor saw much potential political gain from solving the case and acted accordingly, and neither he nor the police had any affection for the guards. There were no clear answers. Dead Heads rightly complained about the abusive attitudes of Meadowlands security, and many implicitly came to blame the band and its management for the death.

Built to Last was released on October 31, along with another Gutierrez video, this one based on the work of Georges Méliès, a French turn-of-the-century filmmaker, for the song "Foolish Heart." The album deserved, and got, a middling reception. Everything that had put energy into *In the Dark*—mature songs recorded nearly live with consummate enthusiasm—was absent, and the versions of Garcia's and Weir's songs lacked fire. Since he had contributed four of the nine songs, Brent was more visible, and thus more vulnerable, and many reviews singled out the emotionalism and literalness of his works. Ironically, what may have been the best song recorded for the album was not included. "Believe It or Not" was a first-rate Hunter-Garcia country-western song that came, as Hunter remarked, out of hearing a tavern jukebox about 1947; Garcia chose to leave it off. Overall, *Built to Last* was not one of Garcia's triumphs as a producer. The band was fortunate, really. Another hit and they'd never have been able to tour again.

Adam Katz's death was a mystery; the death of another Dead Head, Patrick Shanahan, was not. Shortly after the third show of a December run at the Forum in Los Angeles, Shanahan found himself uncomfortable with his LSD trip and went looking for medical aid outside the building. Instead, he was surrounded by five or six police officers. He grew agitated, and they found it necessary to subdue him with their nightsticks, leaving bruises virtually everywhere on his body "as much as an inch deep," said the coroner. The district attorney ruled it a justifiable killing. The band quickly decided to stop patronizing the Forum, but their feelings of responsibility, no matter how hard they tried to deny them, lingered.

Three days later, Scrib and road manager Cameron Sears were at 5th and Lincoln when word came that Brent Mydland had overdosed on some drug—morphine, it was speculated. His wife called 911. The arriving EMTs reported his drug possession, and he was arrested. Scrib and Sears bailed him out and then took him home to an empty house, sitting up with him for much of the night and listening to him deny, deny, deny his profound personal anguish. A day or two later he would go to Gary Gutierrez's Colossal Films to shoot the band's second video for *Built to Last,* his own "Just a Little Light." The decade was ending in dark confusion.

49

Interlude: "Noble but Lame"

(THE GRATEFUL DEAD ON THE G.D.)

esh, 1981: "The Dead is, of course, noble but lame."

Lesh, 1967: "If you want coherence, gentlemen, you've come to the wrong place."

Garcia, 1970: "I just see us as a lot of good-time pirates. I'd like to apologize in advance to anybody who believes we're something really serious."

(Do you see yourself as some kind of guiding light?)

Garcia, 1970: "Fuck, no. We're just musicians. On a good night our music will be clear and won't scare anybody and won't hurt anybody."

Weir, date unknown: "We're a band. We felt free. We still do . . . We're a lot like the circus . . . we won't give up until we feel we've achieved something."

Garcia, 1972: ". . . anybody in the Grateful Dead could draw you a picture of the Grateful Dead, man. It's got like six or seven weird legs, mismatched pairs, and one moth-eaten eagle wing and one bat wing, you know, and it snorts fire and it's cross-eyed . . . And it jumps up and kicks around and laughs real loud."

John Barlow, 1988: "They do something that nobody else does: they create mass hysteria of a very benign sort which makes people hear and see things that cannot be heard and should not be seen."

Lesh, 1981: "We became the Grateful Dead when we started playing for the acid tests. That's it, man. It's like Galileo: recant or be punished. They can burn me, man. They won't burn nothing but the body."

Kreutzmann, 1982: "Bobby would like it to be a Bob Weir band . . . that's the only lapse that I can see in his commitment . . . With the Grateful Dead, there's more possible than you could ever dream of—even I could ever dream of. That's what's frustrating."

Lesh, 1981. "But I don't get bored with being in the Grateful Dead. To me, the Grateful Dead is life—the life of the spirit . . . [and] the mind, as opposed to standing in line and marking time in the twentieth century."

Lesh, date unknown: "I've always called what we play electric chamber music. It's closely interlocked. Chamber music has been called the music of friends . . . Those hookups are like living things . . . like cells in the body of this organism. That seems to be the transformation taking place in human beings. To learn to be cells as well as individuals. Not just cells in society but cells in a living organism."

Dan Healy, 1982: "For me it's a vehicle that enables an aggregate of people to experiment with musical and technical ideas; it's a workshop and a breadboard as well as a dream and a treat . . . I don't hassle destiny—there's some reason why I'm here."

Garcia, 1974: "It's embarrassing to be considered part of the entertainment scene. And weird to be so popular. That's a mystery. Maybe it's because we stuck at it for so long. When the dust clears, there's still the Grateful Dead . . . we don't consciously play what they want to hear. Or what they need. Just what we can remember."

Garcia, 1972: "I think basically the Grateful Dead is not for cranking out rock and roll, it's not for going out and doing concerts or any of that stuff, I think it's to get high . . . To get really high is to forget yourself. And to forget yourself is to see everything else. And to see everything else is to become an understanding molecule in evolution, a conscious tool of the universe . . . [not] unconscious or zonked out, I'm talking about being fully conscious . . . the Grateful Dead should be sponsored by the government or something. It should be a public service, you know, and they should set us up to play at places that need to get high."

Garcia, date unknown: "Coming to see the Grateful Dead is like getting a kit from Radio Shack—" Weir: "Yeah. The audience gets to help put it together." Garcia: "And it might not work."

Garcia, 1971: "Ugly but honest, that's us. Hey, there's a good title for you, 'Ugly But Honest.' A'course, we ain't all that honest, either. Maybe just 'Ugly' is good enough."

50

A Deadicated Life

(1/90–9/92)

A combination of sheer profitability and the Dead's honest efforts to hold the parking lot scene down to a dull roar kept most facilities interested in booking the band. In 1990, to paraphrase a remark once made about Frank Sinatra, it seemed at tour time that it was the Dead's world and everyone else just lived in it. By and large, the media and local decision-makers had enough respect for the band's venerability and the uniqueness of its imprint to shrug at the audience's excesses. The fact that the parking lot and interior of every Dead concert were a no-holds-barred orgy of pot, LSD, nitrous oxide, and other substances seemed to worry only curmudgeonly columnists and the occasional small-town-minded police department (Louisville, Kentucky, comes to mind). Even the Nassau Coliseum, where the police had long ago alienated Dead Heads with an aggressive attitude, had by now acquired a new manager, Neil Sulkes, who wanted the Dead, and worked very hard to make the relationship succeed. Every show got its local reporter, who consistently fell in love with the decency and pleasantness of most Dead Heads, while marveling at the flagrant drug consumption. Most cops shrugged. "It's silly for us to be out here," said a female undercover officer in North Carolina. "We may try to look like them, but they know we're not like them. I'd have to wear no bra and no underwear."

The tours had achieved the inexorable reliability of the seasons, and from within the efficient cocoon of Deadworld, the only differences were the weather and the occasional special blips in the passing parade, as when Dead Heads mingled with the nabobs of the TV industry, the National Association of Broadcasters, on an Atlanta plaza—both Heads and executives seemed amused by each other—or when the Dead Heads shared a (very large) parking lot in Louisville with a Jehovah's Witness encampment. Nineteen ninety brought two final horror stories. One involved a young woman who bought some LSD in the parking lot of an L.A. show and then drove off hallucinating fire, causing a fatal auto accident. The other incident, in Denver, ended in the death of a homeless person with a concert ticket in his pocket after he so terrified a family that a man felt obliged to kill him.

Yet the soft colossus rolled on, with the crazies who were the Dead being treated as serious people. After nearly twenty years of trying to save his home, John Perry Barlow had finally been forced off the Bar Cross Ranch by foreclosure, and had become, as he put it, the Cicero of Cyberspace, establishing the Electronic Frontier Foundation with Lotus software developer Mitch Kapor. Weir was involved in a variety of social concerns, from a celebrity roast of 49er star Ronnie Lott on behalf of the Special Olympics to his more serious environmental lobbying efforts, which included writing a fine *New York Times* op-ed piece on the sale of a Montana forest that spring. When the newly freed South African anti-apartheid hero Nelson Mandela came to the Bay Area in June, Mickey Hart was invited to put on a musical welcome that would include Garcia and Weir and (of course!) many, many drummers.

Early in the year the Rex Foundation made a grant to David "Dawg" Grisman. When David discovered that Garcia was responsible, he called him to say thanks. Because of Grisman's legitimate anger at his treatment by Grateful Dead Records and Garcia's inability to deal with his own embarrassment, they had not spoken for many years after Old and in the Way had ceased playing. Now Grisman invited him to come by and play. Garcia showed up, sat down, and said, "What we should do is make a record, 'cause that'll give us something to focus on." They had their first tune, "Louis Collins," in the can before Dawg's recording engineer, Decibel Dave Dennison, could arrive. Over the next few years, Garcia would visit Grisman's tiny basement studio dozens of times and make a tremendous amount of wonderful music. The material Garcia laid down with

David in the nineties was the best acoustic playing of his life, with Grisman's gifted and creative discipline influencing Garcia for the best. There was a tremendous purity to their music making. Garcia would arrive at one, they'd smoke a fat joint, and sit in a tiny basement room playing. It was a quiet, almost meditative approach.

Many members of the Dead scene viewed this with dark suspicion, not only because Grisman was amassing hours of valuable tape, but also because—well, just because. There had always been a generalized suspicion of people with access to Garcia, and by now these misgivings were accentuated by the ongoing anguish occasioned by his resumption of opiate use. His drug habits were like the weather; everyone talked about them, but no one felt the slightest ability to do anything about it. "[Garcia] just goes over there because he can do what he wants and nobody busts him," grumbled John Cutler. Of course, nobody really busted Garcia at Front Street, either. Periodically, Cutler would tearfully harangue Garcia—it was a measure of Jerry's love for John that he tolerated even that much intrusion on his life—and every once in a while the band would stage an intervention, but Garcia mixed a large ego and grand intelligence with his weakness. Challenging him on a personal matter was, as he put it, a "generally futile pursuit."

Garcia sampled a number of projects at this time. Bob Weir's duo partner, bassist Rob Wasserman, was making an album of trios. Together with singer Edie Brickell, he and Garcia improvised a tune called "Zillionaire." Garcia was deeply ambivalent when Wasserman used a take that had Jerry playing piano, but Edie Brickell's ability to improvise vocally thrilled him, and he looked forward to working with her again. At the other end of the sociomusical spectrum, Garcia recorded the title track for Warren Zevon's *Transverse City,* a song cycle about a grim and ugly technofuture. Zevon was bemused by him, telling the *Boston Globe,* "[Garcia's] a virtuoso, and he played nonstop for about five hours. He said, 'I'll play it as much as you want, and you stop me when you have to go'—the most generous musician I've ever met . . . [He] baffles me. Why did this guy go to all this trouble for me?"

The finest musician to fall into the Dead's orbit at this time did so at a Dead concert. Late in the spring 1990 tour, Phil Lesh was sitting with a friend of a friend who happened to know the great jazz saxophonist Branford Marsalis, and asked if Phil had a message for Branford. "Yeah, tell him to sit in with us at Nassau." At first, the band was cautious, and "auditioned" Marsalis by asking him to sit in on "Bird Song," late in the first set. Never did a musician prove his brilliance faster, and about one verse in, Garcia and Marsalis were trading licks as though they were old friends. "You *will* stick around for the second set, won't you, Branford?" "Love to."

They flew off the planet to a "Dark Star," skated along the heavens with "Eyes of the World," and generally played one of the finest shows with a visiting musician the Dead had ever managed. Since the Dead actually listened and reacted to their guests, an outsider almost always held them back. But Branford was exactly *there* with them and pushed them straight to their strength—highly innovative improvisation. He had played with Sting and knew rock musicians, but this was something new for him. "Those guys can play *music.* They're much better than most people give them credit for. They have big ears and real chops, and they've got 18,000 tie-dyes dancing along. I'd never seen anything like it. Most rock shows are just like versions of MTV, but not the Dead—they're into jazz, they know Coltrane, they're American musical icons . . . They're *fantastic.*" In a note to the band, he wrote, "On Thursday night I had the best time I've had in my entire life. I now know that playing rock and roll can be all that I have envisioned it would be." The admiration was entirely mutual, and Marsalis would be a welcome guest a number of times over the next years. In addition to his towering gifts as a player, he brought to the shows a sweetness of disposition that made even the grumpiest drummer smile when told that Branford was coming.

It was a soggy summer, with the band generally playing very well to reward audiences dancing in the pouring rain. The surreal march through straight America acquired a new twist in Boston, where the local police called in the National Guard to assist them in their pursuit of dope dealers. In a gross violation of the U.S. Constitution, Operation Yankee Scout used forty-five Guardsmen, some in uniform, a guard helicopter, night-vision goggles, super binoculars, and military communications gear to arrest thirty people in a crowd that was estimated at around 100,000.

Three days after the tour ended, Scrib went to work at 5th and Lincoln and was greeted by bookkeeper Mary Jo Meinolf, who sobbed, "They just called. Brent's dead." After various DUI arrests, he was facing time in jail and then a spell of chemical monitoring, and had been chasing one last binge; it was his sheer inexperience that caused him to overdose on a mixture of morphine and cocaine. "He was willing to die just to avoid" the jail time, Garcia believed. "Brent was not a real happy person." It wasn't, Garcia said, that he'd been treated as the new guy all that much. "It's something he did to himself. But it's true that the Grateful Dead is tough

to . . . I mean, we've been together so long." After twenty-five years of being "the Kid," Weir had finally found someone who'd have to listen to
him. He often scrapped with Brent, and they'd had more than one dressing room wrestling match. But the real problem was always a certain hol-
lowness in Brent, a lack of faith in his music and self, in the value of his
own life. "And he could have gotten better," Garcia once said, "but he just
didn't see it. He couldn't see what was good about what he was doing." He
had no intellectual resources and lacked any intellectual perspective.
Growing up in Concord had left him with nothing at the center. Once, he
and Hart had bickered, and Mickey was aghast when he looked out the
window of their New York hotel and watched Brent walk out into Manhattan traffic, his eyes closed, crossing and recrossing the street until finally Mickey went down and gently asked him to come back inside. No
one in the Dead touring party would ever be able to enter the elevator at
the Four Seasons Hotel in Washington, D.C., without thinking of Brent.
Drunk, he had reached up and slugged the hanging crystal light fixture
there, laying his hand wide open. Heavily bandaged, he managed to play
the next show.

His death devastated the band. That afternoon Scrib met alone with
them—the manager, Cameron Sears, was in New York on business—to
draft a statement. Weir's profound frustration was revealed in a powerful
anger, an anger that would torment him for some time. He was so distraught that it was an effort for him to agree to allow the conciliatory line,
"We have lost a brother in music and we grieve for him and his family."
Not that he had any alternative, in any case. The Grateful Dead monster
had claimed another victim, and Garcia could feel it. In a side room at the
funeral home, John Barlow watched the band metaphorically whistle past
the graveyard, engaging in "juvenile grab-ass" joking, stuck in their roles,
unwilling to confront the Reaper. Alone with Garcia in the limousine to
the cemetery, Barlow remarked that he'd come to prefer the Dead Head
side of the proscenium arch, because "they play a straighter game." Garcia
answered, "Man, I would [go there]. If I could do that, I'd go out there
right away."

Though he clearly had greater personal resources than Brent, Garcia
could neither join the audience nor confront what was happening to all of
them. Authentic communication had shut down, leached by time, by the
encompassing pressure of audience demand, by the responsibilities of too
many people's livelihoods. There was still a phenomenal joy in the playing, but only in the playing. Later, Candace Brightman wondered aloud
why she had put up with the frustrations of working for the Dead, from

the sometimes uncooperative crew to the endless depression of watching Garcia slowly crumble. She certainly had other options. So why? " 'Cause I loved the Grateful Dead, Jerry's guitar . . ." During the hiatus she'd worked in film and with other bands, but nothing was as good as the Dead. And she, along with almost all of the people who worked for the band, tried to give the trip 100 percent every night. The love for Garcia endured the horror. David Kemper was the Garcia Band's drummer for ten years, and one day without warning, and for no particular reason other than a desire for change, he was dismissed. Yet he bore no grudge. He said the audience "didn't care if they were hearing fast music or slow . . . it didn't matter if it was good or bad or who he had onstage with him . . . And I don't blame them. Being in the same room with Jerry was a pretty damn wonderful place to be."

The Dead reacted to Brent's death by dealing with it as little as humanly possible. They didn't talk about it, didn't try to use it emotionally. They were stuck in their roles as members of the Dead. Drugs and fame had lured them into forgetting that the Grateful Dead, which had a mission from God to perform, was something to be serious about. But each individual was, of course, just another bozo, and nothing to be too pompous about. Alas, over time, that distinction between the serious whole and the less-than-serious parts proved desperately difficult to maintain. "Why," asked Candace Brightman later, "did they take themselves soooo seriously? One of the reasons I got shit from the crew was that I lacked the proper reverence for the band."

As far back as the previous Christmas, when Brent had overdosed, Garcia had put in a call to his friend, the pianist, singer, and composer Bruce Hornsby, thinking of him as a possible replacement. Hornsby and his band the Range had opened for the Dead in 1987 and several times after, and Garcia had recorded tracks on Hornsby's *Night on the Town* and *Harbor Lights* albums since then. It was convenient that Bruce had played in a Dead cover band as a youth, but far more important, he was a gifted pianist who could make a solid contribution. In December, Garcia only reached Bruce's answering machine, and they never spoke. In the wake of Brent's death, Garcia and Lesh went to see Bruce at a Bay Area concert and eventually invited him to join the band. But Hornsby had a booming solo career, and while happy to fill in, was reluctant to commit completely. In Dead fashion the band decided to include Bruce where and when available, but also search for a permanent new keyboard player.

The next tour was only a month away when they arrived at Front Street to audition new musicians. Because they were emotionally gutted, they had no energy for the process, and after listening to three or four players, including T. Lavitz, Tim Gorman, and Pete Sears, they settled on the first player who seemed able to cover the keyboard parts and high harmonies, Vince Welnick, formerly of the Tubes. The swiftness of his selection did neither him nor the Dead any good at all. Vince was a decent fellow and a more-than-competent player, but he had been a lifetime supporting player, and his fundamental perception of music did not really fit the Dead, where everyone was a lead player. His life had been near the bottom when he joined the band—he'd been sleeping in a barn, about to declare bankruptcy—and the swift turnaround of his financial fortunes complicated his relationship to the band; the enthusiasm with which he grasped prosperity seemed inappropriate to men who were by now used to money.

That September, the band released *Without a Net,* a live album recorded between fall 1989 and spring 1990, which among other things served to document the massive contributions of "Clifton Hanger," the dedicatee and Brent's road alias. The fall tour began in Cleveland, and on the first night, Vince got a hint of what it was like to be in the Dead. Just before the show was to begin, Harry Popick went over to check Vince's microphone and sat down on his bench, which promptly collapsed. By the time Vince got to the stage, the bench was fixed and all he saw was the sticker that Dead Heads had printed up and passed around in welcome: "Yo Vinnie!"

A few nights later, at Madison Square Garden, they were joined by Bruce Hornsby, who would play acoustic piano with the band for most of the next two years. He had a more detailed idea of the structure of Dead songs, as well as the philosophy of playing them, than Welnick. Bruce was at times a little busy in his playing, and the combination with Vince was sometimes too much. At other times, it was brilliant. Vince's real introduction to the Dead may well have been at the next show after the Garden run, in Stockholm, a truly abysmal night. Despite three days' rest after the flight from home, the band was jet-lagged. Garcia had eaten a chunk of hashish and was useless. At the drum break, Vince went to visit the facilities and then stood backstage, wretched, when Scrib came up to him and recognized his dismay. "Vince, you don't understand. It's not you. This is a band that *really* sucks sometimes, and tonight's the night. Don't worry about it."

The Dead had not been in Europe in nine years, and they were effectively starting over with a promotional tour. Working in halls of between seven thousand and ten thousand, they probably sold 80 percent of their tickets on the continent and 90 percent in England. The press coverage was fabulous. The shows varied in quality, but after the nadir in Stockholm they were at least decent, and Saturday night in Paris was as good as it could get. The tour ended in London, and with a synchronistic tip to the future, they played "(I Ain't Gonna Work on) Maggie's Farm" not only for the reigning prime minister, Margaret Thatcher, but also for a future one, Tony Blair, one of a number of members of Parliament who were guests. Yet because the band brought every tour member's family, putting fifty people into first-class hotels, they lost money on the tour. The thinking had been to establish a viable alternative to U.S. tours, but the band was not in a building mood; it would be the last tour of Europe.

The year 1990 ended with one sweet bonus. In an effort to professionalize the national radio broadcast that now accompanied New Year's Eve, Healy had suggested that Ken Nordine, creator of Word Jazz, be invited to host the affair. Nordine had been blessed with a silken basso profundo that had given him a great radio voice-over career, but in the 1950s he'd hung out in jazz clubs and begun working up spoken poetry to music, which became the *Word Jazz* album. He was a real hero to Garcia and Healy, and his presence was not only a marvelous opportunity for everyone to connect with their roots but also a chance to meet a truly lovable man. With Branford's quartet opening, and Branford sitting in with the Dead, 1990 ended well.

The new year began with war, and it sucked Robert Hunter right in. Over the past decade he'd opened up his work life tremendously, first translating Rilke's *Duino Elegies,* published in 1987 by Hulogosi, Alan Trist's Eugene, Oregon, company, and then publishing his own poems in *Idiot's Delight* (1990) and *Night Cadre* (1991) in New York. He'd even cautiously stepped out onstage to read poetry for the first time, and he'd been warmly received not only by Dead Heads but also by poets and poetry critics. And so as the Gulf War of January–March 1991 began, he responded with two hundred pages of open verse called *A Strange Music.* For two months he sat in front of the television, looking at Baghdad through the green of night-vision cameras. And the result, aside from many dead Iraqi soldiers and lots of American chest-pounding?

> *We must change*
> *& we can't*
> *We never could*

Individuals alone
can change
I can change
You can change
They cannot
You & I will
never be them.
They may be us
but never can
they be you or me.

So long as Americans separated themselves from the fortunes of the rest of the world's inhabitants, there would be trouble.

Hunter was not the only published member of the band. The previous fall Mickey Hart had published his memoir, *Drumming at the Edge of Magic.* The book and accompanying CD did well, setting the stage for a second volume, *Planet Drum,* in 1991. It also led to a percussion summit: Hart and his cohorts in the band Planet Drum, Zakir Hussain—Babatunde Olatunji, Airto Moreira, Giovanni Hidalgo, Sikiru Adepoju, and Flora Purim, among others—played at the American Booksellers Association's convention at the Marriott Marquis in the heart of Times Square. A drum and stick were placed at each table setting in the vast ballroom, and at the end of the performance, the band led the entire audience in a thunderous samba line down a number of escalator flights, through the lobby, and out onto Broadway—where Hart leaped into a limo and vanished. Around this time he also engaged in an even more profound adventure. His ethnomusicological studies had led him to produce a series of field recording albums. He was working on one release, a compilation from New Guinea called *Voices of the Rainforest,* which had environmental angles, so a liaison from the environmental movement came to have a talk with him. The liaison was a member of the San Francisco Public Defender's Office named Caryl Orbach, and when Mickey turned from the mixing board in his home studio to greet her, he was instantly and completely smitten. They married in 1991, and their partnership was enlarged by the arrival of a daughter, Reya, in 1993. Hart was a fulfilled man.

In April Arista brought out *Deadicated,* an album of Dead songs performed by other musicians; the company had wanted to direct some attention to the Dead as musicians rather than the band's crowd control problems, and had supported the efforts of an independent producer named Ralph Sall. The resulting album did an excellent job of serving that purpose. Elvis Costello's "Ship of Fools" delighted both Garcia and Hunter, who called it "exquisite . . . he's inside the song so much, he's telling it to me." Many other songs were superb, but the clear winner for many was the most outré take, Jane's Addiction's version of "Ripple," with the lyrics sung over the rhythm of "The Other One."

The summer tour season began in late April with the first outdoor Las Vegas shows, and the local newspapers estimated that the weekend brought $23 million to the local economy. The touring rock business was down that summer, and the Dead had the only stadium tour in America. Money talks. The Dead talked their way across the country, and mostly the responding sound was accommodation. One of the favorite new venues of the nineties was Deer Creek, an amphitheater in the countryside outside Indianapolis. At first, the nearest small town, Noblesville, had been terrified of the Dead Heads. After the first year, though, the town began to charge for camping in the local park. Soon it was basing its yearly park-and-rec budget on the profits from four days of Dead Heads. Money talks, especially through Dead tickets: on June 13, three days before two shows at Giants Stadium, FBI agents burst into Nino's Printing in Queens to arrest Jaime Nino and Joseph "Joe Fish" Dire, who had two thousand counterfeit tickets to the shows, ready for sale, stacked next to the press.

The summer tour ended in Denver, where the band sat down with Garcia in a major intervention, and he responded positively. He spent August driving himself to a methadone clinic every morning, standing in line with everyone else to receive his allocation, seemingly committed to getting healthy. He made other changes in his private life. For the first time since Stinson Beach, he purchased a home, on Palm Court in San Rafael. It featured an Olympic-size swimming pool, which cost $1,200 a month to heat, and, oddly, rental units. For some time, Alice Giblin, once part of the Dead's office staff, had taken care of Garcia's personal business. But she had roused deep suspicions in Garcia's increasingly possessive mate, Manasha, and was let go, replaced by Vince Di Biase, a New York Dead Head who'd been involved in making holographic art. In the early eighties he'd met Garcia and eventually done business with G.D. Merchandising. Despite being burned by the Dead when they'd signed with the merchandising company Brockum in the early nineties—his poster rights were taken away in violation of his contract with the comment "Sorry, we owe you one"—Vince had stuck around. His wife, Gloria, had become Garcia's daughter Keelin's full-time nanny in 1989, and early in 1991, Garcia called in Vince to ask him to manage the property, and ultimately take over his art business from Nora Sage, who annoyed Garcia with her aggressive commercial instincts.

By the fall of 1991 the Dead had hit a certain peak. Coverage of the tour phenomenon verged on the overwhelming, and even their side projects now received respectful, well-deserved notice. That summer the *Independent,* a reputable English publication, had taken note of the Rex Foundation's Lesh-guided grants to avant-garde English composers like Havergal Brian and Robert Simpson, gleefully reporting that the Rex gave as much in some years as the British Arts Council. A few weeks later Mickey Hart appeared before a U.S. Senate Special Committee on Aging to recommend drum circles as a form of music therapy, particularly for the elderly. But *the* media frenzy of the year centered on the band's return to downtown Boston. Ten years before, the Garden's management had decided that basketball, hockey, and the circus were enough. Now the new boss, Larry Moulter, stuck his neck out and invited the band. Their six nights in September came accompanied by days of front-page coverage in both the liberal and traditionally friendly *Globe* and the tabloid *Herald.* When the *Herald* announced on the front page that "Hub Grateful for Dead invasion," predicting the visit would pump $10 million into the Hub's depressed tourist economy, the deal was done. Moulter had anticipated everything, even setting up a merchant's hot line for complaints about Dead Head behavior. The line was used once in the six-night run, when someone wanted to buy some tickets.

The least satisfactory aspect of the visit was the shows, which were generally mediocre. They followed a Madison Square Garden run in which Garcia's playing was so uninspired—in Bruce Hornsby's word, "languorous"—that Hornsby actually protested to Garcia. "I resent you coming to the gig and being there but not being there. You're not bringing what you can to the show every night." Not used to being challenged, Garcia replied, "Well, you don't understand twenty-five years of burnout, man." Though the conversation was cathartic, and Garcia responded with a little more energy in his playing, he was clearly still subpar.

In Boston the *Globe's* Steve Morse visited Garcia onstage and got a tired, cranky interview that lacked Jerry's usual generosity. "Yeah. I can't stand it backstage. Too many geeks." Self-deprecating as ever, he remarked, "I don't go onstage with some kind of messianic vision or anything. I'm basically going out there hoping my guitar is in tune." When the talk turned to Brent, he grew serious. "It's always a blow to lose a friend and I find myself losing them more and more frequently now . . . It's just pain . . . We're now talking about taking some serious time off . . .

So it looks like a hiatus is going to happen." In fact, though Garcia had long grumbled about being overworked, the interview was more of a warning shot to the band than a report on a decision made, since 1992 was as fully booked as ever.

More pain. On October 25, Bill Graham and his lover, Melissa Gold, attended a Huey Lewis and the News show at Concord Pavilion, arriving in a helicopter piloted by his longtime employee Steve "Killer" Kahn. It was a stormy night, and on their way home, the chopper was caught in a sudden downdraft and crashed into an enormous electricity tower near the town of Sonoma, killing all three instantly. It was an insane night to fly, and Graham's hubris in insisting on doing so was absurd. "But what a way to go," said Weir. "Like something out of Wagner."

The Dead's four-show Halloween run began just two days later, and the press was there. The band talked about Bill, going for the laughs, as they always did in a group setting.

GARCIA: "We miss the personal thing—the guy who understands us. That's what hurts. As far as the other stuff, the way of going about things, Bill and us differed a lot of times, but . . ."

WEIR: "That's 'cause we were right and he was wrong."

GARCIA: "Right! We also knew how to get the best out of each other . . . The big loss is this guy who was like our uncle . . ."

WEIR: "Our thieving, conniving uncle . . ."

GARCIA: [laughs] "The guy who was respectable enough to talk to the rest of the world while we were out on the fringe." . . .

WEIR: "But we're not going to have to play 'Sugar Magnolia' every New Year's now."

Instead, they opened their show that night with it, and then on November 3 joined Carlos Santana, CSN&Y, John Fogerty, Neil Young, Aaron Neville, prima ballerina Evelyn Cisneros, and 300,000 San Franciscans at the Polo Field in Golden Gate Park to say good-bye. It had been twenty-four years since the Be-In.

November had become personal tour month, but this year the Jerry Garcia Band went out to work arenas, not bars. The coolest tour of the fall by far was Planet Drum's. The album would sell stunningly well and win the first World Music Grammy, and the tour would crest at Carnegie Hall on the night before Thanksgiving, with a full house and all umpteen backlit tiers of applauding fans calling for encores. Mickey Hart was a long, long way from Flatbush.

Absorbing the new keyboard players had made working up new material even more difficult than usual. Finally, in the first shows of the new year 1992, in February, each vocalist brought out a new song. Throughout the spring tour, each singer would perform with a music stand in front of him as they continued to learn the material. Three of the songs were less than enthusiastically received: Vince's "Long Way to Go," Lesh's "Wave to the Wind," and "Corinna," written by Hart, Hunter, and Weir, although the last would improve with age. Garcia's "So Many Roads" hinted at his exhaustion, and his emotional stance in singing it gave it great authority. Ten years before, Hunter had listened to Garcia playing changes on the piano and recorded them. On listening to the tape once more, he'd set them to words. At first, Garcia said he liked the words but demurred at his music. Hunter told him to run through it anyway, and they both liked the results.

> *Wind inside & the wind outside*
> *Tangled in the window blind*
> *Tell me why you treat me so unkind*
> *Down where the sun don't shine*
> *Lonely and I call your name*
> *No place left to go, ain't that a shame?*
>
> *So many roads I tell you*
> *New York to San Francisco*
> *All I want is one*
> *to take me home*

Two changes marked the early part of the year. Bruce and Kathy Hornsby's twin sons, Keith and Russell, had been born in January, and when Hornsby visited home in the middle of the spring tour, they didn't seem to know him. By that time, he felt "Vinny had really figured it out," and that his job as a bridge from Brent to Vince was complete. The fact that, primarily due to Garcia's playing, the music remained less than fabulous was also a factor. In March he stopped performing regularly with the band. The other important change of the summer was technical, and, from the audience point of view, not entirely positive.

Twenty-seven years of amplified music had noticeably damaged the band members' hearing, ranging from major damage (Mickey and Jerry most, but Phil and Bobby close behind) to only somewhat damaged (Billy; the relatively young keyboard players weren't so badly affected). At first for health reasons, the band switched to ear monitors that summer. This meant that each musician had a custom-molded earpiece in each ear, looking something like hearing aids and virtually invisible, in which he could hear what he wanted. Lesh, in fact, would step over to the monitor mixing board and mix to suit himself. A side effect of ear monitors was that with them, the sound crew could mike all the instruments directly into the system, giving Healy a much purer palette to work with, with no sounds bleeding through other sounds onstage. But the real reason for the ear monitors was that the members of the Dead didn't really want to listen to each other anymore. After three decades of trying to mix so that everyone could hear everything, the technicians found out that most of the band members mostly wanted to hear themselves; only Mickey actually listened to the entire band.

They returned home from the summer tour to new worries about Garcia. On his return to Marin from the summer tour, he and Manasha had moved into a grand new house, this time a ten-acre, 7,500-square-foot mansion near George Lucas's Skywalker ranch, with marble fireplaces, a media room, and a pool. Late in July Garcia had gone to Southern California for a quick run of Garcia Band shows, and on his birthday, August 1, he remarked that he felt weird, as though he'd been dosed. He returned home that day, and the next day he lay comatose, his lips blue and his legs swollen. His heart was enlarged, his lungs were diseased, and he had borderline diabetes. Compounding everyone's distress, Manasha initially refused to let anyone from the band—or any conventional doctor—near him, preferring her acupuncturist Yen Wei and a Santa Cruz hippie, Dr. Randy Davis, whose general air of Dead Head deference to Garcia inspired no faith in the Dead office scene. Garcia's collapse had been easy to anticipate. His weight had ballooned, and he had no energy; on tour he would ask people to carry his rather light briefcase up the stage stairs for him.

It was a querulous August for the Dead family. Manasha's devotion to Garcia was unquestioned, but her manner was dazed and frequently oblivious, and she was generally thought to be a "space case." Her hotel room was always stuffed with icons and candles, and her beliefs were unclear but undoubtedly esoteric. Her habit of having a limousine waiting in front of the hotel for an entire day, just in case she wanted it, was not well thought of. Any date with her was subject to a thousand changes of plans, and more than once her lateness caused herself, Garcia, Keelin, and her nanny to miss a plane bound for Hawaii because she'd changed her mind. Her whims controlled their lives to a remarkable and maddening degree. But she responded to this crisis with a new focus and coherence, and it was certainly true that Garcia would rather have died than go to a hospital. As August passed, he went on a strict vegetarian diet and declared to Parish and other visitors his awareness that unless he changed his ways, his ways would end. At least for a while, he seemed to understand.

51

Interlude:
"Can't Stop for Nothin'"
(ENCORE/NEW YEAR'S EVE)

New Year's Eve, Oakland Coliseum

There was no subject on which Dead Heads and the Dead so diverged as that of New Year's Eve. For the Heads it was heaven. For the band and most of the staff it was hell, the night the most distant cousins came out of the closet demanding tickets, a night invariably played by six exhausted guys with colds or worse, so put off by the borderline hysteria of the audience that it was impossible to work up any genuine enthusiasm. It was like the Super Bowl, so often a mediocre game because of the excessive preceding tension. Factor in that the Dead Heads in this case were represented by Bill "This Is My Goddamn Best Moment of the Year and You Can't Stop Me" Graham, and the atmosphere was even more complicated.

As usual, it is misty gray in the parking lot as Clyde "Willie" Williams, BGP's ageless security guard, lines the audience up to enter the building. Once the doors open, half of the "handicapped" people in line, who enter first, will miraculously heal. The band and staff's closest friends use their all-access laminated passes, but one way or the other, everyone's gotta get in early to save seats. Scrib and BGP's Bob Barsotti bark futilely at the more obvious abusers to try to keep things fair, but they might as well spoon back the tide. Backstage is a little more crowded than usual, because space has been taken to build a studio for the radio broadcast. Radio is where Healy began, and this show and broadcast is one of Healy's favorite things. Over the eighties and early nineties he builds an amazing once-a-year network.

Midnight. Bill Graham has been producing New Year's Eve moments for many years, but 1979's was best. The lights dropped, the crowd noise built, and then the spotlights picked out a shrouded object on the arena floor. The coverings flew off to reveal a wood and fabric "truck," marked "Dead Head Trucking," complete with a happy hippie driver. Then the top of the truck blew off, and into the air ascended Bill Graham, Father Time dressed as a butterfly. He rose all the way to very near the ceiling, flew the length of the hall, and landed onstage. This from a man who hated heights. All the while, Garcia was playing, solo, Aaron Copland's "Fanfare for the Common Man."

On another year, or yet another year, or any year, the ritual is generally the same. The seconds count down, 3, 2, 1, and Father Time lands on the stage, the balloons drop—God, how the musicians hate them, the visual distraction as they come down, and the aural distractions when they're popped—and the band slams into "Sugar Magnolia." It's an ideal song to close a show. Played right, it sounds like the Rolling Stones, sweeping guitars crashing up to a rock and roll Valhalla. It even has a traditional rock subject matter, since it is a tribute to love and the ladies. The coda "Sunshine Daydream" gives the band a chance to build the tension.

This being New Year's Eve—any New Year's—they satisfy Bill Graham's plea; "Sugar Magnolia" is his favorite Dead song, so instead of ending the show with it, they begin with it, and go into a truncated third set. Tonight they cruise out of "Sugar Magnolia" and into "Terrapin." It is an odd song. It is one of their greatest, the product of incredible simultaneous inspiration, and also one of their most formal, the song least subject to variation. It is a modest symphony, really, and it builds a rolling power that can be stunning. The story plays out, the cautious soldier and the impetuous sailor compete for the favors of the lady with the fan; the sailor wins, or does he? Ultimately, our concern is for the narrator, for he has become us.

Inspiration move me brightly
light the song with sense and color,
hold away despair
More than this I will not ask

faced with mysteries dark and vast
statements just seem vain at last
some rise, some fall, some climb
to get to Terrapin

Terrapin, of course, is the goal that we all define for ourselves, possibly a poetic tribute to Gary Snyder's *Turtle Island,* but otherwise the promised land of hearts' dreams. And a hard, bloody hard place to get to. The music is ecstatic, thunderous, overwhelming. Garcia reaches for the final notes, and the audience joins him, all caught up in the moment so deeply that only a scream is possible:

Terrapin—I can't figure out
Terrapin—if it's an end or the beginning
Terrapin—but the train's got its brakes on
Terrapin—and the whistle is screaming: TERRAPIN

Beyond words and into a maelstrom, six men make a symphony and it works beautifully. The song climaxes, ends, and trails away. Time to go. Lesh steps to his rack, takes a sip of water, hits a switch, and leads a deft segue into "Touch of Grey" to end the show. It was the hit that almost killed the band, but a damn good rock song nonetheless, although Garcia never felt terribly comfortable with his performance of it. He wanted a rock and roll snap to it, like the opening of the Stones tune "Shattered," but that is not what the band would play, and he always thought the song was too melodic, lacking in bite. The anthemic chorus took it in another direction. Yet what it also contains is the faith that saves us from ourselves, from despair and age and tragedy.

Scrib's in the photographer's pit in front of the stage, happy the night's over, relaxing now. Next to him is the photographer Susana Millman, his love, and Garcia sings "Oh well a touch of grey / kind of suits you anyway, / that is all I meant to say / it's all right." Scrib carefully pushes a particularly long lens out of the way, and they embrace, and smile, and with sixteen thousand hearts furious with joy, they know that life is very weird and very beautiful and sometimes, as Weir used to say about the equipment, just exactly perfect.

52

Interlude:
Packed and Gone

(LOAD-OUT)

Some month, Somewhere in America

The last notes of the encore are still bouncing around the ceiling as Phil Lesh, always first, clatters down the stage stairs to take his accustomed shotgun seat in the first of the two vans parked in the tunnel behind the stage. Sears and his assistant Jan Simmons stand by, making sure that every band member is accounted for before they hop in. Next to the two of them is a member of the catering crew, handing each band member a postshow made-to-order shopping-bag-size lunch/snack, which might include a good bottle of wine, a salad, a full meal, or Lesh's regular peanut butter and jelly sandwiches. Garcia clomps stolidly along, then jumps in the front bench behind Lesh. Weir brings up the rear. By the time the house lights are fully up and the security guards have started the old chant, "You don't have to go home, but you can't stay here," the vans are halfway to the airport. They'll run out on the tarmac, the band will get on the plane, and at the other end the process will reverse. Less than two hours after the show, the band will be in the next gig's hotel. Security will still be emptying the parking lot. Ecstatic Dead Heads dreamily find cars, grab each other for last hugs, and go off to their chosen rest.

That is the universal; one particular is worth retelling. In 1987 the band played an afternoon show in Telluride, Colorado, leaving around 6 P.M. for the next show, in Phoenix. Because of the altitude at the Telluride airfield, they were not in their usual luxurious G-3 charter airplane, where the arrangements had them sitting on couches that faced in. Instead, they were in something that resembled a plane from the 1930s, with one seat on each side of the aisle, which meant that each seat had a window. After boarding, the pilot inquired as to whether anyone wanted to be a tourist. The beers were out, and fat joints had been sucked down on the ride to the airfield, so the answer was a resounding yes. "The Black Canyon of the Gunnison or Monument Valley?" "Monument Valley!" everyone chorused. The famous buttes of the valley rise approximately two thousand feet above the valley floor, and the plane went in at one thousand feet. It was near sunset, and the sandstone of the buttes was bleeding color. Garcia sat happily giving a film history lecture on John Ford and his Monument Valley efforts. Mickey Hart's brand-new acquisition, a Burmese python named Charley, went up and down the plane depositing various horrible residues on people's shoes—or at the very least scaring the residue out of them. Mickey's son Taro sat in the pilot's lap. The passengers together were a speck in the Creator's infinite universe, enjoying a view of Her handiwork so fantastic, so beyond words, that Scrib later realized it was undoubtedly the most remarkable offstage experience he would ever share with the band.

Onstage, "load-out" resembles the end of *Alice in Wonderland*, a film run in reverse, almost as though the pieces of equipment are leaping back into their cases on their own. As the band's crew packs the instruments, the sound crew gathers the microphones and mike cables, carefully coiling them with a practiced twist of the wrist so they'll be easy to use the next day. The heaviest things begin to leave the stage for the truck, Parish directing traffic at the top of the ramp, Mike Fischer inside the truck.

Parish wants to be on his way, and growls at the truck, "Come on, or I'm gonna come in there and get crazy," and Ram Rod snickers, "You don't have to go in there to get crazy."

As the stage gear clears, Parish grabs a box to make sure it's stable, then asks the monitor man, "Harry, where do you want it?" Word comes up the ramp: "All the lights just blew out in the fuckin' truck." After a few minutes the lights come back on, and the flow of equipment resumes. Forty minutes after the show, the stage is clear of band gear. The hoists have brought the speakers down to the stage, and local guys under Ultra Sound's direction are sending them to the relevant truck. The lighting guys are pulling their storage cases out from under the stage. Parish has moved nearer to the truck and calls to a union stagehand, "Try a new section with the K20A on top of the organ—line it up, now. Push it low, it'll go in smooth."

Ten minutes later, the Dead's crew members have their coats on. Parish, fatherly, passes out T-shirts and hats to the local loaders, and they are delighted.

Taylor and Ram Rod gather next to the truck to watch the final stacking. "Rodriguez," Taylor asks, "did you make the walk?"

"I wouldn't be out here if I hadn't," says Rod, because for nearly thirty years, he won't leave until he's watched the last piece of equipment, the drum risers, enter the truck. The crew exits, bound for their jet to the next town. Taylor remains, supervising the load-out of the sound and lights, setting schedules, worrying over the details.

Day off tomorrow, then another load-in.

"I Guess It Doesn't Matter, Anyway"

(10/92–4/96)

By the time Garcia returned to the stage with the Garcia Band on Halloween, 1992, he had undergone a considerable metamorphosis, losing seventy pounds, although as always he was shy about the attention the transformation earned him. At the beginning of December he and the Dead went to Denver, and the pace of change in his private life accelerated dramatically. Early in the year Barbara "Brigid" Meier, his girlfriend from 1961, had sent Robert Hunter a copy of her first published book of poetry, *The Life You Ordered Has Arrived*, and he and Garcia had sat in the kitchen at 5th and Lincoln, sharing poems and fond memories. They were both sure that one poem, "El Gran Coyote," referred to Garcia, although it didn't.

Brigid had settled in Boulder, Colorado, and in the mid-eighties she'd been contacted by Scrib, acting as the band's biographer. She'd come to a Red Rocks concert and naturally wanted to say hello to Garcia afterward, but riven with guilt over his drugged state, he'd begged off. In mid-1992 Garcia had met with her to do an interview for the Buddhist magazine *Tricycle*, and the old attraction was clearly there. Still an extraordinarily beautiful woman, she looked not terribly different from the nineteen-year-old model of thirty years before. In December their conversation resumed.

Over the years of their relationship, Manasha had grown increasingly possessive, deeply suspicious of Garcia's behavior. Came six o'clock at a Grisman session, and she'd be on the phone wanting to know where he was. By Denver, there were actual reasons for her doubts about his fidelity. In the time since Jerry and Brigid had first reconnected in the summer, they'd maintained an increasingly close relationship by telephone. Now, in a carefully concealed backstage room, Brigid challenged Garcia's personal passivity with an ultimatum: she was ready to make a life change, and she would either go off with Garcia or travel outside the country. They threw the I Ching and found the "Joyous" hexagram, with no changes. Garcia agreed, but said that he could not make the break with Manasha until after Christmas.

On December 30 Brigid flew to San Francisco. Because Bill Graham was no longer able to insist upon it, the Dead were not playing a New Year's show, so Garcia was miraculously unoccupied. He told Manasha he was going out for cigarettes and went to Robert Hunter's home, where he'd been spending time songwriting of late, to meet Brigid. Coincidentally, the Leshes were there for dinner. Garcia got cold feet, and revealed his doubts to his friends; their response seemed to him somewhat in the nature of a drug intervention, as they made clear their concerns over the suffocating nature of his relationship with Manasha. He came to agree. His emotional cowardice surfaced when he decided to have Vince Di Biase tell Manasha that the relationship was over. The women there convinced him to at least write a personal note. Jerry and Brigid went off to Hawaii, and on their return in January, moved to a condo in Marin.

Late in the month he was interviewed there by a *New Yorker* writer, Bill Barich. Over a supper of low-fat Chinese food and a laserdisc of *Naked Lunch*, Jerry was his usual charming self, a "wonderful talker, in fact, and converses in much the same way that he plays, constantly improvising and letting his thoughts lead where they may." Barich described him as the "most improbable pop-culture idol, somebody in whom the playing matters more than the posing," for whom "the absence of style is a style itself and suggests an inability to abide by anybody else's rules. He's the rebellious child grown up, not so much above his youthful audience as insistently a part of it. In refusing to be adulated, he inspires a kind of love."

The tour year 1993 began as usual with a February run, but this year was made special by the presence of Ornette Coleman. He and his band Prime Time opened the Mardi Gras show, and he sat in with the Dead for a good part of the second set. Their reverence for him showed. Even more significant, the run saw the debut of a number of new songs. Lesh sang Robbie Robertson's "Broken Arrow" to good effect, and Weir brought out "Eternity," a darkly brilliant number he'd written with Rob Wasserman and the legendary Willie Dixon. Hunter and Garcia produced three songs. "Liberty" was a traditional Dead anarchist plaint. "Lazy River Road" was a classic Dead shuffle with a southern, Hoagy Carmichael flavor.

> *Moonlight wails us hound dogs bay*
> *but never quite catch the tune*
> *Stars fall down in buckets like rain*
> *till there ain't no standin' room*
> *Bright blue boxcars train by train*
> *clatter while dreams unfold*
> *Way down*
> *down along*
> *Lazy River Road*

Both songs were solid contributions, and if that had been all, it would have been a good week. But Hunter had been deeply inspired by seeing his old friend Brigid again, and the seeming breakthrough in Garcia's life had given him hope. He poured it all into the third song, "Days Between." Garcia's music for it was anything but standard, a sort of drone that put the focus purely on Hunter's splendid lyrics, which were the sort of work T. S. Eliot might have done if he'd heard rock and roll. It premiered on a night the band was playing badly. The sound was crap. But in the middle of the rubble was a masterpiece.

> *There were days*
> *and there were days*
> *and there were days between*
> *Summer flies and August dies*
> *the world grows dark and mean*
> *Comes the shimmer of the moon*
> *on black infested trees*
> *the singing man is at his song*
> *the holy on their knees*
> *the reckless are out wrecking*
> *the timid plead their pleas*
> *No one knows much more of this*
> *than anyone can see / anyone can see . . .*

There were days
and there were days
and there were days between
polished like a golden bowl
the finest ever seen
Hearts of Summer held in trust
still tender, young and green
left on shelves collecting dust
not knowing what they mean
valentines of flesh and blood
as soft as velveteen
hoping love would not forsake
the days that lie between / lie between

Garcia's romance with Brigid was not meant to be. Early in March he ran into Deborah Koons, his lover from the seventies, at a health food store in Mill Valley, and was summarily enchanted. Brigid was a sensitive soul, and knew immediately that something was not altogether kosher. The band left for Chicago to begin the spring tour, and on the last night there she confronted Garcia, who came clean and conceded that their relationship was at an end. The next day was to be an off-day in Chicago, but an incoming blizzard made it necessary to gather up everyone early. On the plane Garcia was relieved, listening to the old rock tune "I Fought the Law" on his Discman and chortling about how good a song it was. Though he spent much time on the phone with Deborah for the rest of the tour, he was presumably alone for the first time in years. That didn't last, either. For much of the tour he would involve himself in a seemingly archetypal May–December romance with a young woman named Shannon Jeske. He would also spend an hour or two after every show of that tour in the hotel bar, which produced the predictable crush of Dead Heads.

The blizzard hit and the tour party got a day off due to a canceled show in Cleveland, most of which was spent in the movie theater next door. The only people who really cared about the blizzard were Scrib and Mickey Hart, because the next town was Washington, and they had an event planned for D.C. Mickey had initiated a relationship with the Library of Congress, one of the world's great repositories of music as well as printed material, and was about to release *The Spirit Cries*, the first item from the library's Endangered Music Project. Since the release consisted of chants and percussion in a language understood by few living persons,

Scrib had suggested that the only way to sell it would be to let the Dead and its friends in Congress shill for it, and all had agreed. It was a new era in Washington. For the first time in many years, a Democrat, Bill Clinton, was in the White House. More important, Clinton was the same age as the band members. In December Garry Trudeau's *Doonesbury* comic strip had celebrated the ascendance of a new political generation by having the character Joanie Caucus apply for a job with the administration. She was required to take a "Clinton Aptitude Test" ("CAT Scan"), and her question was "Who's the Bass Player for the Grateful Dead?"

Washington was not used to deep snow, and it was truly remarkable that the gathering came off. Aided mightily by Dead Heads with Capitol Hill clout, including Diane Blagman, a congressional chief of staff, and a lobbyist, Tim Scully, Mickey and Scrib gathered up various politicians, including Senator Patrick Leahy, and a goodly collection of media, and then mixed in the band. The bonds among the band members might have tarnished since 1965, but they weren't gone. Every band member gladly showed up at the library and helped make it a special event for Mickey, the library, and the band itself.

A few days after the Library of Congress event, a group that included Garcia, Mountain Girl (in town traveling), the Leshes, the Harts, and others visited the White House and met Vice President Al Gore. Impeccable in his elegant suit, he walked everyone through the Oval Office—the president was absent that day—and showed off John Kennedy's desk, chatting animatedly with Garcia, who wore sweatpants and looked even worse than the proverbial unmade bed. Neither man seemed to pay much attention to the other's appearance. Though the Clinton administration was to prove far more centrist than was expected in March 1993, the generational bond between it and the Dead was profound. Garcia had been pleased by Clinton's election, remarking that he wouldn't mind paying his taxes if he thought they'd be used for something other than weapons. Clinton's enemy Newt Gingrich had declared 1967 the year "America fell apart," and despite Clinton's pathetic "I didn't inhale" rationale, it was clear that by age alone, he represented a connection to the sixties. After all, Tipper Gore, once the maven of the effort to label music via the Parents Media Resource Council, was also proud of her background as a drummer in a rock band, the Wildcats. After their visit at the White House, the group went over to Tipper's office at the Old Executive Office Building to talk for quite a bit longer.

———

Deborah Koons was a filmmaker, then finishing a fine romantic film, *Poco Loco,* and she wanted to research a new movie that would be set in Ireland. That summer, after an excellent stadium tour that included Sting as the opening act, Garcia set off for Ireland with Deborah, her cinematographer, and her costumier. Wanting balance, Garcia called his old friend Chesley Millikin and invited him along. They had a wonderful time, with the women going one way and the men another. The contrasts made for great fun. In Dublin they stayed across the street from St. Stephen's Green at the elegant Shelbourne Hotel, where the clerk was so appalled by Garcia's grubby appearance that he balked at checking them in until he discovered that Garcia could afford to reserve the hotel's finest space, the Grace Kelly Suite. At one site the women got out to look at some ruins, and Jerry and Chesley sat in their van across the road from a gathering of tinkers, Irish gypsies with horse-drawn caravans. Garcia pulled out the banjo Chesley had inveigled him into bringing, and a crowd collected to listen, no one having any idea who he was. Perhaps it was memories of his grandfather Pop Clifford, but there was something about Ireland that gave Garcia a continuing string of déjà vu feelings, and he raved about Galway, Connemara, Sligo, and the Burren upon his return.

Unfortunately, the trip ended with a grim reminder of the boundaries of his life. While in Ireland he'd spoken frequently about how much he was anticipating an upcoming trip to Japan, his first. He'd been offered $1 million to make appearances there on behalf of his art. On his return to San Francisco, the band and its staff pointed out to him the risks of the journey—the lack of time before an upcoming tour, the danger to his health—and he canceled. Aside from feeling guilty about what this put his art manager, Vince Di Biase, through, he felt weighted down by all of his responsibilities. The more the Dead made, and by now they were extremely prosperous, the more they needed him.

For many in New York in the early nineties, it wasn't fall until the Dead hit the Garden. In 1993, the band sold out the usual six nights, grossing nearly $3 million on 105,000 tickets. Backstage guests ranged from Tony Bennett to opera star Kiri Te Kanawa to Jets quarterback Glenn Foley, and the amenities included "smart" high-protein/amino-acid drinks with names like Orbit Juice, and virtual-reality game machines. The Boston visit was especially sweet, with superior shows that made up for the tired mediocrity of '91 and the canceled shows of '92. After the tour the band scattered to their private lives. Weir underwent successful surgery for nodes on his vocal cords, while Kreutzmann set off on a monthlong ocean odyssey to the Revillagigedo islands off Mexico on the *Argosy Venture*, an elegant 101-foot motor sailing ketch owned by Bill Belmont. Twenty-five years after first road-managing the Dead, and after years of advising them on foreign music business affairs and helping lead the 1990 tour of Europe, Belmont was still taking care of the Dead.

Two events in the fall were potent markers of the future for Dead Heads. The season saw the first *Almanac*, edited by Gary Lambert, which swiftly grew to an unpaid circulation of around 200,000, offering news as well as merchandise from the band. By far the most significant merchandise, of course, would be music, and on November 1 the band released the first of a series of (by and large) complete shows from the vault, "Dick's Picks." It was an important step. Dick—archivist Dick Latvala—was the ultimate true believer in psychedelics and the Dead's music. Baptized in the Fillmore, raised up at the Avalon, he'd washed his spirit in "Dark Star" and pledged his soul to the cause. After a brief spell as a Berkeley postal carrier, he'd moved to Hawaii to grow pot and make tapes. In the 1980s he'd bribed the crew with enough fine Hawaiian Green to gain access, and eventually he'd become the studio gofer. He'd come to impress band members with his knowledge and diligent meticulousness, and he'd eventually supplanted Willy Legate as the vault's archivist. "Dick's Picks" was the ultimate fulfillment of his dream, although it came with a full load of Dead politics, pain, and disagreements. What Dick, as a Dead Head, thought was a great show did not match the notions of, say, Phil Lesh or John Cutler. Eventually, Lesh and the band would see the wisdom of having two separate series—the two-track, funky "warts and all" "Dick's Picks," and the multitrack "Vault" series.

On January 19, 1994, the Dead were inducted into the Rock and Roll Hall of Fame, along with Bob Marley, John Lennon (as an individual), Rod Stewart, the Band, and the Animals. Having always subscribed to the (Groucho) Marxist dictum "I would never be a member of a club that would have me," Garcia chose not to attend the gathering at the Waldorf-Astoria Grand Ballroom. Instead, the rest of the band brought along a life-size cardboard cutout of him. When asked why Garcia was a no-show, Mickey Hart said, "I thought he was out looking for his sense of humor." Kreutzmann approached the podium, notes in hand, and remarked, "In Grateful Dead tradition I'm gonna read this." After tearing his notes in half, he noted the changes in hair color, but said that he still felt good. "Looking good, Bill," chimed in Lesh. "I'm really doing this tonight 'cause I like to play music," said Bill. "Anyway, I want to say one thing very important to me. I miss Pig Pen, Keith, and Brent . . . [Pig] was our first lead player. He, before Garcia had all the spotlights at him, Ron was our boy, he did it all. So thanks a lot." Lesh added, "It's been long, it's been strange, it's definitely been a trip . . . Also, I'd like to say to the thousands of Heads who are currently serving maximum sentences that there's still hope for a miracle in America. And so keep the faith, keep the change, and keep watching the skies."

At least one thing on Garcia's mind was his impending marriage to Deborah Koons, on Valentine's Day, in a lovely Episcopal church in Sausalito. Garcia was quite dapper in a dark suit, black shirt and vest, and looked a bit like a riverboat gambler. Married or not, though, he and Deborah lived apart, and never seemed to spend the night together. Late as it might get, Garcia would either drift off to John Kahn's place in San Francisco—Kahn shared his seemingly permanent taste for opiates—or return home to his funky new house at Audrey Court, high up on the Tiburon ridge. Surrounded by five TVs, one in almost every room, feeding off two satellite dishes with all of the English-language channels in the world, he spent most of his time playing CD-ROM computer games like Myst, Hellcab, and Journeyman, or working on his art. Between the Dead, the Garcia Band, and his art, he had what he thought were far too many responsibilities, but he seemed unable to cut them down to size. When old friends asked for his time on recording projects, he would always say yes, and then turn to his personal manager, Steve Parish, and say, "Get me out of this." There was a sign above his computer, and it read, "Nothing You Know Is True, but It's Exactly the Way Things Are."

After some early March shows in Phoenix, the band met and decided to fire Dan Healy. Since Healy had spent at least a couple of years muttering, "When are they gonna fire me?" it did not come as a total surprise. To some band employees, he appeared bored with the band's music, and a good deal of his efforts with the sound system seemed mostly for his own amusement. Healy was irascible and at times terribly difficult. But he was also heart and soul a brother, and to be fired with a phone call from the manager after so many years was a profound statement of the band's emotional cowardice. His departure did little good. His replacement, John Cutler, got more bass to work with from Lesh, and in general went for a less radically stereo sound that probably served the audience's interests better, but Cutler's studio orientation and stubborn refusal to sacrifice his hearing led to audience chants of "Turn It

Up." It did not help John that Garcia spent the tour with his head slumped in opiated relaxation, and was the victim of radical diabetes-induced mood swings offstage.

On May 11, Phil Lesh guest-conducted the Berkeley Symphony Orchestra in a fund-raiser for music in Berkeley schools, and both Garcia and Weir attended in support. Afterward Garcia called Phil and told him that he'd done some sketches while at the show, a personal gesture that touched Phil and pleased everyone. Contrarily, during the spring tour the band had been forced to cancel a show when Kreutzmann returned to California for a day to say good-bye to his gravely ill father. Though there seemed to be no lack of support for his decision, only Weir bothered to speak to Kreutzmann about it. Aside from their emotional deep-freeze, none of them were all that healthy. Late in April, Weir had fallen into a profound state of exhausted depression in New Orleans, and although he rebounded quickly, he did not confront whatever demons had led to the crack-up. During the spring tour, everyone in the band underwent physical examinations for an insurance policy connected to the mortgage on a new Club Front, the first building the band would ever own. Weir and Vince had throat nodes, Kreutzmann had high cholesterol readings, Phil had gout and hepatitis C, Mickey had *something*, and Jerry had everything. Every one of them failed the physical. Then in late May Garcia was unable to return to the stage to finish a Garcia Band show in Phoenix. By now, those on the tour were simply waiting for the other shoe to drop.

The World Cup of soccer had taken over many of the band's regular stadium venues for the month of June, so the summer tour began late. It was 120 degrees in the shade on the floor of the Silver Bowl in Las Vegas, and it was a miracle of BGP logistics and Dead Head common sense—"It's too hot to get high!"—that no one died. They returned home to play at Shoreline Amphitheatre, where Weir's ancient complaints about the drummers rushing the tempo reached a new peak when he refused to play an encore. The next day, Saturday, he wrote up a manifesto that said playing out of time was torture to him, argued with Garcia, and got nowhere.

The East Coast summer tour began in Highgate, Vermont, so far north that the border patrol's offices were next door to the backstage area. Flying under the Dead Head radar, the show was a success because not too many of the ticketless came. It foretold the whole summer, which passed quietly.

Two surreal moments would stay with the participants. In Washington, Senators Patrick Leahy and Barbara Boxer invited the band to lunch at the Senate Dining Room. As the group entered and sat at a table near the door, everyone noted the presence of the 1948 segregationist Dixiecrat candidate for president, South Carolina's very senior senator Strom Thurmond. He, of course, noted Senator Leahy's party, and as he passed the table on his way out, turned to Garcia with the remark "I undahstand you're the leadah of this heah organization." Jerry Garcia and Mickey Hart shaking hands with Strom Thurmond was something the wildest acid trip could never have included. Garcia's birthday came on a gig night in Detroit, where Deborah threw a birthday party for him, inviting the crew, staff, and band, which everyone was now calling the "world's most dysfunctional family." Those who came were stiff and Garcia seemed embarrassed. He waved a towel at the candles to put them out, and left within five minutes. The tour ended a few days later, and twelve limousines were lined up on the tarmac in San Francisco when the band's charter plane landed.

Despite the increasingly frozen emotional landscape, the band was still capable of playing brilliantly. And by now there was more than sufficient new material for a good CD. In November, they went into a studio called the Site, near Skywalker Ranch, but the sessions came to nothing; Garcia sat in a corner grumbling about whatever caught his attention, but never really settled down to work.

When three Garcia Band shows in San Francisco were canceled in February 1995, the first after the audience had already entered, Dead Heads feared the worst. For a change, it wasn't all that bad, merely a hand injury. Ever since his 1961 car accident, Garcia had had occasional problems with a pinched nerve and numbness in his hand, and thirty years of hanging a heavy guitar off one shoulder hadn't helped. While on a diving vacation in the Caribbean, he'd exacerbated the problem, but it healed swiftly. He was actually in a pretty pleasant mood.

Later that week, in a van in Salt Lake City going back to the hotel after the first Dead shows of 1995, Scrib remarked that their promoter had once managed the Osmond Brothers, and Garcia affably entered into a thoughtful discourse on the nature of family singing acts, from the bluegrass Stanley Brothers and the pop Mills Brothers to the Boswell Sisters. It had been a good night. Much to the concern of Dead Heads, the band had introduced TelePrompTers, which the musicians generally ignored, but in Salt Lake City Garcia used his to deliver a tremendous, heart-wrenching performance of Dylan's "Visions of Johanna" that was very possibly the musical high point of the year for him. And for sheer charm, it was hard to top the reception the band got once back at the hotel. They'd been sharing the place for three days with the University of Michigan women's gymnastic team, whose big competition was that night. Both groups converged in the lobby, with the gymnasts ecstatic over their standings, and even the oft-grumpy Garcia was pleased to pose for pictures with the fifteen delightful young women.

The spring tour was so-so musically but logistically tolerable because it avoided the Northeast and hit some new places, like Memphis. As they prepared for the summer 1995 tour, it was clear that Garcia's physical and emotional health was at an alarmingly low level. Toward the end of the spring tour, in Birmingham, he had become extremely agitated when he discovered that his room could not be locked. A puzzled hotel maintenance man, unable to understand why a man needed to lock a room only his wife had access to, installed one, even as Garcia tried to minimize the oddness of his needs. Unfortunately, he had begun the spring tour with his blood sugar at truly astronomical levels, and then early in May had lost his helpers, Vince and Gloria Di Biase, when they were fired by Deborah, who was gradually attempting to impose order on Garcia's chaotic financial affairs. Order was Garcia's enemy, even when the source was his wife. Clearly the process was distressing to him. And even when he made plans, he imposed limits. He and his old pal Paddy Moloney of the Chieftains had been talking about recording one of Paddy's songs, "Jerry's Tune," to which Paddy had set as lyrics the Yeats love poem "Crazy Jane on God." Jerry was willing, but told him to get someone else to play. "I just want to sing."

The summer 1995 tour began in Vermont, and the decision to go twice to the well was revealed as a bad one. Though management had begged the town of Highgate to ban camping and vending in the area near the show site, the itch to make a profit on the visit led to a circus. With a place to stay, and all the nitrous and beer they could buy, at least twenty thousand people without tickets showed up, and the gates were opened so that no one would get hurt. A week later, on June 21, in Albany, Garcia could not start the second set without Weir telling him what to play, sitting zombielike in a total meltdown, blaming whatever was wrong on Parish, on his guitar, on anything but his confused mental state. Four days later, in Washington, D.C., three Dead Heads in the parking lot were hit by lightning, and the first whispers of a "cursed tour" went up. It wasn't just logistics or Garcia. Kidd Candelario had taken umbrage with Candace Brightman, and was refusing to turn on the sensor attached to Lesh's belt that ran the new automated follow spotlights. Two young women with a crew member's laminate had been accused of pistol-whipping someone on the Mall in Washington, and the police were back-stage at the next show looking for them. Parish learned that John Scher had violated protocol by speaking to Dylan and Garcia about a possible joint acoustic tour without first talking to him, and was frothing at the mouth.

The tour moved on to Detroit, and with Deborah temporarily absent, it was almost impossible to get Garcia out of his room. Even the optimistic Parish now spoke of Garcia needing a rehab or hospital stay after the tour. Three Rivers Stadium, Pittsburgh: in the middle of a pouring rainstorm, the band played the Beatles' "Rain," "Box of Rain," "Samba in the Rain," and "Looks Like Rain," and it all felt goofily good for a moment. Then the band moved on to Deer Creek, in Indiana, and hit the wall. The first show was scheduled for Sunday, July 2, and as the band arrived that afternoon, Ken Viola took them aside to play them a phone message left with the local police that promised an attempt on Garcia's life. Jerry shrugged, and told Viola not to be ridiculous. "My wife isn't going to like this," said Lesh, but he planned to play. Weir made a speech about standing up to terrorists. There were metal detectors at the gates and trained plainclothes officers in the area in front of the stage, and the house lights stayed up.

Unfortunately, given the holiday weekend and the dearth of excitement in central Indiana, there were twenty thousand people without tickets outside, and around five thousand of them decided to break into the show. Audience members assisted them by kicking giant holes in the fence, and as the intruders poured over and through the fence, a good part of the audience cheered. The band was stunned. More than a little worried, Sears sent the band's guests out in vans before the end of the show, with band and crew to leave in one of the production buses. Slowly pushing through the parking lot, trying not to hit the dozens of kids who pounded on the side of the bus or played some sort of stoned game of chicken with it, the bus finally reached the narrow web of back roads around the facility, where in peace and quiet a mile or two down the road, it got stuck on an impossible turn. Ram Rod, Billy Grillo, and a local farmer with a minitractor tried but failed to dig it out, and during the wait for a tow truck, the laughs came out. The next morning the police informed management that they would not endanger themselves a second time; they would direct traffic, but not work inside the facility. And so the show was canceled, the first such decision caused by the audience in thirty years.

The first show in the next city, St. Louis, went well, but later in the evening, about twenty miles away at a campground, more than a hundred Dead Heads crowded onto the veranda of a lodge to escape a gully-washing downpour, and the porch roof caved in. One hundred and eight people went to the hospital, most with bruises, but one man was paralyzed. By noon of the next day, all three TV networks had sent crews to St. Louis. Nothing happened in St. Louis, but the media were on a "deathwatch." The tour moved on to its final stop, Chicago's Soldier Field, and eleven TV crews asked to cover the shows. It was futile to point out that trouble happened outside shows and that it would take the 101st Airborne to break into Soldier Field. The media came, and nothing happened, and the tour ended, to nearly universal relief, on July 9. As had become traditional, the show ended with a spectacular Soldier Field fireworks display. Candace Brightman figured that the Dead got a better deal for their pathetic $10,000 than the city got on the Fourth of July for eight times as much. As the rockets boomed, Weir went over to give an end-of-tour hug to Garcia, who chirped, "Always a hoot, man. Always a hoot." And they went their separate ways.

A couple of days after he got home, on Thursday, July 13, Garcia called David Grisman and said, "What's happening in your studio? I got this recording session for you, I gotta record a Jimmie Rodgers song. You'll get paid. Can you do it today?" "No, how about Sunday the sixteenth?" "Okay, I'm leaving Monday." Bob Dylan had been working on a tribute album to Rodgers, "the singing brakeman" and one of the creators of country music, and Garcia wanted to participate. He added, "John Kahn's got a percussionist, can you get that chick dobro player [Sally Van Meter]?" He confirmed on Sunday, but added that they needed a drummer, and Grisman got George Marsh. By 11 A.M. they'd gathered at Dawg's studio. "[Garcia] didn't look that good," Grisman thought, although he was "upbeat and into it." Over the next few hours they recorded Rodgers's "Blue Yodel #9." Decibel Dave, the engineer, slated take one and they began, but Garcia stopped them, saying that the tempo was too fast. "Down from the bottom, brother," he said. "Say way down from Dixie now. That's it, that's the feel. Nothing is moving on the river." Garcia's playing was fair, but his vocals, especially the yodels, were weak, as though he lacked enough breath. "Talk to me, David," he said. "You should talk to me a little bit in my solo." "Hi, Jerry. Nice solo you're playing."

Upstairs, Deborah told Grisman's wife, Pam, where Jerry was going on Monday, which was the Betty Ford Clinic in Southern California. Of course, what Garcia's reluctance to deal with doctors had long concealed was that his drug use not only medicated depression and anxiety but masked major physical illnesses, including raging diabetes, a congested heart, and lungs destroyed by thirty-five years of cigarettes and fifteen years of smoked hard drugs. He did not appear to have received any treatment for them. As they left Grisman's studio, Garcia turned to Grisman and said, "Can you finish this up?" Grisman would learn only later that Garcia had already signed a contract identifying Kahn and Grisman as coproducers.

Garcia's stay at the Betty Ford Clinic was painful and hot, and after two weeks he sent for Deborah and Parish to bring him home. Just after his return, he had a long, sweet phone conversation with Bruce Hornsby, regaling him with stories about meeting an old associate of Django Reinhart's there, as well as plenty of ideas and plans for the future. Garcia was clean and clear, and once back in Marin County, cheerful. He went to some AA meetings, met with a recovery psychiatrist, worked on his visual memoir *Harrington Street,* and decided to check into a local substance-abuse clinic, Serenity Knolls, at least in part because he mistakenly thought it was on the site of Camp Lagunitas, where he had spent part of the magical summer of 1966. Close enough; it was perhaps half a mile down the road. The day before he was to check in, he went by Sue Stephens's office at the annex across the street from 5th and Lincoln. He spent an hour and a half there, reminiscing, and telling her that he felt "shaky, and his willpower wasn't up to par, and he could tell how much his body had aged now that he was more or less straight." Still, he intended to "take a big bite out of the apple this time." There were other calls, including an unusually affectionate one to Hunter. He also visited a Wendy's fast-food restaurant for what was doubtless an orgy of cholesterol before settling in at Serenity Knolls on August 8.

That night Robert Hunter's wife, Maureen, found it difficult to sleep, anxiously awakening about 4 A.M. Weir, who was in New Hampshire touring with his band RatDog, was deep in a dream about that time. "I was on the road with RatDog, and we were backstage and I'd discovered some invisible paint, and we were playing with it. And in the middle of the dream, Jerry showed up. Dressed in a long dark cape, his hair was black, he looked regal and Castilian, like a tall Spanish nobleman. He was very purposeful, and he wasn't interested in this invisible paint. I couldn't understand why he wouldn't want to fool around with the paint . . . He seemed preoccupied." Weir woke up to pee, and noticed it was a little after 7 A.M. in New Hampshire.

At 4:23 A.M. on August 9, a nurse passed by Garcia's room, and she became aware that his stentorian snores were no longer audible. She went to check, and discovered him dead of what proved to be a heart attack. He had a smile on his face.

The mayor of San Francisco flew a tie-dye flag at half-mast over City Hall. Dead Heads gathered at the corner of Haight and Ashbury. President Clinton paid tribute with respectful remarks. Even more effectively, so did Bob Dylan. "He is the very spirit personified of whatever is muddy river country at its core and screams up into the spheres. He really had no equal . . . There are a lot of spaces and advances between the Carter Family, Buddy Holly, and, say, Ornette Coleman, a lot of universes, but he filled them all without being a member of any school. His playing was moody, awesome, sophisticated, hypnotic and subtle."

The open-casket funeral was at St. Stephen's Church in Belvedere, Marin County, and David Grisman played "Amazing Grace" before slipping a pick into Jerry's coat pocket. Hornsby flew in from Virginia, Dylan from Los Angeles. Hunter read a wonderful poem, Parish made heartfelt remarks, and daughter Annabelle told the truth, as her father would have loved: "He was a shitty father, and a great man." In her pain, Deborah repeated a mantra she would clutch in the years after, a belief that had led her to ban her "enemy" Mountain Girl from the funeral: Deborah, and Deborah alone, was the love of Garcia's life. "He said-a dat to me," said Barbara Meier, who'd slipped into the church with the Hunters. "He said-a dat to me," said Sara Ruppenthal Katz, ditto. Bit by bit the band struggled to cope. They vetoed the idea of a performed memorial, and twenty thousand Dead Heads gathered in Golden Gate Park a couple of days after the funeral to listen to taped music and oral testimony. Once again, it was Annabelle who got off the best line. "We love each and every one of you because you put us through college and we didn't have to work at Dairy Queen."

The band finally met in December, and Kreutzmann told his brothers that he could not tour. In solidarity, they agreed that the name "Grateful Dead" would never again appear in connection with a live performance, and left the rest to the gods. The decision particularly devastated Vince Welnick, who'd been seriously depressed ever since Garcia's death. Late in the month Sears announced that Weir and Hart would do some sort of summer tour, briefly nicknamed Deadapalooza and later the Furthur Festival. He failed to inform Phil Lesh of this announcement in advance, however, and over the next years the Furthur Festival would ignite a division between Lesh and the rest of the band. When the band wasn't quarreling within, the heirs of the estate of Jerry Garcia were quarreling without. He had left behind $30,000 worth of comic books, a quarter million in instruments, some furnishings, fine arts, and computers, two cars and a Honda scooter—and royalties and a share of Grateful Dead Productions. Taken altogether, there was so much division that the band and Deborah couldn't even agree on a day to scatter Garcia's ashes.

Early in April 1996 Weir and Deborah went to Benares, India, to scatter a small portion of the ashes in the Ganges. Being a filmmaker, Deborah naturally hired a local film crew to record the proceedings, and news of the event spread swiftly from Indian newspapers to the United States. Though Weir later swore that he had tried to call Annabelle before his departure, the news hit Garcia's daughters and ex-wife, M.G., with a devastating impact, for they were convinced that *all* the ashes had been strewn and that they'd been totally excluded from the memorial ritual. On April 12, Bruce Hornsby passed through San Francisco and played the Fillmore, and both Weir and Lesh sat in, an event only somewhat complicated by the fact that their relationship was quite strained, at least from Weir's point of view.

Finally, on Monday, April 15, the last tour gathered at a dock in Marin to carry Garcia home to the sea on the motor-sailer ketch *Argosy Venture.* The vessel was captained by Bill Belmont, piloted by Janice Belmont, and crewed by Randy Waggoner and Allen Gross. Jerry's brother, Tiff, and his oldest friend, Laird Grant, were there, Ram Rod and Frances Shurtliff, Steve Parish and his old friend Angelo Barbera, and Garcia Band crew members David Faust and Corky Varra. Annabelle, Theresa, Sunshine, and Jerry's firstborn daughter, Heather Katz, boarded. Sue Stephens, his loyal assistant. Cameron Sears and Cassidy Law. Scrib. Bob Weir and his future wife, Natascha Muenter. Phil and Jill Lesh.

In a sign of rifts to come, Mickey had been so exasperated by a phone call that day from the Leshes, who were planning a benefit, that he elected not to come. After Deborah Garcia boarded, M.G. stood on the dock and asked to join them. Deborah denied her. In pain, Theresa said, "Deborah, she's my mother." Deborah replied with the meaningless but clearly malevolent "Are you sure?" Then she shouted to get the boat under way or she'd leave. Weir tried to talk with her, got nowhere, and was about to leap off the boat as it pulled away. Past the Golden Gate Bridge the ocean was choppy, with seas of six feet and swells to ten. The skies were gray, spitting a light rain, appropriate weather for a solemn day. Halfway between Land's End, the northwest corner of San Francisco, and Point Bonita, the southwest corner of Marin County, at the entrance to the Golden Gate, they stopped.

Parish opened the plastic bag that contained Garcia's remains. All who so desired reached in and helped tip the bag over. Garcia was gone, the Grateful Dead with him.

Finale: Metaphysics and Other Humorous Subjects

ithout its unifying center, the band's individual members largely sought independent directions. Initially, Kreutzmann and Lesh retired, while Weir worked with a blues band called RatDog and Mickey Hart experimented with various configurations oriented toward world music, first with Mystery Box and then a new Planet Drum. The one attempt at a revival of the basic Grateful Dead model, "The Other Ones" in 1998, included Hart, Lesh, Weir, Hornsby, and friends John Molo, Steve Kimock, Mark Karan, and Dave Ellis. It was a smashing success in terms of musical satisfaction and audience appeal, but—again, without the unifying center—its internal dynamics could not find any functional equilibrium. A possible repeat in 1999 was deferred when Phil Lesh underwent major surgery, receiving a liver transplant, and after his recovery, he went his own way, establishing a band called Phil and Friends that would focus on the progressive improvisation that was his favorite aspect of the Dead's music. Weir's RatDog would turn into a rock band and naturally enough orient itself toward his repertoire, while Hart would dally briefly with a rock and rollish Mickey Hart Band before, in 2001, establishing Bembé Orisha as his world music-oriented performance outlet. In the interval, he had become a national figure in music preservation and a trustee of the American Folklife Center at the Library of Congress. After dabbling with lower-profile ensembles in his Hawaiian retirement, Kreutzmann in 2001 returned to the mainland to organize the Trichromes with Journey veterans Neil Schon and Sy Klopps.

But the primary legacy of the Grateful Dead, at least at the time of writing, appeared to lie in four parts: stylistic and social influence on other bands, the philosophical underpinnings that Dead Heads will carry with them to their graves, and the recorded music itself that the band left behind. No other American band, before or since, has united the improvisational nature of jazz with rock modalities in quite the same way, but a flock of bands—the so-called jam bands—have adopted improvisation as their first stylistic bulwark. Moreover, many of these bands, from Phish to Widespread Panic to String Cheese Incident and on and on, have consciously patterned their social behaviors, their relationship with each other and with their audience, after the Dead. That will continue.

But the Dead's ultimate legacy is their audience and their music itself. First with Dick Latvala and John Cutler and later with David Lemieux and Jeff Norman as the guides, the contents of the band's legendary vault have poured forth, many vault releases and twenty-three "Dick's Picks" by late 2001, and many tens of thousands of Dead Heads and other listeners continue to appreciate this music as an extraordinarily profound document of American electronic folk music in the late twentieth century. By the late 2001 release of the epic *Golden Road* box set, the band's body of work could lay serious claim to comparison with that of Ives, Gershwin, Ellington, and (Miles) Davis, or any of the other great American composer/performers. So long as there are people who listen to music, there will be Dead Heads. And so long as there are Dead Heads, they will be guided by the principles of freedom, spontaneity, caring for each other and their planet, fellowship, and fun.

> *It all rolls into one*
> *and nothing comes for free*
> *There's nothing you can hold*
> *for very long*
> *And when you hear that song*
> *come crying like the wind*
> *it seems like all this life*
> *was just a dream . . .*
>   —*"Stella Blue"*

Dan Healy: "I've discovered over the years that two things are true. One is that what you like is what you like, and two, it isn't necessarily the medium that you use—it's what you do with it."

Garcia: "Say you were the first supreme being and there was no real reason for you to manifest life in the universe, except for it to have the ability to surprise and delight you. For it to be something out of your direct control, and something you couldn't have a lot of knowledge about, or predict. That's what I'd want."

Garcia: "There's an old Prankster proverb that goes, 'The mind believes what the mind believes.' Our experience has been the more the merrier."

Willy Legate: "Everyone around here [the Front Street studio] knows that he could be wrong—but everyone around here knows that everybody's right."

Garcia: "Basically I prefer the light . . . What I do know is that we need the All."

There is no Grateful Dead philosophy, but if there were, a central tenet would be Jung's concept of synchronicity, a "series of events connected by simultaneity and meaning . . . a peculiar interdependence of objective events among themselves as well as the subjective (psychic) states of the observer or observers." Dreams are a definite evocation of synchronicity.

Garcia: "We know from our own experience that enough things happen that *aren't* the result of signals or planning or communication that we're aware of, but that are miraculous manifestations, that keep proving it out, that there's no way to deny it. We're just involved in something that has a very high incidence of synchronicity. You know, the Jungian idea of synchronicity? Well, shit, that's day-to-day *reality* for us."

Garcia: "Synchronicity. There's a large element of what we do that we have no control over. We have to beg off from what's happening—it isn't us that's doing it, we're only like the tools through which it's happening. And it's okay. We have faith . . . Our music is never counting. For us the One is always Now. In time—whether it's 7/4 time, 4/4 time, or whatever—we're always coming back to the One."

Two passing flashes of Grateful Dead synchronicity: In 1982 the band came to Centennial Coliseum, Reno, Nevada, for a show. As Dead Heads approached the venue, they passed the Golden Road Motel, Uncle John's

Restaurant, and the Answer Man hardware store in the space of two blocks, each name a fragment from a Dead song. In October 1978, the Dead showed slides of their journey to Egypt at Winterland during a concert, and as they played "Eyes of the World," three slides flashed in perfect synchronization to the song's lyrics: Mickey on a white Arabian stallion looking dashing on the dunes—"And sometimes we ride on your horses"—Garcia watching the sun rise from the top of the Great Pyramid—"sometimes we walk alone"—and the band on stage singing—"Sometimes the songs that we hear are just songs of our own."

Garcia: "Uncertainty is what's happening to me. Are we living out some predetermined script in which the ending is already known? If so, why are we doing it? . . . Or is it possible that the gift of consciousness has a direct relationship to the atoms of the sense and purpose in the design of organisms, you know. I mean, we're surrounded by artifacts of the mind, things we've invented. All these things are metaphors—they're telling me something about what my mind is . . . It's furious manipulation, man, and it's coming from my mind. It's what separates us from IT. I'm curious because I've had my fucking mind blown. What is IT?"

Garcia: "It's an imperfect universe."

Robert Hunter: "You hear the same sound going out as coming in. The difference is that now you know it's music."

Garcia: "But what the fuck do I know, anyway?"

Notes

All quotations are from the source to the author, or in the presence of the author, except where otherwise noted. "Band" means information gathered from all or virtually all members of the Grateful Dead.

Abbreviations: JB—John Perry Barlow. TC—Tom Constanten. JG—Jerry Garcia. MG—Carolyn "Mountain Girl" Adams Garcia. BG—Bill Graham. MH—Mickey Hart. DH—Dan Healy. RH—Robert Hunter. BK—Bill Kreutzmann. WL—Willy Legate. PL—Phil Lesh. JM—Jonathan McIntire. BM—Brent Mydland. SP—Steve Parish. BP—Bobby Peterson. DR—Danny Rifkin. RS—Rock Scully. RR—Ram Rod Shurtliff. OS—Owsley Stanley. AT—Alan Trist. BW—Bob Weir.

Opening epigraphs: "When the going": Hunter Thompson, *Shark*, p. 53. "Look, there are two curves": Robinson Jeffers, "Diagram," *Selected Poems*, p. 88. "That's why the Lord": Robert Hunter, "CD," p. 4.

Chapter 1. "Why would the universe . . . figure it all out": JG in Gans, *Conversations*, p. 79.

Chapter 2. "For our country": "Epilogue," in Karman, p. 3. JG childhood and adolescence: JG, Clifford Garcia, Dr. Dan Grayson, Lenore Garcia Ross, Mary Brydges Boggess, Laird Grant. "You will run": *S.F. Call-Bulletin* clipping, n.d., courtesy of Clifford Garcia. Rock and Roll: see Palmer for overview. Martin Luther King Jr.: see Viorst. Art Institute: Wally Hedrick, Elmer Bischoff, Ann Besig Forwand, Laird Grant. "serious Buddhism . . . own car": Michael McClure, "Painting Beat by Numbers," in George-Warren.

"kind of easy-listening . . . version": JG in Stuckey, "Jerry Garcia." Folk overview: see von Schmidt and Rooney.

PL childhood: PL, Bob Hanson. "Philip, would you": PL. "Absorbed in the work . . . innocence": Peckham, p. 150. CSM: Mike Lamb. CSM jazz: Dick Crest, Lenny Lasher, Al Molina, Buddy Powers, Bobby Petersen. "blocks of granite": PL in Harrison, *The Dead*, p. 30.

Chapter 3. Palo Alto and Chateau scene: JG, RH, AT, PL, WL, Danya Veltfort, Marshall Leicester, Joan Simms, Lester Hellums, David McQueen, Norman Fontaine, Karen Huntsberger. "Here, take the heavy . . . take you around": JG to John McLaughlin. Paul Speegle: JG, AT, Paul Speegle Sr. "That's the way I'm": AT. St. Michael's Alley: JG, RH, AT, Vern Gates. "The dialogue's beginning . . . *our home*": RH, "Trumpet," pp. 18–20. RH bio: RH. AT bio: AT. Kepler's: JG, RH, AT, Willy Legate, Roy Kepler, Ira Sandperl. "said a great deal . . . right idea after all": RH, "Trumpet," pp. 77–78. "thought is the most ductile": JB. Brigid Meier bio: Brigid Meier. "He speaks of": unpublished poem by Brigid Meier, courtesy of author.

Early folk scene: Debbie Green Anderson, Hoyt Axton, Peter Berg, Gert Chiarito, Ted Claire, Earl Crabb, Dave and Vera Mae Frederickson, Charlie Frizzell, Lou Gottlieb, David Guard, Tom Hobson, Jorma Kaukonen, John Lundberg, Barry Olivier, Mary Ann Pollar, Chris Strachwitz. "dippy folk songs": JG in Reich, p. 30. "Tell you a story about": unrecorded song by RH and JG, courtesy of RH. Harry Smith: see Marcus, *Invisible Republic*. "The next number is an old": RH, "Trumpet," p. 60. "Man, all I wanna do": JG to Norman Van Maastricht. "shiftless": Marshall Leicester. Cadillac Hotel: JG, Brigid Meier. Boar's Head: JG, RH, Rodney Albin, Peter Albin, Suze Wood, Marshall Leicester. "Sure, man . . . Tell everybody": David Nelson.

Ron McKernan: Mrs. Esther McKernan, Carol McKernan, Tawny Jones, John Manusos, Roger "Cool Breeze" Williams, Brigid Meier, Ted Claire, Lester Hellum, Sally Gist. "Don't tell anybody": Ted Claire. "real pixie . . . sweetheart": JG to John McLaughlin. "apocalyptic . . . this planet": AT. "Hey, babe . . . fuck": RH, "Trumpet," p. 22. "could walk on your mind": RH. "come up with knuckle-busting": Rick Melrose. "Music stopped being": TC. PL at Cal: PL, TC, BP; see Constanten, *Between Rock*. KPFA: PL, JG, Gert Chiarito.

Chapter 4. Lundberg's: John Lundberg, Ken Frankel. RH and LSD: RH and RH notes. "Sit back picture . . . to remain insane": RH notes, courtesy of RH.

"that incredible clarity": JG in Jones and Pickard. Bluegrass: Ken Frankel, Joe and Jim Edmonston, JG, RH, Scott Hambly, Marshall Leicester, Neil Rosenberg, Sandy Rothman, Mayne Smith. "imbued the sixties generation": Raskin, p. 45. "We make music in . . . hours to tune": JG, from a recording courtesy of Rodney Albin. CSM Folk Festival: recording, JG, RH, David Nelson, Norman Van Maastricht, Mike Jonas, Rick Melrose. "Let's get loaded . . . this stuff works": David Nelson, Rick Melrose.

Tangent: JG, RH, Stu Goldstein, David and Julie Schoenstadt, Jorma Kaukonen, Rodney Albin, Butch Waller, Herb Pedersen. Romance and wedding with Sara Ruppenthal: JG, Sara R. Katz, RH, WL, David Nelson, PL. PL in Las Vegas: PL, TC. Monterey Folk Festival: JG, RH, Sara R. Katz, Ken Frankel, Suze Wood. Bob Dylan: see Scaduto, Kramer. JG as music teacher: Sara R. Katz, Randy Groenke. "I tried to teach": JG in Reich, p. 33. "How long . . . feel like it": Randy Groenke. Zodiacs: JG, Troy Weidenheimer, BK. Black Mountain Boys: JG, RH, Eric Thompson, Sara R. Katz, David Nelson, letter from Sara R. Katz to Stu Goldstein, 10/3/63. "sort of a weasel . . . mind him": Sara R. Katz to Stu Goldstein, 10/28/63. Offstage: Paul Foster, Paul Kantner, David Freiberg, Jorma Kaukonen. Birth of Heather: Sara R. Katz, JG, RH. Ashgrove gig: JG, Ken Frankel, Marshall Leicester, RH. "Shut up and": RH.

Chapter 5. "anarchic oligarchy": RH. "I am not an artist": JG on "I Believe." "a matter of sensibility": Marshall Leicester. "Avoidance of confrontation": PL to David Gans. "Default and digression": Scully and Dalton, p. 45. "The question is . . . more fun": JG in Reich, p. 110. Ron Rakow to Richard Nixon, in Grateful Dead Record Company newsletter, 9/74. Meeting entries from G.D. meeting minutes taken by Sue Stephens. "Badmouthing someone . . . are coming": unpublished note from Willy Legate. "Well, I can't say . . . rave awhile": Hal Kant.

Chapter 6. 12/31/63: BW, JG, Bob Matthews. BW bio: BW, Wendy Weir, Sue Swanson, Bob Matthews. "eyes open wide": Watrous, "Night." Jug band: JG, BW, RH, Bob Matthews, Sara R. Katz, Dave Parker, Michael Wanger. "practically lived": Sara R. Katz to Stu Goldstein, 3/23/64. Beatles: see Philip Norman. Scientology: RH, Willy Legate, David Nelson. Event III: PL, TC, Ramon Sender, Steve Reich. Mime Troupe: Peter Berg, Peter Coyote. "dockworkers, college students . . . until she did": Coyote, p. 17. "Hat size . . . pretty small": PL.

Southern trip: JG, Sara R. Katz, Sandy Rothman, Scott Hambly, Neil Rosenberg, Mayne Smith, Roland White, Bill Keith, Marshall Leicester. Chrysler Imperial: Loyal Gould in Joseph, p. 27. "little model of good . . . still make it": JG in Reich, p. 38.

Chapter 7. Rolling Stones: see Booth, *True Adventures*. "see that blind man": quoted in ibid., p. 111. "The only drummer . . . total imp": JG to John McLaughlin. BK bio: BK, Brenda Kreutzmann, Lee Anderson. "Bill, you have to leave": BK. LSD experience: JG, Sara R. Katz, RH, David Nelson, Rick Shubb, Butch Waller, Eric Thompson. "Yeah, this is what . . . even more": JG to Alderson. "There's more than": JG to Mary Eisenhart. "Do you always jump": David Nelson. "It's all right": Sara R. Katz. "and just rapped insanely on television": JG in Gleason, *Jefferson Airplane*, p. 325. "Using a blowtorch": Richard Fariña in Eisen, p. 205. "That he not busy": Dylan, "It's Allright Ma," *Writings*, p. 171. Warlocks: JG, BW, BK, Sue Swanson, Connie Bonner, Bob Matthews. "unkempt monkey": PL. "We are witness": David Meltzer, unpublished MS. "Listen, man": PL. "I was so excited": PL in *ZigZag*. "See those bottom . . . you go, man": PL. "decided I just . . . the instruments": Dana Morgan Sr. in Donnelly. "wooden . . . real stiff": PL in *ZigZag*.

Chapter 8. Dylan at Newport: Nick Gravenites, von Schmidt and Rooney. Group LSD trip: JG, PL, BW, Sue Swanson. "The whole world": JG in Reich, p. 41. "The bathrooms alone": Raechel Donahue. Jefferson Airplane: see Gleason, *Jefferson Airplane*; Selvin, *Summer of Love*; Jorma Kaukonen, Bill Thompson. "You better be": Gleason, *Jefferson Airplane*, p. 127. "entirely possible that": Gleason, *Chronicle*, 8/20/65. In Room: JG, BW, PL, BK, Dale O'Keefe, Maruska Nelson, Herb Greene. "looked so young . . . rendered him beautiful": McClanahan, "Grateful Dead." "a part that fetches": Sturgeon, p. 107. "Surrendering . . . why not?": JG in Gleason, *Jefferson Airplane*, p. 326. "longer and longer . . . in bluegrass": JG to Rowland, "Elvis Costello." "one of the reasons": Jones,

Blues People, p. 75. Influence of Coltrane: JG, PL, BW, BK. "There was something . . . influenced us": JG in Blair Jackson, "Pigpen Forever." "You guys . . . too weird": PL and BW.

Red Dog Saloon: Chandler Laughlin, Luria Castell, Mary Works film. Family Dog: Luria Castell, Alton Kelley. "San Francisco can be . . . super-uptite plastic": Gleason, *Jefferson Airplane,* p. 3. "from velvet Lotta": ibid., p. 6. "They can't bust": Selvin, *Summer of Love,* p. 28. San Francisco band origins: see Selvin. "Lady, what this . . . in drag": JG.

"a piano player": Raechel Donahue. Autumn Records: see Selvin; Raechel Donahue, Florence Nathan, Bobby Freeman, Carl Scott. Emergency Crew: JG, PL, BW, BK. Pierre's. PL. "David Grisman found": Israel Young, "Frets." First photo session: JG, BW, Herb Greene, Maruska Nelson, Sara R. Katz. "How dare you": Alton Kelley. Mime Troupe benefit: see Gleason, *Jefferson Airplane;* Graham and Greenfield. "coins and raisins": Anthony, p. 53. "Frank [Sinatra]'s flying": Graham and Greenfield, p. 125. Choosing name "Grateful Dead": JG, PL, BW, BK. "Everything else on the page": JG in Lydon, p. 117. "However you spell it": Pauline Swain.

Chapter 9. "the primitive terror": T. S. Eliot, "The Dry Salvages," in *Four Quartets.* Origins of LSD: see Albert Hofmann. "Acid lowers . . . *is* important": Gaskin, *Haight Street,* p. 12. "It's a language . . . of experience": Kleps, p. 15. "When LSD hit . . . an overview": JG to Alderson. "If one's thesis": Kleps, p. 40. Band and McKenna: JG, Alan Trist, Frances Shurtliff. "spun a myth . . . biocosmic symphony": McKenna, *Hallucinations,* pp. xii, 5, 194.

Chapter 10. "one hundred per cent . . . an art form . . . being conscious": JG to author and Al Aronowitz. "Others can talk": Foster, p. 50. Neal Cassady bio: see McNally, Plummer. "the yoga of a man": Kesey, *Garage,* p. 223. Bus trip: see Wolfe, *Kool-Aid;* Paul Perry, *Bus.* Carolyn Adams bio: Carolyn Adams. "secret meanings": Foster, p. 42. "We're working on": Carolyn Adams. First acid test: JG, PL, BW, Sue Swanson, Connie Bonner. "History had kicked": Kesey in Graham and Greenfield, p. 73. "We always thought": Ken Babbs in ibid. "The idea . . . something of it": JG in Lydon, p. 119. Mime Troupe benefit: see Gleason, *Jefferson Airplane;* JG, BW, PL, BK, Bill Graham. "Goodwill cum": Gleason, *Jefferson Airplane,* pp. 12–13. Big Beat: JG in Reich, JG, BW, PL, BK, Stewart Brand, Foster. "Where's Pigpen": Stewart Brand. "like pigs being": Foster, p. 185. "Suddenly people . . . old armors again": Kesey, *Garage,* p. 175. "Freedom had a lot . . . to get in": JG to Alderson. "tremendously funny": JG in "What Was That?" radio documentary. "Voices coming out": JG in Lufkin, "The Dead." "He would pick": Wavy Gravy in Plummer, p. 139. "the guy who was": JG in ibid., p. 140. "The tips, Captain": Denise Kaufman in Perry, p. 148. "Are you . . . the movie": BK. Owsley Stanley bio: OS. "If Bear decided": Frances Shurtliff. "Just like the big time . . . commercial": Kesey in *Garcia,* editors of *Rolling Stone,* p. 7.

Portland: JG, PL, BK, BW; see also 3/9/67 tape. Matrix: JG, PL, BK, BW, Ray Andersen, Darby Slick, pp. 84–86. California Hall: Luria Castell, Danny Rifkin, Rock Scully. Fillmore Acid Test: BK, JG, BW, PL, RH, Sara R. Katz, Brian Rohan, John Warnecke, Paul Foster. "like the backstage crowd": Gleason, "Fillmore." "An hour or so": Scully and Dalton, p. 10. "Who's in charge . . . dog police": JG in "What Was That?" radio documentary. "They're pretty fast . . . quick-witted, too": BK. "Come on . . . come down": BW.

Trips Festival: Ramon Sender, Stewart Brand, BG, JG, PL, BK, BW, Sara R. Katz, Graham and Greenfield. "in his infinite wisdom": Gottlieb, "Glorious." Kesey arrest: Brian Rohan. "Well, I'm an Angel": Vera Mae Frederickson. "Outside is inside": RH in Allen, *Aces,* p. 140. "Lights flashing . . . beautiful magic": JG to Lydon, pp. 120–21. "It was open . . . something new": JG to Reich, p. 48. "It was music . . . was warping": PL in Harrison, *The Dead,* p. 26. "Jerry Garcia, plug in": BW. "Who's this asshole": BW in Graham and Greenfield, p. 139. BG and Angels: Ramon Sender. "In the clutch": Dusheck, "Abandon." "The Acid Test is at its best": "Mr. Jones," *Daily Cal,* 2/10/66. "a woman in a negligee": "Happenings," *Time.* "Cut out this": Ray Andersen. "No, I wouldn't . . . more fun": OS in Gans, *Conversations,* p. 305. "Ocean ocean": MG.

Chapter 11. L.A.: Jean Mayo Millay, Julius Karpen, Florence Nathan, Sara R. Katz, John Manusos. "Great to see you . . . don't hide": Julius Karpen. Watts: JG, BW, PL, BK, MG, Sara R. Katz, Wavy Gravy. "I'm so high . . . can comprehend": Paul Perry, p. 164. Wavy Gravy bio: Wavy Gravy. "I wanna know . . . talkin' about now": acid-test tape transcription by Nicholas Meriwether, in Getz and Dwork, pp. 99–100. "dynamic . . . paying attention": JG to Alderson.

Pink House: JG, BW, PL, BK, Sara R. Katz, Brenda Kreutzmann, MG, OS, RS, DR, Florence Nathan (later Rosie McGee), Sue Swanson, Tim Scully. "The band is my body": Florence Nathan. Rock Scully bio: RS, Annie Corson. Danny Rifkin bio: DR, BW. "not a small world": Ray Sewell. Ron Rakow bio: Danny Rifkin, Lydia d'Fonsecca Rakow. Sound matters: Tim Scully, OS, PL, DR. Pranksters in L.A.: MG, Julius Karpen. Early Fillmore: Chet Helms, BG, Graham and Greenfield. "Hey, man . . . early . . . production end": Gleason, *Jefferson Airplane,* p. 289. Bill Graham bio: BG, Graham and Greenfield. "He is ambitious": Wasserman, "Hard-Driving." "dances are being . . . Graham": Wenner, "Pranksters'." "Wait a minute . . . let 'em in": BG in Gleason, *Jefferson Airplane,* pp. 286–87. "misdirected and highly unfair": "The Fillmore Auditorium Case," *S.F. Chronicle,* 4/21/66. "Why are you . . . right here": Maitland Zane, "Cops Bust."

Haight scene: Chet Helms, Rodney Albin, DR; see Caserta. Band review: see Selvin, *Summer of Love,* "walking horror . . . walkin' around": JG on 3/9/67 tape.

Chapter 12. History of Olompali: California State Park display. Olompali: JG, BW, BK, Brenda Kreutzmann, PL, DR, RS, Tim Scully, 3/9/67 tape. First party: JG, BW, PL, Julia "Girl Freiberg" Brigden, Herbie Greene, Darby Slick, DR, RS, Tangerine, Florence Nathan, Jorma Kaukonen, Barry Melton. "rock star . . . to be true": Jorma Kaukonen. "Grace really . . . or split": Darby Slick, p. 108. "That's Neal . . . counterprogramming": Grace Slick, pp. 100, 27. "I closed my eyes . . . big joke": JG to Alderson.

Fillmore/Avalon: band, Chet Helms, BG. "who never appeared . . . opening night": JG in "What Was That?" "no longer down": "Rock 'n' Roll: Going to Pot." "Turn off your": "Tomorrow Never Knows." "Dope, fuck": PL in 3/9/67 tape. "cocky . . . better than cowboys": John Cipollina. Olema and Quicksilver: band, John Cipollina, David Freiberg, Ron Polte. Estribou Recording: band, Gene Estribou. Vancouver: PL, RS, Laird Grant. "got screwed around": JG in Gleason, *Jefferson Airplane,* p. 326. Bear's departure: band, OS, Tim Scully. "a really solid": JG in Reich, p. 69. Dan Healy bio: DH, and see Nash, *Music and Sound Output.* "People are starving": BW. "the most successful": Gleason, "All That Jazz." Kelley/Mouse bio: Alton Kelley, Stanley "Mouse" Miller. "20th century teenage": Stanley Miller in McDonough, p. 55.

Chapter 13. 710 Ashbury: band, Sue Swanson, Veronica Barnard Grant, Michael McClure, DR, RS, Allen Cohen, Mary Ann Pollar. "a fantastic universal sense": Hunter Thompson, *Shark,* pp. 104–5. Oracle: Allen Cohen. "We'll talk and screech": from McKernan's "Crazy Peace of Mind," as quoted in Brandelius, p. 51. Diggers: Peter Berg, Peter Coyote. "Far more dangerous . . . the *culture*": Coyote in Graham and Greenfield, p. 184. "The antidote": Coyote, p. 64. "It's yours . . . sacred": Peter Coyote. "a mature street": BG in Graham and Greenfield, p. 187. "Why don't you guys": DR. "Fire, fire": Glenn McKay. "Got any juice": Maruska Nelson. "You're the manager": RS to Joel Selvin. Love Pageant Rally: see Charles Perry; Allen Cohen, Peter Coyote, Laird Grant. Ken Kesey arrest: Brian Rohan. "The Dead are . . . our ethics": Ron Polte. Halloween: Ron Polte, DR, Brian Rohan, Julius Karpen. "That whole [acid test] scene . . . out now": JG to author and Al Aronowitz, 6/73.

Chapter 14. "There is no new . . . Founding Fathers stuff": Felton and Dalton, "Year of the Fork." "anxious to believe": Christgau, *Grown Up,* p. 67. "out of step": Spencer Dryden in Gleason, *Jefferson Airplane,* p. 224. "Everybody looked like": Lydon, p. 114. " 'cause we know . . . without it": Marty Balin in Gleason, *Jefferson Airplane,* p. 101. "It's not what you play": Jorma Kaukonen. Signing with Warner Bros.: band, DR, RS, Brian Rohan, Joe Smith. "Tom, I don't think": Joe Smith in Selvin, *Summer of Love,* p. 94. Warner background: Joe Smith, Stan Cornyn. "Brian, keep the publishing": Brian Rohan. Contract: Joe Smith, Brian Rohan. "It's like dealing": Scully and Dalton, p. 62. *Sons and Daughters:* band, Jon Hendricks. "It's our responsibility": JG in Jon Carroll, "A Conversation." "rapidly gaining . . . sustained genius": Sculatti, "San Francisco Bay." "the newest adventure . . . originality is unmistakable": no author, "Nitty Gritty Sound." 710 Thanksgiving: band, Sue Swanson. "This is the bossest": Gleason, "Thanksgiving." "Dead Silverfish": Barry Melton. "Rabble-rousing is their very": Scully and Dalton, p. 77. Doors: see Hopkins and Sugarman. "unique Be-In . . . we shared": Charles Perry in Lynda Obst, p. 188. "I'd never seen": JG to Randy Groenke. "I've lost . . . smoking grass": Julius Karpen. "Now, pay attention . . . very important": DR. "Like, all that . . . my stomach": JG in Jon Carroll, "A Conversation." "swinging . . . day was full": Gleason, "Tribes."

Chapter 15. First album: band. Mountain Girl: MG, BW. "Whyn't you try it": Michael Lydon. Wenner interview: 1/26/67, courtesy of Joel Selvin. "Those I met": Wainwright, "New Love Land." "Man, you gonna . . . pig": Eldridge Cleaver in Lynda Obst, pp. 192–93. Panthers: see Seale. "We want land": Seale, p. 66. Recording first album: band, Kelley/Mouse, Joe Smith, Stan Cornyn. Reviews: Ralph Gleason, *Chronicle,* 5/7/67; Paul Williams, *Crawdaddy!,* 7–8/67; Richard Goldstein, "Popeye," *Village Voice,* 4/13/67. "pointless . . . Too much": JG to Randy Groenke, 3/67, courtesy of Randy Groenke. "student guitarist . . . rowdy thing": Gleason, *Jefferson Airplane,* p. 312. *Teen Set* session: Jim Marshall. "Alien" photo: Bob Seidemann. 3/20 party: band, DR, RS, Stan Cornyn, Joe Smith. "I want to say . . . Records to the world": Stan Cornyn. Health department: Power, "Hippies Get." Easter Sunday: Allen Cohen. KMPX: Raechel Donahue in Lynda Obst, p. 216. Goodman, p. 37. PL. Screen Actors Guild: comments of Richard Masur, president, SAG, 10/27/97, reported in *Screen Actor,* 1/98. Otto Preminger: MG, BW, Sue Swanson. "No way, man . . . big difference": Ray Manzarek, in Robble, "Reflections"; McClure. Moby Grape: see Selvin, *Summer of Love. Olompali Sunday Times:* G.D. archives. "Pretty little 16": Charles Perry, p. 181. "Jerry's got . . . the teachers": John Cassady in *San Jose*

Metro, Dec. 18–24, 1997. HALO: Brian Rohan. "I never was . . . a process": JG in Brown and Novick, p. 58. "personal liberation": Raskin, p. xv. Russian River: band, John Warnecke.

Chapter 16. "some artifact": RS in *Creem,* 1/74. "functioned not only": Goldstein, "Scenes," *Village Voice,* 6/15/67. Goldstein bio: Richard Goldstein. "if the industry . . . every artery": Goldstein, *Greatest Hits,* p. 119. Group Image: see McNeill, p. 88; Goldstein, *Village Voice,* 6/22/67 New York visit: band, Laird Grant, DR, RS, Richard Goldstein, Howard Klein, Paul Williams, Sandy Pearlman. "That's right": Dave Barry to Joel Selvin. "a shaggy lot . . . with the music": Peter R. Borrelli, *Time* files. "the way to make": PL. "hippies armed . . . by wires": *New York Times,* 6/9/67. Hoffman wedding: Raskin, p. 97. "I am leaving": Freeman House. "I sense violence . . . the fuck": JB. Millbrook: band, JB. "colorful patronness . . . Mellon family": Leary, p. 126. "vaudeville for the mind": Christgau, *Grown Up,* p. 116. *Crawdaddy!:* Paul Williams, Sandy Pearlman. "the problem is": Christgau, *Any Old,* p. 36. "Most hippie rock": ibid., pp. 40–41. "Rock was not intended": Landau, p. 131.

Monterey: see Selvin, *Monterey Pop;* Lou Adler in Joe Smith; Derek Taylor; Phillips (for laughs); Graham and Greenfield; Coyote; Adler in Rosen; Christgau, *Any Old;* band, DR, RS, Ron Polte, Julius Karpen, Peter Coyote. "Judgement reserved": Derek Taylor, p. 111. "to rifle the coatroom . . . not happening": Coyote, p. 99. "Are you gonna . . . pay expenses": Christgau, *Any Old,* p. 19. "to come in peace": Phillips, p. 229. "1,100 people . . . many colors": Derek Taylor, pp. 84–86. "You won't be able": BW. "We have to follow": Florence Nathan. "You know what foldin' " . . . let them in anyway": Christgau, *Any Old,* pp. 29–30. "the English and American . . . mad, no": *Monterey Pop* (film). "and wear some flowers": DR. "Promoters, hustlers . . . or screwed": Hunter Thompson, *Shark,* p. 99. "Pigpen, Captain Trips": *Vancouver Sun,* 7/14/67. "We start off sympathetic": John Wasserman, *S.F. Chronicle,* 7/24/67. "simian . . . to shreds": Kareda, "Jefferson Airplane." Toronto: band, MG, Jorma Kaukonen. Bonnie Dobson: Jackson, "Roots," *Golden Road.* Montreal: band, Bill Thompson, Jorma Kaukonen, Jack Casady. "25,000 hippies": *Montreal Gazette.* 8/7/67 (no title; Jefferson Airplane Scrapbook). "stop playing so": JG. "Are you sure": DR. "a patron": Rakow in Greenfield, p. 79. Chelsea Hotel: DR. Sinclair: RS. "at their best": "The Hippie Temptation," ABC.

Chapter 17. "What happened . . . were nuts": SP. "Everyone is gonna": Joe Winslow. "If you're looking": JG in Henke. "For sure": Harrison, *The Dead,* p. 126. "We're part . . . the hall": Charles Perry, "A New Life."

Chapter 18. RH bio: RH. "Look for a while . . . years . . . sunflower": courtesy RH. "Shall we go, then": T. S. Eliot, *Collected Poems,* p. 3. Straight Theater: Hillel Resner. "Learn body movement": Straight poster. "What I would like": Gleason, "A Most Unusual." "You wanna . . . any drums": MH. MH bio: MH. "I haven't seen you . . . gotta meet him": MH. "whipped into a": Hart and Stevens, p. 135. "We are going to become": MH. 710 bust: band, Florence Nathan, DR, Marilyn Harris Kriegel; see also Raudebaugh, "Cops Raid Pad." "That's what ya get": Wenner, *Rolling Stone.* "Oh, so you're": DR. "I got 'em": Florence Nathan. Press conference: DR; see Wenner, "The Dead." "But if [hippiedom] . . . fashion": Herb Caen, *S.F. Chronicle,* 10/15/67. "The media cast . . . attend services": Digger archives. Death of Hippie: Peter Berg, Peter Coyote, Ron Thelin,

Marilyn Harris Kriegel, DR. March on Pentagon: Lee and Shlain, p. 205. Ellsberg: Raskin, p. 124. *Rolling Stone:* Baron Wolman, Chet Helms, Michael Lydon. "This is not a counterculture": Baron Wolman. "When I woke up . . . cloudy day": early draft of lyrics, courtesy BW. "Certainly they are . . . gobble you up": Lydon, p. 117. "That sounds like . . . meditation": DR. "I hear you're looking": DR. RR bio: RR and Frances Shurt-liff. "Matthews is fired . . . What": RR. "You're killing yourself": MH. New Year's in Omaha: BK, RR. "almost immediately . . . fun and games": Joe Smith to Danny Rifkin, 12/27/67, G.D. archives. "Oh, boy . . . just personalities": JG in Graham and Greenfield, p. 202.

Chapter 19. "negative status . . . cheap to fix": Spence, "Van." "uncut, vilely . . . they stink": Cahill, p. 16. Iowa story: Patrick Stansfield. Parking lot cuisine: see Zipern.

Chapter 20. Tour of the Northwest: band, Brian Rohan, RS, Ron Polte, John Cipol-lina. "pot orgy": John Cipollina. "The Dead never played": RS in Portland State *Vanguard,* 1/26/68. "phenomenal . . . nitroglycerin": ibid. (no title). Crystal Ballroom: see Hills. Un-derground press: see Peck, Pepper. "disregard for time-honored": Biskind, p. 45. Closing of Haight Street: band, RS, Jim Marshall, John Warnecke. "Hey, here we are . . . great": PL. Carousel: band, Dan Healy, Lydia Rakow, Bert Kanegson, Jon Riester, Brian Rohan, Ru-bin Glickman, Bob Matthews, Annie Corson, JM. "McIntire! What . . . exactly": JM. KMPX/KSAN: see Raechel Donahue in Lynda Obst; also Nisker. "What a strange . . . things": MH. "In no way encourages": Kleps, p. 26. Recording of *Anthem:* band, DH in Sandy Troy, "Soundman." "You had to set it": DH, ibid. "How can we make it": JG, ibid. "We really mixed": JG in ibid. Charles Ives: BW, PL. "No tricks, just music . . . frenzied": Annie Fisher, "Riffs," *Village Voice,* 5/16/68. "The coasts linked": McNeill, "East Is West." "are extremely driving": John Kifner, *New York Times,* 5/6/68. Olompali: MH, Don Mc-Coy. GUSS: Jacky Watts Sarti.

End of Carousel: Jon Riester, Lydia Rakow. "1. free identity . . . the myth": Digger papers, courtesy of Peter Berg. St. Louis: Jorge Martinez. Fillmore East: Bill Graham, Jerry Pompili, Amalie Rothschild, Candace Brightman. "got up when . . . you know": Jerry Pompili. Barsalona: see Goodman. "It's real estate . . . Constitution": Jon Riester. "What do you want . . . losing the place": JM. "It's beautiful . . . great": "The Very Grateful Dead," *S.F. Chronicle,* 6/5/68.

Chapter 21. "We had the set-up . . . represent you": Larry Magid to Sam Cutler, 10/18/73, G.D. files. "In the years to come": Sam Cutler to Larry Magid, n.d., G.D. files. "People forcing me . . . a businessman": Graham and Greenfield, p. 342. "It would cost": Lisa Shaftel. "It's true, I can't . . . acrimonious": John Scher. "Jerry stood up . . . Evah": BG.

Chapter 22. "an extraordinary event": Jim Miller, *Rolling Stone,* 9/28/68. "It's so com-pletely": *New Musical Express* review, as quoted in *Spiral Light* 27, p. 27. "Anthem" name: PL. "Well, I guess": Bill Walker. "Dark Star" single sales: Warner Bros. Records, courtesy of Joel Selvin. "perfect two-and-a-half-minute": Williams, *Rock and Roll,* p. 136. Chicago: see Joseph, Raskin, Peck, David Obst. "We are dirty": David Obst, p. 100. Post-Carousel: band, Bert Kanegson, DH, OS, RS, JM. "the situation as it exists . . . Oh, yeah, right": recording, G.D. archives. New songs: JG, RH. Hartbeats: JG, PL, MH. Avalon: Chet

Helms, Bob Cohen. Millard Agency: BG, JM, RS, Janet Soto Knudsen. TC's arrival: band. London run: Cookie Eisenberg, RS, DR, Peter Coyote, Jon Riester, Sue Swanson, Frankie Azzara. "Derek, Adolf Hitler": Philip Norman, p. 439. Ampex: Ron Wickersham. "Fuck it": Ron Wickersham.

"Are you foxing . . . be nice": Barry Melton. "It was the Fillmore West": Jimmy Page in Yorke, p. 64. "garter belts sliding": DesBarres, p. 133. Shoot-out with Led Zep: band, Herb Greene. "filled with mindless": Constanten, "Between Rock," p. 77. *Playboy:* band, OS, Jon Riester. "I want to thank": PL, BK. "Ten minutes after takeoff": Lydon, p. 129. "I wonder how long . . . away from me": Joe Winslow. "We're not gonna": Jon Riester. "caused so much confusion . . . disturb other passengers": letter from Dale W. Bauer, United Airlines, to Tom Sorce, Andrews Travel Agency, Berkeley, 1/27/69, G.D. archives. "I hear you have a problem": Bill Belmont. "Jerry Garcia told me . . . the pressure": Joplin in *Rolling Stone,* 3/15/69.

Chapter 23. "Or there's the one": PL in Gans, *Conversations,* p. 163. "Play a slow number . . . I want": BK. "the *only* one that": John Barlow, *Swing 51.*

Chapter 24. "We were after": JG in Reich, p. 94. "made it into a one-man . . . up again": Gleason, "All That Jazz." "not a lesson but a course": BW on WMMR, 9/8/76. Joe Smith cracks: RS, Brian Rohan, Joe Smith. "Mountains of the Moon": special thanks to Judy Shoaf for help in tracing the mythology. "I'm dying . . . fantastic": JG in Reich, p. 144. Black and White Ball: band, JM, Wendy Weir. "the most beautiful girl . . . so I left": Herb Caen, *S.F. Chronicle,* 3/16/69. Doors: see Hopkins and Sugarman. "They're the same type . . . pop music": "Miami Bans GD Show," *S.F. Chronicle,* 3/19/69. FBI and Columbia: see Peck, pp. 175–77. "It's him or me": MH.

Lenny Hart arrives: band, RR, JM, RS. "I am the Reverend . . . the spirit": JM. "I had no control . . . scare them": RS to Joel Selvin. "We're doing the devil's . . . do this": PL. "Do you want to take": RH to Joel Selvin. "Satan in our midst . . . good goddamn": Lydon, p. 128. "There's no cause worth": John Lennon in Fawcett, p. 53. "But y'know, I dug . . . to be had": JG in Lydon, p. 110. "I don't really care to": MH, PL. "Nero burning . . . people being sick": Frankie Azzara.

Chapter 25. "But I know this . . . voice began": B.B. King in Lydon, p. 6. "Every night when . . . to discover": BW in Sutherland, "Acid Daze." "[Playing is] like being": JG in Mark Rowland, "Bring Me." "The jams are . . . the leader": BW in Alson, "Bob Weir." "For me, a real important": JG in Gans, *Conversations,* p. 66. "Eventually, if I have . . . by any means": JG. "America's longest-running . . . verbal sense": PL in Gans, *Conversations,* p. 166. "So I like to play": PL in *ZigZag.* "I've gone through": JG in Gans, *Conversations,* pp. 58–59. "Intimacy, by the way": BW on WMMR, 3/28/76. "occurs in a mediumistic . . . too well": JG in Haas. "We used to believe . . . 'it' ": PL in Gans, *Conversations,* p. 164. "We've chosen . . . play music": JG to Alderson.

Chapter 26. "I can touch that . . . subconscious": RH in Gilbert. "a road for traveling": Whitman, p. 157. "After all these years . . . is what": Scully and Dalton, p. 168. CSN at the Ranch: David Crosby, MH. "Well, you do . . . own method": BW. The Band: see Helm and Davis. "We didn't know if he . . . couldn't tell": Robbie Robertson in Marcus, *Invisible,* p. xvi. "pretty good musical picture . . . singsongy thing": JG on WFMT, 9/78.

Scientology benefit: TC, BW. "with a spirit . . . atmosphere": Truscott, *Village Voice.* "proceeded to turn . . . better word": *Variety,* 6/25/69.

Wild West Festival: Ron Polte, Bert Kanegson, Barry Olivier, RS, Bill Thompson, Joel Selvin, MH; see also Selvin, *Summer.* "No one's talking . . . revolution": Basic Notes from Breakfast Discussion of Music Festival at Airplane House, 3/12/69, in *Bill Graham Scrapbooks.* "This used to be . . . scares them": *Easy Rider.* "There must be good . . . the spirit": Music Council Notes, *Bill Graham Scrapbooks.* "Nobody talked to me . . . their weight": Wasserman, "Sick and Tired." "You guys have lost . . . I guess": Bill Belmont. "I'm fucking sick . . . to my choice": Wasserman, "Sick and Tired." "Bill, we've heard . . . it was better": JG. "I find it difficult . . . set them up": Selvin, *Summer of Love,* p. 239. "Apparently there is no": Gleason, "The Cancellation."

Chapter 27. "tunneling from one vacuum": Dalton, *Janis,* p. 28. "Thousands of tie-dyed . . . and dice": Rense, "Dead Dance." "A shoe store . . . sell shoes": Sue Klein. "I had a cat": RH in Gans, *Conversations,* p. 24. "I can almost . . . I sign": Blumenfeld, "Dead Mystique."

Chapter 28. Woodstock: band, Jon McIntire, OS, Bert Kanegson, Paul Williams, Bill Belmont; see also Spitz and Santelli. "It's nice to know": JM. "You wanna good movie": Wavy Gravy. "No one honks . . . unnatural": Gail Sheehy, *New York.* "Wow, man . . . my butt": JG in Dallas Taylor, p. 16. "Guess what . . . Take over": Wavy Gravy in Lynda Obst, p. 274. "Hog Farm politics": Hoffman, *Nation,* p. 132. "Sly is not ready . . . Bill Graham": Bill Belmont. "little more sanity . . . astonishingly well": "Nightmare In the Catskills," *New York Times,* 8/18/69. "I think you people . . . for it": Max Yasgur, Woodstock record. Logo: OS, Bob Thomas.

New Orleans Pop: see Santelli. "I wish we had . . . on trial": Rubin, *Everywhere,* p. 14. Warner Bros. contract: Joe Smith. Rock Scully bust: RS, Nicki Scully, Chesley Millikin. "Up against the wall": Paul Kantner, "We Can Be Together." "explains why the Dead . . . or two": Lenny Kaye, *Rolling Stone,* 2/7/70. "Scully was wearing . . . convincing": Booth, *True Adventures,* p. 284. "an opportunist without": BG in Graham and Greenfield, p. 293. "I love the Grateful": Gail Turner Helland. Belli: *Gimme Shelter.*

Chapter 29. "Yeah, it's possible": Sam Cutler. "We don't police . . . we like beer": William Fritsch in Coyote, pp. 120–21. "Charlie Manson Memorial": Ron Wickersham. "passing joints": Leary, p. 283. "the weirdos too . . . medieval, or millennial": Lydon, *Folk,* pp. 193–94. "I didn't go . . . of the word": Sonny Barger in *Gimme Shelter.* "During our set . . . whole time": Carlos Santana in *Rolling Stone,* 1/21/70. "I'd like to mention": Paul Kantner in *Gimme Shelter.* "You talkin' to me": Sonny Barger, ibid. "there's no control": Booth, *True Adventures,* p. 258. "burst of water": Lydon, *Folk,* p. 195. "Many in the audience . . . the violence": op. cit, p. 260. Show dialogue: *Gimme Shelter.* "black hat, black": Booth, *True Adventures,* p. 506. "We believed . . . *organize it*": Mick Jagger in Gilmore, p. 88. "Altamont was the": JG in Reich, p. 116. "I wanted to stand back . . . conscious decision": RH in Gilmore, p. 368. "an overreaction . . . little bit dire": JG in Reich, p. 82. "If a musical experience . . . no one": JG in Lydon, "An Evening." "I recognized how smoothly . . . and jaded": Christgau, *Any Old,* p. 221. Ian Stewart's flight: Bill Belmont.

"Pig, this guy . . . don't worry": JM. T.C. departure: TC, PL, RH. "Those guys are plainclothes": MH. Bust: band, JM. "Hey, you—buddy": JG. Jim Garrison: Joe Smith. "and we have some things . . . anytime soon": Joe Smith.

Chapter 30. "My relationship . . . see him": JG in Rheingold. "We're all siblings . . . neglect": BW, ibid. "GD music has been": BW to Steve Morse, *Boston Globe,* 5/8/80. "Being around . . . that vulnerable": JG to Sue Klein.

Chapter 31. Recording *Workingman's:* band, Bob Matthews, Sam Cutler. "kind of the Workingman's": RH. End of Lenny management: band, RR, RS, JM, Gail Turner, MG. "It's him or me . . . do without him": JG. "Everything turned black . . . suicidal": MH to Joel Selvin. "Karma'll get him": Gail Turner Helland. "a good old band": JG in Reich, p. 95. New structure: band, RS, JM, Sam Cutler, Dave Parker. "I'm a direct descendant": Alice Polesky. "Look, Hunter . . . a beat": RH in Jackson, "Hunter/Garcia." "I don't ever want to hear . . . just heard": PL in Platt, *Lode.* "didn't have shit . . . blew them out": Davis and Troupe, p. 301. "it was sorcery": Gleason, *S.F. Chronicle,* 4/13/70. "They didn't study it . . . Bill Evans": Davis and Troupe, p. 302. "open playing . . . do play": JG in Zimmerman and Zimmerman, "Gavin."

"Lush Life": JG. College demographics: Sale, p. 20. Wesleyan: band, John Barlow. Kent State: see Viorst, pp. 534–37; Peck. "one of the great musical": Francis, "A Sunday." "all of a sudden this jet plane": PL in *Album Network.* "the hillside of people . . . their music": Childs, "History." *Workingman's* cover: Alton Kelley. "I was a little frightened . . . simple spite": RH, "Dark Star." "When we first . . . in the South": JG in Rainier, "Interview." Toronto: see Yorke, "G.D. Surprise." "We demand . . . the community": ibid. Great Train Ride: band, RH, Sam Cutler; see also Dalton, *Janis.* "cautious, almost morosely . . . birch trees": Dalton, *Janis,* pp. 132, 135. "Daddy, daddy": PL. "If I could remember": Dalton, *Janis,* p. 137. "I got the Dead drunk . . . Your Honor": ibid., p. 118.

Chapter 32. Death of Bobbie Garcia: JG, MG, Clifford Garcia. "every vocal nuance": RH, *Box of Rain,* p. 26. "heated the lyrics": RH in Gans, *Conversations,* p. 70. "You can't do . . . my song": BW. "Hey, man, I got": David Grisman. "Good . . . our record": Ned Lagin in Skidmore, "Ned Lagin."

"impact on the audience": *Cashbox,* 10/3/70. "I never saw him": JG in Fedele, "Fuck No." "Comfort is made of . . . everyday life": Dalton, *Janis,* p. 40. College tour: band, Ron Rainey, Sam Cutler. "they were afraid . . . taken over": Charles Klein, Queens College newspaper, 10/12/70. "Last night was . . . of it all": Schwartz, "Grateful Dead." "Hey, man . . . shit in it": show tape. Albany rip-off: see Wilcock, "Ungrateful." *American Beauty:* band, Alton Kelley, JM, RH. "degree of talent . . . the happier he got": David Crosby to Joel Selvin. Trist return: JG, AT, JM.

Chapter 33. "is a compilation . . . went before it": Dan Hupert to author. "one of the most enlightened . . . it's not music": JB in Gilboa, "Getting Gray." "No, that's Sting . . . for the president": Senator Patrick Leahy. "I just didn't . . . Dionysian Festival": Sam Keane. "magicians . . . accord": Joseph Campbell to BW, MH, 1/1/87. "25,000 people . . . atom bomb": Joseph Campbell. "The great thing about . . . really sensual": unnamed student, *Boston University Terrier,* 11/20/70, G.D. archives. "obnoxious religious": Mark Saltveit in Gans, *Not Fade Away,* p. 45. "Dear Jerry . . . past December": author deleted, G.D. archives. "The Grateful Dead represents . . . higher consciousness": Jack Romanski to Jan Rasmussen (Bill Graham Presents), 10/20/80. "never experienced . . . their grace": JG in *Playboy,* 10/80. "Mickey, you're responsible . . . so much": MH.

Chapter 34. Dream Experiment: band, Stanley Krippner; see Krippner, *Song,* and Krippner, "An Experiment." "You are about . . . my neck": Krippner, "An Experiment." Hart departure: MH, Stanley Krippner. Hunter and Weir: BW, RH, JB. Marina Maguire: see Polk, "Drug-Drenched Path." "Barlow, you wrote . . . he's yours": JB. Panther benefit: Sam Cutler, BW.

Crew: SP, Joe Winslow. "more like travel": JG in Reich, p. 112. "there was room . . . anarchistic principles": "Purple Lights." "Sam, give it": Eric Greenspan. "a great document . . . abusive press": David Felton, *Rolling Stone,* 8/5/71.

JG outside band: JG, SP, John Kahn, Howard Wales, Merl Saunders, Freddie Herrera. "John and I played . . . are we in": JG in Sievert, "Jerry Garcia." "Go out and bring": SP. "I played big fat . . . conventional player": JG in Sievert, "Jerry Garcia." "You bored . . . this weekend": BW. Hérouville: band, Rosie McGee, JM, Bob Matthews. "Monsieur, *look*": Rosie McGee in Brandelius, p. 72. "He told us that . . . need much": Coyote, p. 228.

Chapter 35: Stinson Beach: JG, MG, JM, AT, Richard Loren, David Grisman, Sue Stephens, Goldie Rush. "Being able to move . . . anything like that": JG in Peacock, "Jerry Garcia." Solo album: JG, RH, RS, RR, BK, Bob Matthews. "I just succumbed": "GD Bust," *Rolling Stone,* 9/2/71. "The Lord has forgiven . . . big ones": Joe Smith. "100 percent level . . . design": AT, "Notes Toward Deadpatch," G.D. archives. "the twelve principles . . . give it a try": JG in Reich, pp. 214, 222. *Skullfuck:* JG, PL, JM. "I didn't like anybody . . . an attitude": PL in Haas, "Drink." "It's not me, Joe . . . to you": JM in Jackson, "Jon McIntire." "We've set up the tables . . . all prisoners": Scully and Dalton, p. 209. "Oh, we wanted . . . our part": JG in Hunt, "Jerry Garcia." "not only great American . . . Dead fan": Bangs, "Review."

"we spurred him toward": BW to Gary Lambert. Keith Godchaux: Donna Jean Godchaux MacKay, JM, PL. "My husband and I . . . there's this guy": Donna Jean Godchaux MacKay. "It had to happen . . . a vision": Keith Godchaux in G.D. program, 4/72. "I had a dream . . . only direction": Donna Jean Godchaux, ibid. "Regulars greeted": Christgau, *Any Old,* p. 277.

Chapter 36. "Having been born . . . music heard": Willy Legate, *Dead Head Newsletter.* "Rock Scully's Ground . . . for them anyway": G.D. archives. "almost-daily telephone . . . at a time": Catherine Peters, "Dead Ahead." "not merely as the manager": Derek Sutton in Scherman, "Capitalism." "very organized": Clive Davis. "There is scarcely one . . . music field": Dannen, p. 143. Hal Kant: Hal Kant.

Chapter 37. *Europe '72* cover: Alton Kelley. Tour: band, MG, Jim Furman, Dennis Leonard, AT, RS, Sam Cutler. "Fuck it": SP. "Look out . . . molecular": Scully and Dalton, p. 216. "Y'know, a lot . . . interesting": Candace Brightman. "my only vices": Kent, *Melody Maker.* "There's a sort of peak . . . hang out there": JG in Peacock, "Jerry Garcia." Record company rap in London: Peacock, "Jerry Garcia." "held their madness": AT in Wembley program. Geomancy: JG, PL, AT. "buses which came . . . raison d'etre": Willy Legate essay, liner notes, *Europe '72.* "surrealism as metaphor": Willy Legate to AT, 10/82. "Is hypnocracy not": ibid. "it's considered bad . . . fuck ups": Charles Perry, "A New Life." "Here ya are": Jerry Hopkins, "The Beautiful Dead." "Dead had offered safe": Mark Cooper, "Dead but Unburied." "Hey, you guys . . . rental car": PL. "Those things run . . . running": MG. "Hal, we have a problem . . . $15,000": Hal Kant.

"trying to pass themselves": Elman, p. 12. "Alla Rakha": Christgau, *Any Old*, p. 250. Roosevelt: Ron Rainey, John Scher. "Hey, Keith, d'ya": Aronowitz, "Moon Jasmine." Return of Bear: OS, SP. "Sunshine Daydream": Phil DeGuere. "Amnesty, Abortion": Thompson, *Shark*, p. 259. "I'll get elected . . . marijuana": JG. "Which freezes first": BW, BK. "Fuck you, pig": BW. "In the realms of hip . . . separate ways": Carr, "Real Good Hamburger." "Clive, are you sure . . . hear it right": Michael Klenfner. "It was an incredible": Clive Davis, p. 187.

Chapter 38: "I don't want you around": Veronica Barnard Grant. "Seems like there's . . .": Grateful Dead Archives. Pigpen's death: DH, Dave Parker. "If there's one thing": BW.

Old and in the Way: JG, David Grisman, Richard Loren. "We need a bass": David Grisman. "Shit, why don't . . . is fun": JG in Grissim, "Garcia Returns." "At this point . . . around then": Joel Selvin, "Garcia Returns." New Jersey arrest: JG, RH, Sam Cutler, John Scher. "You know I can't let": RH. "tired of working": RH, "Not Necessarily," p. 6. Formation of record company: band, Hal Kant, AT, RS; see Charles Perry, "A New Life." "maximally enthused . . . events going on": Ron Rakow in Greenfield, pp. 142, 144. "Ron is such a weak . . . think he could": Hal Kant in Greenfield, p. 144. "It's the most exciting . . . with us": JG in Grissim, "Garcia Returns."

Out of Town Tours: Sam Cutler, Gail Turner, Rita Gentry. Record company: band, JM, RS, Steve Brown, Bob Seidemann, Chesley Millikin, Emily Craig, Eileen Law. "Don't you understand": DR. Sound system: Ron Wickersham, DH, OS, Bob Matthews, John Curl. Watkins Glen: band, Sam Cutler, JM, DR, Jim Koplik, Jim Furman; see Helm and Davis. "Who are you . . . work with the Grateful Dead": Jim Koplik. "We have four or five . . . are great": John Swenson, "The Sound." "I remember that Jerry . . . we left": Butch Trucks in Gilmore, p. 134. "And the sea gave up": Revelation 20:13. "Right now, somehow . . . more interesting": JG in Charles Perry, "A New Life."

Chapter 39: "What's the dumbest . . . That": Alex Bennett, WMCA, 9/16/70. "When I'm really getting": JG in Territo, *Marin IJ*. "When the Dead are playing . . . responsibility": RH, "Dark Star." "Suddenly the music . . . are clear": Lydon, p. 133. "Music heard so deeply": T. S. Eliot, "The Dry Salvages," *Four Quartets*. "The barriers on the world . . . Pied Piper": Lydon, p. 134.

Chapter 40: "taking a vacation": band meeting minutes, 1/14/74, G.D. archives. Hell's Angel message: Rita Gentry. *Compliments:* JG, John Kahn, Richard Loren. Money from February gigs: 1/2/74 band meeting minutes, G.D. Archives. "Like piloting . . . soundwave": PL in Wasserman, "The Dead." "the ultimate derivation": DH in Wasserman, "The Dead." "quite an acceptable": Alembic Notes, G.D. Archives. "physical model": JG in Block.

"The Book": G.D. archives. "Dear Guerrilla": G.D. archives. "The way they describe it . . . your head": JG in "Interview," *Circus*. "a virtually infinite": PL in *ZigZag*. "so musically inbred": BW in Gans, *Conversations*, p. 120. "I am as coked up . . . but what": Scully and Dalton, p. 238. "The most rewarding . . . people through this": JG in *Melody Maker*, 9/14/74. "What are you looking . . . Mercedes-Benzes": Chesley Millikin. "There was a

bench . . . to get there": Hal Kant. "to rest, recuperate": Herb Caen, *S.F. Chronicle,*
9/17/74. "The kids are walking . . . all the groups": BG in *The Grateful Dead Movie.* Hart's
return: MH, Jerilyn Brandelius, BK. "Well, we'll put . . . you got that": Jerilyn Brandelius.
"This is the first time": MH. "Listen, if there's one . . . didn't work": Stokes, "Death." "We
falter and . . . a relief": RH, 5/74 Dead Head mailer, G.D. archives.

Chapter 41. Hiatus: band, Hal Kant, Richard Loren, David Parker, Eileen Law, DR,
Sue Swanson, AT, Joe Winslow, Jim Furman. Private lives: JG, Deborah Jahnke, Goldie
Rush, BW, Frankie Azzara, Eileen Law.
Blues for Allah: band, Robbie Taylor, DH, RS. "wasn't listening to things . . . different
sensibility": JG to Gans, 4/28/81. "power-rock raver": JG in Timothy White, "From the
Beatles." "Look, I'm political . . . abstruse": Barry Melton. "Listen, I need a song": JB.
"Dear Guerrilla": 1/27/75 letter to Dead Heads from G.D. Records, G.D. archives. "A
horrible bummer": PL in Platt, *Lode.*
"[Garcia] and I talked . . . great, man": David Crosby in Zimmer, p. 180. Show at
Great American Music Hall: band, Mort Feld. "Dear Dead Heads: After going": band letter to Dead Heads, 8/75, G.D. archives. "and a decision that vacationing . . . for sure":
band letter to Dead Heads, 1/76, G.D. archives. "if we get lucky": JG on KSAN, 1/23/76.
"the survival of . . . else either": JG in Weitzman, "A Chat." "Should my daughter . . .
backstage, man": Ron Rakow in Greenfield, p. 176. Musical Christmas card: MH. "I'll
show you . . . looks up": Laird Grant. Rakow and United: see Rakow in Greenfield, pp.
178–79. "I was the family . . . was Hal Kant": ibid, p. 177. "We had sixteen tracks . . .
pissed on his shoes": PL in Block, "Garcia." Mixing "Diga": MH. "Or do I make sure":
Rakow to Greenfield, pp. 178–79. "I'm cutting out . . . strangle Jerry": PL.

Chapter 42. "John, explain to people": John Scher. Moon story: JG, BW. Arista:
band, Clive Davis, Michael Klenfner. "Shitty . . . how to do it": JG in Rainier, "Interview."
"and I say I don't think . . . the transformation": JM in Jackson, "Jon McIntire." "It seemed
to most": BW on "Album Network" radio special. "This might be an off-the-wall . . . I understand": Clive Davis to JG c/o Richard Loren, 4/11/78, G.D. archives. "Garcia never
made it": Keith Olsen in Selvin, "Guiding Hand." "it freaked me . . . loved it": BW in "Album Network" radio special. "about as close": RH letter to JG on the anniversary of his
death, 8/9/96, G.D. archives. "two years of incredible doubt . . . depressed": JG to Charles
Young, "The Awakening." "I wanted elegantly . . . conception": JG in Block, "Garcia."
"Our willingness": ibid. "You're going to distribute . . . this is the Grateful Dead": John
Scher. "Aural excitement": Lawrence Van Gelder, *New York Times,* 6/3/77. "which, as a
short . . . its audience": Wasserman, "GD Film." "justifies itself visually . . . his magic":
Robert Christgau, *Village Voice,* 6/13/77.
"I hope you have been . . . you know": Hart and Stevens, *Edge,* p. 181. "sparse": JG to
Mary Eisenhart. "put the Grateful Dead": MH. "incongruous": PL in "Album Network"
radio special. "Fuck 'em": JG in Block, "Garcia." "so rude, so outrageous . . . public alike":
Saporita, p. 79.

Chapter 43. "Have you ever played . . . right there": PL. Origins of trip: PL, AT,
Richard Loren, Goldie Rush. Appeal to Graham: PL, MH. "No, Bill": MH. "Two count
them": telegram to Sue Stephens, 3/21/78, G.D. archives. "Mix in your mind . . . Cairo
Cacophany": Kesey, *Demon Box,* p. 101. "an unlit boulevard . . . thighcarts": ibid., p. 99.

"Burned": Nichols. "Everyone seemed to be yelling . . . Baksheesh": Nichols, pp. 40–41. "I have the heart . . . woman": ibid., p. 71. "indefinite sustain": DH on WBCN, 11/14/78. "It's a multidimensional": Kesey, *Demon Box,* p. 144. "This place has really . . . normal sense": JG in Watts, *Melody Maker.* "Here it's okay": Jeff Boden. "It makes me feel": MH. "R'all yew guys": Max Bell, "Pyramid Prank." "give me, as they must": Ashraf Ghorbal to Jerry Garcia, 10/10/78, G.D. archives.

Chapter 44: "amazing. It had . . . was the same": Coppola, p. 278. "In the beginning . . . live with": Hart and Stevens, *Edge,* p. 10. "People play music . . . consciousness": MH in Jackson, "Drums and Dreams," 24. "drumming . . . madness": Linda Ellerbee.

Chapter 45. "the victory party": Hirshey, *Rolling Stone.* "You can do it": BK. *SNL:* Tom Davis. "No . . . I don't care": Tom Davis. "We stink": MH. "You know the conga . . . sucked": MH. "You're the promoter": Jim Koplik. "The bulk of the space . . . my collection": BG to Richard Loren, 11/9/78, G.D. archives. "there is 100 times . . . Miami": BG in Selvin, *S.F. Chronicle,* 12/21/78. "invited too many bikers . . . problems backstage": BG in Graham and Greenfield, p. 423. Departure of Keith and Donna: Donna Jean Godchaux MacKay. Brent Mydland bio: BM.

California-ization: see Ciotti, "Revenge"; Blake Green, "California"; Saltus, "Continental." "It is no coincidence . . . *into* shape": Haas, "Drink." "They came together . . . faith in it": JB in *Swing 51.* "Clive Davis actually . . . kill myself": PL in Platt, *Lode.* "Mediocrity on the march": *Playboy,* 8/80. "uninspired fluff": J. DeMatteis, *Rolling Stone,* 8/7/80. "We do not want to be": Timothy Wachtel in Grushkin, p. 11. "Record more than": MH.

"right slide projector . . . a sale": BG notes, G.D. archives. Sound development: DH, Don Pearson, Howard Danchik, John Meyer.

Chapter 47. "You're just a . . . sheer reasonableness": Morley, "What a Long." "Dear sir and brother": PL, G.D. archives. "limitless capacity for denial": Frances FitzGerald, *New Yorker,* 12/24/90. "Why are you asking . . . unhappy with you": Hal Kant. "The other night I experienced . . . complete": Dorris, "Concert Sound." "teaching occasionally . . . order to exist": JM in Jackson, "Jon McIntire." "Get [Scrib] to do it . . . that shit": Mary Jo Meinolf. "Come in, sit down": Tom Davis. "Twilight Zone": Phil DeGuere, MH, Merl Saunders, Hal Kant. "Man, I *live*": JG to Merl Saunders.

"I started feeling like . . . the hospital": JG to Brown and Novick, *Voices,* p. 69. "Jerry's in the bathroom . . . 911": BW. "My main experience . . . like my bloodstream": JG to Brown and Novick, *Voices,* p. 68. "Be tactful . . . Beethoven": MG in Greenfield, p. 217. "taunted and derided . . . to hear that": letter from RH to JG, 8/9/86, G.D. archives.

Chapter 48. JG recovery: JG, MH, Merl Saunders, Laird Grant, MG, Sandy Rothman. "It took a while . . . all that": JG to Sievert, "Jerry Garcia." "kind of like a father . . . together for me": JG to Marre, "At the Edge." "Those lyin' sons . . . don't agree": JG in Marcus and Gans. "vast and it's hopeless . . . other side": RH to Silberman, "Standing." "I just want to know . . . lately": BW in "Album Network" radio special. "Another year, another classic": Randolph Smith, *Hampton Daily Press,* 3/24/87. "The Dead and Garcia": Steve Morse, *Boston Globe,* 4/3/87. "radder, riskier . . . save your life": Gehr, "Dead Zone."

"Lemme ask you . . . Not me": Sean Coakley. "nostalgia mongers": Dave Marsh in Gilmore, "New Dawn." "[It] bespeaks an effortlessness . . . in years": Browne, "Bob Dylan." "The best Dead songs . . . to every rule": Jon Pareles, "The Grateful Dead." "There were plenty . . . different way": BW in Sutherland, "Acid Daze." "It was easy to suspect": Derk Richardson, *Bay Guardian*, 8/5/87. "taught me to look inside . . . at the time": Bob Dylan in *Mojo*, 2/98. "Too literal": Len Dell'Amico in Jackson, "The Making of *So Far.*" 14. Garcia Band on Broadway: JG, SP, David Nelson, Sandy Rothman. "This is great . . . somewhere": David Nelson. "I see more light . . . understanding": JG to Mary Eisenhart. "When I hear his playing . . . sounds right": JG in Sievert, "Jerry Garcia." "I wouldn't say we've got . . . propriety": Voelpel, "Dead Heads." "Well, it's a hideous . . . to play": JG in *Golden Road* 18.

"Fuck 'em . . . if I want": JG to Hal Kant. "potential riot": Cameron Cosgrove in Billiter, "Amphitheatre." "Give it to her . . . her lights": Candace Brightman. "We create a deadline . . . hellish": BW in Timothy White, "From the Beatles." "But what the concert . . . with conviction": Pareles, "Just What." "as much as an inch": Lacey, "Police."

Chapter 49. "If you want coherence": PL to Frost and Wanger, radio. "I just see us . . . won't hurt anybody": JG in Fedele, "Fuck No." "We're a band . . . something": BW to ? "anybody in the Grateful . . . real loud": JG in Reich, p. 160. "They do something": JB in Ken Hunt, "John Barlow." "I've always called . . . organism": source unknown. "For me it's a vehicle . . . I'm here": DH in Gans, p. 160. "It's embarrassing . . . remember": JG in *Boston Phoenix*, 1974. "I think basically . . . to get high": JG in Reich, pp. 127, 86. "Coming to see . . . not work": JG and BW in Gans, *Conversations*, p. 13. "Ugly but honest . . . good enough": JG in Haas, "Drink."

Chapter 50. "It's silly for us . . . no underwear": Barron, "Few Drug Arrests." "What we should do": David Grisman. "[Garcia's] a virtuoso . . . for me": Warren Zevon to Steve Morse, *Boston Globe*, in *Golden Road* 22. "Those guys can play . . . *fantastic*": Branford Marsalis in Pooley, "Raising." "On Thursday night . . . would be": Marsalis in G.D. archives.

"He was willing to die . . . what he was doing": JG in Henke, "Jerry Garcia." "didn't care if they . . . place to be": David Kemper in Barry Smolin, *Dupree's Diamond News*, spring 1997.

"We must change": unpublished MS, courtesy of Robert Hunter. "exquisite": RH to Selvin, "Dead Songwriters." "Yeah. I can't stand it . . . going to happen": JG in Steve Morse, *Boston Globe*, 9/25/91.

Chapter 53. JG: JG, Brigid Meier, PL, RH, Vince Di Biase. "a wonderful talker . . . a kind of love": Barich, "Still Truckin'." "I just want to sing": Paddy Moloney. "Always a hoot": BW. "What's happening . . . dobro player": David Grisman. "Down from the bottom . . . you're playing": session tape, courtesy of David Grisman. "Can you finish": David Grisman. "shaky, and his willpower . . . this time": Sue Stephens. "He is the very spirit . . . and subtle": Bob Dylan in *Rolling Stone* (eds.), *Garcia*, p. 30. "He said-a dat . . . to me": Barbara Meier and Sara Katz, in Greenfield, p. 337.

Chapter 54. "I've discovered . . . with it": Dan Healy in Gans, *Conversations*, p. 158. "Say you were . . . I'd want": JG in Territo, *Marin IJ*. "There's an old Prankster . . . the merrier": JG in Tamarkin, "Jerry Garcia." "Basically I prefer . . . the All": JG in Stoddard. "series of events": Krippner, *Siren,* p. 24. "We know from our own . . . for us": JG in Haas, "Drink." "Synchronicity . . . to the One": JG in Stoddard. "Uncertainty is what's . . . IT": JG in Haas, "Drink." "You hear the same sound": RH, "Endless Parenthesis," *Night Cadre,* p. 77.

Bibliography

Aldrich, Michael R. *A Brief Legal History of Marihuana.* Do It Now Foundation, n.d.

Allen, Scott. *Aces Back to Back: A Guide to the Grateful Dead.* New York: Pierce-Axiom, 1992.

Anson, Robert Sam. *Gone Crazy and Back Again: The Rise and Fall of the Rolling Stone Generation.* Garden City, N.Y.: Doubleday & Co., 1981.

Anthony, Gene. *The Summer of Love.* Millbrae, Calif.: Celestial Arts, 1980.

Babbs, Ken, ed. "Spit in the Ocean," vol. 1, no. 1, "Old in the Streets." Pleasant Hill, Ore., 1974.

Balfour, Victoria. *Rock Wives.* New York: Beech Tree Books, William Morrow, 1986.

Bane, Michael. *Willie.* New York: Dell, 1984.

Barger, Sonny. *Hell's Angel.* New York: William Morrow, 2000.

Barnes, Richard. *The Who: Maximum Rhythm & Blues.* New York: St. Martin's Press, 1982.

Bell, Dale, ed. *Woodstock.* Studio City, Calif.: Michael Wiese Productions, 1999.

Bettemeyer, Peter. *How My Heart Sings.* New Haven, Conn.: Yale University Press, 1998.

Bill Graham Presents Scrapbooks.

Biskind, Peter. *Easy Riders, Raging Bulls.* New York: Simon & Schuster, 1998.

Blush, Margaret, et al. "The Demography of the Haight-Ashbury, June 1969." Unpublished group research project, U.C. Berkeley School of Social Welfare. Fitzhugh Ludlow Memorial Library.

Bockris, Victor. *Keith Richards.* New York: Poseidon Press, 1992.

Booth, Stanley. *Keith.* New York: St. Martin's Press, 1995.

———. *The True Adventures of the Rolling Stones.* New York: Vintage Books, 1985.

Boyd, Douglas. *Rolling Thunder.* New York: Dell, 1974.

Brandelius, Jerilyn. *Grateful Dead Family Album.* New York: Warner Books, 1989.

Brook, Danae, ed. *The Book of the DEAD.* London: Warner Brothers Records, 1972.

Brown, David Jay, and Rebecca McClen Novick. *Voices from the Edge.* Freedom, Calif.: Crossing Press, 1995.

Bugliosi, Vincent, with Curt Gentry. *Helter Skelter.* New York: Bantam Books, 1975.

Burch, Claire. *Dead Heads: Rago & Friends.* Berkeley, Calif.: Art & Education Media, 1992.

Butler, Dougal. *Full Moon.* New York: William Morrow, 1981.

Cahill, Thomas. *How the Irish Saved Civilization.* New York: Doubleday, 1995.

Caserta, Peggy (as told to Dan Knapp). *Going Down with Janis.* New York: Dell, 1973.

Christgau, Robert. *Any Old Way You Choose It.* Baltimore: Penguin Books, 1974.

———. *Grown Up All Wrong.* Cambridge, Mass.: Harvard University Press, 1998.

Cohen, Tom. *Hungry i Revisited.* Transcripts from the film, including interviews with Mort Sahl, Stan Wilson, Lou Gottlieb, etc. Hammermark Productions, P.O. Box 802, Mill Valley, CA.

Constanten, Tom. "Between Rock and Hard Places: An Autobiopsy." Unpublished MS, 1985.

———. *Between Rock and Hard Places: A Musical Autobiodyssey.* Eugene, Ore.: Hulogosi Books, 1992.

———. "Music Lists." Unpublished MS, June 9, 1989.

Cooper, Michael, et al. *The Early Stones.* New York: Hyperion, 1992.

Copeland, Alan, ed. *People's Park.* New York: Ballantine Books, 1969.

Coppola, Eleanor. *Notes.* New York: Simon & Schuster, 1979.

Cornyn, Stan. *Exploding.* New York: HarperEntertainment, 2002.

Coupland, Douglas. *Generation X.* New York: St. Martin's Press, 1991.

Coyote, Peter. *Sleeping Where I Fall.* Washington, D.C.: Counterpoint, 1998.

Crone, Richard. *Hippi Hi.* Self-published, San Francisco, n.d.

Crosby, David, and Carl Gottlieb. *Long Time Gone.* New York: Doubleday, 1988.

Dalton, David. *Janis.* New York: Popular Library, 1971.

Dannen, Fredric. *Hit Men.* New York: Times Books, 1990.

Davis, Clive, with James Willwerth. *Clive: Inside the Record Business.* New York: Ballantine, 1974.

Davis, Miles, with Quincy Troupe. *Miles.* New York: Simon & Schuster, 1989.

Davis, R. G. *The San Francisco Mime Troupe: The First 10 Years.* Palo Alto, Calif.: Ramparts Press, 1975.

DeCurtis, Anthony, et al. *The Rolling Stone Illustrated History of Rock and Roll.* New York: Random House, 1992.

DeRogatis, Jim. *Let It Blurt.* New York: Broadway Books, 2000.

DesBarres, Pamela. *I'm with the Band.* New York: William Morrow, 1987.

de Wilde, Laurent. *Monk.* New York: Marlowe & Co., 1997.

Dickstein, Morris. *Gates of Eden.* New York: Basic Books, 1975.

DiFranco, J. Philip, ed. *The Beatles: A Hard Day's Night.* New York: Penguin, 1978.

Downing, David. *Jack Nicholson.* New York: Stein & Day, 1984.

Draper, Hal. *Berkeley: The New Student Revolt.* New York: Grove Press, 1965.

Duberman, Martin. *Black Mountain.* Garden City, N.Y.: Anchor Press, 1973.

Dylan, Bob. *Writings and Drawings.* New York: Alfred A. Knopf, 1973.

Echols, Alice. *Scars of Sweet Paradise.* New York: Metropolitan Books, Henry Holt & Co., 1999.

Editors of Dupree's Diamond News. Garcia: A Grateful Celebration, 1995.

Ehrlich, Dimitri. *Inside the Music.* Boston: Shambhala, 1997.

Eisen, Jonathan, ed. *The Age of Rock.* New York: Vintage Books, 1969.

Eliot, T. S. *Collected Poems.* New York: Harcourt Brace Jovanovich, 1963.

Elliott, Anthony. *The Mourning of John Lennon.* Berkeley, Calif.: University of California Press, 1999.

Elman, Richard. *Uptight with the Stones.* New York: Charles Scribner's Sons, 1972.

Epstein, Jason. *The Great Conspiracy Trial.* New York: Random House, 1970.

Evans-Wentz, W. Y., ed. *The Tibetan Book of the Dead.* Oxford University Press, 1960.

Farina, Richard. *Been Down So Long It Looks Like Up to Me.* New York: Dell, 1966.

Farr, Jory. *Moguls and Madmen.* New York: Simon & Schuster, 1994.

Fawcett, Anthony. *John Lennon One Day at a Time.* New York: Grove Press, 1976.

Felton, David, ed. *Mindfuckers.* San Francisco: Straight Arrow Books, 1972.

Fitch, Bob. *Hippie Is Necessary.* San Francisco: Glide Urban Center, 1967.

Fong-Torres, Ben. *The Hits Just Keep on Coming.* San Francisco: Miller Freeman, 1998.

Formento, Dan. *Rock Chronicle.* New York: Putnam Publishing Group, 1982.

Foster, Paul. *The Answer Is Always Yes.* Eugene, Ore.: Hulogosi Books, 1995.

Frame, Pete. *Rock Family Trees.* London and New York: Omnibus Press, 1980.

Franzosa, Bob. *Grateful Dead Folktales.* Orono, Maine: Zosafarm Publications, 1989.

Friedman, Myra. *Buried Alive.* New York: William Morrow, 1973.

Fulbright, J. William. *The Arrogance of Power.* New York: Vintage, 1966.

Gans, David. *Conversations with the Dead.* New York: Citadel Press, 1991.

———, ed. *Not Fade Away.* Thunder's Mouth Press, 1995.

Garcia, Jerry. *Harrington Street.* New York: Delacorte Press, 1995.

———. *Paintings, Drawings & Sketches.* Berkeley, Calif.: Celestial Arts, 1992.

Garcia, Jerry, and Tom Davis. *The Sirens of Titan.* Unpublished film script, 1988.

Garcia, Jerry, Charles Reich, and Jann Wenner. *Garcia: The Rolling Stone Interview.* San Francisco: Straight Arrow Books, 1972.

Gardner, June Ericson. *Olompali: In the Beginning.* Fort Bragg, Calif.: Cypress House Press, 1995.

Gaskin, Stephen. *Free.* Talk at Longshoremen's Hall, San Francisco, 12/10/76. Self-published.

———. *Haight Street Flashbacks.* Berkeley, Calif.: Ronin, 1990.

———. *Hey Beatnik!* Summertown, Tenn.: The Book Publishing Co., 1974.

George-Warren, Holly, ed. *The Rolling Stone Book of the Beats.* New York: Hyperion, 1999.

Gerould, Gordon H. *The Grateful Dead: The History of a Folk Story.* David Nutt, 57 Long Acre, London, 1908.

Getz, Michael, and John Dwork. *The Deadhead's Taping Compendium V. I.* New York: Henry Holt & Co., 1998.

Gilmore, Mikal. *Night Beat.* New York: Doubleday, 1998.

Gleason, Ralph J. *The Jefferson Airplane and the San Francisco Sound.* New York: Ballantine Books, 1969.

Goldrosen, John. *The Buddy Holly Story.* New York: Quick Fox Books, 1979.

Goldstein, Richard. *Goldstein's Greatest Hits.* Englewood Cliffs, N.J.: Prentice-Hall, 1970.

Goodman, Fred. *The Mansion on the Hill.* New York Times Books, 1997.

Gordon, Max. *Live at the Village Vanguard.* New York: Da Capo Press, 1980.

Graham, Bill, and Robert Greenfield. *Bill Graham Presents.* New York: Doubleday, 1992.

The Grateful Dead Movie. Unpublished shooting script, 1974.

Green, Justin. *The Binky Brown Sampler.* San Francisco: Last Gasp, 1995.

Greene, Herb. *Book of the Dead.* New York: Delacorte Press, 1990.

———. *Dead Days.* Petaluma, Calif.: Acid Test Productions, 1994.

Greenfield, Robert. *Dark Star.* New York: William Morrow, 1996.

Gregory, Dick. *Write Me In!* New York: Bantam Books, 1968.

Griffith, Robert. *The Politics of Fear.* Hayden, 1970.

Grissim, John, Jr. *We Have Come for Your Daughters.* New York: William Morrow, 1972.

Grogan, Emmett. *Ringolevio.* New York: Avon, 1972.

Grushkin, Paul, et al. *Grateful Dead: The Official Book of the Dead Heads.* New York: Quill, 1983.

Halberstam, David. *The Best and the Brightest.* New York: Fawcett Crest, 1972.

Hamill, Pete. *Why Sinatra Matters.* Boston: Little, Brown & Company, 1998.

Hansberry, Lorraine. *The Movement.* New York: Simon & Schuster, 1964.

Harris, Marvin. *America Now.* New York: Simon & Schuster, 1981.

Harrison, Hank. *The Dead.* Millbrae, Calif.: Celestial Arts, 1980.

———. *The Dead Book.* New York: Links Books, 1973.

Hart, Mickey, and Fredric Lieberman, with D. A. Sonneborn. *Planet Drum.* San Francisco: HarperSan Francisco, 1991.

Hart, Mickey, with Jay Stevens. *Drumming at the Edge of Magic.* San Francisco: HarperSan Francisco, 1990.

Helm, Levon, and Stephen Davis. *This Wheel's on Fire.* New York: William Morrow, 1993.

Henderson, David. *Jimi Hendrix: Voodoo Child of the Aquarian Age.* Garden City, N.Y.: Doubleday, 1978.

Hennesey, Mike. *Klook: The Story of Kenny Clarke.* Pittsburgh: University of Pittsburgh Press, 1990.

Hill, Sam, and Glenn Rifkin. *Radical Marketing.* New York: HarperBusiness, 1999.

Hills, Tim. "Crystal Ballroom History." Unpublished MS, 1996.

Hirsh, Diana. *The World of Turner 1775–1851.* New York: Time-Life Books, 1969.

Hoffman, Abbie. *Woodstock Nation.* New York: Time-Life Books, 1969.

Hofmann, Albert. *LSD: My Problem Child.* Los Angeles: J. P. Tarcher, 1983.

Hopkins, Jerry. *Hit and Run.* New York: Perigee, 1983.

Hopkins, Jerry, and Danny Sugerman. *No One Here Gets Out Alive.* New York: Warner Books, 1980.

Hoskyns, Barney. *Beneath the Diamond Sky.* London: Bloomsbury Publishing, 1997.

Hunter, Robert. *A Box of Rain.* New York: Viking Press, 1990.

———. *Glass Lunch.* New York: Penguin Poets, 1997.

———. *Night Cadre.* New York: Viking, 1991.

———. *The Silver Snarling Trumpet.* Unpublished MS.

———. *A Strange Music.* Unpublished MS, draft #3, 3/4/91.

Jackson, Phil, and Hugh Delehanty. *Sacred Hoops.* New York: Hyperion, 1995.

Jeffers, Robinson. *Selected Poems.* New York: Vintage Books, 1964.

Jefferson Airplane Scrapbooks. San Francisco: The Airplane House, 1965–1980.

Jones, Leroi. *Black Music.* New York: William Morrow, 1968.

———. *Blues People.* New York: William Morrow, 1963.

Joseph, Peter. *Good Times.* New York: Charterhouse, 1976.

Kael, Pauline. *Reeling.* New York: Warner Books, 1976.

Kandel, Lenore. *Word Alchemy.* New York: Grove Press, 1967.

Karman, James. *Robinson Jeffers: Poet of California.* Brownsville, Ore.: Story Line Press, 1995.

Katzman, Allen. *Our Time.* EVO interviews. New York: Dial Press, 1972.

Kearns, Doris. *Lyndon Johnson and the American Dream.* New York: Signet, 1976.

Kelly, Linda. *Deadheads.* New York: Citadel Press, 1995.

Kesey, Ken. *Demon Box.* New York: Viking, 1986.

———. *The Further Inquiry.* New York: Viking/Penguin, 1990.

———. *Garage Sale.* New York: Viking, 1973.

———. *One Flew over the Cuckoo's Nest.* New York: Viking, 1962.

———. *Sometimes A Great Notion.* New York: Bantam Books, 1963.

Kleps, Art. *Millbrook.* Oakland, Calif.: Bench Press, 1975.

Knight, Curtis. *Jimi.* New York: Praeger, 1974.

Koller, James. *Like It Was.* Noblesboro, Maine: Blackberry Books, 1999.

Kornbluth, Jesse, ed. *Notes from the New Underground.* New York: Viking, 1968.

Kosinsky, Jerzy. *Pinball.* New York: Bantam Books, 1982.

Kramer, Daniel. *Bob Dylan.* N.J.: Castle Books, 1967.

Krassner, Paul. *How a Satirical Editor Became a Yippie Conspirator in Ten Easy Years.* New York: G. P. Putnam's Sons, 1971.

Krippner, Stanley. *Song of the Siren.* New York: Harper Colophon Books, 1977.

Kunen, James Simon. *The Strawberry Statement.* New York: Avon, 1970.

Landau, Jon. *It's Too Late to Stop Now.* Straight Arrow Books, 1972.

Landy, Elliott. *Woodstock 1969.* Santa Rosa, Calif.: Squarebooks, 1994.

Lasch, Christopher. *The New Radicalism in America.* New York: Vintage Books, 1965.

Leary, Timothy. *Flashbacks.* New York: G. P. Putnam's Sons, 1983.

Lee, Martin A., and Bruce Shlain. *Acid Dreams.* New York: Grove Press, 1985.

Lehman, Alan. "Music as Symbolic Communication: The Grateful Dead and Their Fans." Ph.D. diss., University of Maryland, 1994.

Lichtenstein, Grace. *Desperado.* New York: Dial Press, 1977.

Litweiler, John. *Ornette Coleman.* New York: Da Capo Press, 1992.

Lomax, Alan. *The Land Where the Blues Began.* New York: Pantheon Books, 1993.

Lydon, Michael. *Rock Folk.* New York: Delta, 1973.

Marcus, Greil. *Invisible Republic.* New York: Henry Holt & Co., 1997.

———. *Mystery Train.* New York: Dutton, 1976.

Marcus, Greil, ed. *Rock and Roll Will Stand.* Boston: Beacon Press, 1969.

Marks, J. *Mick Jagger.* New York: Curtis Books, 1973.

Marsh, Dave. *Born to Run: The Bruce Springsteen Story.* New York: Dell, 1981.

McClelland, Gordon. *Rick Griffin.* Paper Tiger, 1980.

McClure, Michael. *The Adept.* New York: Delacorte Press, 1971.

———. *Lighting the Corners.* Albuquerque: University of New Mexico Press, 1993.

McDonough, Jack. *San Francisco Rock.* San Francisco: Chronicle Books, 1985.

McKenna, Terence. *Food of the Gods.* New York: Bantam Books, 1992.

———. *True Hallucinations.* San Francisco: HarperSan Francisco, 1993.

McNally, Dennis. *Desolate Angel: Jack Kerouac, the Beat Generation, and America.* New York: Random House, 1979.

McNeill, Don. *Moving Through Here.* New York: Alfred A. Knopf, 1970.

Meadoff, Jan, ed. *The Hippies.* San Francisco: Meadoff and Rosenberg, Michael Idlewild Publishing Co., 1967.

Medved, Michael, and David Wallechinsky. *What Really Happened to the Class of '65?* New York: Ballantine Books, 1976.

Meier, Barbara. *The Life You Ordered Has Arrived.* Berkeley, Calif.: Parallax Press, 1988.

Meltzer, David. "Rock Tao." Unpublished MS.

Meltzer, R. *The Aesthetics of Rock.* New York: Something Else Press, 1970.

Millard, Andre. *America on Record.* New York: Cambridge University Press, 1995.

Miller, James. *Flowers in the Dustbin.* New York: Simon & Schuster, 1999.

Miller, Stanley, and Alton Kelley. *Mouse and Kelley.* New York: Delta, 1979.

Mingus, Charles. *Beneath the Underdog.* Penguin Books, 1980.

Mountain Girl. *The Primo Plant.* Berkeley, Calif.: Leaves of Grass, Wingbow Press, 1977.

Mouse, Stanley. *Freehand: The Art of Stanley Mouse.* Berkeley, Calif.: SLG Books, 1993.

Myrus, Donald, ed. *Law and Disorder.* ACLU, 1968.

Neer, Richard. *FM.* New York: Villard, 2001.

Newfield, Jack. *The Prophetic Minority.* New York: New American Library, 1966.

Nichols, Robert. *Truckin' with the Grateful Dead.* San Rafael, Calif.: Moonbow Press, 1984.

Nisker, Wesley "Scoop." *If You Don't Like the News.* Berkeley, Calif.: Ten Speed Press, 1994.

Norman, Gurney. *Divine Right's Trip.* New York: Bantam, 1972. First appeared in *The Last Whole Earth Catalogue*, 1971.

Norman, Philip. *Shout! The Beatles in Their Generation.* New York: Warner Books, 1981.

Obst, David. *Too Good to Be Forgotten.* New York: John Wiley & Sons, 1998.

Obst, Lynda Rosen. *The Sixties.* New York: Random House/Rolling Stone, 1977.

Oliver, Paul. *The Meaning of the Blues.* New York: Collier Books, 1960.

Palmer, Robert. *Rock and Roll.* New York: Harmony Books, 1994.

Peck, Abe. *Uncovering the Sixties.* New York: Pantheon Books, 1985.

Peckham, Morse. *Beyond the Tragic Vision.* New York: George Braziller, 1962.

Perry, Charles. *The Haight Ashbury.* New York: Random House, Rolling Stone Press, 1984.

Perry, Paul. *On the Bus.* New York: Thunder's Mouth Press, 1996

Petersen, Bobby. *Collected Poems.* Eugene, Ore.: Hulagosi Press, 1992.

Phillips, John. *Papa John.* New York: Dell, 1986.

Playboy. Playboy's Music Scene. Playboy Press, 1972.

Plummer, William. *The Holy Goof.* Englewood Cliffs, N.J.: Prentice-Hall, 1981.

Pollack, Dale. *Skywalking: The Life and Films of George Lucas.* Ballantine Books, 1983.

Pollock, Bruce. *When Rock Was Young.* New York: Holt, Rinehart & Winston, 1981.

Rader, Dotson. *I Ain't Marchin' Any More.* New York: Paperback Library, 1969.

Raskin, Jonah. *For the Hell of It: The Life and Times of Abbie Hoffman.* Berkeley, Calif.: University of California Press, 1996.

Reeves, Richard. *A Ford, Not a Lincoln.* New York: Harcourt Brace Jovanovich, 1975.

Reim, Terry, ed. *The Daily Planet Almanac.* Berkeley, Calif.: And/Or Press, 1969.

Reynolds, Frank (as told to Michael McClure). *Freewheelin' Frank, Secretary of the Angels.* New York: Grove Press, 1967.

———. *666.* Self-published, 1968.

Reynolds, Graham. *Turner.* New York: Harry N. Abrams, 1969.

Rinzler, Alan. *Bob Dylan: The Illustrated Record.* New York: Harmony Books, 1978.

Rocco, John, ed. *Dead Reckonings.* New York: Schirmer Books, 1999.

Rohde, H. Kandy. *The Gold of Rock and Roll (1955–1967).* New York: Arbor House, 1978.

Rolling Stone. Garcia. New York: Little, Brown & Co., 1995.

Rolling Stone Record Review, V. II. New York: Pocket Books, 1974.

Romney, Hugh. *The Hog Farm and Friends.* Links, 1974.

Rooney, James. *Bossmen: Bill Monroe and Muddy Waters.* New York: Dial, 1971.

Rothman, Sandy. "Rambling in Redwood Canyon: The Routes of Bay Area Bluegrass." Unpublished MS.

Rowes, Barbara. *Grace Slick: The Biography.* Garden City, N.Y.: Doubleday, 1980.

Rubin, Jerry. *Do It.* New York: Simon & Schuster, 1970.

———. *Growing (Up) at 37.* New York: Warner, 1976.

———. *We Are Everywhere.* New York: Harper & Row, 1970.

Sale, Kirkpatrick. *SDS.* New York: Vintage, 1974.

Sanchez, Tony. *Up and Down with the Rolling Stones.* New York: William Morrow, 1979.

Sander, Ellen. *Trips.* New York: Charles Scribner's Sons, 1973.

Santelli, Robert. *Aquarius Rising: The Rock Festival Years.* New York: Dell, 1980.

Saporita, Jay. *Pourin' It All Out.* Secaucus, N.J.: Citadel Press, 1980.

Sarlin, Bob. *Turn It Up! (I Can't Hear the Words).* New York: Simon & Schuster, 1973.

Scaduto, Anthony. *Bob Dylan.* New York: New American Library, 1971.

———. *Mick Jagger: Everybody's Lucifer.* New York: Berkley Medallion Books, 1974.

Scott, Mary, and Howard Rothman. *Companies with a Conscience.* New York: Carol Publishing Group, 1992.

Sculatti, Gene, and David Seay. *San Francisco Nights.* New York: St. Martin's Press, 1985.

Scully, Rock, with David Dalton. *Living with the Dead.* Boston: Little, Brown, 1996.

Seale, Bobby. *Seize the Time.* New York: Random House, 1970.

Selvin, Joel. *Monterey Pop.* San Francisco: Chronicle Books, 1992.

———. *The Musical History Tour.* San Francisco: Chronicle Books, 1996.

———. *Sly and the Family Stone: An Oral History.* New York: Avon Books, 1998.

———. *Summer of Love.* New York: Dutton, 1994.

Sewall-Ruskin, Yvonne. *High on Rebellion.* New York: Thunder's Mouth Press, 1998.

Shea, Robert, and Robert Anton Wilson. *Illuminatus, Part I: The Eye in the Pyramid.* New York: Dell, 1975.

Shenk, David, and Steve Silberman. *Skeleton Key.* New York: Doubleday, 1994.

Shepard, Sam. *Rolling Thunder Logbook.* New York: Viking Press, 1977.

Slick, Darby. *Don't You Want Somebody to Love.* Berkeley, Calif.: SLG Books, 1991.

Slick, Grace, and Andrea Cagan. *Somebody to Love?* New York: Warner Books, 1998.

Smith, Joe. *Off the Record.* New York: Warner Books, 1988.

Snyder, Gary. *Left Out in the Rain.* San Francisco: North Point Press, 1986.

———. *The Old Ways.* San Francisco: City Lights Books, 1977.

Spitz, Robert Stephen. *Barefoot in Babylon: The Creation of the Woodstock Music Festival, 1969.* New York: Viking, 1979.

Stallings, Penny. *Rock 'n' Roll Confidential.* Boston: Little, Brown & Co., 1984.

Stokes, Geoffrey. *Star Making Machinery.* New York: Vintage Books, 1977.

Stone, I. F. *Polemics and Prophecies.* New York: Vintage Books, 1972.

Sturgeon, Theodore. *More Than Human.* New York: Bantam Books, 1954.

Taylor, Dallas. *Prisoner of Woodstock.* New York: Thunder's Mouth Press, 1994.

Taylor, Derek. *As Time Goes By*. San Francisco: Straight Arrow Books, 1973.

Thomas, J. C. *Chasin' the Trane*. New York: Da Capo, 1975.

Thompson, Hunter. *The Great Shark Hunt*. New York: Fawcett Popular Library, 1979.

Thompson, Toby. *Positively Main Street*. New York: Coward McCann, 1971.

Trist, Alan. *The Water of Life*. Eugene, Ore.: Hulogosi, 1989.

Trubitt, Rudy. *Concert Sound*. Hal Leonard Publishing, 1993.

van Estrik, Robert, and Arie de Revs. *Concerted Efforts*. Privately published, Holland, December 1982.

Vassal, Jacques. *Electric Children: Roots and Branches of Modern Folkrock*. New York. Taplinger Publishing, 1976.

Viorst, Milton. *Fire in the Streets*. New York: Simon & Schuster, 1979.

Von Hoffman, Nicholas. *We Are the People Our Parents Warned Us Against*. Chicago: Quadrangle Books, 1968.

Vonnegut, Kurt. *The Sirens of Titan*. New York: Dell, 1959.

von Schmidt, Eric, and Jim Rooney. *Baby Let Me Follow You Down*. Garden City, N.Y.: Anchor Press, 1979.

Walton, Bill. *Nothing but Net*. New York: Hyperion, 1994.

Wavy Gravy [Hugh Romney]. *The Hog Farm and Friends*. New York: Links, 1974.

Wenner, Jann S., ed. *Twenty Years of Rolling Stone*. New York: Straight Arrow Publishers, 1987.

White, Charles. *The Life and Times of Little Richard*. New York: Harmony Books, 1984.

White, Timonthy. *Catch a Fire: The Life of Bob Marley*. New York: Holt, Rinehart, 1983.

Whitman, Walt. *Leaves of Grass*. New York: W. W. Norton, 1973.

Williams, Paul. *Outlaw Blues*. New York: Pocket Books, 1970.

———. *Rock and Roll: The 100 Best Singles*. New York: Carroll & Graf, 1993.

Wolfe, Tom. *The Electric Kool-Aid Acid Test*. New York: Bantam Books, 1968.

———. *The Right Stuff*. New York: Farrar, Straus & Giroux, 1979.

Wolman, Baron. *Classic Rock and Other Rollers*. Santa Rosa, Calif.: Squarebooks, 1992.

Womack, David. *The Aesthetics of the Dead*. Palo Alto, Calif.: Flying Public Press, 1991.

Woodward, Bob. *Wired*. New York: Simon & Schuster, 1984.

Wyman, Bill, with Ray Coleman. *Stone Alone*. New York: Da Capo, 1997.

Yorke, Ritchie. *The Led Zeppelin Biography*. Toronto: Methuen, 1976.

Zimmer, Dave. *Crosby, Stills & Nash*. New York: St. Martin's Press, 1984.

Zipern, Elizabeth. *Cooking with the Dead*. New York: St. Martin's Paperbacks, 1995.

Articles, Etc.

Abbott, Lee. "Hamburger Metaphysics". *Crawdaddy!*, 3/79.

Adamson, Dale. "Jerry Garcia," *Houston Chronicle*, 1/7/79.

Aikens, Jim. "Grateful Dead, Wired for Sound." *Guitar Player*, 7–8/73.

Albin, Peter. Interview. *Comstock Lode* 9.

Alexander, Lex. "Coliseum Grateful for Dead." *Greensboro News & Record*, 4/17/89.

Allan, Mark. "Dead Journey Still a Long, Wonderful Trip." *Indianapolis Star*, 6/7/91.

Allen, Henry. "The Dead Mystique . . . Jerry Garcia, the Man of Aging Fantasies." *Washington Post*, 6/28/93.

Alson, Bob. "Bob Weir Lets It Grow." *Relix*, 5–6/78.

Alvarez, A. "Good Use." *New Yorker*, 11/26/90.

———. "The Storyteller Speaks (Garcia Transcript)." *Spiral Light* 23, 6/91.

Arnold, Gina. "Nights of the Living Dead." *San Jose Mercury News*, 9/30/88.

Aronowitz, Alfred G. "Moon Jasmine: The Night Jerry Garcia Forgot to Tell Me Something and I Forgot to Ask." From *The Blacklisted Masterpieces of Al Aronowitz* (self-published).

Aronowitz, Alfred G., and Marshall Blonsky. "Three's Company: PPM." *Saturday Evening Post*, 5/20/64.

Bangs, Lester. "Review of 'Grateful Dead.' " *Creem*, 11/71.

———. "The Dead: Dead or Alive?" *Newsday*, 5/18/77.

Barich, Bill. "Still Truckin'." *New Yorker*, 10/11/93.

Barlow, John. Interview. *Swing 51*. 41 Bushey Rd., Sutton, Surrey, SM1 1QR, England, Scribe Printing Ltd., Rochester, Kent.

Barnes, Harper. "Live Dead." *Everyday Magazine, St. Louis Post-Dispatch*, 7/22/94.

———. "Pigpen: Gratitude for the Dead." *Real Paper*, 4/4/73, pp. 14–17.

Barnes, Tom. "Grateful Dead Promoters Agree to Pay $50,000 Fee." *Pittsburgh Post-Gazette*, 5/24/90.

Barrette, Greg. Interview: Steve Brown. *Sacramento Rock 'n' Roll News*, 4/77.

Barron, David. "Few Drug Arrests Made Before Show." *Raleigh News & Observer*, 7/11/90.

Barton, David. "Power to the Music." *Sacramento Bee*, 5/26/93.

Bell, Max. "The GD's First Annual Pyramid Prank." *NME*, 9/30/78.

———. "The Man Who Really Did Keep on Truckin'." *Sunday Telegraph*, London, 10/28/90.

———. "Return of the Living Dead." *Evening Standard*, 10/31/90.

Benchley, Peter. "Face East (or West) Toward Mecca." *Camden Courier Post*, 5/31/69.

Bennett, John. "Dead-Dylan in the Summer of Love." *Clinton St. Quarterly*, winter 1987.

"Best of the Blues." *Time*, 72:39, 9/1/58.

Bianco, Robert. "Stations Respond Slowly to Brutality Issue in Grateful Dead Melee." *Pittsburgh Press*, 4/11/89.

Bilello, Suzanne. "Concerts Will Cost County." *Newsday*, 4/1/90.

Billiter, Bill. "Amphitheatre to Be Urged to Ban the Grateful Dead." *Los Angeles Times* (Orange County), 5/1/89.

Bishop, Bill. "Dead Fest Ends on Mellow Note." *Eugene Register Guard*, 6/25/90.

Bliss, Gil. "Foxboro Concert Might Have Been Eulogy for the Dead." *New Bedford Standard Times*, 7/16/90.

Block, Adam. "Garcia on Garcia '77." *BAM*, 12/77 and 1/78.

Blumenfeld, Laura. "The Dead Mystique, Alive . . . for Deaf Fans . . ." *Washington Post*, 6/28/93.

Bream, Jon. "The Dead." *Minneapolis Star*, 5/31/80.

Brown, Andrew. "Cold Dead Heads." Lesh interview. *Spiral Light* 25.

Brown, G., and David Gans. "Forever Grateful for 'the Dead.' " *Denver Post*, 9/6/83.

Brown, Toni. "Dan Healy." *Relix*, 8/91.

Browne, David. "Bob Dylan/Grateful Dead." *Rolling Stone*, 9/10/87.

Bryant, Judy. "143 Arrested at Grateful Dead Concert." *Louisville Courier-Journal*, 7/7/90.

Cage, Buddy. "The Festival Express." *Relix*, 4/84.

Canter, Donald. "Dame Judith's Cultural Plea for the Hippies." *San Francisco Examiner,* 9/12/67.

Carlini, John. "Jerry Garcia and David Grisman." *Guitar Extra,* fall 1991.

Carlton, Jim. "Fans of Dead Make It Lively for Police." *Los Angeles Times* (Orange County), 4/26/88.

Carr, Patrick. "Grateful Dead." *Grapevine,* 5/17/72.

———. "The Grateful Dead Makes a Real Good Hamburger." *New York Times,* 3/11/73.

Carrier, Jim. "Six Scenes in the Life of a Rock 'n' Roll Rancher." *Denver Post Magazine,* 10/85.

Carroll, Jerry. "Introducing Garcia Lite." *S.F. Chronicle,* 12/9/92.

Carroll, Jon. "A Conversation with JG." *Playboy Electronic Entertainment Guide,* spring/summer 1982.

Carter, Malcolm. "Will Success Spoil Howard Stein." *Riverside (Calif.) Press,* 3/24/74.

Chapin, William. "Hippies and Cops." *S.F. Chronicle,* 1/25/67.

Charters, Sam. "The Great Jug Bands." The Origin Jazz Library.

———. "The Jug Bands." Folkways RF 6, 1963.

Childs, Andy. "The History of the Grateful Dead Part 2." *ZigZag* 36, vol. 3, no. 12.

Christgau, Robert. "Dead—Very Much Alive." *Newsday,* 3/16/73.

Ciotti, Paul. "Revenge of the Nerds." *California,* 7/82.

Coliver, Bob. "Stay Healthy, Keep Fit." Jerry Garcia interview. *Spiral Light* 27, 10/92.

Considine, J. D. "World Music on the Hill." *Rolling Stone,* 4/29/93.

Constanten, Tom. Interview. "Conversation Pieces Part 2. Fandango and Chaconne . . . Anthems and Palindrome Syndrome 2." *Swing 51.*

Cooper, Mark. "Dead but Unburied Dreams of the Sixties." *Independent on Sunday,* London, 10/90.

Cotter, John, and Bob Sutherland. "Red Flag of Peace Waves over Peaceful Festival." *New Orleans Times-Picayune,* 9/3/69.

Coughlan, Robert. "The Chemical Mind Changers." *Life,* 3/15/63.

Coupland, Douglas. "Polaroids from the Dead." *Spin,* 4/92.

Crawford, Mary. "Acid King's Help Sought by Marin." *San Francisco Chronicle,* 9/3/67.

Currie, Mark. "The Winning and Losing of New Year's." *Relix,* 4/85.

Daly, Michael. "A Splendid Time for All." *Mojo,* 8/67.

"The Dead and Dylan." *New Yorker,* 7/27/87.

"The Dead Did Get It: Reporters and Cops." *Rolling Stone,* 11/9/67.

"Dead Set on Regaining Control." *Pollstar,* 6/11/90.

DeCurtis, Anthony. "Jerry Garcia: The Road Goes On Forever." *Rolling Stone,* 9/2/93.

Dedic, Stuart. "Friend: Driver Refused to Stop Car." *Torrance Daily Breeze,* 5/10/90.

Del Priore, Joe. "Forever Dead." *Village Voice,* 11/14/89.

Denison, Paul. "Dylan Raises Dead to New, Inspiring Heights." *Eugene Register Guard,* 7/20/87.

DeVault, Russ. "Grateful Dead Prove They're 'Built to Last' at the Omni." *Atlanta Journal & Constitution,* 3/28/89.

Diebel, Linda. "And 2,000 Enjoy a Free Concert." *Toronto Telegram,* 6/29/70.

Diehl, Digby. "The Henry Ford of Acid." *Cheetah,* 1/68.

Doering, Chris. "Electric Guitar: A Brief History." *Rolling Stone,* 2/18/82.

Doerschuk, Robert. "Keyboards in the Grateful Dead." *Keyboard,* 3/91.

Donato, Maria. "Hanging Out." *Chicago Tribune,* 4/28/88.

Donnelly, Kathleen. "What a Long Strange Trip It's Been." *Palo Alto Weekly*, 5/4/88.

Dorris, Frank. "The Concert Sound of the Grateful Dead." *Absolute Sound*, summer 1993.

Dougherty, Tim. "Deadhead Invasion Brings Big Bucks." *Saratogian*, 6/28/88.

"Dropouts with a Mission." *Newsweek*, 2/6/67.

"Drug Raid Nets 19 in French Quarter." *New Orleans Times-Picayune*, 2/1/70.

Dupree, Tom. "Grateful Dead: Hipper Than the Average Corporation." *Zoo World*, 1/31/74.

Dusheck, George. "Abandon Was Abandoned." *S.F. Examiner*, 1/23/66.

Dustin, Randy. "City Is Grateful for Peaceful Exit of 25,000 Rockers." *Lewiston Sun*, 9/8/80.

Eisenhart, Mary. "G.D. Lyricist's Solo Tales." *BAM*, 8/10/84.

———. "Gray Heirs." *BAM*, 12/18/87.

———. "Robert Hunter." *Golden Road*, fall 1984.

———. "Truckin' in Style." *Microtimes*, 7/6/92.

Elwood, Philip. "The Good Old Grateful Dead Is Back." *S.F. Examiner*, 9/26/80.

Epand, Len. "A Most Informal Group." *Rolling Stone*, 6/20/74.

———. "State of the Artful Dead." *Zoo World*, 8/15/74.

Fahey, Jym. "Gregg Allman." *Relix*, 8/93.

Fedele, Frank. "Fuck No, We're Just Musicians." Jerry Garcia interview. *Berkeley Organ*, 11/70.

Felton, David, and David Dalton. "Year of the Fork, Night of the Hunter." *Rolling Stone*, 6/70.

Feris, Mark. "The Dead Leaves Its Fans . . . Well . . . Grateful." *Akron Beacon Journal*, 9/8/90.

Finn, Melanie. "500,000 Reasons to Be Grateful." *Times* (London), 10/24/90.

Flaum, Eric. "The Grateful Dead." *Gold Mine*, 7/17/87.

"The Foggy, Foggy, Don't." *Time*, 77:69, 4/21/61.

"Folk Song As It Is." *Newsweek*, 4/18/58.

Fong Torres, Ben. "Fifteen Years Dead." *Rolling Stone*, 8/7/80.

———. "FM Underground Radio: Love for Sale." *Rolling Stone*, 4/2/70.

———. "Love Is Just a Song . . ." *Rolling Stone*, 2/26/76.

———. "New Riders in the Circus Circus." *Rolling Stone*, 9/2/71.

———. "Not-So-Good Old Dead Records." *Rolling Stone*, 10/28/71.

———. "What a Long, Strange, Trip." *America*, spring 1988.

France, Kim, "My Life as a Deadhead." *Sassy*, 4/90.

Francis, Miller, "A Sunday Afternoon." *Great Speckled Bird*, 5/18/70.

Frank, Allan Dodds. "And the Beat Goes On." *Forbes*, 5/18/87.

Fricke, David. "America's Greatest Hits." *Rolling Stone*, 9/18/97.

Gans, David. Transcripts of Gans's interviews with Bob Weir, 8/9/77, at L'Hermitage Hotel, Beverly Hills, during recording of "Heaven Help the Fool" and between shows at the Roxy, L.A., 2/17/78.

Gans, David, and Peter Simon. Edited by John Dorrance. "The Grateful Dead Turn 20." *San Francisco*, 6/85.

Garcia, Jerry. *Playboy Supplement*, 10/80.

———. "Interview," *Circus*, 9/74.

Gehr, Richard. "The Dead Zone." *Village Voice*, 4/21/87.

Gilbert, Matthew. "While Garcia & Co. Rock the Garden, the Lyricist Gratefully Works at Home." *Boston Globe,* 9/20/91.

Gilboa, Netta. "Getting Gray with John Perry Barlow." *Gray Areas,* fall 1992.

Gilmore, Mikal. "Could Rock 'n' Roll Be the Night Stalker's Last Victim?" *S.F. Examiner,* 9/11/85.

———. "The New Dawn of the Grateful Dead." *Rolling Stone,* 6/16/87.

Gleason, Ralph J. "All That Jazz and Rock Paid Off." *S.F. Chronicle,* 9/13/66.

———. "The Cancellation of the Wild West Festival." *S.F. Chronicle,* 8/15/69.

———. "Carnival Barker Ruse Not for Concerts." *S.F. Chronicle,* 10/23/68.

———. "The Fillmore Acid Test." *S.F. Chronicle,* 1/10/66.

———. "Lesson for S.F. in the Mime Benefit." *S.F. Chronicle,* 12/13/65.

———. "The Matrix: Social Blues via the JA." *S.F. Chronicle,* 8/20/65.

———. "The Month of the Dead." *S.F. Chronicle,* 10/17/71.

———. "A Most Unusual Dancing Class." *S.F. Chronicle,* 10/2/67.

———. "An Old Joint That's Really Jumping." *S.F. Chronicle,* 7/20/66.

———. "Thanksgiving at the Fillmore." *S.F. Chronicle,* 11/28/66.

———. "The Tribes Gather for a Yea-Saying." *S.F. Chronicle,* 1/16/67.

———. "Why Bill Graham Is Leaving the City." *S.F. Chronicle,* 8/8/69.

Goddard, Peter. "Far Out! Groovy, Man! Bands Resurrect 1966." *Toronto Star,* 11/3/77.

"Going to Pot." *Time,* 88:56–57, 7/1/66.

Goldberg, Danny. "California Rock Enters a New Phase." *Circus,* 4/71.

Goldberg, Michael. "Garcia: Truckin' Again." *Rolling Stone,* 1/21/93.

———. "Performance." *Rolling Stone,* 2/21/80.

Goldstein, Richard. "Hurok of Haight Street." *LAT West,* 8/27/67.

———. "A Reason for Hippies." *S.F. Chronicle,* 6/5/67. (*New York Times/Washington Post* service)

Goodman, Fred. "The Dead Again . . . and Again . . . and Again." *M,* 2/92.

———. "The End of the Road?" *Rolling Stone,* 8/23/90.

———. "Jerry Garcia." *Rolling Stone,* 11/30/89.

Gormley, Mike. "Grateful Dead Sell Out the Knick." *Albany Times Union,* 2/24/90.

Gottesman, Stephen N. "Tom Dooley's Children." Paper for 1976 Popular Culture Association.

Gottlieb, Lou. "Glorious Electricity." *S.F. Chronicle,* 1/18/66.

"Grateful Dead Bust Their Dad." *Rolling Stone,* 9/2/71.

"Grateful Dead's Defense on Pot." *S.F. Chronicle,* 10/4/67.

Green, Blake. "California Has Finished Growing Up." *S.F. Chronicle,* 3/11/82.

Green, Susan. "Life Among the Dead." *Burlington Free Press,* 5/14/78.

Greuber, Mike, Charles Beichman, Rex Browning, and Hank Baig. *Harvard Independent,* Mar. 4–10, 1971.

Grieg, Michael. "Cops Seize Love Poster." *S.F. Chronicle,* 3/10/67.

———. "Death of the Hippies." *S.F. Chronicle,* 10/7/67.

Grissim, John. "Garcia Returns to Banjo: Splendor in the Bluegrass." *Rolling Stone,* 4/26/73.

Gross, Elaine. "Where Are the Chickens, Alice?" *Rolling Stone,* 10/15/70.

Gross, Jane. " 'Deadheads' in an Idolatrous Pursuit." *New York Times,* 5/18/88.

"Guard Hunted Dealers at Concert." *Boston Herald,* 7/19/90.

Gust, Kelly. "Deadheads Make Effort to Placate Neighborhood," *Oakland Tribune*, 1/31/89.

———. "Neighbors Resume Push to Ban Dead Concerts," *Oakland Tribune*, 2/11/89.

Haas, Charles. "Drink Down a Bottle and You're Ready to Kill." *New West*, 9/79.

Hall, John. "True Confessions in Hartford." Jerry Garcia interview. *Relix*, winter 1977, vol. 4, no. 6.

Hambly, Scott. "San Francisco Bay Area Bluegrass and Bluegrass Musicians: A Study in Regional Characteristics." *JEMF* 16, no. 59 (fall 1980).

Hansen, Barry. "First Annual Monterey Pop Festival." *Down Beat*, 8/10/67.

"Happenings Are Happening." *Time*, 3/4/66.

Harris, Mark. "The Flowering of the Hippies." *Atlantic*, 9/67.

Hartman, Janelle. "Deadheads Were Too Mellow to Make Trouble." *Eugene Register Guard*, 6/24/90.

Healy, Dan. "Raising the Dead." *EQ*, 4/91.

"Hear That Big Sound." *Life*, 5/21/65.

Heckman, Don. "Garcia Versatile with His Guitar." *New York Times*, 1/23/71.

———. "GD in Concert Retain Their Magic Glow." *New York Times*, 3/21/72.

Henke, James. "Jerry Garcia." *Rolling Stone*, 10/31/91.

Hentoff, Nat. "The Crackin', Shakin', Breakin' Sounds." *New Yorker*, 10/24/64.

Herbst, Peter. "Nothing Exceeds Like Success." *Boston After Dark*, 11/19/74.

Herron, Jim. "The Deadhead Dilemma." *East Bay Express*, 3/11/88.

Herzog, Brad. "The Legend of 5/8/77." *Cornell Magazine*, 5–6/97.

"Hey Jerry." *New Musical Express*, 9/21/74.

Hibbert, Tom. "California Uber Alles." *Q*, 1/91.

Hilburn, Robert. "At Grateful Dead Concert, the Fans Are the Most Fun." *Los Angeles Times*, 2/13/89.

———. "Bob Dylan, the Grateful Dead . . ." *L.A. Times Calendar*, 7/13/87.

———. "Do Sting and the Dead Mix." *Los Angeles Times*, 5/17/93.

"Hippies' Mystery Walk-In." *S.F. Chronicle*, 4/3/67.

Hippler, Mike. "Deadheads." *Bay Area Reporter*, 8/20/87.

Hirshberg, Charles. "The Ballad of A. P. Carter." *Life*, 12/91.

Hochman, Steve. "Mickey Hart's Long Field Trip." *Escape*, n.d.

———. "Performance." *Rolling Stone*, July 8–22, 1993.

Hoekstra, Dave. "Grateful Dead Keeps on Droning at the Horizon." *Chicago Sun-Times*, 4/13/89.

Hoey, Dennis. "Grateful Dead Rock Band Raises Citizens' Blood Pressure." *Lewiston Sun*, 8/27/80.

"Hoots and Hollers on the Campus." *Newsweek*, 11/27/61.

Hopkins, Jerry. "The Beautiful Dead." *Rolling Stone*, 5/72.

———. "Sympowowsium: What Comes After Woodstock?" *Rolling Stone*, 11/69.

"Hungry Star-Makers." *Newsweek*, 6/6/60.

Hunt, Dennis. "Grateful Dead at Berkeley Concert." *S.F. Chronicle*, 8/16/71.

Hunt, Ken. "Dead on Arrival." *City Limits*, 10/25/90.

———. "John Barlow." *Relix*, 6–8/85.

———. "Jerry Garcia." *Swing 51*, issue 11, 1987.

———. "Mickey Hart." *Swing 51*, issue 13, 1989.

Hunter, Robert. "GD CD Set—Not Necessarily an Intro." Unpublished MS.

———. "Robert Hunter, Dark Star." *Crawdaddy!*, 1/75.

Hurwitz, Miles. "Mickey Hart: Up the River and Other Tales." *BAM*, 8/29/80.

———. "A World of Drums." BK and MH interviews. *BAM*, 8/17/79.

Isaacson, David. "Life After the Dead." *Jerusalem Post*, 8/2/96.

Jackson, Blair. "The Airplane House." *BAM*, 2/2/79.

———. "Dead Heads: A Strange Tale . . ." *BAM*, 4/4/80.

———. "Drums and Dreams." *Golden Road*, fall 1990.

———. "Hunter/Garcia—Words/Music." *Golden Road*, fall 1990.

———. "The Making of *So Far.*" *Golden Road*, summer 1987.

———. "Jon McIntire." *Golden Road*, summer 1988.

———. "Pigpen Forever." *Golden Road*, 1993 annual.

———. "Roots." *Golden Road*, winter 1984.

Jackson, Blair, and Dennis Erokan. "Bill Graham, Rock's Godfather." *BAM*, 2/2/79.

Jackson, Blair, and Regan McMahon. "Howie: On a Life in Music and Art That Matters." *BAM*, 7/15/83.

Jahn, Mike. "Grateful Dead Draws Far-Out Fans." *New York Times*, 4/29/71.

"Jailhouse Rock." *Time*, 73:48, 4/20/59.

"Jerry Garcia's G.D. Pass the True Acid Test: They're Still Playing." *People*, 7/4/76.

Jones, Greg, and Andrew Pickard. Jerry Garcia interview. *Banjo Newsletter*, 3/91.

Junod, Tom. "Oh, What a Night." *Life*, 12/1/92.

Kahn, Alice. "Local Boy Makes Bad." *San Jose Mercury News West Magazine*, 12/30/84.

Kamin, Ira. "Sex and Drugs." *S.F. Examiner Image Magazine*, 12/4/88.

Kamiya, Gary. "Night of the Living Dead." *S.F. Examiner Image Magazine*, 1/27/91.

Kane, Mari. "The Tie-Dyes That Bind." *California*, 12/90.

Kanzer, Adam. "Misfit Power, the First Amendment and the Public Forum . . ." *Columbia Journal of Law and Social Problems* 3, 1992.

Kareda, Urjo. "The Jefferson Airplane: Man, It Was Wild." *Toronto Globe and Mail*, 8/1/67.

Katzman, Allen. "Bill Graham, Rock's Robber Baron." *Other Scenes*, 11/70.

Kava, Brad. "Dead Right." *San Jose Mercury News Eye*, 12/11/92.

Kaye, Lenny. Review of *Grateful Dead. RSR*, vol 2.

Keating, Brian. "Something About Integrity." *Village Voice*, 1/8/70.

Kelley, Alton. Interview. "Art for Fun's Sake." *Golden Road*, 3/84.

Kellogg, Mary Alice. "A Farewell to Nirvana." *Newsweek*, 3/15/76.

Kelp, Larry. " 'Dylan and the Dead' Fails to Fulfill Its Potential." *Oakland Tribune*, 2/7/89.

———. "Garcia and Grisman Steal the Show amid Circus Atmosphere." *Oakland Tribune*, 5/9/92.

Kennedy, Rob. "Khaftans Under the Stars." *Relix*, 6–8/85.

Kent, Bill. "The GD Is Just Circling." *Camden Courier Post*, 8/29/80.

Kent, Robert. "The Dead Arrive." *Melody Maker*, 5/4/72.

Kesey, Ken. "On the Passing of John Lennon." *Rolling Stone*, 3/5/81.

———. "Revisiting the Pyramids," in *Rolling Stone* (eds.), *Garcia*.

Koch, Ed. "What a Long Strange Trip It's Been: A Profile." *Poker World*, 3/96.

Kopkind, Andrew. "The Sixties and the Movement." *Ramparts*, 2/73.

Kot, Greg. "Grateful Dead Still Breezing Along with Their Musical Magic." *Chicago Tribune*, 7/28/90.

Krassner, Paul. "An Impolite Interview with Ken Kesey." *Realist*, 5–6/71.

Krewen, Nick. "It Just Feels Like We're Getting Started." *Hamilton Spectator*, 3/22/90.

Krippner, Stanley, Charles Honorton, and Montague Ullman. "An Experiment in Dream Telepathy with 'The Grateful Dead.' " *Journal of the American Society of Psychosomatic Dentistry and Medicine* 20, no. 1 (1973).

Lacey, Marc. "Police Cleared of Wrongdoing in Youth's Death at Concert." *Los Angeles Times*, 1/10/90.

Lattin, Don. "The Guitar That Speaks for God." *S.F. Chronicle*, 12/31/91.

Lebrecht, Norman. "The Grateful and the Dead." *Independent Magazine*, 6/22/91.

Lefkowitz, Eric. "The Madcap '60s TV Band—Then and Now." *BAM*, 5/4/84.

Leibovitz, Annie. "Night of the Dead." *Rolling Stone*, 12/5/74.

Lem, Ernest. "Teen Dope Users a Worry Here." *S.F. Chronicle*, 1/2/67.

Lemon, Richard. "Daddy Is a Hippy." *Saturday Evening Post*, 7/2/66.

Lesh, Philip. Interview. *ZigZag* 46, vol. 5, no. 1.

Levin, Phyllis Lee. "The Sound of Music?" *New York Times Magazine*, 3/14/65.

Levine, David. "The Peaceable Kingdom . . ." *Washington Post*, 7/13/89.

Liberatore, Paul. "Group Plays Famous Eastern Gig." *Marin Independent Journal*, 8/30/73.

———. "Staying Power." *Marin Independent Journal*, 10/1/89.

"The Limpid Shambles of Violence." *Life*, 7/3/64.

Lipner, Ariel. "The Grateful Dead Nears the '90s." *Worcester Evening Telegram & Gazette*, Apr. 7–8, 1988.

"London: The Swinging City." *Time*, 4/15/66.

Ludlow, Lynn. "Former LSD Maker Tim Scully Triumphs over Prison." *S.F. Examiner & Chronicle*, 6/17/79.

Lueth, Kristen Parrish. "Just Who Are the Grateful Dead?" *Omaha Metropolitan*, 1/11/89.

Lufkin, Liz. "The Dead—Just Becoming Alive." *S.F. Examiner & Chronicle*, 7/19/81.

———. "Ten Freeform Years on the Edge." *BAM*, 5/19/78.

Lydon, Michael. "An Evening with the Grateful Dead." *Rolling Stone*, 9/17/70.

———. "Good Old Grateful Dead." *Rolling Stone* 40, 8/23/69.

———. "Has Frisco Gone Commercial?" *New York Times*, 11/24/68.

———. "The Producer of the New Rock." *New York Times Magazine*, 12/15/68.

"The Magic Dragon." *Newsweek*, 4/8/63.

Magid, Marion. "The Death of Hip." *Esquire*, 6/65.

Marre, Jeremy. "At the Edge." Jerry Garcia interview. *Spiral Light* 28, 2/92.

Marsh, David. "Can the Dead Survive Putting Out Their Own Records?" *Newsday*, 11/18/73.

Martin, Ralph. "Better Dead Than Deadhead." *Albany Times Union*, 3/31/90.

Masters of Rock. New Morning Productions. Various issues of periodical magazine. #6, spring 1991, "Grateful Dead." #7, winter 1992, "Psychedelic '60s."

Mawson, Dave. "On the Dead, Deadheads, and Headaches." *Worcester Evening Gazette-Telegram*, Apr. 7–8, 1988.

McClanahan, Ed. "Grateful Dead I Have Known." *Playboy*, 8/72.

McIntyre, Tom. "Millennium Witness." *S.F. Examiner Magazine*, 10/9/94.

McLaughlin, Sheila. "Judge Is Upset over Concert." *Cincinnati Enquirer*, 4/11/89.

McKeon, Michael. "Deadheads Get Good Reviews." *Albany Times Union*, 3/27/90.

McNeil, Legs. "Jerry Speaks!" *High Times*, 2/89.

McNeill, Don. "Autumn in the Haight: Where Has Love Gone?" *Village Voice*, 11/30/67.

———. "East Is West—a Ritual of Energy." *Village Voice*, 5/16/68.

———. "The Youthquake and the Shook-Up Park." *Village Voice*, 6/8/67.

Mehlman, Lisa. "Grateful Play into the Dead of Night." *Disc & Music Echo*, 8/1/70.

Meier, Barbara. "Jerry Garcia." *Tricycle*, spring 1992.

Meltzer, Richard. "Jerry Garcia, Guitar." *Circus*, 3/71.

Menocal, Maria Rosa. "The Burial Grounds." Unpublished MS., Yale University.

Miley, Scott. "Deadheads May Have to Pay to Camp Before Concerts." *Indianapolis Star*, 7/28/90.

Moffat, Frances. "Black and White and Very San Francisco." *S.F. Chronicle*, 7/16/69.

Mogensen, Mark. "Welfare Rolls Increase After Concert." *Lewiston Sun*, 9/16/80.

Muhl, Bruce. "Rising Ticket Fees Pad Concert Profits." *Boston Globe*, 9/29/92.

Morgan, David. "The Rock Is Acid at Party Given by the Grateful Dead." *Redding Record-Searchlight*, 10/19/66.

Morley, Paul. "What a Long, Predictable Trip It's Become." *New Musical Express*, 3/28/81.

Morrison, Jim. "The Dead, Alive and Well at Hampton." *Norfolk Virginian-Pilot*, 3/28/88.

Morse, Steve. "Dead, Dylan 'Wing It' '60s-style." *Boston Globe*, 7/5/87.

———. "Grateful Dead: The Trip Is Over." *Boston Globe*, 12/9/95.

———. "New Age Dead Ready to Play . . ." *Boston Globe*, 9/28/93.

———. "The New Dawn of the Dead." *Boston Globe*, 9/19/93.

Morse, Steve, and Matthew Gilbert. "Forever Dead: Should the GD have Continued After Jerry Garcia?" *Boston Globe*, 12/15/95.

"Mr. 'Tapes' of Brooklyn: He Rules the GD Tape Empire." *Rolling Stone*, 10/11/73.

"The Music Is Hip in Central Park: 450 at the Bandshell Hear Electric Guitar Combos." *New York Times*, 6/9/67.

Myers, Donald P. "Deadheads Forever." *Newsday Magazine*, 9/9/90.

Nash, Michael. "Been Here So Long They've Got to Calling It Home." *Daily Californian*, 11/2/84.

———. "Grateful Tapers." *Audio*, 1/88.

———. "The Long Strange Trip Continues." *California Executive*, 7/88.

———. "Soundman Dan Healy's 30-Year Trip with the Grateful Dead." *Music & Sound Output*, 6/88.

"Newport Blues." *Time*, 76:47, 7/18/60.

"The New Rock." *Life*, 6/28/68.

Night Owl Reporter. *New York Daily News*, 11/18/70.

"The Nitty Gritty Sound." *Newsweek*, 12/19/66.

Noriyuki, Duane. "One Long Trip." *Detroit Free Press*, 4/12/88.

O'Harrow, Robert, Jr. "A 'Trip' down Memory Lane: LSD Makes a Comeback." *Washington Post*, 7/7/91.

Oldfield, Mike. "Dead to the World." *Guardian*, 10/25/90.

———. "Interview with Bob Weir." *Spiral Light* 22, spring 1991.

Palmer, Robert. "The Beat According to Bo Diddley." *S.F. Chronicle*, 9/2/82. (*New York Times* service)

Pareles, Jon. "The Grateful Dead, Most Alive on the Stage." *New York Times*, 7/26/87.

———. "Just What the Tie-Dyed Crowd Wanted." *New York Times*, 10/14/89.

———. "The Sixties Reinvented: Only the Beat Goes On." *New York Times*, 2/5/89.

Parker, Tom. "In One Day." *S.F. Chronicle*, 2/9/85.

Peacock, Steve. "Jerry Garcia." *Rock*, 7/17/72.

Pelletiere, Steve. "Rock Club Closes—Police Pressure." *S.F. Chronicle*, 10/6/67.

Pepper, Thomas. "Underground Press: Growing Rich on the Hippie." *Nation*, 4/29/68.

Perry, Charles. "Alembic." *Rolling Stone Audio Supplement*, 9/27/73.

———. "The Deadhead Phenomenon," *RS College Papers*, winter 1980. In *Rolling Stone* (eds.), *Garcia*.

———. "From Eternity to Here." *Rolling Stone*, 2/26/76.

———. "A New Life for the Dead." *Rolling Stone*, 11/22/73.

———. "The News Reaches SF." *RSR*, 10/29/70.

Peters, Catherine. "Dead Ahead." *Marin Sun*, Feb. 13–19, 1981.

Peters, Steve. "Built to Last." *Relix*, 12/89.

Piccarella, John. "The GD Peddle Their Record." *Village Voice*, 1/15/79.

Piccoli, Sean. "Deadheads." *Washington Times*, 3/15/90.

"Pickin' Scruggs." *Time*, 77:53, 6/30/61.

"Pied Pipers of the New Generation." *Look*, 1/31/61.

Platt, John, ed. Interviews with Lesh, Hart. *Comstock Lode* 9, autumn 1981.

Polk, Peggy. "The Drug-Drenched Path to Porterville." *Philadelphia Daily News*, 1971. (AP service)

Pooley, Eric. "Raising the Dead." *New York*, 4/16/90.

"Pop's Bad Boys." *Newsweek*, 11/2/65.

Pothier, Dick. "City Closes JFK Stadium." *Philadelphia Inquirer*, 7/12/89.

Power, Keith. "Hippies Get 'Clean' Bill of Health." *S.F. Chronicle*, 3/29/67.

"Purple Lights." *New Yorker*, 4/17/71.

Puterbaugh, Parke. "Fans Steal Show." *Greensboro News & Record*, 3/31/89.

Rainier, Pat. "Interview with Jerry Garcia of the Dead." *Tennessee Roc*, 8/70.

Rainey, James. "Police Say 'Deadhead' on LSD Caused Fatal Crash." *Los Angeles Times*, 5/8/90.

Ramsey, Frederic, Jr. "Newport's Stepchildren." *Saturday Review* 44:44–45, 6/29/61.

Raposa, Laura, and Jeffrey Krasner. "Hub Grateful for Dead invasion." *Boston Herald*, 9/20/91.

Raudebaugh, Charles. "Cops Raid Pad of GD." *S.F. Chronicle*, 10/3/67.

———. "Grateful Dead's Defense on Pot." *S.F. Chronicle*, 10/4/67.

Read, Jeani. "The GD Are Best Seen Alive." *Vancouver Sun*, 6/23/73.

Reiterman, Tim. "FBI's Tricks Surprise Savio." *S.F. Sunday Examiner*, 7/6/82.

Rense, Rip. "Back from the Dead." *L.A. Times Calendar*, 4/19/87.

———. "Childhood Memories, Grown-Up Memories." *Los Angeles Times*, 12/3/93.

———. "The Dead Dance in the Land of Chance." *Los Angeles Herald Examiner*, 3/29/83.

———. "Jerry Garcia Is Taking Better Care of Himself." *Mix*, 7/87.

Rheingold, Howard. "The Grateful." *Interview*, 7/91.

Richards, Brian. "Touch of Grey." *Film and Video Production*, 10/80.

Richards, Lowell. "Blues Outclasses Rock at Sky River Festival." *Down Beat*, 10/31/68.

Richter, Volkmar. "Kids Dance in the O'Keefe's Aisles." *Toronto Star*, 8/1/67.

"The Ride for Rights." *Life*, 5/26/61.

Rifkin, Glenn. "Lessons from the Grateful Dead." *Strategy & Business* 6, 1997.

Robble, Andrew. "Gettin' Down with Nick Gravenites." *Relix*, 10/93.

———. "Reflections on Ron 'Pigpen' McKernan, Part II." *Relix*, 8/93.

———. "Reflections on Ron 'Pigpen' McKernan, Part III." *Relix*, 10/93.

Robins, Wayne. "In a Frenzy for the Dead." *Newsday*, 9/19/90.

"Rock 'n' Roll: Going to Pot." *Time*, 7/1/66.

"Rock 'n' Roll Message Time." *Time*, 9/17/65.

Rockwell, John. "Dead's Fans Know Who a Friend Is." *New York Times*, 7/3/74.

———. "G.D. Returns to N.Y. in Triumph." *New York Times*, 6/16/76.

Rodgers, Jeffrey Pepper. "In the Dawg House." *Acoustic Guitar*, 1–2/94.

Rogers, Dennis. "Joining the Dead Lifts the Spirits." *Raleigh News & Observer*, 7/16/90.

Rood, Jonathan. "Life with the Hippies." *S.F. Chronicle*, 1/3/67.

Rossman, Michael. "Inside the Free Speech Movement." *California Monthly*, 12/74.

Roswell, Clint. "G.D. Bring the Coliseum Alive." *New York Daily News*, 1/14/79.

"Rowan and Martin—Verrry Interesting . . . but Wild." *Time*, 10/11/68.

Rowland, Mark. "Bring Me the Head of JG." *St. Louis Post-Dispatch*, 8/14/80.

———. "Days of the Living Dead." *Musician*, 10/96.

———. "Elvis Costello and Jerry Garcia." *Musician*, 3/91.

Rubeck, Jack. Frank Werber interview. *Gold Mine*, 7/81.

Ruhlman, William. "Robert Hunter." *Relix*, 10/87.

Sacks, Oliver. "The Last Hippie." *New York Review of Books*, 3/26/92.

Saltus, Richard. "Continental Drift." *California Living*, 10/3/82.

Sandalow, Marc. " 'Deadheads' Anger Concert Neighbors." *S.F. Chronicle*, 3/18/88.

———. "Oakland Bummed Out, So the Dead Cancels 3 Gigs." *S.F. Chronicle*, 2/24/89.

"The San Francisco Sound." *Time*. Records. 7/7/67.

Scherman, Tony. "Rocking Capitalism: Force of the Styx." *S.F. Chronicle*, 8/23/81.

Schlosser, Eric. "Fast-Food Nation." *Rolling Stone*, 9/3/98.

Schneider, Howard. "Confrontation at the Coliseum." *Newsday*, 3/16/73.

Schwartz, Bert. "Grateful Dead Rocks Audience." *Philadelphia Evening Bulletin*, 10/17/70.

Scott, Jane. "The GD Liven Things Up." *Cleveland Plain Dealer*, 10/16/70.

Sculatti, Gene. "S.F. Bay Rock." *Crawdaddy*, 11/66.

Selvin, Joel. "Dead Songwriters Get Life." *S.F. Chronicle & Examiner*, 4/21/91.

———. "Garcia Returns to a First Love." *S.F. Chronicle*, 3/14/73.

———. "The Grateful Dead Decides to Try a Guiding Hand." *S.F. Chronicle*, 7/28/77.

———. "Hills Are Alive with the Dead." *S.F. Chronicle*, 5/11/87.

———. "Jerry Garcia: New Life for the Grateful Dead." *S.F. Chronicle*, 12/14/92.

———. "The Last Post." *Mojo*, 10/85.

———. "Musical Stars Shine for Salvador." *S.F. Chronicle*, 1/25/88.

———. "The Naked Dead at the Warfield." *S.F. Chronicle*, 9/29/80.

———. "On the Town." *S.F. Chronicle*, 3/14/73.

Shank, Gary. "The Logic of the Grateful Dead." Paper for Popular Culture Association, Las Vegas, 3/26/96.

———. "Qualitative Research, Semiotics, North Beach, South of Market, Jack London and the Grateful Dead." Paper for American Educational Research Association, 4/95.

Shank, Gary, and Eric Simon. "The Grammar of the Grateful Dead." Paper for International Association for Semiotic Studies, 1994.

Shaw, Arnold. "Gitars, Folk Songs, and Halls of Ivy." *Harper's*, 11/64.

Shelton, Robert. "Freedom Songs." *Nation*, 7/27/63.

Sherman, Robert. "Sing a Song of Freedom." *Saturday Review* 46:65–67, 9/28/63.

Siegel, Jessica. "Color of Money Retools Deadheads' Tie-Dyed Image." *Chicago Tribune*, 7/23/90.

Siegel, Joel. "Watkins Glen Jam Tops Woodstock." *Rolling Stone*, 8/30/73.

Sievert, Jon. "Bob Weir: More Than Rhythm Guitarist for the Grateful Dead." *Guitar Player*, 8/81.

———. "Garcia and Grisman." *Guitar Player*, 9/91.

———. "Jerry Garcia." *Guitar Player*, 7/88.

Silag, Mark. "The GD in Concert." *Modern Recording and Music*, 2/81.

Silberman, Steve. "Standing in the Soul: An Interview with Robert Hunter." *Poetry Flash*, 12/92.

Simonds, C. H. "Playing It Straight." *National Review*, 1/12/71.

"600,000 Jam Watkins Glen: Rockfest Outdraws Woodstock." *New York Daily News*, 7/29/73.

Skaggs, Steven. "The Transitive Nightfall of Diamonds: Eco and the Aesthetics of Transcendence." Unpublished paper presented at the Conference of the Semiotic Society of America.

Skidmore, Mick. "Ned Lagin." *Relix*, 4/91.

Skow, John. "In California: The Dead Live On." *Time*, 2/11/85.

"Sky River Rock Groove." *Rolling Stone*, 10/12/68.

Smith, Dana. "Interview with a Champ: Hal Kant." *Card Player*, 8/20/99.

Snider, Burr. "The Dead Bite the Apple." *S.F. Examiner Image*, 10/30/88.

———. "The Dead Heads." *Oui*, 8/80.

———. "Dead Heads Don't Wear Plaid." *S.F. Examiner Image*, 6/30/91.

Soiffer, Bill. "Origin of the T-shirt Uncovered." *S.F. Chronicle*, 7/29/81.

Spence, Steve. "The Van of Aquarius." *Car and Driver*, 3/92.

Spiegel, Joseph. "In the Ear with Grateful Dead . . ." *Pro Sound News*, 8/92.

Stack, Peter. "Back in Force." *S.F. Chronicle & Examiner Datebook*, 1/26/97.

———. "Glitz and Rock at the Bammies." *S.F. Chronicle*, 3/14/88.

———. "The Times They Are A'Changin'." *S.F. Chronicle*, 7/23/80.

Starr, Mark. "Dead's Performance Elegant." *Rochester Democrat-Chronicle*, 4/1/73.

Stearns, David. "GD Not Ready Yet for the Shroud." *Rochester Times-Union*, 9/4/79.

Stepanian, Michael. Interview. *High Times*, 6/67.

"Still Doin' That Rag." *Eugene Register Guard*, 6/22/90.

Stoddard, Martin. "Psychedelic Reviver." *Avant Garde*, 3/81.

Stokes, Geoff. "Death of the Dead?" *Village Voice*, 10/31/74.

Storch, Thomas. "A Period of Transition." Bill Kreutzmann interview. *Spiral Light* 26, 7/92.

Strand, Alf. "It's Just the Music, Man, Not the Body, That Rocks." *Vancouver Sun*, 7/14/66.

Strugatz, Elizabeth Lynn. "The Grateful Dead Phenomenon: A Qualitative Approach." Master's thesis, Kent State University, 1991.

Stuckey, Fred. "Jerry Garcia." *Guitar Player*, 4/71.

Sumrall, Harry. "Dylan, Dead Live LP Is Dead." *San Jose Mercury News*, 2/12/89.

Sutherland, Steve. "Acid Daze." *Melody Maker*, 5/6/89.

———. "Bone Idols." *Melody Maker*, 10/27/90.

———. "Furthur Ahead." *Melody Maker*, 5/13/89.

———. No title. *Melody Maker*, 3/28/81.

Svetkey, Benjamin. "Is Dead God?" *Entertainment Weekly*, 3/12/93.

Swanton, David. "A Beatle Does His Thing." *S.F. Chronicle*, 8/8/67.

Sweeting, Adam. "Dance of the Dead." *Guardian*, 11/1/90.

Swenson, John. "Back from the Dead." *Guitar World*, 12/87.

————. "Grateful Dead Lyricist Back on His Own Again." *Wheeling (W. Va.) News-Register*, 5/29/88. (UPI service)

Synopwich, Peter. "Rock and Roll Comes of Age." *Toronto Star Sun*, 8/26/67.

Tamarkin, Jeff. "Jack Casady." *Relix*, 10/92.

————. "Marty Balin." *Relix*, 4/93.

————. "Jerry Garcia." *Relix*, 8/80.

————. "Paul Kantner." *Relix*, 8/92.

"Der Tanz der Blumenkinder." *Stern*, 10/18/90.

Teepen, Tom. "The Deadheads Rolled in with All Their Old Pizazz." *Atlanta Journal and Constitution*, 3/30/89.

Territo, Joseph. "Jerry Garcia." *Marin Independent Journal*, 6/82.

"They Finally Did It." *Life*, 6/19/64.

Thompson, Hunter. "Third Rate Romance, Low-Rent Rendezvous." *Rolling Stone*, 6/3/76.

Torassa, Ulysses. "Gathering of Deadheads Create a Dead Calm." *Cleveland Plain Dealer*, 9/8/90.

"A Trio in Tune Makes the Top." *Life*, 8/3/59.

Troy, Sandy. "The Soundman Sounds Off." *Relix*, May–June, August 1978.

Truscott, Lucian IV, *Village Voice*, 6/26/69.

Uhlenbrock, Tom. "Gratefully Back from the Dead." *St. Louis Post-Dispatch*, 8/87.

"The Unbarbershopped Quartet." *Newsweek*, 11/18/63.

Uris, Joe. "Grateful Dead Isn't Just Some Cult." *Portland Oregonian*, 7/24/87.

Van Matre, Lynn. "Voice of the Dead." *Chicago Tribune*, 4/10/88.

Vaughn, Chris. "Dead Fingers Talk." *Spin*, 1987.

————. "Rhythm Devils." *Down Beat*, 11/87.

Voelker, Tom. "Roll Over and Play Live." *NOLA*, 2/16/70.

Voelpel, Dan. "Deadheads: They Seem to Find Much to Be Grateful About." *Tacoma News Tribune*, 8/27/88.

Wainwright, Loudon. "The Strange New Love Land of the Hippies." *Life*, 3/31/67.

Wallace, Bill. "FBI's Harassment of Berkeley Leftists Detailed." *S.F. Chronicle*, 7/7/82.

Walters, Barry. "True Horror: Night of the Living Dead." *S.F. Examiner*, 2/10/89.

Warden, Billy. "And the Band Played On." *Raleigh News & Observer*, 7/12/90.

"War of Sexes Is Reversed in Police Court." *S.F. Call Bulletin*, 4/14/16.

Wasserman, John L. "Bill Graham—Sick and Tired." *S.F. Chronicle*, 8/5/69.

————. "The Dead: Committed to Sound Perfection." *S.F. Chronicle*, 3/22/74.

————. "GD Film a Unique Experience." *S.F. Chronicle*, 7/22/77.

————. "Hard-Driving Producer with a Doomsday Air." *S.F. Chronicle*, 3/18/66.

————. "Hollywood Eyes the Hippies." *S.F. Chronicle*, 7/26/67.

————. "When the Music Finally Stopped." *S.F. Chronicle*, 7/5/71.

Watrous, Peter. "Night of the Grateful Dead." *Musician*, 12/89.

Watts, Michael. No title. *Melody Maker*, 9/23/78.

Weddle, David. "When Worlds Collide." *L.A. Village View*, 7/7/95.

Weitzman, Steve. "Bob Weir: Afternoon with the Living Dead." *Drummer*, 10/2/73.

————. "A Chat with Jerry Garcia," in *Rolling Stone* (eds.), *Garcia*.

Welding, Pete. "NLCR." *Sing Out!* 2, no. 5, 12/61–1/62.

Wenner, Jann. "Blues with a Feeling." *Daily Cal*, 1/12/67.

————. "The Dead Did Get It." *Rolling Stone*, 11/67.

———. "The Pranksters' Last Prank." *Daily Cal,* 3/31/66.

White, Timothy. "From the Beatles to Bartok . . ." *Gold Mine,* 11/2/90.

Wieder, Robert S. "Has Success Spoiled Rock Hustler?" *New West,* 4/10/78.

Wilcock, Donald E. "Ungrateful Dead." *Lotus-Nexus,* 11/19–12/3/70.

Wilgoren, Rachel. "The Dead Live On." Senior thesis, Brandeis University, 1995.

Wood, Sam. "Live, with the Dead." *Philadelphia Inquirer,* 9/11/90.

Woody, Todd. "Jerry Garcia's Heirs Truckin' to Court." *Legal Times,* 3/18/96.

Wright, Charles. "Cold Philly Rock Night." *Village Voice,* 1/23/69.

Wright, Jeff. " 'Dead' Pays off for UO; Some Critics Not Grateful." *Eugene Register Guard,* 6/20/90.

Wright, Robert A. "200,000 Attend Coast Rock Fete." *New York Times,* 12/7/69.

"Yes, I Remember It Well." *Rolling Stone,* 2/16/84.

York, Michael. "Restrictions End Static over Grateful Dead." *Washington Post,* 6/18/89.

———. "Winter Moves to Pull Plug on Grateful Dead Concert Here." *Washington Post,* 6/13/89.

Yorke, Ritchie. "G.D. Surprise." *Toronto Telegram,* 6/29/70.

Young, Charles. "The Awakening of the Dead." *Rolling Stone,* 6/16/77.

Young, Israel. "Frets and Frails." *Sing Out!* 115, no. 5, 11/65.

Zane, J. Peder. "Who Else Would Name a Foundation for a Roadie?" *New York Times,* 6/26/94.

Zane, Maitland. "The Cops Bust Kids for Dancing." *S.F. Chronicle,* 4/23/66.

———. "Police Ban on Fillmore Dance." *S.F. Chronicle,* 4/17/66.

Zimmerman, Kent, and Keith Zimmerman. "Gavin Gets Dead." *Gavin Report,* 10/27/89.

Zorn, Eric. "The Kingston Trio Lives." *Chicago Tribune,* 2/21/82.

Material from Peter Berg, including film *Nowsreal* on Digger, Free City activities.

General files of Fitzhugh Ludlow Memorial Library.

David and Vera Mae Frederickson's collection of interviews and materials on Berkeley folk scene.

Files of Ralph J. Gleason (courtesy Jean Gleason).

Files of *Golden Road* (courtesy Blair Jackson and Regan McMahon).

Collection of materials of Greg Hoffman.

Files of the *San Francisco Chronicle.*

Files of the *San Francisco Examiner.*

Orme School files.

Marty Otelsberg files, Universal Attractions.

Joel Selvin files.

Interviews

Jerry Abrams
Peter Albin
Rodney Albin
David Allen
Ray Andersen
Debbie Green Anderson
Gene Anthony
Hoyt Axton
Frankie Azzara (Weir)

Ken Babbs
Enrico Banducci
Veronica Barnard (Grant)
Stephen Barncard
Bob Barsotti
Peter Barsotti
Bill Belmont
LuVell Benford
Peter Berg (musician)
Peter Berg (Digger)
Elmer Bischoff
Jeff Boden

Mary B. Boggess
Connie Bonner (Mosley)
Boots
Stewart Brand
Julia "Girl Freiberg" Brigden
Candace Brightman
Joan Brown
Michael Brown
Steve Brown
Toni Brown

Joseph Campbell
Bill Candelario
Melissa Cargill
Sandy Carroll
Luria Castell
Gert Chiarito
John Cipollina
Ted Claire
Sean Coakley
Allen Cohen
Bob Cohen

Kate E. Cole
Tom Constanten
Stan Cornyn
Annie Corson
Jim Corson
Peter Coyote
Earl Crabb
Emily Craig
Dick Crest
David Crosby
John Curl
Bill Cutler
John Cutler
Sam Cutler

Clive Davis
Judy Davis
Tom Davis
John Dawson
Paul de Barros
Phil DeGuere
Gloria Di Biase
Vince Di Biase
Raechel Donahue
Al Dotoly

Jim Edmonston
Cookie Eisenberg
Linda Ellerbee
Gene Estribou

Cyrus Faryar
Mort Feld
Norman "Pogo" Fontaine
Ann Besig Forwand
Gary Foster
Paul Foster
Ken Frankel
Dave Frederickson
Vera Mae Frederickson
Bobby Freeman
David Freiberg
Charlie Frizzell
Jim Furman

Carolyn Adams Garcia
Clifford Garcia

Jerry Garcia
Vernon Gates
Ted Gehrke
Rita Gentry
Nancy Getz-Evans
Jerry Gilmore
Sally Gist
Rubin Glickman
Richard Goldstein
Stu Goldstein
Lou Gottlieb
Chuck Gould
Bill Graham
Laird Grant
Nick Gravenites
Dr. Dan Grayson
Herb Greene
Eric Greenspan
Randy Groenke
Allen Gross
David Guard

Terry Hallinan
Scott Hambly
Bob Hanson
Mickey Hart
Dan Healy
Wally Hedrick
Lester Hellum
Chet Helms
Jon Hendricks
Walter "Herbie" Herbert
Freddie Herrera
David Hillis
Tom Hobson
Freeman House
Lynne Hughes
Robert Hunter
Karen Huntsberger

Erik Jacobsen
Deborah Jahnke
Annie Johnston
Mike Jonas
Kim (Niven) Jones
Tawny Jones

John Kahn
Bert Kanegson
   (Sat Sanh Tokh Khalsa)
Hal Kant
Paul Kantner
Julius Karpen
Sara Ruppenthal Katz
Jorma Kaukonen
Sam Keane
Bill Keith
Alton Kelley
Michael Kennedy
Roy Kepler
Howard Klein
Sue Klein
Michael Klenfner
Janet Soto Knudsen
Jim Koplik
Paul Krassner
Bill Kreutzmann
Bill Kreutzmann, Sr.
Brenda Kreutzmann
Shelly Kreutzmann (Quinn)
Marilyn Harris Kriegel
Dr. Stanley Krippner

Charles Michael Lamb
Candace Lambrecht
Lenny Lasher
Chandler Laughlin (Travus T. Hipp)
Don Law
Patrick Leahy
Willy Legate
Marshall Leicester
David Leiken
Dennis "Wizard" Leonard
Phil Lesh
Richard Loren
Roy Lott
John Lundberg
Michael Lydon

Donna Jean Godchaux MacKay
John "Bug" Manusos
Steve Marcus
Jim Marshall
Buzz Marten

Jorge Martinez
Bob Matthews
Mary Anne Mayer
Michael McClure
Don McCoy
Rosie McGee (Florence Nathan)
Jon McIntire
Glenn McKay
Carol McKernan
Mrs. Esther McKernan
David McQueen
Barbara "Brigid" Meier
Mary Jo Meinolf
Rick Melrose
Barry Melton
David Meltzer
John and Helen Meyer
Jean Mayo Millay
Chesley Millikin
Al Molina
Paddy Moloney
Brent Mydland
Max Myerson

David Nelson
Robert Nelson
Bob Nichols

Bill O'Farrell
Dale H. O'Keefe
Barry Olivier

Ruth Pahkala
Steve Parish
David Parker
Judy Parry
Sandy Pearlman
Don Pearson
Herb Pedersen
Bobby Petersen
Jane Petersen
Alice Polesky
Courtney Pollack
Mary Ann Pollar
Ron Polte
Jerry Pompili
Harry Popick

Buddy Powers
Zev Putterman

Bill Quarry

Ron Rainey
Basia Raizene
Lydia d'Fonsecca Rakow
Lee Reeves
Steve Reich
Hillel Resner
Sam Ridge
Jon Riester
Danny Rifkin
Brian Rohan
Neil Rosenberg
Lenore Garcia Ross
Sandy Rothman
Amalie Rothschild
Goldie Rush
Frank Russo

Ira Sandperl
Jacky Watts Sarti
Randy Sarti
Merl Saunders
John Scher
David Schoenstadt
Julie Schoenstadt
Ginger Jackson Schuster
Steve Schuster
Carl Scott
Chloe Scott
Nicki Scully
Rock Scully
Tim Scully
Jeanette Sears
Pete Sears
Bob Seidemann
Joel Selvin
Ramon Sender
Ray Sewell
Lisa Shaftel
Edmund Shea
Bruce Sherman
Rick Shubb
Frances Shurtliff

Lawrence "Ram Rod" Shurtliff
Joan Simms
David Singer
Joe Smith
Mayne Smith
Paul Speegle, Sr.
Owsley (Bear) Stanley
Patrick Stansfield
Jody Stecher
Sue Stephens
Chris Strachwitz
Paula Sunstadt
Pauline Swain
Sue Swanson

Tangerine
Ron Thelin
Bob Thomas
Bill Thompson
Eric Thompson
Alan Trist
Gail Turner
Rick Turner
Randi Tuten

Suzie Wood Urbick

Norman Van Maastricht
Danielle "Danya" Veltfort

Howard Wales
Bill Walker
Butch Waller
Michael Wanger
John Carl Warnecke, Jr.
Wavy Gravy (Hugh Romney)
Troy Weidenheimer
Bob Weir
Wendy Weir
Roland White
Ron Wickersham
John Ramsey Williams
Paul Williams
Roger Williams
Vern Williams
Stan Wilson
Wes Wilson

Joe Winslow   Michael Zagaris
Baron Wolman

Other Interviews

Album Network, interviews with Phil Lesh and Bob Weir by Marty Martinez and David
  Gans, "100 Year Hall," 9/7//95
Jeremy Alderson, interview with Jerry Garcia, 7/3/89
John McLaughlin, Palo Alto Historical Society, 1994, with Jerry Garcia
Aronowitz, Al, and Dennis McNally with Jerry Garcia, New York, 6/73
DiPietro, Ben, AP, interview with Jerry Garcia, at Moana Surfrider Hotel, 5/10/90
Eisenhart, Mary, interview with Jerry Garcia, 11/87
Lambert, Gary, with BW, 7/28/77
Marcus, Steve, and David Gans with Garcia, 10/14/86
Entire band, unknown source, 3/9/67
Garcia, Jerry, interview, "I Believe," KPIX-TV, San Francisco, 1968
Band on Alex Bennett, WMCA, New York, 9/16/70
Band meeting, 8/68
Bob Weir and Donna Jean Godchaux, WNEW, Passaic, N.J. 11/8/78
Jerry Garcia, WPLJ, New York, 9/74
Jerry Garcia, WLIR, New York, 1/11/79
Jerry Garcia, WRNW, Worcester, Mass., 11/9/82
Mickey Hart, Bill Kreutzmann, Dan Healy, WBCN, Boston, 11/14/78
Jerry Garcia with Bonnie Simmons, KSAN, San Francisco, 1/23/76
Mickey Hart, KSJO, San Jose, 8/80
Good Morning America, 1/23/80
Bob Weir, WMMR, Philadelphia, 9/8/76
Jerry Garcia, WMMR, Philadelphia, 11/27/78
Jerry Garcia, WFMT-FM, Chicago, with Studs Terkel, 12/17/78
Frost, Vance, and Michael Wanger, "Golden State Documentary" (radio), 1969
Gans, David, transcripts of his interviews with Bob Weir, 8/9/77, at L'Hermitage Hotel,
  Beverly Hills, during recording of "Heaven Help the Fool" and between shows at the
  Roxy, Los Angeles, 2/17/78
Jerry Garcia interview, "What Was That?" KSAN, San Francisco, 1976
Works, Mary, *The Life and Times of the Red Dog Saloon* (film)

Index

Abrams, Jerry, 324
Acid tests, 107–28, 129–30, 137, 168
  "Space" jams and, 536–38
Adams, Lee, 23–24, 37
Adler, Lou, 202, 203, 208
Agency for the Performing Arts (APA), 405
Albin, Peter, 45, 125, 151
Albin, Rodney, 34, 45, 95
Album covers, 185, 234–35, 274, 382, 410, 424,
  459, 473, 487, 504–5, 523, 561
Albums and CDs. *See also* Recording sessions
  American Beauty (1970), 377–78, 382, 383,
    395, 468, 566
  Anthem of the Sun (1968), 228–36, 258–60,
    273–74
  Aoxomoxoa (1969), 278–79, 300–301, 303,
    316
  Bear's Choice compiled by Bear Stanley
    (1972), 444
  bluegrass *Pistol Packin' Mama* (1975), 486
  Blues for Allah (1975), 482–86
  Built to Last (1989), 573–74, 575
  changeover to CDs, 562–63
  counterfeit, 460
  Deadicated (1991), 587–88
  Dead Reckoning (1980), 534
  Dead Set (1980), 534, 541
  Diga (1976), 488, 490–91, 494

Europe '72 (1972), 443–44
J. Garcia's solo *Cats Under the Stars* (1977),
  504, 506–7
J. Garcia's solo *Garcia*, 404–7
J. Garcia's solo *Garcia/Compliments*, 469
Golden Road, 618
Go to Heaven, 528, 531–32, 544–45, 562
The Grateful Dead (1967), 181–88
Grateful Dead (Skullfuck) (1971), 409–10
Grateful Dead from the Mars Hotel (1974),
  471, 473
M. Hart's *Fire on the Mountain*, 438
M. Hart's *Rolling Thunder* (1972), 437–38
M. Hart's *Voices of the Rainforest*, 587
In the Dark (1987), 462, 561–67
P. Lesh and N. Lagin's *Seastones* (1974), 474,
  486
Live Dead (1969), 299–300, 301, 339, 360
Old and in the Way (1975), 486
Shakedown Street (1978), 522–23
Steal Your Face (1976), 490
Terrapin Station (1977), 497–98, 504–5
Wake of the Flood (1973), 458–60, 559
R. Weir's *Ace* (1972), 415–16, 437, 438–39
R. Weir's *Heaven Help the Fool*, 504
Without a Net (1990), 585
Workingman's Dead (1970), 361, 362, 366,
  369–70, 468, 561, 566

Alchemy, 118
Alembic, 309
    Grateful Dead concert as, 1–5
Alembic (band), 309, 375
Alembic sound company, 426, 455, 471
Allarakha, Ustad, 258, 518
Allman, Duane, 382, 397–98
Allman Brothers (band), 355, 456, 457, 458
All Our Own Equipment Company, 253
Almanac (Lambert), 606
Alpert, Richard (Ram Dass), 111, 177, 463
Altamont Raceway free concert (1969), 342,
    343–50
American culture and politics, 25–26, 51,
    260–61, 305
    assassinations, 51, 53, 79, 260, 263
    California trends and computers in 1980s,
        530
    Chicago Eight, 338, 339, 367
    civil rights movement, 12, 31–32, 53, 71,
        79–80, 149, 185, 338
    Cuban Missile Crisis, 44–45
    Democratic Party convention (1968), 274–75
    environmental movement, 194
    Free Speech Movement, Berkeley, 74
    Gulf War (1991), 586–87
    hippies, 88, 176, 186, 208–9
    Jim Jones and Guyana mass death, 525
    moon walk (1969), 322
    social unrest, 152, 209, 367
    student protests, 367–68
    Vietnam War and antiwar movement,
        173–74, 177, 191, 227–28, 251, 275, 338,
        341, 367–68
Anderson, Lee, 78
Anderson, Signe Toly, 87
Animal production company, 94
Antonioni, Michelangelo, 361, 405–6
Apocalypse Now (film), 518–19
Arista Records, 423, 495–97, 504, 561, 562–63,
    564, 567, 587. *See also* Davis, Clive
Aronowitz, Al, 439–40
Art, 156–57, 256, 337, 369, 535. *See also* Album
    covers
Artist's Liberation Front, 150
Asphalt Jungle Mountain Boys, 73
Atlantic Records, 452
Avalon Ballroom, San Francisco, 148–49, 156,
    280
    live recording at, 299–300

Babbs, Ken, 111, 112, 116, 130, 137
Badwater Valley Boys, 54
Baez, Joan, 32, 45, 48–49, 53, 74, 485, 544
Balin, Marty, 87, 170, 346, 382
Band, The (band), 320, 456, 457, 458
Bangs, Lester, 410
Bank of Boston, financing for recording
    company, 452, 489
Barger, Sonny, 346, 348

Barich, Bill, 601
Barlow, John Perry, 57, 63, 64, 200, 367, 386,
    392, 393–95, 421, 519, 531, 569–70
    compositions by, 297, 394, 414–16, 459,
        484–85, 497, 503–4, 531, 545, 570, 571
    foundation established by, 580
    on Grateful Dead, 577–78, 583
    shooting incident and, 503
Barnard, Veronica "Vee," 161, 166, 225, 280–81,
    447
Barncard, Steve, 378
Barnett, Danny, 37, 42
Barratta, Paul, 380
Barsalona, Frank, 264
Barsotti, Bob, 506, 529, 535
Baxter, Loose Bruce, 308, 362
Bay Area Music Awards, 568
Beat Generation, 14–15, 20–21, 37, 82, 161
Beatles, 67–68, 76, 150, 190, 201, 283
Bell Records, 495. *See also* Arista Records
Belmont, Bill, 287–88, 324, 336, 340
Belushi, John, 521, 522
Ben & Jerry's Cherry Garcia ice cream, 423, 562
Bennett, Alex, 462
Bennett, Christine, 225, 454
Berg, Peter, 162, 163, 200, 202
Berio, Luciano, 38–39
Bessent, Malcolm, 391–92
Big Beat (club), 114
Big Brother and the Holding Company, 123,
    124, 125, 142, 150–51, 176, 188, 205, 208,
    252, 263, 265
Bill Graham Presents (BGP), 217–18, 267,
    269–70, 271, 494, 525–26, 529, 533–34
Black Mountain Boys, 52, 68, 70
Black Panthers, 185, 261, 265, 338, 342, 367,
    379, 395
Bluegrass music, 44, 52–54, 69–73, 80, 448–50,
    454, 486
Blues Brothers (band), 521
Boar's Head (club), 34–35
Bonner, Connie, 81, 112–13, 155, 192, 256
Booth, Stanley, 340, 347
Borden, Bob, 282
Boston Garden concert, Boston, 463–65
Bourne, Christie, 30, 383
Bowen, Michael, 177
Boxer, Barbara, 608–9
Brand, Steward, 115, 123, 124, 126, 166
Brickell, Edie, 581
Brightman, Candace (lighting director), 5, 215,
    239, 242, 425, 435, 442, 464, 512–13,
    610–11
    lighting work of, in 1980s, 572–73
    on working for Grateful Dead, 583–84
British Columbia Festival (1966), 153
Bromberg, David, 439, 440
Brown, Steve (album production coordinator),
    452–53
Bruce, Lenny, 73–74, 98, 146, 149

Bullfrog Festival, Oregon (1969), 337
Buses in English tour, Bolo Bus and Bozo Bus,
    428–29
Butterfield Blues Band, 140, 141
Byrds (band), 85

Caen, Herb, 304, 477–78
Cafe au Go Go (club), New York, 198–99, 201,
    338
Cal Expo Amphitheater, Sacramento,
    California, concert, 297–98
California Hall, San Francisco, 120–21
Campbell, Joseph, 387–88, 519, 551
Candelario Bill "Kidd" (crewman), 2, 215, 238,
    256, 299, 396, 433, 456, 610
Cantor, Betty (sound crew), 255, 300, 360, 426,
    494
Capitol Centre concerts, 299, 517–20
Capitol Theater, Port Chester, New York,
    391–95
Carousel Ballroom, San Francisco, 247–48, 251,
    252–57, 262–66, 276
Carr, Patrick, 444
Casady, Jack, 87, 175, 380
Cassady, Neal, 82, 107–10, 112, 115, 119–20,
    131, 146, 229, 250, 357, 415, 440
Castell, Luria, 93, 94, 121, 141
CDs. See Albums and CDs
Chamberlain, Owen, 387
Charlatans (band), 94, 95, 121, 134, 141, 142,
    188
Chieftains (band), 450
Chords (band), 16
Christgau, Robert, 201–2, 350, 414, 438, 502
Clements, Vassar, 454
Clifford, Tillie and Bill, 7, 8–9
Clinton, Bill, 604, 614
Close Encounters of the Third Kind (film), 506
Coakley, Sean, 562
Cohen, Allen, 160, 177
Colby, Eric, 327–28
Coleman, Ornette, 568, 601
Coltrane, John, 91–92, 119, 209
Columbia Records, 338, 444
Compton Terrace, Phoenix, concert, 538
Concert Associations, 342
Concert Halls Managers' Association, 305
Concerts. See also Festivals; Tours and touring,
        Grateful Dead
    acid tests, 107–28, 129, 137, 168
    Alaska (1980), 532
    Altamont (1969), 342, 343–50
    archetypal Grateful Dead, 291–98, 326–31,
        356–59, 461–67, 517–20, 536–40, 594–99
    Black and White Ball (1969), 304–5
    Breakfast in Bed with the Grateful Dead
        (1982), 546
    cancelled, at Roosevelt Raceway (1974),
        474–75
    on college campuses, 198, 261–62, 309

Dead Head tapes of, 385–86
    drum duet in, 517–20
    Egypt, 508–16
    An Evening with the Grateful Dead series,
        366–67
    experience of Grateful Dead, 1–5
    free, 339, 340, 341, 342, 371
    Human Be-In (1967), 177–80, 184, 193
    Hyde Park, London (1969), 339–40
    Invisible Circus (1967), 185
    Las Vegas, 328–29, 588
    lighting and, 239–40, 242, 293–94, 537
    Memphis (1970), 370
    New Orleans (1970), 351–55
    setting stage for, 237–46
    SNACK benefit (1975), 485
    sound system for (see Sound system)
    "Space" jams, 536–38
    Warfield Theater (1980), 533–35
Constanten, Tom "T. C." (band member), 38,
        53, 69, 260, 281, 352
Coppola, Francis, 518–19
Cornyn, Stan, 316
Country Joe and the Fish (band), 142, 284, 285,
        288, 370
Country music, 318–20
Cow Palace, San Francisco, 470
Coyote, Peter (Cohon), 162, 163, 164, 202, 274,
        282, 401
Crawdaddy! (periodical), 174, 186, 198, 201, 228
Creedence Clearwater Revival (band), 339
Crew, 213–18, 396, 475
    Bear Stanley's problems with, 440
    role of, in concerts, 1–5
    setting of concert stage by, 237–46
Crosby, David, 47, 85, 319, 320, 485
Crosby, Stills, and Nash (band), 319–20, 339,
        347, 406
Crutcher, Susan, 499
Cutler, John, 60, 561, 581, 607–8, 618
Cutler, Sam (road manager), 268, 339, 340–41,
        361, 379, 397, 448, 450
    Altamont concert and, 343, 344, 347, 349
    booking agency of, 424, 437, 453, 468, 469
    firing of, 468–69
    as Grateful Dead road manager, 363, 370,
        381–82, 398, 421, 425, 430, 437, 458

Dalton, David, 169, 372
Dane, Barbara, 32
Danko, Rick, 320
Dannen, Frederic, 422
Davis, Angela, 338
Davis, Clive, 338, 444, 562, 566
    management style of, 495–97, 531
Davis, Miles, 37, 260, 365–66, 537
Davis, R. G. "Ronnie," 69, 150
Davis, Tom, 521–22, 551
Dawson, John "Marmaduke," 318–19, 321, 365,
        372

DeadBase, 562

Dead Heads, 3, 237, 241–42, 244, 328, 385–90, 414, 532, 541, 579–80, 614, 618
  band message to, about counterfeiting, 460
  camping of, at concerts, 529–30
  deaths of, 574–75
  letter from R. Hunter to, 568–69
  problems at concerts and, 569, 572, 574–75, 611, 612

Death of a Hippie Ceremony, 227

Deaths, 337, 574–75

DeGuere, Phil, 441, 552

Dennison, Dave, 580

D'Fonseca, Johnny, 308

D'Fonseca, Lydia (bookkeeper), 254, 308

Di Biase, Vince, 588, 601, 605, 610

Dick's Picks, 606, 618

Diga Rhythm Band (band), 487

Diggers, 162–64, 176, 177, 185, 192–93, 197, 199, 200, 202, 208–9, 211, 227, 256, 261, 263, 282, 401

Dixon, Willie, 602

Donahue, Tom "Big Daddy," 96, 171, 190, 322, 325, 374–75

Doobie Brothers, 485

Doors (band), 178, 305

Dream Experiment, 391–92

Dreyer, Julia, 146

Drug busts, 225–27, 265, 339, 450, 552, 575–76
  New Orleans (1970), 351–55

Drugs and drug use, 13, 176, 336, 475, 522
  cocaine, 321, 393–94, 450, 475
  by Dead Heads, 579–80
  declining, in 1980s, 555
  hashish, 512
  heroin, 500–501
  LSD, 29, 42–43, 80, 86, 93, 102–6, 126, 166, 311, 333, 339 (*see also* Acid tests)
  marijuana, 82, 225
  nitrous oxide, 301, 303
  STP, 301

Drumming at the Edge of Magic (Hart), 519, 587

Dylan, Bob, 50, 53, 80–81, 85–86, 149, 150, 334, 556, 611, 612, 614
  collaboration of, with The Band, 320
  early folk career of, 50
  playing of, with Grateful Dead, 563, 565–66

Easy Rider (film), 322, 349

Eaton, Thor, 370–71

Ed-Din, Saad, 508, 509, 510

Edmonston, Joe, 41, 42, 73

Egypt, 483
  Grateful Dead visit to, 508–16

Eisenberg, Cookie, 282, 308

Electric Kool-Aid Acid Test (Wolfe), 107

Electronic Frontier Foundation, 580

Environmental concerns, Grateful Dead and, 570–71, 580

Epic Records, 339

Evening with the Grateful Dead concerts, 366–67

Event III, 68–69

Extrasensory perception experiments, 391–92

Faisal, Saudi Prince, 483

Family Dog, 93, 95, 99, 148, 323–24

Family Dog on the Great Highway (FDGH), 360–61

Fan Club newsletter, 453–54. *See also* Dead Heads

Felton, David, 169

Festival Express (1970), 370–73

Festivals. *See also* Concerts; Tours and touring, Grateful Dead
  British Columbia (1966), 153
  Bullfrog, Oregon (1969), 337
  Festival Express, Canada (1970), 370–73
  folk, 45, 50
  Free Freedom Three Days, France (1971), 400
  Further Festival, 614
  Monterrey Pop (1967), 202–8
  Sky River Rock, 278
  Trips (1966), 123–27, 166
  US Festival (1982), 546
  Vancouver Pop (1969), 337
  violence at, 322
  Watkins Glen, New York (1973), 455–58
  Wild West Festival (1969), 322–25
  Woodstock (1969), 332–37
  World Music Festival (1982), 546

Field, Sam, 441

Fillmore Auditorium (Fillmore West), San Francisco, 113, 120–22, 139–42, 266, 285, 304, 311, 325, 348, 365, 375, 400, 401

Fillmore East, New York, 264, 283, 289, 321, 334, 338, 355, 373, 379, 397–98, 439

Film, 9, 11, 74, 190–91, 209, 322, 361, 374–75, 416, 438, 506, 518–19, 551
  Fillmore auditoriums, 401–2
  Grateful Dead Movie, 478–79, 488–89, 497–502
  Merry Prankster's team, 441
  of Monterrey Pop, 202–3, 208
  of Rolling Stones concert, 341
  of Woodstock festival, 374

Financial affairs, 276, 288, 289, 301, 418–19
  debt problems, 524
  Lenny Hart as manager and, 305–7, 310, 338–39, 341
  Lenny Hart's thievery, 360–63
  management and, 419–23
  recording company and, 452
  women in charge of, 418–19

Finkel, Shelley (promoter), 439, 456, 457

Fischer, Michael "Fish" (crewman), 237

Fleetwood Mac (band), 352, 354

Flowers, Annette, 419

Fly By Night Travel, 453

Flying Burrito Brothers, 346
FM Productions, 458
Folk music, 17, 32–36, 41–50
Fontaine, Norman "Pogo," 30
Foster, Paul, 108, 130
Frankel, Ken, 41–42, 462
Franken, Al, 522
Franklin, Dale, 364
Free City Collective. *See* Diggers
Freiberg, David, 146, 313
Fritsch, Billy "Sweet William," 202, 282, 344,
    490–91
Front Street Sheiks (band), 488
Furman, Jim, 456, 481
FWAPS (Far West Action Picture Services),
    441

Garbet, Michael, 66
Garcia, Annabelle, 355, 481, 614
Garcia, Carolyn "Mountain Girl" ("M. G.")
    Adams (wife of Jerry Garcia), 110–11,
    124, 166, 182–84, 348, 357, 512, 556
  banning of, from J. Garcia's funeral and ash
    scattering, 614–15
  birth of child Annabelle and, 355
  birth of child Trixie and, 481
  marriage of, to J. Garcia, 544
  Sans Souci Stinson Beach home of, 403–4,
    449
  separation and divorce of, from J. Garcia,
    481, 489, 494
  song "Dire Wolf" and 316
Garcia, Deborah Koons (wife of Jerry Garcia),
    481, 501, 603, 605–6, 608, 609, 612, 613,
    614–15
  marriage of, to J. Garcia, 607
Garcia, Heather, 54, 131
Garcia, Jerry Jerome John (band member), 2
  as apolitical, 32, 75, 174, 177, 186–87
  as artist, 12, 14, 15, 559
  bluegrass music and, 44, 52–54, 69–73, 80,
    448–50, 454, 486
  book on, 408
  car crash of (1961), 23–25
  childhood and family of, 6–17
  compositions by, 32, 97, 98, 182, 230, 301–3,
    316–18, 321, 327, 349, 350–51, 360, 364,
    376–77, 395, 406, 413, 439, 446, 471,
    497–98, 523, 528, 531, 545–46, 560, 570,
    571, 581, 591
  country music and, 317, 318–20
  death of, 614
  drug busts and, 450, 552
  on drugs, 184
  drug use of, 13, 80, 86, 105–6, 147–48,
    500–501, 523–24, 552, 581, 588, 608,
    612–13
  on Egyptian trip, 511–12, 514
  folk music and, 17, 41–50
  as gunsmith, 308
  health problems of, 9, 525, 552, 556–59, 592,
    605, 610, 613
  interest of, in film, 9, 74, 361, 405–6, 478,
    506, 551
  interviews with, 184–87, 427, 460, 476, 488,
    542, 554, 589–90, 601
  jazz music and, 91–92, 365–66, 581–82, 586
  Jefferson Airplane recording and, 170
  jug band music and, 66–69, 73, 79
  marriages, divorces, and children of, 54, 355,
    481, 494, 567, 607
  memorial service and scattering of ashes of,
    614–16
  military stint of, 16–17, 21
  musical groups of, 31–42, 47–49, 51–54, 66,
    67, 70, 73, 279–80, 318–19, 321, 399, 449,
    454, 480, 488 (*see also* Grateful Dead)
  on music and playing music, 187, 463, 476,
    546–47
  as musician, 12–14, 16, 79, 80
  pedal steel guitar and, 318, 321
  philosophy and attitudes of, 3–4, 32, 55–57,
    131–32, 186–87, 311, 350, 408, 542,
    619–20
  on playing music with Grateful Dead,
    314–15, 577–78
  pranks of, 435
  Prankster nickname "Captain Trips," 116
  psychology and personality of, 7–8, 10, 14,
    24–25, 39, 377, 469, 500–501, 584
  on recording companies, 495
  relationships of, with women, 7–8, 10, 37–38,
    44, 166, 182–84, 481, 500–501, 567, 588,
    592–93, 600–601, 603
  Sans Souci Stinson Beach home of, 403–4
  solo albums of, 404–7, 504, 506–7
  trip of, to France, 400–401
  as Warlock band member, 76–100
  on women and art, 358
  on Woodstock festival, 335–36
Garcia, Keelin, 567
Garcia, Manuel (father of Jerry Garcia), 6, 7
Garcia, Theresa "Trixie," 481, 615
Garcia: Signpost to New Space (Reich), 408
Garris, Philip (artist), 487
Garrison, Jim, 354
Gaskin, Stephen, 103–4, 325, 349, 534
Gast, Leon, 498
Geomancy, band members' interest in, 427–28,
    483, 508
George, Lowell, 523
Getz-Evans, Nancy, 437
Giants Stadium, East Rutherford, New Jersey,
    concert, 329–30
Giblin, Alice, 588
Gillespie, Dizzy, 179
Gilmore, Mikal, 564
Ginsberg, Allen, 14, 20, 99, 100, 109, 111, 160,
    177
Glassberg, Barry, 385

Gleason, Ralph, 88, 94, 121, 127, 141, 170, 175, 179–80, 186, 197, 202, 203, 322, 324, 325, 339, 349

Godchaux, Donna Jean (band member), 411–12, 414, 431–32, 470, 479, 486, 487, 488, 494, 505, 524, 526–28

Godchaux, Keith, 411–13, 431, 470, 479, 486, 487, 488, 524, 526–28, 541

Godfather (film), 416

Gold, Melissa, 590

Golden Road (periodical), 562

Goldfinger, Ken, 311, 312, 351

Goldman, Elliot, 496

Goldstein, Richard (critic), 186, 196–97

Gore, Tipper, 604

Gottlieb, Suzanne, 419

Graham, Bill, 60, 99–100, 113–14, 122, 123, 126–27, 128, 139–42, 148, 156, 175, 203, 209–10, 211–12, 235, 264, 283, 322, 340–41, 342, 348, 365, 456, 493–94, 520, 546, 561, 567. *See also* Bill Graham Presents
  and closing of Fillmore auditoriums, 397, 400, 401–2
  crowd control by, 268, 458
  death of, 590
  early life and career of, 140, 268–72
  as Grateful Dead promoter, 280, 287–88, 305, 529, 533–34, 535
  New Year's Eve concerts of, 176, 555, 594–96
  problems of, with labor unions, 151, 217–18, 323–25
  SNACK concert organized by, 485
  trip of, to Egypt with Grateful Dead, 509, 515
  Wild West Festival and, 322–25

Graham Central Station (band), 485

Grant, Laird (stage manager), 10, 22, 83, 153, 216–17, 256, 351, 558

Grateful Dead (band). *See also names of individual members*
  acid test concerts of (*see* Acid tests)
  albums of (*see* Albums and CDs)
  as apolitical, 174, 177, 251
  band meetings of, 55–61, 276–78, 310
  concerts and festivals of (*see* Concerts; Festivals)
  country and acoustic music and, 318–20
  crew of (*see* Crew)
  as dance band, 206–7
  drugs and (*see* Drugs and drug use)
  "family" of, 356–59
  Fifth and Lincoln home/office of (San Rafael), 364, 418–23, 452
  in film, 190–91, 307
  financial affairs of (*see* Financial affairs)
  flight over Monument Valley by, 598
  Front Street office of (San Rafael), 480
  J. Garcia's central role in, 3–4, 55–57, 544

growing audience and prosperity of, in 1980s, 555, 561–62, 564, 567

Haight-Ashbury home of, 158–95

hearing damage among members of, 591–92

hiatus of (1974–1976), 474–75, 480–92

hiatus of (1986), 558–59

improvisation of, 103

induction of, into Rock and Roll Hall of Fame, 606–7

Lagunitas home of, 150–57

legacy of, 617–20

logo for, 337

mail-order ticket office for, 547–48

management of, 419–23

Marin County home of, 262, 279–80

media and (*see* Media)

musicians' bonds and internal band dynamics of, 90–91, 183–84, 273, 276–78, 463–65, 475–79, 501

music publishing company of (Ice Nine), 383, 419

Olompali home of, 144–50

on playing music together, 313–15, 320, 577–78

political songs and support of, 544–45, 570–71

postmodernism and music of, 530

recording company of (*see* Grateful Dead Records)

recording contracts of, 171–73, 495–96 (*see also* Arista Records; Warner Brothers)

recording sessions of (*see* Recording sessions)

relationship of, with audience, 119, 388–90, 618 (*see also* Dead Heads)

setting stage for, 237–46

sojourn in Los Angeles and return to San Francisco of (1966), 129–43

songs of (*see* Songs)

sound system of (*see* Sound system)

synchronicity, philosophy, and, 619–20

tours of (*see* Tours and touring, Grateful Dead)

videos of (*see* Videos)

on voices and vocalizing, 320

Warlocks as precursor to, 76–101

Grateful Dead Movie (film), 478–79, 488–89, 497–502

Grateful Dead Records, 444, 480
  financial problems and failure of, 481, 489–92
  formation of, 451–52
  messages to fans from, 473–74, 485–86, 487–88

Great Society (band), 95, 146–47, 155

Greek Theater, Berkeley, California, concert, 356–59

Greene, Herb, 98, 285

Greenspan, Eric, 397

Griffin, Rick, 554

Grillo, Billy (crewman), 2

Grisman, David, 72, 98, 379, 404, 405, 614
  childhood, family, and early career of, 448–49

musical relationship of, with J. Garcia, 379,
448–50, 486, 580–81, 612, 613
Groenke, Randy, 79, 186–87
Grogan, Emmett, 162, 163, 164, 200, 202, 208,
211, 274, 340, 344, 507
Grossman, Albert, 140, 205, 208, 252
Group Image, 197, 199, 208, 234
Gutierrez, Gary, 499, 563, 575
Gyuto Monks, 553

Haas, Charlie, 530
Haddy, Grace Marie, 31
Hagen, John (crewman), 299, 396
Haight-Ashbury Legal Organization (HALO),
193–94, 226
Haight-Ashbury neighborhood, 94–96, 158–60,
188–89, 192–94, 211, 227, 251–52, 401
Haight Commune, 323, 325
Hallinan, 172
Hambly, Scott, 73
Hard Day's Night (film), 74, 82, 184, 190
Hard Truckers (crew company), 481
Haring, Keith, 387
Harris, Marilyn, 164, 165, 226
Harrison, Hank, 82, 98
Hart, Lenny, 223–24
    conviction and sentencing to jail of, 407
    death of, 486
    financial treachery of, 360–63
    as manager of Grateful Dead finances, 305–7,
        310, 338–39, 341
Hart, Mickey (Michael Steven) (band member),
    2, 213, 215, 277, 281, 333, 334, 339, 359,
    390, 478, 482, 532, 558, 583, 606
    books by, 519, 587
    childhood and family of, 222–25 (*see also*
        Hart, Lenny)
    compositions of, 438, 523, 591
    damaru drum and subsequent accidents,
        502–3
    Diga album of, 488, 490–91, 492, 494
    drug use of, 224, 228–29
    on drum circles as music therapy, 589
    drum duet of, with B. Kreutzmann, 517–20
    on hiatus from Grateful Dead, 392
    impact of Lenny Hart's thievery on, 361–62
    life on ranch belonging to, 307–9, 319, 392
    musical groups of, 279–80, 319, 321, 487, 519
        (*see also* Grateful Dead)
    musicianship and musical interests of,
        229–30, 258, 487, 515, 517, 553, 603–4
    on music of Grateful Dead, 538
    New Orleans drug bust and, 354
    relationships of, with women, 282, 308, 544,
        587
    San Diego arrest of, 532
    solo album *Fire on the Mountain* of, 438
    solo album *Rolling Thunder* of (1972),
        437–38
    temper and pranks of, 284, 287, 523

trip of, to Egypt, 513, 515
Hartbeats (band), 279, 284
Hart Valley Drifters (band), 42, 45, 46
Hassinger, Dave, 181, 182, 233
Haynie, Jim, 176
Head Lights (band), 248, 323
Healy, Dan (sound crew), 5, 154–55, 215,
    235, 259, 276, 286, 345, 351, 429–30,
    500, 506
    concert in Egypt and, 513
    departure of, from Grateful Dead, 607
    on Grateful Dead, 578
    influence of, on Grateful Dead sound,
        445–46, 471, 529, 530, 534, 549
Heard, Sonny (crewman), 375, 394
Hedrick, Wally, 14, 15
Hefner, Hugh, 285–86
Heider, Wally, 378
Hellman, David, 452, 491
Hell's Angels, 87, 111, 163, 176–77, 179, 308
    Altamont concert and, 340, 343–50
    London Run and, 282
Hellum, Lester, 37, 38
Helm, Levon, 320
Helms, Chet, 95, 139–40, 148–49, 156, 254,
    361, 380
    Wild West Festival and, 323–25
Hendricks, Jon, 173–75
Hendrix, Jimi, 206, 207–8, 337, 379
Herrera, Freddie, 399
Hertzberg, Rick, 175
HIP (Haight Independent Proprietors), 189
Hippies, 88, 176, 186, 208–9, 227
Hitchcock, Peggy, 200–201, 211, 228
Hoffman, Abbie, 199, 275, 336
Hofmann, Albert, 103
Hog Farm at Woodstock Festival, 336
Hollingsworth, Ambrose, 178
Hopkins, Nicky, 488
Hornsby, Bruce, musical relationship of, with
    Jerry Garcia, 584–85, 589, 591, 614
Hot Tuna (band), 380
House, Linn (Freeman), 200
Hudson, Garth, 320
Humphrey, Hubert, 275
Hunter, George, 93
Hunter, Meredith, 348, 349
Hunter, Robert (lyricist), 25, 32–33, 42–43, 44,
    45, 46, 51, 68, 86, 87, 479
    childhood and family of, 26–28
    compositions by, 32, 219–21, 296, 301–3,
        316–18, 321, 327, 349, 350–51, 360,
        364–65, 372, 375–77, 378, 392–94, 413,
        439, 446, 462, 471, 482–84, 497–98, 523,
        528, 531, 545–46, 560, 571, 591
    dropped from bluegrass group, 52, 68
    drug bust and (1973), 450
    on Grateful Dead's music, 465
    on J. Garcia, 55
    letter to Dead Heads from, 568–69

poetry of, 195, 586–87
solo album *Tiger Rose* of, 486
Ten Commandments of Rock and Roll by,
    57–58
Hupert, Dan, 385
Hussain, Zakir, 518
Huxley, Aldous, 78

Ice Nine, Grateful Dead's music publishing
    firm, 383, 419
Ienner, Don, 562, 563
Improvisation, 91–92, 103
In Room (club), 88–92
Instant Action Jug Band (band), 95
International Famous (Ashley Famous) booking
    agency, 380

Jackson, Blair, 564
Jackson, Rex (crewman), 217, 299, 340, 375,
    393–94, 475
    death of, 494, 500
    foundation formed in memory of (*see* Rex
        Foundation)
    New Orleans drug bust and, 354–55
Jackson, Rudy, 37
Jagger, Mick, 113, 283, 345, 346, 347, 348–49,
    350
Jahnke, Deborah, 481
James, Etta, 546
Jarrad, Rick, 170
Jazz, 19, 91–92, 98, 173–74, 185, 581–82, 586
    jazz-rock fusion, 365–66
Jefferson Airplane (band), 87–88, 95, 99, 128,
    142, 145, 156, 170, 188, 205, 210, 211,
    252–53, 262, 322, 339, 346–47, 382
Jefferson Starship (band), 485, 488
Jensen, Rhonda, 308, 503
Jensen, Sherry, 308
Jensen, Vickie, 308, 568
Jerry Garcia Band (band), 494, 546, 559, 590,
    592, 600
Jeske, Shannon, 603
Jobs, Steven, 530
Johnson, Dwight, 12
Johnson, Jill, 544
Johnson, Robert, 317–18
Jones, Tawny, 36
Joplin, Janis, 47, 145, 151, 161, 175, 191, 205,
    253, 265, 289, 312, 327, 339, 372–73, 380
Jug band music, 66–69, 73, 79

Kahn, John, 398, 399, 449, 454, 469, 559, 567,
    607
Kahn, Steve "Killer," 590
Kanegson, Bert, 256, 263, 279, 322, 344, 345,
    347
Kant, Hal (Grateful Dead attorney), 61,
    422–23, 435, 451–52, 475, 478, 489, 491,
    495, 496, 553, 558
    on *The Grateful Dead Movie*, 498–99, 501–2

on ticket sales and Ticketmaster, 547–48
Kantner, Paul, 47, 87, 346
Kaplan, Karen "K. K.," 30
Kapor, Mitch, 580
Katz, Adam, 574–75
Katz, Sara Ruppenthal Garcia (wife of Jerry
    Garcia), 48–51, 53–54, 66, 74, 80, 113,
    115, 121, 124–25, 126, 131, 133, 182, 441
Kaufman, Toni, 225
Kaukonen, Jorma Jerry, 47, 65, 70, 87, 145–46,
    170–71, 333, 380, 382
Keith, Bill, 72, 73
Kelley, Alton (artist), 156, 185, 256, 369, 382,
    410, 424, 473, 504
Kennedy, John F., 25, 31, 51, 53
Kepler, Roy, 28–29
Kerouac, Jack, 15, 109, 313, 338
Kesey, Ken, 43, 78, 87, 107, 109–12, 118, 123,
    124, 128, 166, 167–68, 172, 177, 183, 282,
    440–41, 555
    trip of, to Egypt with Grateful Dead, 509,
        510–11, 513, 515
Kesey, Sunshine, 183, 404, 481, 511
Keystone Corner (club), 399
King, Martin Luther, Jr., 12, 25, 53
Kingfish (band), 487
Klein, Howie, 198
Klein, Sue, 358
Klenfner, Michael, 444
Kleps, Art, 104
Knell, Frisco Pete, 282, 344
Knickerbocker Arena, Albany, New York,
    concert, 294–95
Koplik, Jim (promoter), 439, 455–57, 458
Kornfeld, Artie, 333–34, 335
Krassner, Paul, 275, 336, 512
Kreutzmann, Bill (band member), 2, 52, 79,
    120, 224, 352, 365, 394, 442, 443, 507,
    522, 551, 605–6, 608, 614
    childhood and family of, 77–79
    drug use of, 106, 116
    drum duet of, with Mickey Hart, 517–20
    on eruption of Mt. St. Helens while playing
        "Fire on the Mountain," 532
    on European tour, 430, 432
    horse ranch of, 486
    marriages and children of, 79, 357
    musical groups of, 79, 279–80, 406 (*see also*
        Grateful Dead)
    on playing music, 315, 501, 539
    on playing with the Grateful Dead, 578
    as Warlock band member, 76–100
Kreutzmann, Brenda, 133, 150, 184
Kreutzmann, Shelly, 357
Krippner, Stanley, 392
Kweskin, Jim, 66

Lagin, Ned, 368, 379, 470, 471, 485
    Seastones album with P. Lesh, 474, 486
Lambert, Gary, 606

Lang, Michael, 333–34, 335
Larkin, Dennis, 535
Last Days of the Fillmore (film), 401
Latvala, Dick, 606, 618
Law, Cassidy, 243, 297, 375, 419, 494
Law, Eileen, 243, 297, 375, 419, 494
Leahy, Patrick, 387, 604, 608–9
Leary, Timothy, 104, 160, 177, 179, 200, 201,
    345
Led Zeppelin (band), 285
Legate, Willy, 51, 60, 68, 420, 429
    R. Hunter on, 29–30
    liner notes written by, 443
Legends (band), 79
Legion of Mary (band), 480
Leicester, Marshall, 33–34, 42, 43, 72
Leiken, David, 441
Lennon, John, 150, 228, 283, 310–11, 541
Lenzer, Don, 498
Leonard, Andy (recording company employee),
    453
Leonard, Dennis "Wizard" (sound crew), 214
    on European tour, 426, 431, 435, 436
Lesh, Jill, 357
Lesh, Phil (band member), 2, 38–40, 43, 49, 53,
    61, 68–69, 82, 125, 127, 155, 207, 235,
    463, 470, 488, 608, 614–15
    childhood and family of, 18–21, 377
    on Clive Davis at Arista, 531
    compositions of, 69, 364, 377, 471, 591
    drug use of, 105–6, 111, 112, 311
    on European tour, 431
    interest of, in geomancy, 427–28, 483
    musical groups of, 279–80, 321 (*see also*
    Grateful Dead)
    musicianship of, 19–21, 471
    on playing music with Grateful Dead, 315,
    319, 388, 544, 577–78
    relationships of, with women, 357, 544
    Seastones album of, with N. Lagin, 474, 486
    on tours, 286–87
    trip of, to Egypt, 508–16
    as Warlock band member, 82–100
Lester, Richard, 74, 190–91
Lewis, Roger, 308
Library of Congress Endangered Music Project,
    603
Light Artists Guild (LAG), 323–25
Lighting, concert, 239–40, 242, 293–94, 537
Lille, France, concert (1972), 432, 434
Lipset, Hal, 361
London, England, countercultural scene in, 88,
    281–83
London Run, 282–83
Longshoremen's Hall, San Francisco, 95–96, 99,
    123, 138, 139, 191
Loren, Elaine, 509
Loren, Richard (booker/manager), 270–71,
    404–5, 420, 449, 468, 483, 493–94, 496,
    500

departure of, from Grateful Dead, 543, 547
    trip of, to Egypt, 508–10
Los Angeles, Grateful Dead's sojourn in (1966),
    129–39
Lott, Roy, 561, 562
Lovell, Vic, 43, 78
Lovin' Spoonful (band), 86
Lydon, Michael, 170, 184, 286, 347, 465
    story on Grateful Dead by, 309–11

McCauley, Rich, 62, 65
McClure, Michael, 14, 124, 148, 161, 177
McCoy, Paula, 282
McGee, Rosie (Florence Nathan), 116, 133,
    158, 225, 357–58, 401, 432, 453
McGovern, George, 441, 442
McIntire, Jon (manager), 4, 253–55, 276, 312,
    335, 363, 380, 381, 496
    confrontation of, with J. Garcia about drug
    use, 552
    departure of, from Grateful Dead (1974), 476
    hiring of A. Trist by, 383–84
    hiring of D. Franklin as assistant by, 364
    as manager, 307, 420, 421, 437, 452, 453, 562
    New Orleans drug bust and, 351–52
    and rejoining Grateful Dead (1984), 550–51
    reservations of, about Lenny Hart, 306
    trip of, to France (1971), 400–401
McKay, Glenn, 323
McKenna, Terence, 104, 105
McKernan, Ron "Pigpen" (band member)
    35–36, 52, 67, 130–31, 151, 225, 265
    concert singing of, 300
    death of, 447–48
    firing of, by Grateful Dead, 276–78
    health problems of, 410, 413, 426, 439,
    446–47
    jug band music and, 66, 67
    New Orleans drug bust and, 352
    poetry of, 160–61
    relationship of, with Vee Barnard, 161, 166,
    280–81
    as Warlock band member, 76–100
McNally, Dennis "Scrib" (publicist and
    biographer), 3, 60, 243, 313, 389, 390, 461,
    462, 463, 466, 536, 541, 546, 549, 551,
    558, 560, 562, 564, 566, 575, 582, 583,
    585, 596, 600, 608
McNichols Arena, Denver, concert, 536–38
McQueen, Dave, 22, 37
Madison Square Garden, New York, concert,
    461–62
Maguire, Marina, 308, 394
Maharishi Mahesh Yogi, 231
Mallonee, Nancy, 419
Malone, Joe and Lois, 509, 510
Maloney, Mike, 172
Mamas and the Papas, The (band), 149–50, 207
Management of Grateful Dead, 419–23
Manilow, Barry, 496

Manson, Charles, 342
Manuel, Richard, 320
Marin Veterans' Auditorium concert (1987), 560
Marsalis, Branford, 581–82, 586
Matheson, Manasha, 567, 588, 601
Matrix (club), 87–88, 120, 127, 279, 398
Matthews, Bob (crewman), 62, 65, 66, 81, 192, 225, 233, 255, 265, 300, 360, 396, 401, 426, 440, 460
Matusiewicz, Ruth Marie "Bobbie" Clifford Garcia (mother of Jerry Garcia), 6–10, 12–13, 49, 377
Matusiewicz, Wally, 10, 13
Mayer, Mary Ann, 432, 453
May Fourth Movement (M4M), 471
Maysles, Al, 498
Media, 127
   alternative, 87, 160, 251
   Grateful Dead's relations with, 184–90, 226–27, 309–10, 426–27, 462, 554
Medicine Ball Caravan (film), 374–75
Meier, Barbara "Brigid", 30–31, 34, 37–38, 44, 600–601, 602, 603
Meinolf, Mary Jo, 419, 551, 582
Melton, Barry, 147, 484
Meltzer, David, 82
Meltzer, Richard, 198, 201
Merchandising, Grateful Dead, 167, 454
Merry Pranksters, 87, 130, 166–68, 232, 409
   acid tests and, 109–28, 129, 137, 168
   film team, 441
Metropolitan Entertainment, 241, 267
Meyer, John (sound crew), 529, 534
Miami, Florida, concert, 326–28
MIBS (Men in Black Suits), 508–10
Miller, Stanley "Mouse" (artist), 156, 185, 369, 424, 473, 504
Millikin, Chesley, 339, 422, 437, 468, 476–77, 492
Minault, Kent, 162
Mingus, Charles, 199
Moby Grape (band), 191–92
Moffat, Frances, 304
Monk, Peter, 345
Monroe, Bill, 448
Monterrey Pop Festival (1967), 202–8
Moon, Keith, 495
Morgan, Dana, Jr., 77, 79, 82, 83
Morris, John, 336
Morrison, Jim, 178, 232, 305, 405
Morse, Steve, 589–90
Mother McCree's Uptown Jug Champions, 67, 79
Mother's (club), 86, 97
MTV (television), 543, 564
Muldaur, Maria D'Amato, 448, 490, 491
Mydland, Brent (band member), 2, 420, 527–28, 566
   alcohol problem of, 555–56

compositions by, 531, 555, 570, 571, 572
drug overdose and arrest of, 575–76
drug overdose and death of, 582–84

Nash, Graham, 319, 336
Nathan, Florence. See McGee, Rosie
Nelson, David, 45, 46, 49, 51, 65, 67, 68, 80, 86, 365, 559, 567
Nelson, Robert, 195
Newman, Laraine, 358
New Orleans, concerts and drug bust in (1970), 351
New Orleans Pop Festival (1969), 337–38
New Riders of the Purple Sage (band), 318–19, 321, 364, 366, 380, 384, 413, 415
Nixon, Richard, 56
Nordine, Ken, 586

Oakland Auditorium, concerts at, 529
Oakland Coliseum, concerts at, 291–94, 538–40, 560, 594–96
Offstage (club), 53
Old and in the Way (band), 449, 450, 454
Oldham, Andrew Loog, 76–77
Olivier, Barry, 322, 325
Olompali Sunday Times, 192
Olsen, Keith (record producer), 497, 503, 504–5
Omni, Atlanta, concert, 295–96
Ono, Yoko, 310
Oops Concert, Amsterdam (1981), 543
Oracle (periodical), 160, 162, 166, 177
Orbach, Caryl, 587
Ostin, Morris "Mo," 171
Out of Town Tours (OOT), 424, 437, 453, 468, 469

Pahkala, Ruth, 83
Parcels, Jon, 574
Parish, Steve (stage manager), 2, 213, 214, 217, 240, 291, 292, 313, 322, 423, 457, 463
   death of wife and daughter of, 551–52
   and joining Grateful Dead, 396, 399
Parker, Bonnie, 86, 363, 435, 451, 555, 558
Parker, Dave, 66, 67, 74, 80, 82, 86, 363
Parker, Elaine, 503
Pasaro, Alan, 348, 349
Pearlman, Sandy, 198, 201
Pearson, Don, 534
Peckham, Debbie, 65
Pederson, Herb, 80
People's Park benefit concert, 310–11
Percussion, 517–20. See also Hart, Mickey; Kreutzmann, Bill
Perry, Charles, 429
Peter, Paul, and Mary, 50
Petersen, Bobby, 38, 82, 321
Petulia (film), 199–200
Phillips, John, 202, 203–4
Photo sessions, 98–99
Pierre's (club), 98

Pigpen. *See* McKernan, Ron "Pigpen"
Pigpen Look Alike Contest (1969), 316
Planet Drum (band), 519, 590
Planet Drum (Hart), 519, 587
Police, 122, 189, 193, 252, 284, 285, 370, 400
  drug busts and, 225–27, 352, 354, 582
  in Egypt, 514
  in Europe, 431
  San Diego arrests and, 532
Politics. *See* American culture and politics
Polte, Ron, 152, 252, 322, 325
Pomeroy, Wes, 334
Popick, Harry (sound crew), 293, 331, 518, 529, 585
Portland, Oregon, acid test, 119, 120
Potrero Theater, San Francisco, 258
Press. *See* Media
Price, Jay, 79
Pritzker, John, 547
Promoters, 267–72. *See also* Graham, Bill

Questing Beast (club), 128
Quicksilver Messenger Service (band), 95, 142, 150, 151–52, 179, 188, 248, 252–53, 284, 307, 379, 380

Radio, 190, 251, 257, 342, 369–70, 380, 434, 525, 561–62
Radio City Music Hall concert (1980), 535
Radner, Gilda, 358
Rainey, Ron (agent), 380–81, 439, 456
Raizene, Basia, 419
Raizene, Sparky, 396, 440
Rakow, Emily, 358
Rakow, Ron (Grateful Dead recording company president), 56, 135, 211, 247, 358, 479
  Grateful Dead Records and role of, 444, 451–52, 468–69, 473, 489–92, 500
  as manager of Carousel, 252, 253–57, 262–66
Ram Dass (Richard Alpert), 111, 177, 463
Ramparts (periodical), 184–85
Reagan, Ronald, 545
Recording company. *See* Grateful Dead Records
Recording contracts. *See* Arista Records; Warner Brothers
Recording sessions. *See also* Albums and CDs
  live (1971), 408–9
  live, at Avalon Ballroom (1969), 299–300
  live, in Europe (1972), 424
  studio (1967), 181–84
  studio (1968), 230, 233–36, 258–60
  studio (1969), 278–79, 300–301, 303
  studio (1970), 360, 361, 362
  studio (late 1970), 377–78
  studio (1973), 458
  studio (1974), 471
  studio (1975), 482–86
  studio (1984), 548–49
  studio (1989), 573–74
Redding, Otis, 175

Red Dog Saloon (club), 93
Reich, Charles, 408
Reich, Steve, 68
Rense, Rip, 328
Rex Foundation, 60, 297, 589
  founding of, 548
  grant to D. Grisman from, 580
RFK Stadium, Washington D.C., concert, 330–31
Richard, Keith, 345, 347, 348
Richfield Coliseum, Cleveland, Ohio, concert, 462–63
Riester, Jonathan (road manager), 254, 276
  London Run and, 281–83
  reservations about Lenny Hart and departure from Grateful Dead of, 306–7
  on tours, 286–89
Rifkin, Danny (road manager), 57, 121, 134–35, 145, 163, 191, 215, 225–26, 340, 453, 481
  as manager, 159, 191, 203, 269–70, 326, 420, 421, 475, 547–48, 550
  San Diego arrests and, 532
Roberts, John, 334
Robertson, Robbie, 320
Rock and roll music, 11–12, 16, 77, 80, 85, 93, 175
  San Francisco sound, 169–71, 197
Rohan, Brian, 124, 172, 173, 193–94, 225, 247, 253
Rolling Stone (periodical), 228, 339, 362, 408, 429, 565
  Grateful Dead cover stories, 309–10, 564
Rolling Stones (band), 76–77, 85, 112–13, 283, 339, 340
  Altamont concert and, 347–50
  U.S. tours, 340, 436–37, 574
Rolling Thunder (John Pope), 309, 414–15
Romney, Hugh (Wavy Gravy), 115, 130, 131, 334, 336–37
Rosen, Fred, 547–48
Rosenberg, Neil, 71, 72
Rosenman, Joel, 334, 335
Rothman, Sandy, 70–73, 559, 567
Round Records, 452, 486, 492
Rowan, Peter, 449
Rowan Brothers (band), 404, 405
Rubin, Jerry, 177, 179, 275, 338
Rubinson, David, 170, 322
Rudolph, Nicki, 335, 339
Rush, Goldie, 116, 404, 509, 511, 512

Sage, Nora, 524, 589
Salter, Tom, 475
Sands, Bobby, 542
San Francisco, 6, 317
  countercultural scene in, 93–96, 127, 142, 149, 158–60, 169–80, 192–94, 212, 227
  musical sound from, 169–71, 197, 339
San Francisco Mime Troupe, 68–69, 87, 99, 113, 123

San Francisco Music Council, 322
Santana (band) and Carlos Santana, 335–36,
    337, 339, 346, 485, 558, 568
Sarti, Randy, 326, 510
Saturday Night Live (television), 506
    Grateful Dead on, 521–22
Saunders (Washington), Merl, 399, 405, 450,
    485, 552, 553, 558, 559
Scher, John (promoter), 267, 270–71, 439, 450,
    458, 494, 502, 505, 525
Scher, Richard, 494
Scientology, 68, 321, 352
Scrib. *See* McNally, Dennis "Scrib"
Scully, Rock (manager), 56, 121, 173, 225, 265,
    322, 335, 340, 523
    Altamont concert and, 340, 343, 348, 349
    departure of, from Grateful Dead, 550
    drug use and, 339, 523, 524, 550
    financial affairs and, 306
    on Grateful Dead, 56, 319
    on J. Garcia's solo album, 407
    London drug bust of, 339
    London Run and, 281–83
    on management problems, 420–21
    as manager of Grateful Dead, 134, 159,
        197–98, 203, 247, 249, 252, 253, 276–78,
        288, 326, 363, 409, 437, 475, 546
Scully, Tim (sound crew), 136–37, 154
Sears, Cameron (road manager), 420, 538,
    575
Sebastian, John, 86, 336, 448
Security
    at Altamont concert (1969), 344–50
    at Grateful Dead concerts, 241, 245, 472–73
Seidemann, Bob (photographer, art director),
    57, 188, 265, 446, 453, 500
Sex Pistols (band), 506, 527
Shanahan, Patrick, 575
Shankar, Ravi, 204, 205–6, 258
Shelton, Gilbert, 523
Shoreline Amphitheater concert, 296
Shorter, Wayne, 568
Shubb, Rick, 80, 86
Shurtliff, "Ram Rod" Larry (crew chief), 2, 57,
    61, 213, 215, 217, 232, 233–34, 285, 299,
    340, 361, 442, 466
    New Orleans drug bust and, 354–55
    role of, in Grateful Dead family, 232, 287
Silent Flute (film), 438
Silver Stadium, Las Vegas, concert, 328–29
Simon, Paul, 203, 205, 471
Sirens of Titan (film), 551
Sky River Rock Festival, 278
Sleepy Hollow Hog Stompers (band), 43–44
Slick, Darby, 95, 146–47, 155–56
Slick, Grace, 95, 146–47, 155–56, 346–47, 382,
    491
Slick, Jerry, 95, 146
Smith, Harry, 33
Smith, Joe (Warner Brothers executive), 171,

    172, 173, 182, 188, 233, 234–35, 301,
        362–63, 407, 409, 438, 495
Snyder, Gary, 160, 177, 179, 302, 401, 596
So Far (video), 462, 463, 553, 559, 566–67
Songs
    "Alabama Getaway," 531
    "Alligator," 219, 235, 258, 260, 278, 518
    "Althea," 528
    "Attics of My Life," 376–77
    "Barbed Wire. . . .", 279
    "Believe It or Not," 575
    "Bending Your Mind," 98
    "Bertha," 395, 408, 413
    "Bird Song," 327, 406
    "Black Cat," 32
    "Black Muddy River," 388
    "Black Peter," 351, 362, 539
    "Black-Throated Wind," 415
    "Blind John," 438
    "Blood Red Diamonds," 393, 415
    "Blow Away," 570
    "Blues for Allah," 483–84, 487
    "Bombs Away," 504
    "Born Cross-Eyed," 233, 235, 274
    "Box of Rain," 377
    "Brokedown Palace," 376
    "Brown Eyed Woman," 413
    "Casey Jones," 321, 360, 362, 522
    "Cassidy," 297, 414, 415
    "China Cat Sunflower," 249, 278, 303,
        329–30
    "China Doll" ("The Suicide Song"), 446, 471
    "Comes a Time," 413
    "Corinna," 591
    "Cosmic Charley," 278, 493
    "Crazy Fingers," 483
    "Cream Puff War," 182
    "Cryptical Envelopment," 230, 235
    "Cumberland Blues," 351, 362
    "Dark Star," 219–21, 232, 274, 278, 300, 333,
        355, 369, 526, 582
    "Days Between," 602–3
    "Deal," 395, 406
    "Death Don't Have No Mercy," 300
    "Dire Wolf," 316–18, 362
    "Doin' That Rag," 302
    "Dupree's Diamond Blues," 302
    "Easy to Love You," 531
    "Easy Wind," 362
    "Eep Hour," 571
    "The Eleven," 249, 258, 300
    "Estimated Prophet," 388–89, 497, 505
    "Eternity," 602
    "Eyes of the World," 446, 458, 582, 620
    "Far From Me," 531
    "Feedback," 300
    "Feel Like a Stranger," 531
    "Fire on the Mountain," 438, 515, 523, 532
    "Foolish Heart," 570, 575
    "Franklin's Tower," 462–63, 483

"Friend of the Devil," 364, 379
"Gentlemen, Start Your Engines," 570
"Gomorrah," 504
"Good Lovin'," 522, 523
"Greatest Story Ever Told," 393, 438
"Heaven Help the Fool," 504
"Hell in a Bucket," 561, 571
"Help on the Way," 482–83
"He's Gone," 542
"High Time," 321, 362
"I Can't Come Down," 97
"I Need a Miracle," 522, 523
"I Will Take You Home," 572
"If I Had the World to Give," 523
"Jack Straw," 413
"Just a Little Light," 571, 576
"Keep Your Day Job," 545, 549
"The Last Time," 388
"Lazy Lightning," 493
"Lazy River Road," 602
"Liberty," 602
"Long Way to Go," 591
"Loose Lucy," 446, 471
"Loser," 406
"Lost Sailor," 529
"Louis Collins," 580
"Marshmallow Road," 438
"Maybe You Know," 555–56
"Mexicali Blues," 295–96, 394, 413, 414
"Might as Well," 372, 493
"Minglewood Blues," 523
"Mission in the Rain," 488
"Morning Dew," 182, 436, 539
"Mountains of the Moon," 286, 302–3
"Music Never Stopped," 485
"My Brother Essau," 545, 549
"New Potato Caboose," 187, 235, 260
"New Speedway Boogie," 349, 350, 362, 545
"No Place Here," 364
"One More Saturday Night," 393, 414
"The Only Time Is Now," 97
"The Other One," 229, 230, 235, 249–50, 260, 537, 554
"Passenger," 505
"Picasso Moon," 571
"Playing in the Band," 392, 393, 395, 414, 463–65, 531
"Pride of Cucamonga," 471
"Pump Song," 438
"Ramble on Rose," 296, 413
"Ripple," 376, 379, 571
"Rubin & Cherise," 504
"Sage and Spirit," 485
"Saint of Circumstance," 531
"St. Stephen," 249, 258, 278, 300, 303, 333, 493, 526
"Scarlet Begonias," 471–72
"Shades of Grey," 504
"Ship of Fools," 470, 471
"Slipknot," 483

"So Many Roads," 591
"Standing on the Moon," 571
"Stella Blue," 364, 390, 439, 539, 618
"Stones," 539
"Sugaree," 294, 406, 413
"Sugar Magnolia," 358, 375, 378, 394, 395, 595
"Sunrise," 494
"Tennessee Jed," 413
"Terrapin Flyer," 505
"Terrapin Station," 497–98, 595–96
"Throwing Stones," 538, 545
"To Lay Me Down," 406, 407
"Touch of Grey," 461, 545–46, 560, 561, 564, 566, 596
"Truckin'," 292–93, 364, 375, 382, 436
"(Turn on Your) Lovelight," 300
"Uncle John's Band," 350–51, 360, 362, 369, 370, 465–67, 531
"U.S. Blues," 446, 470, 471, 499
"Victim or the Crime," 569
"Viola Lee Blues," 182
"Walk in the Sunshine," 416
"Wave to the Wind," 591
"Weather Report Suite," 459, 529
"We Can Run," 571
"West L. A. Fadeaway," 545
"Wharf Rat," 408, 413
"What's Become of the Baby," 303
"Wheel," 406–7
"Zillionaire," 581
Sopwith Camel (band), 142, 191
Soto-Knudsen, Janet, 57, 419
Sound system, 1–3, 208, 293, 381, 395–96, 534, 549–50, 560–61
    Beam sounds, 520
    D. Healy's influence on, 445–46, 529, 534, 549
    live recordings and, 299–300
    pink noise and, 445
    problems with, at Woodstock festival, 332–33
    stage set up and, 238–45
    Wall of Sound, 460, 470–71, 472–73
Spectrum, Philadelphia, concert, 465–67
Speegle, Paul, 23–25
Spence, Skip, 87
Stanley, Augustus Owsley III "Bear" (sound crew), 130
    album Bear's Choice compiled by, 444
    in band Alembic, 309
    childhood and family of, 117–18
    as Grateful Dead soundman, 127–28, 135–37, 276, 299–300, 345
    impact of, on Grateful Dead, 132–34
    as LSD manufacturer, 104, 118–19, 138–39, 204
    New Orleans drug bust and, 354
    and rejoining Grateful Dead after jail, 440
Stecher, Jody, 73
Stein, Howard, 321

Stepanian, Michael, 193
Stephens, Sue (bookkeeper), 524, 550
Stewart, Ian "Stu," 350
Stills, Stephen, 319, 336
Stone, Sly, 336
Stone, Tom, 66
Stonehenge, band members' visit to, 428
Straight Theater, San Francisco, 221–22, 226, 252
Sulkes, Neil, 579
Swanson, Sue, 65, 81, 112–13, 155, 182, 192, 225, 233, 256, 282, 334, 481

Tangent (club), 47, 48, 67
Taylor, Dallas, 336, 527
Taylor, Derek, 202, 283, 438–39
Taylor, Robbie (production manager), 2, 3, 216, 291, 327, 482, 520, 527
Television, 506, 521–22, 543, 552
Thomas, Bob, 118, 309, 337
Thompson, Bill, 252, 335, 351
Thompson, Bob, 322
Thompson, Eric, 52, 65, 73, 80
Thompson, Hunter, 110, 160, 208, 442, 494
Thunder Mountain Tub Thumpers (band), 41–42
Thurmond, Strom, 609
Tibetan monks, 502–3, 553
Ticketmaster, 547–48
Tickets for Grateful Dead concerts, 547–48, 588
Tours and touring
    J. Garcia's bluegrass, 70–73, 454
    Merry Prankster's 1964 bus, 109–10
    Rolling Stones, in United States, 340, 347–50, 436–37
Tours and touring, Grateful Dead, 56–57. *See also* Concerts; Festivals
    1969, 284–90, 309, 380–82
    1972, 441–42
    1973, 445–46
    1974, 472–73, 474
    1974–76 hiatus, 480–92
    1976 return to, 493–95
    1977 and 1978, 502, 505–7
    1989, 571–72
    1991, 588–90
    1993, 602–3
    1995, 609, 610–12
    in Canada, 209–11, 370–73
    of colleges (1969), 309, 380–82
    in England, 368–69, 425–29, 433, 435–36
    in Europe (1972), 424–36
    in Europe (1974), 475–77
    in Europe (1981), 542–44
    in Europe (1990), 585–86
    flights and hotels, 326–28
    of Great Northwest (1968), 247–50
    Great Train Ride of 1970, 370–73, 493
    of Midwest, 281, 413
    in New York, 196–202, 211, 234, 261–62,

264, 321–22, 338, 355, 379–82, 391–92, 396–97, 535, 566, 589, 605
    in Southern states, 397–98
    in Texas, 284–85
Townsend, Arnold, 323
Trips Festival (1966), 123–27, 135, 166
Trist, Alan, 25, 28–29, 36–37, 104–5, 376, 383–84, 407, 408, 427, 469, 481, 496, 550
    car crash of (1961), 23–25
    on European tour, 427, 428, 429
    as manager of Ice Nine, 419
    trip of, to Egypt, 508 10
Tulku, Tarthang, 502
Turner, Gail, 341, 361, 437
Turner, Rick, 309
Twilight Zone (television), 552–53

Ultra Sound company, 529
Uncalled Four (band), 65
Underground (club), 318
United Artists, 481, 484, 489, 490
United States. *See* American culture and politics
Up Against the Wall Motherfuckers (UAWMF), 283
US Festival (1982), 546

Valenti, Dino, 47, 142
Vancouver Pop Festival (1969), 337
Van Maastricht, Norm, 45
Velvet Underground (band), 198–99
Vicious, Sid, death of, 527
Videos
    Built to Last, 575, 576
    In the Dark, 563
    So Far, 462, 463, 553, 559, 566–67
    Touch of Grey, 564
Village Voice (periodical), 196–97, 200
Viola, Ken, 241
Vitt, Bill, 399

Walden, Phil, 494
Wales, Howard, 398, 410
Walker, Bill, 49, 274
Waller, Butch, 80
Wall of Sound, 460, 470–71, 472–73
Walton, Bill, 387, 463, 510, 512
Warfield Theater concerts, 533–35
Warlocks (band), 76–100
Warner Brothers, 171–73, 234–35, 259, 273, 301, 338–39, 368–69, 382, 409, 431, 444, 495. *See also* Smith, Joe
Waronker, Lenny, 171
Washington, Eddie, 478, 481
Wasserman, John, 502
Wasserman, Rob, 581, 602
Watkins Glen, New York, rock festival (1973), 455–58
Watts, Alan, 160
Watts Acid Test, Compton, 129–31

Wavy Gravy (Hugh Romney), 115, 130, 131, 334, 336–37
Weatherman faction, SDS, 338
Weidenheimer, Troy, 51, 65
Weir, Frankie Azzara, 282, 312, 318, 348, 358–59, 375, 453, 481
Weir, Robert Hall "Bob" (band member), 2, 62, 77, 204–5, 225, 234, 261–62, 265, 378, 426, 442, 443, 463, 475, 487, 605, 608, 613, 615
  Ace's recording studio of, 481–82
  childhood and family of, 62–65, 395
  compositions by, 230, 249–50, 295–96, 364, 375, 392–94, 413, 414–16, 459, 485–86, 497, 503–4, 529, 531, 538, 545, 569, 571, 591, 602
  drugs and, 160
  firing of, by Grateful Dead, 276–78
  on Grateful Dead family, 356–59
  jug band music of, 66–69
  musical groups of, 65, 66, 67, 318–19, 480, 527 (see also Grateful Dead)
  as musician, 63–65, 120, 206, 464, 537
  New Orleans drug bust and, 354
  on playing music with Grateful Dead, 314, 315
  relationships of, with women, 358, 481
  San Diego arrest of, 532
  shooting incident with J. Barlow and, 503
  solo album Ace of (1972), 296, 437, 438–39
  solo album Heaven Help the Fool of, 504
  trip of, to France (1971), 400–401
  twenty-first birthday of, 280
  wake for Pigpen at home of, 447–48
  as Warlock band member, 76–100

Welnick, Vince, 585, 591, 614
Wenner, Jann, 113, 127, 141, 184, 228, 322, 363, 408
Werber, Frank, 322
Who, The (band), 206, 267, 334, 494–95
Wickersham, Ron, 299–300, 309, 446, 455
Wild West Festival (1969), 322–25
Wildwood Boys (band), 47, 49, 52
Williams, Paul, 103, 186, 201, 274
Williams, Roger, 36
Winslow, Joe (crewman), 214, 217, 396–97, 458, 472, 481
Winterland concerts, 163, 310, 379–80, 399–400, 470, 502, 525–26
Wolfe, Tom, 107
Women in Grateful Dead family, 30–31, 182–84, 356–59
  financial management by, 418–19
Woodstock Music and Art Fair (1969), 332–37
World Music Festival (1982), 546
Wozniak, Stephen, 530, 546
Wyn-Ellis, Alana, 447–48

Yasgur, Max, 332, 334, 337
Yippies (Youth International Party), 275
Young, Israel, 448
Young, Neil, 485

Zabriskie Point (film), 361, 405–6
Zachariah (film), 307
Zappa, Frank, 99, 199
Zeavon, Warren, 507, 581
Zellman, Diane, 105
Zimmels, Peter "Monk," 544
Zodiacs (band), 51–52

Permissions

The author wishes to thank the following people and organizations for their willingness to share material.

All songs quoted are courtesy of Ice Nine Music Publishing except where otherwise noted.

"It's Alright, Ma (I'm Only Bleeding)" is © 1965 by Warner Bros. Inc., copyright renewed 1993 by Special Rider Music. All rights reserved. International copyright secured. Reprinted by permission.

"Morning Dew," by Bonnie Dobson and Tim Rose, Warner Tamerlane Publishing, used by permission.

"We Can Be Together," by Paul Kantner, used by permission of Icebag Music.

Material from an article by Frank Dorris in *Absolute Sound,* used by permission of Absolute Media.

Harcourt Brace, for a portion of T. S. Eliot's "The Four Quartets."

Material from *The Collected Poems of Bobby Petersen,* used by permission of Hulagosi Press.

For "Diagram." From *The Selected Poems of Robinson Jeffers* by Robinson Jeffers, copyright 1925, 1929 and renewed 1953, 1957 by Robinson Jeffers. Used by permission of Random House, Inc.

Material from an interview with Jerry Garcia by Paul Morley in *New Musical Express,* used by permission of IPC Media.

Material from a 1973 article by Patrick Carr and a 1987 article by Jon Pareles in the *New York Times,* used by permission of the *New York Times.*